1995-96 Official Guide and Record Book
The New York Rangers Hockey Club

RANGERS 1995-96 MEDIA GUIDE

Table of Contents

(Rangers received
National Hockey League
franchise on May 15, 1926)
(All Contents Copyrighted)

**The Players
16-89**

**1994-95 In Review
94-132**

BROOKS THOMAS   **JOHN ROSASCO**   **ROB KOCH**
Managing Editor   Editor   Associate Editor

Editorial Assistants: Ann Marie Gilmartin, Frank Buonomo,
Elena Cizmaric, John O'Sullivan and Ron Tumpowsky
Photography: Bruce Bennett Studios
Printed by Command Color Press - Roger Young and Dan Pyne, Production Coordinators

Binghamton Rangers
134-137

Career Records
140-154

In The Past
158-288

NEW YORK RANGERS DIRECTORY

Madison Square Garden
2 Penn Plaza, New York, New York 10121
(212) 465-6000

EXECUTIVE MANAGEMENT

President and General Manager ....Neil Smith
Executive Vice President and General Counsel ....Kenneth W. Munoz
Vice President and Business Manager ....Francis P. Murphy
Governor..Charles Dolan
Alternate Governors ....Neil Smith, David W. Checketts,
Kenneth W. Munoz, Rand Araskog, James Dolan

HOCKEY CLUB PERSONNEL

Assistant General Manager\Player Development ....Larry Pleau
Head Coach ....Colin Campbell
Assistant Coaches..Mike Murphy, Dick Todd
Development Coach ....George Burnett
Assistant Development Coach ....Mike Busniuk
Goaltending Analyst ....Sam St. Laurent
Scouting Staff ....Darwin Bennett, Tony Feltrin, Herb Hammond,
Kevin McDonald, Martin Madden, Christer Rockstrom
Director of Business Administration ....John Gentile
Director of Team Operations ....Matthew Loughran
Scouting Manager...Bill Short
Executive Administrative Assistant...Barbara Cahill
Senior Secretary..Nicole Wetzold

MEDICAL\TRAINING STAFF

Team Physician and Orthopedic Surgeon ....Dr. Barton Nisonson
Assistant Team Physician...Dr. Anthony Maddalo
Medical Consultants......................................Drs. Howard Chester, Frank Gardner, Ronald Weissman
Team Dentists...Dr. Irwin Miller and Dr. Don Soloman
Sports Physiologist ....Howie Wenger
Medical Trainer...Jim Ramsay
Equipment Manager...Mike Folga
Massage Therapist..Bruce Lifrieri
Video Assistant ....Jerry Dineen
Staff Assistant ....Brad Kolodny

PUBLIC RELATIONS DEPARTMENT

Director of Public Relations...Brooks Thomas
Assistant Director of Public Relations...John Rosasco
Public Relations Assistant ....Rob Koch
Administrative Assistant...Ann Marie Gilmartin

MARKETING DEPARTMENT

Vice President of Marketing ....Kevin Kennedy
Director of Community Relations...Rod Gilbert
Promotions Manager ....Caroline Calabrese
Manager of Marketing Operations ....Jim Pfeifer
Manager of Event Presentation...Jeanie Baumgartner

ADDITIONAL INFORMATION

Executive Offices...Madison Square Garden
Home Ice ....Madison Square Garden
Seating Capacity 18,200
Largest Crowd 18,200
Press Facilities..33rd Street
Television Facilities ....31st Street
Radio Facilities ....33rd Street
Rink Dimensions..200 feet x 85 feet
Ends and Sides of Rink..Plexiglass (8 feet)
Club Colors...Blue, Red White
Uniforms...Home- Base color white, trimmed with blue and red
Road- Base color blue, trimmed with red and white
Practice Facility ....Rye, New York

1995-96 RANGERS SCHEDULE

OCTOBER

Sun	Mon	Tue	Wed	Thu	Fri	Sat
1	2	3	4	5	6	7 HFD
8	9	10	11 WPG	12	13	14 TOR
15	16 HFD	17 NYI	18	19	20 BUF	21
22 OTT	23	24 VAN	25	26 T.B.	27	28
29 TOR	30	31 SJ				

NOVEMBER

Sun	Mon	Tue	Wed	Thu	Fri	Sat
			1	2 LA	3 ANA	4
5	6 CGY	7	8 T.B.	9	10 NYI	11 HFD
12	13	14 ST. L	15	16 CHI	17 WPG	18
19	20	21 PIT	22 PIT	23	24	25 DET
26	27 NJ	28	29 BUF	30		

DECEMBER

Sun	Mon	Tue	Wed	Thu	Fri	Sat
					1 COL	2 OTT
3	4 ANA	5	6 CHI	7	8 DET	9 MTL
10	11 DAL	12	13 BOS	14	15 BUF	16 WSH
17	18 WSH	19	20	21 PHI	22 HFD	23
24 / 31 CGY	25	26 OTT	27	28 VAN	29	30 EDM

JANUARY

Sun	Mon	Tue	Wed	Thu	Fri	Sat
	1	2	3 MTL	4	5 WSH	6
7	8 WSH	9	10 SJ	11	12	13 PHI
14 ST. L	15	16	17	18	19	20 ALL-STAR GAME BOS
21	22 LA	23	24 PHI	25	26	27 BOS
28	29	30	31 DAL			

FEBRUARY

Sun	Mon	Tue	Wed	Thu	Fri	Sat
				1	2	3 COL
4	5	6 NYI	7	8 NYI	9	10 NJ
11 T.B.	12	13	14	15 MTL	16	17 OTT
18 PIT	19	20	21	22 NYI	23	24 FLA
25	26	27	28 BOS	29		

MARCH

Sun	Mon	Tue	Wed	Thu	Fri	Sat
					1 BUF	2
3	4 NJ	5	6	7 T.B.	8	9 WSH
10	11	12	13 FLA	14	15	16 MTL
17	18	19 EDM	20	21	22	23 BOS
24 PIT / 31 NYI	25	26	27 FLA	28	29	30

APRIL

Sun	Mon	Tue	Wed	Thu	Fri	Sat
	1	2 NJ	3	4 PHI	5 PHI	6
7 NJ	8 FLA	9	10 WSH	11	12 T.B.	13
14 FLA	15	16	17	18	19	20

Rangers home starting time is 7:30 PM, except:
10/22, 7:00 PM; 10/29, 6:00 PM; 1/14, 3/24, 8:00 PM;
Season Subscription   (212) 465-6073
Group Sales   (212) 465-6080

TICKETMASTER
(212) 307-7171   (609) 520-8383
(201) 507-8900   (914) 454-3388
(516) 888-9000   (203) 624-0033

HOME   **AWAY**

5

NEIL SMITH

PRESIDENT and
GENERAL MANAGER

Born: January 9, 1954
Toronto, Ontario

Through the first six years of his tenure at the helm of the Rangers, Neil Smith has become one of the most successful men to ever run the club in the history of the franchise.

During his tenure, the Rangers have posted an overall record of 230-173-53, ranking sixth among all NHL teams through the six year stretch. New York has captured three divisional titles, two Presidents' Trophies, and one Stanley Cup Championship.

In 1993-94, Neil's diligence and persistence to build the Rangers into a Stanley Cup Championship winning club came to fruition on June 14 when the team captured the fourth Stanley Cup in franchise history, defeating Vancouver four games to three. The championship was the culmination of a record setting season in which New York set a club record with 52 wins and 112 points. The Rangers captured their second Presidents' Trophy in three years and became the first team since the Presidents' Trophy was established to win it, along with the Conference Championship and Stanley Cup in the same year.

Following the season, Neil was awarded with the *Hockey News* Executive of the Year Award. Neil was also honored by the New Jersey Sports Writer's Associations' as their Executive of the Year.

In his first three seasons as general manager after joining the Rangers on July 17, New York finished in first place twice, including the 1991-92 Presidents' Trophy and second place once, marking the best three consecutive finishes in club history.

Neil's outstanding accomplishments with the Rangers in 1991-92 were recognized following the season with two tremendous honors.

First, he was named the NHL Executive of the Year by *The Sporting News*, as voted by NHL general managers and governors, becoming the first Rangers executive to ever capture the award.

Then on June 19, 1992, he was promoted to the position of president and general manager, becoming the ninth president in Rangers history and the first president to also hold the title of general manager.

Neil has built the Rangers through his extraordinary ability to recognize talent and by making bold moves when necessary.

Through the NHL Entry Draft, Neil has added players like Sergei Nemchinov, Alexei Kovalev, and Mattias Norstrom to the Rangers roster, while loading the organization's depth chart with top prospects at every position: goaltenders Dan Cloutier, and Jamie Ram; defensemen Eddy Campbell, Mike Martin, Eric Cairns, Scott Malone, Lee Sorochan, Adam

Smith, Maxim Galanov and forwards Peter and Chris Ferraro, Niklas Sundstrom, Dimitri Starostenko, Rudolf Vercik, Christian Dube, Marc Savard and Vladimir Vorobiev.

In addition, when given an opportunity to improve the club through trades or signing free agents, Neil has acted quickly to add even more talent to the Rangers lineup. He has made deals to acquire Mark Messier, Luc Robitaille, Ulf Samuelsson, Jeff Beukeboom, Kevin Lowe, Glenn Healy, Pat Verbeek and Nathan LaFayette and signed Adam Graves as a free agent. Neil made perhaps the boldest moves of his tenure on March 21, 1994, making trades to acquire Glenn Anderson, Craig MacTavish, Brian Noonan and Stephane Matteau at the deadline to help lead the team to the Stanley Cup.

During the off season, Neil continued to improve the club by adding free agents Ray Ferraro, Bruce Driver and Wayne Presley, while acquiring Robitaille, Samuelsson and Doug Lidster in trades.

A native of Toronto, Ontario, Smith played junior hockey at Brockville, Ontario, before entering Western Michigan University, where he became an All-America defenseman as a freshman and team captain in his second year. In September of 1991, Neil was inducted into the school's Hall of Fame, the first hockey player ever given the honor.

After being selected by the New York Islanders in the NHL Amateur draft and playing two seasons in the International Hockey League, Neil joined the Islanders scouting department during the 1980-81 season.

Following two seasons in that capacity, he joined the Detroit Red Wings in 1982 as director of professional scouting and soon after became director of their entire farm system.

Smith was then named director of scouting, and general manager/governor of the Adirondack Red Wings of the AHL, where he won two Calder Cup championships.

Neil, who is a board member of the National Child Abuse Prevention Center and with Ice Hockey in Harlem, was recently named to the board at DISHES, a charity for pediatric AIDS. He lives with his wife, Katia, in New York City.

COLIN CAMPBELL

HEAD COACH

**Born: January 28, 1953
London, Ontario**

Colin Campbell begins his second season as head coach of the Rangers after being named to the post on August 9, 1994. He was promoted to the position after serving in various capacities in the organization over the previous five years, including assistant coach, associate coach and half of the 1992-93 season as head coach of the Rangers American Hockey League affiliate at Binghamton. Colin made his head coaching debut on January 20 vs. Buffalo and earned his first NHL victory on January 21 vs. Montreal.

Campbell, 42, began his coaching career in 1985-86 with the Detroit Red Wings, following his retirement as a player after the 1984-85 season. He worked a total of five seasons as a Red Wings assistant coach, including one season under coach Harry Neale and four seasons under coach Jacques Demers.

The native of London, Ontario, joined the Rangers organization in August of 1990 as an assistant coach to Roger Neilson. He served in that role until January 4, 1993, when he became head coach of the Binghamton Rangers. He guided Binghamton to a record of 29-8-5, helping them set AHL records for wins (57) and points (124) in a single season.

On June 21, 1993, Campbell was promoted to associate coach of New York, under head coach Mike Keenan, helping the Rangers set team records for wins (52) and points in a season (112), while capturing the Presidents' Trophy and the Stanley Cup.

Before joining the coaching ranks, Campbell played 12 seasons of professional hockey as a defensive defenseman. After being drafted by the Pittsburgh Penguins as their third choice, 27th overall, in the second round of the 1973 Amateur Draft, he opted to join the Vancouver Blazers of the World Hockey Association where he was coached by former Rangers Phil Watson and Andy Bathgate.

Following one season in the WHA, he went on to play 11 seasons in the National Hockey League beginning with the Penguins in 1973-74. After two seasons with Pittsburgh he was dealt to the Colorado Rockies and played there for one year before being dealt back to Pittsburgh.

After two more years in Pittsburgh, he was claimed in the 1979 Expansion Draft by the Edmonton Oilers where he was teammates with Mark Messier and Kevin Lowe. Following his only season in Edmonton he was claimed by the Vancouver Canucks in the NHL Waiver draft where he played for two seasons. In 1981-82 he helped the Canucks to the Stanley Cup Finals under coach Roger Neilson, playing in 16 of 17 post-season matches.

Colin signed as a free agent with Detroit in July of 1982 and played for three seasons with the Red Wings before becoming an assistant coach with the club. He played in a total of 636 NHL contests, collecting 25 goals and 103 assists for 128 points along with 1,292 penalty minutes.

"Colie", who is a licensed pilot, owns and operates the Colin Campbell Hockey School in Tillsonburg, Ontario for three weeks each summer. He and his wife Heather reside in Rye, New York with their three children; daughters, Lauren and Courtney and son Gregory.

8

LARRY PLEAU

ASSISTANT GENERAL MANAGER/ PLAYER DEVELOPMENT

Larry Pleau, who joined the Rangers organization in August of 1989, enters his seventh season as the club's assistant general manager/player development.

Pleau assists Neil Smith, the team's president and general manager, with the development of all amateur players in the organization, while he also oversees the day-to-day operation of the Rangers scouting department. In addition, he works closely with Smith on player transactions and the selection of players at the NHL Entry Draft. Last season, Larry added the duties of general manager of New York's American Hockey League affiliate at Binghamton.

Pleau, who served as the assistant general manager for the 1991 United States Canada Cup Team, travels extensively throughout the year to Europe, Canada and across the United States to prepare for the draft and check on the development of Rangers prospects playing in high school, college, junior hockey or in Europe.

Pleau, 48, played three seasons with the Montreal Canadiens (1969-70 - 1971-72) in the National Hockey League, before being the first player signed by the Hartford Whalers of the World Hockey Association. He was a center/left wing for the Whalers from 1972 until his retirement in 1979. He played in a total of 468 regular-season games for Hartford, accumulating 157 goals and 215 assists for 372 points. In 66 playoff contests, he registered 29 goals and 22 assists for 51 points.

During his time with the Whalers, Larry scored 25 goals or more on four occasions and was selected to play in the WHA All-Star Game three times (1973, 1974 and 1975).

Pleau also played for the 1968 United States Olympic Team, the 1969 U.S. National Team and for Team USA in the 1976 Canada Cup Tournament.

A native of Lynn, Massachusetts, Larry became an assistant coach with the Whalers in 1979. He remained in that position until Feb. 20, 1981, when he took the reins as head coach.

The following season he added to his responsibilities as head coach and became the club's director of hockey operations. During his tenure the Whalers drafted many current NHL players including; Ray Ferraro, Kevin Dineen, Ulf Samuelsson and Sylvain Cote.

After two seasons in that position and a year as assistant general manager under Emile Francis, Pleau became director of hockey operations and head coach of the Binghamton Whalers of the American Hockey League in 1984-85.

In his first season at Binghamton, he led the team to a first-place finish with a record of 52-20-8 and in his third season (1986-87) he guided the club to a mark of 47-26-7, as he was named the AHL's Coach of the Year.

Larry remained in Binghamton for three and a half seasons before returning to Hartford as head coach for the remainder of the 1987-88 campaign and all of the 1988-89 season.

Larry and his wife, Wendy reside in Seabrook, New Hampshire with their son, Steve, and daughter, Shannon. Steve recently completed his junior year at the University of New Hampshire, where he played on the school's hockey team.

ASSISTANT COACHES

Mike Murphy

Mike Murphy enters his second year as an assistant coach with the Rangers, following a three year stint as assistant coach with the Toronto Maple Leafs. Murphy was named to the post on August 24, 1994.

Murphy, 44, began his coaching career as an assistant coach with the Los Angles Kings on January 30, 1984. Murphy served briefly as a a special assistant to the general manager after his retirement as a player with the Kings in October of 1983 before joining the coaching staff.

The native of Toronto, Ontario worked as an assistant to head coach Pat Quinn for three seasons until January 10, 1987 when he took over as the club's head coach. Murphy signed on as an assistant coach with Vancouver on March 3, 1988 following his career with Los Angeles. He was named head coach of the Canucks International Hockey League affiliate in Milwaukee for the 1990-91 season and guided the Admirals for one season before joining the Maple Leafs coaching staff.

Murphy was originally drafted by the Rangers in the second round, 25th overall, in the 1970 NHL Amateur Draft. He was named the CHL Rookie-of-the-Year with the Ranger minor league affiliate in Omaha in 1970-71. He was dealt to St. Louis in 1971 -72 and then dealt back to New York in March of 1973. After appearing in 31 games with New York, tallying six goals and five assists, Murphy was then traded to Los Angeles on November 30, 1973 where he played for 10 and a half seasons, including six as the team captain. The right-winger tallied 238 goals and 318 assists for 556 points in 831 career matches.

Mike and his wife Yvonne reside in Aurora, Ontario with their four children; Sean, Ryan, Breeann and Patrick.

Dick Todd

Dick Todd begins his third season as an assistant coach with the Rangers. Todd joined the Rangers on July 7, 1993 following a 21 year career with the Peterborough Petes, including the last 12 as head coach.

The native of Peterborough, Ontario posted a career record of 477-239-53 along with a .655 winning percentage. Under Todd's guidance, Peterborough won four Leyden Division Championships, two OHL Playoff Championship and advanced to two Memorial Cup Finals. In his 12 seasons behind the bench, the Petes have finished lower than third only one time. In his last two seasons, the Petes' compiled a record of 87-33-12 for a .705 winning percentage.

Todd, 50, led Team Canada to a gold medal at the 1991 World Junior Tournament in Saskatoon and in 1990, he was the assistant coach for Team Canada when they earned a silver medal at the World Junior Championships in Helsinki, Finland. In 1987-88 he was selected by his peers as the OHL Coach of the Year.

Over the past two decades, Todd held many different positions with the Petes, including trainer, head coach, and general manager. He began his coaching career halfway through the 1981-82 season, replacing Dave Dryden. He remained as head coach through '92-93 season when he led Peterborough to a 46-15-5 record, finishing with the best record in the OHL and winning the OHL Playoff Championship.

In his 12 years behind the bench for the Petes, Todd coached numerous players who have since gone on to the NHL including: Steve Yzerman, Mike Ricci, Chris Pronger, Kay Whitmore, Kris King, Jody Hull, Tie Domi, Terry Carkner, Randy Burridge, Bob Errey, Ron Tugnutt and Luke Richardson.

Dick currently resides in Rye with his wife, Mary. Their daughter, Terri-Anne, is a teacher in Peterborough.

SCOUTING STAFF

Darwin Bennett
Entering his third year with the Rangers ... Primarily scouts players in the Ontario Hockey League and Western Hockey League ... Joined the scouting staff on August 4, 1993 after spending the previous eight seasons as a scout with the Quebec Nordiques ... Promoted to the position of assistant to the chief scout in 1989 ... Joined the Nordiques scouting staff in 1986, following four seasons scouting for the Prince Albert Raiders of the Western Hockey League ... Worked for 13 years in the Saskatchewan government, including six years as the director of personnel prior to joining the Nordiques in 1986 ... Single.

Tony Feltrin
Beginning his 10th year as a scout with New York after retiring as a player in September of 1986 ... Primarily scouts players in the Western Hockey League, while also evaluating talent in the Ontario Hockey League and Quebec Major Junior Hockey League ... Played parts of four seasons in the National Hockey League, including 10 games with New York during the 1985-86 season ... Suffered a severe eye injury on Dec. 31, 1985, while playing with New Haven of the American Hockey League ... Married: wife, Kelly; children, Kurt and Carli.

Herb Hammond
Enters his seventh season with the Rangers ... Is responsible for scouting U.S. colleges and high schools ... Worked at Brown University from 1982-89 ... Was school's head coach from 1982 to 1988 and served as assistant athletic director in 1988-89 ... Coached prep schools in Albany and North Yarmouth beginning in 1958 ... Moved to the college coaching ranks in 1968 and guided Plattsburgh and Oswego State Colleges before going to Brown ... Earned his Bachelor's degree in history and physical education and his Master's degree in counseling from Springfield College ... Married: wife, Patricia; daughters, Leslie and Heather.

Martin Madden
Begins his fifth season with New York ... Is responsible for scouting Quebec, Ontario and Western Canada ... Joined the Rangers scouting staff in 1990 as a part time scout in the Quebec area ... Served as General Manager of Quebec Nordiques from 1988 to February of 1990 ... Worked as the chief scout of Quebec from 1981 to 1988 ... Coached the Quebec Ramparts from 1978 to 1980 ... Worked with Central Scouting from 1975-78 ... Was a scout for the Philadelphia Flyers from 1969 to 1975 ... Married: wife, Nicole; children, Martin Jr. and Karen ... Martin Jr. joined the staff as a part time scout last season.

Christer Rockstrom
Beginning his seventh year as the Rangers European scout ... Covered Sweden and part of Europe for the Detroit Red Wings from 1984 to 1989 ... Is one of the most highly regarded evaluators of European talent in the NHL ... Has tremendous knowledge of players at all levels and in different areas including Sweden, Finland, Russia and Czechoslovakia ... Makes his home in Stockholm, Sweden ... Single.

TRAINING STAFF

Mike Folga — Equipment Manager

Beginning his third season with the Rangers ... Served as one of the trainers for the 1994 NHL All-Star Game at MSG ... Joined the Rangers after working as head trainer for the Indianapolis Ice (IHL) in '92-93 ... Served as the head trainer for the St. Louis Blues from '87-88 through '90-91 ... Graduated from Mercyhurst College with a Bachelor of Science in Sports Medicine ... Played minor league baseball in the St. Louis Cardinals organization in '80 and '81 ... Head baseball coach at Behrend College following his baseball career ... Resides in Rye, New York ... Son, Dakota.

Bruce Lifrieri — Massage Therapist

Bruce "The Masseuse" enters his third season as a full time member of the Rangers training staff ... Worked with the club on a part-time basis from 1986-87 to 1992-93 ... Worked the 1994 NHL All-Star Game at MSG ... Attended Westchester Community College and Pace University ... Attended the Dr. Victor Scherer Academy of Physiotherapy ... Is a lifelong resident of Westchester county ... Single.

Jim Ramsay — Medical Trainer

Begins his second season with the Rangers after spending the last five seasons with the Winnipeg Jets ... Was selected to be part of the training staff for the Western Conference team at the 1994 NHL All-Star Game held at MSG on Jan. 22 ... Began his career with the Jets in 1989 after working two years in a private sports medicine practice in Winnipeg ... Graduated with honors from the University of Manitoba ... Played junior hockey in Manitoba and was teammates with Vancouver Canucks center Mike Ridley ... Married the former Anita Rhodes on July 14 ... Son, Mason.

Howie Wenger — Sports Physiologist

Begins his third year with the Rangers ... Joined the staff last year after serving as a consultant with the Los Angeles Kings from 1986 to 1993 ... Has also worked as a consultant with Edmonton ('78-'80), and Vancouver ('81-'83) and the 1991 Canadian Team in the Canada Cup Tournament ... Received his Ph.D. in Exercise Physiology from the University of Alberta ... Currently teaches exercise physiology courses at the University of Victoria ... Married; wife, Jan; sons, Matthew and Dave; daughter, Sonja.

IN MEMORIAM

Benny Petrizzi, a lockerroom assistant at the Rangers training facility in Rye, N.Y. for the past 13 seasons, passed away in September at the age of 82. He is survived by his wife, Fannie; son, Robert; and two grandchildren, Sara and Torrey.

THE PLAYERS

JEFF BEUKEBOOM

23

6-5 • 230 • Shoots Right
Born: March 28, 1965
Ajax, Ontario
Off-Season Home:
Dunsford, Ontario

DEFENSE

1994-95: Appeared in 44 of the 48 matches ... Registered his only goal of the season on Apr. 26 vs. Tampa Bay ... Notched an assist on Steve Larmer's shorthanded goal on Apr. 12 vs. Buffalo ... Registered an assist on Darren Langdon's first NHL goal on February 18 at Montreal ... Skated in his 500th NHL match on Feb. 8 vs. Washington ... New York was 0-4 in the four games he missed due to injury ... Registered a plus or even rating in 24 of his last 29 games with a plus eight rating over the span ... Rangers were 3-1-0 when he registered a point.

NHL CAREER: 1985-86: Began the season in Edmonton after a solid training camp, but was sent to Nova Scotia (AHL) on Oct. 15 before seeing any action ... Recalled on Feb. 10, but did not play and was returned the following day ... Made his NHL debut in a playoff game against Vancouver on Apr. 10. **1986-87:** Started the campaign with the Oilers and appeared in his initial regular-season contest on Oct. 17 vs. Detroit and notched his first NHL point with an assist on a goal by Jari Kurri ... Sent to Nova Scotia on Nov. 3 and played in 14 games ... Recalled on Dec. 3 and remained with Edmonton for the rest of the season... First NHL goal was a game-winning, power play tally in 7-3 win at Vancouver on Dec. 30. **1987-88:** Produced career highs in assists (20), points (25) and penalty minutes (201) in his first full season in NHL ... Registered the longest point scoring streak of his career, four games, from Jan. 11-Jan. 18 ... Accumulated a career high three assists in Buffalo on Nov. 29. **1988-89:** Suspended for 10 games in the beginning of the season for leaving the bench in a pre-season contest ... Sent to Cape Breton for conditioning on Nov. 17, returning on Nov. 30 ... Missed 11 games with knee injury suffered in Chicago on Jan. 16. **1989-90:** Appeared in 46 games, collecting 13 points. **1990-91:** Plus six rating ranked fourth among club defensemen and 150 PIM placed fourth on the team ... Was unsuccessful on the first penalty shot of his career in the season opener on Oct. 6, when he was stopped by Winnipeg's Richard Tabaracci. **1991-92:** Obtained from Edmonton on Nov. 12 in exchange for David Shaw as future considerations from the Mark Messier trade ... Played in his 300th NHL game on Dec. 21 at Pittsburgh ... Compiled a plus 19 rating in 56 games with New York ... Missed four games due to suspension and one game to injury ... Tallied his first goal as a Ranger on Jan. 6 vs. Winnipeg. **1992-93:** Appeared in 82 games in his first full season with New York ... Placed third on the team and first among backliners with a plus nine rating ... Tied a career high for points and

assists in game, with three vs. Tampa Bay on Dec. 9. **1993-94:** Set a career-high, tallying eight goals ... Notched his first power play goal since Jan. 18, 1988 at Montreal, while with Edmonton, on Jan. 3 vs. Florida ... Notched his first career two-goal game, including his 100th career point on Nov. 13 vs. San Jose ... Tied for fifth on the club with a plus 18 rating ... Rangers were 12-2-1 when he registered a point and 5-1-0 when he scored a goal. **1994 PLAYOFFS:** Tallied six assists in 21 matches, notching five of the six on the road ... Tallied a pair of assists, including one on Glenn Anderson's game-winning goal, and a plus four rating in Game Three of the Finals on June 4 at Vancouver ... Placed second on the team and second in the NHL with a plus 17 rating.

AHL CAREER: Played a total of 99 American Hockey League games in three different stints ... Spent almost the entire '85-86 season with Nova Scotia, where the leading scorer of the club was former Rangers center Mike Rogers ... Played 14 games with Nova Scotia in '86-87 and eight games in a conditioning stint with Cape Breton in 88-89.

JUNIOR CAREER: Played three seasons with the Sault Ste. Marie Greyhounds of the Ontario Hockey League from 1982 to 1985 ... Named as the OHL's best defenseman by the league's coaches in 1984-85 ... Named an OHL first-team All-Star and earned a spot on the Emms Division All-Star team in 1985.

INTERNATIONAL COMPETITION: Was a member of Canadian team that won the World Junior tournament in Finland in 1985.

BACKGROUND: Was a member of three Stanley Cup teams with Oilers... Selected by Edmonton in the first round of the 1983 Entry Draft, he is the only first-round pick ever selected in the first round who did not score a goal in year prior to draft... His brother, John, played with the Adirondack Red Wings (AHL) and Kalamazoo Wings (IHL) in 1986-87 ... Wore uniform number six with Edmonton ... Is a nephew of former NHL'er Ed Kea ... Enjoys fishing and golfing in the off-season ... Married: wife, Sherri; daughter, Tyson and son, Brock.

CAREER TRANSACTIONS: *June 8, 1983 —* Edmonton's first round choice (19th overall) in the 1983 NHL Entry Draft. *Nov. 12, 1991 —* Traded by Edmonton to New York in exchange for David Shaw as the future considerations in the Mark Messier trade made on Oct. 4.

J
E
F
F

23

B
E
U
K
E
B
O
O
M

CAREER HIGHLIGHTS

MOST GOALS, GAME: 2, Nov. 14, 1993 vs. S.J., **MOST ASSISTS, GAME:** 3 (twice) last- Dec. 9, 1992 vs. T.B., **MOST POINTS, GAME:** 3 (twice) last- Dec. 9, 1992 vs. T.B., **MOST PIM, GAME:** 26, Oct. 8, 1991 vs. L.A., **MOST SHOTS, GAME:** 5 (3 times) last- Jan. 3, 1994 vs. Fla., **MOST SHOTS, SEASON:** 76, 1987-88, **HIGHEST +/-, SEASON:** 27, 1987-88, **FIRST NHL GAME**: Oct. 17, 1986 vs. Det., **FIRST NHL GOAL:** Dec. 30, 1986 at Van. (Brodeur)

AMATEUR AND PROFESSIONAL RECORD

Season	Club	Lea	GP	G	A	PTS	PIM	GP	G	A	PTS	PIM
			Regular Season					**Playoffs**				
1981-82	Newmarket	OPJHL	49	5	30	35	218	—	—	—	—	—
1982-83	Sault Ste. Marie	OHL	70	0	25	25	143	16	1	4	5	46
1983-84	Sault Ste. Marie	OHL	61	6	30	36	178	16	1	7	8	43
1984-85	Sault Ste. Marie	OHL	37	4	20	24	85	16	4	6	10	47
1985-86	Edmonton	NHL	—	—	—	—	—	1	0	0	0	4
1985-86	Nova Scotia	AHL	77	9	20	29	175	—	—	—	—	—
1986-87	Edmonton	NHL	44	3	8	11	124	—	—	—	—	—
1986-87	Nova Scotia	AHL	14	1	7	8	35	—	—	—	—	—
1987-88	Edmonton	NHL	73	5	20	25	201	7	0	0	0	16
1988-89	Edmonton	NHL	36	0	5	5	94	1	0	0	0	2
1988-89	Cape Breton	AHL	8	0	4	4	36	—	—	—	—	—
1989-90	Edmonton	NHL	46	1	12	13	86	2	0	0	0	0
1990-91	Edmonton	NHL	67	3	7	10	150	18	1	3	4	28
1991-92	Edmonton	NHL	18	0	5	5	78	—	—	—	—	—
1991-92	Rangers	NHL	56	1	10	11	122	13	2	3	5	47
1992-93	Rangers	NHL	82	2	17	19	153	—	—	—	—	—
1993-94	Rangers	NHL	68	8	8	16	170	22	0	6	6	50
1994-95	Rangers	NHL	44	1	3	4	70	9	0	0	0	10
NHL Totals			534	24	95	119	1248	73	3	12	15	157
Rangers Totals			250	12	38	50	515	44	2	9	11	107

BRUCE DRIVER

33

6-0 • 185 • Shoots Left
Born: April 29, 1962
Toronto, Ontario
Off-Season Home:
Toronto, Ontario

DEFENSE

1994-95: Signed with the Rangers as an unrestricted free agent on Aug. 24 ... Skated in 41 games with New Jersey, tallying four goals and 12 assists for 16 points last season ... Registered a plus or even rating in 29 of his 41 matches ... Skated in his 700th NHL match on Apr. 26 vs. Pittsburgh ... Collected one goal and six assists for seven points while appearing in 17 of New Jersey's 20 playoff matches and capturing his first Stanley Cup Championship ... Tied for the club lead with a plus 13 rating.

NHL CAREER: 1983-84: Joined the Devils following his participation in the 1984 Winter Olympics with Team Canada ... Made his NHL debut on Mar. 2 vs. Vancouver and tallied his first NHL point with an assist. **1984-85:** Placed second among Devils defensemen with nine goals and 32 points in his first full season in the NHL ... Missed 13 games due to a sprained knee suffered on Mar. 5 at Washington ... Notched assists (seven) in four consecutive games from Dec. 8 to Dec. 15 ... Tallied four assists on Dec. 15 vs. Quebec, tying the franchise record for assists in a game by a defenseman and establishing the record for assists in a game by a rookie. **1985-86:** Began the season with New Jersey before being sent to Maine on Jan. 2 ... Was recalled on Feb. 3 and tallied eight points in 15 games before suffering a season ending shoulder separation on Mar. 9. **1986-87:** Led Devils defensemen with 28 assists and 34 points while appearing in 74 games ... Established a team record for points in a game by a defenseman with five (one goal, four assists) in an 8-5 loss vs. the Rangers at MSG ... Notched his first career point for points on Jan. 12 vs. Hartford. **1987-88:** Led New Jersey backliners with 15 goals, 40 assists and 55 points ... Tied the team record for assists by a defenseman with 40 ... Posted a six game scoring streak (one goal, seven assists) from Jan. 21 to Feb. 1 ... Placed second on the club with 34 points on the power play ... Collected three goals and seven assists for 10 points while appearing in all 20 post-season matches, helping New Jersey reach the Conference Finals. **1988-89:** Appeared in only 27 games after sustaining a fractured right fibula suffered in a collision with Washington's Lou Franceschetti on Dec. 7. **1989-90:** Led New Jersey defensemen with 53 points while appearing in a career high 75 games ... Also notched a career high 46 assists ... Notched a four-game scoring streak (one goal, nine assists) from Nov. 17 to Nov. 24 ... Led the team with 18 power play assists ... Set a club record with 12 shots on goal on Feb. 17 at Toronto ... Collected 11 multiple point games, including a four assist effort at Pittsburgh on Nov. 22 ...**1990-91:** Led New Jersey defense-

men with 45 points ... Tied a career high with seven ppg's ... Posted a five-game scoring streak (one goal, five assists) from Oct. 6 to Oct. 13 ... Missed seven games due to a rib injury suffered on Jan. 8 vs. St. Louis. **1991-92:** Named team captain at the beginning of the season ... Tallied three goals and 13 assists on the power play and one goal and four assists while shorthanded ... Tallied four assists in seven playoff matches vs. the Rangers. **1992-93:** Led New Jersey rearguards with 14 goals and placed second among backliners with 54 points while appearing in a career high 83 games ... Relinquished captaincy following the arrival of Scott Stevens and served as an alternate ... Placed second on the team with 24 power play points ... **1993-94:** Suffered a shoulder injury on Dec. 5 at MSG and missed 14 games ... Notched three goals and 14 assists on the power play ... Posted a career best, plus 29 rating ... Registered a point in seven of the Devils 20 post-season matches, registering three goals and five assists.

AHL CAREER: Joined the Maine Mariners after a four-game stint with New Jersey following the 1984 Winter Olympics ... Tallied 10 assists in 16 playoff matches, helping the Mariners to the Calder Cup Championship ...

COLLEGE CAREER: Played three seasons at the University of Wisconsin from 1980-81 to 1982-83 ... Teammates included Islanders winger Patrick Flatley ... Tallied seven goals and 37 assists for 44 points in 46 matches, helping the Badgers to the NCAA championship ... Earned honors as a WCHA First Team All-Star in 1982 and was also selected to the NCAA All-Tournament Team that year.

INTERNATIONAL CAREER: Tallied three goals and one assist for Team Canada in the 1984 Winter Olympics in Yugoslavia ... Played for Team Canada in the 1987 World Championships.

BACKGROUND: Captured the Devils "Unsung Hero" Award in 1990-91 and was awarded the "Good Guy" Award for cooperation with the media in 1991-92 ... Wore number 32 in his first season with New Jersey and then switched to number 23 ... Was New Jersey's nominee for the Masterton Trophy in 1989-90 ... Married: wife, Tracy; daughter, Whitney Amanda Williams; son, Dillon.

CAREER TRANSACTIONS: *June 10, 1981* — Rockies' sixth round choice (108th overall) in the 1981 NHL Entry Draft. *August 24, 1995* — Signed by the Rangers as an unrestricted free agent.

CAREER HIGHLIGHTS

MOST GOALS, GAME: 2, (3 times) last, Feb. 5, 1995 vs. Pit., **MOST ASSISTS, GAME:** 4, (2 times) last, Nov. 22, 1990 vs Minn., **MOST POINTS, GAME:** 5, Dec. 23, 1986 at NYR., **MOST PIM, GAME:** 17, Jan. 2, 1990 vs Buf., **MOST SHOTS, GAME:**, 12, Feb. 17, 1990 at Tor., **MOST SHOTS, SEASON:** 205, 1991-92, **HIGHEST +/-, SEASON:** 13, 1994-95, **FIRST NHL GOAL:** Mar. 2, 1984 at Van., **FIRST NHL GOAL:** Oct. 19, 1984 vs. Tor. (Bester)

BRUCE 33 DRIVER

AMATEUR AND PROFESSIONAL RECORD

SEASON	CLUB	LEAGUE	Regular Season					Playoffs				
			GP	G	A	PTS	PIM	GP	G	A	PTS	PIM
1978-79	Royal York	OPJHL	45	13	36	49	—	—	—	—	—	—
1979-80	Royal York	OPJHL	48	23	49	72	—	—	—	—	—	—
1980-81	Wisconsin	WCHA	42	5	15	20	42	—	—	—	—	—
1981-82	Wisconsin	WCHA	46	7	37	44	84	—	—	—	—	—
1982-83	Wisconsin	WCHA	49	19	42	61	100	—	—	—	—	—
1983-84	Canadian National		52	8	15	23	22	—	—	—	—	—
1983-84	Canadian Olympic		7	3	1	4	10	—	—	—	—	—
1983-84	New Jersey	NHL	4	0	2	2	0	—	—	—	—	—
1983-84	Maine	AHL	12	2	6	8	15	16	0	10	10	8
1984-85	New Jersey	NHL	67	9	23	32	36	—	—	—	—	—
1985-86	New Jersey	NHL	40	3	15	18	32	—	—	—	—	—
1985-86	Maine	AHL	15	4	7	11	16	—	—	—	—	—
1986-87	New Jersey	NHL	74	6	28	34	36	—	—	—	—	—
1987-88	New Jersey	NHL	74	15	40	55	68	20	3	7	10	14
1988-89	New Jersey	NHL	27	1	15	16	24	—	—	—	—	—
1989-90	New Jersey	NHL	75	7	46	53	63	6	1	5	6	6
1990-91	New Jersey	NHL	73	9	36	45	62	7	1	2	3	12
1991-92	New Jersey	NHL	78	7	35	42	66	7	0	4	4	2
1992-93	New Jersey	NHL	83	14	40	54	66	5	1	3	4	4
1993-94	New Jersey	NHL	66	8	24	32	63	20	3	5	8	12
1994-95	New Jersey	NHL	41	4	12	16	18	17	1	6	7	8
NHL Totals			702	83	316	499	83	82	10	32	42	57

RAY FERRARO

21

5-10 • 185 • Shoots Left
Born: Aug. 23, 1964 • Trail,
British Columbia
Off-Season Home:
Trail, British Columbia

CENTER

1994-95: Signed by the Rangers as an unrestricted free agent on Jul. 19 ... Appeared in 47 games with the Islanders last season, and led the team with 22 goals and 43 points ... Tied for first on the team with 21 assists ... Also, tied for 18th in the NHL with 22 goals and ranked fourth in the league with a 23.4% shooting percentage ... Tallied 20 of his 22 goals at even strength ... Registered his 300th career assist on Feb. 7 vs. Tampa Bay ... Registered eight multiple-point games, including a four point effort (two goals, two assists) vs. Philadelphia on Feb. 2 ... Posted an eight game scoring streak from Jan. 28 to Feb. 14 (seven goals, seven assists) and recorded a seven game scoring streak from Mar. 26 to Apr. 8 (four goals, five assists).

NHL CAREER: 1984-85: Began the season with the Binghamton Whalers (AHL) ... Was recalled in Dec. and made his NHL debut on Dec. 19 vs. Boston ... Recorded his first NHL goal on Dec. 22 at Montreal and also added three assists ... Was returned to Binghamton and was recalled by Hartford on Feb. 5 and remained with the club for the rest of the season ... Recorded a pair of hat tricks, on Mar. 23 vs. Boston and on Mar. 29 vs. Edmonton ... Also, added a pair of assists on Mar. 29 vs. Edmonton, tying a club record for points in game when he scored with five ... **1985-86:** Tied for second on the team in scoring with 77 points in his first full season in the NHL ... Ranked second on the club with 47 assists and led the Whalers with 14 ppg's and a 22.7% shooting percentage ... Posted a team high eight game scoring streak from Mar. 5 to Mar. 20 (three goals, 11 assists) ... Posted 20 multiple point games ... Notched a point in seven of the club's 10 playoff outings. **1986-87:** One of four Whalers to appear in all 80 games ... Placed fourth on the team in scoring with 59 points ... Ranked first in the NHL with a 28.1 shooting percentage ... Led the club for the second consecutive season with 14 ppg's ... Notched his third career hat trick on Feb. 18 at New Jersey and his first of two four point efforts. **1987-88:** Tied for third on the club with 50 points ... Notched 18 of the 50 (six goals, 12 assists) on the power play. **1988-89:** Placed third on the Whalers in scoring and became the first Hartford player to reach the 40 goal plateau since Mike Rogers in 1980-81 ... Led the Whalers with seven game-winning goals. **1989-90:** Ranked fifth on the Whalers in scoring with 54 points ... Notched a career high 109 penalty minutes ... Equaled his career high with five points (three goals, two assists) vs. New Jersey on Dec. 9. **1990-91:** Began the season with Hartford and appeared in 15 games before being dealt to the Islanders on Nov. 13 ... Collected 35 points with the Islanders in 61 games ... Tallied two goals in his debut with the team on Nov. 15 vs. Calgary. **1991-92:** Skated in all 80 games for the third time in his career ... Tied for the team lead with 40 goals and notched a career high 80 points ... Ranked second on the club in scoring and also ranked second with a plus 25 rating ... Ranked third in the NHL with a 26.0% shooting percentage ... Named as an alternate captain mid-way through the season ... Tied for first on the team in even strength scoring with 66 points ... Recorded a pair of hat tricks, including a career high, four-goal game on Jan. 7 at Detroit ... Represented the Islanders at the NHL All-Star game in Philadelphia. **1992-93:** Skated in his 600th NHL game on Nov. 14 vs. Buffalo ... Suffered a fractured right fibula on Dec. 10 vs. Chicago ... Did not return until Mar. 9 ... Led the team and ranked sixth in the NHL in playoff scoring with 20 points in 18 matches ... Placed second in the NHL behind Wayne Gretzky (15) with 13 goals ... Netted two overtime game winners in games three and four of the Division Semi-Finals vs. Washington ... Joined Mike Bossy as the only Islanders players to tally four goals in a playoff match after netting four vs. Washington in Game Five. **1993-94:** Finished the season with a six game scoring streak (four goals, three assists) helping the club secure a playoff spot ... Placed seventh on the team in scoring ... Notched his 700th career penalty minute on Apr. 13 at Tampa Bay.

AHL CAREER: Made his professional debut with the Binghamton Whalers of the AHL in 1984-85 ... Tallied 20 goals and 13 assists in 37 games and was recalled by Hartford in February.

JUNIOR CAREER: Appeared in one season with the Portland Winter Hawks and collected 90 points ... Tallied 14 goals and 10 assists in 14 playoff matches, while leading the team to the Memorial Cup Championship ... Was dealt to the Brandon Wheat Kings the following season and recorded a WHL record 108 goals ... Led the league with 192 points and set CHL records with 15 hat tricks and 43 power play goals ... Tallied seven goals on Jan. 5, 1984 vs. Prince Albert ... Was named a first team All-Star and won the WHL MVP Award.

BACKGROUND: Has twice received the "Good Guy Award" as voted by the Professional Hockey Writers' Association, with the Whalers in 1988 and the Islanders in 1992 ... Was drafted by Rangers Assistant General Manager Larry Pleau who was General Manager of the Whalers in 1982 ... Also played for Pleau at Binghamton in 1984-85 and in 1988-89 with Hartford ... Wore number 26 with the Whalers and number 20 with the Islanders ... Was a member of the 1976 Canadian Little League Championship team from Trail, B.C. ... Played for Team Canada at the World Championships in 1989 ... Does considerable charitable work and was the Islanders nominee for the NHL Bud Light Man of the Year Award ... Is a fan of the Boston Red Sox and Seattle Seahawks ... Married; wife, Tracey; sons, Matthew and Landon.

CAREER TRANSACTIONS: *June 9, 1982 —* Whalers' fifth round choice (88th overall) in the 1982 NHL Entry Draft. *November 13, 1990 —* Traded by Hartford to the Islanders for Doug Crossman. *July 19, 1995 —* Signed as a free agent by the Rangers.

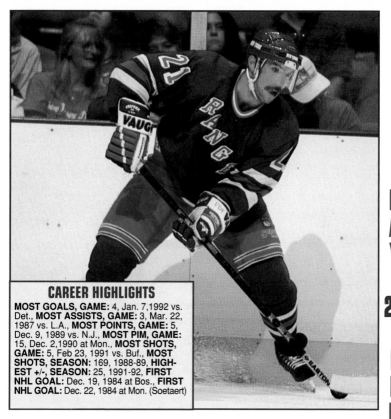

CAREER HIGHLIGHTS

MOST GOALS, GAME: 4, Jan. 7,1992 vs. Det., **MOST ASSISTS, GAME:** 3, Mar. 22, 1987 vs. L.A., **MOST POINTS, GAME:** 5, Dec. 9, 1989 vs. N.J., **MOST PIM, GAME:** 15, Dec. 2,1990 at Mon., **MOST SHOTS, GAME:** 5, Feb 23, 1991 vs. Buf., **MOST SHOTS, SEASON:** 169, 1988-89, **HIGHEST +/-, SEASON:** 25, 1991-92, **FIRST NHL GOAL:** Dec. 19, 1984 at Bos., **FIRST NHL GOAL:** Dec. 22, 1984 at Mon. (Soetaert)

R A Y 21 F E R R A R O

AMATEUR AND PROFESSIONAL RECORD

Season	Club	Lea	Regular Season					Playoffs				
			GP	G	A	PTS	PIM	GP	G	A	PTS	PIM
1982-83	Portland	WHL	50	41	49	90	39	14	14	10	24	13
1983-84	Brandon	WHL	72	108	84	192	84	11	13	15	28	20
1984-85	Hartford	NHL	44	11	17	28	40	—	—	—	—	—
1984-85	Binghamton	AHL	37	20	13	33	29	—	—	—	—	—
1985-86	Hartford	NHL	76	30	47	77	57	10	3	6	9	4
1986-87	Hartford	NHL	80	27	32	59	42	6	1	1	2	8
1987-88	Hartford	NHL	68	21	29	50	81	6	1	1	2	6
1988-89	Hartford	NHL	80	41	35	76	86	4	2	0	2	4
1989-90	Hartford	NHL	79	25	29	54	109	7	0	3	3	2
1990-91	Hartford	NHL	15	2	5	7	18	—	—	—	—	—
1990-91	NY Islanders	NHL	61	19	16	35	52	—	—	—	—	—
1991-92	NY Islanders	NHL	80	40	40	80	92	—	—	—	—	—
1992-93	NY Islanders	NHL	46	14	13	27	40	18	13	7	20	18
1992-93	Capital District	AHL	1	0	2	2	2	—	—	—	—	—
1993-94	NY Islanders	NHL	82	21	32	53	83	4	1	0	1	6
1994-95	NY Islanders	NHL	47	22	21	43	30	—	—	—	—	—
NHL Totals			783	373	316	589	730	55	21	18	39	48

ADAM GRAVES

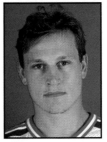

9

6-0 • 210 • Shoots Left
Born: April 12, 1968
Toronto, Ontario
Off-Season Home:
Tecumseh, Ontario

LEFT WING

1994-95: Was awarded the "Players' Player" Award for the third time in his four seasons with New York, for being the best "team player" as voted by his teammates ... Tied for first on the team with 17 goals and ranked fifth on the team in scoring with 31 points ... Collected five goals and six assists for 11 points in the final 11 games and registered 15 points (six goals, nine assists) in the last 17 games ... Tallied three assists on April 14 vs. the Bruins, including one on the power play and one on the game-winner ... Led the team with nine power play goals ... Rangers were 8-4-0 when he scored a goal and 12-7-1 when he tallied a point ... Registered a plus or even rating in 12 of the last 14 games, posting a plus eight over the span and led the team with a plus nine rating ... Also, placed first on the team and fifth in the NHL with 185 shots on goal ... Tallied 22 of his 31 points at MSG and led the team with 11 goals at MSG ... Tied for second on the club with six goals on the road ... Six of his last 12 goals were collected on the road, after recording his first five at MSG ... Notched his fifth career hat trick, including the game winning goal, and added an assist while registering a plus four rating on January 30 vs. Ottawa ... Missed the February 11 game at Tampa Bay due to injury, marking the first game he had missed since December 9, 1990 while with Edmonton ... Had played in 311 consecutive games ... The streak ranked as the second longest streak in the NHL, trailing Trevor Linden ... Had not missed a game with the Rangers, totaling 259 games ... Tallied four goals and four assists in 10 playoff matches.

NHL CAREER: 1987-88: Began the season with the Detroit Red Wings ... Made his NHL debut in the Wings' second game, October 9 in Edmonton ... Collected his initial NHL point on October 23 vs. Pittsburgh with an assist on a goal by Shawn Burr ... Returned to the OHL on November 18. **1988-89:** Began the season with Detroit and remained there until being sent to Adirondack on February 24 ... Returned to Detroit for the final two regular-season games and five playoff matches ... Sent back to Adirondack after Detroit's playoffs ... Potted his first NHL goal on October 15 ... Notched his first two-goal game on November 9 at Minnesota. **1989-90:** Dealt to Edmonton on November 2 ... Played in first game for Oilers and collected an assist on November 3 ... Recorded first career hat trick on December 17 at Chicago ... Accumulated

five goals and six assists in 22 playoff games, helping Edmonton win the Stanley Cup ... Played with Joe Murphy and Martin Gelinas to form "The Kid Line" during the playoffs ... Scored a goal in four consecutive playoff contests from May 10-May 18. **1990-91:** Ranked fifth on the club with 127 PIM and sixth with 126 shots on goal ... 18 of his 25 points were notched in second half of season ... Appeared in all of team's 18 playoff outings and tied for the team lead with a plus eight rating. **1991-92:** Signed by the Rangers as a free agent in September ... Won the Steven McDonald Award and the "Players' Player" Award ... Scored 26 goals, surpassing his career total of 23 in his first 217 games ... Set career highs with 33 assists and 59 points ... Notched 26 goals and 32 assists for 58 points in last 65 games, after collecting only one assist in first 15 outings ... Placed fourth on the team with 228 shots and recorded at least one shot in 79 of his 80 contests ... Was one of three Rangers to appear in all 80 contests. **1992-93:** Won the team's Most Valuable Player award as voted by the media and for the second consecutive year and captured the "Players' Player" Award ... Winner of the Steven McDonald "Extra Effort" Award for the second consecutive season ... Tallied a career-high four assists on March 19 vs. San Jose ... Registered 36 goals, placing second on the team and led the club with six game-winning goals, while also assisting on two game-winners ... Notched a career-high five points (three goals, two assists) at Pittsburgh on November 25 ... Was one of only two Rangers to play in all 84 contests. **1993-94:** Named an NHL Second-Team All-Star following the season ... Established a team record for goals in a single season, notching 52, breaking Vic Hadfield's 22 year-old club record of 50 ... Tallied goals 50 and 51 only 2:54 apart at Edmonton on March 23 ... The 52 goals ranked fifth in the NHL and set a career high for goals in a season, surpassing his previous high of 36 set in 1992-93 ... Received the King Clancy Memorial Trophy following the season, becoming the first Rangers player to be so honored ... The award is given to the player who best exemplifies leadership qualities on and off the ice and has made a noteworthy humanitarian contribution to his community ... Also captured three of the team's five post-season awards, winning his third consecutive Steven McDonald "Extra Effort" Award given to the player "who goes above and beyond the

call of duty" as voted by the fans, along with his second straight Rangers MVP award as voted by the media and the Rangers Fan Club's Frank Boucher Trophy awarded to the team's most popular player on and off the ice ... Was one of only two players to appear in all 84 contests ... Tied John Ogrodnick (1989-90) and Pierre Larouche (1983-84) for the fifth highest single season power play goal total after potting his 20th on March 16 vs. Hartford ... Tied for third on the team in scoring with 79 points ... The Rangers were 33-5-2 when he tallied a goal and 40-8-3 when he recorded a point ... Registered a plus or even rating in 67 of the 84 matches and placed second on the team with a plus 27 rating ... Tied for first on the club with 24 multiple point games ... Recorded his fourth career hat trick (third with New York) on February 2 vs. the Islanders ... Made his first NHL All-Star Appearance on January 22 at MSG, collecting a pair of assists ... Led all players in the game with eight shots on goal. **1994 PLAYOFFS:** Placed third on the team and fifth in the NHL with 10 goals ... Notched the third highest single post-season goal total in club history, trailing Mark Messier (12) and Brian Leetch (11), also set in 1994 ... Ranked fifth on the team in scoring with 17 points and also ranked fifth with a plus 12 rating ... Notched a goal and added an assist on Mark Messier's Cup-winning goal in Game Seven of the Finals vs. Vancouver on June 14 ... Led the team with four goals vs. Washington in the Conference Semifinals ... Placed second on the team with three power play goals.

AHL CAREER: Made his AHL debut in the 1987 playoffs ... Appeared in 14 regular season games for Adirondack in '88-89 and registered 10 goals and 11 assists ... Returned to Adirondack for the playoffs that season and helped them win the Calder Cup with 11 goals and seven assists in 14 outings.

JUNIOR CAREER: Played two and a half seasons with Windsor of the OHL, totalling 100 goals and 124 assists for 224 points in 165 matches ... Recorded 45 goals and 55 assists for 100 points in '86-87 ... Was

Windsor's leading scorer in the playoffs all three seasons ... Captained the Spitfires to the OHL championship in 1988, before losing in the finals of the Memorial Cup ... That season, he led the OHL in playoff scoring with 14 goals and 18 assists for 32 points in 12 games.

INTERNATIONAL COMPETITION: Was a member of the Gold Medal winning, Canadian Junior team at the World Junior Championships in 1988 ... Captain of Team Canada at the 1993 World Championships in Munich, Germany, collecting three goals and three assists in eight games.

BACKGROUND: Serves as an active celebrity chairman for Family Dynamics, a New York City child abuse agency and for the Greater New York City Ice Hockey League ... "Gravy" makes several appearances with each organization during the season ... Won the Crumb Bum award in 1992-93 for work with New York youngsters ... Also captured the Good Guy award for cooperation with media presented by the New York chapter of the Professional Hockey Writers' Association ... Runs a hockey school each summer in Windsor ... Wore uniform number 11 in his Rangers debut, but switched to number nine for the second game, following the arrival of Mark Messier ... Wore uniform number 12 with Red Wings and Oilers ... Played organized soccer for 12 years as a youngster ... Favorite team is the Toronto Blue Jays ... Enjoys the music of U2 and Bruce Springsteen ... Married: wife Violet; daughter, Madison, was born on July 28.

CAREER TRANSACTIONS: *June 21, 1986* — Detroit's second round choice (22nd overall) in the 1986 Entry Draft. *November 2, 1989* — Traded by Detroit to Edmonton along with Petr Klima, Joe Murphy and Jeff Sharples in exchange for Jimmy Carson, Kevin McClelland and a 1991 fifth round draft choice. *September 3, 1991* — Signed by New York as a group one free agent (compensation was Troy Mallette).

NHL & RANGERS AWARDS AND HONORS

KING CLANCY MEMORIAL TROPHY, 1993-94

Given annually to the NHL player who best exemplifies leadership qualities on and off the ice and has made a noteworthy humanitarian contribution to his community. Graves is the only Rangers player to ever receive the award.

NHL ALL STAR TEAM

Skated in his first NHL All-Star Game on January 22, 1994 at Madison Square Garden. Named to the post-season NHL All-Star Second Team, Left Wing in 1993-94.

STEVEN McDONALD AWARD, 1991-92, 1992-93, 1993-94

Given annually to the Rangers player who goes "above and beyond the call of duty". The award is named after paralyzed New York City police officer Steven McDonald and is voted on by the fans.

PLAYERS' PLAYER AWARD, 1991-92, 1992-93, 1994-95

Given annually to the best "team player" as voted on by the players.

RANGERS MOST VALUABLE PLAYER AWARD, 1992-93, 1993-94

Given annually to the Rangers most valuable player as voted by the media.

RANGERS GOOD GUY AWARD, 1992-93

Given annually by the New York chapter of the Professional Hockey Writer's Association for cooperation with the media.

FRANK BOUCHER TROPHY, 1993-94

Given annually by the Rangers Fan Club to the most popular player on and off the ice.

MISCELLANEOUS

USA WEEKEND "MOST CARING ATHLETE" AWARD, 1994

Graves along with tennis player Michael Chang, Kevin Johnson of the Phoenix Suns, Kirby Puckett of the Minnesota Twins and Chris Zorich of the Chicago Bears were honored for their charitable and community service efforts.

CAREER HIGHLIGHTS

MOST GOALS, GAME: 3, (five times) last-Jan. 30, 1995 vs. Ott., **MOST ASSISTS, GAME:** 4, Mar. 19, 1993 vs. S.J., **MOST POINTS, GAME:** 5, Nov. 25, 1992 at Pit., **MOST PIM, GAME:** 22, Oct. 6, 1990 vs. Wpg., **MOST SHOTS, GAME:** 9, Jan. 27, 1994 at L.A., **MOST SHOTS, SEASON:** 291, 1993-94, **HIGHEST +/-, SEASON:** 27, 1993-94, **FIRST NHL GAME:** Oct. 9, 1987 at Edm., **FIRST NHL GOAL:** Oct. 15, 1988 vs. Tor. (Bester)

AMATEUR AND PROFESSIONAL RECORD

Season	Club	Lea	Regular Season					Playoffs				
			GP	G	A	PTS	PIM	GP	G	A	PTS	PIM
1985-86	Windsor	OHL	62	27	37	64	35	16	5	11	16	10
1986-87	Windsor	OHL	66	45	55	100	70	14	9	8	17	32
1986-87	Adirondack	AHL	—	—	—	—	—	5	0	1	1	0
1987-88	Detroit	NHL	9	0	1	1	8	—	—	—	—	—
1987-88	Windsor	OHL	37	28	32	60	107	12	14	18	32	16
1988-89	Detroit	NHL	56	7	5	12	60	5	0	0	0	4
1988-89	Adirondack	AHL	14	10	11	21	28	14	11	7	18	17
1989-90	Detroit	NHL	13	0	1	1	13	—	—	—	—	—
1989-90	Edmonton	NHL	63	9	12	21	123	22	5	6	11	17
1990-91	Edmonton	NHL	76	7	18	25	127	18	2	4	6	22
1991-92	Rangers	NHL	80	26	33	59	139	10	5	3	8	22
1992-93	Rangers	NHL	84	36	29	65	148	—	—	—	—	—
1993-94	Rangers	NHL	84	52	27	79	127	23	10	7	17	24
1994-95	Rangers	NHL	47	17	14	31	51	10	4	4	8	8
NHL Totals			512	154	140	294	796	88	26	24	50	97
Rangers Totals			295	131	103	234	465	43	19	14	33	54

GLENN HEALY

30

5-10 • 190 • Catches Left
Born: August 23, 1962
Pickering, Ontario
Off-Season Home:
Pickering, Ontario

GOALTENDER

1994-95: Started in four of the last seven matches ... Turned aside 24 shots on Apr. 30 at Philadelphia, notching his eighth career shutout (first of the season, third with the Rangers) ... Ranked eighth in the NHL with a 2.24 GAA ... Posted a four game winning streak and five game unbeaten streak from February 2 to March 6 ... Nine of his 13 starts came on the road ... Allowed two or fewer goals in eight of his 13 starts ... Seven of his eight victories were posted following a loss in the Rangers previous game ... Posted a 2-1 record in the post-season, making three starts and two appearances in relief.

NHL CAREER: 1985-86: Called up by Los Angeles on Nov. 21 during a suspension to Bob Janecyk ... Made his NHL debut six days later, relieving Darren Eliot on Nov. 27 vs. Hartford ... Returned to New Haven on Dec. 2. **1987-88:** Started his first NHL contest on Oct. 25 vs. Boston, suffering a 3-2 defeat ... Earned his first NHL victory on Oct. 28, defeating the Rangers, 4-3 at MSG ... Notched his initial NHL shutout on Feb. 28 at Vancouver ... Co-winner of Kings Rookie of the Year Award ... Started four of five playoff games. **1988-89:** Appeared in 48 games, leading L.A. and led the team with 25 wins ... Played in 45 of the first 61 games, going 25-16-2 ... Recorded a four-game winning streak from Nov. 5 and Nov. 15. **1989-90:** Appeared in 39 games with the Islanders, after signing as a free agent with the club in August ... Notched second career shutout on Jan. 16, defeating Vancouver, 3-0 ... Earned second shutout of the season on Feb. 4 at Buffalo, 1-0 ... Started four of Isles five playoff matches. **1990-91:** Goaltender of record in 18 of the Isles 25 victories and in nine of the team's 10 ties, playing in a career-high 53 games. **1991-92:** Recorded Isles only shutout of the season, blanking N.J., 7-0 in the season finale ... Posted a career-high, five-game winning streak Feb. 2, to Feb. 20 ... Missed 28 games due to injury, including 13 games in March after severing his finger during practice. **1992-93:** Led the Islanders to the Wales Conference Finals with his outstanding playoff performance ... Finished fourth in the NHL for the post-season with nine wins and a 3.19 goals against average, while starting all 18 playoff matches ... Stopped 42 shots in 4-3 victory, in Game Seven of the division finals at Pittsburgh ... Led Islanders with 22 victories during the regular season, 3.30 GAA was the best mark of his career ... Notched his fifth career shutout and only Islanders shutout of the season Mar.16 at San Jose, 6-0 ... Earned his 100th NHL victory Mar. 27 vs. San Jose ... Began the season with a five game unbeaten streak (4-0-1), Oct. 10 to

Oct. 23. **1993-94:** Made his Rangers debut on Oct. 7, posting a 5-4 victory vs. Tampa Bay ... Registered his sixth career shutout, stopping 20 shots at Washington on Dec. 23 ... Turned aside 28 shots and notched his second shutout of the season (seventh career) on Feb. 3 at Boston ... Allowed two or fewer goals in seven of his 17 starts and allowed three or fewer in 11 of the 17 ... 14 of his last 15 starts came on the road. **1994 PLAYOFFS:** Appeared in two playoff matches, both in relief ... Made his first post-season appearance with New York on May 7 in Game Four of the Conference Semifinals at Washington ... Did not allow a goal and did not figure in the decision ... Relieved Mike Richter in the first period on May 21 in Game Four of the Conference Finals at New Jersey ... Allowed one goal and did not figure in the decision.

COLLEGE CAREER: Played four seasons at Western Michigan University ... Improved his win totals and GAA each season, posting a 21-14-2 record with a 3.26 average in his senior season ... Earned honors as an All-American in his final season.

AHL CAREER: Appeared in 43 games for New Haven in 1985-86, his first professional season ... Posted a record of 21-15-4 with a 3.98 GAA ... Named as the team's MVP ... Established himself as the Nighthawks top net-minder in '86-87, notching 21 wins for the second consecutive season ... Named Nighthawks MVP for the second consecutive season.

BACKGROUND: Has done extensive work with handicapped children for the National Center for Disability Services and has sold autographed pictures to benefit the Leukemia Society ... Has also worked with the Apple Institute, a drug rehabilitation center on Long Island ... Majored in business at Western Michigan University, the same school Rangers President and General Manager Neil Smith attended... 1991 recipient of the Long Island chapter of the PHWA's Good Guy award ... Married: wife, Susie.

CAREER TRANSACTIONS: *June 13, 1985 —* Signed as a free agent by Los Angeles. *August 16, 1989 —* signed as a free agent with the New York Islanders. *June 24, 1993 —* Claimed by Anaheim in phase one of the NHL Expansion Draft. *June 25, 1993 —* Claimed by Tampa Bay in phase two of the NHL Expansion Draft. *June 25, 1993 —* Traded to the Rangers by Tampa Bay in exchange for a return of Tampa Bay's third round draft choice in the 1993 NHL Entry Draft.

G L E N N

30

H E A L Y

AMATEUR AND PROFESSIONAL RECORD

Season	Club	Lea	GP	W	L	T	MINS	GA	SO	AVG	GP	W	L	MINS	GA	SO	AVG
							Regular Season							Playoffs			
1981-82	W. Michigan	CCHA	27	7	19	1	1569	116	0	4.44	—	—	—	—	—	—	—
1982-83	W. Michigan	CCHA	30	8	19	2	1732	116	0	4.01	—	—	—	—	—	—	—
1983-84	W. Michigan	CCHA	38	19	16	3	2241	146	0	3.90	—	—	—	—	—	—	—
1984-85	W. Michigan	CCHA	37	21	14	2	2171	118	0	3.26	—	—	—	—	—	—	—
1985-86	Los Angeles	NHL	1	0	0	0	51	6	0	7.06	—	—	—	—	—	—	—
1985-86	New Haven	AHL	43	21	15	4	2410	160	0	3.98	2	0	2	49	11	0	5.55
1986-87	New Haven	AHL	47	21	15	0	2828	173	1	3.67	7	3	4	427	19	0	2.67
1987-88	Los Angeles	NHL	34	12	18	1	1869	135	1	4.33	4	1	3	240	20	0	5.00
1988-89	Los Angeles	NHL	48	25	19	2	2699	192	0	4.27	3	0	1	97	6	0	3.71
1989-90	NY Islanders	NHL	39	12	19	6	2197	128	2	3.50	4	1	2	166	9	0	3.25
1990-91	NY Islanders	NHL	53	18	24	9	2999	166	0	3.32	—	—	—	—	—	—	—
1991-92	NY Islanders	NHL	37	14	16	4	1960	124	1	3.80	—	—	—	—	—	—	—
1992-93	NY Islanders	NHL	47	22	20	2	2655	146	1	3.30	18	9	8	1109	59	0	3.19
1993-94	Rangers	NHL	29	10	12	2	1368	69	2	3.03	2	0	0	68	1	0	0.88
1994-95	Rangers	NHL	17	8	6	1	888	35	1	2.36	5	2	1	230	13	0	3.39
NHL Totals			305	121	134	27	16686	1001	8	3.60	36	13	15	1910	108	0	3.39
RangersTotals			46	18	18	13	2256	104	3	2.77	7	2	1	298	14	0	2.82

ALEXANDER KARPOVTSEV

25

6-1 • 205 • Shoots Right
Born: April 7, 1970
Moscow, Russia
Off-Season Home:
Moscow, Russia

DEFENSE

1994-95: Tallied his fourth goal of the season on April 20 vs. Hartford, eclipsing his previous high of three from 1993-94... Also established a career high with 82 shots on goal ... Tallied three goals and seven assists in his last 29 games after registering one goal and one assist in his first 16 games ... Rangers were 3-1-0 when he scored a goal and 7-3-0 when he tallied a point ... Collected a goal and three assists on the power play and registered one shorthanded assist ... Tallied the game-winning goal on February 21 at Florida .. Registered a pair of assists on March 1 at Hartford and March 8 vs. New Jersey .... Skated in his 100th NHL match on April 1 at Boston ... Appeared in 47 of the 48 matches, missing one game due to injury ... Tallied one goal while appearing in eight post-season matches.

NHL CAREER: 1993-94: Appeared in 67 games, tallying three goals and 15 assists for 18 points in his first season in the National Hockey League ... Acquired from Quebec on September 9 in exchange for Mike Hurlbut ... Made his NHL debut on October 9 at Pittsburgh ... Collected his first NHL goal, potting the game winner on the power play, on October 13 vs. Quebec ... Registered a plus or even rating in 51 of his 67 matches and finished the season with a plus 12 rating ... Notched 10 of his 15 assists on the road ... Saw time on the power play and penalty killing units and registered four power play assists and one shorthanded assist ... Collected a pair of assists on April 8 vs. Toronto, notching his first multiple-point game ... Missed 11 games due to injury. **1994 PLAYOFFS:** Appeared in 17 of the 23 playoff matches, tallying four assists ... Made his initial NHL playoff appearance on April 17 in Game One of the Conference Quarterfinals vs. the Islanders ... Recorded his first point of the post-season with an assist on Stephane Matteau's goal on April 18 in Game Two vs. the Islanders ... Three of his four assists were collected during the Conference Semifinals vs. Washington ... Four assists tied for fourth among NHL rookies.

RUSSIAN CAREER: Played four seasons with Dynamo Moscow in the Russian Elite League ... Had his best offensive production in his last year with the club (1992-93), notching three goals and 11 assists for 14 points in 40 games while serving as the team captain ... Led the entire Russian Elite League with 100 penalty minutes in '92-93 ... Skated in eight games for the Russian team at the 1993 World Championships in Munich, Germany, collecting one assist ... Collected three goals and two assists in 28 matches in 1991-92 helping lead the club to a 25-2-3 record and the regular season and playoff championship ... Teammates included Alexei Kovalev, Alexei Zhamnov (Wpg.), Alexander Semak (NYI), Igor Koralev (Wpg.), Yan Kaminsky (NYI), Dimitri Yushkevich (Tor.), Alexei Yashin (Ott.), Darius Kasparaitis (NYI).

BACKGROUND: Nickname is "Pottsy" ... His hobbies include playing tennis, fishing, and playing pool ... Lists tennis star Andrei Medvedev as his favorite athlete ... His brother Andrei played briefly with Moncton in the AHL ... Enjoys listening to the music of Aerosmith ... Married, wife Janna; daughter Dasha.

CAREER TRANSACTIONS: *June 16, 1990* — Quebec's seventh round choice (158th) overall in the 1990 NHL Entry Draft. *September 9, 1993* — Traded to the Rangers by Quebec for Mike Hurlbut.

CAREER HIGHLIGHTS

MOST GOALS, GAME: 1 (7 times) last- Apr. 20, 1995 vs. Hfd., **MOST ASSISTS, GAME:** 2, (3 times) last- Mar. 8, 1995 vs. NJ, **MOST POINTS, GAME:** 3, Apr. 8, 1994 vs. Tor., **MOST PIM, GAME:** 4, (10 times) last- Mar. 30, 1995 vs. Que., **MOST SHOTS, GAME:** 8, Oct. 19, 1993 vs. Ana., **MOST SHOTS, SEASON:** 82, 1995, **HIGHEST +/-, SEASON:** 12, 1993-94, **FIRST NHL GAME:** Oct. 9, 1993 at Pit., **FIRST NHL GOAL:** Oct. 13, 1993 vs. Que. (Fiset)

AMATEUR AND PROFESSIONAL RECORD

Season	Club	Lea	Regular Season					Playoffs				
			GP	G	A	PTS	PIM	GP	G	A	PTS	PIM
1989-90	Dynamo Moscow	Sov. Elite	35	1	1	2	27	—	—	—	—	—
1990-91	Dynamo Moscow	Sov. Elite	40	0	5	5	15	—	—	—	—	—
1991-92	Dynamo Moscow	CIS	28	3	2	5	22	—	—	—	—	—
1992-93	Dynamo Moscow	CIS	40	3	11	14	100	—	—	—	—	—
1993-94	Rangers	NHL	67	3	15	18	58	17	0	4	4	12
1994-95	Rangers	NHL	47	4	8	12	30	8	1	0	1	0
NHL and Rangers Totals			114	7	23	30	88	25	1	4	5	12

JOE KOCUR

26

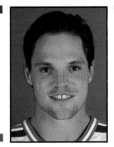

6-0 • 208 • Shoots Right
Born: December 21, 1964
Calgary, Alberta
Off-Season Home:
Highland, Michigan

RIGHT WING

1994-95: One of four players to skate in all 48 matches ... Placed second on the club with 71 PIM's ... Collected his first goal of the season on Mar. 1 at Hartford ... Registered his 2,200th career penalty minute on Apr. 7 vs. the Islanders and ranks 15th on the All-Time Penalty Minutes List with 2,202 ... Registered a plus or even rating in 39 of the 48 matches ... Appeared in each of the ten playoff matches.

NHL CAREER: 1984-85: Spent bulk of campaign with Adirondack (AHL) before being called up by Detroit on Feb. 18 ... Made his NHL debut two nights later in a 3-2 victory vs. St. Louis ... Collected his initial fighting major in his second outing ... Tallied his first NHL goal on Mar. 9 vs. New Jersey (Glenn Resch) with assists from Gerard Gallant and Brad Park. **1985-86:** Spent first nine games of the season with Adirondack before call-up on Oct. 29 ... After going scoreless in first 26 outings with Detroit, notched two goals and one assist in 6-5 triumph against Toronto on Jan. 5 while playing on a line with Steve Yzerman and Petr Klima ... Had another three-point performance on Feb. 14 against the Rangers, two goals and one assist ... Led the NHL and set a Detroit club record with 377 penalty minutes while appearing in 59 games ... Set a Red wings club record for PIM in a single game with 42 on Nov. 2 against St. Louis. **1986-87:** Played entire season with Red Wings, leading the club in PIM for second straight year with 276 ... Potted a pair of goals at Toronto on Jan. 31 ... Two goals and three assists in 16 playoff appearances, along with 71 penalty minutes, still a Wings record. **1987-88:** Was second on team in PIM with 263 ... Missed total of 16 games with four different injuries ... Missed final six playoff outings with a separated right shoulder. **1988-89:** Potted nine goals for the third time in four seasons while also adding nine assists ... Second on Red Wings with 213 PIM ... Missed total of 17 games due to injuries and illness. **1989-90:** Posted a career high 36 points, 16 goals and 20 assists ... Tied for second on team with five game-winning goals, including his first career overtime score on Mar. 17 in 4-3 victory at St. Louis ... Best offensive stretch was a three-game span from Jan. 27-Feb. 2 when he notched four goals and three assists ... Team leader with 268 PIM. **1990-91:** Obtained from Detroit at the trading deadline ... Made his Rangers debut in Quebec on Mar. 7 playing in his 400th NHL contest ... Appeared in only five games with New York after trade due to an injury and a pair of suspensions ... Ranked fifth in NHL with 289 PIM ... Final goal as a Red Wing came on a penalty shot on Nov. 29 in Chicago. **1991-92:** Collected seven goals in his first full season in New York ... Missed 28 games due to injury, including 13 straight from Jan. 30 to Feb. 25, due to a shoulder injury suf-

fered on Jan. 28 against San Jose ... Notched his first goal as a Ranger on Nov. 11 vs. Penguins ... Scored two goals at Detroit on Dec. 6 ... Recorded eight of his 11 points on the road ... Played in 12 of New York's 13 playoff matches and ranked second on the team with 38 penalty minutes. **1992-93:** Became the 19th player in NHL history to surpass the 2,000 mark in career penalty minutes on Apr. 4 at Washington ... Played in his 500th NHL match on Feb. 10 vs. Pittsburgh ... Collected two goals and one assist on the power play ... Six of his eight points were scored on the road. **1993-94:** Appeared in 71 games, tying the second highest mark of his career and his most since joining the Rangers in 1991 ... Placed fourth on the team with 129 penalty minutes. **1994 PLAYOFFS:** Appeared in 20 of the 23 matches, including six of the seven games in the Finals ... Missed three matches due to injury ... Tallied an assist in Game One of the Conference Semifinals on May 1 vs. Washington ... Tallied his only goal of the playoffs in Game Two of the Conference Semifinals vs. Washington.

AHL CAREER: Made his AHL debut in the 1984 playoffs, appearing in five contests ... Split the next season (1984-85) between Adirondack and Detroit, notching 12 goals in 47 AHL games ... Played first nine games with Adirondack in 1985-86 before being called up to Detroit.

JUNIOR CAREER: Joined the Saskatoon Blades of the WHL from the Yorkton Terriers of the Saskatchewan Junior Hockey League and notched 23 goals and 40 points in his rookie season ... The next season he doubled his point production with 40 goals and 41 assists for 81 points ... Ranked second on the team with 40 goals and 81 points and fourth with 41 assists ... Led team in penalty minutes each season.

BACKGROUND: Born in Calgary but moved to Kelvington, Saskatchewan at very early age ... Is a distant cousin of Colorado's Wendel Clark and his first cousin, Kory Kocur was Detroit's first pick in '88 Entry Draft ... Wore uniform number 26 during his entire career with Red Wings ... Is a scratch golfer and lists Pebble Beach as his favorite place to visit ... Also enjoys fishing during the off-season ... A big country music fan, his favorite singer is Garth Brooks and his favorite group is Alabama ... Is a fan of college football with his favorite team being the Michigan Wolverines ... Has a golden retriever named "Molson" ... Married: wife, Kristen; daughter Kendall.

CAREER TRANSACTIONS: *June 8, 1983 —* Detroit's sixth choice (fifth round, 91st overall) in the 1983 Entry Draft ... *Mar. 5, 1991 —* Traded by Detroit along with Per Djoos to Rangers for Kevin Miller, Dennis Vial and Jim Cummins.

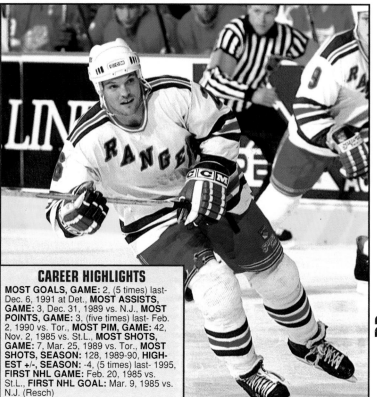

CAREER HIGHLIGHTS

MOST GOALS, GAME: 2, (5 times) last- Dec. 6, 1991 at Det., **MOST ASSISTS, GAME:** 3, Dec. 31, 1989 vs. N.J., **MOST POINTS, GAME:** 3, (five times) last- Feb. 2, 1990 vs. Tor., **MOST PIM, GAME:** 42, Nov. 2, 1985 vs. St.L., **MOST SHOTS, GAME:** 7, Mar. 25, 1989 vs. Tor., **MOST SHOTS, SEASON:** 128, 1989-90, **HIGHEST +/-, SEASON:** -4, (5 times) last- 1995, **FIRST NHL GAME:** Feb. 20, 1985 vs. St.L., **FIRST NHL GOAL:** Mar. 9, 1985 vs. N.J. (Resch)

J O E

26

K O C U R

AMATEUR AND PROFESSIONAL RECORD

Season	Club	Lea	Regular Season GP	G	A	PTS	PIM	Playoffs GP	G	A	PTS	PIM
1982-83	Saskatoon	WHL	62	23	17	40	289	6	2	3	5	25
1983-84	Saskatoon	WHL	69	40	41	81	258	—	—	—	—	—
1983-84	Adirondack	AHL	—	—	—	—	—	5	0	0	0	20
1984-85	Detroit	NHL	17	1	0	1	64	3	1	0	1	5
1984-85	Adirondack	AHL	47	12	7	19	171	—	—	—	—	—
1985-86	Detroit	NHL	59	9	6	15	377	—	—	—	—	—
1985-86	Adirondack	AHL	9	6	2	8	34	—	—	—	—	—
1986-87	Detroit	NHL	77	9	9	18	276	16	2	3	5	71
1987-88	Detroit	NHL	64	7	7	14	263	10	0	1	1	13
1988-89	Detroit	NHL	60	9	9	18	213	3	0	1	1	6
1989-90	Detroit	NHL	71	16	20	36	268	—	—	—	—	—
1990-91	Detroit	NHL	52	5	4	9	253	—	—	—	—	—
1990-91	Rangers	NHL	5	0	0	0	36	6	0	2	2	21
1991-92	Rangers	NHL	51	7	4	11	121	12	1	1	2	38
1992-93	Rangers	NHL	65	3	6	9	131	—	—	—	—	—
1993-94	Rangers	NHL	71	2	1	3	129	20	1	1	2	17
1994-95	Rangers	NHL	48	1	2	3	71	10	0	0	0	8
NHL Totals			640	69	68	137	2202	80	5	9	14	179
Rangers Totals			240	13	13	26	488	48	2	4	6	84

ALEXEI KOVALEV

27

6-0 • 210 • Shoots Left
Born: February 24, 1973
Togliatti, Russia
Off-Season Home:
Mamaroneck, New York

RIGHT WING

1994-95: Registered seven goals in the last 15 games and eight goals and three assists for 11 points in the last 18 games ... Collected nine goals and seven assists for 16 points in the last 27 games ... Registered three two goal games (Feb. 2 vs. Tampa Bay, Apr. 1 at Boston and Apr. 5 at Florida) and notched six multiple-point games ... Tallied a shorthanded goal on April 7 vs. the Islanders ... Led the team with 11 goals at even strength and tied for second with 21 even strength points ... 17 of his 28 points (six goals, 11 assists) were registered at MSG ... Seven of his last eight goals were tallied on the road after notching his first five goals at MSG ... Led the team with eight goals on the road ... Rangers were 11-9-2 when he tallied a point ... Registered an assist on Feb. 4 at Ottawa, for his 100th career point ... Placed third on the team in scoring in the post-season with four goals and seven assists for 11 points in 10 out-ings ... Tallied a point in seven of the 10 playoff matches ... Notched three assists on May 8 in Game Two at Quebec.

NHL CAREER: 1992-93: Made his NHL debut at MSG vs. Hartford on Oct. 12 and tallied his first NHL goal (Sean Burke) ... Registered his first NHL assist and his first career multiple-point outing vs. Washington on Oct. 21 ... Began the season with New York, tallying two goals and four assists in 14 games, before being assigned to Binghamton on Nov. 23 ... Was recalled on Dec. 6 and collected 10 goals and eight assists in his next 20 contests ... Recorded his first career hat trick on Dec. 27 vs. Boston, including the game-winner with :36 remaining ... Tallied a goal and three assists for a career-high four points vs. Montreal on Dec. 13. **1993-94:** Established career highs in games played and all offensive categories in his first full season in the NHL ... Began the season at his natural position of right wing but was shifted to center in March ... Responded by tallying 13 goals and six assists for 19 points in his last 20 games ... Registered an 11-game point scoring streak from Mar. 16 - Apr. 8, col-lecting 10 goals and five assists and tying Mark Messier for the longest point scoring streak on the team ... Also registered a career-high, four-game goal scoring streak from Mar. 27 - Apr. 2 ... Potted 16 goals in his last 36 games after notching seven in his first 40 matches ... Ranked second on the team with 27 assists and 43 points at even strength ... Registered a plus or even rating in 55 of his last 66 matches, recording a plus 26 rating over the span. **1994 PLAYOFFS:** Placed third on the team in scor-ing with nine goals and 12 assists for 21 points in 23 matches ... Tied with Mark Messier for

second on the club in scoring during the Finals, collecting two goals and five assists ... Set a club record, notching his fifth power play goal of the post-season, in Game Six of the Finals ... Notched a point in each of the last five games of the Finals ... Recorded a goal and tallied a pair of assists on Messier's game-tying and game-winning goals on in Game Six of the Conference Finals ... Notched a point in each of the first seven playoff matches (four goals, seven assists) ... Registered a goal in each of the four Conference Quarterfinal matches vs. the Islanders, tying Pavel Bure for the longest goal scoring streak during the playoffs.

RUSSIAN CAREER: In 1988 was invited to Dynamo Moscow ... Played two seasons for Dynamo's junior team ... Made his debut on senior team at the end of the 1989-90 season, at the age of 17 ... In last two seasons, he received two gold medals for winning national championships ... Became a regular with Dynamo Moscow in 1991-92 after appearing in two pre-season contests with Rangers ... Played in 26 games and collected 16 goals and eight assists for 24 points ... Won national title with the team for the second straight year.

INTERNATIONAL CAREER: Made his debut with the national team on Aug. 14, 1991, in an exhibition game vs. Sweden ... Was in training camp of the national team before Canada Cup, but did not make the team ... Won title with the team at the World Junior Championships ... Collected five goals and five assists for 10 points in seven games ... Was the top scorer on the team and fifth overall in the league... Was named to the tournament's All-Star team ... Was a key member of the Russian team that won the gold medal at the 1992 Olympic Games ... Played at the World Championships in Czechoslovakia, appearing in six games, col-lecting one assist... Played two years at European Junior Championships ... Played at World Junior Championships, Olympics and World Championships in 1991-92.

BACKGROUND: Is the first Soviet player ever taken in the first round of the NHL Entry Draft ... Lists Wayne Gretzky as his hockey hero ... Has recently become an avid golfer ... Favorite actor is Saveli Kramarov ("Moscow on Hudson"), the former Soviet comedy actor ... Always keeps a troll with him for good luck ... Married: wife, Euginia.

CAREER TRANSACTIONS: *June 9, 1991* — Rangers' first round choice (15th overall) in 1991 Entry Draft.

ALEXEI 27 KOVALEV

CAREER HIGHLIGHTS

MOST GOALS, GAME: 3, Dec. 27, 1992 vs. Bos., **MOST ASSISTS, GAME:** 3, (twice) last-Dec. 26, 1993 vs. N.J., **MOST POINTS, GAME:** 4, (twice) last-Dec. 26, 1993 vs. N.J., **MOST PIM, GAME:** 21, Jan. 6, 1992 at Ott., **MOST SHOTS, GAME:** 8, (twice) last- Mar. 19,1993 vs. S.J., **MOST SHOTS, SEASON:** 184, 1993-94, **HIGHEST +/-, SEASON:** 18, 1993-94, **FIRST NHL GAME:** Oct. 12, 1992 vs. Hfd., **FIRST NHL GOAL:** Oct. 12, 1992 vs. Hfd. (Burke)

AMATEUR AND PROFESSIONAL RECORD

Season	Club	Lea	Regular Season					Playoffs				
			GP	G	A	PTS	PIM	GP	G	A	PTS	PIM
1989-90	Dynamo Moscow.....Sov. Elite		1	0	0	0	0	—	—	—	—	—
1990-91	Dynamo Moscow.....Sov. Elite		18	1	2	3	4	—	—	—	—	—
1991-92	Unified Olympic Team............		8	1	2	3	—	—	—	—	—	—
1991-92	Dynamo Moscow.....Sov. Elite		33	16	9	25	20	—	—	—	—	—
1992-93	Rangers ....NHL		65	20	18	38	79	—	—	—	—	—
1992-93	Binghamton ....AHL		13	13	11	24	35	9	3	5	8	14
1993-94	Rangers.........................NHL		76	23	33	56	154	23	9	12	21	18
1994-95	Rangers.........................NHL		48	13	15	28	30	10	4	7	11	10
NHL and Rangers Totals.........................			189	56	66	122	263	33	13	19	32	28

NICK KYPREOS

19

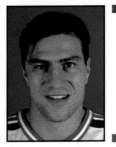

**6-0 • 207 • Shoots Left
Born: June 6, 1966
Toronto, Ontario
Off-Season Home:
Willowdale, Ontario**

LEFT WING

1994-95: Led the team with 93 penalty minutes ... Skated in each of the last 17 games and appeared in 26 of the last 29 matches ... Registered his only goal of the season to open the scoring on Feb. 4 at Ottawa ... Registered a plus or even rating in 37 of his 40 matches ... Rangers were 20-17-3 when he was in the lineup ... Tallied two assists and a plus three rating in 10 playoff matches.

NHL CAREER: 1989-90: Claimed by Washington from Philadelphia in the Waiver Draft, following an impressive training camp with the Flyers ... Made his NHL debut on Oct. 6 vs. Philadelphia ... Tallied his first NHL goal on Nov. 29 at Detroit ... Two of his five goals were game-winners ... Posted a three-game scoring streak from Dec. 5 to Dec. 9, collecting two goals and two assists over the span ... Registered a plus three rating and 82 penalty minutes in 31 games ... Sent to Baltimore on Mar. 8 after undergoing minor knee surgery ... Skated in his first NHL playoff game vs. the Rangers on Apr. 21 at Madison Square Garden. **1990-91:** Played in 79 games after not dressing for the opener ... Collected three game-winning goals ... Registered his only multiple-point game of the season at Edmonton on Mar.10 ... Placed third on the club with 196 penalty minutes ... Tied a career-high with a three-game scoring streak from Jan. 1 to Jan. 5. **1991-92:** Recorded 206 penalty minutes, placing second on the team while playing in his first season with Hartford ... Notched his first career two-goal game on Jan. 1 vs. the Islanders. **1992-93:** Posted career-highs with 17 goals, 10 assists, 27 points and a team-leading 325 penalty minutes ... Ranked fourth in the league in penalty minutes ... Recorded two goals vs. the Islanders on Feb. 28 ... Three of his 17 goals were game-winners ... Whalers were 13-7-3 when he recorded a point and 10-40-2 when he didn't ... Missed the final seven games of the season with an abdominal muscle strain. **1993-94:** Acquired from Hartford on Nov. 2 ... Played in 10 games with the Whalers prior to the trade ... Collected three goals and five assists in 46 games with New York ... Notched his first point with the Rangers on Dec. 13 vs. Buffalo, assisting on Sergei Nemchinov's game winning goal ... Tallied his first goal as a Ranger on Jan. 10 vs. Tampa Bay. **1994 PLAYOFFS:** Appeared in three playoff matches, including Game Seven of the Stanley Cup Finals vs. Vancouver on June 14 ... Skated in Games Three and Four of the Conference Quarterfinals at Long Island.

AHL CAREER: Joined the Hershey Bears following his final season with North Bay and appeared in 10 games in 1986-87 ... Recorded 24 goals and 20 assists for 44 points along with 101 penalty minutes in his first full professional season with Hershey in 1987-88 ... Skated in 12 playoff matches as Hershey captured the 1988 Calder Cup ... Missed the first 52 games of the 1989-90 season and was limited to 28 games due to preseason knee injury ... Recorded two goals and three assists on Mar. 16, 1990 vs. New Haven while playing with Baltimore.

JUNIOR CAREER: Played four seasons with the North Bay Centennials of the Ontario Hockey League ... Led the club in with 62 goals and 97 points and was named a first team OHL All-Star in 1985-86 ... Placed second on the team in scoring in 1986-87 with 90 points despite playing in only 46 games ... Earned honors as a second team OHL All-Star ... Recorded 11 goals and five assists in 24 games as North Bay went to the finals of the OHL playoffs before losing to the Oshawa Generals.

BACKGROUND: Majored in marketing at Candore College ... Enjoys playing soccer and baseball ... Received the Shawmut Bank Favorite Whaler Award as voted by the fans and also captured the Whalers Heavy Hitter Award in 1992-93 ... Following the team's Cup victory, he went with teammates Brian Leetch and Mark Messier to throw out the first pitch at Yankee Stadium, appeared in MTV's *This Week in Rock* with Glenn Healy and went to MTV's Summer Beach House in the Hamptons ... Does considerable charitable work and appearances ... Single.

CAREER TRANSACTIONS: *September 30, 1984* — Signed as a free agent by Philadelphia. *October 2, 1989* — Claimed by Washington in NHL Waiver Draft. *June 15, 1992* — Traded to Hartford by Washington for Mark Hunter and future considerations (Yvon Corriveau). *November 2, 1993* — Traded by Hartford to Rangers along with Steve Larmer, Barry Richter and a 1994 draft choice (Yuri Litvinov).

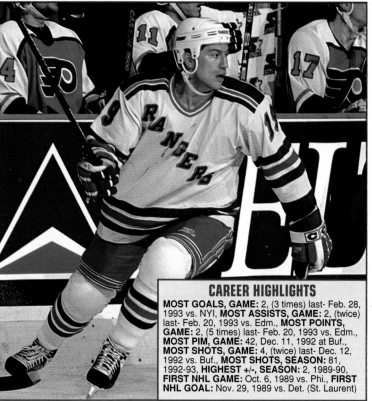

CAREER HIGHLIGHTS

MOST GOALS, GAME: 2, (3 times) last- Feb. 28, 1993 vs. NYI, **MOST ASSISTS, GAME:** 2, (twice) last- Feb. 20, 1993 vs. Edm., **MOST POINTS, GAME:** 2, (5 times) last- Feb. 20, 1993 vs. Edm., **MOST PIM, GAME:** 42, Dec. 11, 1992 at Buf., **MOST SHOTS, GAME:** 4, (twice) last- Dec. 12, 1992 vs. Buf., **MOST SHOTS, SEASON:** 81, 1992-93, **HIGHEST +/-, SEASON:** 2, 1989-90, **FIRST NHL GAME:** Oct. 6, 1989 vs. Phi., **FIRST NHL GOAL:** Nov. 29, 1989 vs. Det. (St. Laurent)

AMATEUR AND PROFESSIONAL RECORD

Season	Club	Lea	Regular Season GP	G	A	PTS	PIM	Playoffs GP	G	A	PTS	PIM
1983-84	North Bay	OHL	51	12	11	23	36	4	3	2	5	9
1984-85	North Bay	OHL	64	41	36	77	71	8	2	2	4	15
1985-86	North Bay	OHL	64	62	35	97	112	—	—	—	—	—
1986-87	Hershey	AHL	10	0	1	1	4	—	—	—	—	—
1986-87	North Bay	OHL	46	49	41	90	54	24	11	5	16	78
1987-88	Hershey	AHL	71	24	20	44	101	12	0	2	2	17
1988-89	Hershey	AHL	28	12	15	27	19	12	4	5	9	11
1989-90	Washington	NHL	31	5	4	9	82	7	1	0	1	15
1989-90	Baltimore	AHL	14	6	5	11	6	7	4	1	5	17
1990-91	Washington	NHL	79	9	9	18	196	9	0	1	1	38
1991-92	Washington	NHL	65	4	6	10	206	—	—	—	—	—
1992-93	Hartford	NHL	75	17	10	27	325	—	—	—	—	—
1993-94	Hartford	NHL	10	0	0	0	37	—	—	—	—	—
1993-94	Rangers	NHL	46	3	5	8	102	3	0	0	0	2
1994-95	Rangers	NHL	40	1	3	4	93	10	0	2	2	6
NHL Totals			346	39	37	76	1041	29	1	3	4	61
Rangers Totals			86	4	8	12	195	13	0	2	2	8

DANIEL LACROIX

37

6-2 • 205 lbs. • Shoots Left
Born: March 11, 1969
Montreal, Quebec
Off-Season Home:
Montreal Quebec

CENTER

1994-95: Began the season with Boston after being acquired from the Rangers in exchange for Glen Featherstone on August 19 ... Appeared in 23 games with the Bruins, collecting one goal ... Registered a plus or even rating in 19 of his 23 matches with the Bruins ... Skated in 40 games with Providence (AHL), tallying 15 goals and 11 assists along with 277 penalty minutes ... Made his only appearance with the Rangers on April 5 at Florida after being claimed off waivers from Boston on March 23.

NHL CAREER: 1993-94: Made his National Hockey League debut on October 5 vs. Boston ... Was returned to Binghamton on October 7 ... Was recalled from Binghamton on January 29 and appeared in three consecutive games from January 31 to February 3 ... Was returned to Binghamton on February 4.

MINOR LEAGUE CAREER: Made his professional debut with Denver of the International Hockey League in 1988-89, following the completion of Granby's season ... Tallied one assist in two games and also collected an assist in two playoff matches ... Registered 12 goals and 16 assists for 28 points along with 128 penalty minutes in 61 games with Flint (IHL) in his first professional season in 1989-90 ... Appeared in 54 games with Binghamton of the American Hockey League in 1990-91, tallying seven goals and 12 assists for 19 points along with 237 penalty minutes, ranking second on the club ... Collected 12 goals and 20 assists for 32 points in 52 games with Binghamton in 1991-92 ... Posted his best offensive season in 1992-93, collecting 21 goals and 22 assists for 43 points along with 255

penalty minutes which ranked second on the club ... Did not appear in the playoffs due to injury ... Matched his career high with 43 points in 1993-94, registering 20 goals and 23 assists for 43 points along with 278 penalty minutes, placing second on the club.

JUNIOR CAREER: Played three seasons with Granby of the Quebec Major Junior Hockey League ... Began his career with the Bisons in 1986-87, playing on a checking line and becoming one of the team's top enforcers, registering 311 penalty minutes ... Improved throughout the season and skated on the first line with Pierre Turgeon for the final quarter of the season ... Improved his offensive totals to 24 goals and 50 assists for 74 points along with a team leading 468 penalty minutes ... Collected 45 goals and 49 assists for 94 points along with 320 penalty minutes in 70 games in his final season with Granby in 1988-89 and was named to the QMJHL first All-Star team.

BACKGROUND: Earned honors as the QMJHL's Student Athlete of the Year in 1988-89 ... Also captured the Guy Lafleur Excellence and Merit Award that season for his excellence on and off the ice ... Majored in creative photography .. Hobbies include photography, drawing and sculpting ... Married: wife, Manon; daughter, Daphne; son, Cedric.

CAREER TRANSACTIONS: *June 13, 1987* — Rangers' second round choice (31st overall) in the 1987 NHL Entry Draft. *August 19, 1994* — Traded by the Rangers to Boston for Glen Featherstone. *March 23, 1994* — Claimed by the Rangers off waivers from Boston.

CAREER HIGHLIGHTS

MOST GOALS, GAMES: 1, Jan. 22, 1995 vs. Phi., **MOST ASSISTS, GAME:** none, **MOST POINTS, GAME:** 1, Jan. 22, 1995 vs. Phi., **MOST PIM, GAME:** 9, Feb. 17, 1995 at Fla., **MOST SHOTS, GAME:** 5, Feb 17, 1995 at Fla., **MOST SHOTS, SEASON:** 14, 1995, **HIGHEST +/-, SEASON:** E., 1993-94, **FIRST NHL GAME:** Oct. 5, 1993 vs. Bos., **FIRST NHL GOAL:** Jan. 22, 1995 vs. Phi. (Roussel).

D A N I E L

37

L A C R O I X

AMATEUR AND PROFESSIONAL RECORD

Season	Club	Lea	Regular Season					Playoffs				
			GP	G	A	PTS	PIM	GP	G	A	PTS	PIM
1986-87	Granby ....QMJHL		54	9	16	25	311	8	1	2	3	22
1987-88	Granby ....QMJHL		58	24	50	74	468	5	0	4	4	12
1988-89	Granby ....QMJHL		70	45	49	94	320	4	1	1	2	57
1988-89	Denver ....IHL		2	0	1	1	0	2	0	1	1	0
1989-90	Flint............................IHL		61	12	16	28	128	4	2	0	2	24
1990-91	Binghamton ....AHL		54	7	12	19	237	5	1	0	1	24
1991-92	Binghamton ....AHL		52	12	20	32	149	11	2	4	6	28
1992-93	Binghamton ....AHL		73	21	22	43	255	—	—	—	—	—
1993-94	Rangers ....NHL		4	0	0	0	0	—	—	—	—	—
1993-94	Binghamton ....AHL		59	20	23	43	278	—	—	—	—	—
1994-95	Providence ....AHL		40	15	11	26	266	—	—	—	—	—
1994-95	Boston.......................NHL		23	1	0	1	14	—	—	—	—	—
1994-95	Rangers ....NHL		1	0	0	0	0	—	—	—	—	—
NHL Totals.............................			28	1	0	1	48	—	—	—	—	—
Rangers Totals.......................			5	0	0	0	0	—	—	—	—	—

NATHAN LaFAYETTE

22

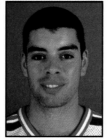

6-1 • 200 • Shoots Right
Born: February 17, 1973
New Westminster, B.C.
Off-Season Home:
Mississauga, Ontario

CENTER

1995: Acquired from Vancouver on April 7 in exchange for Corey Hirsch ... Made his Rangers debut on April 9 at New Jersey and skated in each of the last 12 matches ... Registered a plus or even rating in 10 of his 12 matches and posted a plus one rating with New York ... Tallied four goals and four assists for eight points along with a plus two rating in 27 games with Vancouver ... Collected a shorthanded goal on April 1 vs. Edmonton ... Registered a plus or even rating in 19 of his 27 games with the Canucks and was plus or even in 11 of his last 12, posting a plus eight rating over the span ... Skated in eight post-season matches.

NHL CAREER: 1993-94: Was called up by St. Louis from Peoria (IHL) on December 1 and made his NHL debut on December 2 vs. Toronto ... Skated in six games before returning to Peoria ... Was recalled on January 3 and remained with the Blues until March 23 ... Recorded his first NHL point with an assist on January 13 vs. Edmonton ... Potted his first NHL goal on February 3 vs. Quebec ... Collected two goals and three assists for five points in 38 matches with the Blues ... Was acquired by Vancouver on March 21 along with Jeff Brown and Bret Hedican in exchange for Craig Janney ... Tallied one goal and one assist in 11 games with the Canucks ... Notched his first point with Vancouver in his Canucks debut on March 23 , tallying an assist at Los Angeles ... Registered his first goal with Vancouver on April 1 vs. Winnipeg. **1994 PLAYOFFS:** Collected two goals and seven assists for nine points in 20 playoff matches ... Skated in the last 20 post-season matches, including all seven games in the Stanley Cup Finals, after not dressing for the first four games ... Placed second among NHL rookies with nine points ... Was tied for first on the team and ranked fourth in the NHL with a plus 13 rating.

AHL CAREER: 1993-94: Began his professional career with Peoria (IHL), tallying 13 goals and 11 assists for 24 points in 27 matches.

JUNIOR CAREER: Played four years in the Ontario Hockey League, beginning his career with Kingston in 1989-90 ... Appeared in 53 games in his rookie season, collecting six goals and eight assists for 14 points ... Tallied 13 goals and 13 assists for 26 points in 35 games with Kingston in 1990-91 before being traded to Cornwall ... Registered 16 goals and 22 assists for 38 points in 28 games with the Royals ... Placed third on Cornwall in scoring in 1991-92 with 73 points and was tied for second on the club with 28 goals ... Also placed third on the club in post-season scoring with two goals and five assists in six matches ... Led Newmarket with 49 goals in his final junior season in 1992-93 ... Placed third on the Royals in scoring for the second consecutive year, posting a career best 87 points in 58 games ... Collected four goals and five assists for nine points in seven play-off outings ... Teammates included Jason Bonsingore, Edmonton's first choice, fourth overall in 1994 and Grant Marshall, Toronto's second pick, 23rd overall in 1992.

INTERNATIONAL CAREER: Collected three goals and one assist for four points, helping lead Team Canada to the Gold Medal at the 1993 World Junior Championships ... Three goals tied for third on the team ... Teammates included; Paul Kariya (Ana.), Jason Dawe (Buf.), Jeff Shantz (Chi.), Alexandre Daigle (Ott.), Chris Gratton (T.B.), Mike Rathje (S.J.), Chris Pronger (St.L.), Jason Smith (N.J.) and Rob Niedermayer (Fla.).

BACKGROUND: Was awarded the Bobby Smith Trophy as the OHL's top scholastic player and the Canadian Major Junior Scholastic Player of the Year in 1992, after earning straight A's in computer science at York University ... Was selected as the top skater in the Leyden Division by OHL coaches in 1992 ... Nathan's father David played briefly with the B.C. Lions of the Canadien Football League ... Played baseball, rugby and participated in track and field at Lorne Park High School in Mississauga ... Was selected to the All-Ontario Rugby team one season ... Enjoys golfing and off-road mountain biking ... Single.

CAREER TRANSACTIONS: *June 22, 1991* — St. Louis' third choice (65th overall) in the 1991 NHL Entry Draft. *March 21, 1994 —* Traded by St. Louis with Jeff Brown and Bret Hedican to Vancouver for Craig Janney. *April 7, 1995 —* Traded by Vancouver to the Rangers for Corey Hirsch.

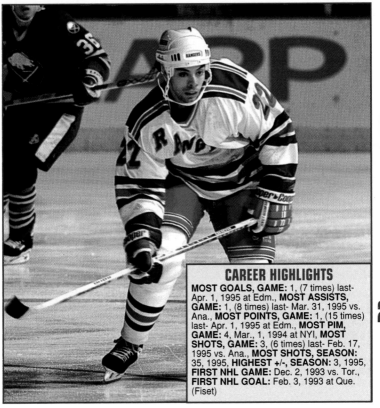

NATHAN 22 LAFAYETTE

CAREER HIGHLIGHTS

MOST GOALS, GAME: 1, (7 times) last- Apr. 1, 1995 at Edm., **MOST ASSISTS, GAME:** 1, (8 times) last- Mar. 31, 1995 vs. Ana., **MOST POINTS, GAME:** 1, (15 times) last- Apr. 1, 1995 at Edm., **MOST PIM, GAME:** 4, Mar., 1, 1994 at NYI, **MOST SHOTS, GAME:** 3, (6 times) last- Feb. 17, 1995 vs. Ana., **MOST SHOTS, SEASON:** 35, 1995, **HIGHEST +/-, SEASON:** 3, 1995, **FIRST NHL GAME:** Dec. 2, 1993 vs. Tor., **FIRST NHL GOAL:** Feb. 3, 1993 at Que. (Fiset)

AMATEUR AND PROFESSIONAL RECORD

Season	Club	Lea	Regular Season					Playoffs				
			GP	G	A	PTS	PIM	GP	G	A	PTS	PIM
1989-90	Kingston	OHL	53	6	8	14	14	7	0	1	1	4
1990-91	Kingston	OHL	35	13	13	26	110	—	—	—	—	—
1990-91	Cornwall	OHL	28	16	22	38	25	—	—	—	—	—
1991-92	Cornwall	OHL	66	28	45	73	26	6	2	5	7	15
1992-93	Newmarket	OHL	58	49	38	87	26	7	4	5	9	19
1993-94	St. Louis	NHL	38	2	3	5	14	—	—	—	—	—
1993-94	Peoria	IHL	27	13	11	24	20	—	—	—	—	—
1993-94	Vancouver	NHL	11	1	1	2	4	20	2	7	9	4
1994-95	Syracuse	AHL	27	9	9	18	10	—	—	—	—	—
1994-95	Vancouver	NHL	27	4	4	8	30	—	—	—	—	—
1994-95	Rangers	NHL	12	0	0	0	0	8	0	0	0	10
NHL Totals			88	7	8	15	48	28	2	7	9	14
Rangers Totals			12	0	0	0	0	8	0	0	0	10

DARREN LANGDON

15

6-1 • 200 • Shoots Left
Born: Jan. 8, 1971 • Deer
Lake, Newfoundland
Off-Season Home: Deer
Lake, Newfoundland

LEFT WING

1994-95: Began the season with Binghamton of the American Hockey League where he tallied six goals and 14 assists for 20 points along with 296 penalty minutes in 55 games ... Notched his first career two-goal game on February 12 at Hershey ... Collected a pair of assists for the third time during the season on February 3 vs. Rochester ... Also notched a goal in that game, marking his first career three-point match ... Tallied four goals and three assists in five games prior to being called up to New York ... Posted his best offensive production during that stretch while playing on a line with Andrei Kudinov and Dimitri Starostenko ... Ranked second in the AHL with 296 penalty minutes at the time of his recall to New York ... Was called up by New York on February 17 ... Made his National Hockey League debut the following night at the Montreal Forum and registered his initial NHL goal ... Tallied his first NHL assist on March 5 at Washington on a goal by Sergei Nemchinov ... Appeared in 18 matches with New York, tallying a goal and an assist along with 62 penalty minutes before being returned to Binghamton on April 10 ... Skated in 11 playoff matches with Binghamton, collecting a goal and three assists along with a team leading 84 penalty minutes.

AHL CAREER: 1992-93: Was loaned to Binghamton February 17 from Dayton after appearing in 54 games with the Bombers ... Skated in his first AHL match on February 19 at Rochester ... Recorded his first American Hockey League point on February 21, registering a goal in a 5-1 victory vs. Hamilton at the Broome County Coliseum ... Collected three goals and four assists for seven points along with 115 penalty minutes, while appearing in 18 matches ... Appeared in eight playoff matches, tallying one assist and 14 penalty minutes ... Signed by the Rangers as a free agent on August 16. 1993-94: Collected two goals and seven assists for nine points in 54 matches ... Led the team and placed second in the AHL with 327 penalty minutes.

ECHL CAREER: 1992-93: Began his professional career with the Dayton Bombers ... Appeared in his first game on October 18 vs. the Wheeling Thunderbirds ... Registered his first professional goal in that match ... Tallied 23 goals and 22 assists for 45 points in 54 games ... Led the team and placed second in the league with 429 penalty minutes, ranking second on the ECHL's all time list.

JUNIOR CAREER: Earned MVP honors in the Maritime Junior Hockey League in 1991-92 with Summerside ... Tallied 34 goals and 49 assists for 83 points in 44 games and led the league with 441 penalty minutes.

BACKGROUND: Nickname "Langer" ... Ranks third on Binghamton's all-time franchise penalty minute list with 738 in 127 career matches ... Trails only Peter Fiorentino and Daniel Lacroix ... Single

CAREER TRANSACTIONS: *August 16, 1993* — Signed as a free agent by the Rangers.

CAREER HIGHLIGHTS

MOST GOALS, GAME: 1, Feb. 18, 1995 at Mtl., **MOST ASSISTS, GAME:** 1, Mar. 5, 1995 at Wsh., **MOST POINTS, GAME:** 1 (twice), last- Mar. 5, 1995 at Wsh., **MOST PIM, GAME:** 19, Feb. 26 at Buf., **MOST SHOTS, GAME:** 2, Feb. 28, 1995 vs Fla., **MOST SHOTS, SEASON:** 6, 1994-95, **HIGHEST +/-, SEASON:** E., 1994-95, **FIRST NHL GAME:** Feb. 18, 1995 at Mtl., **FIRST NHL GOAL:** Feb. 18, 1995 at Mtl. (Roy)

AMATEUR AND PROFESSIONAL RECORD

Season	Club	Lea	Regular Season					Playoffs				
			GP	G	A	PTS	PIM	GP	G	A	PTS	PIM
1991-92	Summerside	MJHL	44	34	49	83	441	—	—	—	—	—
1992-93	Binghamton	AHL	18	3	4	7	115	8	0	1	1	14
1992-93	Dayton	ECHL	54	23	22	45	429	3	0	1	1	40
1993-94	Binghamton	AHL	54	2	7	9	327	—	—	—	—	—
1994-95	Binghamton	AHL	55	6	14	20	296	11	1	3	4	84
1994-95	Rangers	NHL	18	1	1	2	62	—	—	—	—	—
NHL and Rangers Totals			18	1	1	2	62	—	—	—	—	—

D A R R E N 15 L A N G D O N

BRIAN LEETCH

2

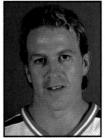

5-11 • 190 • Shoots Left
Born: March 3, 1968
Corpus Christi, Texas
Off-Season Home: New York, New York

DEFENSE

1994-95: Placed fourth in the NHL in scoring among defensemen and ranked second on the team with 41 points ... Recorded 12 shots on goal on April 28 vs. the Islanders ... Tallied three goals and 13 assists for 16 points in the last nine games ... Registered a goal and two assists on April 23 at Boston, moving past Camille Henry into ninth place on the Rangers All-Time Scoring list with 480 points ... Notched a career-high, five assists on April 18 at Pittsburgh, tying a Rangers record for assists in one game and becoming the first defenseman to reach the mark ... Don Maloney last accomplished the feat on January 14, 1987 at Calgary ... With the five assists, he moved past James Patrick into sixth place on the Rangers All-Time Assist list with 367 ... Tallied 19 points (five goals, 14 assists) in the last 10 games and registered 22 points (five goals, 17 assists) in the last 13 games ... Led the team with 21 power play points and 18 power play assists ... Was on the ice for 38 of the Rangers 40 power play goals and for 84 of the 139 overall ... Posted at least one shot on goal in 47 of the 48 games and placed second on the team and sixth in the NHL with 182 shots on goal ... 24 of his 41 points (four goals, 20 assists) were tallied vs. the Northeast Division ... Ranked second on the team with 12 assists and 15 points on the road ... Registered his 350th career assist on February 16 vs. Montreal ... Was one of four players to appear in all 48 games ... Led the team with six goals and eight assists for 14 points in 10 post-season matches .... Recorded his first career hat trick on May 22 in Game Two of the conference semi-finals at Philadelphia, becoming the 11th player in team history and first defenseman to register a playoff hat trick ... Tallied an assist on May 21 in Game One at Philadelphia, moving past Rod Gilbert into first place on the Rangers all-time playoff scoring list with 68 points.

NHL CAREER: 1987-88: Made his NHL debut on February 29 after competing with the U.S. Olympic Team at the games in Calgary ... Initial point was an assist in his first game vs. St. Louis ... Notched his first NHL goal and collected two assists on March 24 vs. Edmonton. **1988-89:** Won the Calder Trophy as the League's Rookie of the Year, becoming the first Ranger to win the award since Steve Vickers in '72-73 ... Led all league freshman in points (71), assists (48) and shots (268) ... Fifth among NHL defensemen with the 71 points ... 23 goals set an NHL record for most goals by a rookie defenseman, breaking the mark set by Barry Beck (22 in '77-78) ... Broke Ranger rookie defenseman records for most goals, assists and points in a season, all held by Reijo

Ruotsalainen ... 13 shots on January 4 against Washington set a Ranger record for a defenseman ... Five points and four assists on February 17 vs. Toronto matched the team mark for a rookie in a single contest ... **1989-90:** Played in team's first 71 contests before suffering a fractured left ankle at Toronto on March 14 ... Led Rangers defensemen in assists (45) and shots (222) and was second among club backliners in goals (11) and points (56) ... Represented the Rangers in the All-Star Game. **1990-91:** Established team records for most assists in a season, 72, breaking Mike Rogers' mark of 65 set in '81-82 and for most points in a season by a defenseman with 88, breaking Brad Park's mark of 82 set in '73-74 ... Only Ranger to play in all 80 contests ... Appeared in second consecutive All-Star Game ... Named team MVP by members of the media. **1991-92:** Winner of the Norris Trophy as the NHL's best defenseman, becoming the first Ranger to capture the award since Harry Howell in '66-67 ... Named an NHL First-Team All-Star ... Broke his own club records for assists in a single season (80) and points by a defenseman in a single season (102) ... Became only the fifth defenseman in league history to collect 100 points in a season ... Recorded the longest point scoring streak in team history, notching a point in 17 consecutive contests from November 23 to December 31 ... The streak was the third longest for a defenseman in league history ... Also collected the longest assist streak in team history, 15 consecutive games, from November 29 to December 31, becoming only the fourth player in NHL history to tally a 15-game assist streak ... Established team record for most ppg's by a defenseman with 10 ... Led all NHL defensemen with 102 points, while placing ninth in the NHL ... 80 assists ranked third in the NHL ... Played in all 80 games for the second straight season ... Appeared in his third consecutive All-Star Game. **1992-93:** Missed 48 games due to injury, including 34 with a neck injury from December 17 to March 9 ... Suffered a fractured right ankle on March 19 and missed the final 13 games of the season ... Rangers were 20-13-3 when he was in the lineup and 14-26-8 when he was injured ... Opened the season with a seven-game point scoring streak (two goals, eight assists) ... Tied a team-high for the season with 11 shots vs. Edmonton on March 17 ... Voted by fans as a starter for the Wales Conference in the NHL All-Star game, but missed the game due to injury ... Was tops among all team blueliners with 36 points despite playing in only 36 games. **1993-94:** Named an NHL Second-Team All-Star following the season ... Tied for third on the team in

scoring and placed fourth among NHL defensemen with 79 points ... Tied his career high with 23 goals, equalling the mark he set in 1988-89 as a rookie ... The mark is tied for the third highest single season goal total by a defenseman in club history ... Led the team and notched a career-high 323 shots on goal ... Ranked second in the NHL with 53 power play points, finished fourth with 26 power play assists and was on the ice for 87 of the Rangers 96 power play goals ... Rangers were 36-9-6 when he tallied a point ... Tallied a pair of goals, including the 100th of his career on March 25 at Vancouver, becoming the third defenseman in club history to reach the plateau, joining Ron Greschner and James Patrick ... Tallied a pair of assists, including the 300th of his career on November 6 at Quebec ... Skated in his 400th NHL match on January 27 at Los Angeles ... Tied a career high with four assists vs. Washington on March 9 at Halifax ... Collected his 400th NHL point with an assist on December 4 at Toronto ... Registered a 10-game point scoring streak (four goals, 10 assists) from November 14 to December 5 ... Was voted as a starter and appeared in his fourth All-Star Game on January 22 at MSG.
1994 PLAYOFFS: Led the NHL in scoring with 11 goals and 23 assists for 34 points in 23 matches and was awarded the Conn Smythe Trophy as the most valuable player in the postseason, becoming the first American-born player to ever capture the award ... 34 points is the second highest total by a defenseman in playoff history, trailing only Paul Coffey's 37 in 1985 ... Is the first Ranger to lead the league in scoring since Pentti Lund in 1949-50 ... Led the team with five goals and six assists in the Finals and opened the scoring in Game Seven on June 14 ... Moved into second place on the Rangers all-time playoff scoring list with 58 points ... Set team playoff records for goals by a defenseman (11), points (34), assists (23), game-winning goals (four), and tied the club mark for power play goals with four ... Led the NHL with a plus 19 rating ... Was on the ice for 61 of the team's 81 goals, including 19 of the 22 power play tallies ... Collected a point in each of the first nine playoff matches and tallied a point in 19 of the 23 games overall.

INTERNATIONAL CAREER: Served as captain of the 1988 U.S. Olympic Team ... Participated for Team USA in the 1991 Canada Cup tournament ... Competed in the 1989 World Championships in Stockholm, Sweden, and was voted as the best player on Team USA ... Played with the 1987 National Team and the 1985, 1986, and 1987 National Junior Teams ... Named to the first All-Star Team at the 1987 World Junior Championship.

COLLEGE CAREER: Played one season (1986-87) for Boston College before leaving to play in the Olympics, and won the Hockey East Player of the Year and Rookie of the Year awards ... Led B.C. to the Hockey East Championship, while being tabbed an All-America and named to the All-Hockey East team ... Was a finalist for the Hobey Baker Memorial Award, symbolic of college hockey's best player, becoming the first freshman to ever be nominated for the award.

HIGH SCHOOL CAREER: Collected M.V.P. honors two consecutive seasons at Avon Old Farms ... All-New England Prep School selection and New England Prep School's Player of the Year in 1985-86.

BACKGROUND: Named the winner of the 1993-94 "Good Guy" award for cooperation with the media ... Does extensive work for the Leukemia Society and the Ronald McDonald House and is the Celebrity Chairman for the Ice Hockey in Harlem program ... "Leetchie" was a pitcher in high school with a fastball that was clocked at 90 miles an hour ... He, along with Mark Messier and Nick Kypreos, took batting practice with the Yankees while bringing the Stanley Cup to Yankee Stadium following the Rangers Stanley Cup Championship in 1994 ... Also, appeared along with Messier and Mike Richter on The Late Show with David Letterman following the team's Cup-victory, as well as The Today Show, Late Night with Conan O'Brien and The Howard Stern Show... Idol growing up was Ray Bourque ... His father, Jack, also played hockey for Boston College ... Enjoys fishing, tennis and golf ... Single.

CAREER TRANSACTIONS: June 21, 1986 — Rangers' first round choice (ninth overall) in the 1986 Entry Draft.

RANGERS RECORDS OWNED OR SHARED BY BRIAN LEETCH

REGULAR SEASON RECORDS

INDIVIDUAL RECORDS
Most Assists, One Season: 80, 1991-92
Longest Consecutive Point Scoring Streak: 17, November 23 thru December 31, 1991
(five goals and 24 assists)

INDIVIDUAL ROOKIE RECORDS
Most Assists, One Season: 48, 1988-89
Most Goals by a Defenseman, One Season: 23, 1988-89
Most Assists by a Defenseman, One Season: 48, 1988-89
Most Points by a Defenseman, One Season: 71, 1988-89
Most Assists, One Game: 4 (tied with three others) - February 17, 1989 against Toronto
at Madison Square Garden.
Most Points, One Game: 5, (tied with two others) - February 17, 1989 against Toronto
at Madison Square Garden.
Most Shots, One Season: 268, 1988-89

INDIVIDUAL DEFENSEMAN RECORDS
Most Assists, One Season: 80, 1991-92
Most Assists One Game: 5, April 18, 1995 at Pittsburgh*
Most Points, One Season: 102, 1991-92
Most Points, One Game: 5, (twice) April 18, 1995 at Pittsburgh and February 17, 1989
against Toronto at Madison Square Garden.
Most Power Play Goals, One Season: 17, 1993-94
Most Shorthanded Goals, One Season 3, 1988-89
Most Shots, One Season: 328, 1993-94
Most Shots, One Game: 13, January 4, 1989 against Washington at Madison Square Garden.
Longest Consecutive Assist Scoring Streak: 15, November 29 thru December 31, 1991
(23 assists during the streak).
Longest Consecutive Point Scoring Streak: 17, November 23 thru December 31, 1991
(five goals and 24 assists over the span).
* One of five players to tally five assists in one game and is the first defenseman.

PLAYOFF RECORDS

INDIVIDUAL PLAYER RECORDS
Most Goals, One Game: 3 (tied with 10 others) - May 22, 1995
against Philadelphia at Philadelphia
Most Assists, One Year: 23, 1993-94
Most Points, One Year: 34, 1993-94
Most Assists, One Period: 3, (tied with two others) - May 9, 1994
vs. Washington at Madison Square Garden during the first period.
Most Goals by a Defenseman, One Year: 11, 1993-94
Most Assists by a Defenseman, One Year: 23, 1993-94
Most Points by a Defenseman, One Year: 34, 1993-94
Most Points by a Defenseman, One Game: 4, twice (tied with two others) -
May 9, 1994 vs. Washington at Madison Square Garden (one goal and three assists);
June 7, 1994 vs. Vancouver at Vancouver (one goal and three assists).
Most Game-Winning Goals, One Year: 4, (tied) 1993-94
Most Power Play Goals, One Game: 2, (tied with seven others) - May 22, 1995
against Philadelphia at Philadelphia
Most Power Play Goals, One Period: 2, (tied with two others) - May 22, 1995
against Philadelphia at Philadelphia

CAREER PLAYER RECORDS
Most Assists: 47 (five playoffs)
Most Points by a Defenseman: 72 (five playoffs)
Most Points: 72 (five playoffs)
Most Power Play Goals:10 (tied with Rod Gilbert)

BRIAN 2 LEETCH

CAREER HIGHLIGHTS

MOST GOALS, GAME: 2, (13 times) last-Mar. 30, 1995 at Phi., **MOST ASSISTS, GAME:** 5, Apr. 18, 1995 at Pit., **MOST POINTS, GAME:** 5, (twice) last- Apr. 18, 1995 at Pit., **MOST PIM, GAME:** 15, Oct. 22, 1993 at T.B., **MOST SHOTS, GAME:** 13, Jan. 4, 1989 vs. Wsh., **MOST SHOTS, SEASON:** 328, 1993-94, **HIGHEST +/-, SEASON:** 28, 1993-94, **FIRST NHL GAME:** Feb. 29, 1988 vs. St.L., **FIRST NHL GOAL:** Mar. 24, 1988 vs. Edm. (Fuhr)

AMATEUR AND PROFESSIONAL RECORD

Season	Club	Lea	Regular Season GP	G	A	PTS	PIM	Playoffs GP	G	A	PTS	PIM
1984-85	Avon Old Farms	H.S.	26	30	46	76	15	—	—	—	—	—
1985-86	Avon Old Farms	H.S.	28	40	44	84	18	—	—	—	—	—
1986-87	Boston College	H.E.	37	9	38	47	10	—	—	—	—	—
1987-88	U.S. National Team		60	13	61	74	38	—	—	—	—	—
1987-88	U.S. Olympic Team		6	1	5	6	4	—	—	—	—	—
1987-88	Rangers	NHL	17	2	12	14	0	—	—	—	—	—
1988-89	Rangers	NHL	68	23	48	71	50	4	3	2	5	2
1989-90	Rangers	NHL	72	11	45	56	26	—	—	—	—	—
1990-91	Rangers	NHL	80	16	72	88	42	6	1	3	4	0
1991-92	Rangers	NHL	80	22	80	102	26	13	4	11	15	4
1992-93	Rangers	NHL	36	6	30	36	26	—	—	—	—	—
1993-94	Rangers	NHL	84	23	56	79	67	23	11	23	34	6
1994-95	Rangers	NHL	48	9	32	41	18	10	6	8	14	8
NHL and Rangers Totals			485	112	375	487	255	56	25	47	72	20

DOUG LIDSTER

6

6-1 • 190 • Shoots Right
Born: Oct. 18, 1960
Kamloops, British
Columbia
Off-Season Home:
Burnaby, British Columbia

DEFENSE

1994-95: Was aquired from St. Louis on July 31 … Skated in 37 matches with St. Louis, collecting two goals and seven assists for nine points and registered a plus nine rating ... Recorded a plus or even rating in 28 of his 37 games ... Amassed a plus six rating in four playoff contests.

NHL CAREER: 1983-84: Made his NHL debut on Feb. 28 at Washington following his participation for Team Canada in the 1984 Olympic Games at Sarajevo, Yugoslavia ... Played in eight regular season matches and two playoff games. **1984-85:** Appeared in 78 of 80 games in his first full campaign and ranked third on the team among defensemen with six goals and 24 assists for 30 points ... Led Canucks blueliners and was second overall on the team in plus/minus rating ... Captured the Premier Trophy as the team's most valuable defenseman as voted on by local media, along with the Fred J. Hume Award given to the Canucks' unsung hero as voted on by the media. **1985-86:** Skated in 78 games for the second consecutive season, doubling his goal output from the previous season, tallying 12 assist goals along with 16 assists for 28 points...Won his second consecutive Premier Trophy and Akai Cup as the team's top defenseman. **1986-87:** Finished seventh in the NHL in scoring among defensemen, notching a career-best 63 points, scoring 12 goals and 51 assists ... The 63 points set a record for points in a season by a Canucks defenseman ... Only Canucks player to appear in all 80 contests ... Posted 15 multiple-point games ... Led the team in power play scoring with three goals and 30 assists ... Captured the Premier Trophy and Akai Cup as the club's best defenseman for the third consecutive season. **1987-88:** Missed 16 games due to a knee injury suffered on Jan. 24 at Chicago... The injury halted his streak of 178 consecutive games ... Tallied four goals and 32 assists in 64 outings ... Two of his four goals were collected on the power play ... Led Canucks defensemen with 133 shots on goal. **1988-89:** Missed 17 games due to three different injuries, including a hyperextended elbow (3), hand fracture (5), and broken cheekbone (9) ... Appeared in each of Vancouver's seven playoff tilts. **1989-90:** Finished the season with eight goals and 28 assists for 36 points while appearing in all 80 games ... Along with Garth Butcher, was one of only two Canucks to skate in every game...Became the third defenseman in Canucks history to reach the 200 point plateau ... Potted a career-best two goals on Jan. 7 vs. Montreal. **1990-91:** Led Canucks blueliners in goals (6), assists (32), and points (38) while capturing the Babe Pratt Trophy as the club's top defenseman ... Named as team co-captain at the start of the season ... Collected four goals and 16 assists on the power play ... Skated in his 500th NHL contest Jan. 23 vs. Edmonton ... Nominated as the Canucks representative for the Bill Masterson Trophy. **1991-92:** Finished second on the team among backliners with six goals and 23 assists for 29 points ... Plus nine rating was third on the team

among defensemen ... Missed 13 games with a separated shoulder ... Collected three of his six goals on the power play, while two of the six were game-winners. **1992-93:** Appeared in 71 games for the Canucks, tallying six goals and 19 assists for 25 points along with a plus nine rating ... Placed fourth on the team in scoring among defensemen and was tied for second among backliners with six goals ... Moved into fourth place on the Canucks all-time games played list, playing in his 614th regular season contest on Mar. 4 at Boston...Tallied an assist on Feb. 22 vs. Toronto, moving him into ninth place on team's all-time point scoring list with 305...Skated in each of Vancouver's 12 playoff contests, recording three assists and a plus three rating. **1993-94:** The team was 22-9-3 with him in the lineup and they won both games he tallied a point. **1994 PLAYOFFS:** Notched two goals during the Stanley Cup Finals vs. Vancouver ... Appeared in the final nine playoff matches, including the Finals and Game Six and Game Seven of the Conference Finals vs. New Jersey.

TEAM CANADA: Played for the Canadian National Team after completing his college career and went on to help Canada finish fourth in the 1984 Olympics ... Teammates on Canadian blueline with James Patrick ... Helped lead Team Canada to silver medals in the 1989 and 1985 World Championships.

COLLEGE CAREER: Played four seasons at Colorado College in the WCHA ... Collected 18 goals and 25 assists for 43 points in his freshman campaign, 1979-80 ... Led the team in scoring with 15 goals and 41 assists for 56 points in his senior year and was named team MVP following the season ... His 56 points tied the school record for most in a season ... Earned honors as a first team WCHA selection ... Finished his college career with 56 goals and 118 assists for 174 points in 145 career matches.

BACKGROUND: Has served as Honorary Chairman of the British Columbia Special Olympics since 1987...Ranks fourth on Canucks all-time games played list with 666, places fifth with 242 assists, and is ninth in points with 307 ... Has never played in a minor league game ... Is the youngest of seven ... Also played baseball and soccer in high school in Kamloops...Enjoys fishing, golf, and water skiing ... Married: wife, Joanne, sons: Ryan and Colin; daughter, Brianna.

CAREER TRANSACTIONS: *June 11, 1980* — Vancouver's seventh round choice (133rd overall) in the 1980 Entry Draft. *June 24, 1993* — Traded to the Rangers by Vancouver as the future considerations in the John Vanbiesbrouck trade. *July 24, 1994* — Traded to St. Louis along with Esa Tikkanen in exchange for Petr Nedved. *July 31, 1995* — Traded from St. Louis to the Rangers for Jay Wells.

D O U G 6 L I D S T E R

CAREER HIGHLIGHTS

MOST GOALS, GAME: 2, Jan. 7, 1990 at Wpg., **MOST ASSISTS, GAME:** 3, Jan. 31, 1986 vs. Min., **MOST POINTS, GAME:** 6, Nov. 27, 1992 at Edm., **MOST PIM, GAME:** 4, Jan. 31, 1986 vs. Min., **MOST SHOTS, GAME:** 15, Oct. 18, 1985 vs. L.A., **MOST SHOTS, GAME:** 6, Jan. 13, 1990 vs. Buf., **MOST SHOTS, SEASON:** 176, 1986-87 **HIGHEST +/-, SEASON:** 10, 1992-93, **FIRST NHL GAME:** Feb. 28, 1984 at Wsh., **FIRST NHL GOAL:** Oct. 31, 1984 vs L.A. (Janecyk)

AMATEUR AND PROFESSIONAL RECORD

Season	Club	Lea	GP	G	A	PTS	PIM	GP	G	A	PTS	PIM
			REGULAR SEASON					**PLAYOFFS**				
1979-80	Colorado	WCHA	39	18	25	43	52	—	—	—	—	—
1980-81	Colorado	WCHA	36	10	30	40	54	—	—	—	—	—
1981-82	Colorado	WCHA	36	13	22	35	32	—	—	—	—	—
1982-83	Colorado	WCHA	34	15	41	56	30	—	—	—	—	—
1983-84	Canadian Olympic Team		59	6	20	26	28	—	—	—	—	—
1983-84	Vancouver	NHL	8	0	0	4	2	0	1	1	0	—
1984-85	Vancouver	NHL	78	6	24	30	55	—	—	—	—	—
1985-86	Vancouver	NHL	78	12	16	28	56	3	0	1	1	2
1986-87	Vancouver	NHL	80	12	51	63	40	—	—	—	—	—
1987-88	Vancouver	NHL	64	4	32	36	105	—	—	—	—	—
1988-89	Vancouver	NHL	63	5	17	22	78	7	1	1	2	9
1989-90	Vancouver	NHL	80	8	28	36	36	—	—	—	—	—
1990-91	Vancouver	NHL	78	6	32	38	77	6	0	2	2	6
1991-92	Vancouver	NHL	66	6	23	29	39	11	1	2	3	11
1992-93	Vancouver	NHL	71	6	19	25	36	12	0	3	3	8
1993-94	Rangers	NHL	34	0	2	2	33	9	2	0	2	10
1994-95	St. Louis	NHL	37	2	7	9	12	4	0	0	0	2
NHL Totals			737	67	251	318	568	54	4	10	14	46
Rangers Totals			34	0	2	2	33	9	2	0	2	10

KEVIN LOWE

4

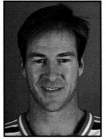

6-2 • 195 • Shoots Left
Born: April 15, 1959
Lachute, Quebec
Off-Season Home: Tappen,
British Columbia

DEFENSE

1994-95: Tallied a power play goal on Apr. 16 at Long Island, his first PPG since Nov. 11, 1990 at Washington ... Five of his seven assists and six of his eight points were collected on the road ... Four of his seven assists were tallied vs. the Northeast Division ... Registered a plus or even rating in 32 of his 44 matches ... Tallied assists in four consecutive games from Jan. 30 to Feb. 4 ... Missed three games due to injury ... Was given the New York Chapter of the Professional Hockey Writers' Associaton "Good Guy" Award for cooperation with the media ... Became the fifth player in NHL history to skate in 200 playoff matches on May 22 in Game Two of the conference semi-finals at Philadelphia.

NHL CAREER: 1979-80: Went directly to the Oilers, without playing a minor league game, after being selected by Edmonton as their first choice (20th overall) in the 1979 draft ... Scored the first NHL goal in the history of the club in his initial NHL game on Oct. 10 in Chicago ... **1980-81:** Played in 79 games which was tied for third on the club ... Scored a career high 10 goals ... **1981-82:** One of five Oilers to play in all 80 contests ... Of his nine goals, two were game-winners ... **1982-83:** One of seven Oilers to play in all 80 matches ... Collected a career high five assists and six points on Feb. 19 at Pittsburgh ... **1983-84:** Played in all 80 outings for the third consecutive season ... Recorded a career high 42 assists and 46 points ... Appeared in his first NHL All-Star Game ... **1984-85:** Appeared in 80 games for the fourth straight season and played in his second All-Star Game ... **1985-86:** Consecutive game streak came to an end at 420 straight outings when he suffered a finger injury and missed six games ... The streak is still an Oilers record ... Played in his third All-Star Game ... **1986-87:** Named as an alternate captain on Mar. 6 after Lee Fogolin was traded ... Accumulated a seven-game point-scoring streak from Jan. 28 to Feb. 8 ... Plus 41 rating placed fourth on the team. **1987-88:** Missed 10 games with a wrist injury ... Played in his fourth NHL All-Star Game ... Scored overtime goal at Winnipeg on Feb. 3. **1988-89:** Plus 26 rating was second on the club and his 25 points were second among team defensemen ... Played in his fifth All-Star Game ... **1989-90:** Ranked second among Oilers defensemen with 33 points and placed fourth on the team with a plus 18 rating ... Played in his sixth All-Star Game ... **1990-91:** Missed seven games with an ankle injury. **1991-92:** Named team captain before the start of the season, replacing Mark Messier, who was traded to New York. **1992-93:** Obtained from Edmonton on Dec. 11 ... Made his Rangers debut on Dec. 15 vs. Calgary ...

Recorded his first goal with New York on Dec. 23 vs. New Jersey ... Collected his 300th NHL assist on Jan. 9 at Philadelphia ... Tallied an assist in the NHL All-Star game on Feb. 6 while making his seventh All-Star appearance ... Skated in his 1,000th NHL game on Mar. 11 in 4-1 victory at Chicago. **1993-94:** Skated in 71 games in his first full season with New York ... Tallied a pair of assists, including his 400th NHL point, on Jan. 25 at San Jose ... Collected four of his 14 assists on game winning goals ... Four of his five goals and 13 of his 19 points were registered on the road ... Rangers were 15-2-0 when he collected a point. **1994 PLAY-OFFS:** Appeared in 22 of the 23 playoff matches, collecting a goal on Apr. 18 in Game Two of the Conference Quarterfinals vs. the Islanders ... Moved past Denis Potvin into second place on the NHL's all-time games played list among defensemen on May 31 in Game One of the Finals.

INTERNATIONAL CAREER: Played for Team Canada in the 1982 World Championships and the 1984 Canada Cup.

JUNIOR CAREER: Played three seasons of junior hockey with the Quebec Remparts of the Quebec Major Junior Hockey League, serving as team captain in his final year ... Named a QMJHL Second-Team All-Star in '78-79.

BACKGROUND: Won the King Clancy Memorial Trophy for his leadership qualities on and off the ice and for his humanitarian contribution to the community and the BUD Light/NHL Man Of The Year award as a positive role model in the local community through his conduct on and off the ice in 1990 ... Completed his 13-year career with Edmonton as their all-time leader in games played in the regular season (966) and the playoffs (170) ... His total of 1,164 minutes in penalties are the second most in Oilers history ... Wore uniform number four during his career in Edmonton ... Member of five Stanley Cup Championship teams in Edmonton ... His brother, Ken, is the Oilers athletic trainer ... Married Olympic skier Karen Percy on June 16, 1990 ... Daughter, Devyn; son, Keegan.

CAREER TRANSACTIONS: *August 19, 1979* — Edmonton's first choice (21st overall) in the 1979 Entry Draft. *December 11, 1992* — Traded to Rangers by Edmonton in exchange for Roman Oksiuta and a third round draft choice in 1993.

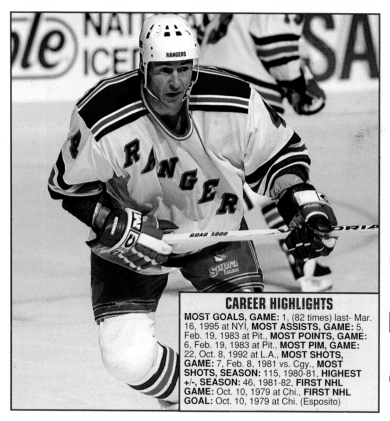

CAREER HIGHLIGHTS

MOST GOALS, GAME: 1, (82 times) last- Mar. 16, 1995 at NYI, **MOST ASSISTS, GAME:** 5, Feb. 19, 1983 at Pit., **MOST POINTS, GAME:** 6, Feb. 19, 1983 at Pit., **MOST PIM, GAME:** 22, Oct. 8, 1992 at L.A., **MOST SHOTS, GAME:** 7, Feb. 8, 1981 vs. Cgy., **MOST SHOTS, SEASON:** 115, 1980-81, **HIGHEST +/-, SEASON:** 46, 1981-82, **FIRST NHL GAME:** Oct. 10, 1979 at Chi., **FIRST NHL GOAL:** Oct. 10, 1979 at Chi. (Esposito)

AMATEUR AND PROFESSIONAL RECORD

Season	Club	Lea	GP	G	A	PTS	PIM	GP	G	A	PTS	PIM
			Regular Season					**Playoffs**				
1977-78	Quebec ....QJHL		64	13	52	65	86	4	1	2	3	6
1978-79	Quebec ....QJHL		68	26	60	86	120	6	1	7	8	36
1979-80	Edmonton..................NHL		64	2	19	21	70	3	0	1	1	0
1980-81	Edmonton..................NHL		79	10	24	34	94	9	0	2	2	11
1981-82	Edmonton..................NHL		80	9	31	40	63	5	0	3	3	0
1982-83	Edmonton..................NHL		80	6	34	40	43	16	1	8	9	10
1983-84	Edmonton..................NHL		80	4	42	46	59	19	3	7	10	16
1984-85	Edmonton..................NHL		80	4	22	26	104	16	0	5	5	8
1985-86	Edmonton..................NHL		74	2	16	18	90	10	1	3	4	15
1986-87	Edmonton..................NHL		77	8	29	37	94	21	2	4	6	22
1987-88	Edmonton..................NHL		70	9	15	24	89	19	0	2	2	26
1988-89	Edmonton..................NHL		76	7	18	25	98	7	1	2	3	4
1989-90	Edmonton..................NHL		78	7	26	33	140	20	0	2	2	10
1990-91	Edmonton..................NHL		73	3	13	16	113	14	1	1	2	14
1991-92	Edmonton..................NHL		55	2	8	10	107	11	0	3	3	16
1992-93	Rangers ....NHL		49	3	12	15	58	—	—	—	—	—
1993-94	Rangers ....NHL		71	5	14	19	70	22	1	0	1	20
1994-95	Rangers ....NHL		44	1	7	8	58	10	0	1	1	12
NHL Totals 1130				82	330	412	1350	202	10	44	54	184
Rangers Totals 164				9	33	42	186	32	1	1	2	32

STEPHANE MATTEAU

32

**6-3 • 215 • Shoots Left
Born: Sept. 2, 1969
Rouyn-Noranda, Quebec
Off-Season Home: Rouyn-
Noranda, Quebec**

LEFT WING

1994-95: Registered three goals and five assists in 42 matches ... All three of his goals were tallied at MSG, while three of his five assists were tallied on the road ... Rangers were 5-2-1 when he registered a point ... Missed three games due to injury ... Tallied one assist in nine playoff matches.

NHL CAREER: 1990-91: Placed second on the Flames among rookies in goals (15), assists (19) and points (34) ... Led club rookies and tied for first in the NHL among rookies with a plus 17 rating ... Made his NHL debut on October 4 vs. Vancouver ... Registered his first NHL goal on October 8 at Winnipeg ... Tallied one shorthanded goal and assisted on four shorthanded scores ... Was plus or even in 60 of his 78 matches ... Recorded a five-game point-scoring streak from February 15 to February 23, collecting three goals and two assists over the span. **1991-92:** Began the season with Calgary, appearing in four games before being dealt to Chicago in exchange for Trent Yawney on December 6 ... Missed 43 games due to a bruised thigh ... Made his Blackhawks debut on January 23 vs. Quebec ... Tallied his first point with the Blackhawks on January 27 at Calgary ... Potted his first goal with Chicago on March 10 vs. San Jose ... Placed fifth on the team with four playoff goals and ranked seventh with 10 points in 18 playoff matches. **1992-93:** Equaled his career-high of 15 goals, set in his rookie season with Calgary ... Recorded a pair of power play goals and two game-winning goals along with a plus six rating ... Registered nine of his 15 goals at home. **1993-94:** Acquired from Chicago along with Brian Noonan on March 21 ... Collected four goals and three assists along with a plus six rating in 12 games with New York ... Established career highs with 19 goals and 38 points ... Recorded the game tying goal with 14 seconds remaining on March 22 at Calgary while making his Rangers debut ... Rangers were 8-2-2 with him in the lineup and 4-1-1 when he scored a goal ... Tallied 15 goals and 26 assists for 31 points, along with a plus 10 rating in 65 games with Chicago ... Notched a career-high three points on March 18 vs. the Rangers at Madison Square Garden. **1994 PLAYOFFS:** Tallied six goals and three assists while appearing in all 23 matches ... Potted the game-winning and series clinching goal at 4:24 of the second overtime period in Game Seven of the Conference Finals vs. New

Jersey ... Tallied the game-winning goal at 6:13 of the second overtime period on May 19 in Game Three at New Jersey and is one of only four players, including Mel Hill, Maurice Richard and Petr Klima to tally two double-overtime goals.

IHL CAREER: Joined Salt Lake for the 1989 playoffs, following the completion of his junior career ... Registered four assists in nine play-off outings ... Notched 23 goals and 35 assists for 58 points along with 130 penalty minutes in 81 games with Salt Lake in his first professional season ... Ranked fifth on the club in goals and points ... Tallied six goals and three assists along with 38 penalty minutes in 10 playoff matches.

JUNIOR CAREER: Played four seasons with the Hull Olympiques (QMJHL) ... Appeared in his first season with Hull in 1985-86, collecting six goals and eight assists in 60 matches ... Recorded 27 goals and 48 assists for 75 points along with 113 penalty minutes in 69 games in 1986-87 ... Collected five goals and 14 assists for 19 points in 18 playoff matches in 1988, leading Hull to the Memorial Cup Tournament ... Tied for the team lead in scoring in 1988-89 with 44 goals and 45 assists for 89 points in 59 matches ... Also notched 202 penalty minutes ... Registered eight goals and six assists for 14 points in nine playoff matches to finish his junior career with 16 goals and 27 assists in 44 playoff matches.

BACKGROUND: Serves as the celebrity chairman for the "Street Rangers" youth street hockey program ... Returns to Rouyn-Noranda in the off-season ... Skated on a line with Chicago's Jeremy Roenick and Vancouver's Martin Gelinas while with Hull ... Boyhood friends with the Canadiens Pierre Turgeon, the two played hockey and organized baseball together, including the 1982 Little League World Series ... Married: wife Natalie; son, Stephane Jr.

CAREER TRANSACTIONS: *June 13, 1987* — Calgary's 2nd choice (25th overall) in the 1987 NHL Entry Draft. *December 6, 1991* — Traded to Chicago from Calgary in exchange for Trent Yawney. *March 21, 1994* — Traded to the Rangers from Chicago with Brian Noonan in exchange for Tony Amonte and Matt Oates.

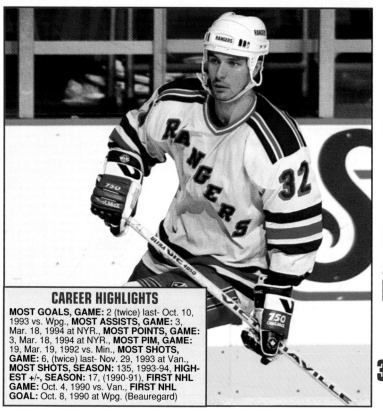

CAREER HIGHLIGHTS

MOST GOALS, GAME: 2 (twice) last- Oct. 10, 1993 vs. Wpg., **MOST ASSISTS, GAME:** 3, Mar. 18, 1994 at NYR., **MOST POINTS, GAME:** 3, Mar. 18, 1994 at NYR., **MOST PIM, GAME:** 19, Mar. 19, 1992 vs. Min., **MOST SHOTS, GAME:** 6, (twice) last- Nov. 29, 1993 at Van., **MOST SHOTS, SEASON:** 135, 1993-94, **HIGHEST +/-, SEASON:** 17, (1990-91), **FIRST NHL GAME:** Oct. 4, 1990 vs. Van., **FIRST NHL GOAL:** Oct. 8, 1990 at Wpg. (Beauregard)

AMATEUR AND PROFESSIONAL RECORD

Season	Club	Lea	Regular Season					Playoffs				
			GP	G	A	PTS	PIM	GP	G	A	PTS	PIM
1985-86	Hull	QMJHL	60	6	8	14	19	4	0	0	0	0
1986-87	Hull	QMJHL	69	27	49	75	113	8	3	7	10	8
1987-88	Hull	QMJHL	57	17	40	57	179	18	5	14	19	94
1988-89	Hull	QMJHL	59	44	45	89	202	9	8	6	14	30
1988-89	Salt Lake	IHL	—	—	—	—	—	9	0	4	4	13
1989-90	Salt Lake	IHL	81	23	35	58	130	10	6	3	9	38
1990-91	Calgary	NHL	78	15	19	34	93	5	0	1	1	0
1991-92	Calgary	NHL	4	1	0	1	19	—	—	—	—	—
1991-92	Chicago	NHL	20	5	8	13	45	18	4	6	10	24
1992-93	Chicago	NHL	79	15	18	33	98	3	0	1	1	2
1993-94	Chicago	NHL	65	15	16	31	55	—	—	—	—	—
1993-94	Rangers	NHL	12	4	3	7	2	23	6	3	9	20
1994-95	Rangers	NHL	41	3	5	8	25	9	0	1	1	10
NHL Totals			299	58	69	127	337	58	10	12	22	56
Rangers Totals			53	7	8	15	27	32	6	4	10	30

MARK MESSIER

11

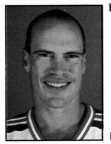

6-1 • 205 • Shoots Left
Born: January 18, 1961
Edmonton, Alberta
Off-Season Home: Hilton Head, South Carolina

CENTER

1994-95: Led the team and tied for 10th in the NHL with 53 points ... Also led the club with 39 assists, ranking fifth in the NHL ... Tied for third on the club with 14 goals and tied for second on the team with a plus eight rating ... Registered three assists on Apr. 26 vs. Tampa Bay, tying John Bucyk for seventh place on the NHL's All-Time Scoring List with 1,369 points ... Posted an assist in eight consecutive games from Apr. 12 to Apr. 26, tallying 19 assists over the span ... The streak tied for the longest in the NHL ... The streak also tied the longest assist streak of his career ... Collected a pair of assists on the power play on Apr. 24 vs. Washington, moving past Phil Esposito into eighth place on the NHL's All-Time Assist list with 874 ... Tallied four assists on Apr. 18 at Pittsburgh ... Tallied four assists on Apr. 14 vs. Boston, moving past Guy Lafleur into eighth place on the NHL's All Time Scoring list ... Tallied 25 points (three goals, 22 assists) in his last 15 games and 35 points (six goals, 29 assists) in his last 25 matches ... Registered his third shorthanded goal of the season on Mar. 15 vs. Philadelphia and tied for third in the NHL with three shorthanded goals ... Collected a point in 30 of his 46 matches ... Rangers were 18-10-2 when he registered a point and 3-12-1 when he didn't ... Registered two game-winning goals and assisted on seven game-winners, ranking first on the team with nine points on game-winning goals ... Led the club with 15 multiple-point games ... Led the team with 16 assists and 25 points vs. the Atlantic Division ... Placed second on the team with 13 points in the post-season, tallying three goals and 10 assists ... Tallied a goal on May 24 in Game Three of the conference semi-finals vs. Philadelphia, tying Jari Kurri for second place on the NHL's all-time playoff goal scoring list with 102 ... Also, passed Don Maloney for third place on the Rangers playoff scoring list with 57 points.

NHL CAREER: 1979-80: Played his first NHL game, at 18 years old, on Oct. 10 vs. Chicago and registered his first NHL goal on Oct. 13 vs. Detroit ... Sent to Houston of the Central Hockey League from Oct. 30 to Nov. 8 ... Brief, four-game, stint with the Apollos are the only games he has played in the minors. **1980-81:** Improved his point totals from 33 to 63 ... 35 of the 63 were scored in his final 24 games ... Collected first NHL three-point effort (all assists) on Jan. 28 vs. Montreal and notched his first four-point outing (two goals, two assists) on Mar. 3 vs. the Islanders ... Potted his first hat trick on Mar. 16 vs. Pittsburgh ... Helped Edmonton to a three-game sweep of

Montreal in the first round of the playoffs. **1981-82:** Blossomed into one of the NHL's premier players, scoring 50 goals and being tabbed as the NHL's First-Team All-Star left wing. **1982-83:** Scored over 100 points for the first time, collecting 48 goals and 58 assists for 106 points, placing seventh in the NHL and second on Edmonton, behind Wayne Gretzky ... Tabbed as the NHL's First-Team All-Star left wing ... Registered his first NHL four-goal game on Dec. 18 vs. Montreal ... Helped Oilers to their first-ever Stanley Cup Finals, despite playing with a sore shoulder ... Led team in playoffs with 15 goals in 15 games, including a four-goal outing vs. Calgary on Apr. 14. **1983-84:** Scored over 100 points for the second consecutive season and was named as the NHL's Second-Team All-Star left wing ... Began playing regularly at center ice on Feb. 15 ... Led the Oilers in PIM with 165 ... Posted a career high six assists vs. Minnesota on Jan. 4 ... Led Edmonton to a record of 57-18-5 for 119 points and on to the first Stanley Cup in team history ... Captured the Conn Smythe Trophy as the playoff's MVP, tallying eight goals and 18 assists for 26 points. **1984-85:** Limited to only 55 games due to a left knee injury suffered on Nov. 4 vs. Winnipeg that caused him to miss 15 contests ... Sat out a 10 game suspension for an altercation with Calgary's Jamie Macoun ... Collected 12 goals and 13 assists for 25 points in 18 playoff matches, helping Edmonton to their second consecutive Stanley Cup. **1985-86:** For the second season in a row his playing time was limited due to injury, as he suffered a left foot injury on Dec. 3 and missed 17 contests. **1986-87:** Went over the 100-point plateau for the third time, tying for third in the NHL's scoring race with 107 points (37 goals, 70 assists) ... 70 assists ranked third in the NHL and placed second on the club ... Member of the NHL team at Rendez-Vous '87 and was named the first star in Game One ... Ranked second in NHL in playoff scoring with 28 points, ... Helped Oilers win their third Stanley Cup. **1987-88:** Notched over 100 points for the fourth time in his career ... Ranked second on Edmonton and fifth in the NHL with 74 assists and 111 points and placed fifth on club with 37 goals ... Registered 33 multiple-point games, including five, four-point games and one, five-point performance on Feb. 23 vs. St. Louis ... Led the team with seven gwg's ... Outstanding playoff performance included a 14-game scoring streak, along with four, four-point efforts ... 23 playoff assists and 34 playoff points were second in NHL along with his 11 goals, helping Edmonton to their fourth Stanley

Cup. **1988-89:** Named captain of the Oilers before the start of the season after Gretzky was traded to L.A. ... Led the club and placed seventh in the NHL with 61 assists, 94 points was third on team ... **1989-90:** Established career highs with 84 assists and 129 points and won the Hart Trophy as the NHL's MVP ... Was also named winner of the Lester B. Pearson Award by the Players Association as the NHL's Outstanding Player, a First-Team NHL All-Star, winner of The Sporting News and Hockey News Player of the Year Awards ... Assist and point totals placed second in NHL, while he led the Oilers in each category, as well as in goals (45) and shots (211) ... Registered at least one point in all but 15 contests and on only one occasion failed to register a point in back-to-back games ... Collected 41 multiple point games inlcuding, a five-point performance (one goal, four assists) on Jan. 25 vs. L.A. ... Appeared in a career high 79 games, resting for the final regular-season contest ... Tied for NHL lead in playoff scoring with 31 points and led NHL with 22 playoff assists ... Also recorded an 11-game point scoring streak in playoffs, leading the Oilers to their fifth Stanley Cup. **1990-91:** Limited to a career low 53 games due to two different injuries ... Injured his left knee on Oct. 16 vs. St. Louis and missed 19 games and fractured his left thumb on Feb. 18, sitting out the next eight games ... Edmonton was 29-20-4 with him in the lineup and 8-17-2 without him. **1991-92:** Swept all of the MVP post season awards, including the Hart Trophy as the NHL's MVP, becoming the first Ranger to win the award since Andy Bathgate in '58-59 ... Captured the Pearson Award as the league's top player as voted by all NHL players, The Sporting News Player of the Year Award and The Hockey News Player of the Year Award, while also earning a first-team All-Star berth ... Acquired from Edmonton on Oct. 4 ... Made Rangers debut the following night at the Montreal Forum and was named team captain before the home opener on Oct. 7 ... Led team in scoring with 107 points, falling two points shy of tying Jean Ratelle's franchise record for most points in a single season ... Set team record for most assists by a center in a season (72), breaking Mike Rogers' mark of 65 set in '81-82 ... Joined Ratelle, Rogers, Vic Hadfield and Brian Leetch as the only players in club history to record 100 points in a season ... Tied for fifth in NHL with 107 points and 72 assists ... Ranked third in the NHL with 65 even-strength points and placed second with nine shorthanded points ... Led club with three hat tricks, including a four-goal game vs. Devils on Mar. 22 ... Registered a career high 15-game point scoring streak from Feb. 5 to Mar. 7 ... Placed third on the club in playoff scoring with 14 points, despite missing two games due to a back injury. **1992-93:** Skated in his 1,000th NHL game at New Jersey on Apr. 7 ... Notched the fourth highest single-season assist total in Rangers history with 66 ... Tied his career-high with six-point effort at Pittsburgh on Nov. 25 ... Ranked first on the team with 66 assists and 91 points ... Led the team with 30 power play points ... Was named to the All-Star team for the 11th consecutive season, but missed the game due to injury. **1993-94:** Placed second on the team with 81 points ... Tied for first on the club with 24 multiple-point games ...

Notched his 800th assist on Dec. 4 at Toronto ... Moved past Alex Delvecchio into 10th place on the NHL's All-Time Scoring list with two points on Jan. 31 vs. Pittsburgh ... Tallied a pair of assists on Mar. 2 vs. Quebec, moving past Delvecchio into 10th place on the NHL's All-Time Assist list ... Registered an 11-game point scoring streak from Jan. 14 to Feb. 9 ... Tied for first in the NHL with seven shorthanded assists ... Assisted on 23 of Adam Graves' club-record 52 goals overall ... Notched four assists for the seventh time in his career on Feb. 2 vs. the Islanders ... Made his 12th NHL all-star appearance on Jan. 22 at MSG, while serving as captain of the Eastern Conference. **1994 PLAYOFFS:** Placed second on the team and third in the NHL with 30 points in 23 matches ... Netted the Stanley Cup clinching goal on June 14 in Game Seven ... Tied for second on the team with seven points in the Finals ... Notched his fourth career playoff hat trick (first as a Ranger), including the game-tying and winning goals on May 25 in Game Six of the Conference Finals at New Jersey ... Set a club record for goals in one playoff year with 12 ... Tallied a point in each of the first 13 matches and in 21 of the 23 post-season matches ... Tied for first in the NHL with four game-winning goals and ranked third in the league with a plus 14 rating ... Registered a goal on Apr. 18 in Game Two of the Conference Quarterfinals vs. the Islanders, moving past Glenn Anderson into third place on the NHL's all-time playoff goal scoring list.

WHA CAREER: Signed as a 17-year old by the Indianapolis Racers after only one year of junior hockey to replace Gretzky, who was sold to the Edmonton Oilers ... After five games with the Racers, he joined the Cincinnati Stingers, where he was teammates with Paul Stewart, a current NHL referee.

INTERNATIONAL COMPETITION: Helped Team Canada to three Canada Cup championships in 1984, 1987 and 1991 ... Also played for Team Canada in the 1989 World Championships at Stockholm, Sweden ... Was a member of the NHL team at Rendez-Vous '87.

BACKGROUND: Has raised over $200,000 for the Tomorrows Children's Fund over the last two seasons after establishing the Mark Messier Point Club in 1993 ... Appeared with teammate Brian Leetch in December of 1991 on the "Late Night with David Letterman" show in a skit that had the pair trying to break a camera with slapshots ... Also appeared with Leetch and Richter with the Stanley Cup on the Late Show with David Letterman following the Stanley Cup Championship in 1994 ... Also, appeared on The Howard Stern Show and threw out the first pitch at Yankee Stadium following the Cup victory ... Became first player in league history to serve as captain for two different Stanley Cup-winning teams ...14 playoff shorthanded goals are an NHL record ... Single.

CAREER TRANSACTIONS: *June 19, 1979* — Edmonton's second choice (third round, 48th overall) in the 1979 Entry Draft. *October 4, 1991* — Traded by Edmonton to New York along with future considerations in exchange for Bernie Nicholls, Steven Rice and Louie DeBrusk.

SCORING STREAKS AND MULTIPLE POINT GAMES

CAREER POINT SCORING STREAKS
(SIX GAMES OR MORE)

(Goals, Assists and Points during streak listed on right)

15	Feb. 5, 1992 -	Mar. 7, 1992	(7-17-24)
14	Oct. 31, 1987 -	Nov. 29, 1987	(11-16-27)
14	Jan. 11, 1983 -	Feb. 14, 1983	(9-17-26)
12	Dec. 11, 1982 -	Jan. 7, 1983	(13-18-31)
12	Feb. 19, 1989 -	Mar. 5, 1989	(8-15-23)
11	Oct. 5, 1991 -	Oct. 26, 1991	(5-11-16)
11	Mar. 1, 1985 -	Mar. 26, 1985	(9- 6-15)
10	Oct. 22, 1983 -	Nov. 12, 1982	(5- 8-13)
10	Dec. 10, 1986 -	Jan. 3, 1987	(4-15-19)
9	Feb. 7, 1990 -	Feb. 25, 1990	(4-14-18)
9	Nov. 25, 1989 -	Dec. 16, 1989	(4-11-15)
9	Mar. 4, 1984 -	Mar. 21, 1984	(9- 8-17)
9	Nov. 8, 1982 -	Nov. 24, 1982	(7- 4-11)
9	Oct. 12, 1992 -	Oct. 29, 1992	(6-10-16)
8	Nov. 3, 1985 -	Nov. 17, 1985	(4- 8- 12)
8	Oct. 19, 1986 -	Nov. 2, 1986	(5-11-16)
8	Oct. 22, 1989 -	Nov. 4, 1989	(5- 9-14)
8	Nov. 19, 1992 -	Dec. 4, 1992	(5-11-16)
8	Feb. 12, 1993 -	Feb. 27, 1993	(2-11-13)
7	Oct. 31, 1991 -	Nov. 13, 1991	(0- 8- 8)
6	Mar. 3, 1990 -	Mar. 10, 1990	(7- 6-13)
6	Jan. 16, 1990 -	Jan. 30, 1990	(8-11-19)
6	Oct. 5, 1989 -	Oct. 18, 1989	(6- 6-12)
6	Mar. 12, 1988 -	Mar. 24, 1988	(2- 9-11)
6	Dec. 16, 1987 -	Dec. 28, 1987	(4- 5- 9)
6	Oct. 9, 1987 -	Oct. 21, 1987	(6- 6-12)
6	Mar. 14, 1986 -	Mar. 28, 1986	(7- 6-13)
6	Feb. 9, 1986 -	Feb. 22, 1986	(1-10-11)
6	Jan. 24, 1986 -	Feb. 1, 1986	(6- 8-14)
6	Nov. 11, 1981 -	Nov. 19, 1981	(3- 4- 7)
6	Feb. 18, 1981 -	Feb. 27, 1981	(3- 6- 9)
6	Nov. 26, 1980 -	Dec. 10, 1980	(4- 4- 8)

GOAL SCORING STREAKS
(MINIMUM OF FOUR)

6	Mar. 14, 1986 -	Mar. 28, 1986	(seven)
5	Jan. 15, 1983 -	Jan. 23, 1983	(seven)
4	Feb. 7, 1992 -	Feb. 14, 1992	(four)
4	Oct. 5, 1990 -	Oct. 13, 1990	(four)
4	Mar. 4, 1987 -	Mar. 11, 1987	(five)
4	Jan. 24, 1986 -	Jan. 31, 1986	(five)
4	Mar. 9, 1985 -	Mar. 17, 1985	(five)
4	Mar. 16, 1983 -	Mar. 23, 1983	(five)
4	Nov. 16, 1982 -	Nov. 24, 1982	(four)
4	Oct. 21, 1981 -	Oct. 27, 1981	(four)
4	Oct. 9, 1981 -	Oct. 16, 1981	(four)

ASSIST STREAKS
(MINIMUM OF FIVE)

8	Feb. 12, 1992 -	Feb. 27, 1992	(11)
8	Feb. 11, 1990 -	Feb. 25, 1990	(14)
7	Nov. 21, 1992 -	Dec. 4, 1992	(11)
7	Oct. 31, 1991 -	Nov. 13, 1991	(eight)
7	Nov. 3, 1985 -	Nov. 16, 1985	(eight)
7	Jan. 22, 1983 -	Feb. 4, 1983	(10)
6	Feb. 9, 1992 -	Feb. 20, 1992	(eight)
6	Oct. 5, 1991 -	Oct. 14, 1991	(eight)
6	Jan. 16, 1990 -	Jan. 30, 1990	(11)
6	Mar. 12, 1988 -	Mar. 24, 1988	(nine)
6	Dec. 10, 1986 -	Dec. 20, 1986	(11)
5	Oct. 12, 1992 -	Oct. 21, 1992	(seven)
5	Jan. 14, 1992 -	Jan. 28, 1992	(seven)
5	Nov. 23, 1991 -	Dec. 6, 1991	(six)
5	Nov. 25, 1989 -	Dec. 3, 1989	(seven)
5	Feb. 11, 1988 -	Feb. 19, 1988	(10)
5	Oct. 31, 1987 -	Nov. 7, 1987	(seven)
5	Dec. 14, 1983 -	Dec. 23, 1983	(seven)
5	Nov. 21, 1983 -	Nov. 30, 1983	(seven)
5	Mar. 21, 1981 -	Mar. 29, 1981	(eight)

ALL-TIME MULTIPLE-POINT GAMES

Two Goal Games	68	(last—Feb. 24, 1993 at Vancouver)
Three Goal Games	12	(last—Dec. 13, 1991 at Washington)
Four Goal Games	4	(last—Mar. 22, 1992 vs. New Jersey)
Two Assist Games	143	(last—Apr. 10, 1993 at Pittsburgh)
Three Assist Games	42	(last—Mar. 24, 1993 vs. Philadelphia)
Four Assist Games	6	(last—Nov. 25, 1992 at Pittsburgh)
Five Assist Games	None	
Six Assist Games	1	(Jan. 4, 1984 vs. Minnesota)
Two Point Games	217	(last—Mar. 10, 1993 at Pittsburgh)
Three Point Games	104	(last—Mar. 24, 1993 vs. Philadelphia)
Four Point Games	28	(last—Jan. 13, 1993 vs. Washington)
Five Point Games	2	(last—Jan. 25, 1990 vs. L.A.)
Six Point Games	2	(last—Nov. 25, 1992 at Pittsburgh)

CAREER HIGHLIGHTS

MOST GOALS, GAME: 4, (four times) last- Mar. 22, 1992 vs. N.J., **MOST ASSISTS, GAME:** 6, Jan. 4, 1984 vs. Min., **MOST POINTS, GAME:** 6, (twice) last- Nov. 25, 1992 at Pit., **MOST PIM, GAME:** 30, Jan. 19, 1980 vs. Pit., **MOST SHOTS, GAME:** 10, Jan. 13, 1993 vs. Wsh., **MOST SHOTS, SEASON:** 237, 1982-83, **HIGHEST +/-, SEASON:** 40, 1983-84, **FIRST NHL GAME:** Oct. 10, 1979 vs. Chi., **FIRST NHL GOAL:** Oct. 13, 1979 vs. Det. (Vachon)

AMATEUR AND PROFESSIONAL RECORD

Season	Club	Lea	Regular Season GP	G	A	PTS	PIM	Playoffs GP	G	A	PTS	PIM
1977-78	Portland	WHL	—	—	—	—	—	7	4	1	5	2
1978-79	Indianapolis	WHA	5	0	0	0	0	—	—	—	—	—
1978-79	Cincinnati	WHA	47	1	10	11	58	—	—	—	—	—
1979-80	Houston	CHL	4	0	3	3	4	—	—	—	—	—
1979-80	Edmonton	NHL	75	12	21	33	120	3	1	2	3	2
1980-81	Edmonton	NHL	72	23	40	63	102	9	2	5	7	13
1981-82	Edmonton	NHL	78	50	38	88	119	5	1	2	3	8
1982-83	Edmonton	NHL	77	48	58	106	72	15	15	6	21	14
1983-84	Edmonton	NHL	73	37	64	101	165	19	8	18	26	19
1984-85	Edmonton	NHL	55	23	31	54	57	18	12	13	25	12
1985-86	Edmonton	NHL	63	35	49	84	68	10	4	6	10	18
1986-87	Edmonton	NHL	77	37	70	107	73	21	12	16	28	16
1987-88	Edmonton	NHL	77	37	74	111	103	19	11	23	34	29
1988-89	Edmonton	NHL	72	33	61	94	130	7	1	11	12	8
1989-90	Edmonton	NHL	79	45	84	129	79	22	9	22	31	20
1990-91	Edmonton	NHL	53	12	52	64	34	18	4	11	15	16
1991-92	Rangers	NHL	79	35	72	107	76	11	7	7	14	6
1992-93	Rangers	NHL	75	25	66	91	72	—	—	—	—	—
1993-94	Rangers	NHL	76	26	58	84	76	23	12	18	30	33
1994-95	Rangers	NHL	46	14	39	53	40	10	3	10	13	8
NHL Totals			1127	492	877	1369	1386	210	102	170	272	222
Rangers Totals			276	100	235	335	264	44	22	35	57	47

SERGEI NEMCHINOV

13

**6-0 • 205 • Shoots Left
Born: January 14, 1964
Moscow, Russia
Off-Season Home: Rye, New York**

CENTER

1994-95: Nine of his 13 points (six goals, three assists) were tallied on the road ... Three of his seven goals were game-winners ... Tied for second on the team with six goals on the road ... Rangers were 5-1-0 when he scored a goal and 8-2-1 when he tallied a point ... All of his 13 points were registered at even strength ... Registered a plus or even rating in nine of the last 12 games and in 13 of the last 18 ... Missed one game due to injury ... Tallied four goals and five assists for nine points in 10 playoff matches and led the team with a plus five rating.

NHL CAREER: 1991-92: Became the first Russian-born player to play for the Rangers in franchise history ... Recorded 30 goals, ranking fourth in the NHL among first-year players and tied for fourth on the club ... Placed third on the team with five game-winning goals ... 24.2 shooting % ranked fifth in the league ... Recorded a six-game goal scoring streak from Dec. 2 to Dec. 14, which was tied for the third longest in the NHL ... First NHL goal was overtime score at Montreal on Oct. 5 ... 28 of his 30 goals and 50 of his 58 points were collected at even-strength... Registered 15 goals and 10 assists at home and 15 goals and 18 assists on the road. **1992-93:** Tallied his 100th NHL point with a goal vs. Islanders on Feb. 12 ... Notched his first career NHL hat trick on Jan. 29 at Buffalo ... Led the team with a plus 15 rating ... Posted a career-high, six-game point scoring streak from Dec. 2 to Dec. 13 ... Team was 13-4-1 when he scored a goal and 23-12-6 when he tallied a point ... Collected 50 of his 54 points at even strength ... Placed third on the team with 50 points at even strength ... Missed the last three games of the season due to injury ... Collected 27 points at MSG and 27 points on the road. **1993-94:** Reached the 20-goal plateau for the third consecutive season, notching 22 along with 27 assists for 49 points in 76 matches ... Placed second on the team with six game-winning goals and also assisted on six game-winners ... Ranked second on the club with 18 even strength goals and was tied for third with 39 points at even strength ... Skated in his 200th NHL game on Jan. 25 at San Jose ... Rangers were 16-1-0 when he scored a goal and 26-8-1 when he scored a point ... Registered 10 multiple-point games, including four three point efforts and six two point games. **1994 PLAYOFFS:** Collected two goals and five assists while appearing in all 23 matches ... Registered his first goal on May 15 in Game One of the Conference Finals vs. New Jersey and collected his second goal in Game Two ... Collected assists in three consecutive games from April 24 to May 5 ... Assisted on Glenn Anderson's game-winning goal on June 4 in Game Three of the Finals at Vancouver.

SOVIET CAREER: Began with the Soviet Wings in 1981-82 at the age of 17 ... Played with the Wings for one season, before joining the Central Red Army team for three years ... Rejoined the Wings for the beginning of the '85-86 season and played there until joining Rangers ... In seven years with the Soviet Wings he totalled 91 goals and 86 assists for 177 points in 279 games and in three seasons with Central Red Army, he accumulated eight goals and nine assists in 62 matches ... Won the Soviet Elite League championship each year with Central Red Army ... Wore uniform number eight with Wings and 14 for Central Red Army ... In 1990-91 he led the Soviet Wings in scoring, reaching career highs in goals (21), assists (24) and points (45) ... 45 points ranked fifth in the league ... Named captain of the Wings for the second straight season ... Added to the Central Red Army team to compete against seven NHL clubs in Super Series '91 ... As part of Super Series, he played against the Rangers at MSG on Dec. 31, recording two assists.

INTERNATIONAL CAREER: Made his debut for the Soviet National team on Apr. 9, 1984 in a game against Finland during Sweden Cup tournament ... Before that he participated in the '81-82 European Junior Championships and the World Junior Championships in '82-83 and '83-84 ... Appeared in five games during Canada Cup '87 and played one game for Soviet team in Rendez-Vous '87 against the NHL All-Stars ... Won gold medal at the World Championships in '89 and '90 and a bronze medal in '91 ... Won gold medal at '89 and '91 European Championships and silver medal in '90 ... Helped Soviet Union to gold medal in Goodwill Game in 1990 ... Teammates on National Team included Sergei Fedorov (Detroit), Alexander Mogilny (Vancouver) and Dimitri Khristich (Los Angeles).

BACKGROUND: Is the first Rangers player to wear uniform number 13 since Bob Brooke was traded in 1986 ... Is one of only two 12th round draft choices to play for the Rangers along with Rudy Poeschek ... Favorite sports teams are the New York Knicks and the New York Yankees ... Was a teammate and roommate with goaltender Vladislav Tretiak while with Central Army ... Enjoys listening to the Beatles, reading history books and playing soccer and volleyball ... Married: wife, Yelena; daughters, Natasha and Elizabeth.

CAREER TRANSACTIONS: *June 16, 1990* — Rangers' 13th choice (12th round, 244th overall) in 1990 Entry Draft.

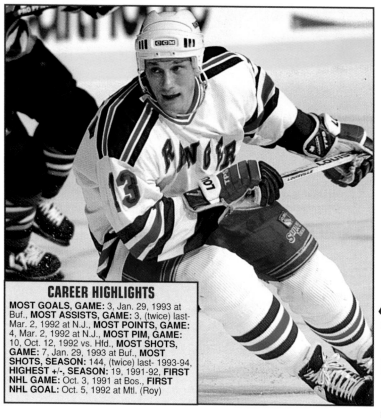

SERGEI 13 NEMCHINOV

CAREER HIGHLIGHTS

MOST GOALS, GAME: 3, Jan. 29, 1993 at Buf., **MOST ASSISTS, GAME:** 3, (twice) last- Mar. 2, 1992 at N.J., **MOST POINTS, GAME:** 4, Mar. 2, 1992 at N.J., **MOST PIM, GAME:** 10, Oct. 12, 1992 vs. Hfd., **MOST SHOTS, GAME:** 7, Jan. 29, 1993 at Buf., **MOST SHOTS, SEASON:** 144, (twice) last- 1993-94, **HIGHEST +/-, SEASON:** 19, 1991-92, **FIRST NHL GAME:** Oct. 3, 1991 at Bos., **FIRST NHL GOAL:** Oct. 5, 1992 at Mtl. (Roy)

AMATEUR AND PROFESSIONAL RECORD

Season	Club	Lea	Regular Season GP	G	A	PTS	PIM	Playoffs GP	G	A	PTS	PIM
1981-82	Soviet Wings	Sov. Elite	15	1	0	1	0	—	—	—	—	—
1982-83	CSKA Moscow	Sov. Elite	11	0	0	0	2	—	—	—	—	—
1983-84	CSKA Moscow	Sov. Elite	20	6	5	11	4	—	—	—	—	—
1984-85	CSKA Moscow	Sov. Elite	31	2	4	6	4	—	—	—	—	—
1985-86	Soviet Wings	Sov. Elite	39	7	12	19	28	—	—	—	—	—
1986-87	Soviet Wings	Sov. Elite	40	13	9	22	24	—	—	—	—	—
1987-88	Soviet Wings	Sov. Elite	48	17	11	28	26	—	—	—	—	—
1988-89	Soviet Wings	Sov. Elite	43	15	14	29	28	—	—	—	—	—
1989-90	Soviet Wings	Sov. Elite	48	17	16	33	34	—	—	—	—	—
1990-91	Soviet Wings	Sov. Elite	46	21	24	45	30	—	—	—	—	—
1991-92	Rangers	NHL	73	30	28	58	15	13	1	4	5	8
1992-93	Rangers	NHL	81	23	31	54	34	—	—	—	—	—
1993-94	Rangers	NHL	76	22	27	49	36	23	2	5	7	6
1994-95	Rangers	NHL	47	7	6	13	16	10	4	5	9	2
NHL and Rangers Totals			277	82	92	174	101	46	7	14	21	16

MATTIAS NORSTROM

14

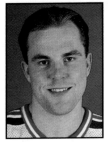

6-1 • 205 lbs. • Shoots Left
Born: January 2, 1972
Stockhom, Sweden
Off-Season Home:
Stockholm, Sweden

DEFENSE

1994-95: Was awarded the Lars-Erik Sjoberg Trophy as the Rangers top rookie in training camp for the second consecutive season ... Began the season with Binghamton and was recalled on March 23 ... Collected his first point of the season with an assist on March 25 at Quebec ... Tallied a pair of assists and a plus four rating on April 5 at Florida ... Appeared in seven of the last 13 matches ... Registered nine goals and 10 assists for 19 points in 63 games with Binghamton ... Ranked fifth on the team with 91 penalty minutes at the time of his recall ... Made his post-season debut on May 14 in Game Five of the Conference Quarterfinals at Quebec.

NHL CAREER: 1993-94: Began the season with New York after an impressive training camp in which he was awarded the Lars-Erik Sjoberg Trophy ... Did not dress for the first two contests and was assigned to Binghamton of the American Hockey League on October 8 ... Was recalled by New York on October 9 ... Made his National Hockey League debut in a 5-2 victory vs. Washington on October 11 ... Skated in one more match on October 13 vs. Quebec before returning to Binghamton on October 21 ... Was recalled on March 11 and skated in four straight matches with New York from March 12 to March 18 ... Registered his first NHL point with an assist on Steve Larmer's game winning goal on March 16 vs. Hartford ... Collected his only other point on April 8 vs. Toronto, registering an assist ... Appeared in seven of New York's final 16 matches ... Remained with the club through the Stanley Cup playoffs but did not make a post season appearance.

AHL CAREER:... Appeared in his first AHL match on October 8, recording an assist in the club's 7-4 opening night victory vs. Hamilton

... Appeared in 55 games with Binghamton, collecting one goal and nine assists along with 70 penalty minutes ... Notched his only multiple point effort on November 24, tallying a pair of assists in a 6-3 win at Providence ... Missed four games in January due to the flu ... Collected his first professional goal on March 9 in Binghamton's 5-3 victory at Cornwall ... Binghamton posted a 7-2-0 record when he tallied a point.

SWEDISH CAREER: Played for two seasons (1991-92 and 1992-93) with AIK in the Swedish Elite League ... Placed third on the club in scoring among defensemen in 1991-92, tallying four goals and four assists for eight points in 39 games in his first season with the club ... Teammates included former NHL all-star defenseman and his childhood idol Borje Salming and Calgary Flames forward Mikael Nylander ... Notched one assist in 22 matches in his second season with the club.

BACKGROUND: Wore number 14 in his first stint with New York in 1993-94 and switched to uniform number 5 after Craig MacTavish was acquired at the trade deadline ... Is an extremely well conditioned athlete, paying strict attention to training and eating habits ... Rangers European scout Christer Rockstrom said of Norstrom, "As far as personality, drive and dedication goes, he along with Detroit's Nicklas Lidstrom are the best defensemen I've ever drafted" ... Had an impressive training camp with the Rangers in 1992 before returning to Sweden ... Single.

CAREER TRANSACTIONS: *June 20, 1992* — Rangers' second round choice (48th overall) in the 1992 NHL Entry Draft.

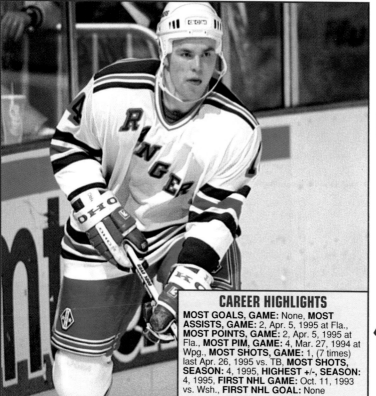

CAREER HIGHLIGHTS

MOST GOALS, GAME: None, **MOST ASSISTS, GAME:** 2, Apr. 5, 1995 at Fla., **MOST POINTS, GAME:** 2, Apr. 5, 1995 at Fla., **MOST PIM, GAME:** 4, Mar. 27, 1994 at Wpg., **MOST SHOTS, GAME:** 1, (7 times) last Apr. 26, 1995 vs. TB, **MOST SHOTS, SEASON:** 4, 1995, **HIGHEST +/-, SEASON:** 4, 1995, **FIRST NHL GAME:** Oct. 11, 1993 vs. Wsh., **FIRST NHL GOAL:** None

AMATEUR AND PROFESSIONAL RECORD

Season	Club	Lea	Regular Season					Playoffs				
			GP	G	A	PTS	PIM	GP	G	A	PTS	PIM
1991-92	AIK ....Swe. Elite		39	4	4	8	28	—	—	—	—	—
1992-93	AIK ....Swe. Elite		22	0	1	1	16	—	—	—	—	—
1993-94	Rangers ....NHL		9	0	2	2	6	—	—	—	—	—
1993-94	Binghamton ....AHL		55	1	9	10	70	—	—	—	—	—
1994-95	Rangers ....NHL		9	0	3	3	2	3	0	0	0	0
1994-95	Binghamton ....AHL		63	9	10	19	91	—	—	—	—	—
NHL and Rangers Totals			18	0	5	5	8	3	0	0	0	0

WAYNE PRESLEY

18

5-11 • 195 • Shoots Right
Born: March 23, 1965
Dearborn, Michigan
Off-Season Home:
Detroit, Michigan

RIGHT WING

1994-95: Signed by the Rangers as an unrestricted free agent on Aug. 2 ... Tallied 14 goals and five assists in 46 games with Buffalo last season ... Ranked third on the team with 14 goals and was tied for second on the club with a plus five rating ... Led the team and ranked second in the NHL with five shorthanded goals and also tied for first in the league with six shorthanded points ... Skated in his 600th NHL match on Apr. 24 vs. Tampa Bay.

NHL CAREER: 1984-85: Called up to the Blackhawks from Sault Ste. Marie (OHL) in Dec. and appeared in three games before being returned to the Greyhounds ... Made his NHL debut on Jan. 26 at Toronto ... Recorded his first NHL point, with an assist on Jan. 26 at Toronto. **1985-86:** Began the season with Nova Scotia (AHL) before being recalled by Chicago on Dec. 13 ... Notched his first NHL goal on Dec. 18 vs. Winnipeg ... Posted a six game scoring streak from Dec. 15 to Dec. 28 ... Tallied five of his seven goals vs. the Norris
• Division. **1986-87:** Recorded career highs with 32 goals, 29 assists and 61 points along with 114 penalty minutes, while playing in all 80 games in his first full season in the NHL ... Ranked second on the team with 32 goals, seven ppg's and four gwg's ... 61 points ranked fourth on the club ... Tallied 14, multiple point games, including a pair of three point efforts on Dec. 10 vs. Buffalo and Feb. 1 vs. Edmonton ... Registered a seven game scoring streak (seven goals, four assists) from Dec. 6 to Dec. 21 ... Notched his first career playoff goal on Apr. 12 vs. Detroit. **1987-88:** Sidelined for 37 games due to a knee injury suffered at Los Angeles on Nov. 25 ... Recorded his first NHL hat trick on Nov. 11 vs. Detroit, tallying all three goals on the power play. **1988-89:** Tied for fifth on the Blackhawks with 21 goals ... Tallied a career high four points (one goal, three assists) on Feb. 1 vs. Winnipeg ... Placed third on the team with three shorthanded goals ... Collected his 100th NHL point on Oct. 6 vs. the Rangers ... Set a team record and tied two NHL records with three shorthanded goals vs. Detroit in the division semi-finals ... Equaled the league marks for shorthanded goals in a series and in a single playoff year. **1989-90:** Tallied six goal and seven assists for 13 points in 49 matches ... Placed second on the team with nine playoff goals and ranked fourth on the club in scoring with 15 points in 19 matches while helping the Hawks to the Conference Finals vs. Edmonton. **1990-91:** Skated in 71 games and posted a career high 122 penalty minutes ... Tallied nine of his 15

goals and 21 of his 34 points at home ... Scored on his first career penalty shot on Feb. 9 at Boston vs. Rejean Lemelin. **1991-92:** Dealt to San Jose on Sept. 20 ... Skated in 47 games with the Sharks, collecting eight goals and 14 assists, before being traded to Buffalo on Mar. 9 ... Recorded his 200th career point on Dec. 3 vs. Los Angeles and notched his 100th NHL goal on Jan. 8 at Calgary ... Placed second on the Sabres with three goals and third in scoring with six points in the postseason. **1992-93:** Tallied 15 goals and 17 assists for 32 points in his first full season with Buffalo ... Registered six multiple point games ... Potted the game winning goal in consecutive games on Feb. 14 vs. Pittsburgh and Feb. 17 at Hartford. **1993-94:** Tied for second in the NHL with a career high, five shorthanded goals ... Suffered a fractured ankle on Dec. 26 and missed 14 games ... Ranked third on the club with a plus 18 rating ... Skated in his 500th NHL match on Oct. 29 vs. Edmonton.

AHL CAREER: Notched six goals and nine assists for 15 points in 29 games with Nova Scotia in his first professional season, in 1985-86. Was recalled by Chicago in January.

JUNIOR CAREER: Appeared in three seasons with the Kitchener Rangers (OHL) before being traded to Sault Ste. Marie where he finished his junior career ... Posted his best offensive season in 1983-84, collecting 63 goals and 76 assists for 139 points ... Was selected to the OHL First All-Star team that year and also captured the Jim Mahon Memorial Trophy as the OHL's top scoring right winger.

BACKGROUND: Was teammates with Jeff Beukeboom in Sault Ste. Marie in 1984-85 ... Became the first American-born player to score 30 goals for Chicago, netting 32 in 1986-87 ... Wore number 17 with Chicago and number 18 with Buffalo ... Is a fan of the Detroit Tigers ... Nickname is "Elvis" and lists "Jailhouse Rock" as his favorite song ... Married; wife, Susan; son, Michael; daughters; Abby Kate and Chloe.

CAREER TRANSACTIONS: *June 8, 1983* — Chicago's second choice (39th overall) in the 1983 NHL Entry Draft. *September 20, 1991* — Traded by Chicago to San Jose for third round draft choice in 1993. *March 9, 1992* — Traded by San Jose to Buffalo for Dave Snuggerud. *August 2, 1995* — Signed by the Rangers as a free agent.

CAREER HIGHLIGHTS

MOST GOALS, GAME: 3, Nov. 11,1987 vs. Det., **MOST ASSISTS, GAME:** 3, Feb. 1, 1989 vs. Wpg., **MOST POINTS, GAME:** 4, Feb. 1 , 1989 vs. Wpg., **MOST PIM, GAME:** 27, Mar. 31, 1991 vs. NJ., **MOST SHOTS, GAME:** 6, Nov. 19, 1983 at Wpg., **MOST SHOTS SEASON:** 167, 1986-87, **HIGHEST +/-, SEASON:** 18, 1993-94, **FIRST NHL GOAL:** Dec. 29, 1984 at Tor., **FIRST NHL GOAL:** Dec. 18, 1985 vs. WPG (Bouchard)

WAYNE 18 PRESLEY

AMATEUR AND PROFESSIONAL RECORD

			Regular Season					Playoffs				
Season	Club	League	GP	G	A	PTS	PIM	GP	G	A	PTS	PIM
1982-83	Kitchener..................OHL		70	39	48	87	99	12	1	4	5	9
1983-84	Kitchener..................OHL		70	63	76	139	156	16	12	16	28	38
1984-85	Chicago....................NHL		3	0	1	1	0					
1984-85	Kitchener..................OHL		31	25	21	46	77					
1984-85	S.S. Marie ....OHL		11	5	9	14	14	16	13	9	22	13
1985-86	Chicago....................NHL		38	7	8	15	38	3	0	0	0	0
1985-86	Nova Scotia..............AHL		29	6	9	15	22					
1986-87	Chicago....................NHL		80	32	29	61	114	4	1	0	1	9
1987-88	Chicago....................NHL		42	12	10	22	52	5	0	0	0	4
1988-89	Chicago....................NHL		72	21	19	40	100	14	7	5	12	18
1989-90	Chicago....................NHL		49	6	7	13	69	19	9	6	15	29
1990-91	Chicago....................NHL		71	15	19	34	122	6	0	1	1	38
1991-92	San Jose ....NHL		47	8	14	22	76					
1991-92	Buffalo......................NHL		12	2	2	4	57	7	3	3	6	14
1992-93	Buffalo......................NHL		79	15	17	32	96	8	1	0	1	6
1993-94	Buffalo......................NHL		65	17	8	25	103	7	2	1	3	14
1994-95	Buffalo......................NHL		46	14	5	19	41	5	3	1	4	8
NHL Totals			664	149	139	288	868	78	26	17	43	140

MIKE RICHTER

35

5-11 • 187 • Catches Left
Born: Sept. 22, 1966
Abington, Pennsylvania
Off-Season Home: New
York, New York

GOALTENDER

1994-95: Finished the season winning four of his last six decisions and five of his last eight ... Stopped 18 shots on Apr. 16 at Long Island for his 124th career win, moving past Chuck Rayner in sole possession of fifth place on the Rangers All-Time Wins list ... Posted his 11th career shutout on Apr. 5 at Florida, turning aside 17 shots in a 5-0 victory, tying Andy Aitkenhead for ninth place on the Rangers All-Time Shutout list ... Allowed two or fewer goals in 15 of his 35 outings and three or fewer in 22 of the 35 ... Stopped his sixth career penalty shot, turning back Steve Konowalchuk in the second period on Mar. 5 at Washington ... Appeared in seven playoff matches, posting a record of 2-5.

NHL CAREER: 1988-89: Although he won the Lars-Erik Sjoberg Award as the best rookie of training camp, he spent most of the season with Denver (IHL) ... Served as New York's back up goalie on two occasions and made his NHL debut as starting goalie in game four of first round playoff series vs. Pittsburgh. **1989-90:** Made his NHL regular-season debut on Oct. 19, defeating the Whalers 7-3 at MSG ... Called up from Flint (IHL) on Dec. 31 to face the Soviet Wings and remained with the team for the rest of the season ... Posted a record of 7-4-2 with a 3.76 GAA in 13 games with Flint ... Lost a 4-3 decision in St. Louis on Jan. 6, then went unbeaten in his next seven games (5-0-2) and was named the NHL's Rookie of the Month for January ... Four of his five losses were by one goal and he allowed more than three goals in only six of his 22 starts ... Stopped two penalty shots during the regular-season and one in the playoffs. **1990-91:** Set an NHL record by alternating starts with John Vanbiesbrouck for the first 76 games of the season ... Started the final four regular season games and all six playoff matches ... Named as a finalist for the Vezina Trophy as the NHL's top goaltender ... .903 save percentage ranked third in the NHL and was the second best in club history ... Recorded a career-high, eight-game unbeaten streak (5-0-3) from Jan. 25 to Mar. 4, including a 59 save performance in 3-3 tie at Vancouver on Jan. 31 that set a team record for saves in a game ... Won several team awards after the season, including the "Players' Player" Award. **1991-92:** Won over 20 games for the second consecutive season, despite missing 12 games from Feb. 1 to Feb.

25 due to injury ... Tied for fifth in the league with .901 save percentage and three shutouts ... Recorded his initial regular season shutout on Nov. 23 at St. Louis, while also posting shutouts vs. Boston on Dec. 8 and against New Jersey on Dec. 23 ... Posted a five game winning streak from Oct. 16 to Nov. 2 ... Played in first career All-Star Game in Philadelphia on Jan. 18 and allowed two goals on 15 shots while playing the third period ... Won the goaltending part of the Skills Competition the night before the All-Star Game ... Notched four of the Rangers' six playoff victories. **1992-93:** Turned aside 29 shots while posting his fourth career shutout at Edmonton on Feb. 27 ... With an assist vs. Ottawa on Jan. 6, he tied the Rangers all-time record for most assists in a season, matching John Vanbiesbrouck's mark of five tallied in '84-85 and again in '87-88 ... Allowed three or fewer goals in 12 of his last 16 decisions ... Completed a five-game conditioning stint at Binghamton on Jan. 23, where he posted a 4-0-1 record with a 1.18 GAA and a .964 save percentage ... Began the season by winning four of his first five starts. **1993-94:** Appeared in a career high 68 matches and established a franchise record for wins in a single season with 42 ... Became the first Rangers goaltender to lead the NHL in wins since Ed Giacomin led the league with 37 in 1968-69 ... Set a career high and tied for fourth in the league with five shutouts ... Placed fifth in the NHL with a career best 2.57 GAA ... Notched his fifth shutout of the season on Apr. 1 vs. Dallas, his 38th victory, setting a club record for wins in a season ... After opening the season with a 0-4-0 mark, he went 42-8-6 with a 2.46 GAA and .913 save percentage in his final 64 outings ... Posted a franchise record 20-game unbeaten streak, going 17-0-3 from Oct. 24 to Dec. 19, surpassing Dave Kerr's club record of 19 (14-0-5) set in 1939-40 ... Started in a career-high 15 consecutive games from Oct. 19 to Nov. 23 ... Was named the NHL Player of the Month for November after posting a record of 9-0-1 with a 2.37 GAA and .917 save percentage in 12 games ... Appeared in his 200th NHL match on Mar. 4 vs. the Islanders ... Recorded his 100th NHL career win on Feb. 28 vs. Philadelphia ... Moved past Gilles Villemure into sixth place on the Rangers all-time wins list on Feb. 18 vs. Ottawa ... Posted a career high eight

game winning streak from Mar. 23 to Apr. 12, surpassing his previous high of seven set from Oct. 30 to Nov. 13, 1993 ... Finished the season with a nine-game unbeaten streak from Mar. 23 to Apr. 14 and was named NHL Player of the Week for the week ending Apr. 3 ... Was named as the MVP in the NHL All-Star Game on Jan. 22 at MSG, stopping 19 of 21 shots in the second period while making his second All-Star appearance ... Was the first goaltender to win the award since Grant Fuhr in 1986 and became the third Ranger to earn the award. **1994 PLAYOFFS:** Started all 23 playoff matches and led the NHL with 16 wins, placed third with a 2.07 GAA and ranked fourth with a .921 save percentage ... Stopped 31 shots in Game Seven double overtime victory in the Conference Finals vs. New Jersey on May 27, setting a club record for wins in one playoff year, with 12 ... Notched his fourth shutout of the playoffs on May 17 in Game Two vs. New Jersey, tying the team and NHL record for shutouts in a single post season ... Stopped Pavel Bure's penalty shot attempt in the second period of Game Four of the Finals on June 7 at Vancouver ... Turned aside 28 shots in Game Seven Stanley Cup clinching victory ... Won his first seven matches, including consecutive 6-0 shutouts in the first two games of the Conference Quarterfinals vs. the Islanders on Apr. 17 and 18 at MSG ... Became the second Rangers player to post back to back shutouts in the playoffs, joining Dave Kerr who blanked the Bruins, 1-0 and 1-0 on Mar. 26 and Mar. 28, 1940.

IHL CAREER: Made his professional debut with the Colorado Rangers on Mar. 1, 1988 just a few days after playing with the U.S. Olympic Team ... Posted a 3-1 victory at Kalamazoo in his initial start and went on to record a 13-3-0 mark during the month to help Colorado win the West Division title ... 2.94 GAA and .905 save percentage during March earned him selection as IHL Player of the Month ... Posted a 5-3 record during playoffs, accounting for five of Colorado's six post season victories ... Spent the entire '88-89 cam-

paign with Denver, leading all IHL goalies in games played (57) and ranking second in minutes (3,031).

COLLEGE CAREER: Played for two seasons at University of Wisconsin, going 14-9-0 in his freshman campaign in '85-86 and 19-16-1 in '86-87 ... Selected as WCHA Freshman of the Year in 1985-86 ... All-Western Collegiate Hockey Association All-Academic selection in 1986-87 ... Among his teammates while playing for the Badgers were Tony Granato (Los Angeles) and Paul Ranheim (Hartford).

INTERNATIONAL CAREER: Member of the 1986 and 1987 U.S. National Teams and 1987 Select Team ... Shared the 1988, 60-game pre-Olympic schedule with Chris Terreri (N.J.), each accumulating a record of 17-7-3 ... Appeared in four matches during the Olympics in Calgary for the U.S. team ... Starting goalie for Team USA in 1991 Canada Cup ... Played in four games with Team USA at the 1993 World Championships in Munich, Germany.

BACKGROUND: Was given two prestigious awards last season, including the Thurman Munson Award for his considerable charitable work and the Sloan Kettering Award of Courage for his work with the hospital ... Took classes at Columbia University for the third consecutive summer ... Appeared with Brian Leetch and Mark Messier on the Late Show with David Letterman, following the team's Stanley Cup victory in 1994 ... Also, appeared on the Howard Stern Show ... Does extensive work with charitable organizations, including serving as honorary hockey chairman of the Children's Health Fund ... Won the 1990-91 "Good Guy" Award for cooperation with the press ... Single.

CAREER TRANSACTIONS: *June 15, 1985* — Rangers' second round draft choice (28th overall) in the 1985 Entry Draft.

RICHTER CAPTURES THURMAN MUNSON AWARD & MEMORIAL SLOAN-KETTERING HOSPITAL'S AWARD OF COURAGE

Mike Richter captured two prestigious awards last season for his extensive work in the community. On February 6, 1995, Mike was one of eight recipients of the Thurman Munson Award. The award is presented annually to athletes, in grateful recognition of "Excellence and Humanitarian Concern." The award was established to commemorate and perpetuate Munson's dedication to helping mentally impaired children and their families.

Richter was also honored with Memorial Sloan-Kettering Hospital's "Award of Courage" for his work with the hospital. The award was conceived by Center volunteer, David Gorin, who successfully fought cancer two and a half years ago. Sloan-Kettering is the world's preeminent and largest private institution devoted to advancing the prevention and treatment of cancer.

From top left, Richter, Jim Brown, Isiah Thomas, John McEnroe, Tracy Austin and Evander Holyfield.

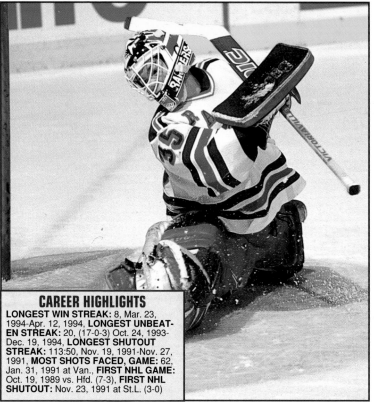

CAREER HIGHLIGHTS
LONGEST WIN STREAK: 8, Mar. 23, 1994-Apr. 12, 1994, **LONGEST UNBEAT-EN STREAK:** 20, (17-0-3) Oct. 24, 1993-Dec. 19, 1994, **LONGEST SHUTOUT STREAK:** 113:50, Nov. 19, 1991-Nov. 27, 1991, **MOST SHOTS FACED, GAME:** 62, Jan. 31, 1991 at Van., **FIRST NHL GAME:** Oct. 19, 1989 vs. Hfd. (7-3), **FIRST NHL SHUTOUT:** Nov. 23, 1991 at St.L. (3-0)

MIKE 35 RICHTER

AMATEUR AND PROFESSIONAL RECORD

Season	Club	Lea	GP	W	L	T	MINS	GA	SO	AVG	GP	W	L	MINS	GA	SO	AVG
				Regular Season								Playoffs					
1985-86	Wisconsin	WCHA	25	14	9	0	1394	92	1	3.96	—	—	—	—	—	—	—
1986-87	Wisconsin	WCHA	36	19	16	1	2136	126	0	3.54	—	—	—	—	—	—	—
1987-88	U.S. National Team		29	17	7	2	1559	86	0	3.31	—	—	—	—	—	—	—
1987-88	U.S. Olympic Team		4	2	2	0	230	15	0	3.91	—	—	—	—	—	—	—
1987-88	Colorado	IHL	22	16	5	0	1298	68	1	3.14	10	5	3	536	35	0	3.92
1988-89	Rangers	NHL	—	—	—	—	—	—	—	—	1	0	1	58	4	0	4.14
1988-89	Denver	IHL	57	23	26	0	3031	217	1	4.30	4	0	4	210	21	0	6.00
1989-90	Rangers	NHL	23	12	5	5	1320	66	0	3.00	6	3	2	330	19	0	3.45
1989-90	Flint	IHL	13	7	4	2	782	49	0	3.76	—	—	—	—	—	—	—
1990-91	Rangers	NHL	45	21	13	7	2596	135	0	3.12	6	2	4	313	14	1	2.68
1991-92	Rangers	NHL	41	23	12	2	2298	119	3	3.11	7	4	2	412	24	1	3.50
1992-93	Rangers	NHL	38	13	19	3	2105	134	1	3.82	—	—	—	—	—	—	—
1992-93	Binghamton	AHL	5	4	0	1	305	6	0	1.18	—	—	—	—	—	—	—
1993-94	Rangers	NHL	68	42	12	6	3710	159	5	2.57	23	16	7	1417	49	4	2.07
1994-95	Rangers	NHL	35	14	17	2	1993	97	2	2.92	7	2	5	384	23	0	3.59
NHL and Rangers Totals			250	125	78	25	14022	710	11	3.04	50	27	21	2914	133	6	2.74

LUC ROBITAILLE

20

6-1 • 195 • Shoots Left
Born: February 17, 1966
Montreal, Quebec
Off-Season Home:
Sherman Oaks, California

LEFT WING

1994-95: Was acquired from Pittsburgh, along with Ulf Samuelsson, on August 31 ... Placed second on the Penguins with 23 goals last season and ranked fourth on the club with 42 points in his first season with the organization after being acquired on July 29 from Los Angeles ... Skated in 46 games, missing two games due to a suspension after high sticking Bruce Driver on February 5 ... Recorded his 400th NHL goal on February 19 vs. Buffalo ... Collected five multiple goal games, including a four-goal effort vs. Hartford on February 16 ... Placed third on the team with five power play goals and was tied for third with three game winners ... Also ranked second on the club with 124 shots on goal ... Registered a point in 28 of his 46 outings ... Collected seven goals and four assists for 11 points in 12 post-season matches.

NHL CAREER: 1986-87: Became the first player in Los Angeles Kings history to capture the Calder Trophy as the NHL's top rookie after leading all rookies with 45 goals and 84 points in 79 outings ... Both totals also placed first on the club, marking the first time a rookie had led the Kings in those categories ... Was named as the NHL's Second Team All-Star Left Wing following the season ... Also earned honors following the season as the Hockey New Rookie of the Year and Second Team All-Star Left Wing ... Tied for first on the team with 18 power play goals ... Registered his first NHL goal in his first NHL game on October 9 vs. St. Louis ... Notched his first NHL hat trick on December 9 at Long Island ... Tallied 26 goals on the road and 19 at home ... Posted a 10 game scoring streak (eight goals, six assists) to finish the season.

1987-88: Led the Kings in scoring for the second consecutive season while playing in all 80 games and set a club record for points (111) and assists (58) by a Kings left wing ... Became the fourth player in Los Angeles history to tally 50 goals in a season, netting numbers 49 and 50 at Calgary on April 1 ... Tallied six points (two goals, four assists) vs. Calgary on March 30 ... Scored a goal on his first NHL penalty shot on Oct. 25 at Winnipeg (Eldon Reddick) ... Posted 11 multiple goal games, including three hat tricks ... Voted as the starting left wing for the NHL All-Star Game at St. Louis and tallied two goals and an assist in the contest, earning second star honors ... Was voted the NHL's First Team All-Star Left Wing following the season ... Was also honored as a First Team All-Star by the Hockey News and the Sporting News. **1988-89:** Ranked first in the NHL in scoring among left wings with 98 points, placing 10th in the

league overall ... Notched his fifth career hat trick, including his 100th NHL goal on October 6 vs. Detroit ... Posted a 13 game point scoring streak (10 goals, 14 assists) from November 27 to December 21 ... Was voted the starting left wing for the Campbell Conference squad at the All-Star Game in Edmonton ... Was voted the NHL's First Team All-Star Left Wing for the second consecutive season. **1989-90:** Led all NHL left wingers in scoring for the third consecutive season with 101 points, placing 12th in the NHL overall ... Led the Kings with 52 goals, 20 power play tallies and seven game winners ... Also led the NHL with a 24.8 shooting percentage ... Played in all 80 games for the second time in his career ... Posted a career high, eight game goal scoring streak (eight goals) from December 13 to December 30 ... Recorded a pair of hat tricks, on November 25 vs. Vancouver and March 10 vs. Pittsburgh ... Was voted as the starting left wing for the Campbell Conference All-Star team for the third consecutive season .... Was also voted as the NHL's First Team All-Star Left Wing for the third straight year ... Tied for the club lead with five playoff tallies and tied for third on the team with 10 points in 10 games. **1990-91:** Led all NHL left wings in scoring for the fourth consecutive season with 91 points ... Tied for the club lead with 45 goals and placed second with 46 assists and 91 points ... Led the team with 229 shots on goal and tied for second on the club with 11 power play tallies ... Surpassed Charlie Simmer (222) as the Kings top all-time goal scorer among left wings on February 2 vs. Vancouver ... Posted 24 multiple point games ... Voted as the starting left wing for the Campbell Conference at the All-Star Game in Chicago ... Named the NHL's First Team All-Star Left Wing for the fourth consecutive season, posting the third longest streak at the position, trailing only Bobby Hull (seven) and Ted Lindsay (five) ... Missed four games due to suspension for a match penalty incurred vs. Edmonton on November 10 ... Led the club with 16 points in the post season and set a Kings record for goals in a single playoff year with 12 ... Tied a club record with eight goals in one series vs. Edmonton ... Tallied a point in 10 of the 12 playoff matches. **1991-92:** Eclipsed the 100-point plateau for the third time in his career, notching 107, while posting a career high 63 assists ... Led the Kings with a club record 26 power play goals, placing second in the NHL ... Tallied a career high four goals, including his second career penalty shot goal, on February 6 vs. Hartford .... Was one of four Kings to play in

all 80 games ... Led the team with 240 shots on goal ... Was voted in as the starting left wing for the Campbell Conference All-Star team ... Was named the NHL's Second Team All-Star Left Wing, marking the sixth time he has been a first or second team All-Star ... Broke Dave Taylor's club record for post season goals (22) notching three for 25 in his career. **1992-93:** Established NHL records for most goals (63) and points (125) in one season by a left wing ... Ranked ninth in the league in scoring overall ... Led the Kings in all offensive categories, including goals, assists (62), points, power play goals (24), game winning goals (eight), shots on goal (265) and shooting percentage (23.8%) ... 63 goals ranks second in Kings history for a single season ... Was named the NHL's First Team All-Star Left Wing for the fifth time in six seasons ... Posted a career-high 10 game goal scoring streak (15 goals) from February 27 to March 20 ... The streak was the second longest in Kings history, trailing only Charlie Simmer's 13 game streak in 1979-80 ... Tallied his 300th NHL goal with a hat trick on Oct. 8 at San Jose ... Notched his 700th career point on March 29 at Detroit ... Was one of two Kings to play in all 84 games ... Served as the Kings captain for the first 39 games while Wayne Gretzky was injured ... Was voted as the starting left wing for the Campbell Conference team at the All-Star Game in Montreal, marking his sixth consecutive start ... Was the Los Angeles Hockey Writers Association nominee for the Masterton Trophy ... Placed third on the team in scoring and fifth in the NHL with 22 points in the post-season, helping the Kings reach the Stanley Cup Finals for the first time in their history ... Tallied four points (one goal, three assists) in Game Six of the Conference Finals vs. Toronto. **1993-94:** Led the Kings in goals for the fifth consecutive season with 44 and placed second on the team with 86 points ... Ranked third in the NHL with 24 power play goals, trailing league leaders Pavel Bure and Brett Hull by one ... Set a Kings record for power play goals in a game, notching four on

November 25 at Quebec ... Missed one game due to a sore ankle, halting his consecutive games played streak at 269 ... Registered an assist on Wayne Gretzky's 802nd NHL goal on March 23 vs. Vancouver.

JUNIOR CAREER: Played three seasons with Hull of the Quebec Major Junior Hockey League ... Placed second on the team in scoring with 85 points in his rookie season, 1983-84, with Hull while also leading the team with 53 assists ... Led the team in all offensive categories the following season, tallying 55 goals and 94 assists for 149 points in 64 contests ... Placed third in the QMJHL scoring race ... Was named QMJHL's Second Team All-Star Left Wing ... Tallied 68 goals and a league leading 123 assists in his final season of junior hockey ... Tied with teammate Guy Rouleau for the QMJHL scoring title ... Was selected as a QMJHL First Team All-Star Left Wing following the season ... Tallied 17 goals and 27 assists for 44 points in 15 playoff outings, leading Hull to the Memorial Cup Finals and was named to the Memorial Cup All-Star Team ... Was named the Canadian Hockey League Player of the Year following the season.

BACKGROUND: Nickname is 'Lucky' ... Is active in many charities, including the Ronald McDonald House and the Star Light Foundation ... Has held charity hockey games to benefit cancer and AIDS research ... Enjoys golfing and horseback riding ... Is an avid movie fan ... Has worn number 20 his entire career ... Married: wife, Stacia; son, Steven.

CAREER TRANSACTIONS: *June 9, 1984—* Kings' ninth round choice (171st overall) in the 1984 NHL Entry Draft. *July 24, 1994—* Traded to Pittsburgh by Los Angeles for Rick Tocchet and a second round draft choice in 1995. *August 31, 1995—* Traded by Pittsburgh to New York along with Ulf Samuelsson for Petr Nedved and Sergei Zubov.

SCORING STREAKS AND MULTIPLE POINT GAMES

CAREER POINT SCORING STREAKS (FIVE GAMES OR MORE)

(Goals, Assists and Points during streak listed on right)

13	Nov. 27, 1988 -	Dec. 21, 1988	(9-14-23)
10	Feb. 27, 1993 -	Mar. 20, 1993	(15-8-23)
10	Oct. 27, 1992 -	Nov. 16, 1992	(10-11-21)
10	Oct. 12, 1991 -	Nov. 2 1991	(8-12-20)
10	Dec. 13, 1989 -	Jan. 2, 1990	(8-8-16)
10	Mar. 19, 1987 -	Apr. 5, 1987	(8-6-14)
9	Nov. 29, 1990 -	Dec. 20, 1990	(8-9-17)
9	Oct. 10, 1987 -	Oct. 28, 1987	(3-10-13)
8	Jan. 30, 1993 -	Feb. 17, 1993	(6-9-15)
8	Dec. 21, 1991 -	Jan. 7, 1992	(3-10-13)
8	Jan. 19, 1989 -	Feb. 4, 1989	(6-7-13)
7	Dec. 8, 1992 -	Dec. 22, 1992	(8-5-13)
7	Feb. 25, 1992 -	Mar. 9, 1992	(5-9-14)
7	Mar. 17, 1991 -	Mar. 31, 1991	(6-6-12)
7	Oct. 4, 1991 -	Oct. 17, 1991	(5-17-12)
7	Nov. 10, 1988 -	Nov. 23, 1988	(6-7-13)
7	Mar. 18, 1988 -	Apr. 3, 1988	(10-10-20)
7	Nov. 21, 1987 -	Dec. 3, 1987	(8-4-12)
7	Nov. 6, 1986 -	Nov. 19, 1986	(2-6-8)
6	Jan. 18, 1994 -	Feb. 5, 1994	(7-3-10)
6	Oct. 13, 1992 -	Oct. 23, 1992	(7-6-13)
6	Jan. 14, 1992 -	Jan. 28, 1992	(3-5-8)
6	Feb. 1, 1992 -	Feb. 11, 1992	(8-3-11)
6	Feb. 10, 1990 -	Feb. 19, 1990	(4-5-9)
6	Oct. 17, 1988 -	Nov. 1, 1988	(4-5-9)
6	Dec. 10, 1987 -	Dec. 22, 1987	(5-3-8)
6	Nov. 4, 1987 -	Nov. 17, 1987	(4-8-12)
6	Nov. 29, 1986 -	Dec. 13, 1986	(7-3-10)
6	Jan. 10, 1987 -	Jan. 21, 1988	(5-5-10)
5	Mar. 15, 1995 -	Mar. 24, 1995	(4-3-7)
5	Oct. 9, 1993 -	Oct. 16, 1993	(5-7-12)
5	Feb. 24, 1991 -	Mar. 5, 1991	(2-3-5)
5	Nov. 4, 1990 -	Nov. 17, 1990	(2-4-6)
5	Nov. 30, 1989 -	Dec. 10, 1989	(6-9-15)
5	Oct. 5, 1989 -	Oct. 13, 1989	(3-4-7)
5	Dec. 30, 1987 -	Jan. 8, 1988	(4-3-7)
5	Feb. 14, 1987 -	Feb. 24, 1987	(5-2-7)
5	Dec. 20, 1986 -	Dec. 30, 1986	(2-5-7)
5	Oct. 19, 1986 -	Oct. 27, 1986	(7-3-10)

GOAL SCORING STREAKS (MINIMUM OF FOUR)

10	Feb. 27, 1993 -	Mar. 20, 1993	(fifteen)
8	Dec. 13, 1989 -	Dec. 30, 1989	(eight)
6	Mar. 19, 1988 -	Apr. 3, 1988	(ten)
6	Nov. 22, 1987 -	Dec. 3, 1987	(eight)
5	Oct. 29, 1992 -	Nov. 8, 1992	(eight)
5	Oct. 13, 1992 -	Oct. 23, 1992	(seven)
5	Feb. 4, 1992 -	Feb. 11, 1992	(eight)
5	Nov. 29, 1990 -	Dec. 11, 1990	(six)
5	Mar. 19, 1987 -	Mar. 26, 1987	(six)
5	Feb. 14, 1987 -	Feb. 24, 1987	(five)
4	Nov. 30, 1993 -	Dec. 8, 1993	(four)
4	Feb. 2, 1993 -	Feb. 11, 1993	(five)
4	Dec. 15, 1992 -	Dec. 22, 1992	(five)

ASSIST STREAKS (MINIMUM OF FOUR)

6	Nov. 5, 1992 -	Nov. 14, 1992	(ten)
6	Oct. 23, 1991 -	Nov. 2, 1991	(nine)
6	Nov. 27, 1988 -	Dec. 8, 1988	(eight)
5	Feb. 25, 1992 -	Mar. 4, 1992	(seven)
5	Oct. 4, 1990 -	Oct. 13, 1990	(five)
5	Nov. 30, 1989 -	Dec. 10, 1989	(nine)
5	Jan. 26, 1989 -	Feb. 4, 1989	(six)
5	Nov. 15, 1988 -	Nov. 23, 1988	(six)
5	Oct. 17, 1988 -	Oct. 30, 1988	(five)
5	Nov. 7, 1987 -	Nov. 17, 1987	(eight)
4	Nov. 30, 1993 -	Dec. 8, 1993	(five)
4	Mar. 15, 1993 -	Mar. 20, 1993	(four)
4	Feb. 11, 1993 -	Feb. 17, 1993	(eight)
4	Dec. 13, 1990 -	Dec. 20, 1990	(six)
4	Dec. 22, 1986 -	Dec. 30, 1986	(five)
4	Nov. 6, 1986 -	Nov. 13, 1986	(four)

ALL-TIME MULTIPLE-POINT GAMES

Two Goal Games	69	(last- Apr. 23, 1995 vs. Hartford)
Three Goal Games	10	(last- Mar. 2, 1995 vs. Hartford)
Four Goal Games	3	(last- Feb. 16, 1995 vs. Ottawa)
Two Assist Games	71	(last- Apr. 15, 1995 vs. Ottawa)
Three Assist Games	13	(last- Nov. 6, 1993 vs. Pittsburgh)
Four Assist Games	3	(last- Feb. 11, 1993 at Anaheim)
Two Point Games	145	(last- Apr. 23, 1995 vs. Hartford)
Three Point Games	55	(last- Apr. 5, 1995 vs. Hartford)
Four Point Games	25	(last- Jan. 12, 1994 vs. Hartford)
Five Point Games	3	(last- Feb. 11, 1993 vs. Detroit)
Six Point Games	1	(last- Mar. 30, 1988 at Calgary)

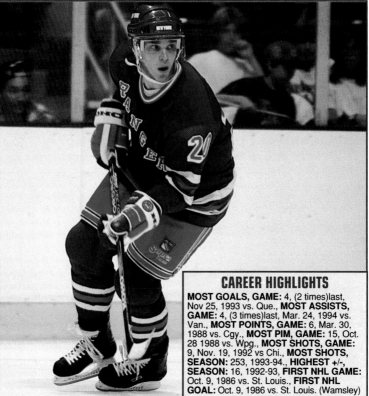

L U C
20
R O B I T A I L L E

CAREER HIGHLIGHTS

MOST GOALS, GAME: 4, (2 times)last, Nov 25, 1993 vs. Que., **MOST ASSISTS, GAME:** 4, (3 times)last, Mar. 24, 1994 vs. Van., **MOST POINTS, GAME:** 6, Mar. 30, 1988 vs. Cgy., **MOST PIM, GAME:** 15, Oct. 28 1988 vs. Wpg., **MOST SHOTS, GAME:** 9, Nov. 19, 1992 vs Chi., **MOST SHOTS, SEASON:** 253, 1993-94., **HIGHEST +/-, SEASON:** 16, 1992-93, **FIRST NHL GAME:** Oct. 9, 1986 vs. St. Louis., **FIRST NHL GOAL:** Oct. 9, 1986 vs. St. Louis. (Wamsley)

AMATEUR AND PROFESSIONAL RECORD

SEASON	CLUB	Lea	REGULAR SEASON					PLAYOFFS				
			GP	G	A	PTS	PIM	GP	G	A	PTS	PIM
1986-87	Los Angeles	NHL	79	45	39	84	28	5	1	4	5	2
1987-88	Los Angeles	NHL	80	53	58	111	82	5	2	5	7	18
1988-89	Los Angeles	NHL	78	46	52	98	65	11	2	6	8	10
1989-90	Los Angeles	NHL	80	52	49	101	38	10	5	5	10	10
1990-91	Los Angeles	NHL	76	45	46	91	68	12	12	4	16	22
1991-92	Los Angeles	NHL	80	44	63	107	95	6	3	4	7	12
1992-93	Los Angeles	NHL	84	63	62	125	100	24	9	13	22	28
1993-94	Los Angeles	NHL	83	44	42	86	86	—	—	—	—	—
1994-95	Pittsburgh	NHL	46	23	19	42	37	12	7	4	11	26
NHL Totals			686	415	430	845	599	85	41	45	86	128

ULF SAMUELSSON

5

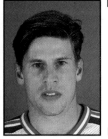

6-1 • 205 • Shoots Left
Born: March 26, 1964
Fagersta, Sweden
Off-Season Home:
Leksand, Sweden

DEFENSE

1994-95: Was acquired from Pittsburgh along with Luc Robitaille on August 31 ... Appeared in 44 games with the Penguins last season, tallying one goal and 15 assists ... Placed second on the club with 113 penalty minutes ... Registered a plus or even rating in 28 of his 44 matches and ranked fifth on the team with a plus 11 rating ... Posted a five game scoring streak (six assists) from Mar. 7 to Mar. 15 ... Skated in his 700th NHL match on Jan. 27 vs. Ottawa ... Missed three games due to surgery performed on Mar. 23 to remove bone chips in his elbow ... Missed the final five playoff games vs. New Jersey due to broken ribs.

NHL CAREER: 1984-85: Made his NHL debut on Oct. 11 vs. the Rangers at MSG ... Appeared in nine more games before being sent to Binghamton (AHL) ... Was recalled along with Ray Ferraro on Feb. 5 and remained with the club for the rest of the season ... Tallied his first NHL goal on Feb. 6 vs. Calgary ... Posted 83 penalty minutes in 41 games, ranking second among Whalers defensemen. **1985-86:** One of only two Whalers to play in all 80 games ... Ranked second on the club with 172 penalty minutes ... Tallied his first career shorthanded goal on Mar. 23 vs. Boston ... Tallied his first career playoff goal, netting the game-winner on Apr. 12 vs. Quebec. **1986-87:** Led the Whalers with a plus 28 rating ... Represented the Whalers along with Kevin Dineen at Rendez-Vous '87 ... Ranked second on the club with 162 penalty minutes ... Was honored as the Whalers best defenseman as voted by the media and also earned honors as a third-team all-star defenseman by The Hockey News. **1987-88:** Led the Whalers with a plus 28 rating ... Posted a nine game scoring streak (one goal, 11 assists) from Jan. 21 to Feb. 6 ... Was voted the Whalers top defenseman by local media for the second consecutive season and was also awarded with the Whalers MVP as voted by the players. **1988-89:** Led the Whalers with a plus 23 rating and tallied a career-high nine goals ... Notched a career high four points including three assists vs. Chicago on Oct. 15 ... Tallied 24 points at home and 10 on the road. **1989-90:** Missed the first 25 games due to knee surgery performed in August after an off-season injury ... Returned to the lineup on Nov. 28 ... Posted a team leading plus 15 rating. **1990-91:** Tallied three goals and 18 assists for 21 points along with 174 penalty minutes in 62 matches with Hartford before being dealt to Pittsburgh on Mar. 4 ... Posted a plus 17 rating, tying for first on the Penguins ... Notched a career-high 211 penalty minutes ... Posted a plus seven rating in 20 playoff matches ... Tallied the Stanley Cup clinching goal in Game Six vs. Minnesota. **1991-92:** Placed second on the Penguins with 206 penalty minutes ... Skated in his 500th NHL game on Dec. 28 at Washington ... Ranked third on the team with a plus seven rating in the post season and ranked second with 39 penalty minutes ...

Skated in all 21 playoff matches, helping the Penguins win their second consecutive Stanley Cup. **1992-93:** Ranked fourth in the NHL with a plus 36 rating ... Notched a plus or even rating in 56 of his 77 matches ... Ranked second among Penguins defensemen in scoring with 29 points ... Notched his first career two-goal game on Oct. 27 at Ottawa ... Posted his second career, three assist effort on Dec. 5 at San Jose ... Placed second on the team with a career-high 249 penalty minutes ... Skated in his 600th NHL game on Mar. 9 vs. Boston ... Skated in all 12 playoff matches and was tied for first on the club with 24 penalty minutes ... Also tied for second on the club with a plus five rating. **1993-94:** Ranked second on the club with a plus 23 rating and led Pittsburgh with 199 penalty minutes ... Notched a plus or even rating in 58 of his 80 games ... Tied a career high with three assists vs. Ottawa on Mar. 24 ... Recorded his 200th career assist on Feb. 7 vs. Montreal ... Was voted as the Penguins Defensive Player of the Year by the local media.

AHL CAREER: Began the 1984-85 season with Hartford and appeared in 10 games before being sent to Binghamton ... Skated in 36 games with the club, tallying five goals and 11 assists along with 92 penalty minutes before being recalled by Hartford on Feb. 5.

SWEDISH CAREER: Played for Leksand in the Swedish Elite League from 1981-82 to 1983-84 ... Notched five goals and 11 assists in 36 games in '83-84 ... Led the team with 72 penalty minutes in '82-83.

INTERNATIONAL CAREER: Was a member of the Swedish Junior National Team in 1981 and play at the World Junior Tournament in Minnesota ... Played with the Swedish National Team in the 1984 Swedish Cup Tournament ... Skated for Team Sweden at the 1989 World Championships at Stockholm, Sweden ... Was a member of Team Sweden at the 1991 Canada Cup Tournament.

BACKGROUND:. Spends the majority of the off-season in Sweden ... Enjoys golfing and tennis ... Has worn number five his entire career ... Was teammates with Ray Ferraro and Pat Verbeek in Hartford ... Lists the New York Mets as his favorite baseball team ... Was drafted by Rangers Assistant General Manger Larry Pleau who was the Whalers Director of Hockey Operations at the time ... Married: wife, Jeanette; sons Phillip and Karl.

CAREER TRANSACTIONS: *June 9, 1982—* Whalers' fourth round choice (67th overall) in the 1982 NHL Entry Draft. *March 4, 1991—* Traded by Hartford with Ron Francis and Grant Jennings to Pittsburgh for John Cullen, Zarley Zalapski and Jeff Parker. *August 31, 1995—* Traded by Pittsburgh to New York along with Luc Robitaille for Petr Nedved and Sergei Zubov.

CAREER HIGHLIGHTS

MOST GOALS, GAME: 2, Oct. 27, 1992 vs OTT., **MOST ASSISTS, GAME:** 3, (2 times) last,Mar. 24, 1994 vs. NJD., **MOST POINTS, GAME:** 3, last Mar. 24, 1994 vs. NJD., **MOST PIM, GAME:** 25, Mar. 31, 1992 at Phi., **MOST SHOTS, GAME:** 5, Nov. 2, 1993 vs. NYR., **MOST SHOTS, SEASON:** 156, 1987-88, **HIGHEST +/-, SEASON:** 36, 1992-93, **FIRST NHL Game:** Oct. 11, 1984 vs. NYR., **FIRST NHL GOAL:** Feb. 6, 1985 vs. Cgy. (La Forest)

AMATEUR AND PROFESSIONAL RECORD

			REGULAR SEASON					PLAYOFFS				
SEASON	CLUB	Lea	GP	G	A	PTS	PIM	GP	G	A	PTS	PIM
1984-85	Hartford	NHL	41	2	6	8	83	—	—	—	—	—
1985-86	Hartford	NHL	80	5	19	24	174	10	1	2	3	38
1986-87	Hartford	NHL	78	2	31	33	162	5	0	1	1	41
1987-88	Hartford	NHL	76	8	33	41	159	5	0	0	0	8
1988-89	Hartford	NHL	71	9	26	35	181	4	0	2	2	4
1989-90	Hartford	NHL	55	2	11	13	177	7	1	0	1	2
1990-91	Hartford	NHL	62	3	18	21	174	—	—	—	—	—
1990-91	Pittsburgh	NHL	14	1	4	5	37	20	3	2	5	34
1991-92	Pittsburgh	NHL	62	1	14	15	206	21	0	2	2	39
1992-93	Pittsburgh	NHL	77	3	26	29	249	12	1	5	6	24
1993-94	Pittsburgh	NHL	80	5	24	29	199	6	0	1	1	18
1994-95	Pittsburgh	NHL	44	1	15	16	113	7	0	2	2	8
NHL Totals			740	42	227	269	1914	97	6	17	23	216

NIKLAS SUNDSTROM

24

6-0 • 185 • Shoots Left
Born: June 6, 1975
Ornskoldsvik, Sweden
Off-Season Home:
Domsgo, Sweden

CENTER/LEFT WING

1994-95: Tallied eight goals and 13 assists for 21 points in 33 matches with MoDo of the Swedish Elite League ... Ranked fourth on the team in scoring and also placed fourth with eight goals ... Tied for second on the club with 13 assists ... Skated in seven games with the bronze medal-winning Swedish team at the 1995 World Junior Championships in Red Deer, Alberta ... Tied for second on the team in scoring, tallying four goals and four assists for eight points ... Tied for third on the team, registering eight penalty minutes.

SWEDISH CAREER: Made his debut in the Swedish Elite League at 16 years of age in 1991-92 with MoDo, appearing in nine games, tallying one goal and three assists ... Became a regular with MoDo the following season in 1992-93, skating in 40 matches, recording seven goals and 11 assists for 18 points while also posting 18 penalty minutes ... Centered a line that included former NHL'er Tommy Lehmann ... Teammates included 1995 Calder Trophy winner Peter Forsberg (Col.) and Markus Naslund (Pit.) along with former Rangers defenseman Miloslav Horova.

INTERNATIONAL CAREER: Made his international debut for Team Sweden at the European Junior Championships in 1991-92 ... Tallied one goal in six outings ... Skated on a line with MoDo teammates, Forsberg and Naslund at the 1993 World Junior Championships in Gavle, Sweden, helping lead Team Sweden to their second consecutive silver medal ... Placed third on the team in scoring, trailing only Forsberg and Naslund, collecting 10 goals and four assists in seven matches... Ranked fourth in the tournament in scoring overall, while placing second in goals and

first in shooting percentage (55%, 10 goals on 18 shots) ... Also played for Team Sweden at the European Junior Championships that year, tying for first overall in scoring in the tournament with 13 points on nine goals and four assists in only five games ... Led the 1994 World Junior Tournament in Ostrava, Czech Republic in scoring, registering four goals and seven assists for 11 points ... Led Sweden to their third consecutive silver medal ... Seven assists led all players, while his 10 penalty minutes tied for first on the team ... Was voted as the tournament's outstanding forward.

BACKGROUND: Was the second European player, following Viktor Kozlov (San Jose) and first Swedish player selected at the 1993 NHL Entry Draft ... Was the top rated European player by Central Scouting ... Is the fifth highest Swede ever drafted, following Mats Sundin (first overall by Quebec in 1989), Bjorn Johansson (fifth overall by California in 1976), Peter Forsberg (sixth overall by Philadelphia in 1991), and Ulf Dahlen (seventh overall by the Rangers in 1986) ... Came to New York in April, 1995 and practiced with the Rangers ... Was coached at MoDo by Peter Forsberg's father, Kent ... Lists former Washington Capitals player Bengt Gustafsson as his favorite player ... Enjoys playing tennis ... Has played both center and left wing during his career in Sweden and has also played on the power play and penalty killing units ... Is very strong on his skates and is extremely well conditioned ... Has above average passing and playmaking skills.

CAREER TRANSACTIONS: *June 26, 1993* — Rangers' first choice, (eighth overall) in the 1993 Entry Draft

NIKLAS 24 SUNDSTROM

AMATEUR AND PROFESSIONAL RECORD

			Regular Season					Playoffs				
Season	Club	Lea	GP	G	A	PTS	PIM	GP	G	A	PTS	PIM
1991-92	MoDo................	Swe. Elite	9	1	3	4	0	—	—	—	—	—
1992-93	MoDo................	Swe. Elite	40	7	11	18	18	3	0	0	0	0
1993-94	MoDo................	Swe. Elite	37	7	12	19	28	11	4	3	7	2
1994-95	MoDo................	Swe. Elite	33	8	13	21	30	—	—	—	—	—

PAT VERBEEK

16

5-9 • 190 • Shoots Right
Born: May 24, 1964
Sarnia, Ontario
Off-Season Home:
Wyoming, Ontario

RIGHT WING

1994-95: Registered a point (10 goals, five assists) in 10 of the last 16 games ... Tied for first on the team with 17 goals ... Registered a goal in six of his 10 matches at MSG (seven goals) and collected a point in 10 of the 19 outings ... Collected 10 goals and five assists for 15 points in 19 matches with the Rangers ... Tallied two game winning goals and assisted on two game winners ... Skated in his 900th NHL game on Apr. 2 at Philadelphia ... Recorded his first goal/point as a Ranger on Mar. 30 vs. Quebec ... Made his Rangers debut on Mar. 23 at Long Island after being acquired from Hartford earlier in the day ... Finished the season playing in his 237th consecutive game ... Tallied four goals and six assists in 10 playoff matches ... Led the team with 20 PIM in the post-season.

NHL CAREER: 1982-83: Called up by New Jersey on Mar. 21, following the conclusion of the OHL season ... Made his NHL debut on Mar. 21 vs. the Rangers ... Potted his first NHL goal on Mar. 23 at Washington. **1983-84:** Placed third on the team in goals (20) and points (47) in his first full season in the NHL ... Registered five ppg's and two game-winners ... Selected as the Devils rookie of the year following the season. **1984-85:** Set a New Jersey club record with 162 PIM ... Posted consecutive two-goal games on Mar. 7 vs. the Islanders and Mar. 9 at Detroit. **1985-86:** Placed second on the club with 25 goals and ranked sixth in scoring with 53 points ... Registered his first NHL hat trick on Mar. 8 vs. Philadelphia, collecting three goals and an assist ... **1986-87:** Led the team with 35 goals and placed fourth on the team in scoring with 59 points ... Set a club record with 17 ppg's ... Recorded his second career hat trick on Mar. 25 at MSG ... Ranked fifth in the NHL in shooting percentage (24.5%) ... Collected 17 points in the first 10 games of the season (10 goals, seven assists) ... Posted a six-game goal-scoring streak (nine goals) from Oct. 18 to Oct. 30. **1987-88:** Established a franchise record with 46 goals ... Also established franchise records with eight game-winning goals, a plus 29 rating and 10 shots on goal on Mar. 29 vs. Pittsburgh ... Posted career highs with 31 assists, 77 points and 227 PIM ... 77 points set a new club record for right wings ... Posted a 12 game scoring streak from Dec. 26 to Jan. 19 (nine goals, 11 assists) ... Tallied four goals on Feb. 28 vs. Minnesota ... Recorded 21 multiple-point games ... Collected four goals and eight assists in 20 playoff outings helping the Devils to the Conference Finals. **1988-89:** Notched his fifth career hat trick on Feb. 13 vs. Toronto. **1989-90:** Played in his first season with Hartford after being acquired from New Jersey ... Led the club in goals (44) and PIM (228), becoming the first

NHL player to lead his team in both categories ... Tallied two goals and three assists on Oct. 8 at Quebec ... Registered a five game goal scoring streak and a six game point scoring streak in Mar. (six goals, seven assists). **1990-91:** Led the Whalers in goals (43) and PIM (246) for the second consecutive year ... Won the team MVP as voted by the players ... Led the team with 11 multiple-goal games and 23 multiple-point games ... Skated in all 80 games for the second consecutive season ... Appeared in his first NHL All-Star Game on Jan. 19 at Chicago. **1991-92:** Led the team in PIM for the third consecutive season with 243 ... Tied for first on the club with 10 ppg's ... Missed four games due to suspension. **1992-93:** Named the ninth captain in Whalers history on Oct. 12 ... Placed second on the team with 39 goals and ranked third on the club with 82 points ... Led the team with six gwg's ... Recorded hat tricks on Feb. 20 vs. Edmonton and Feb. 28 vs. the Islanders ... Tallied his 300th career goal, his 300th career assist and 600th NHL point on Feb. 17 vs. Buffalo ... Registered 24 multiple-point games. **1993-94:** Led the Whalers in scoring with 75 points and tied for first on the club with 15 ppg's ... 37 goals placed second on the club ... Skated in all 84 matches for the second consecutive season ... Recorded his eighth career hat trick on Oct. 14 at Chicago and posted the ninth of his career on Dec. 6 at Washington ... Collected his 700th NHL point with a goal on Mar. 29 at Detroit ... Recorded his 2,000th career PIM on Feb. 26 vs. New Jersey.

JUNIOR CAREER: Played in '81-82 and '82-83 with the Sudbury Wolves of the Ontario Hockey League ... Earned the Simmons award as the league MVP in '81-82 ... Selected by OHL coaches as the league's "Hardest Working Player".

BACKGROUND: Wore number 12 in his first season with New Jersey and then switched to number 16 when he wore in both New Jersey and Hartford ... Worked with both Special Olympics and the Leukemia Society in Hartford ... Is a fan of the Detroit Tigers and Pistons and the Minnesota Vikings ... Nickname "Beeker" ... Is the only NHL player to lead his team in goals and penalty minutes ... Married; wife, Dianne; son, Kyle; daughters, Stephanie, Kendall and Haley.

CAREER TRANSACTIONS: *June 9, 1982* — Devils' third choice (43rd overall) in the 1982 NHL Entry Draft. *June 17, 1989* — Traded by New Jersey to Hartford for Sylvain Turgeon. *March 23, 1995* — Traded by Hartford to the Rangers for Glen Featherstone, Michael Stewart, a 1995 first round draft choice and a 1996 fourth round draft choice.

CAREER HIGHLIGHTS

MOST GOALS, GAMES: 4, Feb. 28, 1988 vs. Min., **MOST ASSISTS, GAME:** 4, Mar. 24, 1990 vs. Mtl., **MOST POINTS, GAME:** 5, (twice) last- Mar. 24, 1990 vs. Mtl., **MOST PIM, GAME:** 30, Nov. 27, 1992 at Bos., **MOST SHOTS, GAME:** 9, Feb. 28, 1984 vs. NYR, **MOST SHOTS, SEASON:** 247, 1990-91, **HIGHEST +/-, SEASON:** 29, 1987-88, **FIRST NHL GAME:** Mar. 21, 1983 vs. NYR, **FIRST NHL GOAL:** Mar. 24, 1983 at Wsh. (Jensen).

AMATEUR AND PROFESSIONAL RECORD

Season	Club	Lea	Regular Season					Playoffs				
			GP	G	A	PTS	PIM	GP	G	A	PTS	PIM
1981-82	Sudbury	OHL	66	37	51	88	180	—	—	—	—	—
1982-83	New Jersey	NHL	6	3	2	5	8	—	—	—	—	—
1982-83	Sudbury	OHL	61	40	67	107	184	—	—	—	—	—
1983-84	New Jersey	NHL	79	20	27	47	158	—	—	—	—	—
1984-85	New Jersey	NHL	78	15	18	33	162	—	—	—	—	—
1985-86	New Jersey	NHL	76	25	28	53	79	—	—	—	—	—
1986-87	New Jersey	NHL	74	35	24	59	120	—	—	—	—	—
1987-88	New Jersey	NHL	73	46	31	77	227	20	4	8	12	51
1988-89	New Jersey	NHL	77	26	21	47	189	—	—	—	—	—
1989-90	Hartford	NHL	80	44	45	89	228	7	2	2	4	26
1990-91	Hartford	NHL	80	43	39	82	246	6	3	2	5	40
1991-92	Hartford	NHL	76	22	35	57	243	7	0	2	2	12
1992-93	Hartford	NHL	84	39	43	82	197	—	—	—	—	—
1993-94	Hartford	NHL	84	37	38	75	177	—	—	—	—	—
1994-95	Hartford	NHL	29	7	11	18	53	—	—	—	—	—
1994-95	Rangers	NHL	19	10	5	15	18	10	4	6	10	20
NHL Totals			915	372	367	739	2105	50	13	20	33	149
Rangers Totals			19	10	5	15	18	10	4	6	10	20

IN THE SYSTEM

SYLVAIN BLOUIN
DEFENSE
6'2"   207 lbs.   Shoots Left
Born: May 21, 1974, Montreal, Quebec
Obtained in Entry Draft, June 28, 1994; fifth choice, 104th overall.

CAREER NOTES:
Won the 1992-93 QMJHL Playoff Trophy (President Cup) with his junior club the Laval Titans ... Was team-mates at Laval with current NHL players Sandy McCarthy (Detroit), Phillipe Boucher (Los Angeles), and Martin Lapointe (Detroit).

Season	Club	League	GP	G	A	PTS	PIM	GP	G	A	PTS	PIM
				Regular Season					Playoffs			
1991-92	Laval	QMJHL	28	0	0	0	23	9	0	0	0	35
1992-93	Laval	QMJHL	68	0	10	10	373	13	1	0	1	66
1993-94	Laval	QMJHL	62	18	23	41	492	21	4	13	17	177
1994-95	Charlotte	ECHL	50	5	7	12	280	3	0	0	0	4
1994-95	Binghamton	AHL	10	1	0	1	46	2	0	0	0	24
1994-95	Chicago	IHL	1	0	0	0	2	—	—	—	—	—

ERIC CAIRNS
DEFENSE
6'5"   230 lbs.   Shoots Left
Born: June 27, 1974, Oakville, Ontario
Obtained in Entry Draft, June 20, 1992; third choice, 72nd overall.

CAREER NOTES:
HIs first professional goal was an overtime winner which clinched the Southern Division Semi-Finals on Apr. 21, 1995 vs. the Rochester Americans ... Was teammates at Detroit (OHL) with Todd Harvey (Dallas) and Pat Peake (Washington) ... MIssed only seven games (including playoffs) in three years with Detroit ... Three of those games were due to suspension.

Season	Club	League	GP	G	A	PTS	PIM	GP	G	A	PTS	PIM
				Regular Season					Playoffs			
1991-92	Detroit	OHL	64	1	11	12	232	7	0	0	0	31
1992-93	Detroit	OHL	64	3	13	16	194	15	0	3	3	24
1993-94	Detroit	OHL	59	7	35	42	204	—	—	—	—	—
1994-95	Binghamton	AHL	27	0	3	3	134	9	1	1	2	28
1994-95	Birmingham	ECHL	11	1	3	4	49	—	—	—	—	—

IN THE SYSTEM

CHRIS FERRARO
CENTER
5'10"   185 lbs.   Shoots Right
Born: January 24, 1973, Port Jefferson, NY
Obtained in Entry Draft , June 20, 1992; fourth choice, 85th overall.

CAREER NOTES:
Skated for the U.S. National Team in 1993-94 ... Selected to the Hockey East All-Rookie team while helping lead the University of Maine Black Bears to their first-ever NCAA National Championship in 1992-93 ... Tied a Hockey East record, tallying 21 goals in 24 conference matches ... Tied the school record for assists in a single game, recording five in an 11-1 win over New Brunswick on Oct. 31, 1992 ... Was a member of the bronze medal winning, Team USA at the World Junior Championships in 1991-92 .... Led the gold medal winning Team South in scoring at the 1992 Junior Olympic Festival ... Was named All-World Right Wing at the select 16's tournament ahead of current Ranger Alexei Kovalev ... Is the "older" of the twins, being born one minute earlier.

Season	Club	League	Regular Season					Playoffs				
			GP	G	A	PTS	PIM	GP	G	A	PTS	PIM
1992-93	U. of Maine	H.E.	39	25	26	51	46	—	—	—	—	—
1993-94	U. of Maine	H.E.	4	0	1	1	8	—	—	—	—	—
1993-94	U.S. National Team		48	8	34	42	58	—	—	—	—	—
1994-95	Atlanta	IHL	54	13	14	27	72	—	—	—	—	—
1994-95	Binghamton	AHL	13	6	4	10	38	10	2	3	5	16

PETER FERRARO
RIGHT WING
5'10"   185 lbs.   Shoots Right
Born: January 24, 1973, Port Jefferson, NY
Obtained in Entry Draft, June 20, 1992; first choice, 24th overall.

CAREER NOTES:
Was a member of the 1994 U.S. Olympic Team ... Won the 1993 NCAA National Championship with the University of Maine ... Played for the US National Junior Team at the 1993 World Junior Championship ... Led bronze medal winning, Team USA in scoring with eight points (three goals, five assists) in seven games at the World Junior Championships ... Competed for Team South at the 1992 Junior Olympic Festival ... Named All-World Center at the 1992 World Junior Championships in Germany ... Joined Brian Leetch, Scott Lachance, Jeremy Roenick, and Scott Young as the only American players to make the World Junior Championship All-Tournament Team ... Is the first New York native to be selected in the first round of the NHL Entry Draft.

Season	Club	League	Regular Season					Playoffs				
			GP	G	A	PTS	PIM	GP	G	A	PTS	PIM
1992-93	U. of Maine	H.E	36	18	32	50	106	—	—	—	—	—
1993-94	U. of Maine	H.E	4	3	6	9	16	—	—	—	—	—
1993-94	U.S. National Team		60	30	34	64	87	—	—	—	—	—
1993-94	U.S. Olympic Team		8	6	0	6	6	—	—	—	—	—
1994-95	Atlanta	IHL	61	15	24	39	118	—	—	—	—	—
1994-95	Binghamton	AHL	12	2	6	8	67	11	4	3	7	51

IN THE SYSTEM

ERIC FLINTON
LEFT WING
6'2"   190 lbs.   Shoots Left
Born: February 2, 1972
Signed as a free agent on August 22, 1995

CAREER NOTES:
Played collegiately at the University of New Hampshire with Assistant General Manager Larry Pleau's son Steven ... Led the club in scoring this past season with 22 goals and 23 assists for 45 points in 36 games.

Season	Club	League	GP	G	A	PTS	PIM	GP	G	A	PTS	PIM
					Regular Season					Playoffs		
1991-92	N. Hampshire	H.E.	36	6	4	10	10	—	—	—	—	—
1992-93	N. Hampshire	H.E.	37	8	8	36	14	—	—	—	—	—
1993-94	N. Hampshire	H.E.	40	16	25	41	36	—	—	—	—	—
1994-95	N. Hampshire	H.E.	36	22	23	45	44	—	—	—	—	—

MAXIM GALANOV
DEFENSE
6'1"   195 lbs.   Shoots Left
Born: March 13, 1974, Krasnoyarsk, USSR
Obtained in Entry Draft, June 26, 1993; third choice, 61st overall.

CAREER NOTES:
Played on the Russian team at the 1993 World Junior Championships ... Was selected for the Russian Junior National Team as an underage 18-year-old ... Was teammates at Lada Togliatti with Denis Tsygurov (Los Angeles).

Season	Club	League	GP	G	A	PTS	PIM	GP	G	A	PTS	PIM
					Regular Season					Playoffs		
1992-93	Togliatti	CIS	41	4	2	6	12	10	1	1	2	12
1993-94	Togliatti	CIS	7	1	0	1	4	12	1	0	1	8
1994-95	Togliatti	CIS	45	5	6	11	54	N/A	0	1	1	12

KEN GERNANDER
CENTER/LEFT WING
5'10"   180 lbs.   Shoots Left
Born: June 30, 1969, Coleraine, Minnesota
Signed as a free agent on September 9,1994.
Originally drafted by Winnipeg as their fourth choice, 96th overall, in the 1987 NHL Entry Draft.

CAREER NOTES:
Ken's father Bob Gernander, is the Chief Scout of the Dallas Stars.

Season	Club	League	GP	G	A	PTS	PIM	GP	G	A	PTS	PIM
					Regular Season					Playoffs		
1987-88	U. Minnesota	WCHA	44	14	14	28	14	—	—	—	—	—
1988-89	U. Minnesota	WCHA	44	9	11	20	2	—	—	—	—	—
1989-90	U. Minnesota	WCHA	44	32	17	49	24	—	—	—	—	—
1990-91	U. Minnesota	WCHA	44	23	20	43	24	—	—	—	—	—
1991-92	Fort Wayne	IHL	13	7	6	13	2	—	—	—	—	—
1991-92	Moncton	AHL	43	8	18	26	98	1	1	2	2	
1992-93	Moncton	AHL	71	18	29	47	20	5	1	4	5	0
1993-94	Moncton	AHL	71	22	35	57	12	6	1	7	0	0
1994-95	Binghamton	AHL	80	28	25	53	24	11	2	2	4	6

IN THE SYSTEM

JON HILLEBRANDT
GOALTENDER
5'10"   185 lbs.   Catches Left
Born: December 18, 1971, Cottage Grove, Wisconsin
Obtained in 1990 Entry Draft, June 16, 1990; 10th choice, 202nd overall.

CAREER NOTES:
Played with the 1993-94 U.S. National Team and traveled with the U.S. Olympic Team to Lillehammer, Norway as the number three goaltender ... Earned All-CCHA Second Team honors in 1992-93 and was the first University of Chicago at Illinois Flames player to be named to the CANSTAR CCHA All-Rookie Team in 1991-92.

Season	Club	League	GP	W	L	T	AVG	GP	W	L	AVG
1990-91	Madison	USHL	28	10	14	3	4.08	—	—	—	—
1991-92	Univ. of Illinois-Chicago	CCHA	31	7	19	—	4.14	—	—	—	—
1992-93	Univ. of Illinois-Chicago	CCHA	33	8	22	2	4.51	5	2	3	4.80
1993-94	Binghamton	AHL	8	0	0	0	0	—	—	—	—
1993-94	U.S. National Team		2	1	1	0	3.9	—	—	—	—
1994-95	Charlotte	ECHL	32	14	11	2	4.05	3	0	2	4.01
1994-95	San Diego	IHL	—	1	0	1	9.00	—	—	—	—
1994-95	Binghamton	AHL	—	—	—	—	—	1	0	0	10.00

BRAD JONES
LEFT WING
6'0"   190 lbs.   Shoots Left
Born: June 26,1970, Sterling Heights, Michigan
Signed as a free agent on August 23, 1995.

CAREER NOTES:
Has played 148 NHL matches with Winnipeg, Los Angeles and Philadelphia ... Was named to the CCHA First All-Star Team in 1987 and the Second All-Star Team in 1986 ... Was voted to the 1987 NCAA West Second All-American Team.

Season	Club	League	GP	G	A	PTS	PIM	GP	G	A	PTS	PIM
1983-84	U. of Michigan	CCHA	37	8	26	34	32	—	—	—	—	—
1984-85	U. of Michigan	CCHA	34	21	27	48	66	—	—	—	—	—
1985-86	U. of Michigan	CCHA	36	28	39	67	40	—	—	—	—	—
1986-87	U. of Michigan	CCHA	40	32	46	78	64	—	—	—	—	—
1986-87	Winnipeg	NHL	4	1	0	1	0	—	—	—	—	—
1987-88	Winnipeg	NHL	19	2	5	7	15	1	0	0	0	0
1987-88	U.S. National		50	27	23	50	59	—	—	—	—	—
1988-89	Winnipeg	NHL	22	6	5	11	6	—	—	—	—	—
1988-89	Moncton	AHL	44	20	19	39	62	7	0	1	1	22
1989-90	Winnipeg	NHL	2	0	0	0	0	—	—	—	—	—
1989-90	Moncton	AHL	15	5	6	11	47	—	—	—	—	—
1989-90	New Haven	AHL	36	8	11	19	71	—	—	—	—	—
1990-91	Los Angeles	NHL	53	9	11	20	57	8	1	1	2	2
1991-92	Philadelphia	NHL	48	7	10	17	44	—	—	—	—	—
1992-93	Ilves	Finland	26	10	7	17	62	—	—	—	—	—
1992-93	New Haven	AHL	4	2	1	3	6	—	—	—	—	—
1994-95	Springfield	AHL	61	23	22	45	47	—	—	—	—	—
	NHL Totals		148	25	31	56	122	9	1	1	2	2

IN THE SYSTEM

PAVEL KOMAROV
DEFENSE
6'2"   190 lbs.   Shoots Left
Born: February 28, 1974, Gorky, USSR
Obtained in Entry Draft, June 26, 1993; 12th Choice, 261st overall.

				Regular Season				Playoffs			
Season	Club	League	GP	G	A	PTS	PIM	GP	G	A	PTS	PIM
1991-92	Nizhny Novg.	CIS	10	0	1	1	0	—	—	—	—	—
1992-93	Nizhny Novg.	CIS	28	0	0	0	25	—	—	—	—	—
1993-94	Nizhny Novg.	CIS	18	1	0	1	20	1	0	0	0	2
1993-94	Binghamton	AHL	1	1	0	1	2	—	—	—	—	—
1994-95	Nizhny Novg.	CIS	26	0	1	1	38	3	0	0	0	0
1994-95	Binghamton	AHL	2	0	0	0	2	—	—	—	—	—

ANDREI KUDINOV
CENTER
6'0"   205 lbs.   Shoots Left
Born: June 28, 1970, Chelyabinsk, CIS
Obtained in Entry Draft, June 26, 1993; 10th round choice, number 242 overall.

				Regular Season				Playoffs			
Season	Club	League	GP	G	A	PTS	PIM	GP	G	A	PTS	PIM
1990-91	Chelyabinsk	Sov. El.	24	2	3	5	20	—	—	—	—	—
1991-92	Chelyabinsk	CIS	36	9	7	16	40	—	—	—	—	—
1992-93	Chelyabinsk	CIS	41	13	23	36	50	8	0	1	1	6
1993-94	Binghamton	AHL	25	3	3	6	6	—	—	—	—	—
1994-95	Binghamton	AHL	65	14	22	36	45	3	0	0	0	0

SCOTT MALONE
DEFENSE
6'1"   195 lbs.   Shoots Left
Born: January 16, 1971, South Boston, Massachusetts
Obtained from the Toronto Maple Leafs along with Glenn Anderson and a 1994 fourth round draft pick (Alexander Korobolin) for Mike Gartner on March 21, 1994. Originally drafted by Toronto as their 10th pick, 220th overall, in the 1990 NHL Entry Draft.

CAREER NOTES:
Was teammates at the University of New Hampshire with Assistant General Manager Larry Pleau's son, Steven.

				Regular Season				Playoffs			
Season	Club	League	GP	G	A	PTS	PIM	GP	G	A	PTS	PIM
1991-92	N. Hampshire	H.E.	27	0	4	4	52	—	—	—	—	—
1992-93	N. Hampshire	H.E.	36	5	6	11	96	—	—	—	—	—
1993-94	N. Hampshire	H.E.	40	14	6	20	162	—	—	—	—	—
1994-95	Binghamton	AHL	48	3	14	17	85	11	0	2	2	12
1994-95	Birmingham	ECHL	8	1	4	5	36	—	—	—	—	—

IN THE SYSTEM

CAL McGOWAN
CENTER
6'1"   185 lbs.   Shoots Left
Born: June 19, 1970, Sydney, Nova Scotia
Signed as a free agent on August 13,1995.

CAREER NOTES:
Named to WHL First All-Star Team in 1991 and ranked third overall in scoring in the WHL, with 139 points.

Season	Club	League	GP	G	A	PTS	PIM	GP	G	A	PTS	PIM
1988-89	Kamloops	WHL	72	21	31	52	44	—	—	—	—	—
1989-90	Kamloops	WHL	71	33	45	78	76	17	4	5	9	42
1990-91	Kamloops	WHL	71	58	81	139	147	12	7	7	14	24
1991-92	Kalamazoo	IHL	77	13	30	43	62	1	0	0	0	2
1992-93	Kalamazoo	IHL	78	18	42	60	62	—	—	—	—	—
1993-94	Kalamazoo	IHL	49	9	18	27	48	4	0	0	0	2
1994-95	Kalamazoo	IHL	1	0	0	0	0	—	—	—	—	—
1994-95	Worcester	AHL	64	22	22	21	32	—	—	—	—	—

JEFF NIELSEN
RIGHT WING
6'0"   195 lbs.   Shoots Right
Born: September 20 ,1971, Grand Rapids, Minnesota
Obtained in Entry Draft, June 16, 1990; fourth choice, 69th overall.

CAREER NOTES:
Led the University of Minnesota Golden Gophers in scoring his senior season (1993-94) with 45 points ... Was teammates at Minnesota with defenseman Chris McAlpine (New Jersey Devils).

Season	Club	League	GP	G	A	PTS	PIM	GP	G	A	PTS	PIM
1987-88	Grand Rapids HS	Minn. HS	21	9	11	20	14	—	—	—	—	—
1988-89	Grand Rapids HS	Minn. HS	25	13	17	30	26	—	—	—	—	—
1989-90	Grand Rapids HS	Minn. HS	28	32	25	57		—	—	—	—	—
1990-91	U. Minnesota	WCHA	45	11	14	25	50	—	—	—	—	—
1991-92	U. Minnesota	WCHA	44	15	16	30	74	—	—	—	—	—
1992-93	U. Minnesota	WCHA	42	21	20	41	80	—	—	—	—	—
1993-94	U. Minnesota	WCHA	41	20	16	45	94	—	—	—	—	—
1994-95	Binghamton	AHL	76	24	13	37	139	7	0	0	0	22

JAMIE RAM
GOALTENDER
5'11"   175 lbs.   Catches Left
Born: January 18, 1971, Scarborough, Ontario
Obtained in Entry Draft, June 22, 1991,10th choice, 213th overall.

CAREER NOTES:
Was on the NCAA West First All-American Team at Michigan Tech. in 1993 and 1994 ... Also named to the WCHA First All-Star Team for those two seasons ... Had the best save percentage in the WCHA in 1990-91 with a .901 mark ... Named the WCHA All-Rookie goaltender in 1990-91 ... Made 26 saves in his first professional shutout (4-0) on 12/7/94 at Adirondack.

Season	Club	League	GP	W	L	T	GAA	GP	W	L	T	GAA
1990-91	Michigan Tech.	WCHA	14	5	9	0	4.14	—	—	—	—	—
1991-92	Michigan Tech.	WCHA	23	9	9	1	4.35	—	—	—	—	—
1992-93	Michigan Tech.	WCHA	36	16	14	5	3.32	—	—	—	—	—
1993-94	Michigan Tech.	WCHA	39	12	20	5	3.20	—	—	—	—	—
1994-95	Binghamton	AHL	26	12	10	2	3.30	11	6	5	1	2.62

IN THE SYSTEM

SHAWN REID
DEFENSE
6'0"   195 lbs.   Shoots Left
Born: September 21, 1970, Toronto, Ontario
Signed as a free agent on July 6, 1994.

CAREER NOTES:
Was a 1994 WCHA First All-Star Team member with Colorado College and a NCAA East Second Team All-Star in 1994 ... Also earned First Team Titan West All American honors while captaining the Tigers to their first regular season championship since 1957.

				Regular Season					Playoffs			
Season	Club	League	GP	G	A	PTS	PIM	GP	G	A	PTS	PIM
1990-91	Colorado	WCHA	38	10	8	18	36	—	—	—	—	—
1991-92	Colorado	WCHA	41	12	22	34	64	—	—	—	—	—
1992-93	Colorado	WCHA	32	3	11	14	54	—	—	—	—	—
1993-94	Colorado	WCHA	39	7	20	27	28	—	—	—	—	—
1994-95	Fort Wayne	IHL	42	4	8	12	28	—	—	—	—	—
1994-95	Binghamton	AHL	18	3	4	7	8	9	0	3	3	6

BARRY RICHTER
DEFENSE
6'2"   205 lbs.   Shoots Left
Born: September 11, 1970, Madison, Wisconsin
Obtained from the Hartford Whalers along with Nick Kypreos, Steve Larmer and a 1994 sixth round draft pick (Yuri Litvinov) for James Patrick and Darren Turcotte. Originally drafted by Hartford as their second round pick, 32nd overall, in the 1988 NHL Entry Draft.

CAREER NOTES:
Was a member of the 1994 U.S. Olympic Team ... Earned NCAA West First Team All-American honors following his senior year ... Participated wtih Team USA at the 1992-93 World Championships in Munich, Germany ... Also skated for Team USA at the 1991-92 World Championships in Czechoslovakia ... Played for Team North at the 1990 U.S. Olympic Festival, tallying one goal and three assists for the gold medal winners ... Participated with Team North at the 1989 U.S. Olympic Festival in Oklahoma ... Collected one goal and three assists while serving as team captain for the U.S. Junior Team at the 1989-90 World Junior Championships in Finland ... His father Pat, is a former Washington Redskins Tight End and the current Athletic Director at the University of Wisconsin.

				Regular Season					Playoffs			
Season	Club	League	GP	G	A	PTS	PIM	GP	G	A	PTS	PIM
1989-90	Wisconsin	WCHA	42	13	23	36	36	—	—	—	—	—
1990-91	Wisconsin	WCHA	43	15	20	35	42	—	—	—	—	—
1991-92	Wisconsin	WCHA	39	10	25	35	62	—	—	—	—	—
1992-93	Wisconsin	WCHA	42	14	32	46	74	—	—	—	—	—
1993-94	Binghamton	AHL	21	0	9	9	12	—	—	—	—	—
1993-94	U.S. Olympic Team		8	0	3	3	4	—	—	—	—	—
1993-94	U.S. National Team		56	7	16	23	50	—	—	—	—	—
1994-95	Binghamton	AHL	73	15	41	56	54	11	4	5	9	12

JEAN-YVES ROY

RIGHT WING
5'10"   175 lbs.   Shoots Left
Born: February 17, 1969, Rosemere, Quebec
Signed as a free agent on July 20, 1992.

CAREER NOTES:
Is the first player in Binghamton's history to record back-to-back 40 goal seasons ... Won the 1994 Silver Medal with the Canadian Olympic Team in Lillehammer, Norway ... Represented Team USA in the 1995 AHL All-Star Game in Providence, Rhode Island ... Is a three-time collegiate All-American at the University of Maine.

Season	Club	League	Regular Season					Playoffs				
			GP	G	A	PTS	PIM	GP	G	A	PTS	PIM
1989-90	Univ. of Maine	H.E.	46	39	26	65	52	—	—	—	—	—
1990-91	Univ. of Maine	H.E.	43	37	45	82	62	—	—	—	—	—
1991-92	Univ. of Maine	H.E.	35	32	24	56	62	—	—	—	—	—
1992-93	Binghamton	AHL	49	13	15	28	21	14	5	2	7	4
1992-93	Canadian National Team		23	9	6	15	35	—	—	—	—	—
1993-94	Binghamton	AHL	65	41	24	65	33	—	—	—	—	—
1993-94	Canadian Olympic Team		8	1	0	1	0	—	—	—	—	—
1993-94	Canadian National Team		6	3	2	5	2	—	—	—	—	—
1994-95	Binghamton	AHL	67	41	36	77	28	11	4	6	10	12
1994-95	Rangers	NHL	3	1	0	1	2	—	—	—	—	—
NHL & Rangers Totals			3	1	0	1	2	—	—	—	—	—

KEN SHEPARD

GOALTENDER
5'10"   195 lbs.   Catches Left
Born: January 20, 1974, Toronto, Ontario
Obtained in 1993 Entry Draft, 10th choice, 216th overall.

CAREER NOTES:
Earned the FW Dinty Moore Trophy which is awarded annually to the OHL rookie goaltender with the lowest goals-against average (3.48) ... Was teammates at Oshawa with NHLers Eric Lindros (Philadelphia), Jason Arnott (Edmonton) and Rangers second choice in the 1995 Entry Draft, Marc Savard.

Season	Club	League	Regular Season					Playoffs				
			GP	W	L	T	AVG	GP	W	L	T	AVG
1991-92	Oshawa	OHL	7	1	2	0	3.62	1	0	0	0	0
1992-93	Oshawa	OHL	31	12	7	4	3.48	11	3	7	0	3.98
1993-94	Oshawa	OHL	45	20	15	5	3.95	5	1	4	0	3.5
1994-95	Oshawa	OHL	42	24	11	3	3.19	5	1	4	0	5.22

IN THE SYSTEM

ANDY SILVERMAN
DEFENSE
6'3"   205 lbs.   Shoots Left
Born: August 23, 1972, Beverly, Massachusetts
Obtained in Entry Draft, June 16, 1990; 11th choice, 181st overall.

CAREER NOTES:
Won the 1993 NCAA National Championship with the University of Maine Black Bears ... Was teammates at Maine with current NHLers Paul Kariya (Anaheim), and Garth Snow (Philadelphia), and Rangers prospects Chris and Peter Ferraro.

Season	Club	League	GP	G	A	PTS	PIM	GP	G	A	PTS	PIM
					Regular Season					Playoffs		
1991-92	Univ. of Maine	H.E.	30	2	9	11	18	—	—	—	—	—
1992-93	Univ. of Maine	H.E.	37	1	7	8	56	—	—	—	—	—
1993-94	Univ. of Maine	H.E.	35	0	3	3	80	—	—	—	—	—
1994-95	Binghamton	AHL	5	0	1	1	2	—	—	—	—	—
1994-95	Charlotte	ECHL	64	3	11	14	57	3	0	0	0	2

LEE SOROCHAN
DEFENSE
5'11"   210 lbs.   Shoots Left
Born: September 9, 1975
Obtained in NHL Entry Draft, June 1993; second choice, 34th overall.

CAREER NOTES:
Was the second youngest player selected in the 1993 NHL Entry Draft on June 26th (17 years, nine months, 17 days) ... Was a member of Canada's Under-18 team that earned the gold medal at the Pacific Cup in 1992 ... Has played on the provincial champion baseball team.

Season	Club	League	GP	G	A	PTS	PIM	GP	G	A	PTS	PIM
					Regular Season					Playoffs		
1991-92	Lethbridge	WHL	67	2	9	11	105	5	0	2	2	6
1992-93	Lethbridge	WHL	69	8	32	40	208	4	0	1	1	12
1993-94	Lethbridge	WHL	46	5	27	32	123	9	4	3	7	16
1994-95	Lethbridge	WHL	29	4	15	19	93	—	—	—	—	—
1994-95	Saskatoon	WHL	24	5	13	18	63	10	3	6	9	34
1994-95	Binghamton	AHL	—	—	—	—	—	8	0	0	0	11

DIMITRI STAROSTENKO
RIGHT WING
6'0"   200 lbs.   Shoots Left
Born: March 18, 1973, Minsk, Russia
Obtained in Entry Draft, June 20, 1992, fifth round choice, number 120 overall.

CAREER NOTES:
Led CSKA Moscow in scoring in 1992-93 with 15 goals and 12 assists for 27 points in 42 contests .... Was teammates with Andrei Kovalenko (Colorado), Valery Kamensky (Colorado), Igor Kravchuk (Edmonton), and Vladimir Malakhov (Montreal) during the 1990-91 season, and with Sergei Zubov (Pittsburgh) in 1991-92.

Season	Club	League	GP	G	A	PTS	PIM	GP	G	A	PTS	PIM
					Regular Season					Playoffs		
1990-91	CSKA	USSR	20	2	1	3	—	—	—	—	—	—
1991-92	CSKA	CIS	32	3	1	4	12	—	—	—	—	—
1992-93	CSKA	CIS	42	15	12	27	22	—	—	—	—	—
1993-94	Binghamton	AHL	41	12	9	21	10	—	—	—	—	—
1994-95	Binghamton	AHL	69	19	22	41	40	5	1	1	2	0

IN THE SYSTEM

RYAN VANDENBUSSCHE
RIGHT WING
5'11"   187 lbs.   Shoots Right
Born: February 28, 1973, Simcoe, Ontario
Signed as a free agent on August 3, 1995.

CAREER NOTES:
Was teammates at Cornwall/Newmarket with Nathan LaFayette ... Captured the "Rookie Fitness Award" at the Ranger's 1995 training camp.

Season	Club	League	GP	Regular Season G	A	PTS	PIM	Playoffs GP	G	A	PTS	PIM
1990-91	Cornwall	OHL	49	3	8	11	139	—	—	—	—	—
1991-92	Cornwall	OHL	61	13	15	28	232	6	0	2	2	9
1992-93	Newmarket	OHL	30	15	12	27	161	—	—	—	—	—
1992-93	Guelph	OHL	29	3	14	17	99	5	1	3	4	13
1992-93	St. John's	AHL	1	0	0	0	0	—	—	—	—	—
1993-94	St. John's	AHL	44	4	10	14	124	—	—	—	—	—
1993-94	Springfield	AHL	9	1	2	3	29	5	0	0	0	16
1994-95	St. John's	AHL	53	2	13	15	239	3	0	0	0	17

RICK WILLIS
LEFT WING
6'0"   188 lbs.   Shoots Left
Born: January 12, 1972, Lynn, Massachusetts
Obtained in Entry Draft, June 16,1990; fifth choice, 76th overall.

CAREER NOTES:
Captained the University of Michigan Wolverines to a CCHA leading 22-4-1 record this past season.

Season	Club	League	GP	Regular Season G	A	PTS	PIM	Playoffs GP	G	A	PTS	PIM
1991-92	U. of Michigan	CCHA	32	1	4	5	42	—	—	—	—	—
1992-93	U. of Michigan	CCHA	39	3	8	11	67	—	—	—	—	—
1993-94	U. of Michigan	CCHA	40	8	5	13	83	—	—	—	—	—
1994-95	U. of Michigan	CCHA	35	3	6	9	78	—	—	—	—	—

NEW YORK RANGERS 1995

Name-Round/Overall-Position/Shoots-Ht.-Wt.-Birthdate-Birthplace

CHRISTIAN DUBE
2/39   C/R   5-11   170   4/25/77   Sherbrooke, Quebec
Tallied 36 goals and 65 assists for 101 points in 71 games with the Sherbrooke
Faucons of the Quebec Major Junior Hockey League ... His 101 points tied him for 10th
in the league in scoring while his 65 assists ranked seventh ... Has played the last two
seasons with Sherbrooke ... Is a skilled forward with soft hands and good scoring ability
... Was a member of the QMJHL select team at the 1995 Chrysler Challenge Cup (CHL
All-Star Game) ... Attended Canada's National Junior Team Evaluation Camp in August
... Was a member of the gold medal winning Jr. Canadian National team in 1994 in
Mexico (tournament for top draft eligible prospects) ... Has very good hockey sense and
uses it in all situations ... Is an unselfish player who is very aggressive around loose
pucks ... Plays a finesse game but is always in the middle of the play and won't back
down in any situation ... Has an easy skating stride combined with good balance, agility
and burst of speed ... Favorite player is Boston Bruins center Adam Oates ... Is excellent at finding open ice to receive a pass or make a play ... Was selected to the QMJHL
Rookie All-Star Team for 1993-94 ... Received the Michel Bergeron Trophy for the
QMJHL Offensive Rookie of the Year in 1993-94 ... Spent 12 years living in Switzerland
... Is the son of former Kansas City Scouts player, Normand Dube.

MIKE MARTIN
3/65   D/R   6-2   204   10/27/76   Stratford, Ontario
A "defensive" defenseman, Martin collected nine goals and 28 assists for 37 points in
53 games with the Windsor Spitfires of the Ontario Hockey League ... Has played the
last three seasons with Windsor ... Was a member of the OHL select team at the 1995
Chrysler Cup Challenge (CHL All-Star Game) ... Was named the Windsor's Best
Defensive Defenseman for the past two seasons ... Is strong and mobile on his skates
with a long stride and good straight-away speed ... Was selected as one of the OHL's
top defensive defensemen in the annual OHL coaches poll in 1994-95 ... Is a solid posi-
tional player who supports his partner and clears out the front of the net ... Plays
rugged and abrasive and won't back down if challenged ... Likes to move up into the
play and is capable of rushing with the puck ... Was Windsor's Scholastic Player of the
Year in 1994-95 ... Was named to the OHL Second All-Star Rookie Team in 1992-93 ...
Is a good competitor and team player who is well respected by his teammates ... Tries
to emulate Scott Stevens in his style of play ... List Wayne Gretzky as his favorite NHL
player.

MARC SAVARD
4/91   C/L   5-10   174   7/17/77   Ottawa, Ontario
Has played the last two seasons with the Oshawa Generals of the Ontario Hockey
League ... Led the OHL in scoring with 43 goals and 96 assists for 139 points in 66
matches with Oshawa ... His 96 assists ranked second in the league ... Is the 10th player in CHL history to win their own league's scoring title in their first year of draft eligibili-
ty joining; Jim Fox, Doug Wickenheiser, Dale Hawerchuk, Pat La Fontaine, Mario
Lemieux, Rob Brown, Keith Primeau, Eric Lindros and Tampa Bay's 1995 first round
selection Daymond Langkow ... Attended the Canadian National Junior Team's evaluation camp in August ... Is a skilled player with very soft hands who is dangerous around
the net ... Was a second team OHL All-Star in 1994-95 ... Member of the OHL team at
the 1995 Chrysler Cup Challenge (CHL All-Star Game) ... Carries the puck well and is
an excellent passer who is always aware of all his options ... Is consistent at winning
faceoffs, he seldom gives the puck away and is used in all game situations ... Is considered one of the smartest players in the OHL by the annual OHL coaches poll ... Won
the 1995 CHL Top Scorer Award ... Favorite player is Wayne Gretzky ... Was selected
as Oshawa's Rookie of the Year in 1993-94 ... Played on the top line for the Under-17
Ontario team at the World Challenge in 1994 ... Was a member of the 1994 gold medal
winning Under-18 national team in Mexico.

ENTRY DRAFT SELECTIONS

Name-Round/Overall-Position/Shoots-Ht.-Wt.-Birthdate-Birthplace

ALEXEI VASILJEV
5/110   D/L   6-1   189   9/1/77   Yaroslavl, Russia
A stay at home defenseman who moves the puck well ... Strong on his skates with excellent mobility, balance and acceleration ... Is poised under pressure and makes smart passes ... Tries to copy the playing style of Sergei Zubov ...Played in the European Championships and the Four Nations Tournament ... Has good hockey sense and plays with a lot of confidence ... Plays both on the power play and penalty killing units ... Is effective in the corners and along the boards and will play tough when needed ... Is defensive partners with Rangers eighth round pick Ilja Gorokhov.

DALE PURINTON
5/117   D/L   6-2   201   10/11/76   Fort Wayne, Indiana
Strong, physical defenseman who collected 291 penalty minutes in his first season of junior hockey with the Tacoma Rockets of the Western Hockey League ... Ranked third in the WHL with 291 penalty minutes ... Tallied eight assists in 65 matches ... Lists Bob Probert as his favorite NHL player ...Teammates with Rangers 1994 draft selections, Adam Smith and Jamie Butt ... Is a very solid checker who likes to hit ... Possesses a good hard shot from the point combined with a quick release ... Can pass equally well on forehand and backhand ... Has excellent desire and attitude ... Likes to get involved and stands up to a challenge ... His father Calvin played for the Fort Wayne Komets of the International League.

PETER SLAMIAR
6/143   RW/R   5-11   174   2/26/77   Zvolen, Slovakia
Began last season with the Zvolen Junior team in the Slovakian League ... Ended the season playing regularly with the Zvolen Senior club ... Is expected to play with the senior team this season ... Improved steadily as the season progressed ... Is considered one of the best skaters among this years draftable players from all of Europe ... Was one of the top players on the Slovak Jr. National team ... Notched five goals and eight assists in five games during the Eurpoean Junior B-Pool Tournament ... Has a great work ethic and was the most physically conditioned athlete on the Slovak Jr. National team according to his coach ... Is a coachable, team-player with a winning attitude ... Lists Sergei Fedorov as his favorite player.

JEFF HEIL
7/169   G/L   6-1   190   9/17/75   Bloomington, Minnesota
Played with River Falls, Wisconsin of the NCAA Division III league this past season ... Is a very agile netminder with skating abilities that are seldom found in a goaltender ... Has above average puckhandling ability for a goaltender of his age ... He reads and reacts well to the play ... Has a solid glove hand and controls his rebounds well.

ILJA GOROKHOV
8/195   D/R   6-1   190   1/16/76   Yaroslavl, Russia
Skated with the Yaroslavl junior team last season ... Is a very controlled, thinking player who moves the puck up ice quickly ... Is a very steady "defensive" defenseman .. An excellent skater with good mobility ... He makes very few mistakes and is hard to beat one on one ... Played in the Four Nations Tournament in February ... Skated in one game with Yaroslavl's senior team and is expected to see substantial playing time with the club this season.

BOB MAUDIE
9/221   C/L   5-11   180   9/17/76   Cranbrook, British Columbia
Collected nine goals and 29 assists for 38 points in 67 games with Kamloops of the Western Hockey League ... Has played the last three seasons with Kamloops ... Is a good skater with balance, speed and acceleration ... Is a consistent player who is used in most game situations ... Was a member of the Memorial Cup championship team in 1993-94 and 1994-95 ... Was Kamloops Scholastic Player of the Year in 1993-94 ... Is good friends with Florida Panthers forward Rob Niedermayer ... Was the British Columbia Juvenile Golf Champion in 1991 and 1993.

Player	Height	Weight	Shoots	Place of Birth
Forwards:				
Ferraro, Chris	5-10	185	R	Port Jefferson, New York
Ferraro, Peter	5-10	185	R	Port Jefferson, New York
Ferraro, Ray	5-10	185	L	Trail, British Columbia
Flinton, Eric	6-2	190	L	William Lake, British Columbia
Gernander, Ken	5-10	180	L	Coleraine, Minnesota
Graves, Adam	6-0	210	L	Toronto, Ontario
Jones, Brad	6-0	195	L	Sterling Heights, Michigan
Kocur, Joe	6-0	208	R	Calgary, Alberta
Kovalev, Alexei	6-0	210	L	Moscow, Russia
Kudinov, Andrei	6-0	205	L	Chelyabinsk, Russia
Kypreos, Nick	6-0	207	L	Toronto, Ontario
Lacroix, Daniel	6-2	205	L	Montreal, Quebec
LaFayette, Nathan	6-1	200	R	New Westminster, British Columbia
Langdon, Darren	6-1	200	L	Deer Lake, Newfoundland
Matteau, Stephane	6-3	215	L	Rouyn Noranda, Quebec
McGowan, Cal	6-1	185	L	Sydney, Nova Scotia
Messier, Mark	6-1	205	L	Edmonton, Alberta
Nemchinov, Sergei	6-0	205	L	Moscow, Russia
Nielsen, Jeff	6-0	200	R	Grand Rapids, Minnesota
Presley, Wayne	5-11	195	R	Dearborn, Michigan
Robitaille, Luc	6-1	195	L	Montreal, Quebec
Roy, Jean-Yves	5-10	195	L	Rosemere, Quebec
Starostenko, Dimitri	6-0	200	L	Minsk, Russia
Sundstrom, Niklas	6-0	185	L	Ornskoldsvik, Sweden
VandenBussche, Ryan	5-11	187	R	Simcoe, Ontairo
Verbeek, Pat	5-9	190	R	Sarnia, Ontairo
Willis, Rick	6-0	188	L	Lynn, Massachusetts
Defensemen:				
Beukeboom, Jeff	6-5	230	R	Ajax, Ontario
Blouin, Sylvain	6-2	207	L	Montreal, Quebec
Cairns, Eric	6-5	230	L	Oakville, Ontario
Driver, Bruce	6-0	185	L	Toronto, Ontario
Galanov, Maxim	6-1	195	L	Krasnoyarsk, Russia
Karpovtsev, Alexander	6-1	205	R	Moscow, Russia
Komarov, Pavel	6-1	190	L	Gorky, Russia
Leetch, Brian	5-11	190	L	Corpus Christi, Texas
Lidster, Doug	6-0	190	R	Kamloops, British Columbia
Lowe, Kevin	6-2	195	L	Lachute, Quebec
Malone, Scott	6-1	195	L	South Boston, Massachusetts
Norstrom, Mattias	6-1	205	L	Mora, Sweden
Reid, Shawn	6-0	195	L	Toronto, Ontario
Richter, Barry	6-2	205	L	Madison, Wisconsin
Samuelsson, Ulf	6-1	205	L	Fagersta, Sweden
Silverman, Andy	6-3	205	L	Beverly, Massachusetts
Sorochan, Lee	5-11	210	L	Edmonton, Alberta
Goaltenders			**Catches**	
Healy, Glenn	5-10	190	L	Pickering, Ontario
Hillebrandt, Jon	5-10	185	L	Cottage Grove, Wisconsin
Ram, Jamie	5-11	175	L	Scarborough, Ontario
Richter, Mike	5-11	187	L	Abington, Pennsylvania
Shepard, Ken	5-10	195	L	Toronto, Ontario

1995-96 ROSTER

		1994-95 Regular Season Statistics				
Birthdate	1994-95 Team	GP	G	A	PTS	PIM
1/24/73	Binghamton (AHL)	13	6	4	10	38
	Atlanta (IHL)	54	13	14	27	72
1/24/73	Binghamton (AHL)	12	2	6	8	67
	Atlanta (IHL)	61	15	24	39	118
8/23/64	N.Y.Islanders	47	22	21	43	30
2/2/72	New Hampshire (HE)	36	22	23	45	44
6/30/69	Binghamton (AHL)	80	28	25	53	24
4/12/68	N.Y. Rangers	47	17	14	31	51
6/26/65	Springfield (AHL)	61	23	22	45	47
12/21/64	N.Y. Rangers	48	1	2	3	71
2/24/73	N.Y. Rangers	48	13	15	28	30
6/28/70	Binghamton (AHL)	65	14	22	36	45
6/4/66	N.Y. Rangers	40	1	3	4	93
3/11/69	N.Y. Rangers	1	0	0	0	0
	Boston	23	1	0	1	38
2/17/73	N.Y. Rangers	12	0	0	0	0
	Vancouver	27	4	4	8	2
1/8/71	Binghamton (AHL)	55	6	14	20	296
	N.Y. Rangers	18	1	1	2	62
9/2/69	N.Y. Rangers	41	3	5	8	25
6/19/70	Worcester (AHL)	64	22	21	43	28
1/18/61	N.Y. Rangers	46	14	39	53	40
1/14/64	N.Y. Rangers	47	7	6	13	16
9/20/71	Binghamton (AHL)	76	24	13	37	139
3/23/65	Buffalo	46	14	5	19	41
2/17/66	Pittsburgh	46	23	19	42	37
2/17/69	Binghamton (AHL)	67	41	36	77	28
	N.Y. Rangers	3	1	0	1	2
3/18/73	Binghamton (AHL)	69	19	22	41	40
6/6/75	Modo (Sweden)	33	8	13	21	30
2/28/73	St.John's (AHL)	53	2	13	15	239
5/24/64	N.Y. Rangers	19	10	5	15	18
	Hartford	29	7	11	18	53
1/12/72	U. of Michigan (CCHA)	35	3	6	9	78
3/28/65	N.Y. Rangers	44	1	3	4	70
5/21/74	Binghamton (AHL)	10	1	0	1	46
	Charlotte (ECHL)	50	5	7	12	280
	Chicago (IHL)	1	0	0	0	2
6/27/74	Binghamton (AHL)	27	0	3	3	134
	Birmingham (ECHL)	11	1	3	4	49
4/29/62	New Jersey	41	4	12	16	18
3/13/74	Lada Togliatti (CIS)	45	5	6	11	54
4/7/70	N.Y. Rangers	47	4	8	12	30
2/28/74	Binghamton (AHL)	2	0	0	0	2
	Torpedo Nizhny (CIS)	26	0	1	1	38
3/3/68	N.Y. Rangers	48	9	32	41	18
10/18/60	St. Louis	37	2	7	9	12
4/15/59	N.Y. Rangers	44	1	7	8	58
1/16/71	Binghamton (AHL)	48	3	14	17	85
1/2/72	N.Y. Rangers	9	0	3	3	2
	Binghamton (AHL)	63	9	10	19	91
9/21/70	Binghamton (AHL)	18	3	4	7	8
	Fort Wayne (IHL)	42	4	8	12	28
9/11/70	Binghamton (AHL)	73	15	41	56	54
3/26/64	Pittsburgh	44	1	15	16	113
8/23/72	Binghamton (AHL)	5	0	1	1	2
	Charlotte (ECHL)	64	3	11	14	57
9/09/75	Lethbridge (WHL)	29	4	15	19	93
	Saskatoon (WHL)	24	5	13	18	63

		GP	W	L	T	AVG
8/23/62	N.Y. Rangers	17	8	6	1	2.36
12/18/71	Charlotte (ECHL)	32	14	11	2	4.05
	San Diego (IHL)	1	0	1	0	10.00
1/18/71	Binghamton (AHL)	26	12	10	2	3.30
9/22/66	N.Y. Rangers	35	14	17	2	2.92
1/20/74	Oshawa (OHL)	42	24	11	3	3.19

On September 15, MSG Network launched a community outreach program called Yes! Make it Count! to benefit children's organizations. Derived from Marv Albert's popular and often imitated phrase—Yes! And it Counts!—MSG Network's program has been established to reach out and touch the lives of children. At MSG Network our goal is to make a difference—for the children of today are the leaders of tomorrow.

This comprehensive program primarily focuses on the following areas: helping to find a cure for birth defects and children's illness and disease; aiding in the prevention of child abuse; and putting homeless children in a safe, educational environment. MSG Network will also join the outstanding efforts of the YMCA in assisting their education/recreation program, participate in events featuring the Special Olympians, and support and reward good students in New York City public schools with visits from MSG Network personalities.

Yes! Make it Count! is a program where each MSG Network announcer serves as an active "Celebrity Chairman/Host" for a specific organization. During the course of the year the announcers will lend their time and energy to help raise awareness and funds for those organizations, by visiting to centers, hosting events, speaking about problems in our community, and conducting sports clinics. In addition to helping each organization raise funds and promote awareness MSG Network will encourage viewers to help in an area that is greatly underrated — volunteering. Many children's organizations desperately need the support of local community volunteers. MSG Network will support all events through the production of Public Service Announcements and extensive on-air publicity.

MSG Network is working with its announcer-affiliated organizations in creating unique events specifically designed to "Make it Count!" For example, MSG Network and the Leukemia Society will host the "MSG Network Tip-an-Announcer Lunch" where eight MSG Network waiters (announcers) will raise funds by not allowing diners to have certain items, such as a fork, until a donation is made. Certain events will be held yearly, like the MSG Network Roast to benefit the March of Dimes. Each year the Roast will "honor" one of our announcers.

MSG NETWORK BROADCAST TEAM

Kenny Albert

Marv Albert

John Davidson

Sal Messina

Sam Rosen

Al Trautwig

Away from the ice and up in the broadcast booth, the Rangers have another star-studded lineup. Whether on radio or on television, at home or on the road, the Rangers are well-covered in the talent department by: Kenny Albert, Marv Albert, John Davidson, Sal Messina, Sam Rosen and Al Trautwig.

Follow the Rangers-and their off-ice lineup-all season long on Madison Square Garden Network and MSG Radio, including WFAN-Radio (660-AM) and WEVD (1050). Consult your local radio and television listings for games being carried, game times, and station information.

SEASON IN REVIEW

NATIONAL HOCKEY LEAGUE
FINAL STANDINGS

EASTERN CONFERENCE

Northeast Division		GP	W	L	T	GF	GA	PTS	PCTG
	QUEBEC	48	30	13	5	185	134	65	.677
	PITTSBURGH	48	29	16	3	181	158	61	.635
	BOSTON	48	27	18	3	150	127	57	.594
	BUFFALO	48	22	19	7	130	119	51	.531
	HARTFORD	48	19	24	5	127	141	43	.448
	MONTREAL	48	18	23	7	125	148	43	.448
	OTTAWA	48	9	34	5	117	174	23	.240

Atlantic Division		GP	W	L	T	GF	GA	PTS	PCTG
	PHILADELPHIA	48	28	16	4	150	132	60	.625
	NEW JERSEY	48	22	18	8	136	121	52	.542
	WASHINGTON	48	22	18	8	136	120	52	.542
	NY RANGERS	**48**	**22**	**23**	**3**	**139**	**134**	**47**	**.490**
	FLORIDA	48	20	22	6	115	127	46	.479
	TAMPA BAY	48	17	28	3	120	144	37	.385
	NY ISLANDERS	48	15	28	5	126	158	35	.365

WESTERN CONFERENCE

Central Division		GP	W	L	T	GF	GA	PTS	PCTG
	DETROIT	48	33	11	4	180	117	70	.729
	ST LOUIS	48	28	15	5	178	135	61	.635
	CHICAGO	48	24	19	5	156	115	53	.552
	TORONTO	48	21	19	8	135	146	50	.521
	DALLAS	48	17	23	8	136	135	42	.438
	WINNIPEG	48	16	25	7	157	177	39	.406

Pacific Division		GP	W	L	T	GF	GA	PTS	PCTG
	CALGARY	48	24	17	7	163	135	55	.573
	VANCOUVER	48	18	18	12	153	148	48	.500
	SAN JOSE	48	19	25	4	129	161	42	.438
	LOS ANGELES	48	16	23	9	142	174	41	.427
	EDMONTON	48	17	27	4	136	183	38	.396
	ANAHEIM	48	16	27	5	125	164	37	.385

TEAM STANDINGS BY CONFERENCE

EASTERN CONFERENCE

	GP	W	L	T	GF	GA	PTS	PCTG
QUEBEC	48	30	13	5	185	134	65	.677
PITTSBURGH	48	29	16	3	181	158	61	.635
PHILADELPHIA	48	28	16	4	150	132	60	.625
BOSTON	48	27	18	3	150	127	57	.594
NEW JERSEY	48	22	18	8	136	121	52	.542
WASHINGTON	48	22	18	8	136	120	52	.542
BUFFALO	48	22	19	7	130	119	51	.531
NY RANGERS	**48**	**22**	**23**	**3**	**139**	**134**	**47**	**.490**
FLORIDA	48	20	22	6	115	127	46	.479
HARTFORD	48	19	24	5	127	141	43	.448
MONTREAL	48	18	23	7	125	148	43	.448
TAMPA BAY	48	17	28	3	120	144	37	.385
NY ISLANDERS	48	15	28	5	126	158	35	.365
OTTAWA	48	9	34	5	117	174	23	.240

WESTERN CONFERENCE

	GP	W	L	T	GF	GA	PTS	PCTG
DETROIT	48	33	11	4	180	117	70	.729
ST LOUIS	48	28	15	5	178	135	61	.635
CALGARY	48	24	17	7	163	135	55	.573
CHICAGO	48	24	19	5	156	115	53	.552
TORONTO	48	21	19	8	135	146	50	.521
VANCOUVER	48	18	18	12	153	148	48	.500
SAN JOSE	48	19	25	4	129	161	42	.438
DALLAS	48	17	23	8	136	135	42	.438
LOS ANGELES	48	16	23	9	142	174	41	.427
WINNIPEG	48	16	25	7	157	177	39	.406
EDMONTON	48	17	27	4	136	183	38	.396
ANAHEIM	48	16	27	5	125	164	37	.385

LEAGUE LEADERS

INDIVIDUAL SCORING LEADERS
FOR ART ROSS TROPHY

PLAYER	TEAM	GP	G	A	PTS
Jaromir Jagr	Pittsburgh	48	32	38	70
Eric Lindros	Philadelphia	46	29	41	70
Alexei Zhamnov	Winnipeg	48	30	35	65
Joe Sakic	Quebec	47	19	43	62
Ron Francis	Pittsburgh	44	11	48	59
Theoren Fleury	Calgary	47	29	29	58
Paul Coffey	Detroit	45	14	44	58
Mikael Renberg	Philadelphia	47	26	31	57
John LeClair	Mtl-Phi	46	26	28	54
Mark Messier	**NY Rangers**	**46**	**14**	**39**	**53**
Adam Oates	Boston	48	12	41	53
Bernie Nicholls	Chicago	48	22	29	51
Keith Tkachuk	Winnipeg	48	22	29	51
Brett Hull	St. Louis	48	29	21	50
Joe Nieuwendyk	Calgary	46	21	29	50
Sergei Fedorov	Detroit	42	20	30	50
*Peter Forsberg	Quebec	47	15	35	50
Owen Nolan	Quebec	46	30	19	49
Teemu Selanne	Winnipeg	45	22	26	48
Mark Recchi	Phi-Mtl	49	16	32	48
Wayne Gretzky	Los Angeles	48	11	37	48
Pierre Turgeon	NYI-Mtl	49	24	23	47
Mats Sundin	Toronto	47	23	24	47
Alexander Mogilny	Buffalo	44	19	28	47

Eric Lindros tied for the league lead in scoring with 70 points.

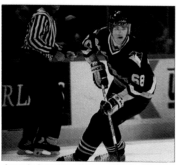

Jaromir Jagr placed second in the NHL with 32 goals.

GOAL SCORING

NAME	TEAM	GP	G
Peter Bondra	Washington	47	34
Jaromir Jagr	Pittsburgh	48	32
Ray Sheppard	Detroit	43	30
Owen Nolan	Quebec	46	30
Alexei Zhamnov	Winnipeg	48	30
Eric Lindros	Philadelphia	46	29
Theoren Fleury	Calgary	47	29
Brett Hull	St. Louis	48	29
Cam Neely	Boston	42	27
John LeClair	Mtl-Phi	46	26
Mikael Renberg	Philadelphia	47	26
Donald Audette	Buffalo	46	24
Pierre Turgeon	NYI-Mtl	49	24
Joe Murphy	Chicago	40	23
Stephane Richer	New Jersey	45	23
Luc Robitaille	Pittsburgh	46	23
Mats Sundin	Toronto	47	23

ASSISTS

NAME	TEAM	GP	A
Ron Francis	Pittsburgh	44	48
Paul Coffey	Detroit	45	44
Joe Sakic	Quebec	47	43
Eric Lindros	Philadelphia	46	41
Adam Oates	Boston	48	41
Mark Messier	**NY Rangers**	**46**	**39**
Joe Juneau	Washington	44	38
Jaromir Jagr	Pittsburgh	48	38
Wayne Gretzky	Los Angeles	48	37
Phil Housley	Calgary	43	35
*Peter Forsberg	Quebec	47	35
Alexei Zhamnov	Winnipeg	48	35
Chris Chelios	Chicago	48	33
Doug Weight	Edmonton	48	33
Brian Leetch	**NY Rangers**	**48**	**32**
Mark Recchi	Phi-Mtl	49	32

Mark Messier's 39 assists were sixth best in the NHL.

LEAGUE LEADERS

DEFENSEMEN SCORING LEADERS

PLAYER	TEAM	GP	G	A	PTS
Paul Coffey	Detroit	45	14	44	58
Ray Bourque	Boston	46	12	31	43
Phil Housley	Calgary	43	8	35	43
Brian Leetch	**NY Rangers**	**48**	**9**	**32**	**41**
Larry Murphy	Pittsburgh	48	13	25	38
Steve Duchesne	St. Louis	47	12	26	38
Chris Chelios	Chicago	48	5	33	38
Gary Suter	Chicago	48	10	27	37
Sergei Zubov	NY Rangers	38	10	26	36
Todd Gill	Toronto	47	7	25	32
Garry Galley	Phi-Buf	47	3	29	32

Brian Leetch placed fourth among defensemen in scoring with 41 points.

ROOKIE SCORING LEADERS

PLAYER	TEAM	GP	G	A	PTS
Peter Forsberg	Quebec	47	15	35	50
Paul Kariya	Anaheim	47	18	21	39
David Oliver	Edmonton	44	16	14	30
Ian Laperriere	St. Louis	37	13	14	27
Todd Marchant	Edmonton	45	13	14	27
Mariusz Czerkawski	Boston	47	12	14	26
Jeff Friesen	San Jose	48	15	10	25
Roman Oksiuta	Edm-Van	38	16	4	20
Todd Harvey	Dallas	40	11	9	20
Brian Savage	Montreal	37	12	7	19
Sergei Krivokrasov	Chicago	41	12	7	19

GOALTENDING LEADERS
GOALS AGAINST AVERAGE

GOALTENDER	TEAM	GPI	MINS	GA	AVG
Dominik Hasek	Buffalo	41	2416	85	2.11
Rick Tabaracci	Wsh-Cgy	13	596	21	2.11
*Jim Carey	Washington	28	1604	57	2.13
Chris Osgood	Detroit	19	1087	41	2.26
Ed Belfour	Chicago	42	2450	93	2.28

WINS

GOALTENDER	TEAM	GPI	MINS	W	L	T
Ken Wregget	Pittsburgh	38	2208	25	9	2
Ed Belfour	Chicago	42	2450	22	15	3
Trevor Kidd	Calgary	43	2463	22	14	6
Curtis Joseph	St. Louis	36	1914	20	10	1
Mike Vernon	Detroit	30	1807	19	6	4
*Blaine Lacher	Boston	35	1965	19	11	2
Martin Brodeur	New Jersey	40	2184	19	11	6
Dominik Hasek	Buffalo	41	2416	19	14	7

Dominik Hasek led the NHL with a .930 save percentage and tied for league best with a 2.11 GAA and 5 Shutouts.

SAVE PERCENTAGE

GOALTENDER	TEAM	GPI	MINS	GA	SA	SPCTG	W	L	T
Dominik Hasek	Buffalo	41	2416	85	1221	.930	19	14	7
Chris Osgood	Detroit	19	1087	41	496	.917	14	5	0
Jocelyn Thibault	Quebec	18	898	35	423	.917	12	2	2
Andy Moog	Dallas	31	1770	72	846	.915	10	12	7
*Damian Rhodes	Toronto	13	760	34	404	.915	6	6	1

SHUTOUTS

GOALTENDER	TEAM	GPI	MINS	SO	W	L	T
Dominik Hasek	Buffalo	41	2416	5	19	14	7
Ed Belfour	Chicago	42	2450	5	22	15	3
*Jim Carey	Washington	28	1604	4	18	6	3
*Blaine Lacher	Boston	35	1965	4	19	11	2
Arturs Irbe	San Jose	38	2043	4	14	19	3
J. Vanbiesbrouck	Florida	37	2087	4	14	15	4

FINAL SCORING

POS	NO.	PLAYER		GP	G	A	PTS	+/-	PIM	PP	SH	GW	GT	S	PCTG
C	11	Mark Messier		46	14	39	53	8	40	3	3	2	0	126	11.1
D	2	Brian Leetch		48	9	32	41	0	18	3	0	2	0	182	4.9
D	21	Sergei Zubov		38	10	26	36	-2	18	6	0	0	0	116	8.6
RW	17	Pat Verbeek	HFD	29	7	11	18	0	53	3	0	0	1	75	9.3
			NYR	19	10	5	15	-2	18	4	0	2	0	56	17.9
			TOTAL	48	17	16	33	-2	71	7	0	2	1	131	13.0
LW	9	Adam Graves		47	17	14	31	9	51	9	0	3	0	185	9.2
RW	28	Steve Larmer		47	14	15	29	8	16	3	1	4	0	116	12.1
RW	27	Alexei Kovalev		48	13	15	28	-6	30	1	1	1	0	103	12.6
RW	16	Brian Noonan		45	14	13	27	-3	26	7	0	1	0	95	14.7
C	10	Petr Nedved		46	11	12	23	-1	26	1	0	3	0	123	8.9
C	13	Sergei Nemchinov		47	7	6	13	-6	16	0	0	3	0	67	10.4
D	25	Alexander Karpovtsev		47	4	8	12	-4	30	1	0	1	0	82	4.9
LW	14	Troy Loney	NYI	26	5	4	9	0	23	2	0	1	0	45	11.1
			NYR	4	0	0	0	-2	0	0	0	0	0	2	.0
			TOTAL	30	5	4	9	-2	23	2	0	1	0	47	10.6
D	24	Jay Wells		43	2	7	9	0	36	0	0	0	0	38	5.3
C	22	Nathan LaFayette	VAN	27	4	4	8	2	2	0	1	0	0	30	13.3
			NYR	12	0	0	0	1	0	0	0	0	0	5	.0
			TOTAL	39	4	4	8	3	2	0	1	0	0	35	11.4
LW	32	Stephane Matteau		41	3	5	8	-8	25	0	0	0	0	37	8.1
D	4	Kevin Lowe		44	1	7	8	-2	58	1	0	0	0	35	2.9
LW	20	Mark Osborne		37	1	3	4	-2	19	0	0	0	0	32	3.1
LW	19	Nick Kypreos		40	1	3	4	0	93	0	0	0	0	16	6.3
D	23	Jeff Beukeboom		44	1	3	4	3	70	0	0	0	0	29	3.4
RW	26	Joey Kocur		48	1	2	3	-4	71	0	0	0	0	25	4.0
D	5	*Mattias Norstrom		9	0	3	3	2	2	0	0	0	0	4	.0
LW	15	*Darren Langdon		18	1	1	2	0	62	0	0	0	0	6	16.7
D	29	Joby Messier		10	0	2	2	2	18	0	0	0	0	4	.0
G	30	Glenn Healy		17	0	2	2	0	2	0	0	0	0	0	.0
RW	8	*Jean-Yves Roy		3	1	0	1	-1	2	0	0	0	0	8	12.5
C	39	*Shawn McCosh		5	1	0	1	1	2	0	0	0	0	2	50.0
C	37	*Dan Lacroix	BOS	23	1	0	1	-2	38	0	0	0	0	14	7.1
			NYR	1	0	0	0	0	0	0	0	0	0	0	.0
			TOTAL	24	1	0	1	-2	38	0	0	0	0	14	7.1
L	18	Mike Hartman		1	0	0	0	0	4	0	0	0	0	0	.0
G	35	Mike Richter		35	0	0	0	0	2	0	0	0	0	0	.0

GOALTENDING RECORDS

NO.	GOALTENDER	GPI	MINS	AVG	W	L	T	EN	SO	GA	SA	SV%	G	A	PIM
30	Glenn Healy	17	888	2.36	8	6	1	0	1	35	377	.907	0	2	2
35	Mike Richter	35	1993	2.92	14	17	2	2	2	97	884	.890	0	0	2
	NYR TOTALS	48	2895	2.78	2	23	3	2	3	134	1263	.894			

*Indicates Rookie

SCORING BREAKDOWN

Player	Home GP	G	A	PTS	Road GP	G	A	PTS	Total GP	G	A	PTS	Gm. Winning G	A	PTS	Gm. Tying G	A	PTS
Jeff Beukeboom	23	1	1	2	21	0	2	2	44	1	3	4	0	0	0	0	0	0
Adam Graves	24	11	11	22	23	6	3	9	47	17	14	31	3	2	5	0	0	0
Glenn Healy	8	0	2	2	9	0	0	0	17	0	2	2	0	0	0	0	0	0
Alexander Karpovtsev	23	2	5	7	24	2	3	5	47	4	8	12	1	1	2	0	0	0
Joe Kocur	24	0	0	0	24	1	2	3	48	1	2	3	0	0	0	0	0	0
Alexei Kovalev	24	6	11	17	24	7	4	11	48	13	15	28	1	3	4	0	0	0
Nick Kypreos	22	0	1	1	18	1	2	3	40	1	3	4	0	0	0	0	0	0
Daniel Lacroix (BOS)	11	1	0	1	12	0	0	0	23	1	0	1	0	0	0	0	0	0
Daniel Lacroix (NYR)	0	0	0	0	1	0	0	0	1	0	0	0	0	0	0	0	0	0
Nathan LaFayette (VAN)	15	3	2	5	12	1	2	3	27	4	4	8	0	0	0	0	0	0
Nathan LaFayette (NYR)	7	0	0	0	5	0	0	0	12	0	0	0	0	0	0	0	0	0
Darren Langdon	8	0	0	0	10	1	1	2	18	1	1	2	0	0	0	0	0	0
Steve Larmer	24	8	10	18	23	6	5	11	47	14	15	29	4	3	7	0	0	0
Brian Leetch	24	6	20	26	24	3	12	15	48	9	32	41	2	1	3	0	0	0
Troy Loney (NYI)	14	3	2	5	12	2	2	4	26	5	4	9	1	0	1	0	0	0
Troy Loney (NYR)	2	0	0	0	2	0	0	0	4	0	0	0	0	0	0	0	0	0
Kevin Lowe	21	0	2	2	23	1	5	6	44	1	7	8	0	1	1	0	0	0
Shawn McCosh	2	0	0	0	3	1	0	1	5	1	0	1	0	0	0	0	0	0
Stephane Matteau	22	3	2	5	19	0	3	3	41	3	5	8	0	1	1	0	0	0
Joby Messier	6	0	2	2	4	0	0	0	10	0	2	2	0	1	1	0	0	0
Mark Messier	23	8	25	33	23	6	14	20	46	14	39	53	2	7	9	0	0	0
Petr Nedved	23	9	10	19	23	2	2	4	46	11	12	23	3	1	4	0	0	0
Sergei Nemchinov	23	1	3	4	24	6	3	9	47	7	6	13	3	1	4	0	0	0
Brian Noonan	23	9	8	17	22	5	5	10	45	14	13	27	1	2	3	0	0	0
Mattias Norstrom	5	0	0	0	4	0	3	3	9	0	3	3	0	0	0	0	0	0
Mark Osborne	17	0	1	1	20	1	2	3	37	1	3	4	0	2	2	0	0	0
Mike Richter	20	0	0	0	15	0	0	0	35	0	0	0	0	0	0	0	0	0
Jean-Yves Roy	2	1	0	1	1	0	0	0	3	1	0	1	0	0	0	0	0	0
Pat Verbeek (HFD)	17	3	6	9	12	4	5	9	29	7	11	18	0	0	0	0	0	0
Pat Verbeek (NYR)	9	7	3	10	10	3	2	5	19	10	5	15	2	2	4	0	0	0
Jay Wells	21	1	6	7	22	1	1	2	43	2	7	9	0	2	2	0	0	0
Sergei Zubov	19	5	17	22	19	5	9	14	38	10	26	36	0	8	8	0	0	0

GOALTENDING BREAKDOWN

	GP	W	L	T	GA	EN	HOME MINS	AVG	SH	SHOTS	SAVES	PERCENTAGE
Glenn Healy	7	3	2	0	12	0	286	2.52	0	124	112	.903
Mike Richter	20	8	8	2	56	1	1097	3.06	1	512	456	.891

	GP	W	L	T	GA	EN	ROAD MINS	AVG	SH	SHOTS	SAVES	PERCENTAGE
Glenn Healy	10	5	4	1	23	0	602	2.29	1	253	230	.909
Mike Richter	15	6	9	0	41	1	896	2.75	1	372	331	.890

Adam Graves collected a team-high 11 goals at MSG.

Alexei Kovalev led the team with seven goals on the road.

SPECIAL TEAMS SCORING BREAKDOWN

	Power Play			Shorthanded			Even Strength			Total		
	G	A	PTS	G	A	PTS	G	A	PTS	G	A	PTS
Beukeboom	0	0	0	0	1	1	1	2	3	1	3	4
Graves	9	6	15	0	1	1	8	7	15	17	14	31
Healy	0	1	1	0	0	0	0	1	1	0	2	2
Karpovtsev	1	4	5	0	1	1	3	3	6	4	8	12
Kocur	0	0	0	0	0	0	1	2	3	1	2	3
Kovalev	1	5	6	1	0	1	11	10	21	13	15	28
Kypreos	0	0	0	0	0	0	1	2	3	1	2	3
Lacroix (BOS)	0	0	0	0	0	0	1	0	1	1	0	1
Lacroix (NYR)	0	0	0	0	0	0	0	0	0	0	0	0
LaFayette (VAN)	0	0	0	1	0	1	3	4	7	4	4	8
LaFayette (NYR)	0	0	0	0	0	0	0	0	0	0	0	0
Langdon	0	0	0	0	0	0	1	1	2	1	1	2
Larmer	3	4	7	1	0	1	10	11	21	14	15	29
Leetch	3	18	21	0	1	1	6	13	19	9	32	41
Loney (NYI)	0	0	0	0	0	0	5	4	9	5	4	9
Loney (NYR)	0	0	0	0	0	0	0	0	0	0	0	0
Lowe	1	0	1	0	0	0	0	7	7	1	7	8
McCosh	0	0	0	0	0	0	1	0	1	1	0	1
Matteau	0	0	0	0	0	0	3	5	8	3	5	8
J. Messier	0	0	0	0	0	0	0	2	2	0	2	2
M. Messier	3	17	20	3	0	3	8	22	30	14	39	53
Nedved	1	3	4	0	0	0	10	9	19	11	12	23
Nemchinov	0	0	0	0	0	0	7	6	13	7	6	13
Noonan	7	4	11	0	1	1	7	8	15	14	13	27
Norstrom	0	0	0	0	0	0	0	3	3	0	3	3
Osborne	0	0	0	0	1	1	1	2	3	1	3	4
Richter	0	0	0	0	0	0	0	0	0	0	0	0
Roy	0	0	0	0	0	0	1	0	1	1	0	1
Verbeek (HFD)	3	0	3	0	0	0	4	11	18	7	11	18
Verbeek (NYR)	6	1	7	0	0	0	4	4	8	10	5	15
Wells	0	2	2	0	0	0	2	5	7	2	7	9
Zubov	6	14	20	0	1	1	4	11	15	10	26	36

Rangers Total Power Play Statistics

HOME				ROAD				TOTAL			
PPGF	ADV	PCTG	RANK	PPGF	ADV	PCTG	RANK	PPGF	ADV	PCTG	RANK
28	111	25.2	2nd	12	89	13.5	19th	40	200	20.0	5th

Rangers Total Penalty Killing Statistics

HOME				ROAD				TOTAL			
PPGA	TSH	PCTG	RANK	PPGA	TSH	PCTG	RANK	PPGA	TSH	PCTG	RANK
18	101	82.2	19th	16	110	85.5	5th	34	211	211	83.9

INDIVIDUAL SCORING VS. EACH DIVISION

Player	ATLANTIC GP	G	A	PTS	NORTHEAST GP	G	A	PTS	TOTAL GP	G	A	PTS
Jeff Beukeboom	21	1	1	2	23	0	2	2	44	1	3	4
Adam Graves	23	8	5	13	24	9	9	18	47	17	14	31
Glenn Healy	8	0	0	0	7	0	2	2	15	0	2	2
Alexander Karpovtsev	24	2	6	8	23	2	2	4	47	4	8	12
Joe Kocur	24	0	0	0	24	1	2	3	48	1	2	3
Alexei Kovalev	24	6	8	14	24	7	7	14	48	13	15	28
Nick Kypreos	20	0	0	0	20	1	3	4	40	1	3	4
Daniel Lacroix (BOS)	13	1	0	1	10	0	0	0	23	1	0	1
Daniel Lacroix (NYR)	1	0	0	0	0	0	0	0	1	0	0	0
Nathan LaFayette (NYR)	7	0	0	0	5	0	0	0	12	0	0	0
Darren Langdon	10	0	1	1	8	1	0	1	18	1	1	2
Steve Larmer	23	9	10	19	24	5	5	10	47	14	15	29
Brian Leetch	24	5	12	17	24	4	20	24	48	9	32	41
Troy Loney (NYI)	10	2	1	3	16	3	3	6	26	5	4	9
Troy Loney (NYR)	4	0	0	0	0	0	0	0	4	0	0	0
Kevin Lowe	20	0	3	3	24	1	4	5	44	1	7	8
Shawn McCosh	2	0	0	0	3	1	0	1	5	1	0	1
Stephane Matteau	20	1	3	4	21	2	2	4	41	3	5	8
Joby Messier	6	0	1	1	4	0	1	1	10	0	2	2
Mark Messier	22	9	15	24	24	5	24	29	46	14	39	53
Petr Nedved	23	3	7	10	23	8	5	13	46	11	12	23
Sergei Nemchinov	24	4	2	6	23	3	4	7	47	7	6	13
Brian Noonan	21	7	5	12	24	7	8	15	45	14	13	27
Mattias Norstrom	7	0	2	2	2	0	1	1	9	0	3	3
Mark Osborne	18	1	2	3	19	0	1	1	37	1	3	4
Mike Richter	17	0	0	0	18	0	0	0	35	0	0	0
Jean-Yves Roy	0	0	0	0	3	1	0	1	3	1	0	1
Pat Verbeek (HFD)	15	2	5	7	14	5	6	11	29	7	11	18
Pat Verbeek (NYR)	11	5	3	8	8	5	2	7	19	10	5	15
Jay Wells	20	0	1	1	23	2	6	8	43	2	7	9
Sergei Zubov	18	3	15	18	20	7	11	18	38	10	26	36

GOALTENDING BREAKDOWN

ATLANTIC

		GP	W	L	T	GA	EN	MINS	SH	SHOTS	SAVES	PERCENTAGE
Healy	HOME	5	1	1	1	9	0	202	0	91	82	.901
	ROAD	5	3	2	0	9	0	298	1	122	113	.926
	TOTAL	10	4	3	1	18	0	500	1	213	195	.915
		GP	W	L	T	GA	EN	MINS	SH	SHOTS	SAVES	PERCENTAGE
Richter	HOME	10	4	4	1	33	1	524	1	237	204	.861
	ROAD	7	3	4	0	17	1	419	1	161	144	.894
	TOTAL	17	7	8	1	50	2	943	2	398	348	.874

NORTHEAST

		GP	W	L	T	GA	EN	MINS	SH	SHOTS	SAVES	PERCENTAGE
Healy	HOME	3	2	1	0	6	0	149	0	61	55	.902
	ROAD	4	2	2	0	11	0	239	0	103	92	.893
	TOTAL	7	4	3	0	17	0	388	0	164	147	.896
		GP	W	L	T	GA	EN	MINS	SH	SHOTS	SAVES	PERCENTAGE
Richter	HOME	10	4	5	1	23	0	573	0	275	252	.916
	ROAD	8	3	4	0	24	0	477	0	211	187	.886
	TOTAL	18	7	9	1	47	0	1050	0	486	439	.903

SEASON TOTALS

	GP	W	L	T	GA	EN	MINS	SH	SHOTS	SAVES	PERCENTAGE
Healy	17	8	6	1	35	0	888	1	377	342	.907
Richter	35	14	17	2	97	2	1993	2	884	787	.890

QUARTER-BY-QUARTER SCORING

	First Quarter				Second Quarter				Third Quarter				Fourth Quarter				Totals			
	GP	G	A	PTS	GP	G	A	PTS	GP	G	A	PTS	GP	G	A	PTS	GP	G	A	PTS
Beukeboom	12	0	1	1	11	0	1	1	9	0	0	0	12	1	1	2	44	1	3	4
Graves	11	5	4	9	12	6	1	7	12	1	3	4	12	5	6	11	47	17	14	31
Healy	3	0	0	0	3	0	1	1	5	0	0	0	6	0	1	1	17	0	2	2
Karpovtsev	12	1	1	2	12	1	4	5	12	1	2	3	11	1	1	2	47	4	8	12
Kocur	12	0	1	1	12	1	1	2	12	0	0	0	12	0	0	0	48	1	2	3
Kovalev	12	3	6	9	12	2	5	7	12	6	2	8	12	2	2	4	48	13	15	28
Kypreos	12	1	1	2	7	0	0	0	9	0	2	2	12	0	0	0	40	1	3	4
Lacroix	12	1	0	0	10	0	0	0	2	0	0	0	0	0	0	0	24	1	0	1
LaFayette	4	1	0	0	12	2	1	3	11	1	3	4	12	0	0	0	39	4	4	8
Langdon	0	0	0	0	10	1	1	2	8	0	0	0	0	0	0	0	18	1	1	2
Larmer	12	5	3	8	12	5	2	7	11	3	6	9	12	1	4	5	47	14	15	29
Leetch	12	1	5	6	12	1	7	8	12	2	6	8	12	5	14	19	48	9	32	41
Loney	11	1	2	3	10	2	2	4	5	2	0	2	3	0	0	0	29	5	4	9
Lowe	12	0	5	5	12	0	2	2	11	0	0	0	9	1	0	1	44	1	7	8
McCosh	5	1	0	1	0	0	0	0	0	0	0	0	0	0	0	0	5	1	0	1
Matteau	11	1	0	1	12	1	4	5	10	0	1	1	8	1	0	1	41	3	5	8
J. Messier	2	0	0	0	6	0	2	2	2	0	0	0	0	0	0	0	10	0	2	2
M. Messier	12	3	7	10	12	5	9	14	12	6	4	10	10	0	19	19	46	14	39	53
Nedved	12	2	3	5	10	1	2	3	12	2	4	6	12	6	3	9	46	11	12	23
Nemchinov	11	3	2	5	12	2	2	4	12	1	0	1	12	1	2	3	47	7	6	13
Noonan	12	2	3	5	12	5	2	7	10	2	4	6	11	5	4	.9	45	14	13	27
Norstrom	0	0	0	0	0	0	0	0	4	0	3	3	4	0	0	0	8	0	3	3
Osborne	11	0	1	1	12	1	1	2	11	0	1	1	4	0	0	0	38	1	3	4
Richter	9	0	0	0	9	0	0	0	10	0	0	0	7	0	0	0	35	0	0	0
Roy	3	1	0	1	0	0	0	0	0	0	0	0	0	0	0	0	3	1	0	1
Verbeek	12	1	5	6	12	4	4	8	12	6	3	9	12	6	4	10	48	17	16	33
Wells	11	0	2	2	11	0	1	1	10	2	2	4	11	0	2	2	43	2	7	9
Zubov	11	2	10	12	7	2	3	5	8	0	5	5	12	6	8	14	38	10	26	36

GOALTENDING BREAKDOWN

	First Quarter				Second Quarter				Third Quarter				Fourth Quarter				Totals			
	GP	W	L	T	GP	W	L	T	GP	W	L	T	GP	W	L	T	GP	W	L	T
Glenn Healy	3	1	1	1	3	3	0	0	5	1	2	0	6	3	3	0	17	8	6	1
Mike Richter	9	4	5	0	9	4	3	2	10	2	7	0	7	4	2	0	35	14	17	2

	GA	SH	SV	SV%	GA	SH	SV	SV%	GA	SH	SV	SV%	GA	SH	SV	SV%	GA	SH	SV	SV%
Glenn Healy	7	73	66	.904	6	63	57	.905	8	89	81	.910	14	152	138	.908	35	377	342	.907
Mike Richter	24	249	225	.904	21	232	211	.909	30	221	191	.864	22	182	160	.879	97	884	787	.890

Kevin Lowe notched five assists in the first quarter of the season.

Stephane Matteau tallied one goal and four assists in the second quarter of the season.

MISCELLANEOUS

WIN/LOSS BREAKDOWN

DIVISION	HOME	ROAD	TOTALS
Atlantic	5-5-2	6-6-0	11-11-2
Northeast	6-5-1	5-7-0	11-12-1
TOTALS	**11-10-3**	**11-13-0**	**22-23-3**

GOALS BY PERIODS

	1st	2nd	3rd	OT	TOTALS
Rangers	41	53	45	0	139
Opponents	40	46	48	0	134

SHOTS BY PERIOD

	1st	2nd	3rd	OT	TOTALS
Rangers	525	538	460	6	1529
Opponents	429	428	396	10	1263

TEAM STATISTICS

Most Goals, Game– 6, (3 times) last- April 26, 1995 vs. Tampa Bay).

Most Goals Allowed, Game– 6, (April 18, 1995 @ Pittsburgh).

Most Goals, Period– 4, (twice) last- April 5, 1995 @ Florida, 3rd period.

Most Goals Allowed, Period– 5, (March 30, 1995 vs. Quebec, 2nd period).

Largest Margin of Victory– 5, (April 5, 1995 @ Florida).

Largest Margin of Defeat– 3, (4 times) last- March 22, 1995 vs. New Jersey.

Most Shots, Game– 48, (April 26, 1995 vs. Tampa Bay).

Most Shots Allowed, Game– 41, (April 26, 1995 vs. Tampa Bay).

Most Shots, Period– 20, (twice) last- May 2, 1995 vs. Florida, 1st period.

Most Shots Allowed, Period– 18, (April 26, 1995 vs. Tampa Bay, 3rd period).

Least Shots, Game– 15, (February 11, 1995 @ Tampa Bay).

Least Shots Allowed, Game– 15, (twice) last- March 23, 1995 @ Islanders.

Least Shots, Period– 2, (March 11, 1995 @ Montreal, 3rd period).

Least Shots Allowed, Period– 2, (March 30, 1995 vs. Quebec, 3rd period).

Most Power Play Goals, Game– 4, (twice) last - February 8, 1995 vs. Washington.

Most Power Play Goals Allowed, Game– 3, (twice) last- February 18, 1995 @ Montreal.

Most Shorthanded Goals, Game– 1, (5 times) last- April 12, 1995 vs. Buffalo.

Most Shorthanded Goals Allowed, Game– 1, (3 times) last- April 7, 1995 vs. Islanders.

Longest Winning Streak– 3, (April 12 to April 16).

Longest Losing Streak– 7, (March 11 to March 30).

Longest Unbeaten Streak–4, (February 26 to March 3, 3-0-1).

Longest Winless Streak– 7, (March 11 to March 30, 0-7-0).

INDIVIDUAL STATISTICS

Most Goals, Game– 3, (twice) - Noonan (March 1, 1995 @ Hartford), Graves (January 30, 1995 vs. Ottawa).

Most Assists, Game– 5, Leetch (April 18, 1995 @ Pittsburgh).

Most Points, Game– 5, Leetch (April 18, 1995 @ Pittsburgh).

Most Shots, Game– 12, Leetch (April 28, 1995 vs. Islanders).

Most Shots, Period– 6, Leetch (April 28, 1995 vs. Islanders, 1st period).

Most Penalty Minutes, Game– 19, Langdon (February 26, 1995 @ Buffalo).

Longest Point Scoring Streak– 8, Messier (April 12 to April 26, 0-19-19).

Longest Goal Scoring Streak– 5, Zubov (April 16 to April 24, five goals).

Longest Assist Streak– 8, Messier (April 12 to April 26, 19 assists).

STATISTICS

MONTHLY RECORD

	GP	W	L	T	GF	GA	PTS
January	6	2	4	0	15	13	4
February	14	7	4	3	36	34	17
March	12	4	8	0	34	40	8
April	15	9	6	0	52	45	18
May	1	0	1	0	3	4	0

QUARTER BY QUARTER

	W	L	T	PTS
1st quarter of season	5	6	1	11
2nd quarter of season	7	3	2	16
3rd quarter of season	3	9	0	6
4th quarter of season	7	5	0	14

RANGERS RECORD

	WON	LOST	TIED
When Scoring First	14	9	1
When Allowing First Goal	8	14	2
When Leading After First Period	9	4	1
When Trailing After First Period	5	10	0
When Tied After First Period	8	9	2
When Leading After Second Period	15	0	1
When Trailing After Second Period	3	11	0
When Tied After Second Period	4	12	2
In Overtime	0	0	3
When Outshooting Opponents	18	16	2
When Outshot by Opponents	4	6	1
When Shots Are Even	0	1	0
In Second Game of back-to back games	5	3	2
On Sundays	3	4	0
On Mondays	4	1	0
On Tuesdays	1	2	1
On Wednesdays	7	4	0
On Thursdays	1	3	2
On Fridays	2	4	0
On Saturdays	4	5	0
In One Goal Games	9	13	-
In Two Goal Games	9	6	-
In Three Goal Games	2	4	-
In Four Goal Games	1	0	-
In Five Goal Games	1	0	-
In Six Or More Goal Games	0	0	-

When Rangers Score

	WON	LOST	TIED
0 Goals	-	3	1`
1 Goal	0	7	0
2 Goals	3	6	1
3 Goals	6	4	1
4 Goals	2	2	0
5 Goals	8	1	0
6 Goals	3	0	0
7 Goals	0	0	0
8 Goals	0	0	0
9 or More Goals	0	0	0

When Opposition Scores

	WON	LOST	TIED
0 Goals	2	-	1
1 Goal	4	1	0
2 Goals	8	6	1
3 Goals	4	2	1
4 Goals	4	9	0
5 Goals	0	4	0
6 Goals	0	1	0
7 Goals	0	0	0
8 Goals	0	0	0
9 or More Goals	0	0	0

HAT TRICKS AND SHORTHANDED GOALS

Hat Tricks

BY RANGERS (2)
Adam Graves vs. Ottawa on January 30. All scored against Don Beaupre.
Brian Noonan vs. Hartford on March 1. All scored against Jeff Reese.

AGAINST RANGERS (2)
Cam Neely, Boston, at Boston on April 23. All scored against Glenn Healy.
Owen Nolan, Quebec at Madison Square Garden on March 30. Two scored against Mike Richter, one scored against Glenn Healy.

Shorthanded Goals

Rangers (5)			Opponents (3)		
Mark Messier	3	(Wsh., Buf., Phi.)	Marc Bureau	1	(T.B.)
Alexei Kovalev	1	(NYI)	Adam Oates	1	(Bos.)
Steve Larmer	1	(Buf.)	Peter Bondra	1	(Wsh.)

Penalty Shots

BY RANGERS
NONE

AGAINST RANGERS
Steve Konowalchuk (3/5/95 vs. Washington - unsuccessful against Mike Richter)

Empty Net Goals

BY RANGERS (6)
Steve Larmer vs. Tampa Bay on Feb. 20 at Tampa Bay. Against the record of Daren Puppa.
Mark Messier vs. Florida on Feb. 21 at Florida. Against the record of John Vanbiesbrouck.
Sergei Zubov vs. Buffalo on Feb. 26 at Buffalo. Against the record of Dominik Hasek.
Brian Noonan vs. Hartford on Mar. 1 at Hartford. Against the record of Jeff Reese.
Mark Messier vs. New Jersey on Mar. 8 at Madison Square Garden. Against the record of Martin Brodeur.
Steve Larmer vs. Buffalo on Apr. 12 at Madison Square Garden. Against the record of Dominik Hasek.

AGAINST RANGERS (2)
Mark Lamb of Montreal on Feb. 28 at Montreal. Against the record of Mike Richter.
Kelly Miller of Washington on Mar. 5 at Washington. Against the record of Mike Richter.

Mark Messier led the club last season with three shorthanded goals.

MANPOWER GAMES LOST
TO INJURY OR ILLNESS

PLAYER	DATE OF INJURY	TYPE OF INJURY	DATES MISSED	GAMES MISSED
Beukeboom	3/5	Neck Spasms	3/5	1
	3/22	Sore Chest	3/22-3/29	3
Graves	2/11	Infected Elbow	2/11	1
Karpovtsev	4/14	Sore Ankle	4/14	1
Larmer	3/23	Sore Back	3/23	1
Lowe	3/18	Flu	3/18	1
	4/23	Pinched Nerve (Neck)	4/24-4/26	2
Matteau	2/1	Flu	2/1	1
	4/24	Back Spasms	4/24-4/26	2
Messier	4/30	Back Spasms	4/30-5/2	2
Nedved	2/28	Abdominal Strain	2/28-3/1	2
Nemchinov	1/30	Bruised Achilles Tendon	1/30	1
Noonan	4/2	Sprained Right Knee	4/5-4/9	3
Norstrom	4/28	Flu	4/28-4/30	2
Osborne	2/8	Flu	2/8	1
	3/18	Flu	3/18	1
Zubov	2/4	Flu	2/4	1
	2/27	Wrist Surgery	2/28-3/21	9

TOTAL MANPOWER GAMES LOST DUE TO INJURY OR ILLNESS: 44
(Includes all traded players)

TRANSACTIONS

January 21 . . . . .   Jean-Yves Roy is recalled from Binghamton.

January 29 . . . . .   Shawn McCosh is recalled from Binghamton.

February 10 . . . . .   Jean-Yves Roy is sent to Binghamton.

February 12 . . . . .   Shawn McCosh is sent to Binghamton.

February 17 . . . . .   Darren Langdon is recalled from Binghamton.

March 8 . . . .   Mike Hartman is loaned to the Detroit Vipers of the International Hockey League.

March 10 . . . . . .   Peter and Chris Ferraro are signed to professional contracts.

March 10 . . . . . .   Jim Hiller is loaned to the Atlanta Knights of the International Hockey League.

March 23 . . . . . .   Pat Verbeek is acquired from the Hartford Whalers in exchange for Glen Featherstone, Michael Stewart, a 1995 first round draft pick and a 1996 fourth round draft pick.

March 23 . . . . . .   Daniel Lacroix is claimed off waivers from Boston.

March 23 . . . . . .   Mattias Norstrom is recalled from Binghamton.

April 7 . . . .   Troy Loney is claimed off waivers from Islanders.

April 7 . . . .   Eddie Olczyk is traded to the Winnipeg Jets in exchange for their 1995 fifth round draft pick.

April 7 . . . .   Nathan LaFayette is acquired from the Vancouver Canucks in exchange for Corey Hirsch.

April 10 . . . .   Darren Langdon and Joby Messier are sent to Binghamton.

Pat Verbeek

1995 OFF-SEASON ACTIVITY

July 7.........................Rangers sign Niklas Sundstrom to a professional contract.

July 7.........................Rangers sign Dan Cloutier to a professional contract.

July 18.......................Rangers name George Burnett as head coach of the Binghamton Rangers.

July 19.......................Rangers sign free agent Ray Ferraro.

July 26.......................Rangers sign Pavel Komarov to a professional contract.

July 26.......................Rangers sign Maxim Galanov to a professional contract.

July 27.......................Rangers agree to terms with Stephane Matteau.

July 31.......................Rangers acquire Doug Lidster from the St. Louis Blues in exchange for Jay Wells.

August 2 ....Rangers sign free agent Wayne Presley.

August 3 ....Rangers sign Ken Shepard to a professional contract.

August 3 ....Rangers sign free agent Ryan VandenBussche.

August 3 ....Rangers agree to terms with Doug Lidster.

August 7 ....Rangers agree to terms with Ken Gernander.

August 13 ....Rangers sign Cal McGowan.

August 21 ....Rangers agree to terms with Sergei Zubov.

August 22 ....Rangers sign free agent Brad Jones.

August 22 ....Rangers sign free agent Eric Flinton.

August 22 ....Rangers agree to terms with Daniel Lacroix.

August 23 ....Rangers sign Rick Willis to a professional contract.

August 24 ....Rangers sign free agent Bruce Driver.

August 31 ....Rangers acquire Luc Robitaille and Ulf Samuelsson from the Pittsburgh Penguins in exchange for Petr Nedved and Sergei Zubov.

September 5 ....Rangers agree to terms with Daniel Lacroix.

September 6 ....Rangers agree to terms with Joe Kocur.

September 12 ....Rangers agree to terms with Peter and Chris Ferraro.

Rangers Birthdays in 1995-96

OCTOBER
18- Doug Lidster (35)

DECEMBER
21- Joe Kocur (31)

JANUARY
2- Mattias Norstrom (24)
8- Darren Langdon (25)
9- Neil Smith (42)
14- Sergei Nemchinov (32)
18- Mark Messier (35)
28- Colin Campbell (43)

FEBRUARY
17- Luc Robitaille (30)
17- Nathan LaFayette (23)
25- Alexei Kovalev (23)

MARCH
3- Brian Leetch (28)
11- Daniel Lacroix (27)
23- Wayne Presley (31)
26- Ulf Samuelsson (32)
28- Jeff Beukeboom (31)

APRIL
7- Alexander Karpovtsev (26)
12- Adam Graves (28)
15- Kevin Lowe (37)
29- Bruce Driver (34)

MAY
24- Pat Verbeek (32)

JUNE
4- Nick Kypreos (30)
6- Niklas Sundstrom (21)

AUGUST
23- Ray Ferraro (32)
23- Glenn Healy (34)

SEPTEMBER
2- Stephane Matteau (27)
22- Mike Richter (30)

(Number in parenthesis indicates age he will become)

GAME-BY-GAME RESULTS

Game No.	Date	Opponent	Score	Result	Rangers Goalie(s)	Winning/ Tying Goal	Team Record	Position in Standings	SF	SA	(Total) GF	GA
1	Jan. 20	Buf	1-2	L	35	Audette	0 - 1 - 0	—	30	24	1	2
2	Jan. 21	Mtl.	5-2	W	35	Messier-1	1 - 1 - 0	—	40	32	6	4
3	Jan. 23	Bos.	1-2	L	35	Sweeney	1 - 2 - 0	—	30	35	7	6
4	Jan. 25	Pit.	2-3	L	35	Stevens	1 - 3 - 0	14T	41	29	9	9
5	Jan. 28	@ Que.	0-2	L	30	Kovalenko	1 - 4 - 0	24T	29	20	9	11
6	Jan. 30	Ott.	6-2	W	35	Graves-1	2 - 4 - 0	17T	26	22	15	13
7	Feb. 1	@ Pit.	3-4	L	35	Sandstrom	2 - 5 - 0	19T	38	31	18	17
8	Feb. 2	T.B.	3-3	T	30	Bureau	2 - 5 - 1	18T	29	28	21	20
9	Feb. 4	@ Ott.	2-1	W	35	Nemchinov-1	3 - 5 - 1	14T	30	17	23	21
10	Feb. 8	Wsh.	5-4	W	35	Leetch-1	4 - 5 - 1	11T	38	26	28	25
11	Feb. 9	@ N.J.	1-4	L	35	Lemieux	4 - 6 - 1	12T	28	33	29	29
12	Feb. 11	@ T.B.	3-2	W	30	Nemchinov-2	5 - 6 - 1	12T	15	25	32	31
13	Feb. 15	@ Buf.	2-1	W	35	Larmer-1	6 - 6 - 1	10T	31	26	34	32
14	Feb. 16	Mtl.	2-2	T	35	Brunet	6 - 6 - 2	8T	34	35	36	34
15	Feb. 18	@ Mtl.	2-5	L	35	Brisebois	6 - 7 - 2	10T	36	23	38	39
16	Feb. 20	@ T.B.	3-1	W	30	Larmer-2	7 - 7 - 2	8T	18	15	41	40
17	Feb. 21	@ Fla.	5-3	W	35	Karpovtsev-1	8 - 7 - 2	6	27	26	46	43
18	Feb. 24	Hfd.	1-2	L	35	Ranheim	8 - 8 - 2	9T	33	25	47	45
19	Feb. 26	@ Buf.	4-2	W	30	Messier-2	9 - 8 - 2	8T	26	24	51	47
20	Feb. 28	Fla.	0-0	T	35		9 - 8 - 3	8T	44	23	51	47
21	Mar. 1	@ Hfd.	5-2	W	35	Noonan-1	10 - 8 - 3	6T	32	23	56	49
22	Mar. 3	Phi.	5-3	W	35	Graves-2	11 - 8 - 3	5T	29	23	61	52
23	Mar. 5	@ Wsh.	2-4	L	35	Hunter	11 - 9 - 3	5T	17	29	63	56
24	Mar. 6	Ott.	4-3	W	30	Nedved-1	12 - 9 - 3	5	33	24	67	59

GAME-BY-GAME RESULTS

Game No.	Date	Opponent	Score	Result	Rangers Goalie(s)	Winning/ Tying Goal	Team Record	Position in Standings	SF	SA	(Total) GF	GA
25	Mar. 8	N.J.	6-4	W	35	Larmer-3	13 - 9 - 3	3T	37	23	73	63
26	Mar. 11	@ Mtl.	1-3	L	35	Brunet	13 - 10 - 3	5T	27	32	74	66
27	Mar. 15	Phi.	3-4	L	35	LeClair	13 - 11 - 3	5T	34	22	77	70
28	Mar. 18	@ Wsh.	1-4	L	30	Konowalchuk	13 - 12 - 3	9T	28	33	78	74
29	Mar. 22	N.J.	2-5	L	35/30	Guerin	13 - 13 - 3	11T	29	29	80	79
30	Mar. 23	@ NYI.	0-1	L	35	Thomas	13 - 14 - 3	11T	37	15	80	80
31	Mar. 25	@ Que.	1-2	L	35	MacDermid	13 - 15 - 3	13T	21	31	81	82
32	Mar. 30	Que.	4-5	L	35/30	Nolan	13 - 16 - 3	15T	40	27	85	87
33	Apr. 1	@ Bos.	3-2	W	30	Kovalev-1	14 - 16 - 3	13T	27	31	88	89
34	Apr. 2	@ Phi.	2-4	L	35	LeClair	14 - 17 - 3	15T	34	22	90	93
35	Apr. 5	@ Fla.	5-0	W	35	Larmer-4	15 - 17 - 3	13T	28	17	95	93
36	Apr. 7	NYI.	3-4	L	35/30	Sutter	15 - 18 - 3	13T	34	28	98	97
37	Apr. 9	@ N.J.	0-2	L	30	Holik	15 - 19 - 3	16T	32	25	98	99
38	Apr. 12	Buf.	3-1	W	35	Verbeek-1	16 - 19 - 3	15T	35	23	101	100
39	Apr. 14	Bos.	5-3	W	35	Verbeek-2	17 - 19 - 3	15T	24	33	106	103
40	Apr. 16	@ NYI.	3-2	W	35	Nedved-2	18 - 19 - 3	13T	25	20	109	105
41	Apr. 18	@ Pit.	5-6	L	35	Francis	18 - 20 - 3	15	34	28	114	111
42	Apr. 20	Hfd.	3-2	W	30	Nedved-3	19 - 20 - 3	11T	40	27	117	113
43	Apr. 23	@ Bos.	4-5	L	30	Neely	19 - 21 - 3	15T	36	28	121	118
44	Apr. 24	Wsh.	5-4	W	35	Nemchinov-3	20 - 21 - 3	12T	32	35	126	122
45	Apr. 26	T.B.	6-4	W	35/30	Graves-3	21 - 21 - 3	12T	48	41	132	126
46	Apr. 28	NYI.	2-4	L	35	Schneider	21 - 22 - 3	12T	47	26	134	130
47	Apr. 30	@ Phi.	2-0	W	30	Leetch-2	22 - 22 - 3	12T	32	24	136	130
48	May 2	Fla.	3-4	L	30	Hull	22 - 23 - 3	13T	34	25	139	134

HOME GAME-BY-GAME RESULTS

Game No.	Date	Opponent	Score	Result	Ranger Goalie(s)	Winning/ Tying Goal	Team Record	Position in Standings	SF	SA	(Total) GF	GA
1	Jan. 20	Buf.	1-2	L	35	Audette	0 - 1 - 0	—	30	24	1	2
2	Jan. 21	Mtl.	5-2	W	35	Messier-1	1 - 1 - 0	—	40	32	6	4
3	Jan. 23	Bos.	1-2	L	35	Sweeney	1 - 2 - 0	—	30	35	7	6
4	Jan. 25	Pit.	2-3	L	35	Stevens	1 - 3 - 0	14T	41	29	9	9
5	Jan. 30	Ott.	6-2	W	35	Graves-1	2 - 4 - 0	17T	26	22	15	13
6	Feb. 2	T.B.	3-3	T	30	Bureau	2 - 5 - 1	18T	29	28	18	16
7	Feb. 8	Wsh.	5-4	W	35	Leetch-1	4 - 5 - 1	11T	38	26	23	20
8	Feb. 16	Mtl.	2-2	T	35	Brunet	6 - 6 - 2	8T	34	35	25	22
9	Feb. 24	Hfd.	1-2	L	35	Ranheim	8 - 8 - 2	9T	33	25	26	2
10	Feb. 28	Fla.	0-0	T	35	None	9 - 8 - 3	8T	44	23	26	24
11	Mar. 3	Phi.	5-3	W	35	Graves-2	11 - 8 - 3	5T	29	23	31	27
12	Mar. 6	Ott.	4-3	W	30	Nedved-1	12 - 9 - 3	5	33	24	35	30
13	Mar. 8	N.J.	6-4	W	35	Larmer-3	13 - 9 - 3	3T	37	23	41	34
14	Mar. 15	Phi.	3-4	L	35	LeClair	13 - 11 - 3	5T	34	22	44	38
15	Mar. 22	N.J.	2-5	L	35/30	Guerin	13 - 13 - 3	11T	29	29	46	43
16	Mar. 30	Que.	4-5	L	35/30	Nolan	13 - 16 - 3	15T	40	27	50	48
17	Apr. 7	NYI.	3-4	L	35/30	Sutter	15 - 18 - 3	13T	34	28	53	52
18	Apr. 12	Buf.	3-1	W	35	Verbeek-1	16 - 19 - 3	15T	35	23	56	5
19	Apr. 14	Bos.	5-3	W	35	Verbeek-2	17 - 19 - 3	15T	24	33	61	56
20	Apr. 20	Hfd.	3-2	W	30	Nedved-3	19 - 20 - 3	11T	40	27	64	58
21	Apr. 24	Wsh.	5-4	W	35	Nemchinov-3	20 - 21 - 3	12T	32	35	69	60
22	Apr. 26	T.B.	6-4	W	35/30	Graves-3	21 - 21 - 3	12T	48	41	75	64
23	Apr. 28	NYI.	2-4	L	35	Schneider	21 - 22 - 3	12T	47	26	77	68
24	May 2	Fla.	3-4	L	30	Hull	22 - 23 - 3	13T	34	25	80	72

ROAD GAME-BY-GAME RESULTS

Game No.	Date	Opponent	Score	Result	Ranger Goalie(s)	Winning/ Tying Goal	Team Record	Position in Standings	SF	SA	(Total) GF	GA
1	Jan. 28	@ Que.	0-2	L	30	Kovalenko	1 - 4 - 0	24T	29	20	0	2
2	Feb. 1	@ Pit.	3-4	L	35	Sandstrom	2 - 5 - 0	19T	38	31	3	6
3	Feb. 4	@ Ott.	2-1	W	35	Nemchinov-1	3 - 5 - 1	14T	30	17	5	7
4	Feb. 9	@ N.J.	1-4	L	35	Lemieux	4 - 6 - 1	12T	28	33	6	11
5	Feb. 11	@ T.B.	3-2	W	30	Nemchinov-2	5 - 6 - 1	12T	15	25	9	13
6	Feb. 15	@ Buf.	2-1	W	35	Larmer-1	6 - 6 - 1	10T	31	26	11	14
7	Feb. 18	@ Mtl.	2-5	L	35	Brisebois	6 - 7 - 2	10T	36	23	13	19
8	Feb. 20	@ T.B.	3-1	W	30	Larmer-2	7 - 7 - 2	8T	18	15	16	20
9	Feb. 21	@ Fla.	5-3	W	35	Karpovtsev-1	8 - 7 - 2	6	27	26	21	23
10	Feb. 26	@ Buf.	4-2	W	30	Messier-2	9 - 8 - 2	8T	26	24	25	25
11	Mar. 1	@ Hfd.	5-2	W	35	Noonan-1	10 - 8 - 3	6T	32	23	30	27
12	Mar. 5	@ Wsh.	2-4	L	35	Hunter	11 - 9 - 3	5T	17	29	32	31
13	Mar. 11	@ Mtl.	1-3	L	35	Brunet	13 -10 - 3	5T	27	32	33	34
14	Mar. 18	@ Wsh.	1-4	L	30	Konowalchuk	13 -12 - 3	9T	28	33	34	38
15	Mar. 23	@ NYI.	0-1	L	35	Thomas	13 -14 - 3	11T	37	15	34	39
16	Mar. 25	@ Que.	1-2	L	35	MacDermid	13 -15 - 3	13T	21	31	35	41
17	Apr. 1	@ Bos.	3-2	W	30	Kovalev-1	14 -16 - 3	13T	27	31	38	43
18	Apr. 2	@ Phi.	2-4	L	35	LeClair	14 -17 - 3	15T	34	22	40	47
19	Apr. 5	@ Fla.	5-0	W	35	Larmer-4	15 -17 - 3	13T	28	17	45	47
20	Apr. 9	@ N.J.	0-2	L	30	Holik	15 -19 - 3	16T	32	25	45	49
21	Apr. 16	@ NYI.	3-2	W	35	Nedved-2	18 -19 - 3	13T	25	20	48	51
22	Apr. 18	@ Pit.	5-6	L	35	Francis	18 -20 - 3	15	34	28	53	57
23	Apr. 23	@ Bos.	4-5	L	30	Neely	19 -21 - 3	15T	36	28	57	62
24	Apr. 30	@ Phi.	2-0	W	30	Leetch-2	22 -22 - 3	12T	32	24	59	62

GAME-BY-GAME POWER PLAY TOTALS

GM	Date	Opponent	PPGF	ADV	PPGF	ADV	PP%	SGA
					Season Totals			
1	1-20-95	Buffalo	1	4	1	4	25.0	0
2	1-21-95	Montreal	4	7	5	11	45.5	0
3	1-23-95	Boston	0	3	5	14	35.7	0
4	1-25-95	Pittsburgh	0	5	5	19	26.3	0
5	1-28-95	@ Quebec	0	3	5	22	22.7	0
6	1-30-95	Ottawa	1	5	6	27	22.2	0
7	2-1-95	@ Pittsburgh	0	4	6	31	19.4	0
8	2-2-95	Tampa Bay	0	3	6	34	17.6	1
9	2-4-95	@Ottawa	0	2	6	36	16.7	0
10	2-8-95	Washington	4	8	10	44	22.7	0
11	2-9-95	@ New Jersey	1	5	11	49	22.4	0
12	2-11-95	@ Tampa Bay	0	4	11	53	20.8	0
13	2-15-95	@ Buffalo	0	3	11	56	19.6	0
14	2-16-95	Montreal	1	3	12	59	20.3	0
15	2-18-95	@ Montreal	1	3	13	62	21.0	0
16	2-20-95	@ Tampa Bay	0	2	13	64	20.3	0
17	2-21-95	@ Florida	1	5	14	69	20.3	0
18	2-24-95	Hartford	1	4	15	73	20.5	0
19	2-26-95	@ Buffalo	0	5	15	78	19.2	0
20	2-28-95	Florida	0	6	15	84	17.9	0
21	3-1-95	@ Hartford	2	3	17	87	19.5	0
22	3-3-95	Philadelphia	2	5	19	92	20.7	0
23	3-5-95	@ Washington	0	6	19	98	19.4	0
24	3-6-95	Ottawa	1	4	20	102	19.6	0
25	3-8-95	New Jersey	1	6	21	108	19.4	0
26	3-11-95	@ Montreal	0	4	21	112	18.8	0
27	3-15-95	Philadelphia	0	6	21	118	17.8	0
28	3-18-95	@ Washington	0	5	21	123	17.1	1
29	3-22-95	New Jersey	1	3	22	126	17.5	0
30	3-23-95	@ NY Islanders	0	2	22	128	17.2	0
31	3-25-95	@ Quebec	0	4	22	132	16.7	0
32	3-30-95	Quebec	2	4	24	136	17.6	0
33	4-1-95	@ Boston	0	5	24	141	17.0	1
34	4-2-95	@ Philadelphia	1	4	25	145	17.2	0
35	4-5-95	@ Florida	0	3	25	148	16.9	0
36	4-7-95	NY Islanders	1	2	26	150	17.3	0
37	4-9-95	@ New Jersey	0	2	26	152	17.1	0
38	4-12-95	Buffalo	0	2	26	154	16.9	0
39	4-14-95	Boston	1	5	27	159	17.3	0
40	4-16-95	@ NY Islanders	5	2	29	164	17.7	0
41	4-18-95	@ Pittsburgh	2	3	31	167	18.6	0
42	4-20-95	Hartford	1	4	32	171	18.7	0
43	4-23-95	@ Boston	1	3	33	174	19.0	0
44	4-24-95	Washington	2	6	35	180	19.4	0
45	4-26-95	Tampa Bay	2	3	37	183	20.2	0
46	4-28-95	NY Islanders	1	6	38	189	20.1	0
47	4-30-95	@ Philadelphia	1	4	39	193	20.2	0
48	5-2-95	Florida	1	7	40	200	20.0	0

GAME-BY-GAME PENALTY KILLING TOTALS

GM	Date	Opponent	PPGA	TSH	Season Totals PPGA	TSH	PK%	SGF
1	1-10-95	Buffalo	0	2	0	2	100.0	0
2	1-21-95	Montreal	2	5	2	7	71.4	0
3	1-23-95	Boston	0	3	2	10	80.0	0
4	1-25-95	Pittsburgh	0	4	2	14	85.7	0
5	1-28-95	@ Quebec	0	3	2	17	88.2	0
6	1-30-95	Ottawa	0	6	2	23	91.3	0
7	2-1-95	@ Pittsburgh	0	4	2	27	92.6	0
8	2-2-95	Tampa Bay	0	5	2	32	93.8	0
9	2-4-95	@ Ottawa	1	4	3	36	91.7	0
10	2-8-95	Washington	3	8	6	45	86.7	1
11	2-9-95	@ New Jersey	2	6	8	51	84.3	0
12	2-11-95	@ Tampa Bay	0	5	8	56	85.7	0
13	2-15-95	@ Buffalo	0	4	8	60	86.7	0
14	2-16-95	Montreal	0	2	8	62	87.1	0
15	2-18-95	@ Montreal	3	6	11	68	83.8	0
16	2-20-95	@ Tampa Bay	0	2	11	70	84.3	0
17	2-21-95	@ Florida	1	6	12	76	84.2	0
18	2-24-95	Hartford	0	3	12	79	84.8	0
19	2-26-95	@ Buffalo	1	7	13	86	84.9	1
20	2-28-95	Florida	0	3	13	89	85.4	0
21	3-1-95	@ Hartford	1	4	14	93	84.9	0
22	3-3-95	Philadelphia	1	3	15	96	84.4	0
23	3-5-95	@ Washington	1	4	16	100	84.0	0
24	3-6-95	Ottawa	1	3	17	103	83.5	0
25	3-8-95	New Jersey	1	4	18	107	83.2	0
26	3-11-95	@ Montreal	0	3	18	110	83.6	0
27	3-15-95	Philadelphia	2	5	20	115	82.6	1
28	3-18-95	@ Washington	1	7	21	122	82.8	0
29	3-22-95	New Jersey	1	5	22	127	82.7	0
30	3-23-95	@ NY Islanders	0	2	22	129	82.9	0
31	3-25-95	@ Quebec	0	5	22	134	83.6	0
32	3-30-95	Quebec	1	4	23	138	83.3	0
33	4-1-95	@ Boston	1	6	24	144	83.3	0
34	4-2-95	@ Philadelphia	0	7	24	151	84.1	0
35	4-5-95	@ Florida	0	6	24	157	84.7	0
36	4-7-95	NY Islanders	1	3	25	160	84.4	1
37	4-9-95	@ New Jersey	1	3	26	163	84.0	0
38	4-12-95	Buffalo	1	5	27	168	83.9	1
39	4-14-95	Boston	0	4	27	172	84.3	0
40	4-16-95	@ NY Islanders	1	3	28	175	84.0	0
41	4-18-95	@ Pittsburgh	0	4	28	179	84.4	0
42	4-20-95	Hartford	0	1	28	180	84.4	0
43	4-23-95	@ Boston	2	5	30	185	83.8	0
44	4-24-95	Washington	2	7	32	192	83.3	0
45	4-26-95	Tampa Bay	1	4	33	196	83.2	0
46	4-28-95	NY Islanders	1	5	34	201	83.1	0
47	4-30-95	@ Philadelphia	0	4	34	205	83.4	0
48	5-2-95	Florida	0	6	34	211	83.9	0
SEASON TOTALS					**34**	**211**	**83.9**	**5**

GAME-BY-GAME HOME ATTENDANCE

NO.	DATE	DAY	VS.	ATTENDANCE	SEASON	SELLOUT	AVG
1	Jan. 20	Fri.	Buffalo	18,200	18,200	1	18,200
2	Jan. 21	Sat.	Montreal	18,200	36,400	2	18,200
3	Jan. 23	Mon.	Boston	18,200	54,600	3	18,200
4	Jan. 25	Wed.	Pittsburgh	18,200	72,800	4	18,200
5	Jan. 30	Mon.	Ottawa	18,046	90,846		18,169
6	Feb. 2	Thu.	Tampa Bay	18,200	109,046	5	18,174
7	Feb. 8	Wed.	Washington	18,200	127,246	6	18,178
8	Feb. 16	Thu.	Montreal	18,200	145,446	7	18,181
9	Feb. 24	Fri.	Hartford	18,200	163,646	8	18,183
10	Feb. 28	Tue.	Florida	18,200	181,846	9	18,185
11	Mar. 3	Fri.	Philadelphia	18,200	200,046	10	18,186
12	Mar. 6	Mon.	Ottawa	18,200	218,246	11	18,187
13	Mar. 8	Wed.	New Jersey	18,200	236,446	12	18,188
14	Mar. 15	Wed.	Philadelphia	18,200	254,646	13	18,189
15	Mar. 22	Wed.	New Jersey	18,200	272,846	14	18,190
16	Mar. 30	Thu.	Quebec	18,200	291,046	15	18,190
17	Apr. 7	Fri.	Islanders	18,200	309,246	16	18,191
18	Apr. 12	Wed.	Buffalo	18,200	327,446	17	18,191
19	Apr. 14	Fri.	Boston	18,200	345,646	18	18,192
20	Apr. 20	Thu.	Hartford	18,200	363,846	19	18,192
21	Apr. 24	Mon.	Washington	18,200	382,046	20	18,193
22	Apr. 26	Wed.	Tampa Bay	18,200	400,246	21	18,193
23	Apr. 28	Fri.	Islanders	18,200	418,446	22	18,193
24	May. 2	Tue.	Florida	18,200	436,646	23	18,194

SCORING OF RANGERS DRAFT CHOICES

CANADIAN HOCKEY LEAGUE

POS	NAME	BORN	HT-WT	RD/YR	CLUB/LEAGUE	GP	G	A	PTS	PIM
LW	Eric Boulton	8/17/76	6-0-201	9b/94	Sarnia (OHL)	24	3	7	10	134
					Oshawa (OHL)	27	7	5	12	125
LW	David Brosseau	1/16/76	6-1-190	6b/94	Granby (QMJHL)	26	9	6	15	37
					Shawnigan (QMJHL)	39	28	20	48	65
LW	Jamie Butt	4/4/76	5-11-180	11a/94	Tacoma (WHL)	44	1	4	5	140
D	Martin Ethier	9/03/76	6-1-180	5/94	Beauport (QMJHL)	68	4	26	30	123
C	Sergei Olympijev	1/12/75	6-3-190	4/93	Kitchener (OHL)	25	4	9	13	27
D	Gary Roach	2/04/75	6-2-190	5/93	North Bay (OHL)	23	2	12	14	21
					Sault Ste. Marie (OHL)	42	5	27	32	41
D	Lee Sorochan	9/09/75	6-1-210	2/93	Saskatoon (WHL)	24	5	13	18	63
					Lethbridge (WHL)	29	4	15	19	93
D	Adam Smith	4/24/76	6-0-190	3/94	Tacoma (WHL)	69	2	19	21	96

POS	NAME	BORN	HT-WT	RD/YR	CLUB/LEAGUE	GP	W	L	T	GAA
G	Dan Cloutier	4/22/76	6-1-182	1/94	Sault Ste. Marie (OHL)	45	15	26	2	4.41
G	Ken Shepard	1/20/74	5-10-192	9/93	Oshawa (OHL)	42	24	11	3	3.19
G	Dave Trofimenkoff	1/20/75	6-1-190	6/93	Prince George (WHL)	17	4	8	2	5.80
					Lethbridge (WHL)	11	4	6	0	4.70

EUROPEANS

POS	NAME	BORN	HT-WT	RD/YR	SCHOOL	GP	G	A	PTS	PIM
C	Vitali Chinakov	1/15/72	5-11-183	11/91	Molot Perm (CIS)	14	2	1	3	4
D	Maxim Galanov	3/13/74	6-1-175	3/93	Lada Togliatti (CIS)	45	5	6	11	54
D	Kim Johnsson	3/16/76	6-1-175	11b/94	Malmo (Sweden)	13	0	0	0	4
D	Pavel Komarov	2/28/74	6-1-180	11a/93	Torpedo Nizhny (CIS)	26	0	1	1	38
RW	Sergei Kondrashikin	4/02/75	6-0-192	7a/93	Cherepovets (CIS)	51	7	2	9	22
D	Alexander Korobolin	3/12/76	6-2-189	4a/94	Mechel (CIS)		Not Available			
RW	Radoslav Kropac	4/5/75	6-0-187	10/94	Slovan Bratislava (Slovakia)	35	17	8	25	38
LW	Alexei Lazarenko	1/03/76	6-1-171	7/94	CSKA Moscow (CIS)	5	0	0	0	0
C	Yuri Litvinov	4/11/76	5-10-165	6a/94	Krylja Sovetov (CIS)	6	0	0	0	8
C	Lubos Rob	8/05/70	5-11-183	5/90	Budejovice	41	15	21	36	0
C	Maxim Smelnitski	3/24/74	6-3-207	11b/93	Chelyabinsk (CIS)	49	9	5	14	22
C	Niklas Sundstrom	6/06/75	6-0-185	1/93	MoDo (Sweden)	33	8	13	21	30
LW	Rudolf Vercik	3/19/76	6-1-191	2/94	Slovan Bratislava (Slovakia)	33	14	9	23	22
RW	Vladimir Vorobiev	11/03/72	6-0-183	10/92	Moscow Dynamo (CIS)	48	9	20	29	78

POS	NAME	BORN	HT-WT	RD/YR	SCHOOL	GP	W	L	T	GAA
G	Vitali Yeremeyev	9/23/75	5-10-167	9a/94	CSKA (CIS)	49	—	—	—	—

NATIONAL COLLEGIATE ATHLETIC ASSOCIATION

POS	NAME	BORN	HT-WT	RD/YR	SCHOOL	GP	G	A	PTS	PIM
D	Dan Brierley	1/23/74	6-2-185	9/92	Yale University	28	5	8	13	44
D	Eddy Campbell	11/26/73	6-2-212	8/93	University of Lowell	34	6	24	30	105
D	Davide Dal Grande	7/08/74	6-5-195	6/92	Notre Dame	36	4	12	16	48
D	Mickey Elick	3/17/74	6-1-180	8/92	University of Wisconsin	43	5	24	29	52
C	Brett Lievers	6/18/71	6-0-170	11/90	St. Cloud State	38	21	27	48	8
D	Brian Lonsinger	7/21/72	6-3-193	7/90	Harvard University	28	8	9	17	12
C	John Rushin	9/12/72	6-5-207	7/91	Notre Dame	31	3	3	6	36
RW	Wayne Strachan	12/12/72	5-10-185	Sp/93	Lake Superior State	41	22	20	42	68
LW	Rick Willis	1/09/72	6-0-185	4/90	University of Michigan	33	3	6	9	78

BRUINS VS. RANGERS, 1994-95

	Overall Record: 2-2-0	at New York 1-1-0		at Boston 1-1-0		
	GP	W	L	T	GF	GA	PTS
Bruins	4	2	2	0	12	13	4
Rangers	4	2	2	0	13	12	4

Jan. 23	Rangers 1, Bruins 2 at New York (Lacher & Richter)
Apr. 1	Rangers 3, Bruins 2 at Boston (Lacher & Healy)
Apr. 14	Rangers 5, Bruins 3 at New York (Lacher/Billington & Richter)
Apr. 23	Rangers 4, Bruins 5 at Boston (Billington/Lacher & Healy)

SCORING

Bruins	GP	G	A	PTS	PIM	S	+\-
Oates	4	2	2	4	2	13	-1
Neely	3	3	0	3	0	21	E
Donato	4	2	1	3	0	4	-1
Naslund	3	0	3	3	0	5	-1
Heinze	2	1	1	2	0	5	E
Sweeney	4	1	1	2	2	6	E
Bourque	4	0	2	2	0	16	E
Kasatonov	4	0	2	2	2	6	-2
Shaw	4	0	2	2	2	1	E
Smolinski	3	1	0	1	8	7	E
Czerkawski	4	1	0	1	4	6	2
Murray	4	1	0	1	6	8	-3
Hughes	3	0	1	1	0	6	1
Rohloff	3	0	1	1	0	3	-1
Stumpel	3	0	1	1	0	2	-1
Lacroix	1	0	0	0	0	1	E
Makela	1	0	0	0	0	0	E
Potvin	1	0	0	0	0	0	E
Stewart	1	0	0	0	0	0	E
Gruden	2	0	0	0	0	2	1
Leach	2	0	0	0	2	3	-1
Reid	2	0	0	0	0	1	1
Knipscheer	3	0	0	0	0	5	-2
Moger	3	0	0	0	0	4	-1
Huscroft	4	0	0	0	8	2	-2

Rangers	GP	G	A	PTS	PIM	S	+\-
Verbeek	3	3	2	5	2	9	1
Leetch	4	3	2	5	0	17	3
Messier	4	0	5	5	4	8	-1
Kovalev	4	3	0	3	2	8	2
Graves	4	0	3	3	2	11	-1
Nedved	4	1	1	2	0	11	1
Zubov	4	1	1	2	0	11	-2
Kypreos	4	0	2	2	2	2	2
Wells	4	0	2	2	6	3	2
Matteau	2	1	0	1	2	5	E
Nemchinov	4	1	0	1	0	4	-1
Olczyk	2	0	1	1	0	2	1
Noonan	4	0	1	1	4	5	-1
Norstrom	1	0	0	0	0	0	-1
Healy	2	0	0	0	2	0	E
LaFayette	2	0	0	0	0	0	E
Karpovtsev	3	0	0	0	2	6	E
Osborne	3	0	0	0	0	1	E
Beukeboom	4	0	0	0	8	2	4
Kocur	4	0	0	0	0	1	E
Larmer	4	0	0	0	0	8	2
Lowe	4	0	0	0	6	3	-1

GOALTENDING

	GP	MINS	GA	EN	AVG	W	L	T
Lacher	4	172	9	0	3.14	2	1	0
Billington	2	67	4	0	3.58	0	1	0

	GP	MINS	GA	EN	AVG	W	L	T
Richter	2	119	5	0	2.52	1	1	0
Healy	2	119	7	0	3.53	1	1	0

Bruins Power Play: 3-18 (16.7%)
Power Play Goals: Neely (2), Donato
Shorthanded Goals: Oates
Game-Winning Goals: Sweeney, Neely
Game-Tying Goals: None

Goals by Period:	1st	2nd	3rd	OT	Total
Bruins	2	4	6	0	12
Rangers	6	4	3	0	13

Last Win at MSG: 1/23/95 (2-1)
Last Win at Bos: 4/23/95 (5-4)

Rangers Power Play: 2-16 (12.5%)
Power Play Goals: Leetch, Zubov
Shorthanded Goals: None
Game-Winning Goals: Kovalev, Verbeek
Game-Tying Goals: None

Shots by Period:	1st	2nd	3rd	OT	Total
Bruins	46	47	34	0	127
Rangers	32	47	38	0	117

Last Win at MSG: 4/14/95 (5-3)
Last Win at Bos: 4/1/95 (3-2)

Last Ranger trade with Boston: August 19, 1994, Bruins traded Glen Featherstone to Rangers for Daniel Lacroix

SABRES VS. RANGERS, 1994-95

	GP	W	L	T	GF	GA	PTS
Overall Record: 3-1-0	at New York 1-1-0			at Buffalo 2-0-0			
Sabres	4	1	3	0	6	10	2
Rangers	4	3	1	0	10	6	6

Jan. 20	Rangers 1, Sabres 2 at New York (Fuhr & Richter)
Feb. 15	Rangers 2, Sabres 1 at Buffalo (Hasek & Richter)
Feb. 26	Rangers 4, Sabres 2 at Buffalo (Hasek & Healy)
Apr. 12	Rangers 3, Sabres 1 at New York (Hasek & Richter)

SCORING

Sabres	GP	G	A	PTS	PIM	S	+\-
Audette	4	1	1	2	2	7	-5
Sweeney	4	1	1	2	0	3	-1
Khmylev	4	0	2	2	2	6	E
Zhitnik	1	1	0	1	0	5	-1
Hawerchuk	3	1	0	1	0	9	E
Huddy	3	1	0	1	2	2	2
Hannan	4	1	0	1	0	4	E
Galley	1	0	1	1	0	3	-1
LaFontaine	1	0	1	1	0	0	-2
Simpson	2	0	1	1	0	0	E
Mogilny	3	0	1	1	0	8	-2
Smehlik	3	0	1	1	2	5	-3
Presley	4	0	1	1	6	8	-1
Astley	1	0	0	0	0	0	-2
Boucher	1	0	0	0	0	3	2
Gordiouk	1	0	0	0	0	3	-2
MacDonald	1	0	0	0	0	0	-1
Melanson	1	0	0	0	2	1	-1
Pearson	1	0	0	0	2	3	E
Sutton	1	0	0	0	0	1	E
Barnaby	2	0	0	0	10	0	E
Houda	2	0	0	0	5	1	E
Dawe	3	0	0	0	0	1	-1
May	3	0	0	0	17	4	E
Muni	3	0	0	0	2	0	-2
Svoboda	3	0	0	0	4	2	-1
Bodger	4	0	0	0	4	6	-3
Plante	4	0	0	0	2	12	-3
Ray	4	0	0	0	17	0	1

Rangers	GP	G	A	PTS	PIM	S	+\-
Larmer	4	3	0	3	0	15	2
Noonan	4	2	1	3	2	11	4
Zubov	4	2	1	3	2	7	4
Nemchinov	4	1	2	3	0	6	2
Leetch	4	0	3	3	2	8	5
Messier	4	1	1	2	4	9	1
Graves	4	0	2	2	5	24	1
Verbeek	1	1	0	1	0	3	1
Beukeboom	4	0	1	1	23	1	3
Kovalev	4	0	1	1	0	6	E
Lowe	4	0	1	1	4	3	2
Matteau	4	0	1	1	2	5	1
Nedved	4	0	1	1	4	9	2
LaFayette	1	0	0	0	0	0	E
Langdon	1	0	0	0	19	0	E
Kypreos	3	0	0	0	0	1	E
Olczyk	3	0	0	0	2	2	E
Osborne	3	0	0	0	0	1	E
Richter	3	0	0	0	2	0	E
Karpovtsev	4	0	0	0	0	6	-2
Kocur	4	0	0	0	4	1	E
Wells	4	0	0	0	4	4	-3

GOALTENDING

	GP	MINS	GA	EN	AVG	W	L	T
Fuhr	1	60	1	0	1.00	1	0	0
Hasek	3	179	7	2	2.35	0	3	0

	GP	MINS	GA	EN	AVG	W	L	T
Richter	3	179	4	0	1.34	2	1	0
Healy	1	60	2	0	2.00	1	0	0

Sabres Power Play: 2-18 (11.1%)
Power Play Goals: Huddy, Sweeney
Shorthanded Goals: None
Game-Winning Goals: Audette
Game-Tying Goals: None

Goals by Period:	1st	2nd	3rd	OT	Total
Sabres	2	1	3	0	6
Rangers	3	2	5	0	10

Last Win at MSG: 1/20/95 (2-1)
Last Win at Buf: 12/31/93 (4-1)

Rangers Power Play: 1-14 (7.1%)
Power Play Goals: Larmer
Shorthanded Goals: Messier, Larmer
Game-Winning Goals: Larmer, Messier, Verbeek
Game-Tying Goals: None

Shots by Period:	1st	2nd	3rd	OT	Total
Sabres	34	31	32	0	97
Rangers	43	39	40	0	122

Last Win at MSG: 4/12/95 (3-1)
Last Win at Buf: 2/26/95 (4-2)

Last Ranger trade with Sabres: March 2, 1992, Sabres traded Jay Wells to Rangers in exchange for Randy Moller.

WHALERS vs. RANGERS, 1994-95

Overall Record: 2-1-0   at New York 1-1-0   at Hartford 1-0-0

	GP	W	L	T	GF	GA	PTS
Whalers	3	1	2	0	6	9	2
Rangers	3	2	1	0	9	6	4

Feb. 24	Rangers 1, Whalers 2 at New York (Burke & Richter)
Mar. 1	Rangers 5, Whalers 2 at Hartford (Reese & Richter)
Apr. 20	Rangers 3, Whalers 2 at New York (Burke & Healy)

SCORING

Whalers	GP	G	A	PTS	PIM	S	+\-
Cassels	3	1	3	4	0	7	2
Sanderson	3	1	2	3	2	7	1
Pronger	3	2	0	2	0	7	1
Ranheim	3	2	0	2	0	8	1
Turcotte	3	0	2	2	0	8	-1
Janssens	3	0	1	1	0	1	-1
Kucera	3	0	1	1	0	6	E
Rice	3	0	1	1	4	2	E
Carson	1	0	0	0	0	1	-1
Chase	1	0	0	0	0	0	E
Chibirev	1	0	0	0	0	0	E
Daniels	1	0	0	0	2	0	E
Featherstone	1	0	0	0	0	1	E
Sandlak	1	0	0	0	0	0	-1
Smyth	1	0	0	0	0	1	E
Drury	2	0	0	0	0	1	E
Glynn	2	0	0	0	0	1	E
Kron	2	0	0	0	0	1	-2
Verbeek	2	0	0	0	4	7	E
Burt	3	0	0	0	4	3	-2
Lemieux	3	0	0	0	6	6	E
McCrimmon	3	0	0	0	0	1	1
Nikolishin	3	0	0	0	0	0	1
Wesley	3	0	0	0	6	7	E

Rangers	GP	G	A	PTS	PIM	S	+\-
Noonan	3	3	1	4	0	9	1
Zubov	2	1	2	3	0	7	-2
Karpovtsev	3	1	2	3	6	11	1
Messier	3	0	3	3	0	6	E
Leetch	3	0	2	2	0	15	E
Nedved	2	1	0	1	0	4	-1
Graves	3	1	0	1	2	8	E
Kocur	3	1	0	1	15	5	E
Kovalev	3	1	0	1	2	9	-1
Healy	1	0	1	1	0	0	E
Larmer	3	0	1	1	0	5	E
Matteau	3	0	1	1	0	4	1
Nemchinov	3	0	1	1	0	3	E
LaFayette	1	0	0	0	0	1	E
J. Messier	1	0	0	0	0	2	1
Verbeek	1	0	0	0	0	3	1
Kypreos	2	0	0	0	0	1	-1
Langdon	2	0	0	0	6	1	1
Olczyk	2	0	0	0	0	4	-1
Osborne	2	0	0	0	0	3	E
Beukeboom	3	0	0	0	0	2	E
Lowe	3	0	0	0	0	1	-1
Wells	3	0	0	0	0	1	1

GOALTENDING

	GP	MINS	GA	EN	AVG	W	L	T
Burke	2	119	4	0	2.02	1	1	0
Reese	1	59	4	1	4.07	0	1	0

	GP	MINS	GA	EN	AVG	W	L	T
Healy	1	60	2	0	2.00	1	0	0
Richter	2	120	4	0	2.00	1	1	0

Whalers Power Play: 1-8 (12.5%)
Power Play Goals: Pronger

Shorthanded Goals: None
Game-Winning Goals: Ranheim
Game-Tying Goals: None

Rangers Power Play: 4-11 (36.4%)
Power Play Goals: Graves, Noonan, Kovalev, Zubov

Shorthanded Goals: None
Game-Winning Goals: Noonan, Nedved
Game-Tying Goals: None

Goals by Period:	1st	2nd	3rd	OT	Total
Whalers	2	3	1	0	6
Rangers	0	4	5	0	9

Last Win at MSG: 2/24/95 (2-1)
Last Win at Hfd: 2/19/94 (4-2)

Shots by Period:	1st	2nd	3rd	OT	Total
Whalers	29	17	29	0	75
Rangers	30	42	33	0	105

Last Win at MSG: 4/20/95 (3-2)
Last Win at Hfd: 3/1/95 (5-2)

Last Ranger trade with Hartford: March 23, 1995, Whalers traded Pat Verbeek to Rangers for Glen Featherstone, Michael Stewart, a 1995 first round draft choice and a 1996 fourth round draft choice.

PANTHERS VS. RANGERS, 1994-95

	Overall Record: 2-1-1		at New York 0-1-1		at Florida 2-0-0		
	GP	W	L	T	GF	GA	PTS
Panthers	4	1	2	1	7	13	3
Rangers	4	2	1	1	13	7	5

Feb. 21	Rangers 5, Panthers 3, at Florida (Vanbiesbrouck & Richter)
Feb. 28	Rangers 0, Panthers 0, at New York (Vanbiesbrouck & Richter)
Apr. 5	Rangers 5, Panthers 0, at Florida (Vanbiesbrouck & Richter)
May 2	Rangers 3, Panthers 4, at New York (Vanbiesbrouck & Healy)

SCORING

Panthers	GP	G	A	PTS	PIM	S	+\-		Rangers	GP	G	A	PTS	PIM	S	+\-
Svensson	2	1	2	3	0	4	1		Messier	3	3	1	4	2	9	3
Hull	4	2	0	2	2	6	E		Zubov	3	1	3	4	2	11	2
Lindsay	4	1	1	2	8	2	1		Verbeek	2	2	1	3	0	7	E
Mellanby	4	1	1	2	4	10	-1		Graves	4	1	2	3	4	17	2
Kudelski	4	1	0	1	0	5	-2		Larmer	4	1	2	3	2	14	2
Woolley	4	1	0	1	2	9	-3		Leetch	4	0	3	3	4	17	4
Barnes	2	0	1	1	0	7	1		Kovalev	4	2	0	2	0	8	E
Laus	2	0	1	1	4	0	-2		Norstrom	2	0	2	2	0	0	2
Lowry	3	0	1	1	11	3	-1		Olczyk	2	1	0	1	0	3	1
Smith	3	0	1	1	2	1	-2		Nedved	3	1	0	1	0	6	-2
Fitzgerald	4	0	1	1	4	6	-1		Karpovtsev	4	1	0	1	4	8	1
Skrudland	4	0	1	1	6	5	-2		Noonan	3	0	1	1	0	8	1
Duchesne	1	0	0	0	0	1	1		Osborne	3	0	1	1	2	5	3
Eakins	1	0	0	0	0	0	-2		Matteau	4	0	1	1	9	5	1
Moller	1	0	0	0	0	2	-3		Lacroix	1	0	0	0	0	0	E
Severyn	1	0	0	0	5	2	E		LaFayette	1	0	0	0	0	1	E
Svehla	1	0	0	0	0	1	3		Loney	1	0	0	0	0	0	E
Benning	2	0	0	0	0	3	-1		J.Messier	1	0	0	0	4	0	E
Garpenlov	2	0	0	0	0	0	-1		Langdon	2	0	0	0	5	2	E
Lomakin	2	0	0	0	0	1	-1		Kypreos	3	0	0	0	4	0	E
Tomlinson	2	0	0	0	0	0	-1		Lowe	3	0	0	0	2	1	E
Cirella	3	0	0	0	2	2	-1		Wells	3	0	0	0	2	3	E
Belanger	4	0	0	0	0	5	-3		Beukeboom	4	0	0	0	8	2	1
Hough	4	0	0	0	0	4	-4		Kocur	4	0	0	0	0	3	1
Murphy	4	0	0	0	4	8	-2		Nemchinov	4	0	0	0	4	3	3
Niedermayer	4	0	0	0	0	4	E									
Vanbiesbrouck	4	0	0	0	2	0	E									

GOALTENDING

	GP	MINS	GA	EN	AVG	W	L	T			GP	MINS	GA	EN	AVG	W	L	T
Vanbiesbrouck	4	245	12	1	2.94	1	2	1		Richter	3	185	3	0	0.97	2	0	1
										Healy	1	59	4	0	4.07	0	1	0

Panthers	Rangers
Panthers Power Play: 1-21 (4.8%)	**Rangers Power Play:** 2-21 (9.5%)
Power Play Goals: Woolley	**Power Play Goals:** Verbeek, Graves
Shorthanded Goals: None	**Shorthanded Goals:** None
Game-Winning Goals: Hull	**Game-Winning Goals:** Karpovtsev, Larmer
Game-Tying Goals: None	**Game-Tying Goals:** None

Goals by Period:	1st	2nd	3rd	OT	Total		Shots by Period:	1st	2nd	3rd	OT	Total
Panthers	4	0	3	0	7		*Panthers*	29	20	37	5	91
Rangers	5	1	7	0	13		*Rangers*	51	42	37	3	133

Last Win at MSG: 5/2/95 (4-3) **Last Win at MSG:** 4/4/94 (3-2)
Last Win at Fla: 3/14/94 (2-1) **Last Win at Fla:** 4/5/95 (5-0)

Last Ranger trade with Florida: March 21, 1994, Panthers traded a ninth round draft choice (Vitali Yeremeyev) in the 1994 NHL Entry Draft in exchange for Peter Andersson.

CANADIENS VS. RANGERS, 1994-95

Overall Record: 1-2-1 at New York 1-0-1 at Montreal 0-2-0

	GP	W	L	T	GF	GA	PTS
Canadiens	4	2	1	1	12	10	5
Rangers	4	1	2	1	10	12	3

Jan. 21	Rangers 5, Canadiens 2 at New York (Roy & Richter)
Feb. 16	Rangers 2, Canadiens 2 at New York (Tugnutt & Richter)
Feb. 18	Rangers 2, Canadiens 5 at Montreal (Roy & Richter)
Mar. 11	Rangers 1, Canadiens 3 at Montreal (Roy & Richter)

SCORING

Canadiens	GP	G	A	PTS	PIM	S	+\-
Schneider	4	0	6	6	4	13	5
Damphousse	4	1	3	4	0	13	2
Recchi	3	3	0	3	0	8	E
Brunet	4	2	1	3	0	6	2
Brisebois	4	1	1	2	0	9	E
Muller	4	1	1	2	0	12	-1
Racine	4	0	2	2	4	9	1
LeClair	1	1	0	1	2	2	E
Conroy	2	1	0	1	0	1	1
Lamb	3	1	0	1	2	4	1
Keane	4	1	0	1	2	7	3
Darby	1	0	1	1	0	0	E
Desjardins	1	0	1	1	0	3	E
Ronan	2	0	1	1	0	1	1
Bellows	3	0	1	1	0	8	2
DiPietro	3	0	1	1	0	8	-1
Brashear	4	0	1	1	7	1	1
Bure	1	0	0	0	0	2	E
Dionne	1	0	0	0	0	0	E
Petrov	1	0	0	0	0	1	-1
Savage	2	0	0	0	4	2	E
Stevenson	2	0	0	0	2	0	-1
Popovic	3	0	0	0	0	0	-3
Sevigny	3	0	0	0	4	0	E
Daigneault	4	0	0	0	6	4	-1
Odelein	4	0	0	0	4	8	4

Rangers	GP	G	A	PTS	PIM	S	+\-
Messier	4	2	2	4	0	14	-3
Leetch	4	0	4	4	0	17	-5
Zubov	3	1	2	3	4	8	-1
Kovalev	4	1	2	3	0	9	E
Wells	3	1	1	2	6	3	2
Noonan	4	1	1	2	2	6	1
Larmer	4	0	2	2	2	8	-3
Nedved	4	0	2	2	2	22	2
Langdon	2	0	2	2	4	1	E
Graves	4	1	0	1	4	14	-1
Karpovtsev	4	1	0	1	2	8	2
Matteau	4	1	0	1	0	2	-1
Beukeboom	4	0	1	1	10	1	-4
Kocur	4	0	1	1	5	1	-1
Featherstone	1	0	0	0	0	2	1
J. Messier	1	0	0	0	0	1	E
Kypreos	3	0	0	0	0	2	E
Olczyk	3	0	0	0	0	2	-1
Lowe	4	0	0	0	2	5	-1
Nemchinov	4	0	0	0	0	7	-1
Osborne	4	0	0	0	0	4	-1

GOALTENDING

	GP	MINS	GA	EN	AVG	W	L	T
Tugnutt	1	65	2	0	1.85	0	0	1
Roy	3	180	8	0	2.67	2	1	0

	GP	MINS	GA	EN	AVG	W	L	T
Richter	4	244	12	0	2.95	1	2	1

Canadiens Power Play: 5-16 (31.3%)
Power Play Goals: Recchi (2), Damphousse, LeClair, Muller
Shorthanded Goals: None
Game-Winning Goals: Brunet, Brisebois
Game-Tying Goals: Brunet

Goals by Period:	1st	2nd	3rd	OT	Total
Canadiens	4	4	4	0	12
Rangers	3	4	3	0	10

Last Win at MSG: 11/6/91 (4-1)
Last Win at Mtl: 3/11/95 (3-1)

Rangers Power Play: 6-17 (35.3%)
Power Play Goals: Messier (2), Karpovtsev, Noonan, Zubov, Graves
Shorthanded Goals: None
Game-Winning Goals: Messier
Game-Tying Goals: None

Shots by Period:	1st	2nd	3rd	OT	Total
Canadiens	41	40	40	1	122
Rangers	52	48	36	1	137

Last Win at MSG: 1/21/95 (5-2)
Last Win at Mtl: 10/5/91 (2-1)

Last Ranger trade with Montreal: January 27, 1988, Canadiens traded Chris Nilan to Rangers in exchange for option to exchange first round draft picks in 1989.

DEVILS vs. RANGERS, 1994-95

	Overall Record: 1-3-0		at New York 1-1-0		at New Jersey 0-2-0		
	GP	W	L	T	GF	GA	PTS
Devils	4	3	1	0	15	9	6
Rangers	4	1	3	0	9	15	2

Feb. 9	Rangers 1, Devils 4	at New Jersey (Brodeur & Richter)
Mar. 8	Rangers 6, Devils 4	at New York (Brodeur & Richter)
Mar. 22	Rangers 2, Devils 5	at New York (Brodeur & Richter/Healy)
Apr. 9	Rangers 0, Devils 2	at New Jersey (Brodeur & Healy)

SCORING

Devils	GP	G	A	PTS	PIM	S	+\-
Broten	3	1	3	4	2	4	1
Albelin	4	1	3	4	6	3	2
Niedermayer	4	1	3	4	2	3	1
Stevens	4	0	4	4	16	6	3
Holik	4	2	1	3	2	9	2
Lemieux	4	2	1	3	14	13	1
Rolston	4	2	1	3	2	7	1
MacLean	4	1	2	3	0	10	2
Driver	4	0	3	3	2	4	2
Brylin	2	1	1	2	0	2	2
Semak	2	1	1	2	2	3	E
Guerin	4	1	1	2	22	9	1
Chorske	4	1	0	1	2	5	-1
Richer	4	1	0	1	2	16	-3
McKay	2	0	1	1	9	5	2
Carpenter	4	0	1	1	0	6	-1
Peluso	4	0	1	1	7	0	2
McAlpine	1	0	0	0	4	0	-2
Millen	1	0	0	0	0	0	E
Modry	1	0	0	0	0	0	E
Chambers	2	0	0	0	0	1	1
Daneyko	2	0	0	0	7	2	E
Dean	2	0	0	0	2	1	1
Simpson	2	0	0	0	10	1	E

Rangers	GP	G	A	PTS	PIM	S	+\-
Larmer	4	2	4	6	0	10	1
Noonan	3	3	1	4	0	9	3
Messier	4	2	2	4	6	12	-1
Nedved	4	1	2	3	4	13	3
Leetch	4	1	1	2	2	15	E
Zubov	3	0	2	2	2	11	-5
Karpovtsev	4	0	2	2	4	9	E
Matteau	3	0	1	1	2	0	1
Kovalev	4	0	1	1	2	10	-3
Featherstone	1	0	0	0	2	0	E
LaFayette	1	0	0	0	0	0	-1
Loney	1	0	0	0	0	1	E
J. Messier	1	0	0	0	0	0	-1
Norstrom	1	0	0	0	0	0	E
Verbeek	1	0	0	0	2	5	E
Langdon	2	0	0	0	12	0	-1
Olczyk	2	0	0	0	0	4	-1
Beukeboom	3	0	0	0	4	2	1
Kypreos	3	0	0	0	15	1	E
Wells	3	0	0	0	0	4	-3
Graves	4	0	0	0	9	11	-3
Kocur	4	0	0	0	26	1	-2
Lowe	4	0	0	0	4	2	-1
Nemchinov	4	0	0	0	0	6	-3
Osborne	4	0	0	0	2	0	-2

GOALTENDING

	GP	MINS	GA	EN	AVG	W	L	T
Brodeur	4	240	8	1	2.00	3	1	0

	GP	MINS	GA	EN	AVG	W	L	T
Healy	2	84	3	0	2.14	0	1	0
Richter	3	155	12	0	4.65	1	2	0

Devils Power Play: 5-18 (27.8%)
Power Play Goals: Niedermayer, Lemieux, Rolston (2), Albelin
Shorthanded Goals: None
Game-Winning Goals: Lemieux, Guerin, Holik
Game-Tying Goals: None

Rangers Power Play: 3-16 (18.8%)
Power Play Goals: Noonan (2), Larmer
Shorthanded Goals: None
Game-Winning Goals: Larmer
Game-Tying Goals: None

Goals by Period:	1st	2nd	3rd	OT	Total
Devils	3	6	6	0	15
Rangers	0	5	4	0	9

Last Win at MSG: 3/22/95 (5-2)
Last Win at NJ: 4/9/95 (2-0)

Shots by Period:	1st	2nd	3rd	OT	Total
Devils	30	49	31	0	110
Rangers	37	43	46	0	126

Last Win at MSG: 3/8/95 (6-4)
Last Win at NJ: 4/2/94 (1-1)

Last Ranger trade with New Jersey: November 2, 1979, Rockies traded Barry Beck to Rangers in exchange for Bobby Crawford, Lucien Deblois, Pat Hickey, Mike McEwen and Dean Turner.

ISLANDERS vs. RANGERS, 1994-95

Overall Record: 1-3-0   at New York 0-2-0   at Islanders 1-1-0

	GP	W	L	T	GF	GA	PTS
Islanders	4	3	1	0	11	8	6
Rangers	4	1	3	0	8	11	2

Mar. 23	Rangers 0, Islanders 1 at Islanders (Soderstrom & Richter)
Apr. 7	Rangers 3, Islanders 4 at New York (Soderstrom & Richter/Healy)
Apr. 16	Rangers 3, Islanders 2 at Islanders (Soderstrom & Richter)
Apr. 28	Rangers 2, Islanders 4 at New York (Soderstrom & Richter)

SCORING

Islanders	GP	G	A	PTS	PIM	S	+\-
Ferraro	4	2	3	5	0	9	2
McInnis	4	2	1	3	0	6	3
Schneider	3	1	2	3	2	10	2
Palffy	3	0	3	3	2	7	2
Green	4	2	0	2	2	8	1
Muller	2	1	1	2	4	1	1
Beers	3	1	1	2	2	5	1
Sutter	3	1	0	1	0	4	1
Thomas	4	1	0	1	2	11	1
Taylor	1	0	1	1	0	1	-1
Turgeon	1	0	1	1	0	2	1
Marinucci	2	0	1	1	2	1	E
Severyn	2	0	1	1	0	1	1
King	4	0	1	1	0	5	E
Luongo	4	0	1	1	5	1	3
Dineen	1	0	0	0	0	1	E
Hogue	1	0	0	0	0	0	E
Lachance	1	0	0	0	2	3	1
Malakhov	1	0	0	0	0	1	1
Pilon	1	0	0	0	2	0	E
Dalgarno	2	0	0	0	2	0	E
Chynoweth	3	0	0	0	9	3	E
Stanton	3	0	0	0	2	0	E
Vaske	3	0	0	0	0	0	-1
Flatley	4	0	0	0	0	6	2
Lindros	4	0	0	0	7	3	-1
Vukota	4	0	0	0	0	0	E

Rangers	GP	G	A	PTS	PIM	S	+\-
Messier	4	1	2	3	4	11	-3
Leetch	4	0	3	3	2	22	-2
Kovalev	4	1	1	2	6	4	-1
Nedved	4	1	1	2	2	8	-1
Zubov	4	1	1	2	0	22	-1
Graves	4	0	2	2	5	16	-1
Noonan	3	1	0	1	0	8	-2
Lowe	4	1	0	1	6	6	1
Matteau	4	1	0	1	2	2	E
Verbeek	4	1	0	1	2	9	-2
Osborne	2	0	1	1	0	4	1
Larmer	3	0	1	1	0	5	E
Karpovtsev	4	0	1	1	2	3	-2
Langdon	1	0	0	0	0	0	E
Loney	1	0	0	0	0	1	-2
Olczyk	1	0	0	0	0	3	E
LaFayette	2	0	0	0	0	1	1
Norstrom	2	0	0	0	0	2	-2
Beukeboom	3	0	0	0	0	3	-1
Kypreos	3	0	0	0	5	4	E
Wells	3	0	0	0	0	0	-1
Kocur	4	0	0	0	2	2	-1
Nemchinov	4	0	0	0	0	7	-3

GOALTENDING

	GP	MINS	GA	EN	AVG	W	L	T
Soderstrom	4	240	8	0	2.00	3	1	0

	GP	MINS	GA	EN	AVG	W	L	T
Healy	1	17	0	0	0.00	0	0	0
Richter	4	220	10	1	2.73	1	3	0

Islanders Power Play: 3-13 (23.1%)
Power Play Goals: Beers, Muller, Schneider
Shorthanded Goals: None
Game-Winning Goals: Thomas, Sutter, Schneider
Game-Tying Goals: None

Goals by Period:	1st	2nd	3rd	OT	Total
Islanders	2	5	4	0	11
Rangers	4	1	3	0	8

Last Win at MSG: 4/28/95 (4-2)
Last Win at NYI: 3/23/95 (1-0)

Rangers Power Play: 4-15 (26.7%)
Power Play Goals: Lowe, Verbeek, Zubov, Noonan
Shorthanded Goals: Kovalev
Game-Winning Goals: Nedved
Game-Tying Goals: None

Shots by Period:	1st	2nd	3rd	OT	Total
Islanders	26	38	25	0	89
Rangers	55	43	45	0	143

Last Win at MSG: 2/12/93 (4-3)
Last Win at NYI: 4/16/95 (3-2)

Last Ranger trade with Islanders: November 14, 1973, Islanders sent cash to Rangers for Ron Stewart.

SENATORS vs. RANGERS, 1994-95

Overall Record: 3-0-0   at New York 2-0-0   at Ottawa 1-0-0

	GP	W	L	T	GF	GA	PTS
Senators	3	0	3	0	6	12	0
Rangers	3	3	0	0	12	6	6

Jan.	30	Rangers 6, Senators 2 at New York (Beaupre & Richter)
Feb.	4	Rangers 2, Senators 1 at Ottawa (Beaupre & Richter)
Mar.	6	Rangers 4, Senators 3 at New York (Beaupre & Healy)

SCORING

Senators	GP	G	A	PTS	PIM	S	+\-
Huard	3	1	1	2	17	3	2
McIlwain	3	1	1	2	0	3	E
Daigle	3	0	2	2	0	4	-2
Bourque	3	1	0	1	0	2	E
Elyniuk	3	1	0	1	2	7	-3
Hill	3	1	0	1	4	10	E
Yashin	3	1	0	1	0	8	-2
Paek	1	0	1	1	4	0	1
Pitlick	1	0	1	1	0	0	E
Dahlquist	2	0	1	1	0	1	-2
Maciver	3	0	1	1	0	5	-5
Murray	3	0	1	1	2	1	1
Demitra	1	0	0	0	0	0	E
Picard	1	0	0	0	2	0	-1
Archibald	2	0	0	0	2	2	-4
Turgeon	2	0	0	0	2	2	-1
Vial	2	0	0	0	10	0	-4
Beaupre	3	0	0	0	2	0	E
Bonk	3	0	0	0	2	2	-2
Cunneyworth	3	0	0	0	2	4	-5
Gaudreau	3	0	0	0	0	3	-2
Huffman	3	0	0	0	2	2	E
Neckar	3	0	0	0	2	4	-1

Rangers	GP	G	A	PTS	PIM	S	+\-
Graves	3	4	1	5	4	11	6
Messier	3	0	5	5	0	7	6
Nedved	3	0	3	3	2	13	1
Leetch	3	1	2	3	0	12	3
Noonan	3	1	2	3	0	7	1
Larmer	3	1	1	2	0	9	3
Kovalev	3	0	2	2	0	5	2
Lowe	3	0	2	2	6	2	1
Wells	3	0	2	2	0	6	2
Nemchinov	2	1	0	1	0	2	E
Kypreos	3	1	0	1	9	1	1
Healy	1	0	1	1	0	0	E
Zubov	1	0	1	1	2	2	3
J. Messier	2	0	1	1	0	0	1
Osborne	3	0	1	1	2	0	E
Langdon	1	0	0	0	0	0	-1
Roy	1	0	0	0	2	1	E
McCosh	2	0	0	0	2	1	E
Beukeboom	3	0	0	0	5	2	2
Karpovtsev	3	0	0	0	4	6	E
Kocur	3	0	0	0	9	0	-1
Matteau	3	0	0	0	2	2	E

GOALTENDING

	GP	MINS	GA	EN	AVG	W	L	T
Beaupre	3	178	12	0	4.04	0	3	0

	GP	MINS	GA	EN	AVG	W	L	T
Richter	2	120	3	0	1.50	2	0	0
Healy	1	60	3	0	3.00	1	0	0

Senators Power Play: 2-13 (15.4%)
Power Play Goals: McIlwain, Yashin
Shorthanded Goals: None
Game-Winning Goals: None

Game-Tying Goals: None

Rangers Power Play: 2-11 (18.2%)
Power Play Goals: Graves, Noonan
Shorthanded Goals: None
Game-Winning Goals: Graves, Nemchinov, Nedved
Game-Tying Goals: None

Goals by Period:	1st	2nd	3rd	OT	Total
Senators	2	3	1	0	6
Rangers	4	5	3	0	12

Last Win at MSG: 3/6/34 (5-4)
Last Win at OTT: 12/23/26 (1-0)

Shots by Period:	1st	2nd	3rd	OT	Total
Senators	25	20	18	0	63
Rangers	25	37	27	0	89

Last Win at MSG: 3/6/95 (4-3)
Last Win at OTT: 2/4/95 (2-1)

Last Ranger trade with Ottawa: March 21, 1994, Senators traded future considerations to Rangers for Phil Bourque.

FLYERS vs. RANGERS, 1994-95

	Overall Record: 2-2-0	at New York 1-1-0		at Philadelphia 1-1-0		
	GP	W	L	T	GF	GA	PTS
Flyers	4	2	2	0	11	12	4
Rangers	4	2	2	0	12	11	4

Mar. 3	Rangers 5, Flyers 3 at New York (Hextall & Richter)
Mar. 15	Rangers 3, Flyers 4 at New York (Roussel & Richter)
Apr. 2	Rangers 2, Flyers 4 at Philadelphia (Hextall & Richter)
Apr. 30	Rangers 2, Flyers 0 at Philadelphia (Roussel & Healy)

SCORING

Flyers	GP	G	A	PTS	PIM	S	+\-	Rangers	GP	G	A	PTS	PIM	S	+\-
Lindros	4	3	4	7	8	18	5	Leetch	4	3	2	5	0	17	-1
Renberg	4	3	4	7	0	8	2	Messier	3	1	4	5	5	13	2
LeClair	4	3	2	5	4	17	2	Larmer	4	2	2	4	0	6	4
Galley	3	0	2	2	0	4	1	Graves	4	3	0	3	4	15	E
Semenov	3	1	0	1	0	4	-1	Noonan	4	0	3	3	2	8	1
Therien	4	1	0	1	4	3	-1	Kovalev	4	1	1	2	6	10	E
Dineen	2	0	1	1	0	4	E	Featherstone	1	1	0	1	0	4	1
DiMaio	3	0	1	1	2	2	E	Verbeek	2	1	0	1	6	9	-2
Dionne	3	0	1	1	0	2	E	J. Messier	1	0	1	1	0	1	1
Haller	3	0	1	1	15	1	3	Zubov	2	0	1	1	0	3	E
Fedyk	1	0	0	0	2	1	-1	Matteau	3	0	1	1	2	4	-2
Montgomery	1	0	0	0	0	0	-1	Karpovtsev	4	0	1	1	2	9	-1
Svoboda	1	0	0	0	0	2	E	Nedved	4	0	1	1	4	9	E
Brown	2	0	0	0	0	0	E	LaFayette	1	0	0	0	0	2	1
Zettler	2	0	0	0	0	0	-1	Loney	1	0	0	0	0	0	E
Antoski	3	0	0	0	7	0	2	Olczyk	1	0	0	0	0	0	-1
Desjardins	3	0	0	0	2	2	E	Langdon	2	0	0	0	0	1	1
Dupre	3	0	0	0	4	3	1	Osborne	3	0	0	0	2	0	-2
Juhlin	3	0	0	0	0	0	-3	Beukeboom	4	0	0	0	2	2	-1
Brind'Amour	4	0	0	0	6	5	-2	Kocur	4	0	0	0	2	4	-1
Dykhuis	4	0	0	0	4	5	1	Kypreos	4	0	0	0	30	0	E
MacTavish	4	0	0	0	0	1	-1	Lowe	4	0	0	0	2	4	1
Podein	4	0	0	0	2	4	-3	Nemchinov	4	0	0	0	4	7	-2
Yushkevich	4	0	0	0	4	6	-3	Wells	4	0	0	0	4	1	E

GOALTENDING

	GP	MINS	GA	EN	AVG	W	L	T		GP	MINS	GA	EN	AVG	W	L	T
Roussel	2	120	5	0	2.50	1	1	0	Healy	1	60	0	0	0.00	1	0	0
Hextall	2	120	7	0	3.50	1	1	0	Richter	3	179	11	0	3.69	1	2	0

Flyers Power Play: 3-19 (15.8%)
Power Play Goals: Renberg (2), Lindros

Shorthanded Goals: None
Game-Winning Goals: LeClair (2)
Game-Tying Goals: None

Goals by Period:	1st	2nd	3rd	OT	Total
Flyers	5	2	4	0	11
Rangers	2	9	1	0	12

Last Win at MSG: 3/15/95 (4-3)
Last Win at Phi: 4/2/95 (4-2)

Rangers Power Play: 4-19 (21.1%)
Power Play Goals: Graves (2), Larmer, Leetch

Shorthanded Goals: Messier
Game-Winning Goals: Graves, Leetch
Game-Tying Goals: None

Shots by Period:	1st	2nd	3rd	OT	Total
Flyers	29	29	33	0	91
Rangers	41	57	31	0	129

Last Win at MSG: 3/3/95 (5-3)
Last Win at Phi: 4/30/95 (2-0)

Last Ranger trade with Philadelphia: August 8, 1991, Flyers traded Don Biggs to Rangers in exchange for future considerations.

PENGUINS vs. RANGERS, 1994-95

Overall Record: 0-3-0   at New York 0-1-0   at Pittsburgh 0-2-0

	GP	W	L	T	GF	GA	PTS
Penguins	3	3	0	0	13	10	6
Rangers	3	0	3	0	10	13	0

Jan.	25	Rangers 2, Penguins 3 at New York (Wregget & Richter)
Feb.	1	Rangers 3, Penguins 4 at Pittsburgh (Wregget & Richter)
Apr.	18	Rangers 5, Penguins 6 at Pittsburgh (Wregget & Richter)

SCORING

Penguins	GP	G	A	PTS	PIM	S	+/-	Rangers	GP	G	A	PTS	PIM	S	+/-
Stevens	3	3	2	5	0	11	1	Leetch	3	0	6	6	2	8	-3
Jagr	3	1	4	5	0	12	5	Messier	3	1	4	5	2	10	E
Francis	3	3	1	4	0	7	4	Graves	3	3	0	3	6	14	1
Sandstrom	3	2	1	3	4	8	-1	Zubov	3	1	2	3	0	14	1
Cullen	3	1	2	3	0	6	E	Kovalev	3	1	1	2	0	10	-2
Robitaille	3	0	3	3	0	0	3	Larmer	3	1	1	2	2	12	-2
Mullen	3	2	0	2	0	5	2	Nedved	3	1	1	2	0	11	-6
Joseph	2	1	1	2	2	3	1	McCosh	1	1	0	1	0	1	1
Straka	2	0	2	2	0	3	2	Roy	1	1	0	1	0	4	E
McEachern	3	0	2	2	0	6	E	Kocur	3	0	1	1	0	2	1
U. Samuelsson	3	0	2	2	6	3	5	Kypreos	3	0	1	1	4	2	E
Maciver	1	0	1	1	0	1	1	Lowe	3	0	1	1	8	3	E
Barrie	3	0	1	1	2	2	E	Nemchinov	3	0	1	1	2	3	-1
Murphy	3	0	1	1	6	7	-1	Noonan	3	0	1	1	2	5	-4
K. Samuelsson	3	0	1	1	8	5	6	Hartman	1	0	0	0	4	0	E
Fitzgerald	1	0	0	0	0	0	1	LaFayette	1	0	0	0	0	0	E
Jennings	1	0	0	0	2	0	E	Verbeek	1	0	0	0	2	1	-1
Murray	1	0	0	0	0	3	E	Matteau	2	0	0	0	2	3	E
Tamer	1	0	0	0	0	0	-1	Osborne	2	0	0	0	0	3	-2
Hawgood	2	0	0	0	2	1	-1	Beukeboom	3	0	0	0	2	2	-3
Hudson	2	0	0	0	6	4	-1	Karpovtsev	3	0	0	0	0	1	-3
McKenzie	2	0	0	0	2	1	E	Wells	3	0	0	0	4	4	-2
Leroux	3	0	0	0	2	0	-1								

GOALTENDING

	GP	MINS	GA	EN	AVG	W	L	T		GP	MINS	GA	EN	AVG	W	L	T
Wregget	3	180	10	0	3.33	3	0	0	Richter	3	178	13	0	4.38	0	3	0

Penguins Power Play: 0-12 (0.0%)
Power Play Goals: None
Shorthanded Goals: None
Game-Winning Goals: Stevens, Francis, Sandstrom
Game-Tying Goals: None

Goals by Period:	1st	2nd	3rd	OT	Total
Penguins	4	4	5	0	13
Rangers	4	4	3	0	10

Last Win at MSG: 1/25/95 (3-2)
Last Win at Pit: 4/18/95 (6-5)

Rangers Power Play: 2-12 (16.7%)
Power Play Goals: Graves, Nedved
Shorthanded Goals: None
Game-Winning Goals: None
Game-Tying Goals: None

Shots by Period:	1st	2nd	3rd	OT	Total
Penguins	28	33	27	0	88
Rangers	39	38	36	0	113

Last Win at MSG: 2/21/94 (4-3)
Last Win at Pit: 11/25/92 (11-3)

Last Ranger trade with Pittsburgh: August 31, 1995, Penguins traded Luc Robitaille and Ulf Samuelsson to Rangers for Petr Nedved and Sergei Zubov.

NORDIQUES vs. RANGERS, 1994-95

Overall Record: 0-3-0   at New York 0-1-0   at Quebec 0-2-0

	GP	W	L	T	GF	GA	PTS
Nordiques	3	3	0	0	9	5	6
Rangers	3	0	3	0	5	9	0

Jan. 28	Rangers 0, Nordiques 2 at Quebec (Fiset & Healy)
Mar. 25	Rangers 1, Nordiques 2 at Quebec (Thibault & Richter)
Mar. 30	Rangers 4, Nordiques 5 at New York (Fiset & Richter/Healy)

SCORING

Nordiques	GP	G	A	PTS	PIM	S	+\-		Rangers	GP	G	A	PTS	PIM	S	+\-
Nolan	3	3	0	3	0	9	2		Messier	3	1	2	3	0	9	E
Forsberg	3	0	3	3	0	3	3		Kovalev	3	1	1	2	0	8	-2
Kamensky	3	0	3	3	4	9	E		Wells	3	1	1	2	2	1	2
Deadmarsh	3	2	0	2	9	4	2		Verbeek	2	1	0	1	0	2	-1
Kovalenko	3	2	0	2	0	6	1		Nedved	3	1	0	1	0	4	E
Bassen	3	1	1	2	0	3	4		Norstrom	1	0	1	1	0	1	1
Miller	1	0	2	2	0	1	2		Graves	3	0	1	1	0	13	E
Krupp	3	0	2	2	2	8	3		Leetch	3	0	1	1	0	10	-2
MacDermid	2	1	0	1	4	2	1		Noonan	3	0	1	1	2	8	-2
Clark	1	0	1	1	0	3	1		Zubov	3	0	1	1	0	8	-6
Gusarov	1	0	1	1	0	1	1		Roy	1	0	0	0	0	3	-1
Corbet	2	0	1	1	0	0	1		Beukeboom	2	0	0	0	2	3	E
Sakic	3	0	1	1	0	7	1		Kypreos	2	0	0	0	0	0	E
Young	3	0	1	1	2	6	E		Langdon	2	0	0	0	2	0	E
Laukkanen	1	0	0	0	0	0	E		Osborne	2	0	0	0	7	3	E
Rucinsky	1	0	0	0	0	0	E		Karpovtsev	3	0	0	0	4	1	E
Simon	1	0	0	0	2	0	E		Kocur	3	0	0	0	6	2	-2
Finn	2	0	0	0	2	0	3		Larmer	3	0	0	0	4	5	-2
Foote	2	0	0	0	0	1	E		Lowe	3	0	0	0	2	2	-5
Lapointe	2	0	0	0	2	4	E		Matteau	3	0	0	0	0	2	-4
Wolanin	2	0	0	0	2	0	-2		Nemchinov	3	0	0	0	4	5	-2
Lefebvre	3	0	0	0	0	4	E									
Leschyshyn	3	0	0	0	0	1	3									
Ricci	3	0	0	0	4	5	E									

GOALTENDING

	GP	MINS	GA	EN	AVG	W	L	T			GP	MINS	GA	EN	AVG	W	L	T
Thibault	1	60	1	0	1.00	1	0	0		Healy	2	89	3	0	2.02	0	2	0
Fiset	2	120	4	0	2.00	2	0	0		Richter	2	90	6	0	4.00	0	1	0

Nordiques Power Play: 1-12 (8.3%)
Power Play Goals: Nolan
Shorthanded Goals: None
Game-Winning Goals: Kovalenko, MacDermid, Nolan
Game-Tying Goals: None

Goals by Period:	1st	2nd	3rd	OT	Total
Nordiques	3	5	1	0	9
Rangers	1	1	3	0	5

Last Win at MSG: 3/30/95 (5-4)
Last Win at Que: 3/25/95 (2-1)

Rangers Power Play: 2-11 (18.2%)
Power Play Goals: Messier, Verbeek
Shorthanded Goals: None
Game-Winning Goals: None

Game-Tying Goals: None

Shots by Period:	1st	2nd	3rd	OT	Total
Nordiques	29	38	11	0	78
Rangers	32	27	31	0	90

Last Win at MSG: 3/2/94 (5-2)
Last Win at Que: 2/14/94 (4-2)

Last Ranger trade with Nordiques: September 9, 1993, Nordiques traded Alexander Karpovtsev to Rangers for Mike Hurlbut.

LIGHTNING vs. RANGERS, 1994-95

Overall Record: 3-0-1   at New York 1-0-1   at Tampa 2-0-0

	GP	W	L	T	GF	GA	PTS
Lightning	4	0	3	1	10	15	1
Rangers	4	3	0	1	15	10	7

Feb.	2	Rangers 3, Lightning 3 at New York (Puppa & Healy)
Feb.	11	Rangers 3, Lightning 2 at Tampa (Puppa & Healy)
Feb.	20	Rangers 3, Lightning 1 at Tampa (Puppa & Healy)
Apr.	26	Rangers 6, Lightning 4 at New York (Puppa/Bergeron & Richter/Healy)

SCORING

Lightning	GP	G	A	PTS	PIM	S	+\-
Bradley	3	2	2	4	2	9	-2
Hamrlik	4	1	2	3	0	9	-6
Klima	4	2	0	2	2	7	-1
Andersson	4	1	1	2	0	6	E
Gratton	4	1	1	2	2	10	-1
Plavsic	1	1	0	1	0	2	E
Bureau	4	1	0	1	4	6	-1
Tucker	4	1	0	1	0	8	-4
Bergevin	3	0	1	1	0	3	-1
Savard	3	0	1	1	0	6	-1
Selivanov	4	0	1	1	2	8	-3
Wiemer	4	0	1	1	2	0	E
Zamuner	4	0	1	1	0	5	E
Myhres	1	0	0	0	0	1	E
Poeschek	1	0	0	0	4	0	E
Semak	1	0	0	0	0	2	-1
Ysebaert	1	0	0	0	0	5	-1
Cummins	2	0	0	0	5	0	-1
Halkidis	2	0	0	0	4	0	E
Chambers	3	0	0	0	2	5	-3
Cole	3	0	0	0	2	5	1
Charron	4	0	0	0	6	6	2
Ciccone	4	0	0	0	2	3	E
Cross	4	0	0	0	2	3	1

Rangers	GP	G	A	PTS	PIM	S	+\-
Messier	4	1	5	6	2	9	5
Larmer	4	4	1	5	2	13	4
Zubov	4	0	5	5	4	4	4
Graves	3	2	1	3	2	13	6
Kovalev	4	2	1	3	8	9	1
Nemchinov	4	2	1	3	2	8	3
Verbeek	1	1	2	3	4	6	1
Beukeboom	4	1	1	2	0	4	1
Nedved	4	1	1	2	8	10	-2
Lowe	3	0	2	2	0	3	3
Noonan	4	1	0	1	0	4	-3
Leetch	4	0	1	1	0	11	-1
Featherstone	1	0	0	0	4	0	1
LaFayette	1	0	0	0	0	0	-1
Langdon	1	0	0	0	5	0	E
Norstrom	1	0	0	0	0	1	2
McCosh	2	0	0	0	0	0	E
Olczyk	2	0	0	0	0	1	E
Kypreos	3	0	0	0	4	1	-2
Matteau	3	0	0	0	0	0	-3
Wells	3	0	0	0	0	1	-1
Karpovtsev	4	0	0	0	0	4	-1
Kocur	4	0	0	0	2	2	2
Osborne	4	0	0	0	4	6	E

GOALTENDING

	GP	MINS	GA	EN	AVG	W	L	T
Bergeron	1	19	1	1	3.16	0	1	0
Puppa	4	224	12	1	3.21	0	2	1

	GP	MINS	GA	EN	AVG	W	L	T
Healy	4	221	7	0	1.90	3	0	1
Richter	1	24	3	0	7.50	0	0	0

Lightning Power Play: 1-16 (6.3%)
Power Play Goals: Bradley
Shorthanded Goals: Bureau
Game-Winning Goals: None

Game-Tying Goals: Bureau

Goals by Period:	1st	2nd	3rd	OT	Total
Lightning	4	4	2	0	10
Rangers	5	7	3	0	15

Last Win at MSG: 1/10/94 (5-2)
Last Win at T.B.: 10/22/93 (4-1)

Rangers Power Play: 2-12 (16.7%)
Power Play Goals: Verbeek, Noonan
Shorthanded Goals: None
Game-Winning Goals: Nemchinov, Larmer, Graves

Game-Tying Goals: None

Shots by Period:	1st	2nd	3rd	OT	Total
Lightning	33	31	41	4	109
Rangers	42	31	35	2	110

Last Win at MSG: 4/26/95 (6-4)
Last Win at T.B.: 2/20/95 (3-1)

Last Ranger trade with Lightning: June 25, 1993, Lightning traded Glenn Healy to Rangers in exchange for a return of Tampa Bay's 1993 third round draft choice.

CAPITALS vs. RANGERS, 1994-95

Overall Record: 2-2-0   at New York 2-0-0   at Washington 0-2-0

	GP	W	L	T	GF	GA	PTS
Capitals	4	2	2	0	16	13	4
Rangers	4	2	2	0	13	16	4

Feb.	8	Rangers 5, Capitals 4 at New York (Tabaracci & Richter)
Mar.	5	Rangers 2, Capitals 4 at Washington (Carey & Richter)
Mar.	18	Rangers 1, Capitals 4 at Washington (Carey & Healy)
Apr.	24	Rangers 5, Capitals 4 at New York (Carey/Kolzig & Richter)

SCORING

Capitals	GP	G	A	PTS	PIM	S	+\-
Bondra	4	5	0	5	0	15	3
Hunter	4	3	2	5	16	9	1
Miller	4	2	3	5	0	8	E
Juneau	4	0	5	5	4	2	1
Cote	4	1	3	4	14	17	E
Johansson	4	0	4	4	2	10	1
Konowalchuk	4	2	0	2	2	6	1
Jones	3	1	1	2	0	9	1
Khristich	4	1	1	2	2	10	1
Peake	2	0	2	2	6	4	1
Slaney	2	0	2	2	4	4	E
Tinordi	3	0	2	2	12	2	E
Johnson	4	0	2	2	10	3	-1
Reekie	4	1	0	1	12	4	3
Berube	3	0	1	1	5	1	-1
Pivonka	4	0	1	1	19	7	2
Allison	1	0	0	0	0	0	E
Eagles	1	0	0	0	0	1	E
Klee	1	0	0	0	0	1	E
Kaminski	2	0	0	0	19	1	-2
Nelson	2	0	0	0	0	0	-2
Pearson	2	0	0	0	6	1	-1
Poulin	2	0	0	0	2	1	-1
Gonchar	4	0	0	0	6	7	1

Rangers	GP	G	A	PTS	PIM	S	+\-
Zubov	2	2	4	6	2	8	1
Graves	4	2	2	4	4	18	-1
Messier	4	1	3	4	11	9	-1
Kovalev	4	0	4	4	4	7	-2
Nemchinov	4	2	1	3	0	6	-1
Karpovtsev	4	1	2	3	0	10	1
Leetch	4	1	2	3	6	13	-1
Noonan	4	2	0	2	12	7	-3
Nedved	4	0	2	2	0	3	2
Olczyk	2	1	0	1	2	8	E
Osborne	2	1	0	1	0	2	1
Langdon	2	0	1	1	9	1	E
Lowe	2	0	1	1	16	0	-1
Wells	4	0	1	1	8	7	1
LaFayette	1	0	0	0	0	0	1
Norstrom	1	0	0	0	2	0	E
Verbeek	1	0	0	0	0	2	E
Featherstone	2	0	0	0	12	0	-3
Beukeboom	3	0	0	0	6	3	E
Matteau	3	0	0	0	2	3	-2
J. Messier	3	0	0	0	14	0	E
Kocur	4	0	0	0	0	1	E
Kypreos	4	0	0	0	20	1	E
Larmer	4	0	0	0	4	6	-3

GOALTENDING

	GP	MINS	GA	EN	AVG	W	L	T
Kolzig	1	54	2	0	2.22	0	1	0
Carey	3	126	6	0	2.86	2	0	0
Tabaracci	1	60	5	0	5.00	0	1	0

	GP	MINS	GA	EN	AVG	W	L	T
Richter	3	180	11	1	3.67	2	1	0
Healy	1	60	4	0	4.00	0	1	0

Capitals Power Play: 7-27 (25.9%)
Power Play Goals: Bondra (3), Khristich, Hunter, Miller, Konowalchuk
Shorthanded Goals: Bondra
Game-Winning Goals: Hunter, Konowalchuk
Game-Tying Goals: None

Rangers Power Play: 6-25 (24.0%)
Power Play Goals: Zubov (2), Graves (2), Olczyk, Leetch.
Shorthanded Goals: Messier
Game-Winning Goals: Leetch, Nemchinov
Game-Tying Goals: None

Goals by Period:	1st	2nd	3rd	OT	Total
Capitals	3	5	8	0	16
Rangers	2	6	2	0	13

Last Win at MSG: 2/7/94 (4-1)
Last Win at Wsh.: 3/18/95 (4-1)

Shots by Period:	1st	2nd	3rd	OT	Total
Capitals	50	35	38	0	123
Rangers	46	44	25	0	115

Last Win at MSG: 4/24/95 (5-4)
Last Win at Wsh.: 3/9/94 (7-5)

Last Ranger trade with Washington: August 27, 1987, Capitals traded a 1988 fifth round draft choice (Martin Bergeron) to Rangers in exchange for Peter Sundstrom.

EASTERN CONFERENCE QUARTERFINALS
NORDIQUES vs. RANGERS

	Overall Record: 4-2		at New York 3-0		at Quebec 1-2	
	GP	W	L	GF	GA	PTS
Nordiques	6	2	4	19	25	4
Rangers	6	4	2	25	19	8

May	6	Rangers 4, Nordiques 5 at Quebec (Fiset & Richter)
May	8	Rangers 8, Nordiques 3 at Quebec (Fiset/Snow & Healy)
May	10	Rangers 4, Nordiques 3 at New York (Fiset & Healy)
May	12	Rangers 3, Nordiques 2 at New York (Thibault & Healy/Richter)
May	14	Rangers 2, Nordiques 4 at Quebec (Thibault & Richter)
May	16	Rangers 4, Nordiques 2 at New York (Thibault/Fiset & Richter)

SCORING

Nordiques	GP	G	A	PTS	PIM	S	+\-	Rangers	GP	G	A	PTS	PIM	S	+\-
Young	6	3	3	6	2	12	3	Kovalev	6	4	5	9	2	18	4
Bassen	5	2	4	6	0	10	2	Leetch	6	2	7	9	6	22	3
Forsberg	6	2	4	6	4	13	2	Nemchinov	6	4	4	8	2	13	8
Sakic	6	4	1	5	0	15	-4	Messier	6	2	5	7	2	14	-4
Nolan	6	2	3	5	6	12	2	Graves	6	4	2	6	4	25	-6
Ricci	6	1	3	4	8	9	4	Verbeek	6	2	4	6	12	20	-1
Clark	6	1	2	3	6	18	-6	Zubov	6	2	4	6	2	24	-3
Simon	6	1	1	2	19	9	-1	Nedved	6	2	2	4	4	19	-2
Wolanin	6	1	1	2	4	8	5	Larmer	6	2	1	3	4	11	-4
Krupp	5	0	2	2	2	13	-2	Kypreos	6	0	2	2	2	4	4
Lefebvre	6	0	2	2	2	7	5	Karpovtsev	6	1	0	1	0	7	E
Kamensky	2	1	0	1	0	2	E	Matteau	5	0	1	1	4	5	1
Laukkanen	6	1	0	1	2	11	-2	Lowe	6	0	1	1	8	2	E
Corbet	2	0	1	1	0	0	1	Loney	1	0	0	0	0	0	E
Leschyshyn	3	0	1	1	4	3	-1	Noonan	1	0	0	0	0	0	E
Finn	4	0	1	1	2	2	-4	Norstrom	1	0	0	0	0	0	E
Deadmarsh	6	0	1	1	0	6	-3	Beukeboom	5	0	0	0	8	5	5
Foote	6	0	1	1	14	6	-3	Osborne	5	0	0	0	2	0	1
Kovalenko	6	0	1	1	2	6	-3	Kocur	6	0	0	0	2	1	E
Huard	1	0	0	0	0	0	-1	LaFayette	6	0	0	0	2	1	E
MacDermid	3	0	0	0	2	1	E	Wells	6	0	0	0	4	3	-3
Lapointe	5	0	0	0	8	0	-1								

GOALTENDING

	GP	MINS	GA	EN	AVG	W	L		GP	MINS	GA	EN	AVG	W	L
Thibault	3	148	8	0	3.24	1	2	Richter	4	227	10	1	2.64	2	2
Fiset	4	209	16	0	4.59	1	2	Healy	3	140	8	0	3.43	2	0
Snow	1	9	1	0	6.67	0	0								

Nordiques Power Play: 2-25 (8.0%)
Power Play Goals: Forsberg, Sakic

Shorthanded Goals: Young, Sakic
Game-Winning Goals: Sakic, Simon

Rangers Power Play: 7-29 (24.1%)
Power Play Goals: Graves (2), Verbeek (2), Messier (2), Nedved

Shorthanded Goals: Larmer
Game-Winning Goals: Leetch, Nemchinov, Messier, Larmer

Goals by Period:	1st	2nd	3rd	OT	Total
Nordiques	8	4	7	0	19
Rangers	9	9	6	1	25

Shots by Period:	1st	2nd	3rd	OT	Total
Nordiques	44	48	66	5	163
Rangers	68	67	57	2	194

EASTERN CONFERENCE SEMIFINALS
FLYERS vs. RANGERS

	Overall Record: 0-4-0	at New York 0-2-0	at Philadelphia 0-2-0			
	GP	W	L	GF	GA	PTS
Flyers	4	4	0	11	12	4
Rangers	4	2	2	12	11	4

May 21	Rangers 4, Flyers 5 (OT) at Philadelphia (Hextall & Richter)
May 22	Rangers 3, Flyers 4 (OT) at Philadelphia (Hextall & Richter)
May 24	Rangers 2, Flyers 5 at New York (Hextall & Richter/Healy)
May 26	Rangers 1, Flyers 4 at New York (Hextall & Healy)

SCORING

Flyers	GP	G	A	PTS	PIM	S	+\-
Renberg	4	3	4	7	0	12	4
LeClair	4	3	2	5	2	11	5
Lindros	4	1	4	5	6	14	3
Desjardins	4	2	2	4	0	10	7
Brind'Amour	4	1	3	4	4	8	7
Dineen	4	2	1	3	4	10	3
Dykhuis	4	2	1	3	4	7	4
Haller	4	2	1	3	2	4	6
Yushkevich	4	1	1	2	6	11	2
DiMaio	4	0	2	2	2	4	3
Fedyk	4	0	2	2	2	2	1
MacTavish	4	0	2	2	2	6	1
Semenov	4	1	0	1	0	2	2
Svoboda	4	0	1	1	4	5	2
Antoski	4	0	0	0	4	1	1
Hextall	4	0	0	0	2	0	E
Juhlin	4	0	0	0	0	4	1
Podein	4	0	0	0	4	2	1
Therien	4	0	0	0	2	7	1

Rangers	GP	G	A	PTS	PIM	S	+\-
Messier	4	1	5	6	6	12	-7
Leetch	4	4	1	5	2	24	-4
Zubov	4	1	4	5	0	10	-6
Verbeek	4	2	2	4	8	9	-7
Graves	4	0	2	2	4	13	-7
Kovalev	4	0	2	2	8	5	-2
Osborne	2	1	0	1	0	2	E
Nedved	4	1	0	1	2	9	-2
Larmer	4	0	1	1	2	3	-1
Nemchinov	4	0	1	1	0	3	-2
Karpovtsev	2	0	0	0	0	1	-1
LaFayette	2	0	0	0	0	0	-1
Norstrom	2	0	0	0	0	1	-1
Beukeboom	4	0	0	0	2	6	-4
Kocur	4	0	0	0	6	0	E
Kypreos	4	0	0	0	4	5	-1
Lowe	4	0	0	0	4	5	-5
Matteau	4	0	0	0	6	4	-2
Noonan	4	0	0	0	8	5	E
Wells	4	0	0	0	4	2	-1

GOALTENDING

	GP	MINS	GA	EN	AVG	W	L	T
Hextall	4	247	10	0	2.43	4	0	0

	GP	MINS	GA	EN	AVG	W	L	T
Healy	2	90	5	0	3.33	0	1	0
Richter	3	157	13	0	4.97	0	3	0

Flyers Power Play: 3-25 (12.0%)
Power Play Goals: LeClair, Brind'Amour, Dykhuis
Shorthanded Goals: Haller
Game-Winning Goals: Desjardins, Haller, Dineen, Dykhuis

Goals by Period:	1st	2nd	3rd	OT	Total
Flyers	4	9	3	2	18
Rangers	4	3	3	0	10

Rangers Power Play: 6-17 (35.3%)
Power Play Goals: Leetch (3), Zubov, Verbeek, Nedved
Shorthanded Goals: None
Game-Winning Goals: None

Shots by Period:	1st	2nd	3rd	OT	Total
Flyers	40	43	29	8	120
Rangers	38	42	36	3	119

RANGERS 1995 FINAL PLAYOFF SCORING

POS	NO.	PLAYER	GP	G	A	PTS	+/-	PIM	PP	SH	GW	OT	S	PCTG
D	2	Brian Leetch	10	6	8	14	1-	8	3	0	1	0	46	13.0
C	11	Mark Messier	10	3	10	13	11-	8	2	0	1	0	26	11.5
R	27	Alexei Kovalev	10	4	7	11	2	10	0	0	0	0	23	17.4
D	21	Sergei Zubov	10	3	8	11	9-	2	1	0	0	0	34	8.8
R	17	Pat Verbeek	10	4	6	10	8-	20	3	0	0	0	29	13.8
C	13	Sergei Nemchinov	10	4	5	9	6	2	0	0	1	0	16	25.0
C	9	Adam Graves	10	4	4	8	13-	8	2	0	0	0	38	10.5
C	10	Petr Nedved	10	3	2	5	4-	6	2	0	0	0	28	10.7
R	28	Steve Larmer	10	2	2	4	5-	6	0	1	1	1	14	14.3
L	19	Nick Kypreos	10	0	2	2	3	6	0	0	0	0	9	.0
L	20	Mark Osborne	7	1	0	1	1	2	0	0	0	0	2	50.0
D	25	A. Karpovtsev	8	1	0	1	1-	0	0	0	0	0	8	12.5
L	32	Stephane Matteau	9	0	1	1	1-	10	0	0	0	0	9	.0
D	4	Kevin Lowe	10	0	1	1	5-	12	0	0	0	0	7	.0
L	14	Troy Loney	1	0	0	0	0	0	0	0	0	0	0	.0
D	5	*Mattias Norstrom	3	0	0	0	1-	0	0	0	0	0	1	.0
G	30	Glenn Healy	5	0	0	0	0	0	0	0	0	0	0	.0
R	16	Brian Noonan	5	0	0	0	0	8	0	0	0	0	5	.0
G	35	Mike Richter	7	0	0	0	0	0	0	0	0	0	0	.0
C	22	Nathan LaFayette	8	0	0	0	1-	2	0	0	0	0	1	.0
D	23	Jeff Beukeboom	9	0	0	0	1	10	0	0	0	0	11	.0
R	26	Joe Kocur	10	0	0	0	0	8	0	0	0	0	1	.0
D	24	Jay Wells	10	0	0	0	4-	8	0	0	0	0	5	.0

GOALTENDING RECORDS

NO.	GOALTENDER	GPI	MINS	AVG	W	L	EN	SO	GA	SA	SV %	G	A	PIM
30	Glenn Healy	5	230	3.39	2	1	0	0	13	93	.860	0	0	0
35	Mike Richter	7	384	3.59	2	5	1	0	23	189	.878	0	0	0
	NYR TOTALS	10	616	3.60	4	6	1	0	37	283	.869			

*Indicates Rookie

1995 STANLEY CUP PLAYOFFS

STANLEY CUP FINALS
New Jersey vs. Detroit
(New Jersey wins series, 4-0)

Sat.	June 17	NJ	2	at DET	1
Tue.	June 20	NJ	4	at DET	2
Thu.	June 22	DET	2	at NJ	5
Sat.	June 24	DET	2	at NJ	5

CONFERENCE FINALS

EASTERN CONFERENCE
New Jersey vs. Philadelphia
(New Jersey wins series, 4-2)

Sat.	June 3	NJ	4	at PHI	1
Mon.	June 5	NJ	5	at PHI	2
Wed.	June 7	PHI	3	at NJ	2 (OT)
Sat.	June 10	PHI	4	at NJ	2
Sun.	June 11	NJ	3	at PHI	2
Tue.	June 13	PHI	2	at NJ	4

WESTERN CONFERENCE
Chicago vs. Detroit
(Detroit wins series, 4-1)

Thu.	June 1	CHI	1	at DET	2 (OT)
Sun.	June 4	CHI	2	at DET	3
Tue.	June 6	DET	4	at CHI	3 (2OT)
Thu.	June 8	DET	2	at CHI	5
Sun	June 11	CHI	1	at DET	2 (2OT)

CONFERENCE SEMIFINALS

EASTERN CONFERENCE
Rangers vs. Philadelphia
(Philadelphia wins series, 4-0)

Sun.	May 21	NY	4	at PHI	5 (OT)
Mon.	May 22	NY	3	at PHI	4 (OT)
Wed.	May 24	PHI	5	at NY	2
Fri.	May 26	PHI	4	at NY	1

WESTERN CONFERENCE
San Jose vs. Detroit
(Detroit wins series, 4-0)

Sun.	May 21	SJ	0	at DET	6
Tue.	May 23	SJ	2	at DET	6
Thu.	May 25	DET	6	at SJ	2
Sat.	May 27	DET	6	at SJ	2

New Jersey vs. Pittsburgh
(New Jersey wins series, 4-1)

Sat.	May 20	NJ	2	at PIT	3
Mon.	May 22	NJ	4	at PIT	2
Wed.	May 24	PIT	1	at NJ	5
Fri.	May 26	PIT	1	at NJ	2 (OT)
Sun.	May 28	NJ	4	at PIT	1

Vancouver vs. Chicago
(Chicago wins series, 4-0)

Sun.	May 21	VAN	1	at CHI	2 (OT)
Tue.	May 23	VAN	0	at CHI	2
Thu.	May 25	CHI	3	at VAN	2 (OT)
Sat.	May 27	CHI	4	at VAN	3 (OT)

CONFERENCE QUARTERFINALS

EASTERN CONFERENCE
Rangers vs. Quebec
(Rangers win series, 4-2)

Sat.	May 6	NY	4	at QUE	5
Mon.	May 8	NY	8	at QUE	3
Wed.	May 10	QUE	3	at NY	4
Fri.	May 12	QUE	2	at NY	3 (OT)
Sun.	May 14	NY	2	at QUE	4
Tue.	May 16	QUE	2	at NY	4

WESTERN CONFERENCE
Dallas vs. Detroit
(Detroit wins series, 4-1)

Sun.	May 7	DAL	3	at DET	4
Tue.	May 9	DAL	1	at DET	4
Thu.	May 11	DET	5	at DAL	1
Sun.	May 14	DET	1	at DAL	4
Mon.	May 15	DAL	1	at DET	3

Washington vs. Pittsburgh
(Pittsburgh wins series, 4-3)

Sat.	May 6	WSH 5	at PIT	4
Mon.	May 8	WSH 3	at PIT	5
Wed.	May 10	PIT	2	at WSH	6
Fri.	May 12	PIT	2	at WSH	6
Sun.	May 14	WSH 5	at PIT	6 (OT)
Tue.	May 16	PIT	7	at WSH	1
Thu.	May 18	WSH 0	at PIT	3

San Jose vs. Calgary
(San Jose wins series, 4-3)

Sun.	May 7	SJ	5	at CGY	4
Tue.	May 9	SJ	5	at CGY	4 (OT)
Thu.	May 11	CGY	9	at SJ	2
Sat.	May 13	CGY	6	at SJ	4
Mon.	May 15	SJ	0	at CGY	5
Wed.	May 17	CGY	3	at SJ	5
Fri.	May 19	SJ	5	at CGY	4 (2OT)

Buffalo vs. Philadelphia
(Philadelphia wins series, 4-1)

Sun.	May 7	BUF	3	at PHI	4 (OT)
Mon.	May 8	BUF	1	at PHI	3
Wed.	May 10	PHI	1	at BUF	3
Fri.	May 12	PHI	4	at BUF	2
Sun.	May 14	BUF	4	at PHI	6

Vancouver vs. St. Louis
(Vancouver wins series, 4-3)

Sun.	May 7	VAN	1	at STL	2
Tue.	May 9	VAN	5	at STL	3
Thu.	May 11	STL	1	at VAN	6
Sat.	May 13	STL	5	at VAN	2
Mon.	May 15	VAN	6	at STL	5 (OT)
Wed.	May 17	STL	8	at VAN	2
Fri.	May 19	VAN	5	at STL	3

New Jersey vs. Boston
(New Jersey wins series, 4-1)

Sun.	May 7	NJ	5	at BOS	0
Mon.	May 8	NJ	3	at BOS	0
Wed.	May 10	BOS	3	at NJ	2
Fri.	May 12	BOS	0	at NJ	1 (OT)
Sun.	May 14	NJ	3	at BOS	2

Toronto vs. Chicago
(Chicago wins series, 4-3)

Sun.	May 7	TOR	5	at CHI	3
Tue.	May 9	TOR	3	at CHI	0
Thu.	May 11	CHI	3	at TOR	2
Sat.	May 13	CHI	3	at TOR	1
Mon.	May 15	TOR	2	at CHI	4
Wed.	May 17	CHI	4	at TOR	5 (OT)
Fri.	May 19	TOR	2	at CHI	5

**BINGHAMTON
RANGERS**

George Burnett
Head Coach

George Burnett enters his first season with Binghamton after being named head coach on July 18, 1995. Burnett joins the Rangers after serving as Head Coach of the Edmonton Oilers last season.

Prior to joining the Oilers, Burnett served as Head Coach of Edmonton's AHL affiliate, the Cape Breton Oilers from 1992 through 1994. During his tenure, Burnett amassed a record of 68-67-25 and led the club to the Calder Cup Championship in 1992-93, posting a 14-2 playoff record.

Before entering the Oilers organization, Burnett was behind the bench as Head Coach of the Niagara Falls Thunder from 1989 through 1991, where he compiled a 97-66-15 record. He was awarded the Matt Leydon Trophy as Coach of the Year for the 1990-91 and 1991-92 seasons. George also served as an assistant coach with the Oshawa Generals of the Ontario Hockey League in 1989-90.

A graduate of McGill University, Burnett played three seasons with the Redman, and was named to the Canadian Interuniversity Athletic Union All-Canadian Team in 1982-83. He played 84 career games with McGill and broke the school's single-season scoring record, recording 81 points in 38 games during the 1982-83 season.

George and his wife reside in Binghamton, with their two children Hanna and Dylan.

Mike Busniuk
Assistant Coach

Mike Busniuk begins his third season with the Binghamton Rangers after being named assistant coach on September 2, 1993.

Busniuk, 45, joined the Rangers coaching staff after spending the previous two seasons as co-coach along with Bob McCammon of the Tri-City Americans of the Western Hockey League.

The native of Thunder Bay, Ontario played in 143 NHL matches with the Philadelphia Flyers from 1979-80 to 1980-81. He was originally drafted in 1971 by the Montreal Canadiens. Busniuk was a member of five Calder Cup Championship teams, two with the Nova Scotia Voyageurs in 1975-76 and 1976-77 and three with Maine in 1977-78, 1978-79 and 1983-84. A graduate

of Denver University, Busniuk finished his playing career spending three seasons in Italy.

Mike and his wife Jan spend the off-season in Thunder Bay with their three children, Jake, Katie and Molly.

BINGHAMTON RANGERS DIRECTORY

President ....James R. McCoy
Vice-President/Governor ....Robert W. Carr Jr.
Secretary/Treasurer/Alternate Governor ....Tom Mitchell
Managing Partner ....Tom Mitchell
General Manager/Alternate Governor ....Larry Pleau
Coach ....George Burnett
Assistant Coach..Mike Busniuk
Medical Trainer ....Chris Felix
Equipment Manager ....Mark Dumas
Vice-President Marketing/Communications..Patrick Snyder
Office Manager ....Sandra L. Wood
Director of Broadcasting..David Miller
Director of Merchandising ....Gary Foodim
Director of Sales/Sponsorship...Ron Mitchell
Administrative Assistant/Assistant Director of Ticketing..Darcie Kocan
Director of Group Sales/Promotions..Kirstin Berg
Administrative Assistant ....Tammy Zorn
Home Ice..Broome County Veterans Memorial Arena
Address..One Stuart Street
Binghamton, NY 13901

Seating Capacity...4,803
NHL Affiliation ....New York Rangers
Phone ....(607) 723-8937
Fax Number...(607) 724-6892

1995-96 BINGHAMTON RANGERS SCHEDULE

OCTOBER
Oct.	7	Carolina
Oct.	10	at Carolina
Oct.	11	at Carolina
Oct.	13	at Syracuse
Oct.	14	Rochester
Oct.	20	at Springfield
Oct.	21	at Hershey
Oct.	27	Providence
Oct.	28	Syracuse

NOVEMBER
Nov.	3	PEI
Nov.	4	PEI
Nov.	5	at Rochester
Nov.	10	Hershey
Nov.	11	Rochester
Nov.	17	Carolina
Nov.	18	Rochester
Nov.	19	at Hershey
Nov.	22	at Adirondack
Nov.	23	Carolina
Nov.	25	Baltimore

DECEMBER
Dec.	1	Hershey
Dec.	2	Baltimore
Dec.	6	at Baltimore
Dec.	8	at Carolina
Dec.	10	at Carolina
Dec.	13	at Baltimore
Dec.	15	at Providence
Dec.	16	Carolina
Dec.	20	at Adirondack
Dec.	22	at Syracuse
Dec.	23	Adirondack
Dec.	26	Baltimore
Dec.	29	at Carolina
Dec.	30	at Carolina
Dec.	31	Springfield

JANUARY
Jan.	3	at Baltimore
Jan.	5	Adirondack
Jan.	6	at Albany
Jan.	10	at Cornwall
Jan.	12	Hershey
Jan.	13	at Hershey
Jan.	14	Albany
Jan.	19	Cornwall
Jan.	20	Rochester
Jan.	21	at Hershey
Jan.	27	at PEI
Jan.	28	at PEI

FEBRUARY
Feb.	2	Albany
Feb.	3	Baltimore
Feb.	4	at Hershey
Feb.	7	at Albany
Feb.	9	at Rochester
Feb.	10	Syracuse
Feb.	17	at Portland
Feb.	18	Baltimore
Feb.	19	at Baltimore
Feb.	21	Albany
Feb.	23	at Rochester
Feb.	24	at Springfield
Feb.	25	Syracuse
Feb.	28	at Baltimore

MARCH
Mar.	1	at Syracuse
Mar.	3	Carolina
Mar.	8	Worcester
Mar.	9	Hershey
Mar.	13	Springfield
Mar.	15	at Worcester
Mar.	16	Cornwall
Mar.	17	at Syracuse
Mar.	20	at Hershey
Mar.	22	Hershey
Mar.	23	Portland
Mar.	24	at Rochester
Mar.	29	at Baltimore
Mar.	30	Syracuse

APRIL
Apr.	2	at Cornwall
Apr.	5	Hershey
Apr.	6	at Albany
Apr.	10	Carolina
Apr.	13	Baltimore

AMERICAN HOCKEY LEAGUE
1994-95 FINAL STANDINGS

SOUTHERN DIVISION

Team	GP	W	L	T	PTS	GF	GA
Binghamton	**80**	**43**	**30**	**7**	**93**	**302**	**261**
Cornwall	80	38	33	9	85	236	248
Hershey	80	34	36	10	78	275	300
Rochester	80	35	38	7	77	300	304
Syracuse	80	29	42	9	67	288	325

NORTHERN DIVISION

Team	GP	W	L	T	PTS	GF	GA
Albany	80	46	17	17	109	293	219
Portland	80	46	22	12	104	333	233
Providence	80	39	30	11	89	300	268
Adirondack	80	32	38	10	74	271	294
Springfield	80	31	37	12	74	269	289
Worcester	80	24	45	11	59	234	300

ATLANTIC DIVISION

Team	GP	W	L	T	PTS	GF	GA
PEI Senators	80	41	31	8	90	305	271
St. John's	80	33	37	10	76	263	263
Fredericton	80	35	40	5	75	274	288
Saint John, NB	80	27	40	13	67	250	286
Cape Breton	80	27	44	9	63	298	342

BINGHAMTON RANGERS FINAL SCORING

PLAYER	GP	G	A	PTS	PIM	PPG	SHG	GWG
Shawn McCosh	67	23	60	83	73	7	0	4
Jean-Yves Roy	67	41	36	77	28	12	1	7
Craig Duncanson	62	21	43	64	105	6	1	2
Dave Smith	77	20	40	60	225	6	3	4
Barry Richter	73	15	41	56	54	7	0	4
Ken Gernander	80	27	25	52	24	7	0	6
Darcy Werenka	73	18	29	47	12	10	1	1
Dmitri Starostenko	69	19	22	41	40	2	0	2
Jeff Nielsen	76	24	13	37	139	10	2	2
Andrei Kudinov	65	14	22	36	45	1	0	2
Jim Hiller	49	15	13	28	44	2	0	0
Mike McLaughlin	60	10	16	26	27	1	0	2
Pete Fiorentino	67	9	16	25	183	1	1	0
Darren Langdon	55	6	14	20	296	1	0	1
Mattias Norstrom	63	9	10	19	91	0	1	1
Scott Malone	48	3	14	17	85	0	0	0
Brad Rubachuk	30	6	8	14	54	0	0	1
Rob Kenny	17	2	9	11	32	0	0	1
Joby Messier	24	2	9	11	36	1	0	0
Chris Ferraro	13	6	4	10	38	0	0	1
Peter Ferraro	12	2	6	8	67	1	0	0
Shawn Reid	18	3	4	7	8	0	0	1
Eric Cairns	27	0	3	3	134	0	0	0
Sylvain Blouin	10	1	0	1	46	0	0	0
Andy Silverman	5	0	1	1	2	0	0	0
Jamie Ram	26	0	1	1	4	-	-	-
Corey Hirsch	57	0	1	1	10	-	-	-
Pavel Komarov	2	0	0	0	2	0	0	0
Jan Benda	4	0	0	0	0	0	0	0

GOALTENDING RECORDS

GOALTENDER	GP	W	L	T	MINS	GA	AVG
Corey Hirsch	57	31	20	5	3372	175	3.11
Jamie Ram	26	12	10	2	1472	81	3.30

BINGHAMTON RANGERS
PLAYOFF RESULTS

Binghamton defeated Rochester four games to one in the opening round of the American Hockey League Playoffs.

April 12	Binghamton 4, Rochester 3 at Binghamton
April 14	Binghamton 3, Rochester 1 at Binghamton
April 15	Binghamton 2, Rochester 3 at Rochester
April 19	Binghamton 8, Rochester 0 at Rochester
April 21*	Binghamton 4, Rochester 3 at Binghamton

The Rangers were defeated by the Cornwall Aces four games to two in the Southern Division Finals.

April 29*	Binghamton 4, Cornwall 5 at Binghamton
May 1	Binghamton 4, Cornwall 2 at Binghamton
May 3	Binghamton 0, Cornwall 2 at Cornwall
May 5	Binghamton 0, Cornwall 6 at Cornwall
May 7	Binghamton 3, Cornwall 2 at Binghamton
May 10	Binghamton 2, Cornwall 4 at Cornwall

*Overtime

BINGHAMTON RANGERS PLAYOFF SCORING

PLAYER	GP	G	A	PTS	PIM	PPG	SHG	GWG
Shawn McCosh	8	3	9	12	6	0	0	1
Jean-Yves Roy	11	4	6	10	12	0	0	0
Barry Richter	11	4	5	9	12	0	0	0
Craig Duncanson	11	4	4	8	16	3	0	0
Peter Ferraro	11	4	3	7	51	1	0	0
Darcy Werenka	11	4	3	7	2	2	0	2
Dave Smith	8	2	4	6	38	1	0	0
Brad Rubachuk	8	2	3	5	33	1	0	1
Chris Ferraro	10	2	3	5	16	0	0	0
Ken Gernander	11	2	2	4	6	2	0	0
Darren Langdon	11	1	3	4	84	0	0	0
Mike McLaughlin	8	0	3	3	0	0	0	0
Shawn Reid	10	0	3	3	6	0	0	0
Dmitri Starostenko	5	1	1	2	0	0	0	1
Eric Cairns	9	1	1	2	28	0	0	1
Scott Malone	11	0	2	2	12	0	0	0
Jamie Ram	11	0	2	2	2	-	-	-
Peter Fiorentino	2	0	1	1	11	0	0	0
Jon Hillebrandt	1	0	0	0	0	-	-	-
Joby Messier	1	0	0	0	0	0	0	0
Sylvain Blouin	2	0	0	0	24	0	0	0
Andrei Kudinov	3	0	0	0	0	0	0	0
Jeff Nielsen	7	0	0	0	22	0	0	0
Lee Sorochan	8	0	0	0	11	0	0	0

GOALTENDING RECORDS

GOALTENDER	GP	W	L	MINS	GA	AVG
Jamie Ram	11	6	5	664	29	2.62
Jon Hillebrandt	1	0	0	6	1	10.00

CAREER RECORDS

PLAYER CAREER RECORDS VS. NHL TEAMS

TEAM	Jeff Beukeboom				Bruce Driver				Ray Ferraro				Adam Graves				Alexander Karpovtsev				Joe Kocur			
	GP	G	A	PTS	GP	G	A	PTS	GP	G	A	PTS	GP	G	A	PTS	GP	G	A	PTS	GP	G	A	PTS
Anaheim	1	0	1	1	2	0	2	2	2	1	1	2	2	0	1	1	2	0	0	0	2	0	0	0
Boston	22	0	1	1	28	4	7	11	55	23	17	40	21	4	6	10	6	0	0	0	24	2	3	5
Buffalo	25	0	9	9	30	5	11	16	60	15	23	38	25	6	8	14	8	1	1	2	28	3	1	4
Calgary	34	2	7	9	23	2	6	8	24	9	6	15	25	5	4	9	1	0	0	0	20	4	1	5
Chicago	16	1	4	5	21	2	11	13	25	8	11	19	19	10	1	11	1	0	0	0	47	7	6	13
Colorado	19	2	5	7	30	6	18	24	56	23	24	47	20	9	7	16	5	1	0	1	26	3	1	4
Dallas	16	0	5	5	20	3	3	6	25	10	12	22	20	2	5	7	2	0	0	0	45	2	8	10
Detroit	20	0	2	2	21	4	5	9	25	14	14	28	13	6	2	8	2	0	0	0	7	3	0	3
Edmonton	5	0	1	1	21	4	10	14	25	11	9	20	9	3	0	3	2	0	1	1	18	3	3	6
Florida	9	2	0	2	7	0	3	3	8	3	1	4	9	3	2	5	7	1	0	1	9	1	0	1
Hartford	23	3	0	3	31	7	12	19	16	4	10	14	24	5	4	9	6	1	3	4	26	3	6	9
Los Angeles	35	2	7	9	24	3	15	18	25	7	10	17	23	3	3	6	2	0	0	0	25	1	2	3
Montreal	20	2	4	6	30	7	8	15	60	21	29	50	24	6	3	9	7	1	0	1	25	1	3	4
New Jersey	28	1	2	3	—	—	—	—	42	20	23	43	31	5	10	15	10	0	2	2	39	4	4	8
NY Islanders	28	2	4	6	57	5	32	37	16	2	8	10	29	14	10	24	8	0	3	3	28	3	1	4
Rangers	11	0	2	2	59	5	38	43	43	17	17	34	5	0	1	1	0	0	0	0	13	2	5	7
Ottawa	9	0	2	2	10	3	3	6	9	1	3	4	10	9	4	13	7	0	2	2	7	0	0	0
Philadelphia	30	0	1	1	56	3	28	31	42	15	17	32	31	11	9	20	8	0	2	2	30	3	2	5
Pittsburgh	28	0	5	5	62	6	42	48	38	16	18	34	31	11	10	21	7	0	1	1	31	1	2	3
St. Louis	20	0	8	8	24	3	8	11	27	8	15	23	19	3	6	9	2	1	0	1	47	4	2	6
San Jose	8	2	1	3	7	1	3	4	6	1	5	6	7	7	5	12	7	0	0	0	6	1	1	2
Tampa Bay	10	1	4	5	11	1	3	4	11	4	2	6	11	7	3	10	7	0	1	1	10	0	0	0
Toronto	16	0	1	1	22	3	11	14	25	12	12	24	17	3	4	7	2	0	2	2	54	12	10	22
Vancouver	37	1	8	9	26	1	13	14	26	5	8	13	25	5	11	16	2	0	1	1	19	2	2	4
Washington	34	2	3	5	57	4	15	19	42	12	12	24	36	13	11	24	8	1	4	5	36	3	3	6
Winnipeg	31	1	8	9	22	2	8	10	25	11	9	20	26	4	10	14	1	0	0	0	18	1	2	3
Totals	534	24	95	119	701	84	315	399	758	273	316	589	512	154	140	294	114	7	23	30	640	69	68	137

PLAYER CAREER RECORDS VS. NHL TEAMS

TEAM	Alexei Kovalev				Nick Kypreos				Daniel Lacroix				Nathan LaFayette				Darren Langdon				Brian Leetch			
	GP	G	A	PTS	GP	G	A	PTS	GP	G	A	PTS	GP	G	A	PTS	GP	G	A	PTS	GP	G	A	PTS
Anaheim	2	0	2	2	1	0	0	0	0	0	0	0	8	0	1	1	0	0	0	0	2	1	1	2
Boston	10	8	0	8	21	1	3	4	2	0	0	0	3	0	0	0	0	0	0	0	21	5	17	22
Buffalo	10	2	2	4	22	1	2	3	1	0	0	0	2	0	1	1	1	0	0	0	22	1	18	19
Calgary	4	0	3	3	10	1	1	2	0	0	0	0	3	0	0	0	0	0	0	0	15	4	6	10
Chicago	4	1	3	4	11	0	0	0	0	0	0	0	5	0	0	0	0	0	0	0	16	1	14	15
Colorado	10	1	3	4	18	4	3	7	2	0	0	0	2	1	0	1	2	0	0	0	20	7	18	25
Dallas	2	1	0	1	10	0	1	1	0	0	0	0	4	0	0	0	0	0	0	0	15	4	11	15
Detroit	3	1	0	1	10	2	0	2	0	0	0	0	6	2	0	2	0	0	0	0	16	6	10	16
Edmonton	3	1	1	2	10	2	4	6	0	0	0	0	5	1	2	3	0	0	0	0	15	3	9	12
Florida	9	2	2	4	5	0	1	1	3	0	0	0	1	0	0	0	2	0	0	0	9	1	5	6
Hartford	10	5	1	6	10	1	0	1	2	0	0	0	2	0	0	0	2	0	0	0	22	8	20	28
Los Angeles	3	1	2	3	10	3	1	4	0	0	0	0	7	0	3	3	0	0	0	0	14	3	10	13
Montreal	12	2	8	10	18	2	3	5	1	0	0	0	1	0	0	0	2	0	1	1	22	1	17	18
New Jersey	14	3	7	10	23	4	2	6	4	0	0	0	2	0	0	0	2	0	0	0	41	12	26	38
NY Islanders	16	4	5	9	24	4	4	8	1	0	0	0	4	0	0	0	1	0	0	0	38	8	24	32
Rangers	0	0	0	0	18	0	1	1	1	0	0	0	2	0	0	0	0	0	0	0	0	0	0	0
Ottawa	9	2	6	8	11	3	0	3	2	0	0	0	1	0	0	0	1	0	0	0	8	1	7	8
Philadelphia	14	4	2	6	28	2	3	5	3	1	0	1	2	0	0	0	2	0	0	0	39	13	26	39
Pittsburgh	11	2	3	5	20	1	3	4	3	0	0	0	2	0	0	0	0	0	0	0	35	10	40	50
St. Louis	4	1	1	2	10	0	2	2	0	0	0	0	0	0	0	0	0	0	0	0	15	0	13	13
San Jose	5	3	0	3	6	0	2	2	0	0	0	0	8	1	0	1	0	0	0	0	5	2	5	7
Tampa Bay	12	5	5	10	7	2	0	2	1	0	0	0	1	0	0	0	1	0	0	0	12	2	6	8
Toronto	2	3	1	4	12	0	1	1	0	0	0	0	7	0	0	0	0	0	0	0	14	1	12	13
Vancouver	4	0	3	3	9	0	0	0	0	0	0	0	3	0	0	0	0	0	0	0	13	7	12	19
Washington	15	3	6	9	11	1	1	2	2	0	0	0	2	2	1	3	2	0	1	1	40	9	31	40
Winnipeg	1	1	0	1	11	4	0	4	0	0	0	0	5	2	1	3	0	0	0	0	16	.2	17	19
Totals	189	56	66	122	346	39	37	76	28	1	0	1	88	7	8	15	18	1	1	2	485	112	375	487

PLAYER CAREER RECORDS VS. NHL TEAMS

TEAM	Doug Lidster				Kevin Lowe				Stephane Matteau				Mark Messier				Sergei Nemchinov				Mattias Norstrom			
	GP	G	A	PTS	GP	G	A	PTS	GP	G	A	PTS	GP	G	A	PTS	GP	G	A	PTS	GP	G	A	PTS
Anaheim	4	1	0	1	1	0	0	0	3	1	0	1	2	2	0	2	2	0	0	0	0	0	0	0
Boston	25	1	9	10	47	1	11	12	11	2	3	5	45	8	34	42	14	2	3	5	1	0	0	0
Buffalo	26	4	12	16	48	4	13	17	13	1	1	2	47	20	35	55	15	6	9	15	0	0	0	0
Calgary	71	5	32	37	97	6	28	34	8	2	4	6	82	32	63	95	6	2	0	2	0	0	0	0
Chicago	32	4	7	11	43	4	16	20	3	1	0	1	41	17	38	55	6	2	1	3	1	0	0	0
Colorado	30	0	11	11	44	4	14	18	12	3	4	7	48	20	36	56	14	2	5	7	2	0	1	1
Dallas	31	3	14	17	35	2	12	14	18	2	4	6	40	14	32	46	6	3	1	4	0	0	0	0
Detroit	28	2	8	10	41	7	11	18	17	5	3	8	39	24	35	59	7	2	2	4	0	0	0	0
Edmonton	68	9	17	26	4	0	0	0	18	5	1	6	6	3	3	6	5	1	0	1	0	0	0	0
Florida	2	0	0	0	7	1	0	1	7	0	2	2	7	3	1	4	9	2	1	3	4	0	2	2
Hartford	24	3	9	12	45	3	9	12	10	3	4	7	43	20	34	54	12	4	5	9	1	0	1	1
Los Angeles	67	5	19	24	94	5	32	37	16	1	3	4	86	43	67	110	6	2	4	6	0	0	0	0
Montreal	26	5	9	14	47	0	8	8	10	2	1	3	50	23	25	48	14	4	5	9	0	0	0	0
New Jersey	24	0	10	10	58	3	22	25	11	2	1	3	59	27	41	68	24	11	11	22	1	0	0	0
NY Islanders	25	0	10	10	49	2	16	18	13	3	3	6	56	20	38	58	22	3	3	6	2	0	0	0
Rangers	24	3	5	8	38	1	11	12	8	1	6	7	35	16	26	42	0	0	0	0	0	0	0	0
Ottawa	3	0	0	0	7	1	2	3	7	0	1	1	10	4	12	16	9	3	5	8	0	0	0	0
Philadelphia	27	0	7	7	47	3	7	10	11	4	4	8	57	21	35	56	21	6	10	16	0	0	0	0
Pittsburgh	26	3	12	15	50	4	22	26	10	2	2	4	55	22	58	80	20	6	5	11	1	0	0	0
St. Louis	25	1	10	11	42	6	11	17	13	2	4	6	39	19	36	55	7	2	6	8	0	0	0	0
San Jose	13	3	1	4	11	0	3	3	10	1	3	4	7	3	5	8	7	4	5	9	0	0	0	0
Tampa Bay	5	0	2	2	8	0	4	4	9	1	4	5	12	5	9	14	12	4	2	6	1	0	0	0
Toronto	27	5	10	15	38	3	6	9	17	2	6	8	39	11	34	45	5	1	0	1	1	0	1	1
Vancouver	3	0	1	1	97	4	28	32	16	3	3	6	85	56	70	126	5	2	0	2	0	0	0	0
Washington	27	0	7	7	47	5	14	19	10	4	0	4	58	17	45	62	23	7	6	13	2	0	0	0
Winnipeg	74	10	29	39	85	13	30	43	18	5	2	7	79	42	65	107	6	1	3	4	1	0	0	0
Totals	737	67	251	318	1130	82	330	412	299	58	69	127	1127	492	877	1369	277	82	92	174	18	0	5	5

PLAYER CAREER RECORDS VS. NHL TEAMS

TEAM	Wayne Presley GP	G	A	PTS	Luc Robitaille GP	G	A	PTS	Ulf Samuelsson GP	G	A	PTS	Pat Verbeek GP	G	A	PTS
Anaheim	2	0	0	0	6	2	3	5	2	0	0	0	2	0	2	2
Boston	28	9	6	15	26	15	16	31	60	5	16	21	58	16	26	42
Buffalo	14	4	2	6	26	17	12	29	57	5	17	22	59	22	26	48
Calgary	21	5	11	16	60	43	42	85	25	2	10	12	29	14	4	18
Chicago	6	1	4	5	27	11	11	22	24	3	8	11	29	7	11	18
Colorado	32	8	8	16	24	28	14	42	61	2	12	14	58	23	28	51
Dallas	43	10	7	17	25	15	14	29	22	2	6	8	31	16	11	27
Detroit	45	14	8	22	24	18	26	44	20	1	4	5	31	16	12	28
Edmonton	17	6	4	10	60	38	44	82	24	1	7	8	30	22	10	32
Florida	6	1	0	1	5	2	2	4	7	1	0	1	9	2	5	7
Hartford	34	11	7	18	26	28	17	45	15	1	5	6	17	8	7	15
Los Angeles	22	4	3	7	—	—	—	—	25	1	6	7	30	16	12	28
Montreal	33	9	0	9	25	15	10	25	62	2	19	21	53	15	23	38
New Jersey	24	5	4	9	25	11	12	23	37	2	4	6	20	9	9	18
NY Islanders	31	6	12	18	24	9	16	25	38	1	18	19	65	28	25	53
Rangers	26	2	4	6	25	11	15	26	39	1	14	15	58	27	18	45
Ottawa	16	3	4	7	8	3	7	10	13	3	8	11	15	6	10	16
Philadelphia	23	5	7	12	25	14	8	22	38	2	10	12	59	23	18	41
Pittsburgh	25	11	4	15	22	12	22	34	17	1	13	14	61	22	29	51
St. Louis	36	12	9	21	25	16	13	29	6	1	5	6	7	1	4	5
San Jose	4	0	2	2	20	14	14	28	25	0	10	10	32	12	12	24
Tampa Bay	9	3	2	5	8	3	7	10	9	0	2	2	9	4	6	10
Toronto	41	4	13	17	26	17	18	35	27	2	6	8	30	20	10	30
Vancouver	23	2	4	6	60	32	39	71	26	2	11	13	30	7	15	22
Washington	23	5	6	11	26	14	17	31	36	0	6	6	61	26	15	41
Winnipeg	20	9	8	17	58	27	31	58	25	1	10	11	32	10	19	29
Totals	604	149	139	288	686	415	430	845	740	42	227	269	915	372	367	739

CAREER BREAKDOWN OF CURRENT RANGERS GOALIES VS. OPPOSITION

GLENN HEALY

TEAM	GP	MINS	GA	SO	AVG	W	L	T
Anaheim	1	59	3	0	3.05	0	1	0
Boston	17	944	57	1	3.62	5	10	2
Buffalo	12	692	39	1	3.38	7	3	1
Calgary	14	721	50	0	4.16	6	6	1
Chicago	10	596	36	0	3.62	3	7	0
Colorado	16	869	45	0	3.11	6	7	2
Dallas	11	559	37	0	3.97	5	4	0
Detroit	9	457	26	0	3.41	3	3	2
Edmonton	14	672	56	0	5.00	3	8	1
Florida	2	89	5	0	3.37	1	1	0
Hartford	9	534	34	0	3.82	4	3	1
Los Angeles	6	356	27	0	4.55	0	6	0
Montreal	8	447	22	0	2.95	2	5	1
New Jersey	21	1189	60	1	3.03	9	5	5
NY Islanders	7	306	20	0	3.92	1	4	0
Rangers	21	1193	72	0	3.62	11	7	1
Ottawa	4	239	11	0	2.76	3	1	0
Philadelphia	22	1230	71	1	3.46	9	9	3
Pittsburgh	16	892	65	0	4.37	4	9	2
St. Louis	10	536	37	0	4.14	3	5	1
San Jose	3	180	7	1	2.33	3	0	0
Tampa Bay	7	388	15	0	2.32	5	1	1
Toronto	10	603	29	0	2.89	6	3	1
Vancouver	15	874	43	2	2.95	8	6	1
Washington	26	1386	89	1	3.85	10	13	1
Winnipeg	14	680	45	0	3.97	4	7	1
Totals	305	16691	1001	8	3.60	121	134	28

MIKE RICHTER

TEAM	GP	MINS	GA	SO	AVG	W	L	T
Anaheim	2	59	4	0	4.07	0	1	0
Boston	8	451	16	1	2.13	4	2	1
Buffalo	13	751	35	1	2.80	8	4	1
Calgary	8	408	28	0	4.12	1	3	2
Chicago	5	304	16	0	3.16	2	2	1
Colorado	12	586	38	0	3.89	5	4	0
Dallas	7	429	14	1	1.96	4	1	2
Detroit	7	311	22	0	4.24	2	3	0
Edmonton	6	365	11	1	1.81	5	0	1
Florida	8	453	13	2	1.72	4	2	1
Hartford	15	902	42	1	2.79	10	4	1
Los Angeles	8	445	18	0	2.43	7	0	7
Montreal	9	547	31	0	3.40	3	3	2
New Jersey	17	958	38	1	2.38	11	4	1
NY Islanders	21	1093	62	0	3.40	5	9	4
Rangers	—	—	—	—	—	—	—	—
Ottawa	7	428	13	1	1.82	7	0	0
Philadelphia	19	1107	59	0	3.20	10	6	2
Pittsburgh	19	1050	74	0	4.23	4	13	1
St. Louis	8	486	22	1	2.72	4	3	1
San Jose	4	246	10	0	2.44	3	0	1
Tampa Bay	6	277	20	0	4.33	2	2	0
Toronto	7	430	21	0	2.93	4	1	2
Vancouver	5	305	13	0	2.56	4	0	1
Washington	25	1390	79	1	3.41	13	10	0
Winnipeg	4	239	8	0	2.01	3	1	0
Totals	250	14020	707	11	3.03	125	78	25

LIFETIME SHUTOUTS OF CURRENT RANGER GOALIES

DATE		OPPONENT	SITE	SCORE	SAVES
GLENN HEALY					
(one with Los Angeles, four with Islanders, three with Rangers)					
Feb. 22,	1988	Vancouver	Vancouver	2-0	13
Jan. 16,	1990	Vancouver	Nassau Coliseum	3-0	51
Feb. 4,	1990	Buffalo	Buffalo	1-0	39
Apr. 15,	1992	New Jersey	Nassau Coliseum	7-0	22
Mar. 6,	1993	San Jose	San Jose	6-0	26
Dec. 23,	1993	Washington	Washington	1-0	20
Feb. 3,	1994	Boston	Boston	3-0	28
Apr. 30,	1995	Philadelphia	Philadelphia	2-0	24
MIKE RICHTER					
Apr. 7,	1991	Washington (Play.)	Washington	6-0	37
Nov. 23,	1991	St. Louis	St. Louis	3-0	24
Dec. 8,	1991	Boston	MSG	4-0	30
Dec. 23,	1991	New Jersey	MSG	3-0	25
Apr. 25,	1992	New Jersey (Play.)	Meadowlands	3-0	33
Feb. 27,	1993	Edmonton	Edmonton	1-0	29
Nov. 13,	1993	Washington	Washington	2-0	21
Dec. 13,	1993	Buffalo	MSG	2-0	28
Feb. 18,	1994	Ottawa	MSG	3-0	24
Mar. 16,	1994	Hartford	MSG	4-0	27
Apr. 1,	1994	Dallas	MSG	3-0	28
Apr. 17,	1994	Islanders (Play.)	MSG	6-0	21
Apr. 18,	1994	Islanders (Play.)	MSG	6-0	29
May 5,	1994	Washington (Play.)	Washington	3-0	21
May 17,	1994	New Jersey (Play.)	MSG	3-0	16
Feb. 28,	1995	Florida	MSG	0-0	23
Apr. 5,	1995	Florida	Florida	5-0	17

Career Assists and Penalty Minutes
of Current Rangers Goalies

	HEALY			**RICHTER**	
	ASSISTS	PIM		ASSISTS	PIM
1985-86	0	0	1989-90	3	0
1987-88	2	6	1990-91	1	4
1988-89	1	28	1991-92	0	6
1989-90	1	7	1992-93	5	2
1990-91	2	14	1993-94	0	2
1991-92	1	18	1994-95	0	2
1992-93	2	2	TOTALS	9	16
1993-94	2	2			
1994-95	2	2			
TOTALS	13	79			

Glenn Healy

Mike Richter

LIFETIME HAT TRICKS BY CURRENT RANGERS

DATE	OPPONENT	SITE	GOALTENDER
RAY FERRARO (5 with Hartford, 3 with Islanders)			
Mar. 23, 1995	Boston	Hartford	Pete Peeters
Mar. 29, 1985	Edmonton	Hartford	Andy Moog (1), Grant Fuhr (2)
Feb. 18, 1987	New Jersey	New Jersey	Alain Chevrier
Nov. 26, 1988	Quebec	Quebec	Mario Gosselin
Dec. 9, 1989	New Jersey	Hartford	Sean Burke
Dec. 10, 1991	St. Louis	Nassau Coliseum	Curtis Joseph
Jan. 7, 1992	Detroit	Detroit	Tim Cheveldae
*Apr. 26, 1993	Washington (4 goals)	Washington	Don Beaupre
ADAM GRAVES (3 with Rangers, 1 with Detroit)			
Dec. 14, 1989	Chicago	Chicago	Alain Chevrier
Feb. 14, 1992	Islanders	MSG	Mark Fitzpatrick
Nov. 25, 1992	Pittsburgh	Pittsburgh	Tom Barrasso (1), Ken Wregget (2)
Feb. 2, 1994	Islanders	MSG	Ron Hextall
Jan. 30, 1995	Ottawa	MSG	Don Beaupre
ALEXEI KOVALEV			
Dec. 27, 1992	Boston	MSG	Andy Moog
MARK MESSIER (16 with Edmonton, 4 with Rangers)			
Mar. 16, 1981	Pittsburgh	Edmonton	Greg Millen
Dec. 2, 1981	Quebec	Quebec	Dan Bouchard
Feb. 17, 1982	Minnesota	Edmonton	Don Beaupre
Dec. 19, 1982	Montreal (4 goals)	Edmonton	Richard Sevigny 3,ENG
Jan. 19, 1983	Vancouver	Edmonton	Richard Brodeur
*Apr. 14, 1983	Calgary (4 goals)	Edmonton	Rejean Lemelin
*Apr. 17, 1983	Calgary	Calgary	Rejean Lemelin (1), Don Edwards (2)
*Apr. 26, 1983	Chicago	Edmonton	Murrary Bannerman
Feb. 25, 1983	Toronto	Edmonton	Allan Bester
Mar. 11, 1984	Vancouver	Edmonton	John Garrett
Feb. 26, 1986	Winnipeg	Winnipeg	Brian Hayward
Feb. 14, 1988	Vancouver	Edmonton	Frank Caprice
Feb. 21, 1989	Hartford (4 goals)	Edmonton	Mike Luit 3, ENG
Nov. 21,1989	Vancouver	Edmonton	Kirk McLean
Jan. 17, 1990	Winnipeg	Edmonton	Bob Essensa
Mar. 3, 1990	Philadelphia (4 goals)	Edmonton	Ron Hextall
Nov. 19, 1991	Vancouver	Vancouver	Kirk McLean
Dec. 13, 1991	Washington	Washington	Don Beaupre 2, ENG
Mar. 22, 1992	New Jersey	MSG	Chad Erickson
*May 25, 1994	New Jersey	New Jersey	Martin Brodeur 2, ENG
SERGEI NEMCHINOV			
Jan. 29, 1993	Buffalo	Buffalo	Tom Draper

LIFETIME HAT TRICKS BY CURRENT RANGERS

WAYNE PRESLEY (2 with Chicago)

Nov. 11, 1987	Detroit	Chicago	Greg Stefan
*Apr. 13, 1989	Detroit	Chicago	Greg Stefan (1), Glen Hanlon (2)

LUC ROBITAILLE (12 with Los Angeles, 1 with Pittsburgh)

Dec. 9, 1986	Islanders	Nassau Coliseum	Billy Smith
Dec. 30, 1987	Winnipeg	Los Angeles	Daniel Berthiaume (2), Eldon Reddick (1)
Feb. 11, 1988	Quebec	Los Angeles	Mario Gosselin
Apr. 3, 1988	Edmonton	Los Angeles	Grant Fuhr
Oct. 6, 1988	Detroit	Los Angeles	Greg Stefan
Nov. 25, 1989	Vancouver	Los Angeles	Steve Weeks
Mar. 10, 1990	Pittsburgh	Los Angeles	Alain Chevier (2), Frank Pietrangelo (1)
*Apr. 26, 1991	Edmonton	Los Angeles	Grant Fuhr
Feb 6, 1992	Hartford (4 goals)	Los Angeles	Kay Whitmore
Nov. 8, 1992	San Jose	San Jose	Arturs Irbe
Mar. 2, 1993	Calgary	Los Angeles	Jeff Reese
Nov. 25, 1993	Quebec (4 goals)	Quebec	Jocelyn Thibault
Feb. 16, 1995	Hartford (4 goals)	Pittsburgh	Jeff Reese

PAT VERBEEK (5 with New Jersey, 4 with Hartford)

Mar. 9, 1986	Philadelphia	New Jersey	Bob Froese (2), Darren Jensen (1)
Mar. 25, 1987	Rangers	MSG	John Vanbiesbrouck(1), Bob Froese (2)
Jan. 10, 1988	Philadelphia	Philadelphia	Mark LaForest
Feb. 28, 1988	Minnesota	Minnesota	Don Beaupre
Feb. 13, 1989	Toronto	Toronto	Allan Bester
Feb. 20, 1993	Edmonton	Hartford	Bill Ranford
Feb. 28, 1993	Islanders	Hartford	Mark Fitzpatrick
Oct. 14, 1993	Chicago	Chicago	Ed Belfour (2), Jeff Hackett (1)
Dec. 7, 1993	Washington	Washington	Rick Tabaracci (2), Don Beaupre (1)

*Playoff hat trick

Pat Verbeek has registered nine hat tricks in his career.

ALL-STAR GAME APPEARANCES

(Current Rangers only)

RAY FERRARO

Season	Club	GP	G	A	PTS
1991-92	Wales All-Stars	1	0	0	0

ADAM GRAVES

Season	Club	GP	G	A	PTS
1993-94	Eastern All-Stars	1	0	2	2

BRIAN LEETCH

Season	Club	GP	G	A	PTS
1989-90	Wales All-Stars	1	0	0	0
1990-91	Wales All-Stars	1	0	0	0
1991-92	Wales All-Stars	1	0	0	0
1992-93	Wales All-Stars	Injured			
1993-94	Eastern All-Stars	1	0	0	0
	Totals	4	0	0	0

KEVIN LOWE

Season	Club	GP	G	A	PTS
1983-84	Campbell All-Stars	1	0	0	0
1984-85	Campbell All-Stars	1	0	0	0
1985-86	Campbell All-Stars	1	0	0	0
1987-88	Campbell All-Stars	1	0	1	1
1988-89	Campbell All-Stars	1	0	0	0
1989-90	Campbell All-Stars	1	0	0	0
1992-93	Wales All-Stars	1	0	1	1
	Totals	7	0	2	2

MARK MESSIER

Season	Club	GP	G	A	PTS
1981-82	Campbell All-Stars	1	0	0	0
1982-83	Campbell All-Stars	1	0	3	3
1983-84	Campbell All-Stars	1	0	0	0
1985-86	Campbell All-Stars	1	0	0	0
1986-87	NHL All-Stars	1	1	0	1
1987-88	Campbell All-Stars	1	0	0	0
1988-89	Campbell All-Stars	1	1	1	2
1989-90	Campbell All-Stars	1	1	0	1
1990-91	Campbell All-Stars	1	0	1	1
1991-92	Wales All-Stars	1	0	1	1
1992-93	Wales All-Stars	Injured			
1993-94	Eastern All-Stars	1	1	2	3
	Totals	11	4	8	12

MIKE RICHTER

Season	Club	GP	MINS	GA	GAA
1991-92	Wales All-Stars	1	20	2	6.00
1993-94	Eastern All-Stars	1	20	2	6.00
	Totals	2	40	4	6.00

LUC ROBITAILLE

Season	Club	GP	MINS	GA	GAA
1987-88	Campbell All-Stars	1	2	1	3
1988-89	Campbell All-Stars	1	1	1	2
1989-90	Campbell All-Stars	1	2	0	2
1990-91	Campbell All-Stars	1	0	0	0
1991-92	Campbell All-Stars	1	0	3	3
1992-93	Campbell All-Stars	1	0	0	0
	Totals	6	5	5	10

ULF SAMUELSSON

Season	Club	GP	G	A	PTS
1986-87	NHL All-Stars	1	0	0	0

PAT VERBEEK

Season	Club	GP	G	A	PTS
1990-91	Wales All-Stars	1	0	1	1

CAREER GOAL BREAKDOWN AND SCORING STREAKS OF CURRENT RANGERS

JEFF BEUKEBOOM

SEASON	PPG	SHG	GWG
1986-87	1	0	1
1987-88	1	0	1
1988-89	0	0	0
1989-90	0	0	0
1990-91	0	0	0
1991-92	0	0	0
1992-93	0	0	0
1993-94	1	0	0
1994-95	0	0	0
Totals	3	0	2

Last PPG: 1/3/94 vs. Fla. (Vanbiesbrouck)
Last SHG: None
Last GWG: 1/6/88 at Hfd. (Liut)
Last 2-Goal Game: None
Longest Point Scoring Streak: 4, 1/11-1/18/88 (1 goal, 3 assists)
Longest Goal Scoring Streak: 2, 11/25-11/27/88 (2 goals)
Longest Assist Streak: 3, (many) last- 10/29-11/2/92 (3 assists)

RAY FERRARO

SEASON	PPG	SHG	GWG
1984-85	6	0	2
1985-86	14	0	0
1986-87	14	0	2
1987-88	6	0	2
1988-89	11	0	7
1989-90	7	0	4
1990-91	6	0	1
1991-92	7	0	4
1992-93	3	0	1
1993-94	5	0	3
1994-95	2	0	1
Totals	81	0	27

Last PPG: 4/4/95 vs. Wsh. (Carey)
Last SHG: None
Last GWG: 2/2/95 at Phi. (Roussel)
Last 2-Goal Game: 4/28/95 at NYR (Richter)
Longest Point Scoring Streak: 10, 2/9-2/28/89 (11 points, 6 assists)
Longest Goal Scoring Streak: 7, 2/9-2/23/89 (9 goals)
Longest Assist Streak: 5, (3 times) last- 3/24-4/2/88 (6 assists)

BRUCE DRIVER

SEASON	PPG	SHG	GWG
1983-84	0	0	0
1984-85	3	1	0
1985-86	1	0	1
1986-87	0	0	0
1987-88	7	0	0
1988-89	1	0	0
1989-90	1	0	0
1990-91	7	0	2
1991-92	3	1	1
1992-93	6	0	0
1993-94	3	1	0
1994-95	1	0	1
Totals	33	3	5

Last PPG: 3/10/95 at T.B. (Puppa)
Last SHG: 1/29/94 at Van. (Whitmore)
Last GWG: 4/5/95 at Ott. (Billington)
Last 2-Goal Game: 2/5/95 vs. Pit. (Wregget)
Longest Point Scoring Streak: 6, 1/21 - 2/1/88 (1 goal, 7 assists)
Longest Goal Scoring Streak: 2, (9 times) last- 2/4 - 2/5/94 (2 goals)
Longest Assist Streak: 6, 1/21 - 2/1/88 (7 assists)

ADAM GRAVES

SEASON	PPG	SHG	GWG
1987-88	0	0	1
1988-89	0	0	0
1989-90	0	0	0
1990-91	2	0	1
1991-92	4	4	4
1992-93	12	1	6
1993-94	20	4	4
1994-95	9	0	3
Totals	47	9	19

Last PPG: 4/24/95 vs. Wsh. (Carey)
Last SHG: 11/10/93 vs. Wpg. (Essensa)
Last GWG: 4/26/95 vs. TB (Puppa)
Last 2-Goal Game: 4/26/95 vs. TB (Puppa)
Longest Point Scoring Streak: 5, (3 times) last- 1/25-2/2/94 (4 goals, 4 assists)
Longest Goal Scoring Streak: 4, (4 times) last- 11/16-11/24/93 (5 goals)
Longest Assist Streak: 4, (3 times) last- 2/28-3/5/94 (4 assists)

ALEXANDER KARPOVTSEV

SEASON	PPG	SHG	GWG
1993-94	1	0	1
1994-95	1	0	1
Totals	2	0	2

Last PPG: 1/21/95 vs. Mtl. (Roy)
Last SHG: None
Last GWG: 2/21/95 at Fla. (Vanbiesbrouck)
Last 2-Goal Game: None
Longest Point Scoring Streak: 3, 3/1-3/5/95 (4 assists)
Longest Goal Scoring Streak: One
Longest Assist Streak: 3, 3/1-3/5/95 (4 assists)

CAREER GOAL BREAKDOWN AND SCORING STREAKS OF CURRENT RANGERS

JOE KOCUR

SEASON	PPG	SHG	GWG
1984-85	0	0	0
1985-86	2	0	0
1986-87	2	0	2
1987-88	0	0	1
1988-89	1	0	1
1989-90	1	0	5
1990-91	0	0	0
1991-92	0	0	2
1992-93	1	0	0
1993-94	0	0	0
1994-95	0	0	0
Totals	7	0	11

Last PPG: 12/2/92 vs. Det. (Cheveldae)
Last SHG: None
Last GWG: 11/23/91 at StL. (Joseph)
Last 2-Goal Game: 12/6/91 at Det. (Cheveldae)
Longest Point Scoring Streak: 3, (4 times) last-1/27-2/2/90 (4 goals, 3 assists)
Longest Goal Scoring Streak: 3, 1/27-2/2/90 (4 goals)
Longest Assist Streak: 2, (4 times) last-12/17-12/19/92 (3 assists)

ALEXEI KOVALEV

SEASON	PPG	SHG	GWG
1992-93	3	0	3
1993-94	7	0	3
1994-95	1	1	1
Totals	11	1	7

Last PPG: 2/24/95 vs. Hfd. (Burke)
Last SHG: 4/7/95 vs. NYI (Soderstrom)
Last GWG: 4/1/95 at Bos. (Lacher)
Last 2-Goal Game: 4/5/95 at Fla. (Vanbiesbrouck)
Longest Point Scoring Streak: 11, 3/16-4/8/94 (10 goals, 5 assists)
Longest Goal Scoring Streak: 4, 3/27-4/2/94 (5 goals)
Longest Assist Streak: 4, (3 times) last- 3/3-3/8/95 (4 assists)

NICK KYPREOS

SEASON	PPG	SHG	GWG
1989-90	0	0	2
1990-91	0	0	3
1991-92	0	0	0
1992-93	0	0	2
1993-94	0	0	1
1994-95	0	0	0
Totals	0	0	8

Last PPG: None
Last SHG: None
Last GWG: 2/14/94 at Que. (Fiset)
Last 2-Goal Game: 2/12/93 vs. Wpg. (Essensa)
Longest Point Scoring Streak: 3, (4 times) last-12/3-12/9/92 (2 goals, 1 assist)
Longest Goal Scoring Streak: 2, (6 times) last-3/16-3/19/93 (2 goals)
Longest Assist Streak: 2, 3/2-3/4/94 (2 assists)

DANIEL LACROIX

SEASON	PPG	SHG	GWG
1993-94	0	0	0
1994-95	0	0	0
Totals	0	0	0

Last PPG: None
Last SHG: None
Last GWG: None
Last 2-Goal Game: None
Longest Point Scoring Streak: One
Longest Goal Scoring Streak: One
Longest Assist Streak: None

NATHAN LaFAYETTE

SEASON	PPG	SHG	GWG
1993-94	0	0	0
1994-95	0	1	0
Totals	0	1	0

Last PPG: None
Last SHG: 4/1/95 vs. Edm. (Ranford)
Last GWG: None
Last 2-Goal Game: None
Longest Point Scoring Streak: 3, 3/29-4/1/95 (1 goal, 2 assists)
Longest Goal Scoring Streak: One
Longest Assist Streak: 2, (twice) last- 3/29-3/31/95 (2 assists)

DARREN LANGDON

SEASON	PPG	SHG	GWG
1994-95	0	0	0
Totals	0	0	0

Last PPG: None
Last SHG: None
Last GWG: None
Last 2-Goal Game: None
Longest Point Scoring Streak: One
Longest Goal Scoring Streak: One
Longest Assist Streak: One

BRIAN LEETCH

SEASON	PPG	SHG	GWG
1987-88	1	0	1
1988-89	8	3	1
1989-90	5	0	2
1990-91	6	0	4
1991-92	10	1	3
1992-93	2	1	1
1993-94	17	1	4
1994-95	3	0	2
Totals	52	6	18

Last PPG: 4/30/95 at Phi. (Roussel)
Last SHG: 3/25/94 at Van. (Whitmore)
Last GWG: 4/30/95 at Phi. (Roussel)
Last 2-Goal Game: 4/30/95 at Phi. (Roussel)
Longest Point Scoring Streak: 17, 11/23-12/31/91 (5 goals, 24 assists)
Longest Goal Scoring Streak: 3, (many) last-3/29-4/2/94 (3 goals)
Longest Assist Streak: 15, 11/29-12/31/91 (23 assists)

CAREER GOAL BREAKDOWN AND SCORING STREAKS OF CURRENT RANGERS

DOUG LIDSTER

SEASON	PPG	SHG	GWG
1983-84	0	0	0
1984-85	2	0	0
1985-86	1	1	0
1986-87	3	0	0
1987-88	2	1	0
1988-89	3	0	0
1989-90	1	0	0
1990-91	4	0	1
1991-92	3	0	2
1992-93	3	0	0
1993-94	0	0	0
1994-95	1	0	0
Totals	23	2	3

Last PPG: 4/11/95 vs. Wpg. (Cheveldae)
Last SHG: 3/3/88 vs. Wpg. (Berthiaume)
Last GWG: 4/11/92 vs. L.A. (Weeks)
Last 2-Goal Game: 1/7/90 at Mtl. (Hayward)
Longest Point Scoring Streak: 8, 12/11-12/27/86
 (2 goals, 11 assists)
Longest Goal Scoring Streak: 2 (4 times) last -
 11/3-11/6/90 (2 goals)
Longest Assist Streak: 8, 12/11-12/27/86
 (11 assists)

KEVIN LOWE

SEASON	PPG	SHG	GWG
1979-80	2	0	0
1980-81	4	0	2
1981-82	1	1	2
1982-83	1	0	0
1983-84	1	0	1
1984-85	1	0	1
1985-86	0	0	0
1986-87	2	2	1
1987-88	2	1	2
1988-89	0	0	1
1989-90	2	1	0
1990-91	0	0	0
1991-92	0	0	0
1992-93	0	0	0
1993-94	0	0	1
1994-95	1	0	0
Totals	17	5	11

Last PPG: 4/16/95 at Islanders (Soderstrom)
Last SHG: 1/17/90 vs. Wpg. (Essensa)
Last GWG: 1/16/94 at Chi. (Belfour)
Last 2-Goal Game: None
Longest Point Scoring Streak: 7, (twice) last-
 1/28-2/8/87 (2 goals, 6 assists)
Longest Goal Scoring Streak: 2, (many) last-
 2/6/-2/8/91 (2 goals)
Longest Assist Streak: 6, 1/28-2/6/87 (6 assists)

STEPHANE MATTEAU

SEASON	PPG	SHG	GWG
1990-91	0	1	1
1991-92	1	0	0
1992-93	2	0	4
1993-94	3	0	2
1994-95	0	0	0
Totals	6	1	7

Last PPG: 3/23/94 at Edm. (Ranford)
Last SHG: 12/16/90 at Van. (Gamble)
Last GWG: 2/6/94 vs. Ana. (Hebert)
Last 2-Goal Game: 10/10/93 vs. Wpg (Beauregard)
Longest Point Scoring Streak: 5, (twice) last-
 3/26-4/12/93 (3 goals, 2 assists)
Longest Goal Scoring Streak: 3, 11/20-11/26/93
 (3 goals)
Longest Assist Streak: 3, 11/5-11/8/92 (3 assists)

MARK MESSIER

SEASON	PPG	SHG	GWG
1979-80	1	1	1
1980-81	4	0	1
1981-82	10	0	3
1982-83	12	1	2
1983-84	7	4	7
1984-85	4	5	1
1985-86	10	5	7
1986-87	7	4	5
1987-88	12	3	7
1988-89	6	6	4
1989-90	13	6	3
1990-91	3	1	2
1991-92	12	4	6
1992-93	7	2	5
1993-94	6	2	5
1994-95	3	3	2
Totals	117	47	58

Last PPG: 3/30/95 vs. Que. (Fiset)
Last SHG: 3/15/95 vs. Phi. (Roussel)
Last GWG: 2/26/95 at Buf. (Hasek)
Last 2-Goal Game: 3/8/95 vs. NJ (Brodeur)
Longest Point Scoring Streak: 15, 2/5-3/7/92
 (7 goals, 17 assists)
Longest Goal Scoring Streak: 6, 3/14/-3/28/86
 (7 goals)
Longest Assist Streak: 8, (3 times) last-
 4/12-4/26/95 (19 assists)

SERGEI NEMCHINOV

SEASON	PPG	SHG	GWG
1991-92	2	0	5
1992-93	0	1	3
1993-94	4	0	6
1994-95	0	0	3
Totals	6	1	17

Last PPG: 2/28/94 vs. Phi. (Roussel)
Last SHG: 11/4/92 vs. Phi. (Beauregard)
Last GWG: 4/24/95 vs. Wsh. (Kolzig)
Last 2-Goal Game: 2/11/95 at TB. (Puppa)
Longest Point Scoring Streak: 11, 12/2-12/26/91
 (9 goals, 4 assists)
Longest Goal Scoring Streak: 6, 12/2-12/14/91
 (6 goals)
Longest Assist Streak: 4, (twice) last- 3/7-3/14/92
 (5 assists)

CAREER GOAL BREAKDOWN AND SCORING STREAKS OF CURRENT RANGERS

MATTIAS NORSTROM

SEASON	PPG	SHG	GWG
1993-94	0	0	0
1994-95	0	0	0
Totals	0	0	0

Last PPG: None
Last SHG: None
Last GWG: None
Last 2-Goal Game: None
Longest Point Scoring Streak: 2, 3/25-4/5/95
  (3 assists)
Longest Goal Scoring Streak: None
Longest Assist Streak: 2, 3/25-4/5/95 (3 assists)

WAYNE PRESLEY

SEASON	PPG	SHG	GWG
1984-85	0	0	0
1985-86	0	0	1
1986-87	7	0	4
1987-88	4	0	1
1988-89	4	3	4
1989-90	1	0	0
1990-91	1	0	3
1991-92	3	0	1
1992-93	0	1	2
1993-94	1	5	1
1994-95	0	5	2
Totals	21	14	19

Last PPG: 2/4/94 at Fla. (Vanbiesbrouck)
Last SHG: 4/23/95 vs. Phi. (Hextall)
Last GWG: 3/5/95 vs. Mtl (Tugnutt)
Last 2-Goal Game: 1/7/90 at Mtl. (Hayward)
Longest Point Scoring Streak: 7, 12/6-12/21/86
  (6 goals, 4 assists)
Longest Goal Scoring Streak: 5, 2/25-3/7/87
  (5 goals)
Longest Assist Streak: 4, (twice) last-
  12/6-12/14/86 (4 assists)

LUC ROBITAILLE

SEASON	PPG	SHG	GWG
1986-87	18	0	3
1987-88	17	0	6
1988-89	10	0	4
1989-90	20	0	7
1990-91	11	0	5
1991-92	26	0	6
1992-93	22	2	7
1993-94	24	0	2
1994-95	5	0	3
Totals	153	2	4

Last PPG: 4/11/95 vs Wsh. (Carey)
Last SHG: 3/2/93 at Hfd. (Burke)
Last GWG: 4/11/95 vs. Wsh. (Carey)
Last 2-Goal Game: 4/23/95 at Hfd. (Burke)
Longest Point Scoring Streak: 13, 11/27-12/21/88
  (9 goals, 14 assists)
Longest Goal Scoring Streak: 10, 2/27-3/20/93
  (13 goals)
Longest Assist Streak: 6, (3 times) last-
  11/5-11/14/93 (10 assists)

ULF SAMUELSSON

SEASON	PPG	SHG	GWG
1984-85	0	0	00
1985-86	0	1	1
1986-87	0	0	0
1987-88	3	0	0
1988-89	3	0	2
1989-90	0	0	0
1990-91	0	0	0
1991-92	1	0	1
1992-93	0	0	0
1993-94	1	0	0
1994-95	0	0	0
Totals	33	3	5

Last PPG: 11/16/93 vs. Phi. (Wregget)
Last SHG: 3/23/86 at Bos. (Riggin)
Last GWG: 12/23/91 at NYI (Healy)
Last 2-Goal Game: 10/27/92 at Ott.
  (Sidorkiewicz / Weeks)
Longest Point Scoring Streak: 9, 1/21-2/6/88
  (1 goal, 11 assists)
Longest Goal Scoring Streak: 2, 3/5-3/8/88
  (2 goals)
Longest Assist Streak: 9, 1/21-2/6/88
  (11 assists)

PAT VERBEEK

SEASON	PPG	SHG	GWG
1982-83	0	0	0
1983-84	5	1	2
1984-85	5	1	1
1985-86	4	1	0
1986-87	17	0	5
1987-88	13	0	8
1988-89	9	0	1
1989-90	14	0	5
1990-91	15	0	5
1991-92	10	0	3
1992-93	16	0	6
1993-94	15	1	3
1994-95	7	0	2
Totals	130	4	41

Last PPG: 5/2/95 vs Fla. (Vanbiesbrouck)
Last SHG: 10/23/93 vs. Buf. (Fuhr)
Last GWG: 4/14/95 vs. Bos. (Billington)
Last 2-Goal Game: 4/14/95 at Bos.
  (Billington/Lacher)
Longest Point Scoring Streak: 12, (twice) last-
  12/29/93-1/24/94 (6 goals, 9 assists)
Longest Goal Scoring Streak: 6, 10/18-10/30/86
  (9 goals)
Longest Assist Streak: 5, 11/28-12/9/93
  (5 assists)

RANGERS MILESTONES IN SIGHT

Jeff Beukeboom
66 games for 600
5 assists for 100
52 PIM for 1300

Bruce Driver
17 goals for 100
1 point for 400
66 PIM for 600

Ray Ferraro
42 games for 800
27 goals for 300
11 points for 600
70 PIM for 800

Adam Graves
46 goals for 200
6 points for 300
4 PIM for 800

Alexander Karpovtsev
36 games for 150
12 PIM for 100

Joe Kocur
61 games for 700
13 points for 150
98 PIM for 2300

Alexei Kovalev
11 games for 200
44 goals for 100
34 assists for 100
78 points for 200
37 PIM for 300

Nick Kypreos
54 games for 400
24 points for 100
59 PIM for 1100

Daniel Lacroix
72 games for 100
62 PIM for 100

Nathan LaFayette
12 games for 100

Darren Langdon
38 PIM for 100

Brian Leetch
15 games for 500
25 assists for 400
13 points for 500
45 PIM for 300

Doug Lidster
63 games for 800
32 points for 350
29 PIM for 600

Kevin Lowe
70 games for 1200
50 PIM for 1400

Stephane Matteau
1 game for 300
42 goals for 100
31 assists for 100
63 PIM for 400

Mark Messier
73 games for 1200
8 goals for 500
23 assists for 900
31 points for 1400
14 PIM for 1400

Sergei Nemchinov
23 games for 300
18 goals for 100
8 assists for 100
26 points for 200

Wayne Presley
46 games for 650
1 goal for 150
12 points for 300
98 PIM for 2300

Mike Richter
50 games for 300
25 wins for 150

Luc Robitaille
14 games for 700
35 goals for 450
20 assists for 450
55 points for 900
1 PIM for 600

Ulf Samuelsson
60 games for 800
23 assists for 250
31 points for 300
86 PIM for 2000

Pat Verbeek
28 goals for 400
33 assists for 400
61 points for 800
95 PIM for 2200

RANGERS GAME NIGHT STAFF

Music Director . . . . Ray Castoldi
Video\Matrix Operations . . . . Rich Carlino, Steve Smith
Press Box Attendants . . . . Paul Clogher, Sal Frasca, Tommy Matthews
Press Room Attendants . . . . Joe Pinto, John Arnone, Anthony Di Giovanni
Game Night Staff . . . . Karin Strelec, Darren Blake, Rob Picarello, Damien Echevarrieta, Bruce Popko
Lockerroom Assistants . . . . Joe Devanney, Tommy Horvath, Joe Vanness, Mike Vanness, Ed Whiteman
Video Staff . . . . Rich Chapman, Ken Watnick
Interpreter . . . . Irina Cytowicz
Public Address Announcer . . . . Bob Galerstein

OFF-ICE OFFICIALS

Supervisor . . . . Frank Koch
Timekeeper and Scoreboard Operator . . . . Anthony Daddario
Goal Judge and Spare Official . . . . Charles Joyce
Game Timekeeper and Scoreboard Operator . . . . Frank Koch
Statistician and Spare Official . . . . Stephen Devaney
Goal Judge and Spare Official . . . . Adam Giever
Statistician and Spare Official . . . . Joseph Leone
Goal Judge and Penalty Timekeeper . . . . Charles O'Donnell
Scorer and Timekeeper . . . . Mark Rubenfeld
Penalty Timekeeper and Spare Official . . . . Bernard Ryan
Statistician and Spare Official . . . . Jim Breidenbach
Goal Judge and Spare Official . . . . Louis Venturino
Video Goal Judges . . . . John Damante and Dennis McKiernan

HOW THE RANGERS WERE BUILT

PLAYER	HOW ACQUIRED
Jeff Beukeboom	From the Edmonton Oilers for David Shaw as the future considerations of the Mark Messier trade on November 12, 1991.
Sylvain Blouin	Rangers fourth round choice, 104th overall, in the 1994 Entry Draft.
Eric Cairns	Rangers third round choice, 72nd overall, in the 1992 Entry Draft.
Bruce Driver	Signed as a free agent on August 24, 1995.
Chris Ferraro	Rangers fourth round choice, 85th overall, in the 1993 Entry Draft.
Peter Ferraro	Rangers first round choice, 24th overall, in the 1993 Entry Draft.
Ray Ferraro	Signed as a free agent on July 19, 1995.
Eric Flinton	Signed as a free agent on August 22, 1995.
Maxim Galanov	Rangers third round choice, 61st overall, in the 1993 Entry Draft.
Ken Gernander	Signed as a free agent on September 9, 1994.
Adam Graves	Signed as a free agent from the Edmonton Oilers on September 3, 1991.
Glenn Healy	From the Tampa Bay Lightning for the return of Tampa Bay's third round draft choice in the 1993 Entry Draft on June 25, 1993.
Jon Hillebrandt	Rangers 10th round choice, 202nd overall, in the 1990 Entry Draft.
Brad Jones	Signed as a free agent on August 22, 1995.
Alexander Karpovtsev	From the Quebec Nordiques in exchange for Mike Hurlbut on September 9, 1993.
Joe Kocur	From the Detroit Red Wings along with Per Djoos in exchange for Kevin Miller, Dennis Vial and Jim Cummins on March 5, 1991.
Pavel Komarov	Rangers 11th round choice, 261st overall, in the 1993 Entry Draft.
Alexei Kovalev	Rangers first round choice, 15th overall, in the 1991 Entry Draft.
Andrei Kudinov	Rangers ninth round choice, 216th overall, in the 1993 Entry Draft.
Nick Kypreos	From the Hartford Whalers with Steve Larmer, Barry Richter, and a 1994 sixth round draft choice (Yuri Litvinov) in exchange for James Patrick and Darren Turcotte on November 2, 1993.
Daniel Lacroix	Claimed off waivers from Boston on March 23, 1995.
Nathan LaFayette	From the Vancouver Canucks in exchange for Corey Hirsch on April 7, 1995.
Darren Langdon	Signed as a free agent on August 16, 1993.
Brian Leetch	Rangers first round choice, ninth overall, in the 1986 Entry Draft.
Doug Lidster	From St. Louis in exchange for Jay Wells on July 31, 1995.
Kevin Lowe	From the Edmonton Oilers in exchange for Roman Oksiuta and the Rangers' third round draft choice in the 1993 Entry Draft on December 11, 1992.
Scott Malone	From the Toronto Maple Leafs with Glenn Anderson and a 1994 sixth round choice (Alexander Korobolin) in exchange for Mike Gartner on March 21, 1994.
Stephane Matteau	From the Chicago Blackhawks along with Brian Noonan in exchange for Tony Amonte and the rights to Matt Oates on March 21, 1994.
Cal McGowan	Signed as a free agent on August 13, 1995.
Mark Messier	From the Edmonton Oilers along with future considerations (Jeff Beukeboom) in exchange for Bernie Nicholls, Steven Rice and Louie DeBrusk on October 4, 1991.
Sergei Nemchinov	Rangers 12th round choice, 244th overall, in the 1990 Entry Draft.
Jeff Nielsen	Rangers fourth round choice, 69th overall, in the 1990 Entry Draft.
Mattias Norstrom	Rangers second round choice, 48th overall, in the 1992 Entry Draft.
Wayne Presley	Signed as a free agent on August 2, 1993.
Jamie Ram	Rangers 10th round choice, 213th overall, in the 1991 Entry Draft.
Shawn Reid	Signed as a free agent on July 6, 1994.
Barry Richter	From the Hartford Whalers with Steve Larmer, Nick Kypreos, and a 1994 sixth round draft choice in (Yuri Litvinov) in exchange for James Patrick and Darren Turcotte on November 2, 1993.
Mike Richter	Rangers second round choice, 28th overall, in the 1985 Entry Draft.
Luc Robitaille	From the Pittsburgh Penguins with Ulf Samuelsson in exchange for Petr Nedved and Sergei Zubov on August 31, 1995.
Jean-Yves Roy	Signed as a free agent on July 20, 1992.
Ulf Samuelsson	From the Pittsburgh Penguins with Luc Robitaille in exchange for Petr Nedved and Sergei Zubov on August 31, 1995.
Ken Shepard	Rangers 10th choice, 216th overall, in the 1993 Entry Draft.
Andy Silverman	Rangers ninth round choice, 181st overall, in the 1990 Entry Draft.
Lee Sorochan	Rangers second round choice, 34th overall, in the 1993 Entry Draft.
Dimitri Starostenko	Rangers fifth round choice, 120th overall, in the 1990 Entry Draft.
Niklas Sundstrom	Rangers first round choice, eighth overall, in the 1993 Entry Draft.
Ryan VandenBussche	Signed as a free agent on August 3, 1995.
Pat Verbeek	From the Hartford Whalers for Glen Featherstone, Michael Stewart and a 1995 first round draft pick and a 1996 fourth round draft pick, on March 23, 1995.

TECHNICALLY SPEAKING, THE ARMY HAS A LOT TO OFFER.

The Army can give you a definite edge on life if you want to learn valuable high-tech skills. We offer hard-to-duplicate, hands-on training in a wide variety of challenging specialties. If you qualify, the Army offers training in the following fields:

- Communications Electronics
- Digital Communications Equipment
- Tactical Satellite Microwave
- Avionics
- Automatic Data Telecommunications
- Tactical Fire Control Systems
- Computers

These are just a few of the high-tech skills in which you can train. There are over 250 specialties to choose from. Technically speaking, the Army has a lot to offer. Your Army Recruiter can tell you even more. Call today.

1-800-USA-ARMY

ARMY.
BE ALL YOU CAN BE®

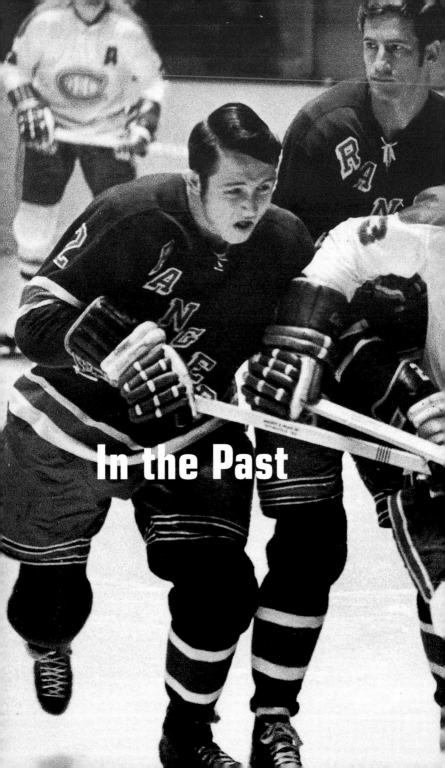

In the Past

RANGERS RECORD AGAINST ALL NATIONAL HOCKEY LEAGUE TEAMS SINCE 1926

New York Rangers vs.	GP	W	L	T	GF	GA	PTS
OVERALL							
Chicago Blackhawks	557	228	233	96	1604	1638	552
Boston Bruins	564	212	258	94	1644	1813	518
Detroit Red Wings (a)	554	206	245	103	1541	1688	515
Toronto Maple Leafs	535	189	252	94	1513	1705	472
Montreal Canadiens	544	165	292	87	1415	1867	417
Philadelphia Flyers	172	70	69	33	540	548	173
Pittsburgh Penguins	158	77	63	18	619	564	172
St. Louis Blues	108	68	27	13	411	283	149
New Jersey Devils (K.C.,Colo.)	123	68	43	12	505	406	148
Dallas Stars (Minn.)	107	62	27	18	399	310	142
Vancouver Canucks	92	66	18	8	402	261	140
New York Islanders	145	61	70	14	509	533	136
Washington Capitals	125	56	55	14	469	470	126
Los Angeles Kings	103	54	35	14	394	324	122
Buffalo Sabres	98	36	45	17	334	358	89
Calgary Flames (Atl.)	87	29	44	14	290	356	72
Ottawa Senators (b)	42	27	6	9	136	81	63
Colorado Avalanche (Que.)	52	26	20	6	214	185	58
Hartford Whalers	51	25	21	5	204	171	55
Winnipeg Jets	45	24	17	4	191	173	52
Edmonton Oilers	44	17	22	5	164	176	39
Tampa Bay Lightning	12	8	3	1	46	43	17
San Jose Sharks	7	6	0	1	37	16	13
Florida Panthers	9	5	3	1	26	18	11
Anaheim Mighty Ducks	2	0	2	0	4	7	0
Defunct Teams (c)	246	152	58	36	811	521	340
Totals	**4582**	**1937**	**1928**	**717**	**14422**	**14515**	**4591**
HOME							
Detroit Red Wings (a)	276	131	87	58	852	710	320
Boston Bruins	284	123	107	54	863	797	300
Chcago Blackhawks	279	117	108	54	827	790	288
Toronto Maple Leafs	268	111	101	56	821	785	278
Montreal Canadiens	272	110	109	53	789	793	273
Philadelphia Flyers	87	40	27	20	293	253	100
New York Islanders	72	43	21	8	286	219	94
St. Louis Blues	53	42	6	5	228	120	89
Pittsburgh Penguins	79	41	31	7	322	276	89
New Jersey Devils (K.C., Colo.)	61	37	16	8	271	194	82
Dallas Stars (Minn.)	54	33	11	10	194	148	76
Vancouver Canucks	47	35	7	5	215	117	75
Washington Capitals	62	32	24	6	256	225	70
Los Angeles Kings	51	31	15	5	207	150	67
Buffalo Sabres	48	22	15	11	168	132	55
Calgary Flames (Atl.)	44	19	20	5	156	160	43
Colorado Avalanche (Que.)	25	16	6	3	107	71	35
Hartford Whalers	26	16	8	2	113	75	34
Ottawa Senators (b)	21	12	4	5	60	42	29
Winnipeg Jets	22	12	8	2	104	89	26
Edmonton Oilers	22	6	12	4	87	90	16
Tampa Bay Lightning	7	4	2	1	29	29	9
San Jose Sharks	3	2	0	1	15	7	5
Florida Panthers	4	2	1	1	9	8	5
Anaheim Mighty Ducks	1	0	1	0	2	4	0
Defunct Teams (c)	123	80	26	17	425	258	177
Totals	**2291**	**1117**	**773**	**401**	**7699**	**6542**	**2635**
ROAD							
Chicago Blackhawks	278	111	125	42	777	848	264
Boston Bruins	280	89	151	40	781	1016	218
Detroit Red Wings (a)	278	75	158	45	689	978	195
Toronto Maple Leafs	267	78	151	45	692	920	194
Montreal Canadiens	272	55	183	34	626	1074	144
Pittsburgh Penguins	79	36	32	11	297	288	83
Philadelphia Flyers	85	30	42	13	247	295	73
Dallas Stars (Minn.)	53	29	16	8	205	162	66
New Jersey Devils (K.C.,Colo.)	62	31	27	4	235	212	66
Vancouver Canucks	45	31	11	3	187	144	65
St. Louis Blues	55	26	21	8	183	163	60
Washington Capitals	63	24	31	8	213	245	56
Los Angeles Kings	52	23	20	9	187	174	55
New York Islanders	73	18	49	6	223	314	42
Ottawa Senators (b)	21	15	2	4	76	39	34
Buffalo Sabres	50	14	30	6	166	226	34
Calgary Flames (Atl.)	43	10	24	9	134	196	29
Winnipeg Jets	23	12	9	2	87	84	26
Edmonton Oilers	22	11	10	1	77	86	23
Colorado Avalanche (Que.)	27	10	14	3	107	114	23
Hartford Whalers	25	9	13	3	91	96	21
San Jose Sharks	4	4	0	0	22	9	8
Tampa Bay Lightning	5	4	1	0	16	14	8
Florida Panthers	5	3	2	0	17	10	6
Anaheim Mighty Ducks	1	0	1	0	2	3	0
Defunct Teams (c)	123	72	32	19	386	263	163
Totals	**2291**	**820**	**1155**	**316**	**6723**	**7973**	**1956**

(a) includes records of Detroit Cougars and Detroit Falcons
(b) includes records of Ottawa Senators
(c) Teams are: Brooklyn and New York Americans, Cleveland Barons (Calif.), Montreal Maroons, Philadelphia Quakers, Pittsburgh Pirates, and St. Louis Eagles

CURRENT STREAKS VS. NHL OPPONENTS

	AT GARDEN	ON ROAD	OVERALL
vs. ANAHEIM	0-1-0	0-1-0	0-2-0
vs. BOSTON	4-4-1	5-2-2	10-7-3
vs. BUFFALO	7-1-1	3-1-0	6-2-0
vs. CALGARY	5-3-1	0-6-3	2-2-3
vs. CHICAGO	5-3-3	3-0-0	5-2-0
vs. COLORADO	7-3-0	2-4-0	4-3-0
vs. DALLAS	6-1-1	1-1-3	7-3-4
vs. DETROIT	4-4-1	1-7-3	2-6-2
vs. EDMONTON	3-4-3	5-1-0	6-3-3
vs. FLORIDA	2-1-1	3-2-0	4-2-1
vs. HARTFORD	9-2-0	3-1-1	13-6-1
vs. LOS ANGELES	5-0-0	5-1-0	10-2-0
vs. MONTREAL	2-0-2	0-6-0	4-10-3
vs. NEW JERSEY	4-1-1	3-2-0	7-3-0
vs. ISLANDERS	5-3-3	2-10-1	3-8-3
vs. OTTAWA	5-0-0	5-0-0	10-0-0
vs. PHILADELPHIA	9-2-2	2-5-0	5-2-1
vs. PITTSBURGH	5-4-0	0-6-0	4-10-0
vs. ST. LOUIS	6-3-1	5-0-1	5-0-0
vs. SAN JOSE	2-0-1	4-0-0	6-0-1
vs. TAMPA BAY	4-1-1	3-0-0	3-0-1
vs. TORONTO	4-1-2	5-4-1	10-6-3
vs. VANCOUVER	6-0-2	7-1-1	12-1-3
vs. WASHINGTON	5-2-0	7-6-0	7-3-0
vs. WINNIPEG	3-0-0	5-3-0	7-3-0

YEAR	Anaheim			Boston			Buffalo			Calgary			Chicago			Colorado			Dallas			Detroit			Edmonton			Florida			Hartford			Los Angeles			Montreal		
	W	L	T	W	L	T	W	L	T	W	L	T	W	L	T	W	L	T	W	L	T	W	L	T	W	L	T	W	L	T	W	L	T	W	L	T	W	L	T
1994-95				2	2	0	3	1	0							0	3	0										2	1	1	2	1	0				1	2	1
1993-94	0	2	0	1	2	1	3	1	0	0	1	1	1	1	0	4	0	0	1	1	0	0	2	0	1	0	1	3	2	0	3	1	0	2	0	0	1	2	1
1992-93				1	1	1	1	2	1	0	1	1	1	1	0	0	4	0	0	1	1	1	0	1	1	1	0				1	1	1	2	0	0	1	2	1
1991-92				2	1	0	2	1	0	2	0	1	3	0	0	3	0	0	3	0	0	1	1	1	1	1	0				2	1	0	2	1	0	2	1	0
1990-91				1	1	1	2	0	1	0	2	1	0	3	0	2	1	0	2	0	1	0	3	0	1	1	1				2	1	0	3	0	0	1	2	0
1989-90				3	0	0	0	2	1	1	2	0	1	0	2	3	0	0	1	1	1	2	0	1	2	0	1				2	1	0	1	2	0	0	3	0
1988-89				0	1	2	0	3	0	1	2	0	2	0	1	2	1	0	2	1	0	0	3	0	1	2	0				1	2	0	2	1	0	0	3	0
1987-88				2	1	0	0	3	0	1	2	0	2	0	1	2	1	0	2	1	0	1	1	1	1	2	0				2	1	0	0	3	0	1	1	1
1986-87				2	1	0	2	1	0	1	2	0	1	1	1	2	1	0	1	1	1	1	2	0	0	3	0				0	3	0	2	0	1	0	2	1
1985-86				2	1	0	0	3	0	1	2	0	0	3	0	0	2	1	1	2	0	3	0	0	2	1	0				1	2	0	2	1	0	2	0	1
1984-85				0	1	2	1	1	1	0	2	1	0	3	0	1	2	0	1	2	0	1	2	0	1	1	1				0	1	2	1	2	0	0	2	1
1983-84				0	2	1	1	1	1	2	1	0	2	1	0	2	0	1	1	1	1	3	0	0	1	2	0				1	2	0	1	0	2	1	2	0
1982-83				0	3	0	0	2	1	2	0	1	0	3	0	1	2	0	2	1	0	2	0	1	0	3	0				2	1	0	1	1	1	1	2	0
1981-82				1	2	0	2	0	1	2	0	1	3	0	0	1	1	1	2	1	0	2	1	0	0	3	0				1	1	1	2	1	0	1	2	0
1980-81				2	2	0	1	2	1	1	2	1	2	1	1	1	1	2	1	1	2	1	2	1	2	1	1				3	1	0	1	3	0	1	2	1
1979-80				2	2	0	1	2	1	0	3	1	1	2	1	2	1	1	1	2	1	3	1	0	3	1	0				2	1	1	3	1	0	0	3	1
1978-79				2	3	0	2	1	1	3	4	1	4	0	0				1	2	1	1	1	2										3	1	0	3	1	0
1977-78				1	4	0	1	2	1	0	6	0	3	1	1				3	0	2	2	1	1										1	3	0	1	3	0
1976-77				0	4	1	0	4	0	1	4	1	2	2	1				5	0	0	3	1	0										0	3	1	1	3	0
1975-76				1	3	0	0	2	3	2	3	1	2	0	3				4	1	0	3	1	0										0	4	0	0	3	1
1974-75				1	3	0	1	4	0	3	3	0	3	1	1				4	1	0	2	1	1										1	1	2	0	2	2
1973-74				1	4	0	2	2	1	2	1	2	1	3	1				4	0	1	3	2	1										2	1	2	2	4	0
1972-73				3	3	0	1	5	0	4	1	0	2	2	1				3	2	0	3	1	1										3	0	2	0	3	2
1971-72				1	5	0	6	0	0				2	1	3				1	3	2	4	1	1										6	0	0	3	1	2
1970-71				2	2	2	4	0	2				3	3	0				6	0	0	4	1	1										4	0	2	3	3	0
1969-70				4	4	0							1	4	3				3	1	2	4	2	2										4	1	1	3	4	1
1968-69				3	3	2							3	4	1				6	1	0	3	4	1										3	3	0	4	3	1
1967-68				2	6	2							4	3	3				2	0	2	5	3	2										2	2	0	4	4	2
1966-67				8	2	4							6	7	2							7	7	0													5	7	2
1965-66				6	7	1							4	9	1							3	7	4													2	12	0
1964-65				8	5	1							3	9	2							2	10	2													2	10	2
1963-64				7	5	2							3	9	2							6	6	2													3	10	1
1962-63				7	4	3							2	10	2							3	9	2													5	5	4
1961-62				10	2	2							6	7	1							5	6	3													1	8	5
1960-61				9	3	2							4	7	3							5	7	2													2	11	1
1959-60				4	8	2							1	11	2							4	4	6													6	6	2

EAR-BY-YEAR

New Jersey		Islanders			Ottawa			Philadelphia			Pittsburgh			San Jose			St. Louis			Tampa Bay			Toronto			Vancouver			Washington			Winnipeg			Defunct			TOTALS		
L	T	W	L	T	W	L	T	W	L	T	W	L	T	W	L	T	W	L	T	W	L	T	W	L	T	W	L	T	W	L	T	W	L	T	W	L	T	W	L	T
3	0	1	3	0	3	0	0	2	2	0	0	3	0							3	0	1							2	2	0							22	23	3
0	0	1	2	2	4	0	0	3	1	1	2	2	0	1	0	1	2	0	0	3	2	0	2	0	0	2	0	0	5	1	0	1	1	0				52	24	8
4	1	2	4	1	3	0	0	2	4	1	2	5	0	3	0	0	2	0	0	2	1	0	1	1	0	0	1	1	4	5	0	2	0	0				34	39	11
3	0	2	4	1				6	1	0	5	2	0	2	0	0	2	1	0				0	1	1	2	0	1	2	5	0	2	1	0				50	25	5
2	2	2	4	1				3	2	2	3	4	0	1	1	1							2	1	0	2	0	1	4	2	1	2	1	0				36	31	13
3	1	3	2	2				5	2	0	1	5	1				0	2	1				1	1	1	3	0	0	3	4	0	1	1	1				36	31	13
4	0	5	2	0				3	3	1	3	3	1				3	0	0				1	1	1	3	0	0	3	2	2	2	1	0				37	35	8
3	0	2	2	3				3	3	1	2	3	2				3	0	0				2	1	0	2	1	0	2	5	0	2	0	1				36	34	10
4	0	3	3	1				4	3	0	3	2	2				1	2	0				1	1	1	2	1	0	4	3	0	1	2	0				34	38	8
2	0	3	3	1				1	6	0	2	4	1				1	1	1				2	1	0	3	0	0	3	3	1	2	1	0				36	38	6
2	0	3	4	0				0	7	0	4	3	0				2	0	1				2	0	1	2	1	0	2	5	0	0	3	0				26	44	10
1	1	4	3	0				4	3	0	5	2	0				2	1	0				1	2	0	1	1	1	3	3	1	2	1	0				42	29	9
3	1	3	4	0				3	4	0	5	1	1				2	0	1				3	0	0	1	1	1	3	3	1	1	1	1				35	35	10
0	1	2	6	0				4	2	2	4	3	1				2	0	1				1	1	1	3	0	0	3	2	3	1	1	1				39	27	14
3	0	2	2	0				1	1	2	1	2	1				0	4	0				2	2	0	2	1	1	2	2	0	3	1	0				30	36	14
1	2	2	2	0				1	2	1	2	2	0				4	0	0				2	2	0	4	0	0	2	2	0	2	2	0				38	32	10
1	0	3	5	0				2	3	3	2	2	0				3	2	0				2	2	1	4	0	0	1	1	2							40	29	11
2	1	2	4	0				0	4	2	0	2	2				4	0	1				1	3	0	4	1	0	2	0	2				3	1	0	30	37	13
1	1	1	4	1				0	2	4	1	2	1				2	2	1				2	1	1	3	2	0	2	2	0				3	0	1	29	37	14
1	0	2	4	0				1	5	0	1	3	0				3	2	0				0	4	0	3	1	1	2	2	0				1	3	0	29	42	9
0	1	3	2	1				2	3	1	2	2	0				3	1	1				1	2	1	3	2	0	2	1	1				2	0	2	37	29	14
		4	1	0				2	1	2	4	1	0				3	1	1				1	2	2	4	1	1							5	0	0	40	24	14
		6	0	0				4	0	1	3	2	0				5	0	0				4	1	0	3	2	0							3	1	1	47	23	8
								6	0	0	3	1	2				5	1	0				2	2	2	5	1	0							4	1	1	48	17	13
								2	3	1	5	0	1				3	2	1				6	1	0	5	1	0							3	2	1	49	18	11
								0	0	6	4	1	1				4	2	0				6	2	0										5	1	0	38	22	16
								3	1	2	5	1	0				3	1	2				4	4	0										5	1	0	41	26	9
								3	1	0	3	0	1				3	1	0				7	3	0										4	0	0	39	23	12
																							6	5	4													30	28	12
																							3	6	5													18	41	11
																							6	4	5													20	38	12
																							3	8	3													22	38	10
																							6	8	1													22	36	12
																							4	9	1													26	32	12
																							2	10	2													22	38	10
																							2	9	3													17	38	15

YEAR	Anaheim W L T	Boston W L T	Buffalo W L T	Calgary W L T	Chicago W L T	Colorado W L T	Dallas W L T	Detroit W L T	Edmonton W L T	Florida W L T	Hartford W L T	Los Angeles W L T	Montreal W L
1958-59		5 6 3			4 7 3			7 6 1					5 8
1957-58		5 6 3			9 4 1			5 4 5					6 6
1956-57		8 5 1			7 1 6			3 10 1					5 8
1955-56		5 7 2			10 3 1			6 5 3					2 8
1954-55		4 5 5			4 5 5			2 9 3					3 10
1953-54		7 7 0			9 3 2			5 6 3					5 9
1952-53		7 5 2			3 10 1			3 7 4					2 7
1951-52		6 4 4			7 5 2			3 9 2					4 9
1950-51		2 4 8			9 2 3			3 8 3					3 5
1949-50		5 5 4			9 4 1			5 7 2					5 7
1948-49		2 8 2			5 6 1			4 7 1					4 5
1947-48		3 7 2			4 6 2			4 5 3					7 3
1946-47		2 8 2			8 4 0			3 6 3					5 6
1945-46		3 6 1			2 5 3			4 4 2					1 8
1944-45		3 4 3			3 3 4			2 6 2					1 9
1943-44		2 7 1			1 7 2			1 8 1					0 9
1942-43		2 8 0			4 4 2			1 7 2					2 6
1941-42		4 4 0			6 2 0			7 1 0					4 4
1940-41		2 4 2			3 4 1			2 3 3					5 2
1939-40		4 2 2			4 4 0			3 2 3					6 1
1938-39		3 5 0			4 3 1			6 2 0					4 1
1937-38		3 5 0			4 3 1			6 1 1					1 3
1936-37		2 3 3			3 4 1			1 5 2					2 4
1935-36		6 2 0			2 5 1			1 4 3					2 1
1934-35		1 3 2			1 3 2			4 2 0					2 3
1933-34		3 2 1			3 2 1			3 3 0					3 2
1932-33		3 3 0			2 2 2			2 4 0					4 1
1931-32		4 2 2			5 1 2			3 3 2					2 3
1930-31		0 4 2			1 4 1			3 2 1					2 2
1929-30		0 5 1			3 1 2			1 2 3					1 2
1928-29		1 5 0			4 0 2			4 1 1					1 1
1927-28		1 2 3			4 2 0			3 2 1					0 4
1926-27		3 2 1			4 2 0			3 1 2					3 1
TOTALS	0 2 0	212 258 94	36 45 17	29 44 14	228 233 96	26 20 6	62 27 18	206 245 103	17 22 5	5 3 1	25 21 5	54 35 14	165 292

* Defunct teams include Brooklyn and New York Americans, Cleveland Barons, California Golden Seals, Montreal Maroons, Philadelphia Quakers, Pittsburgh Pirates and St. Louis
** The Detroit Red Wings totals include the records of the Detroit Cougars and Detroit Falcons. The Ottawa Senators totals include the record of the Ottawa Senators from 1926-27-

New Jersey			Islanders			Ottawa			Philadelphia			Pittsburgh			San Jose			St. Louis			Tampa Bay			Toronto			Vancouver			Washington			Winnipeg			Defunct			TOTALS		
W	L	T	W	L	T	W	L	T	W	L	T	W	L	T	W	L	T	W	L	T	W	L	T	W	L	T	W	L	T	W	L	T	W	L	T	W	L	T	W	L	T
																								5	5	4													26	32	12
																								7	5	2													32	25	13
																								3	6	5													26	30	14
																								9	5	0													32	28	10
																								4	6	4													17	35	18
																								3	6	5													29	31	10
																								2	8	4													17	37	16
																								3	7	4													23	34	13
																								3	10	1													20	29	21
																								4	8	2													28	31	11
																								3	5	4													18	31	11
																								3	5	4													21	26	13
																								4	8	0													22	32	6
																								3	5	2													13	28	9
																								2	7	1													11	29	10
																								2	8	0													6	39	5
																								2	6	2													11	31	8
																								3	4	1											5	2	1	29	17	2
																								3	5	0											6	1	1	21	19	8
																								4	1	3											6	1	1	27	11	10
																								4	3	1											5	2	1	26	16	6
																								4	2	0											9	1	2	27	15	6
																								5	1	0											6	3	2	19	20	9
																								1	3	2											7	2	3	19	17	12
																								4	2	0											10	7	2	22	20	6
						4	1	1																0	3	3											5	6	1	21	19	8
						3	0	3																2	4	0											7	3	2	23	17	8
																								2	4	0											7	4	1	23	17	8
						3	1	0																1	2	1											9	1	4	19	16	9
						2	0	2																0	3	1											10	4	0	17	17	10
						3	1	0																3	1	0											5	4	5	21	13	10
						2	0	2																2	2	0											7	4	3	19	16	9
						0	3	1																2	1	1											10	3	1	25	13	6
	3	12	61	70	14	27	6	9	70	69	33	77	63	18	6	0	1	68	27	13	8	3	1	189	252	94	66	18	8	56	55	14	24	17	4	152	58	36	1937	1928	717

RECENT RECORDS VS.
NHL OPPONENTS

	Last 5 Games	Last 10 Games	Last 15 Games	Last 20 Games
vs. ANAHEIM	0-2-0	- - -	- - -	- - -
vs. BOSTON	2-2-1	4-5-1	6-6-3	10-7-3
vs. BUFFALO	4-1-0	6-3-1	9-5-1	11-6-3
vs. CALGARY	0-2-3	2-4-4	4-7-4	5-11-4
vs. CHICAGO	3-2-0	5-5-0	8-5-2	11-5-4
vs. COLORADO	2-3-0	4-6-0	7-8-0	12-8-0
vs. DALLAS	2-2-1	5-2-3	7-4-4	11-5-4
vs. DETROIT	2-2-1	2-6-2	4-8-3	5-11-4
vs. EDMONTON	3-1-1	5-3-2	7-5-3	8-9-3
vs. FLORIDA	3-1-1	5-3-1	- - -	- - -
vs. HARTFORD	3-2-0	6-3-1	10-4-1	13-6-1
vs. LOS ANGELES	5-0-0	9-1-0	11-4-0	12-7-1
vs. MONTREAL	1-3-1	2-6-2	4-8-3	5-12-3
vs. NEW JERSEY	2-3-0	7-3-0	8-6-1	11-8-1
vs. ISLANDERS	1-4-0	2-6-2	4-8-3	5-11-4
vs. OTTAWA	5-0-0	10-0-0	- - -	- - -
vs. PHILADELPHIA	2-2-1	5-4-1	6-7-2	10-8-2
vs. PITTSBURGH	1-4-0	3-7-0	5-10-0	8-12-0
vs. ST. LOUIS	5-0-0	7-2-1	9-4-2	14-4-2
vs. SAN JOSE	4-0-1	6-0-1	- - -	- - -
vs. TAMPA BAY	3-1-1	7-2-1	8-3-1	- - -
vs. TORONTO	3-2-0	5-3-2	7-5-3	10-7-3
vs. VANCOUVER	2-1-2	6-1-3	11-1-3	14-3-3
vs. WASHINGTON	3-2-0	7-3-0	9-6-0	11-9-0
vs. WINNIPEG	4-1-0	7-3-0	9-5-1	12-6-2

RANGERS LAST SHUTOUT VS. NHL OPPONENTS

	BY RANGERS	VS. RANGERS
ANAHEIM	NONE	NONE
BOSTON	3-0, Feb. 3, 1994 at Bos. (Healy)	4-0, Mar. 20, 1983 at MSG (Peeters)
BUFFALO	2-0, Dec. 13, 1993 at MSG (Richter)	2-0, Mar. 8, 1989 at MSG (Malarchuk)
CALGARY	4-0, Nov. 4, 1991 at MSG (Vanbiesbrouck)	3-0, Dec. 15, 1992 at MSG (Vernon)
CHICAGO	3-0, Jan. 25, 1969 at MSG (Giacomin)	4-0, Nov. 30, 1983 at MSG (Bannerman)
COLORADO	5-0, Oct. 29, 1990 at MSG (Vanbiesbrouck)	2-0, Jan. 28, 1995 at Que. (Fiset)
DALLAS	3-0, Apr. 1, 1994 at MSG (Richter)	7-0, Oct. 10, 1981 at Minn. (Meloche)
DETROIT	5-0, Nov. 27, 1976 at Det. (Davidson)	4-0, Jan. 9, 1980 at Det. (Vachon)
EDMONTON	1-0, Feb. 27, 1993 at Edm. (Richter)	NONE
FLORIDA	5-0, Apr. 5, 1995 at Fla. (Richter)	0-0, Feb. 28, 1995 at MSG (Vanbiesbrouck)
HARTFORD	4-0, Mar. 16, 1994 at MSG (Richter)	5-0, Jan. 20, 1986 at MSG (Weeks)
LOS ANGELES	5-0, Oct. 25, 1985 at MSG (Vanbiesbrouck)	6-0, Dec. 2, 1989 at LA (Hayward)
MONTREAL	3-0, Oct. 12, 1990 at MSG (Vanbiesbrouck)	3-0, Jan. 16, 1993 at Mtl. (Roy)
NEW JERSEY	3-0, Dec. 21, 1992 at NJ (Vanbiesbrouck)	2-0, Apr. 9, 1995 at NJ (Brodeur)
ISLANDERS	0-0, Dec. 9, 1989 at Coliseum (Vanbiesbrouck)	1-0, Mar. 23, 1995 at NYI (Soderstrom)
OTTAWA	3-0, Feb. 18, 1994 at MSG (Richter)	0-0, Dec. 21, 1933 at MSG (Beveridge)
PHILADELPHIA	2-0, Apr. 30, 1995 at Phi. (Healy)	1-0, Apr. 12, 1993 at Phi. (Roussel)
PITTSBURGH	7-0, Nov. 18, 1973 at MSG (Giacomin)	3-0, Feb. 10, 1993 at MSG. (Barrasso)
ST. LOUIS	6-0, Mar. 14, 1992 at St.L. (Vanbiesbrouck)	NONE
SAN JOSE	4-0, Feb. 22, 1993 at SJ (Vanbiesbrouck)	NONE
TAMPA BAY	NONE	NONE
TORONTO	6-0, Dec. 6, 1992 at MSG (Vanbiesbrouck)	6-0, Feb. 15, 1967 at Tor. (Bower)
VANCOUVER	6-0, Jan. 2, 1985 at MSG (Vanbiesbrouck)	3-0, Nov. 20, 1977 at MSG (Maniago)
WASHINGTON	1-0, Dec. 23, 1993 at Wash. (Healy)	2-0, Apr. 14, 1993 at MSG (Tabaracci)
WINNIPEG	3-0, Jan. 12, 1980 at Winn. (Davidson)	NONE

RANGERS ALL-TIME WON-AND-LOST RECORD

Year	G	W	L	T	GF	GA	PTS	Finished*	Division Champion
1926-27	44	25	13	6	95	72	56	1st	**RANGERS
1927-28	44	19	16	9	94	79	47	2nd	Boston
1928-29	44	21	13	10	72	65	52	2nd	Boston
1929-30	44	17	17	10	136	143	44	3rd	Boston
1930-31	44	19	16	9	106	87	47	3rd	Boston
1931-32	48	23	17	8	134	112	54	1st	**RANGERS
1932-33	48	23	17	8	135	107	54	3rd	Boston
1933-34	48	21	19	8	120	113	50	3rd	Detroit
1934-35	48	22	20	6	137	139	50	3rd	Boston
1935-36	48	19	17	12	91	96	50	4th	Detroit
1936-37	48	19	20	9	117	106	47	3rd	Detroit
1937-38	48	27	15	6	149	96	60	2nd	Boston
1938-39	48	26	16	6	149	105	58	2nd	Boston
1939-40	48	27	11	10	136	77	64	2nd	Boston
1940-41	48	21	19	8	143	125	50	4th	Boston
1941-42	48	29	17	2	177	143	60	1st	**RANGERS
1942-43	50	11	31	8	161	253	30	6th	Detroit
1943-44	50	6	39	5	162	310	17	6th	Montreal
1944-45	50	11	29	10	154	247	32	6th	Montreal
1945-46	50	13	28	9	144	191	35	6th	Montreal
1946-47	60	22	32	6	167	186	50	5th	Montreal
1947-48	60	21	26	13	176	201	55	4th	Toronto
1948-49	60	18	31	11	133	172	47	6th	Detroit
1949-50	70	28	31	11	170	189	67	4th	Detroit
1950-51	70	20	29	21	169	201	61	5th	Detroit
1951-52	70	23	34	13	192	219	59	5th	Detroit
1952-53	70	17	37	16	152	211	50	6th	Detroit
1953-54	70	29	31	10	161	182	68	5th	Detroit
1954-55	70	17	35	18	150	210	52	5th	Detroit
1955-56	70	32	28	10	204	203	74	3rd	Montreal
1956-57	70	26	30	14	184	227	66	3rd	Detroit
1957-58	70	32	25	13	195	188	77	2nd	Montreal
1958-59	70	26	32	12	201	217	64	5th	Montreal
1959-60	70	17	38	15	187	247	49	6th	Montreal
1960-61	70	22	38	10	204	248	54	5th	Montreal
1961-62	70	26	32	12	195	207	64	4th	Montreal
1962-63	70	22	36	12	211	233	56	5th	Toronto
1963-64	70	22	38	10	186	242	54	5th	Montreal
1964-65	70	20	38	12	179	246	52	5th	Detroit
1965-66	70	18	41	11	195	261	47	6th	Montreal
1966-67	70	30	28	12	188	189	72	4th	Chicago
1967-68	74	39	23	12	226	183	90	2nd	Montreal
1968-69	76	41	26	9	231	196	91	3rd	Montreal
1969-70	76	38	22	16	246	189	92	4th	Chicago
1970-71	78	49	18	11	259	177	109	2nd	Boston
1971-72	78	48	17	13	317	192	109	2nd	Boston
1972-73	78	47	23	8	297	208	102	3rd	Montreal
1973-74	78	40	24	14	300	251	94	3rd	Boston
1974-75	80	37	29	14	319	276	88	2nd	Philadelphia
1975-76	80	29	42	9	262	333	67	4th	Philadelphia
1976-77	80	29	37	14	272	310	72	4th	Philadelphia
1977-78	80	30	37	13	279	280	73	4th	Islanders
1978-79	80	40	29	11	316	292	91	3rd	Islanders
1979-80	80	38	32	10	308	284	86	3rd	Philadelphia
1980-81	80	30	36	14	312	317	74	4th	Islanders
1981-82	80	39	27	14	316	306	92	2nd	Islanders
1982-83	80	35	35	10	306	287	80	4th	Philadelphia
1983-84	80	42	29	9	314	304	93	4th	Islanders
1984-85	80	26	44	10	295	345	62	4th	Philadelphia
1985-86	80	36	38	6	280	276	78	4th	Philadelphia
1986-87	80	34	38	8	307	323	76	4th	Philadelphia
1987-88	80	36	34	10	300	283	82	5th	Islanders
1988-89	80	37	35	8	310	307	82	3rd	Washington
1989-90	80	36	31	13	279	267	85	1st	RANGERS
1990-91	80	36	31	13	297	265	85	2nd	Pittsburgh
1991-92	80	50	25	5	321	246	105	1st	**RANGERS
1992-93	84	34	39	11	304	308	79	6th	Pittsburgh
1993-94	84	52	24	8	299	231	112	1st	**RANGERS
1994-95	48	22	23	3	139	134	47	4th	Philadelphia

*From 1926-27 through 1937-38, listing refers to American Division only; from 1967-68 to 1973-74, listing refers to East Division only; from 1974-75, listing refers to Lester Patrick Division of Clarence Campbell Conferences; from 1981-82, listing refers to Patrick Divison of Prince of Wales Conference; from 1993-94, listing refers to Atlantic Division of Eastern Conference.
**Finished 1st overall in the league.

WON-AND-LOST RECORD—HOME AND AWAY

Year	G	W	L	Home T	GF	GA	PTS	G	W	L	Away T	GF	GA	PTS
1926-27	22	13	5	4	46	31	30	22	12	8	2	49	41	26
1927-28	22	10	8	4	47	36	24	22	9	8	5	47	43	23
1928-29	22	12	6	4	32	21	28	22	9	7	6	40	44	24
1929-30	22	11	5	6	79	54	28	22	6	12	4	57	89	16
1930-31	22	10	9	3	58	43	23	22	9	7	6	48	44	24
1931-32	24	13	7	4	66	54	30	24	10	10	4	68	58	24
1932-33	24	12	7	5	64	55	29	24	11	10	3	71	52	25
1933-34	24	11	7	6	58	47	28	24	10	12	2	62	66	22
1934-35	24	11	8	5	69	64	27	24	11	12	1	68	75	23
1935-36	24	11	6	7	49	42	29	24	8	11	5	42	54	21
1936-37	24	9	7	8	55	46	26	24	10	13	1	62	60	21
1937-38	24	15	5	4	79	50	34	24	12	10	2	70	46	26
1938-39	24	13	8	3	70	48	29	24	13	8	3	79	57	29
1939-40	24	17	4	3	82	33	37	24	10	7	7	54	44	27
1940-41	24	13	7	4	85	60	30	24	8	12	4	58	65	20
1941-42	24	15	8	1	97	72	31	24	14	9	1	80	71	29
1942-43	25	7	13	5	83	112	19	25	4	18	3	78	141	11
1943-44	25	4	17	4	78	137	12	25	2	22	1	84	173	5
1944-45	25	7	11	7	77	101	21	25	4	18	3	77	146	11
1945-46	25	8	12	5	72	85	21	25	5	16	4	72	106	14
1946-47	30	11	14	5	106	100	27	30	11	18	1	61	86	23
1947-48	30	11	12	7	90	96	29	30	10	14	6	86	105	26
1948-49	30	13	12	5	77	65	31	30	5	19	6	56	107	16
1949-50	35	19	12	4	89	73	42	35	9	19	7	81	116	25
1950-51	35	14	11	10	98	97	38	35	6	18	11	71	104	23
1951-52	35	16	13	6	112	97	38	35	7	21	7	80	122	21
1952-53	35	11	14	10	89	90	32	35	6	23	6	63	121	18
1953-54	35	18	12	5	95	90	41	35	11	19	5	66	92	27
1954-55	35	10	12	13	86	93	33	35	7	23	5	64	117	19
1955-56	35	20	7	8	122	78	48	35	12	21	2	82	125	26
1956-57	35	15	12	8	103	97	38	35	11	18	6	81	130	28
1957-58	35	14	15	6	92	93	34	35	18	10	7	103	95	43
1958-59	35	14	16	5	108	110	33	35	12	16	7	93	107	31
1959-60	35	10	15	10	103	105	30	35	7	23	5	84	142	19
1960-61	35	15	15	5	102	95	35	35	7	23	5	102	153	19
1961-62	35	16	11	8	105	91	40	35	10	21	4	90	116	24
1962-63	35	12	17	6	107	110	30	35	10	19	6	104	123	26
1963-64	35	14	13	8	97	102	36	35	8	25	2	89	140	18
1964-65	35	8	19	8	94	132	24	35	12	19	4	85	114	28
1965-66	35	12	16	7	95	104	31	35	6	25	4	100	157	16
1966-67	35	18	12	5	100	81	41	35	12	16	7	88	108	31
1967-68	37	22	8	7	118	87	51	37	17	15	5	108	96	39
1968-69	38	27	7	4	131	74	58	38	14	19	5	100	122	33
1969-70	38	22	8	8	125	84	52	38	16	14	8	121	105	40
1970-71	39	30	2	7	150	71	67	39	19	16	4	109	106	42
1971-72	39	26	6	7	173	88	59	39	22	11	6	144	104	50
1972-73	39	26	8	5	162	84	57	39	21	15	3	135	124	45
1973-74	39	26	7	6	166	102	58	39	14	17	8	134	149	36
1974-75	40	21	11	8	174	120	50	40	16	18	6	145	156	38
1975-76	40	16	16	8	134	136	40	40	13	26	1	128	197	27
1976-77	40	17	18	5	139	147	39	40	12	19	9	133	163	33
1977-78	40	18	15	7	157	138	43	40	12	22	6	122	142	30
1978-79	40	19	13	8	161	140	46	40	21	16	3	155	152	45
1979-80	40	22	10	8	168	129	52	40	16	22	2	140	155	34
1980-81	40	17	13	10	166	143	44	40	13	23	4	146	174	30
1981-82	40	19	15	6	162	154	44	40	20	12	8	154	152	48
1982-83	40	24	13	3	186	135	51	40	11	22	7	120	152	29
1983-84	40	27	12	1	169	145	55	40	15	17	8	145	159	38
1984-85	40	16	18	6	150	153	38	40	10	26	4	145	192	24
1985-86	40	20	18	2	147	123	42	40	16	20	4	133	153	36
1986-87	40	18	18	4	152	156	40	40	16	20	4	155	167	36
1987-88	40	22	13	5	160	125	49	40	14	21	5	140	158	33
1988-89	40	21	17	2	160	147	44	40	16	18	6	150	160	38
1989-90	40	20	11	9	147	119	49	40	16	20	4	132	148	36
1990-91	40	22	11	7	161	114	51	40	14	20	6	136	151	34
1991-92	40	28	8	4	170	106	60	40	22	17	1	151	140	45
1992-93	42	20	17	5	158	142	45	42	14	22	6	146	166	34
1993-94	42	28	8	6	153	111	62	42	24	16	2	146	120	50
1994-95	24	11	10	3	80	72	25	24	11	13	0	59	62	22
Totals	2291	1118	773	400	7699	6542	2636	2291	819	1155	317	6723	7973	1955

RANGERS YEAR BY YEAR SCORING LEADERS

Year	Goals		Assists		Points	
1926-27	33	Bill Cook	15	Boucher	37	Bill Cook
1927-28	23	Boucher	14	Bun Cook	35	Boucher
1928-29	15	Bill Cook	16	Boucher	26	Boucher
1929-30	29	Bill Cook	36	Boucher	62	Boucher
1930-31	30	Bill Cook	27	Boucher	42	Bill Cook
1931-32	33	Bill Cook	23	Boucher	47	Bill Cook
1932-33	28	Bill Cook	28	Boucher	50	Bill Cook
1933-34	18	Bun Cook	30	Boucher	44	Boucher
1934-35	25	Dillon	32	Boucher	45	Boucher
1935-36	18	Dillon	18	Boucher	32	Dillon
1936-37	22	Keeling	18	N. Colville	31	Dillon
1937-38	21	Dillon	25	Watson	39	Dillon
1938-39	24	Shibicky	23	Heller	41	C. Smith
1939-40	24	Hextall	28	Watson	39	Hextall
1940-41	26	Hextall	28	N. Colville	44	Hextall
					44	Lynn Patrick
1941-42	32	Lynn Patrick	37	Watson	56	Hextall
1942-43	27	Hextall	39	Lynn Patrick	61	Lynn Patrick
1943-44	21	Hextall	33	Hextall	54	Hextall
1944-45	24	DeMarco	30	DeMarco	54	DeMarco
1945-46	20	DeMarco	27	DeMarco	47	DeMarco
1946-47	27	Leswick	25	Laprade	41	Leswick
1947-48	24	O'Connor	36	O'Connor	60	O'Connor
	24	Leswick				
1948-49	18	Laprade	24	O'Connor	35	O'Connor
1949-50	22	Laprade	25	Leswick	44	Laprade
			25	Raleigh	44	Leswick
1950-51	20	Mickoski	24	Raleigh	39	Raleigh
					39	Sinclair
1951-52	26	Hergesheimer	42	Raleigh	61	Raleigh
1952-53	30	Hergesheimer	38	Ronty	59	Hergesheimer
1953-54	27	Hergesheimer	33	Ronty	46	Ronty
1954-55	29	Lewicki	32	Raleigh	53	Lewicki
1955-56	24	Prentice	47	Bathgate	66	Bathgate
	24	Hebenton				
1956-57	27	Bathgate	50	Bathgate	77	Bathgate
1957-58	32	Henry	48	Bathgate	78	Bathgate
1958-59	40	Bathgate	48	Bathgate	88	Bathgate
1959-60	32	Prentice	48	Bathgate	74	Bathgate
1960-61	29	Bathgate	48	Bathgate	77	Bathgate
1961-62	28	Bathgate	56	Bathgate	84	Bathgate
1962-63	37	Henry	46	Bathgate	81	Bathgate
1963-64	29	Henry	41	Goyette	65	Goyette
1964-65	25	Gilbert	36	Gilbert	61	Gilbert
1965-66	29	Nevin	33	Nevin	62	Nevin
1966-67	28	Gilbert	49	Goyette	61	Goyette
1967-68	32	Ratelle	48	Gilbert	78	Ratelle
1968-69	32	Ratelle	49	Gilbert	78	Ratelle
1969-70	33	Balon	50	Tkaczuk	77	Tkaczuk
1970-71	36	Balon	49	Tkaczuk	75	Tkaczuk
1971-72	50	Hadfield	63	Ratelle	109	Ratelle
1972-73	41	Ratelle	59	Gilbert	94	Ratelle
1973-74	36	Gilbert	57	Park	82	Park
1974-75	41	Vickers	61	Gilbert	97	Gilbert
1975-76	36	Gilbert	53	Vickers	86	Gilbert
1976-77	34	Esposito	48	Gilbert	80	Esposito
1977-78	40	Hickey	48	Greschner	81	Esposito
1978-79	42	Esposito	45	Hedberg	78	Esposito
					78	Hedberg
1979-80	34	Esposito	50	Beck	78	Esposito
1980-81	30	Hedberg	41	Greschner	70	Hedberg
	30	Johnstone				
1981-82	40	Duguay	65	Rogers	103	Rogers
1982-83	37	Pavelich	53	Ruotsalainen	76	Rogers
1983-84	48	Larouche	53	Pavelich	82	Pavelich
1984-85	29	Sandstrom	45	Ruotsalainen	73	Ruotsalainen
1985-86	25	Sandstrom	43	Ridley	65	Ridley
1986-87	40	Poddubny	47	Poddubny	87	Poddubny
	40	Sandstrom				
1987-88	38	Poddubny	55	Kisio	88	Poddubny
1988-89	36	Granato	56	Sandstrom	88	Sandstrom
1989-90	43	Ogrodnick	45	Leetch	74	Ogrodnick
1990-91	49	Gartner	72	Leetch	88	Leetch
1991-92	40	Gartner	80	Leetch	107	Messier
1992-93	45	Gartner	66	Messier	91	Messier
1993-94	52	Graves	77	Zubov	89	Zubov
1994-95	17	Graves	39	Messier	53	Messier
	17	Verbeek				

168

RANGERS ALL-TIME SCORING LIST

	PLAYER	GP	Goals	Assists	Points	PIM
1.	Rod Gilbert	1065	406	615	1021	508
2.	Jean Ratelle	862	336	481	817	192
3.	Andy Bathgate	719	272	457	729	444
4.	Walt Tkaczuk	945	227	451	678	556
5.	Ron Greschner	982	179	431	610	1226
6.	Steve Vickers	698	246	340	586	330
7.	Vic Hadfield	838	262	310	572	1036
8.	Don Maloney	653	195	307	502	739
9.	Brian Leetch*	485	112	375	487	255
10.	Camille Henry	637	256	222	478	78
11.	James Patrick	671	104	363	467	541
12.	Dean Prentice	666	186	236	422	263
13.	Frank Boucher	533	152	261	413	114
14.	Phil Esposito	422	184	220	404	263
15.	Anders Hedberg	465	172	225	397	144
16.	Tomas Sandstrom	407	173	207	380	563
17.	Brad Park	465	95	283	378	738
18.	Andy Hebenton	560	177	191	368	75
19.	Bill Cook	475	228	138	366	386
20.	Bryan Hextall	449	187	175	362	227
21.	Bill Fairbairn	536	138	224	362	161
22.	Phil Watson	546	127	233	360	471
23.	Harry Howell	1160	82	263	345	1147
24.	Bob Nevin	505	168	174	342	105
25.	Ron Duguay	499	164	176	340	370
26.	Lynn Patrick	455	145	190	335	240
27.	Mark Messier*	276	100	235	335	264
28.	Phil Goyette	397	98	231	329	51
29.	Don Raleigh	535	101	219	320	96
30.	Mark Pavelich	341	133	185	318	326
31.	Pete Stemkowski	496	113	204	317	380
32.	Reijo Ruotsalainen	389	99	217	316	154
33.	Mike Rogers	316	117	191	308	142
34.	Kelly Kisio	336	110	195	305	415
35.	Jim Neilson	810	60	238	298	766
36.	Dave Maloney	605	70	225	295	1113
37.	Bun Cook	433	154	139	293	436
38.	Mike Gartner	322	173	113	286	231
39.	Cecil Dillon	409	160	121	281	93
40.	Edgar Laprade	500	108	172	280	42
41.	Don Marshall	479	129	141	270	40
42.	Bill Gadsby	457	58	212	270	411
43.	Neil Colville	463	99	166	265	213
44.	Earl Ingarfield	527	122	142	264	198
45.	Pat Hickey	370	128	129	257	216
46.	Darren Turcotte	325	122	133	255	183
47.	John Ogrodnick	338	126	128	254	106
48.	Brian Mullen	307	100	148	248	188
49.	Rod Seiling	644	50	198	248	423
50.	Carol Vadnais	485	56	190	246	690
51.	Pierre Larouche	253	123	120	243	59
52.	Barry Beck	415	66	173	239	775
53	Adam Graves*	295	131	103	234	465
54.	Ed Johnstone	371	109	125	234	319
55.	Grant Warwick	293	117	116	233	179
56.	Ott Heller	647	55	176	231	465
57.	Jan Erixon	556	57	159	216	167
58.	Dave Balon	361	99	113	212	284
59.	Red Sullivan	322	59	150	209	300
60.	Tony Leswick	368	113	89	202	420
61.	Larry Popein	402	75	127	202	150
62.	Alex Shibicky	322	110	91	201	161

* Active Rangers

RANGERS CAREER LEADERS

GOALS

Rod Gilbert	406
Jean Ratelle	336
Andy Bathgate	272
Vic Hadfield	262
Camille Henry	256
Steve Vickers	246
Bill Cook	228
Walt Tkaczuk	227
Don Maloney	195
Bryan Hextall	187
Dean Prentice	186
Phil Esposito	184
Ron Greschner	179
Andy Hebenton	177
Mike Gartner	173
Tomas Sandstrom	173
Anders Hedberg	172
Bob Nevin	168
Ron Duguay	164
Cecil Dillon	160
Bun Cook	154
Frank Boucher	152

GAMES

Harry Howell	1160
Rod Gilbert	1065
Rod Greschner	982
Walt Tkaczuk	945
Jean Ratelle	862
Vic Hadfield	838
Jim Neilson	810
Andy Bathgate	719
Steve Vickers	698
James Patrick	671
Dean Prentice	666
Don Maloney	653
Ott Heller	647
Rod Seiling	644
Camille Henry	637
Dave Maloney	605

WINS

Ed Giacomin	266
Lorne Worsley	204
John Vanbiesbrouck	200
Dave Kerr	157
*Mike Richter	125
Chuck Rayner	123
Gilles Villemure	96
John Davidson	93
John Ross Roach	80
Glen Hanlon	56

ASSISTS

Rod Gilbert	615
Jean Ratelle	481
Andy Bathgate	457
Walt Tkaczuk	451
Ron Greschner	431
*Brian Leetch	375
James Patrick	363
Steve Vickers	340
Vic Hadfield	310
Don Maloney	307
Brad Park	283
Harry Howell	263
Frank Boucher	261
Jim Neilson	238
Dean Prentice	236
*Mark Messier	235
Phil Watson	233
Phil Goyette	231
Anders Hedberg	225
Dave Maloney	225
Bill Fairbairn	224
Camille Henry	222
Phil Esposito	220
Don Raleigh	219
Reijo Ruotsalainen	217
Bill Gadsby	212
Tomas Sandstrom	207
Pete Stemkowski	204

PENALTY MINUTES

Ron Greschner	1226
Harry Howell	1147
Dave Maloney	1113
Vic Hadfield	1036
Nick Fotiu	970
Lou Fontinato	939
Ching Johnson	798
Barry Beck	775
Jim Neilson	766
Don Maloney	739
Brad Park	738
Kris King	733
Carol Vadnais	690
Jack Evans	670
Tomas Sandstrom	563
Tom Laidlaw	561
Troy Mallette	557
Walt Tkaczuk	556
Arnie Brown	545
Jame Patrick	541
Reg Fleming	540
Tie Domi	526
*Jeff Beukeboom	515
Rod Gilbert	508

SHUTOUTS

Ed Giacomin	49
Dave Kerr	40
John Ross Roach	30
Chuck Rayner	24
Lorne Worsley	24
Lorne Chabot	21
John Vanbiesbrouck	16
Gilles Villemure	13
Andy Aitkenhead	11
*Mike Richter	11

*Active Rangers

RANGERS SINGLE SEASON LEADERS

GOALS

*Adam Graves	1993-94	52
Vic Hadfield	1971-72	50
Mike Gartner	1990-91	49
Pierre Larouche	1983-84	48
Jean Ratelle	1971-72	46
Mike Gartner	1992-93	45
Rod Gilbert	1971-72	43
John Ogrodnick	1989-90	43
Phil Esposito	1978-79	42
Jean Ratelle	1972-73	41
Steve Vickers	1974-75	41
Andy Bathgate	1958-59	40
Pat Hickey	1977-78	40
Ron Duguay	1981-82	40
Walt Poddubny	1986-87	40
Tomas Sandstrom	1986-87	40
Mike Gartner	1991-92	40

POINTS

Jean Ratelle	1971-72	109
*Mark Messier	1991-92	107
Vic Hadfield	1971-72	106
Mike Rogers	1981-82	103
*Brian Leetch	1991-92	102
Rod Gilbert	1971-72	97
Rod Gilbert	1974-75	97
Jean Ratelle	1972-73	94
Jean Ratelle	1974-75	91
*Mark Messier	1992-93	91
Steve Vickers	1974-75	89
Sergei Zubov	1993-94	89
Andy Bathgate	1958-59	88
Walt Poddubny	1987-88	88
Tomas Sandstrom	1988-89	88
*Brian Leetch	1990-91	88
Walt Poddubny	1986-87	87
Rod Gilbert	1975-76	86

ASSISTS

*Brian Leetch	1991-92	80
Sergei Zubov	1993-94	77
*Brian Leetch	1990-91	72
*Mark Messier	1991-92	72
*Mark Messier	1992-93	66
Mike Rogers	1981-82	65
Jean Ratelle	1971-72	63
Rod Gilbert	1974-75	61
Rod Gilbert	1972-73	59
*Mark Messier	1993-94	58
Brad Park	1973-74	57
James Patrick	1991-92	57
Andy Bathgate	1961-62	56
Vic Hadfield	1971-72	56
Tomas Sandstrom	1988-89	56
*Brian Leetch	1993-94	56
Jean Ratelle	1974-75	55
Kelly Kisio	1987-88	55
Rod Gilbert	1971-72	54
Jean Ratelle	1972-73	53
Steve Vickers	1975-76	53
Reijo Ruotsalainen	1982-83	53
Mark Pavelich	1983-84	53
Andy Bathgate	1956-57	50
Walt Tkaczuk	1969-70	50
Rod Gilbert	1975-76	50
Walt Poddubny	1987-88	50

GOALS BY A ROOKIE

Tony Granato	1988-89	36
Tony Amonte	1991-92	35
Mark Pavelich	1981-82	33
Don Murdoch	1976-77	32
Darren Turcotte	1989-90	32
Steve Vickers	1972-73	30
Tomas Sandstrom	1984-85	29
Ulf Dahlen	1987-88	29
Wally Hergesheimer	1951-52	26
Mike Allison	1980-81	26

WINS

*Mike Richter	1993-94	42
Ed Giacomin	1968-69	37
Ed Giacomin	1967-68	36
Ed Giacomin	1969-70	35
Lorne Worsley	1955-56	32
John Vanbiesbrouck	1985-86	31
Ed Giacomin	1966-67	30
Ed Giacomin	1973-74	30
Jim Henry	1941-42	29
John Bower	1953-54	29
Chuck Rayner	1949-50	28
Glen Hanlon	1983-84	28
John Vanbiesbrouck	1988-89	28

PIM

Troy Mallette	1989-90	305
Kris King	1989-90	286
Troy Mallette	1990-91	252
Tie Domi	1991-92	246
Barry Beck	1980-81	231
Michel Petit	1987-88	223
Ed Hospodar	1980-81	214
Lou Fontinato	1955-56	202
Rudy Poeschek	1988-89	199
Nick Fotiu	1978-79	190
Dave Maloney	1979-80	186
Tie Domi	1990-91	185
Larry Melynk	1986-87	182
Chris Nilan	1988-89	177
Nick Fotiu	1976-77	174

GOALS BY A DEFENSEMAN

Brad Park	1973-74	25
Brad Park	1971-72	24
*Brian Leetch	1988-89	23
*Brian Leetch	1993-94	23
*Brian Leetch	1991-92	22
Ron Greschner	1977-78	21
Ron Greschner	1979-80	21
Ron Greschner	1980-81	20
Carol Vadnais	1975-76	20
Mike McEwen	1978-79	20
Reijo Ruotsalainen	1983-84	20

SHUTOUTS

John Ross Roach	1928-29	13
Lorne Chabot	1927-28	11
Lorne Chabot	1926-27	10
John Ross Roach	1931-32	9
Ed Giacomin	1966-67	9
Dave Kerr	1935-36	8
Dave Kerr	1937-38	8
Dave Kerr	1939-40	8
Ed Giacomin	1967-68	8
Ed Giacomin	1970-71	8

POWER PLAY GOALS

Vic Hadfield	1971-72	23
Marcel Dionne	1987-88	22
Mike Gartner	1990-91	22
Phil Esposito	1977-78	21
*Adam Graves	1993-94	20
Pierre Larouche	1983-84	19
John Ogrodnick	1989-90	19
*Brian Leetch	1993-94	17
Rod Gilbert	1973-74	16
Jean Ratelle	1974-75	16
Steve Vickers	1974-75	16
Phil Esposito	1975-76	16
Phil Esposito	1976-77	15
Darren Turcotte	1990-91	15
Mike Gartner	1991-92	15

SHORTHANDED GOALS

Don Maloney	1980-81	5
Mike Rogers	1982-83	5
Mike Gartner	1993-94	5
Ron Stewart	1969-70	4
Bill Fairbairn	1971-72	4
Greg Polis	1977-78	4
Tony Granato	1988-89	4
*Adam Graves	1991-92	4
*Mark Messier	1991-92	4
*Adam Graves	1993-94	4
Steve Larmer	1993-94	4

*Active Rangers

RANGERS ALL-TIME LONGEST SCORING STREAKS

Longest All-Time Point Scoring Streaks

17   **Brian Leetch, Nov. 23 to Dec. 31, 1991, (5 goals and 24 assists).**
16   Mike Rogers, Feb. 14 to Mar. 20, 1982, (10 goals and 18 assists).
15   Mark Messier, Feb. 5 to Mar. 7, 1992, (7 goals and 17 assists).
15   Walt Poddubny, Jan. 11 to Feb. 17, 1987, (11 goals and 8 assists).
14   Carey Wilson, Dec. 26 to Jan. 26, 1989, (7 goals and 17 assists).
14   Rod Gilbert, Oct. 7 to Nov. 8, 1972, (11 goals and 12 assists).
14   Brian Leetch, Oct. 7 to Nov. 4, 1991, (4 goals and 16 assists).
14   Reijo Ruotsalainen, Feb. 5 to Mar. 7, 1985, (9 goals and 11 assists).
13   Jean Ratelle, Feb. 3 to Feb. 27, 1972, (16 goals and 12 assists).
13   Jean Ratelle, Mar. 5 to Mar. 30, 1969, (12 goals and 10 assists).
13   Walt Tkaczuk, Dec. 28 to Jan. 28, 1978, (9 goals and 12 assists).
13   Andy Bathgate, Dec. 9 to Jan. 5, 1963, (12 goals and 6 assists).
13   Rod Gilbert, Nov. 8 to Dec. 5, 1968, (5 goals and 12 assists).

Longest All-Time Goal Scoring Streaks

10   **Andy Bathgate, Dec. 15 to Jan. 15, 1963, (11 goals).**
8   Jean Ratelle, Feb. 12 to Feb. 23, 1972, (12 goals).
8   Jean Ratelle, Feb. 15 to Mar. 4, 1973, (10 goals).
8   Phil Esposito, Mar. 22 to Mar. 29, 1978, (8 goals).
7   Rod Gilbert, Jan. 25 to Feb. 7, 1976, (12 goals).
7   Pierre Larouche, Feb. 5 to Feb. 24, 1986, (10 goals).
7   Andy Bathgate, Nov. 8 to Nov. 23, 1958, (9 goals).
7   Mike Gartner, Mar. 12 to Mar. 27, 1990, (8 goals).
7   Eddie Johnstone, Mar. 14 to Mar. 28, 1982, (8 goals).
7   Mike Gartner, Jan. 30 to Feb. 13, 1991, (7 goals).
7   Rod Gilbert, Dec. 12 to Jan. 23, 1964, (7 goals).
7   Bryan Hextall, Feb. 25 to Mar. 16, 1941, (7 goals).

Longest All-Time Assist Streaks

15   **Brian Leetch, Nov. 29 to Dec. 31, 1991, (23 assists).**
10   Rod Gilbert, Mar. 5 to Mar. 26, 1969, (14 assists).
9   Darren Turcotte, Oct. 8 to Oct. 25, 1990, (11 assists).
9   Jean Ratelle, Oct. 25 to Nov. 8, 1972, (10 assists).
8   Mark Messier, Apr. 12 to Apr. 26, 1995, (19 assists).
8   Don Maloney, Mar. 8 to Mar. 24, 1982, (12 assists).
8   Mark Messier, Feb. 12 to Feb 27, 1993, (11 assists).
8   Lynn Patrick, Jan. 1 to Jan. 21, 1943, (11 assists).
8   Mike Rogers, Mar. 4 to Mar. 20, 1982, (10 assists).
8   Babe Pratt, Jan. 6 to Feb. 1, 1942, (10 assists).
8   Earl Ingarfield, Jan. 22 to Feb. 5, 1961, (8 assists).
     Seventeen players are tied with 7.

LONGEST GOAL SCORING STREAKS YEAR-BY-YEAR

(Since 1950)

1994-95	Sergei Zubov	5	Apr. 16 to Apr. 24, 1995	(5 goals)
1993-94	Adam Graves	4	Oct. 11 to Oct. 16, 1993	(4 goals)
		4	Nov. 3 to Nov. 10, 1993	(4 goals)
		4	Nov. 16 to Nov. 24, 1993	(4 goals)
	Alexei Kovalev	4	Mar. 27 to Apr. 2, 1994	(4 goals)
	Mark Messier	4	Oct. 7 to Oct. 13, 1993	(4 goals)
		4	Jan. 25 to Jan. 31, 1994	(6 goals)
1992-93	Mike Gartner	6	Jan. 2 to Jan. 13, 1993	(9 goals)
	Darren Turcotte	6	Nov. 30 to Dec 11, 1992	(7 goals)
	Darren Turcotte	6	Oct. 31 to Nov 11, 1992	(7 goals)
1991-92	Sergei Nemchinov	6	Dec. 2 to Dec. 14, 1991	(6 goals)
1990-91	Mike Gartner	7	Jan. 30 to Feb. 13, 1991	(7 goals)
1989-90	Mike Gartner	7	Mar. 12 to Mar. 27, 1990	(8 goals)
1988-89	Tony Granato	6	Jan. 9 to Jan. 21, 1989	(10 goals)
1987-88	Walt Poddubny	5	Dec. 20 to Dec. 29, 1987	(7 goals)
	Ulf Dahlen	5	Dec. 31 to Jan. 8, 1988	(6 goals)
1986-87	Tomas Sandstrom	5	Jan. 14 to Jan. 26, 1987	(8 goals)
1985-86	Pierre Larouche	7	Feb. 5 to Feb. 24, 1986	(10 goals)
1984-85	Tomas Sandstrom	5	Dec. 30 to Jan. 9, 1985	(6 goals)
1983-84	Pierre Larouche	5	Dec. 12 to Dec. 30, 1983	(7 goals)
	Anders Hedberg	5	Mar. 22 to Mar. 31, 1984	(5 goals)
	Don Maloney	5	Nov. 13 to Nov. 23, 1983	(5 goals)
1982-83	Don Maloney	4	Jan. 3 to Jan. 9, 1983	(5 goals)
	Anders Hedberg	4	Oct. 20 to Oct. 27, 1982	(4 goals)
	Mark Pavelich	4	Oct. 24 to Oct. 31, 1982	(4 goals)
	Don Maloney	4	Nov. 10 to Nov. 17, 1982	(4 goals)
1981-82	Ed Johnstone	7	Mar. 4 to Mar. 28, 1982	(8 goals)
1980-81	Ron Greschner	5	Oct. 25 to Nov. 1, 1980	(5 goals)
1979-80	Phil Esposito	5	Jan. 22 to Feb. 2, 1980	(6 goals)
1978-79	Ron Duguay	6	Jan. 24 to Feb. 3, 1979	(7 goals)
1977-78	Phil Esposito	8	Mar. 22 to Mar. 29, 1978	(8 goals)
1976-77	Rod Gilbert	3	Nov. 22 to Nov. 27, 1976	(4 goals)
	Phil Esposito	3	Oct. 13 to Oct. 17, 1976	(3 goals)
1975-76	Rod Gilbert	7	Jan. 25 to Feb. 7, 1976	(12 goals)
1974-75	Steve Vickers	4	Mar. 19 to Mar. 23, 1975	(6 goals)
	Jean Ratelle	4	Jan. 23 to Jan. 28, 1975	(4 goals)
1973-74	Rod Gilbert	5	Dec. 16 to Dec. 26, 1973	(5 goals)
1972-73	Jean Ratelle	8	Feb. 15 to Mar. 4, 1973	(10 goals)
1971-72	Jean Ratelle	8	Feb. 12 to Feb. 23, 1972	(12 goals)
1970-71	Bruce MacGregor	5	Feb. 27 to Mar. 6, 1971	(6 goals)
	Rod Gilbert	5	Jan. 31 to Feb. 9, 1971	(5 goals)
1969-70	Dave Balon	5	Feb. 1 to Feb. 13, 1970	(7 goals)
1968-69	Reg Fleming	5	Dec. 21 to Dec. 28, 1968	(5 goals)
1967-68	Jean Ratelle	3	Feb. 11 to Feb. 18, 1968	(5 goals)
	Jean Ratelle	3	Feb. 24 to Feb. 29, 1968	(4 goals)
	Vic Hadfield	3	Oct. 21 to Oct. 25, 1967	(4 goals)
	Vic Hadfield	3	Mar. 2 to Mar. 6, 1968	(4 goals)
	Vic Hadfield	3	Dec. 30 to Jan. 3, 1968	(3 goals)
	Phil Goyette	3	Oct. 18 to Oct. 22, 1967	(4 goals)
	Phil Goyette	3	Jan. 13 to Jan. 19, 1968	(3 goals)
	Rod Gilbert	3	Dec. 31 to Jan. 6, 1968	(3 goals)
	Rod Gilbert	3	Feb. 4 to Feb. 11, 1968	(3 goals)
	Bob Nevin	3	Nov. 29 to Dec. 3, 1967	(3 goals)
1966-67	Rod Gilbert	5	Dec. 7 to Dec. 17, 1966	(7 goals)
1965-66	Jean Ratelle	3	Jan. 1 to Jan. 8, 1966	(4 goals)
	Don Marshall	3	Nov. 20 to Nov. 24, 1965	(3 goals)
	Don Marshall	3	Jan. 26 to Jan. 30, 1966	(3 goals)
	Rod Gilbert	3	Oct. 30 to Nov. 6, 1965	(3 goals)
	Rod Seiling	3	Nov. 13 to Nov. 17, 1965	(3 goals)
	Vic Hadfield	3	Jan. 30 to Feb. 5, 1966	(3 goals)
	Reg Fleming	3	Feb. 20 to Feb. 26, 1966	(3 goals)
1964-65	Rod Gilbert	4	Dec. 29 to Jan. 6, 1965	(4 goals)
1963-64	Rod Gilbert	7	Dec. 12 to Jan. 23, 1964	(7 goals)
1962-63	**ANDY BATHGATE**	**10**	**DEC. 15 TO JAN. 5, 1963**	**(11 GOALS)**
1961-62	Johnny Wilson	4	Feb. 15 to Feb. 21, 1962	(5 goals)
1960-61	Andy Hebenton	4	Jan. 8 to Jan. 15, 1961	(4 goals)
	Camille Henry	4	Nov. 13 to Nov. 23, 1960	(4 goals)
1959-60	Andy Bathgate	4	Nov. 18 to Nov. 26, 1959	(6 goals)
	Dean Prentice	4	Nov. 28 to Dec. 5, 1959	(6 goals)
	Andy Hebenton	4	Dec. 27 to Jan. 3, 1960	(4 goals)
1958-59	Andy Bathgate	7	Nov. 8 to Nov. 23, 1958	(9 goals)
1957-58	Andy Bathgate	4	Feb. 23 to Mar. 2, 1958	(6 goals)
1956-57	Andy Hebenton	3	Jan. 9 to Jan. 12, 1957	(5 goals)
	Andy Bathgate	3	Nov. 28 to Dec. 2, 1956	(4 goals)
	Camille Henry	3	Feb. 7 to Feb. 10, 1957	(3 goals)
	Camille Henry	3	Feb. 14 to Feb. 20, 1957	(3 goals)
	Red Sullivan	3	Nov. 14 to Nov. 18, 1956	(3 goals)
1955-56	Andy Bathgate	5	Nov. 27 to Dec. 7, 1955	(6 goals)
1954-55	Danny Lewicki	3	Nov. 13 to Nov. 17, 1954	(5 goals)
	Dean Prentice	3	Dec. 25 to Dec. 30, 1954	(5 goals)
1953-54	Wally Hergesheimer	3	Jan. 17 to Jan. 23, 1954	(4 goals)
1952-53	Nick Mickoski	4	Dec. 28 to Jan. 7, 1953	(4 goals)
1951-52	Camille Henry	3	Nov. 4 to Nov. 11, 1951	(4 goals)
	Camille Henry	3	Dec. 9 to Dec. 12, 1951	(3 goals)
	Don Raleigh	3	Dec. 20 to Dec. 25, 1951	(3 goals)
1950-51	Nick Mickoski	3	Dec. 17 to Dec. 24, 1950	(6 goals)
	Tony Leswick	3	Jan. 13 to Jan. 17, 1951	(3 goals)

LONGEST ASSIST STREAKS YEAR-BY-YEAR

(Since 1950)

Year	Player		Dates	
1994-95	Mark Messier	8	Apr. 12 to Apr. 26, 1995	(19 assists)
1993-94	Brian Leetch	5	Nov. 14 to Nov. 24, 1993	(7 assists)
	Sergei Zubov	5	Oct. 22 to Oct. 31, 1993	(8 assists)
	Sergei Zubov	5	Jan. 14 to Jan. 27, 1994	(8 assists)
1992-93	Mark Messier	8	Feb. 12 to Feb. 27, 1993	(11 assists)
1991-92	**BRIAN LEETCH**	**15**	**NOV. 29 TO DEC. 31, 1991**	**(23 ASSISTS)**
1990-91	Darren Turcotte	9	Oct. 8 to Oct. 25, 1990	(11 assists)
1989-90	Brian Mullen	6	Feb. 21 to Mar. 3, 1990	(10 assists)
1988-89	Brian Leetch	7	Feb. 17 to Mar. 1, 1989	(11 assists)
	Carey Wilson	7	Jan. 9 to Jan. 23, 1989	(9 assists)
1987-88	Kelly Kisio	6	Jan. 19 to Feb. 4, 1988	(8 assists)
	Walt Poddubny	6	Feb. 29 to Mar. 12, 1988	(8 assists)
	Brian Leetch	6	Mar. 22 to Apr. 1, 1988	(7 assists)
1986-87	Pierre Larouche	5	Feb. 7 to Feb. 19, 1987	(7 assists)
	Curt Giles	5	Dec. 21 to Dec. 30, 1986	(6 assists)
1985-86	Mike Ridley	7	Feb. 8 to Feb. 25, 1986	(11 assists)
	Reijo Ruotsalainen	7	Oct. 25 to Mar. 9, 1985	(9 assists)
1984-85	Tomas Sandstrom	5	Dec. 30 to Jan. 9, 1985	(6 assists)
1983-84	Mikko Leinonen	6	Feb. 11 to Feb. 25, 1984	(7 assists)
1982-83	Dave Maloney	7	Nov. 11 to Dec. 12, 1982	(8 assists)
1981-82	Don Maloney	8	Mar. 8 to Mar. 24, 1982	(12 assists)
	Mike Rogers	8	Mar. 4 to Mar. 20, 1982	(10 assists)
1980-81	Tom Laidlaw	5	Feb. 19 to Feb. 28, 1981	(7 assists)
	Steve Vickers	5	Dec. 3 to Dec. 12, 1980	(5 assists)
1979-80	Don Maloney	7	Dec. 3 to Dec. 15, 1979	(6 assists)
1978-79	Ron Greschner	6	Oct. 28 to Nov. 8, 1978	(7 assists)
	Don Maloney	6	Mar. 4 to Mar. 15, 1979	(6 assists)
1977-78	Carol Vadnais	4	Oct. 25 to Oct. 30, 1977	(4 assists)
	Walt Tkaczuk	4	Mar. 8 to Mar. 18, 1978	(4 assists)
1976-77	Rod Gilbert	7	Nov. 28 to Dec. 8, 1976	(10 assists)
1975-76	Rod Gilbert	6	Oct. 8 to Oct. 19, 1975	(8 assists)
1974-75	Rod Gilbert	7	Nov. 27 to Dec. 12, 1974	(8 assists)
1973-74	Rod Gilbert	5	Dec. 1 to Dec. 9, 1973	(6 assists)
1972-73	Jean Ratelle	9	Oct. 25 to Nov. 8, 1972	(10 assists)
1971-72	Jean Ratelle	7	Nov. 28 to Dec. 12, 1971	(14 assists)
	Rod Gilbert	7	Feb. 13 to Feb. 23, 1972	(10 assists)
	Vic Hadfield	7	Oct. 31 to Nov. 14, 1971	(9 assists)
1970-71	Walt Tkaczuk	7	Dec. 19 to Dec. 29, 1970	(9 assists)
1969-70	Rod Gilbert	7	Nov. 22 to Dec. 10, 1969	(10 assists)
1968-69	Rod Gilbert	10	Mar. 5 to Mar. 26, 1969	(14 assists)
1967-68	Rod Gilbert	6	Feb. 4 to Feb. 17, 1968	(10 assists)
	Rod Gilbert	6	Feb. 24 to Mar. 6, 1968	(7 assists)
1966-67	Earl Ingarfield	5	Nov. 20 to Nov. 30, 1966	(6 assists)
	Phil Goyette	5	Feb. 8 to Feb. 26, 1967	(5 assists)
1965-66	Phil Goyette	5	Nov. 17 to Nov. 25, 1965	(7 assists)
1964-65	Rod Gilbert	7	Mar. 14 to Mar. 28, 1965	(10 assists)
1963-64	Phil Goyette	6	Jan. 15 to Jan. 25, 1964	(6 assists)
1962-63	Dean Prentice	5	Dec. 12 to Dec. 31, 1962	(6 assists)
	Andy Bathgate	5	Feb. 12 to Feb. 23, 1963	(5 assists)
1961-62	Andy Bathgate	6	Oct. 11 to Oct. 19, 1961	(8 assists)
	Andy Bathgate	6	Jan. 3 to Jan. 17, 1962	(7 assists)
1960-61	Earl Ingarfield	8	Jan. 22 to Feb. 5, 1961	(8 assists)
1959-60	Andy Hebenton	4	Oct. 24 to Nov. 1, 1959	(4 assists)
	Andy Bathgate	4	Dec. 5 to Dec. 13, 1959	(4 assists)
1958-59	Andy Bathgate	6	Jan. 14 to Jan. 28, 1959	(7 assists)
1957-58	Andy Bathgate	6	Feb. 14 to Feb. 26, 1958	(8 assists)
1956-57	Andy Bathgate	5	Feb. 10 to Feb. 20, 1957	(6 assists)
	Camille Henry	5	Feb. 7 to Feb. 16, 1957	(6 assists)
	Camille Henry	5	Feb. 20 to Mar. 2, 1957	(5 assists)
1955-56	Andy Bathgate	7	Dec. 25 to Jan. 11, 1956	(10 assists)
1954-55	Don Raleigh	6	Feb. 5 to Feb. 16, 1955	(7 assists)
1953-54	Paul Ronty	5	Feb. 14 to Feb. 24, 1954	(6 assists)
1952-53	Wally Hergesheimer	3	Dec. 17 to Dec. 20, 1952	(5 assists)
	Don Raleigh	3	Feb. 1 to Feb. 8, 1953	(4 assists)
	Hy Buller	3	Oct. 19 to Oct. 26, 1952	(3 assists)
	Hy Buller	3	Mar. 5 to Mar. 8, 1953	(3 assists)
	Wally Hergesheimer	3	Oct. 16 to Oct. 19, 1952	(3 assists)
	Paul Ronty	3	Mar. 14 to Mar. 18, 1953	(3 assists)
	Neil Strain	3	Dec. 14 to Dec. 18, 1952	(3 assists)
1951-52	Don Raleigh	4	Dec. 1 to Dec. 9, 1951	(7 assists)
	Steve Kraftcheck	4	Jan. 13 to Jan. 20, 1952	(4 assists)
1950-51	Reg Sinclair	5	Feb. 2 to Mar. 7, 1951	(7 assists)

RANGERS ALL-TIME POINT SCORING STREAKS YEAR-BY-YEAR

(Since 1950)

1994-95	Mark Messier	8	Apr. 12 to Apr. 26, 1995	(19 assists)
1993-94	Alexei Kovalev	11	Mar. 16 to Apr. 8, 1994	(10 goals and 5 assists)
	Mark Messier	11	Jan, 14 to Feb. 9, 1994	(10 goals and 11 assists)
1992-93	Mark Messier	9	Oct. 12 to Oct. 29, 1992	(6 goals and 10 assists)
	Tony Amonte	9	Mar. 6 to Mar. 26, 1993	(3 goals and 11 assists)
1991-92	**BRIAN LEETCH**	**17**	**NOV. 23 TO DEC. 31, 1991 (5 GOALS AND 24 ASSISTS)**	
1990-91	Darren Turcotte	11	Oct. 4 to Oct. 25, 1990	(6 goals and 13 assists)
1989-90	Brian Mullen	12	Feb. 14 to Mar. 10, 1990	(6 goals and 14 assists)
1988-89	Carey Wilson	14	Dec. 26 to Jan. 26, 1989	(7 goals and 17 assists)
1987-88	Walt Poddubny	11	Oct. 12 to Nov. 1, 1987	(9 goals and 9 assists)
1986-87	Walt Poddubny	15	Jan. 11 to Feb. 17, 1987	(11 goals and 8 assists)
1985-86	Pierre Larouche	9	Feb. 5 to Feb. 27, 1986	(10 goals and 4 assists)
1984-85	Reijo Ruotsalainen	14	Feb. 5 to Mar. 7, 1985	(9 goals and 11 assists)
1983-84	Mike Rogers	10	Oct. 10 to Oct. 30, 1983	(3 goals and 9 assists)
1982-83	Don Maloney	10	Nov. 6 to Nov. 27, 1982	(7 goals and 7 assists)
1981-82	Mike Rogers	16	Feb. 14 to Mar. 20, 1982	(10 goals and 18 assists)
1980-81	Don Maloney	7	Nov. 26 to Dec. 10, 1980	(4 goals and 5 assists)
1979-80	Don Maloney	7	Dec. 3 to Dec. 15, 1979	(3 goals and 6 assists)
1978-79	Mike McEwen	5	Oct. 12 to Oct. 21, 1978	(3 goals and 5 assists)
1977-78	Don Murdoch	8	Feb. 23 to Mar. 15, 1978	(7 goals and 6 assists)
1976-77	Rod Gilbert	10	Nov. 20 to Dec. 8, 1976	(7 goals and 11 assists)
1975-76	Rod Gilbert	8	Jan. 23 to Feb. 7, 1976	(12 goals and 3 assists)
1974-75	Rod Gilbert	7	Nov. 27 to Dec. 12, 1974	(7 goals and 8 assists)
1973-74	Rod Gilbert	5	Dec. 1 to Dec. 9, 1973	(5 goals and 6 assists)
1972-73	Rod Gilbert	14	Oct. 7 to Nov. 8, 1972	(11 goals and 12 assists)
1971-72	Jean Ratelle	13	Feb. 3 to Feb. 27, 1972	(16 goals and 12 assists)
1970-71	Rod Gilbert	10	Jan. 20 to Feb. 9, 1971	(9 goals and 3 assists)
1969-70	Walt Tkaczuk	13	Dec. 28 to Jan. 28, 1978	(9 goals and 12 assists)
1968-69	Rod Gilbert	13	Nov. 8 to Dec. 5, 1968	(5 goals and 12 assists)
	Jean Ratelle	13	Mar. 5 to Mar. 30, 1969	(12 goals and 10 assists)
1967-68	Rod Gilbert	10	Dec. 25 to Jan. 17, 1968	(6 goals and 11 assists)
1966-67	Earl Ingarfield	6	Nov. 19 to Nov. 30, 1966	(2 goals and 6 assists)
1965-66	Don Marshall	7	Feb. 19 to Mar. 3, 1966	(5 goals and 5 assists)
1964-65	Rod Gilbert	7	Mar. 14 to Mar. 28, 1965	(2 goals and 10 assists)
1963-64	Rod Gilbert	11	Dec. 29 to Jan. 23, 1964	(8 goals and 7 assists)
1962-63	Andy Bathgate	13	Dec. 9 to Jan. 5, 1963	(12 goals and 6 assists)
1961-62	Dean Prentice	9	Jan. 31 to Feb. 15, 1962	(5 goals and 7 assists)
1960-61	Red Sullivan	8	Jan. 4 to Feb. 18, 1961	(4 goals and 4 assists)
	Earl Ingarfield	8	Jan. 22 to Feb. 5, 1961	(8 assists)
1959-60	Dean Prentice	8	Mar. 6 to Mar. 20, 1960	(6 goals and 6 assists)
1958-59	Andy Bathgate	12	Jan. 10 to Feb. 7, 1959	(8 goals and 11 assists)
1957-58	Andy Bathgate	8	Feb. 14 to Mar. 2, 1958	(8 goals and 9 assists)
1956-57	Camille Henry	11	Feb. 7 to Mar. 2, 1957	(8 goals and 12 assists)
1955-56	Dave Creighton	8	Oct. 7 to Oct. 26, 1955	(4 goals and 8 assists)
1954-55	Danny Lewicki	6	Feb. 5 to Feb. 16, 1955	(4 goals and 5 assists)
	Don Raleigh	6	Feb. 5 to Feb. 16, 1955	(2 goals and 7 assists)
	Dean Prentice	6	Nov. 27 to Dec. 8, 1954	(2 goals and 5 assists)
1953-54	Paul Ronty	5	Feb. 14 to Feb. 24, 1954	(1 goal and 6 assists)
1952-53	Wally Hergesheimer	9	Dec. 7 to Dec. 28, 1952	(3 goals and 9 assists)
1951-52	Hy Buller	6	Jan. 9 to Jan. 20, 1952	(4 goals and 3 assists)
1950-51	Jack McLeod	6	Nov. 5 to Nov. 18, 1950	(3 goals and 4 assists)
	Buddy O'Connor	6	Feb. 1 to Feb. 15, 1951	(3 goals and 4 assists)

RANGERS LAST OVERTIME WIN & LOSS VS. NHL OPPONENTS

	WIN	LOSS
ANAHEIM	NONE	NONE
BOSTON	2-1, Oct. 7, 1991 at MSG (Gartner, 0:31)	2-3, Nov. 5, 1990 at MSG (B. Sweeney, 3:30)
BUFFALO	7-6, Nov. 2, 1992 at MSG (Turcotte, 0:58)	NONE
CALGARY	NONE	NONE
CHICAGO	NONE	4-5, Nov. 11, 1985 at MSG (B. Murray, 0:53)
COLORADO	6-5, Nov. 20, 1983 at MSG (Andersson, 0:08)	2-3, Nov. 25, 1984 at MSG (Hunter, 3:36)
DALLAS	NONE	3-4, Nov. 9, 1993 at Min. (Bjugstad, 2:04)
DETROIT	NONE	5-6, Dec. 6, 1991 at Det. (Fedyk, 4:23)
EDMONTON	NONE	3-4, Mar. 17, 1993 at MSG (MacTavish, 0:32)
FLORIDA	NONE	NONE
HARTFORD	NONE	3-4, Dec 21, 1986 at MSG (K. Dineen, 2:57)
LOS ANGELES	5-4, Jan. 27, 1994 at LA (Messier, 4:58)	NONE
MONTREAL	2-1, Oct. 5, 1991 at Mtl. (Nemchinov, 1:42)	3-4, Feb. 9, 1994 at Mtl. (Desjardins, 1:27)
NEW JERSEY	4-3, Feb. 19, 1990 at MSG (Mullen, 4:47)	4-5, Dec. 23, 1992 at MSG (Richer, 1:33)
ISLANDERS	4-3, Dec. 31, 1986 at MSG (Sandstrom, 4:37)	2-3, Apr. 3, 1993 at MSG (Turgeon, 3:41)
OTTAWA	4-3, Feb. 12, 1994 at Ott. (Gartner, 2:37)	NONE
PHILADELPHIA	2-1, Feb. 23, 1992 at MSG (Amonte, 4:21)	2-3, Feb. 19, 1984 at MSG (Kerr, 1:33)
PITTSBURGH	4-3, Feb. 21, 1994 at MSG (Amonte, 0:08)	4-5, Mar. 21, 1991 at Pit. (Stevens, 0:13)
ST. LOUIS	3-2, Jan. 5, 1991 at Stl. (Nicholls, 3:12)	NONE
SAN JOSE	4-3, Dec. 16, 1991 at MSG (Leetch, 0:23)	NONE
TAMPA BAY	NONE	NONE
TORONTO	NONE	NONE
VANCOUVER	5-4, Jan. 21, 1989 at Van. (Kisio, 1:59)	NONE
WASHINGTON	5-4, Feb. 7, 1987 at Wsh. (Sandstrom, 4:20)	3-4, Dec. 29, 1992 at Wsh. (Pivonka, 1:28)
WINNIPEG	6-5, Mar. 9, 1984 at Wpg. (Osborne, 0:43)	5-6, Jan. 9, 1985 at Wpg. (Hawerchuk, 3:50)

RANGERS MODERN DAY REGULAR SEASON OVERTIME HISTORY (1983-84—1986-87)

DATE	OPPONENT	SCORE / RESULT		GOAL SCORER	GOALTENDER	TIME OF GOAL
1983-84	**5-3-9**					
10-23-83	ISLANDERS	6-5	W	Sundstrom	Melanson	1:13
10-30-83	EDMONTON	4-5	L	Hughes	Weeks	1:18
11-2-83	@ Buffalo	3-3	T			
11-5-83	@ Quebec	4-4	T			
11-19-83	@ Boston	6-6	T			
11-20-83	QUEBEC	6-5	W	Andersson	Bouchard	:08
11-26-83	@ Hartford	3-4	L	Stoughton	Weeks	4:52
11-28-83	VANCOUVER	3-3	T			
1-2-84	@ Washington	2-2	T			
1-4-84	NEW JERSEY	4-3	W	Ruotsalainen	Resch	4:47
2-5-84	@ Los Angeles	3-3	T			
2-9-84	@ Minnesota	4-4	T			
2-11-84	@ Los Angeles	6-6	T			
2-19-84	PHILADELPHIA	2-3	L	Kerr	Hanlon	1:33
2-26-84	PITTSBURGH	4-3	W	Osborne	Herron	2:18
2-28-84	@ New Jersey	3-3	T			
3-9-84	@ Winnipeg	6-5	W	Osborne	Behrend	:43
1984-85	**2-5-10**					
10-11-84	HARTFORD	4-4	T			
11-9-84	ISLANDERS	5-4	W	Ruotsalainen	Melanson	:57
11-25-84	QUEBEC	2-3	L	Hunter	Hanlon	3:36
11-30-84	TORONTO	3-3	T			
12-5-84	CALGARY	4-4	T			
12-7-84	PITTSBURGH	3-4	L	Hillier	Hanlon	1:35
12-12-84	BOSTON	3-3	T			
12-23-84	MONTREAL	3-3	T			
1-5-85	@ Boston	3-3	T			
1-6-85	NEW JERSEY	5-4	W	Sandstrom	Resch	1:14
1-9-85	@ Winnipeg	5-6	L	Hawerchuk	Vanbiesbrouck	3:50
1-12-85	@ St. Louis	4-4	T			
1-16-85	BUFFALO	2-2	T			
2-9-85	@ Hartford	2-2	T			
2-21-85	HARTFORD	3-4	L	Cote	Hanlon	3:45
3-9-85	@ Edmonton	3-3	T			
3-11-85	CHICAGO	3-4	L	B. Wilson	Hanlon	1:36
1985-86	**0-7-6**					
10-13-85	NEW JERSEY	2-3	L	Preston	Kleisinger	3:41
11-2-85	@ New Jersey	5-6	L	Bridgman	Vanbiesbrouck	:50
11-9-85	@ Minnesota	3-4	L	Bjugstad	Scott	2:04
11-11-85	CHICAGO	4-5	L	B. Murray	Vanbiesbrouck	:53
11-16-85	@ Montreal	2-2	T			
11-17-85	EDMONTON	2-3	L	Napier	Vanbiesbrouck	2:06
11-24-85	ISLANDERS	3-4	L	Gilbert	Scott	1:57
12-20-85	ISLANDERS	2-2	T			
1-12-86	ST. LOUIS	2-2	T			
1-27-86	@ Quebec	6-6	T			
3-15-86	@ Pittsburgh	2-2	T			
4-5-86	@ Washington	4-4	T			
4-6-86	PITTSBURGH	4-5	L	Lemieux	Hanlon	:25
1986-87	**5-6-8**					
10-11-86	@ Pittsburgh	5-6	L	Bodger	Vanbiesbrouck	0:50
10-13-86	WASHINGTON	6-7	L	Gartner	Soetaert	3:20
10-15-86	@ Chicago	5-5	T			
10-19-86	ISLANDERS	2-2	T			
10-22-86	LOS ANGELES	5-4	W	Osborne	Eliot	4:34
10-25-86	@ Montreal	3-3	T			
10-26-86	TORONTO	3-3	T			
11-2-86	WINNIPEG	4-5	L	MacLean	Vanbiesbrouck	3:23
11-5-86	@ Detroit	4-5	L	Shedden	Soetaert	2:21
11-12-86	BUFFALO	2-1	W	Poddubny	Barrasso	2:01
11-19-86	@ Edmonton	4-5	L	Anderson	Vanbiesbrouck	1:05
11-29-86	@ Pittsburgh	5-5	T			
11-30-86	PITTSBURGH	2-2	T			
12-21-86	HARTFORD	3-4	L	Dineen	Vanbiesbrouck	2:57
12-31-86	ISLANDERS	4-3	W	Sandstrom	Hrudey	4:37
1-5-87	MINNESOTA	3-3	T			
1-19-87	@ Los Angeles	2-2	T			
2-7-87	@ Washington	5-4	W	Sandstrom	Mason	4:20
3-14-87	@ Pittsburgh	3-2	W	Sandstrom	Riggin	1:05

RANGERS MODERN DAY REGULAR SEASON OVERTIME HISTORY (1987-88—1991-92)

DATE	OPPONENT	SCORE / RESULT		GOAL SCORER	GOALTENDER	TIME OF GOAL
1987-88	**0-1-10**					
10-8-87	PITTSBURGH	4-4	T			
10-15-87	@ Pittsburgh	6-6	T			
10-26-87	PHILADELPHIA	2-2	T			
11-14-87	@ Pittsburgh	2-3	L	Mantha	Vanbiesbrouck	2:04
12-9-87	MONTREAL	2-2	T			
12-29-87	@ Islanders	3-3	T			
1-11-88	CHICAGO	2-2	T			
2-2-88	@ Islanders	2-2	T			
2-14-88	ISLANDERS	4-4	T			
3-26-88	@ Detroit	4-4	T			
4-1-88	@ Winnipeg	6-6	T			
1988-89	**1-1-8**					
10-6-88	@ Chicago	2-2	T			
11-11-88	BOSTON	4-4	T			
11-15-88	@ Philadelphia	3-3	T			
12-10-88	@ Boston	1-1	T			
12-23-88	@ Washington	2-2	T			
1-4-89	WASHINGTON	3-3	T			
1-14-89	@ Pittsburgh	4-4	T			
1-21-89	@ Vancouver	5-4	W	Kisio	McLean	1:59
1-28-89	@ Toronto	1-1	T			
2-1-89	WASHINGTON	3-4	L	Ridley	Vanbiesbrouck	1:51
1989-90	**2-2-13**					
10-17-89	CHICAGO	3-3	T			
10-25-89	EDMONTON	3-3	T			
10-27-89	ISLANDERS	5-5	T			
11-17-89	@ New Jersey	4-5	L	Muller	Vanbiesbrouck	3:37
11-20-89	WINNIPEG	3-3	T			
12-9-89	@ Islanders	0-0	T			
12-20-89	BUFFALO	2-2	T			
12-26-89	NEW JERSEY	4-4	T			
1-10-90	CHICAGO	2-2	T			
1-14-90	PHILADELPHIA	4-3	W	Leetch	Wregget	1:16
1-18-90	@ Pittsburgh	3-3	T			
1-31-90	ST. LOUIS	2-2	T			
2-14-90	PITTSBURGH	3-4	L	Loney	Richter	3:33
2-19-90	NEW JERSEY	4-3	W	Mullen	Burke	4:47
2-21-90	@ Detroit	4-4	T			
3-10-90	@ Minnesota	2-2	T			
3-21-90	TORONTO	5-5	T			
1990-91	**1-2-13**					
11-5-90	BOSTON	2-3	L	B. Sweeney	Vanbiesbrouck	3:30
11-11-90	CALGARY	4-4	T			
11-13-90	@ Philadelphia	1-1	T			
11-19-90	MINNESOTA	2-2	T			
11-21-90	@ Buffalo	5-5	T			
11-24-90	@ Islanders	2-2	T			
12-23-90	BOSTON	5-5	T			
12-30-90	NEW JERSEY	2-2	T			
1-5-91	@ St. Louis	3-2	W	Nicholls	Riendeau	3:12
1-15-91	EDMONTON	2-2	T			
1-31-91	@ Vancouver	3-3	T			
2-21-91	@ Philadelphia	4-4	T			
2-27-91	WASHINGTON	4-4	T			
2-28-91	@ St. Louis	4-4	T			
3-21-91	@ Pittsburgh	4-5	L	Stevens	Vanbiesbrouck	:13
3-26-91	NEW JERSEY	3-3	T			
1991-92	**5-1-5**					
10-5-91	@ Montreal	2-1	W	Nemchinov	Roy	1:42
10-7-91	BOSTON	2-1	W	Gartner	Delguidice	:31
11-8-91	TORONTO	3-3	T			
11-29-91	@ Buffalo	5-4	W	Messier	Draper	:43
12-6-91	@ Detroit	5-6	L	Fedyk	Vanbiesbrouck	4:23
12-16-91	SAN JOSE	4-3	W	Leetch	Hayward	:23
1-22-92	@ Calgary	4-4	T			
2-9-92	DETROIT	5-5	T			
2-17-92	VANCOUVER	3-3	T			
2-23-92	PHILADELPHIA	2-1	W	Amonte	Roussel	4:21
3-18-92	ISLANDERS	1-1	T			

RANGERS MODERN DAY REGULAR SEASON OVERTIME HISTORY (1992-93—1994-95)

DATE	OPPONENT	SCORE / RESULT		GOAL SCORER	GOALTENDER	TIME OF GOAL
1992-93	**2-4-11**					
10-23-92	MONTREAL	3-3	T			
10-24-92	@ Ottawa	3-2	W	Bourque	Sidorkiewicz	4:49
11-2-92	BUFFALO	7-6	W	Turcotte	Puppa	0:58
11-7-92	@ Boston	2-2	T			
11-27-92	@ Minnesota	4-4	T			
12-19-92	@ Hartford	4-4	T			
12-23-92	NEW JERSEY	4-5	L	Richer	Vanbiesbrouck	1:33
12-29-92	@ Washington	3-4	L	Pivonka	Vanbiesbrouck	1:28
1-4-93	NEW JERSEY	3-3	T			
1-11-93	VANCOUVER	3-3	T			
1-19-93	@ Detroit	2-2	T			
2-1-93	@ Islanders	4-4	T			
2-3-93	PHILADELPHIA	3-3	T			
2-26-93	@ Calgary	4-4	T			
3-3-93	BUFFALO	2-2	T			
3-17-93	EDMONTON	3-4	L	MacTavish	Vanbiesbrouck	0:32
4-2-93	ISLANDERS	2-3	L	Turgeon	Richter	3:41
1993-94	**3-1-8**					
10-28-93	MONTREAL	3-3	T			
11-14-93	SAN JOSE	3-3	T			
12-8-93	EDMONTON	1-1	T			
1-27-94	@ Los Angeles	5-4	W	Messier	Hrudey	4:58
2-9-94	@ Montreal	3-4	L	Desjardins	Healy	1:27
2-12-94	@ Ottawa	4-3	W	Gartner	Madeley	2:37
2-21-94	PITTSBURGH	4-3	W	Amonte	Barrasso	0:08
3-4-94	ISLANDERS	3-3	T			
3-10-94	@ Boston	2-2	T			
3-22-94	@ Calgary	4-4	T			
4-4-94	ISLANDERS	4-4	T			
4-14-94	PHILADELPHIA	2-2	T			
1994-95	**0-0-3**					
2-2-95	Tampa Bay	3-3	T			
2-16-95	Montreal	2-2	T			
2-28-95	Florida	0-0	T			

RANGERS MODERN DAY REGULAR SEASON OVERTIME RECORD
(Since 1983-84)

		OVERALL	HOME	AWAY
vs.	Anaheim	0-0-0	0-0-0	0-0-0
	Boston	1-1-8	1-1-3	0-0-5
	Buffalo	3-0-5	2-0-3	1-0-2
	Calgary	0-0-5	0-0-2	0-0-3
	Chicago	0-2-5	0-2-3	0-0-2
	Colorado	1-1-2	1-1-0	0-0-2
	Dallas	0-1-5	0-0-2	0-1-3
	Detroit	0-2-4	0-0-1	0-2-3
	Edmonton	0-4-4	0-3-3	0-1-1
	Florida	0-0-1	0-0-1	0-0-0
	Hartford	0-3-3	0-2-1	0-1-2
	Los Angeles	2-0-3	1-0-0	1-0-3
	Montreal	1-1-7	0-0-5	1-1-2
	New Jersey	3-4-5	3-2-4	0-2-1
	Islanders	3-2-12	3-2-7	0-0-5
	Ottawa	2-0-0	0-0-0	2-0-0
	Philadelphia	2-1-6	2-1-3	0-0-3
	Pittsburgh	3-6-7	2-3-2	1-3-5
	St. Louis	1-0-4	0-0-2	1-0-2
	San Jose	1-0-1	1-0-1	0-0-0
	Tampa Bay	0-0-1	0-0-1	0-0-0
	Toronto	0-0-5	0-0-4	0-0-1
	Vancouver	1-0-4	0-0-3	1-0-1
	Washington	1-3-5	0-2-2	1-1-3
	Winnipeg	1-2-2	0-1-1	1-1-1
	TOTALS	**26-33-104**	**16-20-54**	**10-13-50**

LIFETIME RANGERS SHUTOUTS

	Regular Season	Playoffs	Total		Regular Season	Playoffs	Total
Giacomin	49	1	50	Baker	3	0	3
Kerr	40	7	47	Maniago	2	0	2
Roach	30	5	35	Mio	2	0	2
Rayner	24	1	25	Paille	2	0	2
Worsley	24	0	24	Winkler	2	0	2
Chabot	21	2	23	Hanlon	1	1	2
Vanbiesbrouck	16	2	18	Beveridge	1	0	1
Richter	**11**	**6**	**17**	Froese	1	0	1
Aitkenhead	11	3	14	McAuley	1	0	1
Villemure	13	0	13	McCartan	1	0	1
Davidson	7	1	8	Sawchuk	1	0	1
Bower	5	0	5	Soetaert	1	0	1
Plante	5	0	5	Weeks	1	0	1
Thomas	5	0	5	Miller	0	1	1
Henry	4	1	5		287	31	318
Healy	**4**	**0**	**4**				

MOST DECISIVE VICTORIES

HOME

12-1 — vs. California . . . . Nov. 21, 1971
10-0 — vs. California . . . . Nov. 17, 1974
9-0 — vs. Montreal . . . . . . Feb. 4, 1940
9-0 — vs. Montreal . . . . . Jan. 30, 1949
9-0 — vs. Boston . . . . . . Feb. 23, 1969
9-0 — vs. New Jersey. . . Mar. 31, 1986
11-2 — vs. Detroit. . . . . . . Jan. 25, 1942
8-0 — vs. Los Angeles . . . Jan. 9, 1972
9-1 — vs. St. Louis . . . . . . Jan. 5, 1972
9-1 — vs. Pittsburgh. . . . Dec. 17, 1972
10-2 — vs. Chicago . . . . . Mar. 12, 1952
10-2 — vs. Edmonton . . . . Oct. 24, 1979
10-2 — vs. Detroit. . . . . . Dec. 23, 1985
11-3 — vs. Hartford . . . . . Feb. 23, 1983

ROAD

11-2 — at New Jersey. . . . Oct. 25, 1984
11-3 — at Pittsburgh. . . . . Nov. 25, 1992
7-0 — at NY Americans . Jan. 29, 1928
7-0 — at Montreal . . . . . . Jan. 22, 1935
7-0 — at NY Americans . . Feb. 2, 1939
7-0 — at Toronto. . . . . . . Mar. 22, 1958
8-1 — at Oakland . . . . Nov. 7, 1969
8-1 — at California . . . . . . Nov. 5, 1971
8-1 — at Minnesota . . . . Dec. 30, 1974
9-2 — at Ottawa . . . . Jan. 28, 1933
9-2 — at Minnesota . . . . Feb. 15, 1975
11-4 — at Minnesota . . . . . Dec. 4, 1976
11-4 — at Washington . . . Mar. 24, 1978

MOST DECISIVE DEFEATS

HOME

3-13 — vs. Boston. . . . . Jan. 2, 1944
0-9 — vs. Detroit. . . . . . . Dec. 6, 1950
1-10 — vs. Toronto. . . . . . Mar. 21, 1965
0-8 — vs. Toronto. . . . . . . Mar. 9, 1944
0-8 — vs. Chicago. . . . . . . Apr. 2, 1967

ROAD

0-15 — at Detroit. . . . . Jan. 23, 1944
1-14 — at Toronto . . . . . . Mar. 16, 1957
3-14 — at Boston . . . . Jan. 21, 1945
2-12 — at Detroit . . . . Feb. 3, 1944

RANGERS AND OPPONENTS 10-GOAL GAMES SINCE 1950

RANGERS

Dec. 13, 1992	—	10-5	—	vs. Montreal at MSG
Nov. 25, 1992	—	11-3	—	vs. Pittsburgh at Pittsburgh
Dec. 23, 1985	—	10-2	—	vs. Detroit at MSG
Oct. 25, 1984	—	11-2	—	vs. New Jersey at New Jersey
Feb. 23, 1983	—	11-3	—	vs. Hartford at MSG
Oct. 24, 1979	—	10-2	—	vs. Edmonton at MSG
Mar. 24, 1978	—	11-4	—	vs. Washington at Washington
Dec. 4, 1976	—	11-4	—	vs. Minnesota at Minnesota
Oct. 12, 1976	—	10-4	—	vs. Minnesota at Minnesota
Feb. 18, 1976	—	11-4	—	vs. Washington at MSG
Nov. 17, 1974	—	10-0	—	vs. California at MSG
Nov. 21, 1971	—	12-1	—	vs. California at MSG
Mar. 29, 1967	—	10-5	—	vs. Detroit at MSG
Mar. 12, 1952	—	10-2	—	vs. Chicago at MSG

Opponents

Apr. 10, 1993	—	4-10	—	vs. Pittsburgh at MSG
Mar. 6, 1993	—	2-10	—	vs. Quebec at Quebec
Dec. 31, 1992	—	6-11	—	vs. Buffalo at Buffalo
Feb. 17, 1989	—	6-10	—	vs. Toronto at MSG
Dec. 4, 1988	—	6-10	—	vs. Edmonton at Edmonton
Mar. 7, 1985	—	5-11	—	vs. Calgary at Calgary
Feb. 25, 1985	—	5-12	—	vs. Winnipeg at MSG
Nov. 17, 1984	—	4-10	—	vs. Islanders at Nassau Coliseum
Nov. 13, 1979	—	5-10	—	vs. Islanders at Nassau Coliseum
Mar. 10, 1977	—	3-10	—	vs. Boston at Boston
Apr. 3, 1976	—	2-10	—	vs. Islanders at Nassau Coliseum
Dec. 19, 1974	—	3-11	—	vs. Boston at Boston
Nov. 15, 1973	—	2-10	—	vs. Boston at Boston
Mar. 21, 1965	—	1-10	—	vs. Toronto at MSG
Jan. 21, 1960	—	2-11	—	vs. Montreal at Montreal
Mar. 16, 1957	—	1-14	—	vs. Toronto at Toronto
Feb. 19, 1955	—	2-10	—	vs. Montreal at Montreal

RANGERS 0-0 GAMES SINCE 1950

Oct. 22, 1950 vs. Boston at Boston
Goaltenders: Chuck Rayner and Jack Gelineau
Mar. 5, 1954 vs. Chicago at Chicago
Goaltenders: Johnny Bower and Al Rollins
Jan. 12, 1955 vs. Toronto at Madison Square Garden
Goaltenders: Lorne Worsley and Harry Lumley
Dec. 8, 1956 vs. Toronto at Toronto
Goaltenders: Lorne Worsley and Ed Chadwick
Mar. 8, 1964 vs. Montreal at Madison Square Garden
Goaltenders: Jacques Plante and Charlie Hodge
Mar. 8, 1970 vs. Pittsburgh at Madison Square Garden
Goaltenders: Ed Giacomin and Al Smith
Mar. 30, 1981 vs. Philadelphia at Madison Square Garden
Goaltenders: Steve Baker and Rick St. Croix
Dec. 9, 1989 vs. Islanders at Nassau Coliseum
Goaltenders: John Vanbiesbrouck and Mark Fitzpatrick
Feb. 28, 1995 vs. Florida at Madison Square Garden
Goaltenders: Mike Richter and John Vanbiesbrouck

RANGERS IN THE NHL ALL-STAR GAME

Season	Team	Player	G	Mins/GA A	Pts.
1947-48	NHL All-Stars	Edgar Laprade	0	1	1
	NHL All-Stars	Tony Leswick	0	0	0
	NHL All-Stars	Grant Warwick	1	0	1
1948-49	NHL All-Stars	Neil Colville	0	0	0
	NHL All-Stars	Edgar Laprade	0	0	0
	NHL All-Stars	Tony Leswick	0	0	0
1949-50	NHL All-Stars	Martin Egan	0	0	0
	NHL All-Stars	Edgar Laprade	0	1	1
	NHL All-Stars	Tony Leswick	0	0	0
	NHL All-Stars	Buddy O'Connor	0	0	0
	NHL All-Stars	Chuck Rayner	31:30, 0 GA		
1950-51	NHL All-Stars	Tony Leswick	0	0	0
	NHL All-Stars	Chuck Rayner	31:12, 3 GA		
	NHL All-Stars	Edgar Laprade	0	0	0
1951-52	First Team NHL	Frank Eddolls	0	0	0
	First Team NHL	Don Raleigh	0	1	1
	Second Team NHL	Chuck Rayner	29:28, 1 GA		
	First Team NHL	Reg Sinclair	0	0	0
	First Team NHL	Gaye Stewart	0	1	1
1952-53	Second Team NHL	Hy Buller	0	1	1
	First Team NHL	Leo Riese, Jr.	0	0	0
1953-54	NHL All-Stars	Wally Hergesheimer	2	0	2
	NHL All-Stars	Leo Riese, Jr.	0	0	0
	NHL All-Stars	Paul Ronty	0	1	1
1954-55	NHL All-Stars	Harry Howell	0	0	0
	NHL All-Stars	Don Raleigh	0	0	0
	NHL All-Stars	Paul Ronty	0	0	0
1955-56	NHL All-Stars	Dan Lewicki	0	0	0
1956-57	NHL All-Stars	David Creighton	0	0	0
	NHL All-Stars	Bill Gadsby	0	0	0
	NHL All-Stars	Red Sullivan	0	0	0
1957-58	NHL All-Stars	Andy Bathgate	1	1	2
	NHL All-Stars	Bill Gadsby	0	0	0
	NHL All-Stars	Dean Prentice	1	2	3
1958-59	NHL All-Stars	Andy Bathgate	2	0	2
	NHL All-Stars	Bill Gadsby	0	0	0
	NHL All-Stars	Camille Henry	0	1	1
	NHL All-Stars	Red Sullivan	0	1	1
1959-60	NHL All-Stars	Andy Bathgate	0	0	0
	NHL All-Stars	Bill Gadsby	0	0	0
	NHL All-Stars	Red Sullivan	0	0	0
1960-61	NHL All-Stars	Andy Bathgate	0	0	0
	NHL All-Stars	Bill Gadsby	0	0	0
	NHL All-Stars	Andy Hebenton	1	0	1
	NHL All-Stars	Red Sullivan	0	1	1
1961-62	NHL All-Stars	Andy Bathgate	0	1	1
	NHL All-Stars	Doug Harvey	0	0	0
	NHL All-Stars	Gump Worsley	30:00, 0 GA		
1962-63	NHL All-Stars	Andy Bathgate	0	0	0
	NHL All-Stars	Doug Harvey	0	0	0
	NHL All-Stars	Dean Prentice	0	0	0
	NHL All-Stars	Gump Worsley	20:00, 0 GA		
1963-64	NHL All-Stars	Andy Bathgate	0	0	0
	NHL All-Stars	Camille Henry	0	1	1
	NHL All-Stars	Harry Howell	0	0	0
1964-65	NHL All-Stars	Rod Gilbert	0	0	0
	NHL All-Stars	Camille Henry	0	0	0
	NHL All-Stars	Harry Howell	0	1	1
1965-66	NHL All-Stars	Rod Gilbert	0	0	0
	NHL All-Stars	Vic Hadfield	0	0	0
	NHL All-Stars	Harry Howell	0	0	0
1966-67	NHL All-Stars	Ed Giacomin	30:00, 1 GA		
	NHL All-Stars	Rod Gilbert	0	0	0
	NHL All-Stars	Harry Howell	0	0	0
	NHL All-Stars	Jim Neilson	0	0	0
	NHL All-Stars	Bob Nevin	0	0	0
1967-68	NHL All-Stars	Ed Giacomin	20:00, 1 GA		

RANGERS IN THE NHL ALL-STAR GAME

Season	Team	Player	Mins/GA G	A	Pts.
	NHL All-Stars	Harry Howell	0	0	0
	NHL All-Stars	Don Marshall	0	0	0
1968-69	East	Ed Giacomin	40:00, 2 GA		
	East	Rod Gilbert	0	1	1
	East	Bob Nevin	1	0	1
1969-70	East	Ed Giacomin	30:00, 1 GA		
	East	Rod Gilbert	0	0	0
1969-70	East	Jim Neilson	0	0	0
(con't)	East	Brad Park	0	0	0
	East	Jean Ratelle	0	0	0
	East	Walt Tkaczuk	1	0	1
1970-71	East	Dave Balon	0	1	1
	East	Ed Giacomin	31:00, 2 GA		
	East	Jim Neilson	0	0	0
	East	Brad Park	0	0	0
	East	Jean Ratelle	0	0	0
	East	Gilles Villemure	29:00, 0 GA		
1971-72	East	Rod Gilbert	0	1	1
	East	Vic Hadfield	0	0	0
	East	Brad Park	0	1	1
	East	Jean Ratelle	1	0	1
	East	Rod Seiling	0	1	1
	East	Gilles Villemure	29:26, 0 GA		
1972-73	East	Ed Giacomin	30:44, 3 GA		
	East	Brad Park	0	1	1
	East	Jean Ratelle	0	0	0
	East	Gilles Villemure	29:16, 1 GA		
1973-74	East	Brad Park	0	0	0
1974-75	Campbell	Rod Gilbert	0	0	0
	Campbell	Brad Park	0	0	0
	Campbell	Steve Vickers	0	0	0
1975-76	Campbell	Carol Vadnais	0	0	0
	Campbell	Steve Vickers	1	0	1
1976-77	Campbell	Phil Esposito	1	0	1
	Campbell	Rod Gilbert	0	1	1
	Campbell	Don Murdoch	0	0	0
1977-78	Campbell	Phil Esposito	0	0	0
	Campbell	Carol Vadnais	0	0	0
1978-79	NHL (vs. USSR)	Anders Hedberg	0	0	0
	NHL (vs. USSR)	Ulf Nilsson	0	0	0
1979-80	Campbell	Phil Esposito	0	1	1
	Campbell	Ron Greschner	0	0	0
1980-81	Campbell	Ed Johnstone	0	2	2
1981-82	Wales	Barry Beck	0	1	1
	Wales	Ron Duguay	0	0	0
1982-83	Wales	Don Maloney	1	0	1
1983-84	Wales	Pierre Larouche	2	0	2
	Wales	Don Maloney (MVP)	1	3	4
1984-85	Wales	Anders Hedberg	1	0	1
1985-86	Wales	Reijo Ruotsalainen	0	0	0
1986-87	NHL (vs. USSR)	Tomas Sandstrom	0	0	0
1987-88	Wales	Tomas Sandstrom	1	0	1
1988-89	Wales	Brian Mullen	0	1	1
1989-90	Wales	Brian Leetch	0	0	0
1990-91	Wales	Brian Leetch	0	0	0
	Wales	Darren Turcotte	0	1	1
1991-92	Wales	Brian Leetch	0	0	0
	Wales	Mark Messier	0	1	1
	Wales	Mike Richter	20:00, 2 GA		
1992-93	Wales	Mike Gartner (MVP)	4	1	5
	Wales	Kevin Lowe	0	1	1
	Wales	Brian Leetch	Injured		
	Wales	Mark Messier	Injured		
1993-94	Eastern	Adam Graves	0	2	2
		Brian Leetch	0	0	0
		Mark Messier	1	2	3
		Mike Richter (MVP)	20:00, 2 GA		

RANGERS NHL ALL-STARS

FIRST TEAM

Bill Cook, right wing 1930-31
Lester Patrick, coach 1930-31
Bill Cook, right wing...........................1931-32
Ching Johnson, defense 1931-32
Lester Patrick, coach 1931-32
Frank Boucher, center 1932-33
Bill Cook, right wing 1932-33
Ching Johnson, defense 1932-33
Lester Patrick, coach 1932-33
Frank Boucher, center 1933-34
Lester Patrick, coach 1933-34
Frank Boucher, center 1934-35
Earl Seibert, defense..........................1934-35
Lester Patrick, coach 1934-35
Lester Patrick, coach 1935-36
Cecil Dillon, right wing 1937-38
Lester Patrick, coach 1937-38
Bryan Hextall, right wing 1939-40
Dave Kerr, goal...................................1939-40
Bryan Hextall, right wing 1940-41

Bryan Hextall, right wing 1941-42
Lynn Patrick, left wing........................1941-42
Frank Boucher, coach.........................1941-42
Bill Gadsby, defense 1955-56
Bill Gadsby, defense 1957-58
Bill Gadsby, defense 1958-59
Andy Bathgate, right wing 1958-59
Andy Bathgate, right wing 1961-62
Doug Harvey, defense........................1961-62
Ed Giacomin, goal...............................1966-67
Harry Howell, defense 1966-67
Brad Park, defense..............................1969-70
Ed Giacomin, goal...............................1970-71
Brad Park, defense..............................1971-72
Rod Gilbert, right wing........................1971-72
Brad Park, defense..............................1973-74
John Vanbiesbrouck, goal 1985-86
Mark Messier, center..........................1991-92
Brian Leetch, defense 1991-92

SECOND TEAM

Ching Johnson, defense.....................1930-31
Frank Boucher, center 1930-31
Bun Cook, left wing.............................1930-31
Ching Johnson, defense.....................1933-34
Bill Cook, right wing............................1933-34
Cecil Dillon, right wing........................1935-36
Cecil Dillon, right wing........................1936-37
Dave Kerr, goal 1937-38
Art Coulter, defense 1937-38
Art Coulter, defense 1938-39
Neil Colville, center 1938-39
Art Coulter, defense 1939-40
Neil Colville, center 1939-40
Frank Boucher, coach.........................1939-40
Ott Heller, defense..............................1940-41
Phil Watson, center.............................1941-42
Bryan Hextall, right wing 1942-43
Lynn Patrick, left wing 1942-43
Buddy O'Connor, center 1947-48
Neil Colville, defense...........................1947-48
Chuck Rayner, goal.............................1948-49
Chuck Rayner, goal 1949-50
Tony Leswick, left wing 1949-50

Chuck Rayner, goal.............................1950-51
Hy Buller, defense 1951-52
Danny Lewicki, left wing.....................1954-55
Bill Gadsby, defense 1956-57
Andy Bathgate, right wing 1957-58
Camille Henry, left wing......................1957-58
Dean Prentice, left wing......................1959-60
Andy Bathgate, right wing 1962-63
Don Marshall, left wing 1966-67
Ed Giacomin, goal 1967-68
Jim Neilson, defense...........................1967-68
Rod Gilbert, right wing 1967-68
Ed Giacomin, goal 1968-69
Ed Giacomin, goal 1969-70
Brad Park, defense 1970-71
Vic Hadfield, left wing 1971-72
Jean Ratelle, center.............................1971-72
Brad Park, defense 1972-73
Steve Vickers, left wing 1974-75
Brian Leetch, defense 1990-91
Adam Graves, left wing.......................1993-94
Brian Leetch, defense 1993-94

RANGERS ALL-TIME LONGEST TEAM STREAKS

Overall	Home	Road

Winning Streak

Overall		Home		Road	
10	12/19 — 1/13/40	14	12/19 — 2/25/40	7	1/12 — 2/12/35
10	1/19 — 2/10/73	9	2/10 — 3/14/71	7	10/28 — 11/29/78
8	2/16 — 3/6/74	9	11/10 — 12/15/71	6	10/30 — 11/24/93
8	12/27 — 1/11/75	8	12/13 — 1/14/32	5	1/19 — 2/10/73
7	1/18 — 2/5/42	8	12/31 — 2/15/70	4	(many times)
7	12/11 — 12/23/70	8	2/20 — 3/16/80		last 2/20 - 3/1/95
7	2/20 — 3/5/72	8	10/8 — 10/31/90		
7	10/22 — 11/5/78	7	1/5 — 2/8/69		
7	10/16 — 10/30/88	7	2/9 — 3/5/72		
7	12/13 — 12/26/91	7	2/6 — 3/10/74		
		7	11/17 — 12/15/82		
		7	12/21 — 1/18/84		

Unbeaten Streak

Overall		Home		Road	
19	11/23 — 1/13/40	24	10/14 — 1/31/71	11	11/5 — 1/13/40
16	2/6 — 3/11/72	18	11/28 — 2/25/40	10	11/12 — 1/3/31
16	1/7 — 2/11/73	18	1/5 — 3/30/69	10	12/20 — 2/10/73
14	11/7 — 12/10/69	18	10/17 — 12/29/71	9	2/8 — 3/22/58
14	10/16 — 11/14/71	16	10/24 — 1/5/94	8	2/3 — 3/9/68
14	10/24 — 11/24/93	13	11/25 — 2/5/42	8	12/2 — 1/15/82
13	1/3 — 2/5/35	12	12/28 — 2/25/70	8	12/23 — 1/23/89
11	12/10 — 1/5/32	11	11/7 — 12/12/73	7	1/12 — 2/12/35
11	2/20 — 3/14/71	11	1/6 — 3/10/74	7	10/28 — 11/29/78
10	11/17 — 12/5/63	11	1/14 — 3/1/92		
10	2/10 — 3/6/74	10	11/2 — 12/10/69		
10	11/7 — 11/26/90	10	10/11 — 11/15/72		
		10	1/7 — 2/28/73		

Losing Streak

Overall		Home		Road	
11	10/30 — 11/27/43	7	10/20 — 11/14/76	10	10/30 — 12/23/43
10	1/3 — 1/28/62	7	3/24 — 4/14/93	10	2/8 — 3/15/61
8	10/28 — 11/14/87	6	2/26 — 3/16/46	9	11/27 — 1/8/55
8	3/7 — 3/23/91	5	11/6 — 11/21/43	9	1/19 — 2/13/65
7	12/31 — 1/15/44	5	12/31 — 1/13/44	8	1/23 — 3/4/44
7	1/11 — 1/25/50	5	2/20 — 3/6/55	8	2/9 — 3/16/49
7	3/11 — 3/22/50	5	1/6 — 2/2/57	8	11/15 — 12/26/53
7	10/31 — 11/16/63	5	11/24 — 12/8/58	7	(10 times)
7	4/5 — 4/16/93				last 3/7 - 3/30/91
7	3/11 — 3/30/95				

Winless Streak

Overall		Home		Road	
21	1/23 — 3/19/44	10	1/30 — 3/19/44	16	10/9 — 12/20/52
19	12/31 — 2/20/43	9	12/31 — 2/18/43	13	10/26 — 12/25/63
15	10/30 — 12/11/43	9	11/29 — 1/3/65	12	11/28 — 2/7/46
15	10/19 — 11/19/50	8	11/12 — 12/27/44	11	1/1 — 2/27/43
14	12/1 — 12/26/54	8	12/1 — 12/26/54	11	1/23 — 3/18/44
11	11/25 — 12/18/65	7	2/23 — 3/16/46	11	11/20 — 1/8/55
11	12/9 — 12/31/89	7	10/28 — 11/25/56	11	11/20 — 1/15/66
10	10/28 — 11/21/56	7	12/25 — 1/29/58	10	10/30 — 12/23/43
10	1/14 — 2/3/60	7	3/3 — 3/28/65	10	10/19 — 11/25/50
10	1/3 — 1/28/62	7	10/20 — 11/14/76	10	11/14 — 12/29/51
		7	3/24 — 4/14/93	10	2/8 — 3/15/61
				10	10/18 — 11/22/80

YEAR	WINNING STREAK	UNBEATEN STREAK	LOSING STREAK	WINLESS STREAK
1926-27	5 3/15-3/25	7 3/5-3/25	3 12/23-12/28	3 (twice) last-3/1-3/13
1927-28	4 1/22-1/31	4 (twice) last-2/23-2/29	2 (3 times) last-3/6-3/8	5 2/4-2/16
1928-29	4 12/11-12/20	6 (twice) last-12/30-1/13	3 (3 times) last-3/5-3/10	4 (twice) last-2/5-2/14
1929-30	4 1/14-1/23	4 (twice) last-2/27-3/4	3 1/7-1/12	7 2/18-3/11
1930-31	3 12/23-12/28	5 12/20-12/30	4 1/18-1/29	8 1/11-1/31
1931-32	4 12/22-1/1	11 12/10-1/5	2 (5 times) last-3/15-3/17	5 2/9-2/21
1932-33	3 12/6-12/11	6 12/6-12/17	3 3/16-3/21	4 3/14-3/21
1933-34	5 (twice) last-1/23-1/28	6 12/14-12/28	2 (4 times) last-3/15-3/17	3 (twice) last-3/6-3/11
1934-35	5 1/27-2/5	13 1/3-2/5	4 (twice) last-2/26-3/7	5 2/24-3/7
1935-36	4 3/12-3/22	9 1/28-2/25	4 1/18-1/26	6 2/25-3/10
1936-37	3 12/20-12/29	5 1/24-2/4	3 (3 times) last-3/11-3/16	5 (twice) last-1/28-2/7
1937-38	5 (twice) last-2/1-2/13	7 12/5-12/23	4 (twice) last-2/17-2/22	4 11/21-12/2
1938-39	4 11/13-11/20	4 (3 times) last-1/31-2/5	3 2/26-3/5	4 2/26-3/7
1939-40	10 12/19-1/13	19 11/23-1/13	2 (twice) last-2/18-2/22	4 11/5-11/16
1940-41	5 2/18-3/1	5 2/18-3/1	4 2/11-2/16	4 2/11-2/16
1941-42	7 1/18-2/5	7 (twice) 1/18-2/5	4 (twice) last-2/10-2/17	4 (twice) last-2/10-2/17
1942-43	5 12/25-12/29	3 12/25-12/29	5 1/10-1/21	19 12/31-2/20
1943-44	2 (3 times) last-1/16-1/22	2 (3 times) last-1/16-1/22	11 10/30-11/27	21 1/23-3/19
1944-45	2 (twice) last-2/18-2/22	5 12/31-1/11	3 3/1-3/11	8 2/24-3/11
1945-46	2 3/13-3/17	4 12/30-1/6	6 11/6-1/26	6 (twice) last-12/13-12/26
1946-47	3 (twice) last-1/19-1/25	4 12/1-12/11	6 3/9-3/22	8 11/3-11/21
1947-48	4 11/16-11/30	7 12/6-12/17	5 11/6-11/15	7 (twice) last-3/3-3/16
1948-49	3 12/19-12/25	6 12/12-12/25	5 (twice) last-3/2-3/12	8 3/2-3/16
1949-50	4 (twice) 2/18-2/23	8 2/5-2/23	7 (twice) last-3/11-3/22	9 1/8-1/28
1950-51	3 (twice) last-2/11-2/15	6 12/10-12/24	5 3/14-3/21	15 10/19-11/19
1951-52	3 1/1-1/6	4 (twice) last-2/17-2/24	3 (3 times) last-3/1-3/4	5 (4 times) last-2/27-3/4
1952-53	2 (3 times) last-37-38	4 2/1-2/11	4 10/9-10/18	8 11/27-12/14
1953-54	4 1/1-1/10	4 (twice) last-2/14-2/21	3 (twice) last-12/26-12/29	7 12/2-12/13
1954-55	2 (3 times) last-3/12-3/13	4 2/9-2/16	4 (twice) last-2/27-3/6	14 12/1-12/26
1955-56	3 11/30-12/7	4 11/20-12/7	4 (twice) last-2/18-2/23	4 (4 times) last-2/18-2/23
1956-57	3 2/16-2/20	7 2/24-3/10	6 10/31-11/14	10 10/28-11/21
1957-58	3 (4 times) last-2/23-3/1	9 2/14-3/8	5 12/25-1/5	8 12/25-1/2
1958-59	5 11/8-11/19	6 11/8-11/22	6 2/7-2/18	7 2/7-2/21
1959-60	3 12/5-12/13	5 3/5-3/13	5 1/14-1/23	10 1/14-2/3

YEAR-BY-YEAR

YEAR	WINNING STREAK	UNBEATEN STREAK	LOSING STREAK	WINLESS STREAK
1960-61	2 (5 times) last-2/19-2/22	5 1/8-1/18	5 (twice) last-12/28-1/7	8 10/27-11/13
1961-62	3 12/20-12/25	7 11/8-11/23	10 1/3-1/28	10 1/3-1/28
1962-63	3 11/18-11/22	5 12/27-1/5	3 (7 times) last-3/10-3/17	6 12/2-12/13
1963-64	4 1/1-1/9	5 1/25-2/2	7 10/31-11/16	9 11/28-12/14
1964-65	2 (5 times) last-2/27-2/28	3 (4 times) last-1/16-1/23	6 (4 times) last-2/13-2/20	7 (twice) last-3/6-3/21
1965-66	2 (twice) last-3/2-3/3	6 10/30-11/11	2 (9 times) last-4/1-4/2	11 11/25-12/18
1966-67	5 12/7-12/17	5 (3 times) last-12/7-12/17	3 3/10-3/14	9 2/26-3/18
1967-68	6 2/24-3/6	8 (twice) last-2/3-2/18	3 (twice) last-2/12-2/15	4 3/9-3/14
1968-69	5 1/23-1/30	8 3/2-3/19	3 (twice) 3/11-3/15	6 12/5-12/21
1969-70	5 (twice) last-1/30-2/11	14 11/17-12/10	3 3/18-3/21	9 2/26-3/15
1970-71	7 12/11-12/23	11 2/20-3/14	2 (twice) last-4/1-4/2	4 (twice) last-1/27-2/3
1971-72	7 2/20-3/5	16 2/6-3/11	3 3/24-3/31	6 3/25-4/2
1972-73	10 1/19-2/10	16 1/7-2/11	4 10/20-10/28	5 3/24-4/1
1973-74	8 2/16-3/6	10 (twice) last-2/10-3/6	3 10/31-11/5	4 10/20-10/28
1974-75	8 12/27-1/11	8 12/27-1/11	4 (twice) last-3/20-3/25	4 (twice) 2/16-2/22
1975-76	3 (twice) last-3/27-3/31	7 11/30-12/13	4 2/26-3/5	9 2/20-3/11
1976-77	3 3/19-3/23	9 11/22-12/8		5 1/5-1/13
1977-78	5 3/22-3/29	6 3/19-3/29	6 1/20-2/1	7 (twice) last-1/20-2/4
1978-79	7 10/22-11/5	7 10/22-11/5	2 (7 times) last-4/6-4/8	4 (twice) last-3/25-4/1
1979-80	5 2/24-3/5	7 12/1-12/12	3 (3 times) last-3/19-3/23	5 (3 times) last-3/19-3/28
1980-81	5 12/3-12/12	5 12/3-12/12	4 10/12-10/19	9 10/28-11/14
1981-82	5 3/17-3/26	9 3/8-3/26	4 (twice) last-10/25-10/31	7 11/21-11/29
1982-83	5 11/17-11/27	7 12/30-1/12	4 (twice) last-3/3-3/11	8 1/12-1/27
1983-84	5 10/5-10/13	6 2/4-2/15	4 2/29-3/7	5 (3 times) last-2/28-3/7
1984-85	4 10/20-10/27	4 (twice) last-12/30-1/6	5 1/31-2/7	7 1/31-2/10
1985-86	6 2/8-2/24	6 2/8-2/24	4 10/12-10/19	4 (3 times) last-1/23-1/31
1986-87	4 1/31-2/7	6 10/15-10/26	4 3/15-3/21	5 10/25-11/5
1987-88	4 (twice) last-2/25-3/2	7 12/26-1/6	8 10/28-11/14	9 10/26-11/14
1988-89	7 10/16-10/30	7 (twice) last-12/23-1/7	5 (twice) last-3/26-4/2	5 (twice) last-3/26-4/2
1989-90	4 2/23-3/2	8 10/15-10/28	4 12/10-12/17	11 12/9-12/31
1990-91	6 10/20-10/31	10 11/7-11/26	8 3/7-3/23	8 3/7-3/23
1991-92	7 12/13-12/26	8 (twice) last-3/11-3/24	3 (twice) last-3/4-3/9	3 (twice) last-3/4-3/9
1992-93	4 12/6-12/13	5 10/18-10/26	7 4/5-4/16	7 4/5-4/16
1993-94	7 10/30-11/13	14 10/24-11/24	3 (twice) last-1/5-1/10	3 (3 times) last 3/10-3/14
1994-95	3 4/12-4/16	4 2/26-3/3	7 3/11-3/30	7 3/11-3/30

RANGERS LONGEST HOME STREAKS

YEAR	WINNING STREAK	UNBEATEN STREAK	LOSING STREAK	WINLESS STREAK
1926-27	3 (twice) last-3/20-3/25	6 1/6-1/23	2 2/22-2/24	3 2/22-3/13
1927-28	5 1/22-1/31	4 1/22-2/7	2 (twice) last-2/12-2/16	4 11/22-12/15
1928-29	5 11/25-12/20	5 (twice) last-12/30-1/22	1 (6 times) last-3/29	3 3/10-3/20
1929-30	4 (twice) last-1/14-1/28	7 1/14-2/13	2 2/18-2/23	4 2/18-3/11
1930-31	3 2/22-3/10	4 2/22-3/15	3 1/20-1/29	5 1/11-1/29
1931-32	8 12/13-1/14	8 12/13-1/14	2 1/28-2/2	3 2/16-2/25
1932-33	6 (twice) last-12/25-1/3	6 12/25-1/19	3 1/22-1/31	4 2/9-3/5
1933-34	6 1/2-1/28	8 1/2-2/6	3 3/6-3/15	4 12/7-12/21
1934-35	2 (3 times) last-2/14-2/19	10 12/25-2/3	3 2/28-3/17	4 2/24-3/17
1935-36	2 (4 times) last-3/12-3/17	8 11/19-12/31	3 1/2-1/12	4 2/16-3/8
1936-37	2 (3 times) last-2/18-3/23	9 11/19-1/5	3 3/7-3/16	4 1/28-2/14
1937-38	5 1/18-2/13	9 12/31-2/13	1 (6 times) last-3/13	2 (3 times) last-2/17-2/22
1938-39	5 12/31-1/22	5 12/31-1/22	2 (twice) last-2/26-3/2	4 2/26-3/12
1939-40	14 12/19-2/25	18 11/28-2/25	3 11/12-11/19	3 11/12-11/19
1940-41	5 2/23-3/16	5 (twice) last-2/23-3/16	2 (3 times) last-2/13-2/16	2 (4 times) last-2/13-2/16
1941-42	6 (twice) last-1/6-2/5	13 11/25-2/5	4 11/15-11/23	4 11/15-11/23
1942-43	2 (twice) last-2/21-2/25	2 (5 times) last-3/7-3/14	4 1/10-1/31	9 12/31-2/18
1943-44	3 12/12-12/26	3 12/12-12/26	5 (twice) 12/31-1/13	10 1/30-3/19
1944-45	3 2/15-2/22	4 (twice) last-2/15-2/25	3 (twice) last-3/1-3/11	8 11/12-12/27
1945-46	2 1/6-1/13	4 (twice) last-1/27-2/14	4 12/13-12/26	6 2/3-3/3
1946-47	6 1/12-2/19	7 1/12-2/23	6 2/26-3/16	7 2/23-3/16
1947-48	2 (3 times) last-2/29-3/2	4 12/7-12/17	3 3/14-3/21	5 1/18-2/18
1948-49	3 12/12-12/19	4 (twice) last-12/31-1/9	2 (twice) last-2/10-2/13	5 11/13-12/7
1949-50	5 (twice) last-12/21-1/4	6 (3 times) last-1/29-2/26	4 3/12-3/21	6 10/19-11/13
1950-51	5 12/24-1/7	8 12/13-1/7	3 (twice) last-3/14-3/21	6 10/25-11/19
1951-52	3 12/19-12/26	6 12/19-1/6	3 (twice) last-2/27-3-9	5 1/9-2/10
1952-53	2 (twice) last-2/25-3/1	3 11/19-11/26	2 (twice) last-3/18-3/22	4 (twice) last-3/11-3/22
1953-54	3 (3 times) last-2/17-2/28	5 (twice) last-2/10-2/28	4 (twice) last-12/27-12/29	4 12/2-12/13
1954-55	3 10/20-10/27	7 12/12-1/2	5 2/20-3/6	8 12/1-12/26
1955-56	4 2/26-2/24	9 11/9-12/7	2 2/19-2/22	2 (5 times) last-3/15-3/18
1956-57	5 2/6-2/24	8 (twice) last-2/6-3/10	5 1/6-2/2	7 10/28-11/25
1957-58	4 (twice) last-2/16-2/26	5 2/16-3/2	5 11/24-12/8	7 12/25-1/29
1958-59	4 (twice) last-12/21-12/31	4 (twice) last-2/22-3/8	4 3/11-3/22	4 (twice) last-3/11-3/22
1959-60	3 12/6-12/20	5 11/25-12/20	3 (twice) last-12/23-12/29	6 1/6-2/6

YEAR-BY-YEAR

YEAR	WINNING STREAK	UNBEATEN STREAK	LOSING STREAK	WINLESS STREAK
1960-61	2 (4 times) last-3/1-3/5	5 2/1-2/22	3 (twice) last-12/28-1/4	5 11/27-12/21
1961-62	3 2/10-2/21	9 10/25-12/3	5 12/27-1/28	5 12/27-1/28
1962-63	2 (twice) last-3/20-3/24	4 2/6-2/20	3 (twice) last-1/27-2/3	5 (twice) last-1/6-2/3
1963-64	4 1/4-1/26	6 1/4-2/2	3 3/11-3/22	4 3/8-3/22
1964-65	3 10/28-11/11	3 10/28-11/11	4 12/16-12/29	9 11/29-1/3
1965-66	2 (3 times) last-3/9-3/13	6 2/23-3/13	3 3/16-3/27	6 11/27-12/12
1966-67	4 12/7-12/21	5 10/23-11/16	3 2/26-3/8	5 2/26-3/15
1967-68	4 2/25-3/6	7 12/27-1/28	2 3/10-3/13	3 12/23-12/30
1968-69	7 1/5-2/8	18 1/5-3/30	3 12/15-12/18	4 12/8-12/18
1969-70	8 12/31-2/15	12 12/28-2/25	3 3/15-3/25	6 3/1-3/25
1970-71	9 2/10-3/14	24 10/14-1/31	1 (twice) last-3/21	3 1/27-2/3
1971-72	9 11/10-12/15	18 10-17-12/29	1 (6 times) last-4-2	3 (twice) last-3/26-4/4
1972-73	6 (twice) last-10/25-11/15	10 (twice) last-1/7-2/28	3 3/25-3/28	3 3/25-4/1
1973-74	7 2/6-3/10	11 (twice) last-1/6-3/10	2 (twice) last-3/14-3/20	2 (3 times) last-3/27-3/31
1974-75	6 12/27-1/26	7 12/27-2/2	3 3/2-3/9	3 (twice) last-3/2-3/9
1975-76	3 3/28-4/4	4 2/29-3/17	3 2/4-2/13	5 (twice) last-2/22-3/7
1976-77	7 11/17-12/1	8 11/17-12/22	7 10/20-11/14	7 10/20-11/14
1977-78	2 (4 times) last-3/27-3/29	3 (5 times) last-3/8-3/15	4 1/9-2/1	6 12/28-2/1
1978-79	3 10/22-10/29	7 1/17-3/3	3 3/14-3/25	4 3/14-3/27
1979-80	8 2/20-3/16	8 2/20-3/16	2 11/21-11/25	5 11/21-12/5
1980-81	3 (twice) 2/18-2/25	6 2/18-3/8	3 (twice) last-12/22-12/31	4 3/1-3/11
1981-82	4 (twice) last-1/7-1/20	7 1/7-2/18	3 10/21-10/28	5 11/22-12/9
1982-83	7 11/17-12/15	7 11/17-12/15	4 1/16-1/30	5 1/12-1/30
1983-84	7 12/21-1/18	7 12/21-1/18	3 10/26-10/30	3 (twice) last-11/23-11/30
1984-85	4 1/24-2/17	5 1/16-2/17	3 2/21-2/28	6 11/25-12/7
1985-86	4 2/12-2/27	5 2/12-2/27	3 (twice) last-3/2-3/12	3 (4 times) last-3/2-3/12
1986-87	2 (5 times) last-2/15-2/17	3 (3 times) last-12/23-1/5	3 (5 times) last-4/1-4/5	3 (twice) last-1/5-1/9
1987-88	5 2/25-3/15	6 11/15-12/16	3 10/28-11/10	4 10/26-11/10
1988-89	6 10/16-11/9	7 10/16-11/11	2 (6 times) last-3/26-4/2	3 11/11-11/21
1989-90	5 2/19-3/5	7 10/11-10/27	3 12/10-12/17	6 12/10-12/31
1990-91	8 10/8-10/31	8 10/8-10/31	2 (twice) last-3/13-3/17	3 (2 times) last-1/15-2/3
1991-92	5 12/2-12/23	11 1/14-3/1	2 3/4-3/9	3 (twice) last-3/4-3/9
1992-93	4 10/12-10/31	7 12/27-2/3	7 3/24-4/14	7 3/24-4/14
1993-94	4 (3 times) last-4/1-4/12	16 10/24-1/5	2 1/5-1/10	2 (3 times) last 3/4-3/7
1994-95	5 4/12-4/26	5 4/12-4/26	4 3/15-4/7	4 3/15-4/7

YEAR	WINNING STREAK		UNBEATEN STREAK		LOSING STREAK		WINLESS STREAK	
1926-27	4	1/27-2/12	6	1/27-2/27	3	12/15-12/26	3	12/15-12/26
1927-28	3	11/15-11/29	4	11/15-12/1	3	12/27-1/14	4	2/26-3/10
1928-29	2	(twice) last-1/24-2/3	6	12/6-1/10	3	2/7-2/23	4	(twice) last-2/7-2/28
1929-30	2	11/23-11/28	3	3/1-3/4	3	(twice) last-1/2-1/12	7	1/26-3/8
1930-31	2	2/5-2/10	5	(twice) last-1/31-2/15	2	12/4-12/6	3	(3 times) last-1/13-1/31
1931-32	4	11/12-11/29	10	11/12-1/3	2	3/6-3/22	4	3/6-3/22
1932-33	2	(4 times) last-2/26-3/12	3	(twice) last-1/24-2/2	4	(3 times) last-3/16-3/21	4	12/13-1/10
1933-34	4	12/2-12/24	4	12/2-12/24	4	11/11-11/25	4	11/11-11/25
1934-35	7	1/12-2/12	7	1/12-2/12	4	11/10-12/4	4	11/10-12/4
1935-36	3	3/15-3/22	3	(twice) last-3/10-3/22	4	1/18-1/26	4	(twice) last-2/25-3/10
1936-37	2	(twice) last-12/6-12/12	2	(3 times) last-1/26-2/4	4	2/11-3/4	4	2/11-3/4
1937-38	4	12/11-12/23	4	12/11-12/23	2	11/27-12/2	3	3/6-3/20
1938-39	3	(twice) last-2/2-2/12	3	(3 times) last-2/2-2/12	1	(8 times) last-3/18	4	1/5-1/19
1939-40	3	1/2-1/18	11	11/11-1/13	3	2/11-2/22	6	2/1-2/22
1940-41	3	2/18-3/1	3	2/18-3/1	3	12/13-12/28	5	12/13-1/4
1941-42	3	(3 times) last-1/20-2/3	3	(3 times) last-1/20-2/3	3	12/13-12/23	3	(twice) last-3/3-3/7
1942-43	2	12/25-12/29	3	12/19-12/29	6	1/24-2/7	11	1/1-2/27
1943-44	1	(twice) last-1/22	1	(3 times) last-3/12	10	10/30-12/23	11	1/23-3/18
1944-45	1	(4 times) last-1/24	1	(7 times) last-2/24	3	(4 times) last-3/7-3/10	9	1/27-3/10
1945-46	1	(5 times) last-3/13	3	2/16-2/27	7	1/12-2/27	12	11/28-2/7
1946-47	2	(4 times) last-1/22-1/25	2	(4 times) last-1/22-1/25	5	10/26-11/21	5	10/26-11/21
1947-48	3	11/19-11/30	6	11/19-12/13	5	10/19-11/9	8	2/4-3/13
1948-49	3	12/23-12/25	3	12/18-12/25	8	2/9-3/16	7	2/9-3/16
1949-50	3	2/9-2/23	4	2/5-2/23	4	1/14-1/25	8	1/14-2/5
1950-51	1	(6 times) last-3/1	3	2/4-2/15	6	3/10-3/17	10	10/19-11/25
1951-52	2	2/7-2/9	4	1/17-1/26	6	12/1-12/29	10	11/4-12/29
1952-53	3	(6 times) last-3/7	3	12/20-1/8	6	10/30-11/27	16	10/9-12/20
1953-54	2	(4 times) last-3/13-3/20	3	1/28-2/4	8	11/15-12/26	9	11/8-12/26
1954-55	1	(7 times) last-3/12	3	1/23-1/29	9	11/27-1/8	11	11/20-1/8
1955-56	2	(5 times) last-1/28-1/29	3	(twice) last-1/14-1/17	7	2/4-3/3	7	2/4-3/3
1956-57	2	(twice) last-1/26-1/27	3	(twice) last-3/2-3/9	5	10/14-11/8	6	10/14-11/18
1957-58	3	(twice) last-3/12-3/22	9	2/8-3/22	3	1/25-2/2	4	12/7-12/19
1958-59	3	1/26-2/5	3	(twice) last-1/26-2/5	3	(twice) last-2/8-2/18	7	10/8-11/4
1959-60	1	(7 times) last-3/12	2	(twice) last-3/10-3/12	5	1/14-1/23	7	(twice) last-1/14-1/30

YEAR-BY-YEAR

YEAR	WINNING STREAK		UNBEATEN STREAK		LOSING STREAK		WINLESS STREAK	
1960-61	2	12/4-12/10	4	1/12-1/18	10	2/8-3/15	10	2/8-3/15
1961-62	2	12/25-1/1	2	(4 times) last-12/25-1/1	7	1/3-1/27	7	1/3-1/27
1962-63	2	2/26-2/28	2	(4 times) last-2/26-2/28	4	2/10-2/23	6	12/22-1/13
1963-64	2	1/1-1/9	2	(twice) last-1/25-1/30	7	10/26-11/28	13	10/26-12/25
1964-65	2	(twice) last-2/27-3/4	3	(3 times) last-1/16-1/23	7	1/24-2/24	8	1/23-2/24
1965-66	2	10/30-11/6	3	10/30-11/11	9	1/19-2/13	11	11/20-1/15
1966-67	2	(3 times) last-2/19-2/25	6	11/12-12/17	3	1/21-1/28	7	3/1-4/1
1967-68	4	2/15-2/29	8	2/3-3/9	4	(twice) last-12/7-12/16	4	(twice) last-12/7-12/16
1968-69	3	(twice) last-3/6-3/19	4	3/5-3/19	6	2/1-3/1	7	(twice) last-2/1-3/5
1969-70	3	11/7-11/15	5	11/7-11/22	3	3/6-3/14	8	2/13-3/14
1970-71	3	1/2-1/12	4	(3 times) last-2/20-3/10	3	2/9-2/17	4	1/15-1/30
1971-72	3	(4 times) last-2/22-3/11	8	10/9-11/6	2	11/20-11/27	3	3/23-4/1
1972-73	5	1/19-2/10	10	12/20-2/10	3	10/7-10/14	3	11/23-12/1
1973-74	4	2/16-3/2	5	2/14-3/2	4	12/23-1/10	7	10/20-11/15
1974-75	4	12/30-1/11	4	12/30-1/11	5	3/11-3/29	6	3/11-4/3
1975-76	3	12/5-12/13	4	12/4-12/13	4	(4 times) last-3/16-3/25	4	(4 times) last-3/16-3/25
1976-77	1	(12 times) last-3/19	5	11/22-12/4	4	(twice) last-2/26-3/12	5	(twice) last-1/19-2/3
1977-78	3	3/22-3/25	4	3/19-3/25	4	1/20-2/22	7	1/20-2/22
1978-79	7	10/28-11/29	7	10/28-11/29	3	(3 times) last-3/28-4/6	3	(3 times) last-3/28-4/6
1979-80	4	12/1-12/12	4	12/1-12/12	5	10/20-11/3	5	10/20-11/3
1980-81	4	(twice) last-1/23-1/31	4	(twice) last-1/23-1/31	7	2/5-3/10	10	10/18-11/22
1981-82	4	(twice) last-3/11-3/26	8	12/2-1/15	3	10/9-10/17	3	(4 times) last-2/4-2/10
1982-83	2	(3 times) last-3/29-3/31	3	1/29-2/5	4	10/16-11/5	6	(twice) last-11/28-12/26
1983-84	2	(4 times) last-3/9-3/10	5	2/4-2/11	3	2/9-3/7	8	2/9-3/7
1984-85	3	10/20-10/27	3	10/20-10/27	7	1/19-2/7	9	1/19-2/10
1985-86	4	1/14-1/22	5	1/14-1/27	3	10/12-11/2	4	10/12-11/2
1986-87	2	(4 times) last-3/12-3/14	3	10/15-10/25	3	11/9-11/19	3	(4 times) last-1/19-1/23
1987-88	3	1/22-1/30	4	1/22-2/2	6	10/31-11/19	6	10/31-11/19
1988-89	4	1/18-1/23	8	12/23-1/23	7	3/3-4/1	7	3/3-4/1
1989-90	4	(4 times) last-2/13-2/16	4	2/13-2/23	6	12/16-1/6	8	12/2-1/6
1990-91	3	2/28-1/5	6	11/9-11/24	7	3/7-3/30	6	1/30-2/28
1991-92	4	(twice) last-1/23-2/1	5	1/22-2/1	3	2/7-2/20	3	2/7-2/20
1992-93	3	3/11-4/4	4	12/11-12/21	6	12/26-1/16	7	12/26-1/19
1993-94	6	10/30-11/24	6	10/30-11/24	2	(4 times) last-3/12-3/14	4	3/10-3/22
1994-95	4	2/20 - 3/1	4	2/20 - 3/1	5	3/5 - 3/25	5	3/5 - 3/25

ALL-TIME RANGERS AND OPPONENTS PENALTY SHOTS

PLAYER AND TEAM	DATE	SCORE	GOALTENDER	RESULT
Ebbie Goodfellow, Detroit	11/15/34	NYR 2 at Detroit 8	Percy Jackson	NO
Bun Cook, RANGERS	11/18/34	St. Louis 0 at NYR 5	Bill Beveridge	NO
Armand Mondou, Montreal	12/4/34	NYR 3 at Canadiens 5	Andy Aitkenhead	YES
Bun Cook, RANGERS	12/8/34	NYR 5 at Toronto 2	George Hainsworth	NO
Charlie Conacher, Toronto	12/11/34	Toronto 8 at NYR 4	Andy Aitkenhead	NO
Bert Connolly, RANGERS	1/24/35	Chicago 3 at NYR 3	Lorne Chabot	NO
Bert Connolly, RANGERS	1/31/35	NYR 3 at Toronto 2	George Hainsworth	NO
Bert Connolly, RANGERS	1/16/36	Toronto 0 at NYR 1	George Hainsworth	YES
Hap Emms, NY Americans	12/16/37	Americans 0 at NYR 2	Davey Kerr	NO
Neil Colville, RANGERS	12/16/38	Americans 0 at NYR 2	Earl Robertson	NO
Alex Shibicky, RANGERS	2/1/37	Chicago 1 at NYR 6	Mike Karakas	YES
Paul Thompson, Chicago	2/1/37	Chicago 1 at NYR 6	Davey Kerr	NO
Alex Shibicky, RANGERS	12/8/38	NYR 6 at Candiens 5	Claude Bourque	YES
Mac Colville, RANGERS	12/27/41	NYR 4 at Montreal 3	Paul Bibeault	YES
Sid Abel, Detroit	2/26/42	Detroit 4 at NYR 7	Jim Henry	YES
Bob Goldham, Toronto	3/7/42	NYR 2 at Toronto 4	Jim Henry	YES
Bud Poile, Toronto	11/19/42	Toronto 7 at NYR 3	Steve Buzinski	YES
Ray Getliffe, Montreal	2/20/43	NYR 1 at Canadiens 6	Bill Beveridge	NO
Ab DeMarco, Sr., RANGERS	2/19/44	NYR 2 at Canadiens 5	Bill Durnan	NO
Chuck Scherza, RANGERS	11/30/44	NYR 7 at Montreal 5	Bill Durnan	YES
Fred Thurier, RANGERS	1/18/45	NYR 3 at Detroit 7	Harry Lumley	YES
Alex Shibicky, RANGERS	11/25/45	NYR 4 at Detroit 1	Harry Lumley	YES
Ted Sloan, Toronto	2/17/51	NYR 0 at Toronto 2	Chuck Rayner	NO
Bernie Geoffrion, Montreal	10/16/52	NYR 1 at Montreal 3	Gump Worsley	YES
Gordie Howe, Detroit	3/5/53	NYR 1 at Detroit 7	Gump Worsley	YES
Danny Lewicki, RANGERS	10/24/56	Montreal 2 at NYR 3	Gerry McNeil	YES
Andy Bathgate, RANGERS	3/14/62	Detroit 2 at NYR 3	Hank Bassen	YES
Andy Hebenton, RANGERS	3/21/63	NYR 2 at Boston 2	Eddie Johnston	NO
Don Marshall, RANGERS	11/3/63	Montreal 5 at NYR 3	Charlie Hodge	NO
Rod Gilbert, RANGERS	11/27/63	Detroit 2 at NYR 3	Terry Sawchuk	YES
Bob Nevin, RANGERS	11/5/66	NYR 1 at Toronto 3	Terry Sawchuk	YES
Dallas Smith, Boston	12/21/66	Boston 1 at NYR 5	Ed Giacomin	NO
John Bucyk, Boston	2/4/67	NYR 4 at Boston 3	Ed Giacomin	YES
Ed Joyal, Los Angeles	10/31/67	NYR 6 at Los Angeles 1	Ed Giacomin	NO
Norm Ferguson, Oakland	11/24/68	Oakland 2 at NYR 3	Ed Giacomin	YES
Charlie Burns, Pittsburgh	2/5/69	NYR 2 at Pittsburgh 3	Ed Giacomin	NO
Keith McCreary, Pittsburgh	3/18/70	NYR 2 at Pittsburgh 0	Ed Giacomin	NO
Butch Goring, Los Angeles	2/13/72	Los Angeles 2 at NYR 4	Gilles Villemure	YES
Stan Mikita, Chicago	3/15/72	NYR 1 at Chicago 3	Ed Giacomin	NO
Ron Schock, Pittsburgh	3/10/73	NYR 5 at Pittsburgh 4	Ed Giacomin	NO
Jacques Lemaire, Montreal	3/31/73	NYR 1 at Montreal 5	Ed Giacomin	YES
Paul Henderson, Toronto	10/20/73	NYR 2 at Toronto 3	Gilles Villemure	NO
Yvan Cournoyer, Montreal	12/29/73	NYR 1 at Montreal 7	Ed Giacomin	NO
Greg Polis, RANGERS	2/1/76	Minnesota 2 at NYR 3	Cesare Maniago	NO
Don Murdoch, RANGERS	11/3/76	NYR 6 at Vancouver 1	Curt Ridley	YES
Bill Goldsworthy, RANGERS	11/14/76	Pittsburgh 5 at NYR 1	Dunc Wilson	NO
Don Murdoch, RANGERS	1/9/77	Los Angeles 5 at NYR 4	Rogie Vachon	NO
Don Murdoch, RANGERS	1/28/78	NYR 2 at Islanders 6	Glenn Resch	NO
Claude Larose, RANGERS	1/7/80	Hartford 2 at NYR 5	Al Smith	NO
Rolf Edberg, Washington	2/2/80	NYR 6 at Washington 3	Doug Soetaert	YES
Ron Greschner, RANGERS	10/28/80	NYR 4 at St. Louis 5	Mike Liut	YES
Mike Gartner, Washington	12/10/80	Washington 2 at NYR 6	Wayne Thomas	YES
Bobby MacMillan, Calgary	1/13/81	NYR 4 at Calgary 4	Doug Soetaert	NO
Mike Rogers, Hartford	2/22/81	NYR 5 at Hartford 6	Doug Soetaert	NO
Mike Rogers, RANGERS	12/5/81	NYR 2 at Colorado 1	Glenn Resch	NO
Pierre Larouche, RANGERS	2/16/86	Detroit 1 at NYR 3	Corrado Micalef	NO
Mike Ridley, RANGERS	2/16/86	Detroit 1 at NYR 3	Corrado Micalef	NO
Peter Sundstrom, RANGERS	3/2/86	Washington 4 at NYR 2	Al Jensen	YES
Petr Klima, Detroit	2/17/87	Detroit 2 at NYR 6	John Vanbiesbrouck	NO
Jan Erixon, RANGERS	10/24/87	NYR 5 at Philadelphia 3	Mark Laforest	YES
Pat Verbeek, New Jersey	3/27/88	NYR 2 at New Jersey 7	John Vanbiesbrouck	YES
Ray Bourque, Boston	11/11/88	Boston 4 at NYR 4	John Vanbiesbrouck	NO
Guy Lafleur, RANGERS	11/29/88	NYR 4 at Winnipeg 3	Eldon Reddick	NO
Kevin Dineen, Hartford	10/19/89	Hartford 3 at NYR 7	Mike Richter	NO
Lindy Ruff, RANGERS	11/26/89	Quebec 1 at NYR 3	Mario Brunetta	YES
Pelle Eklund, Philadelphia	1/14/90	Philadelphia 3 at NYR 4	Mike Richter	NO
Kelly Kisio, RANGERS	2/26/90	Boston 1 at NYR 6	Rejean Lemelin	NO
Keith Acton, Philadelphia	3/25/90	Philadelphia 3 at NYR 7	John Vanbiesbrouck	YES
Troy Murray, Winnipeg	11/27/91	NYR 2 at Winnipeg 3	Mike Richter	NO
Darren Turcotte, RANGERS	12/29/91	Pittsburgh 6 at NYR 3	Wendell Young	NO
Paul Broten, RANGERS	1/16/92	Calgary 4 at NYR 6	Mike Vernon	YES
Pavel Bure, Vancouver	2/17/92	Vancouver 3 at NYR 3	John Vanbiesbrouck	NO
Alexei Kovalev, RANGERS	10/5/93	Boston 4 at NYR 3	Jon Casey	NO
Steve Larmer, RANGERS	1/16/94	NYR 5 at Chicago 1	Ed Belfour	YES
Tony Amonte, RANGERS	1/27/94	NYR 5 at Los Angeles 4	Kelly Hrudey	NO
Steve Konowalchuk, Washington	3/5/95	NYR 2 at Washington 4	Mike Richter	NO

THE LAST TIME

RANGERS SHUTOUT OPPOSITION AT HOME: 2/28/95, Rangers 0, Florida 0. Goaltender: Mike Richter.
RANGERS SHUTOUT OPPOSITION ON ROAD: 4/30/95, Rangers 2, Philadelphia 0.
Goaltender: Glenn Healy.
OPPOSITION SHUTOUT RANGERS AT HOME: 2/28/95, Rangers 0, Florida 0.
Goaltender: John Vanbiesbrouck.
OPPOSITION SHUTOUT RANGERS ON ROAD: 4/9/95, Rangers 0, New Jersey 2.
Goaltender: Martin Brodeur.
RANGERS PLAYED A 0-0 GAME: 2/28/95 vs. Florida at Madison Square Garden. Goaltenders: Mike Richter
and John Vanbiesbrouck.
RANGERS WON A 1-0 GAME AT HOME: 3/14/71, Rangers 1, Toronto 0. Goaltender: Eddie Giacomin.
RANGERS LOST A 1-0 GAME AT HOME: 3/25/79, Rangers 0, Montreal 1. Goaltender: Michel Larocque.
RANGERS WON A 1-0 GAME ON ROAD: 12/23/93 Rangers 1, Washington 0. Goaltender: Glenn Healy.
RANGERS LOST A 1-0 GAME ON ROAD: 3/23/95, Rangers 0, Islanders 1. Goaltender: Tommy Soderstrom.
RANGERS HAD TWO CONSECUTIVE SHUTOUTS: 1977, November 30 at St. Louis, Rangers 4, St. Louis 0.
Goaltender: Wayne Thomas. December 3 at Minnesota, Rangers 4, Minnesota 0. Goaltender: John
Davidson.
OPPOSITION HAD TWO CONSECUTIVE SHUTOUTS: 1993, April 12 at Philadelphia, Philadelphia 1 Rangers
0. Goaltender: Dominic Roussel. April 14 at Madison Square Garden, Washington 2, Rangers 0.
Goaltender: Rick Tabaracci.
RANGERS HELD OPPOSITION SHOTLESS FOR ONE PERIOD: 2/25/79 Second period vs.
New York Islanders at Madison Square Garden. Rangers won 3-2.
RANGERS DID NOT HAVE A PENALTY IN A GAME: 1/7/89 vs. Islanders at Nassau Coliseum.
Rangers won 5-1. Referee Bob Myers.
RANGERS AND OPPONENT DID NOT HAVE A PENALTY IN A GAME: 3/13/76 vs. Vancouver Canucks
at Vancouver. Rangers won 7-3. Referee Lloyd Gilmour.
RANGERS SCORED AT LEAST 10 GOALS IN A GAME: 12/13/92 vs. Montreal Canadiens at
Madison Square Garden. Rangers won 10-3.
OPPOSITION SCORED AT LEAST 10 GOALS IN A GAME: 4/10/93 vs. Pittsburgh Penguins at
Madison Square Garden. Penguins won 10-4.
RANGERS SCORED AT LEAST FIVE GOALS IN ONE PERIOD: 4/8/94 vs. Toronto Maple Leafs at MSG.
Rangers scored five goals in the second period and won 5-3.
OPPOSITION SCORED AT LEAST FIVE GOALS IN ONE PERIOD: 3/30/95 vs. Quebec Nordiques at Quebec.
Quebec scored five goals in the second period and won 5-4.
RANGERS HAD AT LEAST 50 SHOTS IN A GAME: 54, 4/14/94 vs. Philadelphia Flyers at
Madison Square Garden. Rangers and Flyers tied 2-2.
OPPOSITION HAD AT LEAST 50 SHOTS IN A GAME: 51, 1/13/93 vs. Washington Capitals at
Madison Sqaure Garden. Rangers won 5-4.
RANGERS HAD AT LEAST 50 SHOTS IN CONSECUTIVE GAMES: 54, January 3, 1994 vs. Florida at MSG.
53, January 5, 1994 vs. Calgary at MSG.
RANGERS HAD AT LEAST 25 SHOTS IN A PERIOD: 26, 11/12/89 vs. Islanders at Madison Square Garden.
Rangers had 26 shots in second and won 4-2.
OPPOSITION HAD AT LEAST 25 SHOTS IN A PERIOD: 28, 1/31/91 vs. Vancouver Canucks at Vancouver.
Canucks had 28 shots in third and game ended in 3-3 tie.
FOUR-GOAL GAME BY A RANGER AT GARDEN: 3/22/92 Mark Messier scored four goals vs.
Chad Erickson of New Jersey Devils. Rangers won 6-3.
FOUR-GOAL GAME BY A RANGER ON THE ROAD: 11/21/86 Tony McKegney scored one goal vs.
Richard Brodeur and three vs. Wendell Young of Vancouver Canucks. Rangers won 8-5.
OPPONENT HAD FOUR-GOAL GAME AT GARDEN: 1/8/90 Mario Lemieux of Pittsburgh Penguins scored
two goals vs. Bob Froese and two vs. John Vanbiesbrouck. Pittsburgh Penguins won 7-5.
OPPONENT HAD FOUR-GOAL GAME ON THE ROAD: 11/21/86 Petri Skriko of Vancouver Canucks scored
four goals vs. John Vanbiesbrouck. Rangers won 8-5.
FIVE-GOAL GAME BY A RANGER AT GARDEN: 2/23/83 Mark Pavelich scored five goals vs. Greg Millen of
Hartford Whalers. Rangers won 11-3.
FIVE-GOAL GAME BY A RANGER ON THE ROAD: 10/12/76 Don Murdoch scored five goals against
Gary Smith of Minnesota North Stars. Rangers won 10-4.
OPPONENT HAD FIVE-GOAL GAME AT GARDEN: 4/9/93 Mario Lemieux of Pittsburgh Penguins scored
three goals vs. Corey Hirsch and two vs. Mike Richter. Pittsburgh won 10-4.
OPPONENT HAD FIVE-GOAL GAME ON THE ROAD: 12/23/78 Bryan Trottier of Islanders scored four goals
vs. Wayne Thomas and one vs. John Davidson. Islanders won 9-4.
RANGERS GOALTENDER ASSISTED ON A GOAL: 4/20/95, Glenn Healy assisted on a goal by Sergei Zubov
at 4:41 of the second period against the Hartford Whalers at Madison Square Garden. New York won 3-2.
RANGERS HAD TWO PENALTY SHOTS IN ONE GAME: 2/16/86 Pierre Larouche and Mike Rogers vs.
Detroit at Madison Square Garden, against Corrado Micalef. Both missed, Rangers won 3-1.
RANGERS AND OPPONENT HAD A PENALTY SHOT IN ONE GAME: 2/1/38 Chicago vs. Rangers at
Madison Square Garden. Alex Shibicky scored against Mike Karakuls and Paul Thompson missed against
Davey Kerr. Rangers won 6-1.
RANGERS HAD TWO HAT TRICKS IN ONE GAME: Ron Duguay and Phil Esposito on March 24, 1978 at
Washington. Rangers won 11-4.
RANGERS HAD HAT TRICKS IN CONSECUTIVE GAMES: Mike Gartner vs. Pittsburgh, at MSG on January
31, 1994 and Adam Graves vs. Islanders, at MSG on February 2, 1994.

RANGERS REGULAR SEASON RECORDS

TEAM RECORDS

MOST VICTORIES, ONE SEASON: 52 1993-94. Home: **30**, 1970-71 (39 games). Road: **24** 1993-94.

FEWEST VICTORIES, ONE SEASON: 6 1943-44 (50-game schedule). Home: **4**, 1943-44 (25 games). Road: **2**, 1943-44 (25 games).

FEWEST VICTORIES, ONE SEASON (Minimum 70-game schedule): 17 1952-53, 1954-55, 1959-60. Home: **8**, 1964-65 (35 games). Road: **6**, 1950-51, 1952-53, 1965-66 (35 games).

FEWEST LOSSES, ONE SEASON: 11 1939-40 (48 games schedule). Home: **2**, 1970-71 (39 games). Road: **7**, 1928-29 (22 games), 1930-31 (22 games), 1939-40 (24 games).

FEWEST LOSSES, ONE SEASON (Minimum 70-game schedule): 17 1971-72. Home: **2**, 1970-71 (39 games). Road: **10**, 1957-58 (35 games).

MOST LOSSES, ONE SEASON: 44 1984-85 (80-game schedule). **39** 1943-44 (50-game schedule). Home: **17**, 1943-44 (25 games). **19**, 1964-65 (35 games). Road: **26**, 1975-76 (40 games), **26** 1984-85 (40 games).

MOST TIES, ONE SEASON: (Minimum 70-game schedule): 21 1950-51 (70-game schedule). Home: **13**, 1954-55 (35 games). Road: **11**, 1950-51 (35 games).

FEWEST TIES, ONE SEASON: (Minimum 70-game schedule): 5 1991-92 (80-game schedule). Home: **1**, 1983-84 (40 games). Road: **1**, 1991-92 & 1975-76 (40 games).

MOST POINTS, ONE SEASON: 112 1993-94. Home: **67**, 1970-71 (39 games). Road: **50**, (twice) 1971-72, 1993-94.

FEWEST POINTS, ONE SEASON: 17 1943-44 (50-game schedule). Home: **12**, 1943-44 (25 games). Road: **5**, 1943-44 (25 games).

FEWEST POINTS, ONE SEASON (Minimum 70-game schedule): 47 1965-66. Home: **24**, 1964-65 (35 games). Road: **16**, 1965-66 (35 games).

MOST GOALS ONE SEASON: 321 1991-92. Home: **186**, 1982-83 (40 games). Road: **155**, 1978-79, 1986-87 (40 games).

FEWEST GOALS , ONE SEASON: 72 1928-29 (44-game schedule). Home: **32**, 1928-29 (22 games). Road: **40**, 1928-29 (22 games).

FEWEST GOALS, ONE SEASON (Minimum 70-game schedule): 150 1954-55. Home: **86**, 1954-55 (35 games). Road: **63**, 1952-53 (35 games).

MOST ASSISTS, ONE SEASON: 540 1988-89.

FEWEST ASSISTS, ONE SEASON: 45 1926-27 (44-game schedule).

FEWEST GOALS AGAINST, ONE SEASON: 65 1928-29 (44-game schedule). Home: **21**, 1928-29 (22 games). Road: **41**, 1926-27 (22 games).

FEWEST GOALS AGAINST ONE SEASON (Minimum 70-game schedule): 177 1970-71. Home: **71**, 1970-71 (39 games). Road: **95**, 1957-58 (35 games).

MOST GOALS AGAINST, ONE SEASON: 345 1984-85 (80-game schedule). Home: **156**, 1986-87 (40 games). Road: **197**, 1975-76 (40 games).

MOST POWER PLAY GOALS, ONE SEASON: 111 1987-88.

MOST POWER PLAY GOALS, ONE GAME: 6 10/13/93 vs. Quebec at Madison Square Garden.

MOST POWER PLAY GOALS ALLOWED, ONE SEASON: 85 1988-89.

MOST SHORTHANDED GOALS, ONE SEASON: 20 1993-94.

MOST SHORTHANDED GOALS, ONE GAME: 3 10/5/83 vs. New Jersey at Madison Square Garden.

MOST SHORTHANDED GOALS ALLOWED, ONE SEASON: 18, 1992-93.

MOST 20-GOAL SCORERS, ONE SEASON: 9 1993-94.

MOST 30-GOAL SCORERS, ONE SEASON: 5 1991-92.

MOST 40-GOAL SCORERS, ONE SEASON: 3 1971-72.

MOST HAT TRICKS, ONE SEASON: 10 1986-87.

MOST PLAYERS USED, ONE SEASON: 46 1986-87.

MOST ROOKIES USED, ONE SEASON: 14 1988-89.

MOST ROOKIES USED, ONE GAME: 9 3/21/90, vs. Toronto and 3/27/90 vs. Quebec.

MOST SCORING POINTS (Goal and Assists), ONE SEASON: 854 1978-79.

FEWEST SCORING POINTS, ONE SEASON: 140 1926-27 (44-game schedule).

MOST PENALTY MINUTES, ONE SEASON: 2018 1989-90.

FEWEST PENALTY MINUTES, ONE SEASON: 253 1943-44 (50-game schedule).

MOST SHUTOUTS, ONE SEASON: 13 1928-29 (44-game schedule). Home: **8**, 1928-29 (22 games). Road: **7**, 1926-27 (22 games).

MOST TIMES SHUT OUT, ONE SEASON: 10 1928-29 (44-game schedule). Home: **5**, 1930-31 (22 games); 1938-39 (24 games). Road: **7**, 1952-53 (35 games).

RANGERS REGULAR SEASON RECORDS

(Team Records, cont.)

LONGEST WINNING STREAK: 10 1939-40. Began 12/19 with 5-2 victory over Montreal. Ended 1/14 when defeated by Chicago, 2-1. (Rangers then won next five games for overall record of 15 wins in 16 games.) **10** 1972-73. Began 1/19 with 6-0 victory over California. Ended 2/11 with 2-2 tie against Montreal.

LONGEST WINNING STREAK AT START OF SEASON: 5 1983-84. Began 10/5 with 6-2 victory over New Jersey. Ended 10/15 when defeated by St. Louis, 6-5. (Rangers then won next four games for overall record of 9-1-0 in first 10 games of season.)

LONGEST HOME WINNING STREAK AT START OF SEASON: 8 1990-91. Began 10/8 with 6-3 victory over Minnesota. Ended 11/2 when defeated by Islanders, 3-2.

LONGEST LOSING STREAK AT START OF SEASON: 11 1943-44. Began October 30 with 5-2 loss to Toronto. Ended November 28 with a 2-2 tie with Montreal. (Rangers then lost next three games for overall record of 0-14-1 in first 15 games before defeating Boston 6-4 on December 12.)

LONGEST HOME WINNING STREAK: 14 1939-40. Began 12/19 with 5-2 victory over Montreal. Ended 2/29 when defeated by Chicago, 2-1.

LONGEST HOME LOSING STREAK AT START OF SEASON: 4 1940-41. Began 11/15 with 2-1 defeat to Boston. Ended with a 5-4 overtime victory over Chicago.

LONGEST ROAD WINNING STREAK: 7 1934-35. Began 1/12 with a 3-1 victory over Americans. Ended 2/16 when defeated by Toronto, 5-1. **7** 1978-79. Began 10/28 with a 2-1 victory over Montreal. Ended 12/2 when defeated by Toronto, 5-2.

LONGEST UNDEFEATED STREAK: 19 1939-40. Won 14 games and tied five. Began 11/23 with 1-1 tie against Montreal. Ended 1/14 when defeated by Chicago, 2-1. (Rangers then won next five games for overall record of 24 victories or ties in 25 games).

LONGEST HOME UNDEFEATED STREAK: 26 Won 19 games and tied seven. Began 3/29/70, with a 4-1 victory over Montreal. Ended 2/3/71, when defeated by Chicago, 4-2. The streak covered the final two games of the 1969-70 season and the first 24 games of the 1970-71 season.

LONGEST ROAD UNDEFEATED STREAK: 11 1939-40. Won six games and tied five. Began 11/5 with 1-1 tie against Detroit. Ended 1/14 when defeated by Chicago, 2-1.

MOST CONSECUTIVE TIE GAMES: 4 1929-30. Tied by Chicago, 1-1, on 2/27; by Toronto, 3-3, on 3/1; by Detroit, 2-2, on 3/2; by Chicago, 2-2 on 3/4. (All overtime games).

LONGEST LOSING STREAK: 11 1943-44. Began 10/30 with 5-2 defeat by Toronto. Ended 11/28 with 2-2 tie against Montreal.

LONGEST HOME LOSING STREAK: 7 1976-77. Began 10/20 with 4-2 defeat by Los Angeles. Ended 11/17 with 3-2 victory over Chicago. **7** 1992-93. Began 3/26 with a 3-1 defeat by Chicago. Continued to end of season.

LONGEST ROAD LOSING STREAK: 10 1943-44. Began 10/30 with 5-2 defeat by Toronto. Ended 12/25 with 5-3 victory over Toronto. **10** 1960-61. Began 2/8 with 5-3 defeat by at Toronto. Continued to end of season.

LONGEST WINLESS STREAK, ONE SEASON: 21 1943-44. Lost 17 games and tied four. Began 1/23 with 15-0 defeat by Detroit. Continued to end of season.

LONGEST HOME WINLESS STREAK, ONE SEASON: 10 1943-44. Lost seven games and tied three. Began 1/30 with 5-3 defeat by Montreal. Continued to end of season.

LONGEST ROAD WINLESS STREAK, ONE SEASON: 16 1952-53. Lost 12 games and tied four. Began 10/9 with 5-3 defeat by Detroit. Ended 12/25 with 2-1 victory over Boston.

MOST CONSECUTIVE SHUTOUTS: 4 1927-28. Rangers were not scored upon for a total of 297 minutes and 42 seconds. Defeated Plttsburgh, 3-0; Chicago, 1-0; tied Detroit, 0-0 (10 minutes overtime); defeated Toronto, 1-0. Streak started on 2/23 and ran until 2/28.

MOST CONSECUTIVE TIMES SHUT OUT: 4 1927-28. Rangers failed to score for 341 minutes and 42 seconds. Tied by Ottawa, 0-0 (twice); lost to Chicago, 3-0; Boston, 2-0. Streak ran 2/7-2/19.

LONGEST NON-SHUTOUT STREAK: 236 Began 12/20/89 with a 2-2 tie with Buffalo. Ended 12/15/92 vs. Calgary (Vernon).

MOST GOALS, ONE GAME: 12 Defeated California, 12-1 11/21/71, at Madison Square Garden.

MOST GOALS, ONE GAME, RANGERS AND OPPONENTS: 19 Defeated by Boston, 10-9, at Boston, 3/4/44.

MOST POINTS ONE GAME, RANGERS AND OPPONENTS: 46 Boston Bruins, at Boston, 3/4/44. Boston won, 10-9. Boston had 15 assists, Rangers 12.

MOST GOALS ALLOWED, ONE GAME: 15 Defeated by Detroit, 15-0, at Detroit, 1/23/44.

GREATEST WINNING MARGIN: 11 Defeated California, 12-1, 11/21/71, at Madison Square Garden.

GREATEST LOSING MARGIN: 15 Defeated by Detroit, 15-0 at Detroit, 1/23/44.

HIGHEST TIE SCORE: 7-7 Tied Minnesota on 3/19/78 at Minnesota. **7-7** Tied Quebec on 3/22/81 at Madison Square Garden.

MOST ASSISTS, ONE GAME: 23 11/21/71. Defeated California 12-1, at Madison Square Garden.

MOST POINTS, ONE GAME: 35 11/21/71, vs. California (12 goals and 23 assists).

MOST GOALS, ONE PERIOD: 8 11/21/71, vs. California (third period).

RANGERS REGULAR SEASON RECORDS

(Team Records, cont.)

MOST POINTS, ONE PERIOD: 23 11/21/71 vs. California (third period). Eight goals and 15 assists.
MOST ASSISTS, ONE PERIOD: 15 11/21/71 vs. California (third period).
MOST GOALS, ONE PERIOD, RANGERS AND OPPONENTS: 10 3/16/39 (third period). Rangers
scored seven goals and Americans three, at Madison Square Garden. Rangers won game, 11-5.
MOST SHOTS, ONE GAME: 65 4/5/70. Defeated Detroit, 9-5, at Madison Square Garden.
LARGEST HOME ATTENDANCE, ONE SEASON: 738,968 1992-93.
FASTEST TWO GOALS BY RANGERS: 4 sec. Kris King at 19:45 and James Patrick at 19:49 of
the third period against the Islanders at Madison Square Garden, 10/9/91 Rangers won 5-3.
FASTEST TWO GOALS BY RANGERS AND OPPONENTS: 4 sec. Denis Savard of Chicago at
19:23 of third period and Mark Pavelich of Rangers at 19:27, 2/24/82 at Madison Square
Garden, Rangers won, 6-4.
FASTEST THREE GOALS BY RANGERS: 28 sec. Doug Sulliman at 7:52, Eddie Johnstone at
7:57 and Warren Miller at 8:20 of first period against Colorado at Madison Square Garden,
1/14/80. Game ended in a 6-6 tie.
FASTEST THREE GOALS vs. RANGERS: 21 sec. Bill Mosienko of Chicago scored all three goals
at 6:09, 6:20 and 6:30 of third period, 2/23/52, at Madison Square Garden. Chicago won, 7-6.
FASTEST THREE GOALS BY RANGERS AND OPPONENTS: 15 sec. Mark Pavelich of Rangers
at 19:18 of second period and Ron Greschner at 19:27 and Willi Plett of Minnesota at 19:33,
2/10/83, at Minnesota. Minnesota won game, 7-5.
FASTEST FOUR GOALS BY RANGERS: 1 min. 38 sec. Mark Pavelich at 15:53, Mike Rogers at
16:18, Ron Greschner at 16:51 and Mike Rogers at 17:31 of first period against Edmonton at
Madison Square Garden, 2/15/85. Rangers won, 8-7.
FASTEST FOUR GOALS vs. RANGERS: 1 min. 20 sec. Bill Thoms of Boston at 6:34 of second
period, Frank Mario at 7:08 and 7:27, and Ken Smith at 7:54, 1/21/45, at Boston. Boston won
14-3.
FASTEST FOUR GOALS BY RANGERS AND OPPONENTS: 1 min. 1 sec. Doug Sulliman of
Rangers at 7:52 of first period, Eddie Johnstone at 7:57, Warren Miller at 8:20 and Rob Ramage
of Colorado at 8:53, 1/14/80, at Madison Square Garden. Game ended in 6-6 tie.
FASTEST FIVE GOALS BY RANGERS: 3 min. 22 sec. Mark Pavelich at 15:53, Mike Rogers at
16:18, Ron Greschner at 16:51, Mike Rogers at 17:31 and Grant Ledyard at 19:15 of first period
against Edmonton at Madison Square Garden, 2/15/85. Rangers won, 8-7.
FASTEST FIVE GOALS vs. RANGERS: 2 min. 55 sec. Bobby Schmautz of Boston at 19:13 of first
period, Ken Hodge at 0:18, Phil Esposito at 0:43, Don Marcotte at 0:58 and John Bucyk at 2:08
of second period, 12/19/74, at Boston. Boston won, 11-3.
MOST PENALTY MINUTES, ONE GAME BY RANGERS: 134 Rangers vs. Pittsburgh, 10/30/88 at
Madison Square Garden.
MOST PENALTY MINUTES, ONE GAME BY RANGERS AND OPPONENT: 292 Rangers vs.
Pittsburgh, 10/30/88 at Madison Square Garden.
MOST PENALTY MINUTES, ONE PERIOD BY RANGERS: 126 Rangers vs. Pittsburgh, 10/30/88
at Madison Square Garden (third period).
MOST PENALTY MINUTES, ONE PERIOD BY RANGERS AND OPPONENT: 272 Rangers vs.
Pittsburgh, 10/30/88 at Madison Square Garden (third period).

**Mike Rogers tallied two goals while Ron Greschner and Mark Pavelich added one goal each
to combine for the fastest four goals in Rangers history when they scored four goals in 1:38
on February 15, 1985.**

RANGERS REGULAR SEASON RECORDS

INDIVIDUAL PLAYER RECORDS

MOST GOALS, ONE SEASON: 52 Adam Graves, 1993-94.

MOST ASSISTS, ONE SEASON: 80 Brian Leetch, 1991-92.

MOST POINTS, ONE SEASON: 109 Jean Ratelle, 1971-72.

MOST GOALS BY A CENTER, ONE SEASON: 48 Pierre Larouche, 1983-84.

MOST ASSISTS BY A CENTER, ONE SEASON: 72 Mark Messier, 1991-92.

MOST POINTS BY A CENTER, ONE SEASON: 109 Jean Ratelle, 1971-72.

MOST GOALS BY A LEFT WING, ONE SEASON: 52 Adam Graves, 1993-94.

MOST ASSISTS BY A LEFT WING, ONE SEASON: 56 Vic Hadfield, 1971-72.

MOST POINTS BY A LEFT WING, ONE SEASON: 106 Vic Hadfield, 1971-72.

MOST GOALS BY A RIGHT WING, ONE SEASON: 49 Mike Gartner, 1990-91.

MOST ASSISTS BY A RIGHT WING, ONE SEASON: 61 Rod Gilbert, 1974-75.

MOST POINTS BY A RIGHT WING, ONE SEASON: 97 Rod Gilbert, 1971-72, 1974-75

MOST POWER PLAY GOALS, ONE SEASON: 23 Vic Hadfield, 1971-72.

MOST SHORTHANDED GOALS, ONE SEASON: 5 Mike Gartner, 1993-94. Don Maloney, 1980-81. Mike Rogers, 1982-83.

HIGHEST SHOOTING PERCENTAGE, ONE SEASON: 29.6 Steve Vickers, 1979-80 (29 goals on 98 shots).

MOST GAME-WINNING GOALS, ONE SEASON: 9 Don Maloney, 1980-81.

MOST POINTS BY A LINE, ONE SEASON*: 302 Vic Hadfield (97)-Jean Ratelle (109)-Rod Gilbert (96) 1971-72.

MOST GOALS BY A LINE, ONE SEASON*: 133 Vic Hadfield (45)-Jean Ratelle (46)-Rod Gilbert (42) 1971-72.

MOST GOALS, ONE GAME: 5 Don Murdoch, 10/12/76 against Minnesota at Minnesota; Mark Pavelich, 2/23/83 against Hartford at Madison Square Garden.

MOST POWER PLAY GOALS, ONE GAME: 3 Mark Messier, March 22, 1992 against New Jersey at Madison Square Garden.

MOST SHORTHANDED GOALS, ONE GAME: 2 Greg Polis, November 4, 1977 against Vancouver at Vancouver. Ron Duguay, January 22, 1980 against Los Angeles at Los Angeles. Don Maloney, February 21, 1981 against Washington at Madison Square Garden. Don Maloney, October 5, 1983 against New Jersey at Madison Square Garden. Don Maloney, January 14, 1987 against Calgary at Calgary.

MOST GOALS, ONE PERIOD: 3 Many: Last time: Adam Graves, November 25, 1992 in third period vs. Pittsburgh at Pittsburgh.

MOST ASSISTS, ONE PERIOD: 4 Phil Goyette. First period on October 20, 1963 against Boston at Madison Square Garden.

MOST ASSISTS, ONE GAME: 5 Walt Tkaczuk on Feb. 12, 1972 against Pittsburgh at Pittsburgh. Rod Gilbert on March 2, 1975 against Pittsburgh at Madison Square Garden and October 8, 1976 against Colorado at Colorado. Don Maloney on January 3, 1987 against Quebec at Quebec. Brian Leetch on April 18,1995 against Pittsburgh at Pittsburgh.

MOST POINTS, ONE GAME: 7 Steve Vickers. Three goals and four assists on Feb. 18, 1976 against Washington at Madison Square Garden.

MOST HAT TRICKS, ONE SEASON: 4 Tomas Sandstrom, 1986-87.

MOST CONSECUTIVE HAT TRICKS: 2 Steve Vickers scored hat tricks against Los Angeles on November 12, 1972 and against Philadelphia on Nov. 15, 1972.

MOST SHOTS ON GOAL, ONE GAME: 16 Rod Gilbert, February 24, 1968 against Montreal at Montreal.

MOST SHOTS ON GOAL, ONE SEASON: 344 Phil Esposito, 1976-77.

*These records computed on basis of having at least two members of line on ice at time of each goal.

RANGERS REGULAR SEASON RECORDS

LONGEST CONSECUTIVE GOAL SCORING STREAK: 10 Andy Bathgate. Dec. 15, 1962 to Jan. 5, 1963 (11 goals during streak).

LONGEST CONSECUTIVE ASSIST SCORING STREAK: 15 Brian Leetch, Nov. 29 to December 31, 1991 (23 assists during the streak).

LONGEST CONSECUTIVE POINT SCORING STREAK: 17 Brian Leetch, Nov. 23 to December 31, 1991 (five goals and 24 assists during the streak).

FASTEST GOAL AT START OF GAME: 9 sec. Ron Duguay, April 6, 1980 at Philadelphia and Jim Wiemer, March 27, 1985, at Buffalo.

FASTEST TWO GOALS: 8 sec. Pierre Jarry. Scored at 11:03 and 11:11 of third period against California on November 21, 1971 at Madison Square Garden. Don Maloney. Scored at 12:48 and 12:56 of third period against Philadelphia on March 12, 1987 at Philadelphia.

FASTEST THREE GOALS: 2 min. 30 sec. Don Maloney scored at 16:41, 18:37 and 19:11 of second period on February 21, 1981 against Washington at Madison Square Garden.

FASTEST THREE ASSISTS: 1 min. 21 sec. Don Raleigh at 5:23; 5:43 and 6:44 of first period on November 16, 1947 against Montreal at Madison Square Garden.

MOST PENALTY MINUTES, ONE GAME: 35 Chris Nilan, October 8, 1989 against Chicago at Chicago.

MOST PENALTY MINUTES, ONE SEASON: 305 Troy Mallette, 1989-90.

MOST GOALS WITH THE RANGERS: 406 Rod Gilbert.

MOST ASSISTS WITH THE RANGERS: 615 Rod Gilbert.

MOST POINTS WITH THE RANGERS: 1,021 Rod Gilbert.

MOST PENALTY MINUTES WITH THE RANGERS: 1,226 Ron Greschner.

MOST GAMES WITH THE RANGERS: 1,160 Harry Howell.

MOST SEASONS WITH THE RANGERS: 18 Rod Gilbert, 1960-61 - 1977-78.

MOST CONSECUTIVE GAMES WITH THE RANGERS: 560 Andy Hebenton. Including playoff games, 22, Hebenton appeared in 582 consecutive games with the Rangers (1955-56 - 1962-63).

MOST 20-GOAL SEASONS WITH THE RANGERS: 12 Rod Gilbert.

MOST 20-ASSIST SEASONS WITH THE RANGERS: 13 Walt Tkaczuk, Rod Gilbert.

MOST 30-POINT SEASONS WITH THE RANGERS: 14 Rod Gilbert.

MOST 30-GOAL SEASONS WITH THE RANGERS: 6 Jean Ratelle.

Jean Ratelle tallied 30 or more goals in six seasons with the Rangers, including 46 in 1971–72.

RANGERS REGULAR SEASON RECORDS

INDIVIDUAL ROOKIE RECORDS

MOST GOALS, ONE SEASON: 36 Tony Granato, 1988-89.
MOST ASSISTS, ONE SEASON: 48 Brian Leetch, 1988-89.
MOST POINTS, ONE SEASON: 76 Mark Pavelich, 1981-82.
MOST GOALS BY A DEFENSEMAN, ONE SEASON: 23 Brian Leetch, 1988-89.
MOST ASSISTS BY A DEFENSEMAN, ONE SEASON: 48 Brian Leetch, 1988-89.
MOST POINTS BY A DEFENSEMAN, ONE SEASON: 71 Brian Leetch, 1988-89.
MOST GOALS, ONE GAME: 5 Don Murdoch, October 12, 1976 against Minnesota at Minnesota.
MOST ASSISTS, ONE GAME: 4 Brad Park, February 2, 1969 against Pittsburgh at Madison Square Garden; Walt Tkaczuk, February 26, 1969 against Chicago at Madison Square Garden; Mark Heaslip, March 12, 1978 against Washington at Madison Square Garden; Brian Leetch, February 17, 1989 against Toronto at Madison Square Garden.
MOST POINTS ONE GAME: 5 Rick Middleton, November 17, 1974 against California at Madison Square Garden; Don Murdoch, October 12, 1976 against Minnesota at Minnesota; Brian Leetch, February 17, 1989 against Toronto at Madison Square Garden.
LONGEST GOAL SCORING STREAK: 7 Darren Turcotte, October 15, 1989-October 28, 1989 (Scored eight goals during streak.)
MOST POWER PLAY GOALS, ONE SEASON: 15 Camille Henry, 1953-54.
MOST SHORTHANDED GOALS, ONE SEASON: 4 Tony Granato, 1988-89.
MOST SHOTS, ONE SEASON: 268 Brian Leetch, 1988-89.
MOST HAT TRICKS, ONE SEASON: 3 Tony Granato, 1988-89.
MOST PENALTY MINUTES, ONE SEASON: 305 Troy Mallette, 1989-90.

INDIVIDUAL DEFENSEMEN RECORDS

MOST GOALS, ONE SEASON: 25 Brad Park, 1973-74.
MOST ASSISTS, ONE SEASON: 80 Brian Leetch, 1991-92.
MOST POINTS, ONE SEASON: 102 Brian Leetch, 1991-92.
MOST GOALS, ONE GAME: 3 (Many) Last time: Reijo Ruotsalainen, March 17, 1982 against Philadelphia at Madison Square Garden.
MOSTS ASSISTS, ONE GAME: 5 Brian Leetch, April 18, 1995 against Pittsburgh at Pittsburgh.
MOST POINTS, ONE GAME: 5 (twice) Brian Leetch, February 17, 1989 against Toronto at Madison Square Garden and April 18, 1995 at Pittsburgh.
MOST POWER PLAY GOALS, ONE SEASON: 17 Brian Leetch, 1993-94.
MOST SHORTHANDED GOALS, ONE SEASON: 3 Brian Leetch, 1988-89.
MOST SHOTS, ONE SEASON: 328 Brian Leetch, 1993-94.
MOST SHOTS, ONE GAME: 13 Brian Leetch, January 4, 1989 against Washington at Madison Square Garden.
MOST PENALTY MINUTES, ONE SEASON: 231 Barry Beck, 1980-81.
LONGEST CONSECUTIVE ASSIST SCORING STREAK: 15 Brian Leetch, Nov. 29 to December 31, 1991 (23 assists during the streak).
LONGEST CONSECUTIVE POINT SCORING STREAK: 17 Brian Leetch, Nov. 23 to December 31, 1991 (5 goals and 24 assists).

INDIVIDUAL GOALTENDER RECORDS

MOST GAMES, ONE SEASON: 70 Johnny Bower, 1953-54. Ed Giacomin, 1968-69 and 1969-70.
MOST WINS, ONE SEASON: 42 Mike Richter, 1993-94.
MOST WINS, ONE SEASON (Including Playoffs): 58 Mike Richter, 1993-94.
LOWEST GOAL-AGAINST AVERAGE: 1.48 John Ross Roach, 1928-29.
MOST SHUTOUTS, ONE SEASON: 13 John Ross Roach, 1928-29.
MOST ASSISTS, ONE SEASON: 5 John Vanbiesbrouck, 1984-85 and 1987-88. Mike Richter, 1992-93.
MOST PENALTY MINUTES, ONE SEASON: 56 Bob Froese, 1986-87.
HIGHEST SAVE PERCENTAGE, ONE SEASON: .910 John Vanbiesbrouck, 1991-92. Mike Richter, 1993-94.
MOST SAVES, ONE GAME: 59 Mike Richter, January 31, 1991 vs. Vancouver at Vancouver. Game ended in 3-3 tie.
MOST ASSISTS ONE GAME: 2 Ed Giacomin, March 19, 1972 vs. Toronto at Madison Square Garden. John Vanbiesbrouck, January 8, 1985 vs. Winnipeg at Winnipeg. Mike Richter, February 23, 1990 vs. Washington at Washington, and October 29, 1992 vs. Quebec at MSG.
MOST ASSISTS, CAREER: 22 John Vanbiesbrouck.
MOST SHUTOUTS, CAREER: 49 Ed Giacomin.
MOST WINS, CAREER: 266 Ed Giacomin.

RANGERS PLAYOFF RECORDS

TEAM RECORDS

MOST VICTORIES, ONE YEAR: 16 1993-94 (23 games).
MOST LOSSES, ONE YEAR: 8 1985-86 (16 games).
MOST TIES, ONE YEAR: 2 1934-35 (4 games).
MOST GOALS SCORED, ONE YEAR: 81 1993-94 (23 games).
MOST GOALS ALLOWED, ONE YEAR: 56 1980-81 (14 games).
MOST ASSISTS, ONE YEAR: 121 1993-94 (23 games).
MOST SCORING POINTS, ONE YEAR: 202 1993-94 (23 games).
MOST PENALTY MINUTES, ONE YEAR: 426 1985-86 (16 games).
MOST SHUTOUTS, ONE YEAR: 4 (twice) 1993-94 (23 games) and 1936-37 (9 games).
MOST SHUTOUTS AGAINST, ONE YEAR: 2 1927-28 (9 games); 1928-29 (6 games); 1930-31 (4 games); 1936-37 (9 games); 1986-87 (6 games).
MOST GOALS SCORED, ONE GAME: 10 April 11, 1981, Rangers defeated Los Angeles, 10-3, at Madison Square Garden.
MOST GOALS ALLOWED, ONE GAME: 8 (5 times) last-April 9, 1987, Philadelphia won game 8-3 in Philadelphia.
MOST GOALS SCORED, ONE PERIOD: 6 April 24, 1979 vs. Philadelphia at Philadelphia. Rangers scored six goals in third period and won game 8-3.
MOST GOALS ALLOWED, ONE PERIOD: 5 (7 times) last-June 9, 1994 by Vancouver at MSG. Canucks scored five goals in the third period and won the game 6-3.
MOST GOALS BY RANGERS AND OPPONENT, ONE PERIOD: 9 April 24, 1979 vs. Philadelphia in the third period at Philadelphia. Rangers scored six goals and the Flyers three.
MOST GOALS THREE-GAMES SERIES: 18 1982-83. Rangers defeated Philadelphia, 3 games to 0.
MOST GOALS FOUR-GAME SERIES: 23 1980-81, Rangers defeated Los Angeles, 3 games to 1.
MOST GOALS FIVE-GAME SERIES: 28 1978-79. Rangers defeated Philadelphia, 4 games to 1.
MOST GOALS SIX-GAME SERIES: 29 1980-81, Rangers defeated St. Louis, 4 games to 2.
MOST GOALS SEVEN-GAME SERIES: 28 1991-92, Rangers defeated New Jersey, 4 games to 3.
MOST SHOTS, ONE GAME: 49 April 9, 1989 vs. Pittsburgh at Madison Square Garden. Pittsburgh won game 4-3.
MOST SHOTS, ONE GAME (OVERTIME): 54 May 31, 1994 vs. Vancouver at Madison Square Garden. Canucks won game 3-2.
MOST SHOTS ALLOWED, ONE GAME: 55 April 11, 1991 vs. Washington at Madison Square Garden. Washington won game 5-4 in overtime.
MOST PENALTY MINUTES, ONE GAME: 142 April 9, 1981 at Los Angeles. Los Angeles had 125 minutes for a total of 267 minutes.
MOST PENALTY MINUTES, ONE PERIOD: 125 April 9, 1981 in first period at Los Angeles. Los Angeles had 104 minutes for a total of 229 minutes.
MOST PENALTIES, ONE GAME: 31 April 9, 1981 at Los Angeles. Los Angeles had 28 penalities for a total of 59 penalties.
MOST PENALTIES, ONE PERIOD: 24 April 9, 1981 in first period at Los Angeles. Los Angeles had 19 penalites for a total of 43.
MOST PENALTY MINUTES, ONE SERIES: 214 1988-89 vs. Pittsburgh (4 games). Pittsburgh had 210 penalty minutes for a total of 424 minutes.
MOST PENALTIES, ONE SERIES: 65 1991-92 vs. New Jersey (7 games). New Jersey had 64 penalities for a total of 129 penalties.

SPECIALTY TEAMS

MOST POWER PLAY GOALS, ONE GAME: 4 April 8, 1982 vs. Philadelphia at Madison Square Garden.
MOST POWER PLAY GOALS, ONE SERIES: 10 1989-90 vs. Islanders.
MOST POWER PLAY GOALS, ONE YEAR: 22 1993-94 8 vs. Islanders, 4 vs. Washington, 4 vs. New Jersey and 6 vs. Vancouver.
MOST SHORTHANDED GOALS, ONE GAME: 2 (5 times) last-May 1, 1992 vs. New Jersey at New York.
MOST SHORTHANDED GOALS, ONE SERIES: 5 1978-79 vs. Philadelphia.
MOST SHORTHANDED GOALS, ONE YEAR: 6 1978-79. 5 vs. Philadelphia and 1 vs. Montreal.

OVERTIME

ALL-TIME OVERTIME RECORD: 27 Wins and **32** Losses, **11-14** at home and **16-18** on road.
LONGEST HOME OVERTIME PLAYED BY RANGERS: 59 min. 25 sec. Mel Hill of the Boston Bruins scored at 19.25 of the third overtime, March 21, 1939. Bruins won 2-1.
LONGEST ROAD OVERTIME PLAYED BY RANGERS: 68 min. 52 sec. Gus Rivers of the Montreal Canadiens scored at 8:52 of the fourth overtime, March 28, 1930 at Montreal. Canadiens won, 2-1.
SHORTEST HOME OVERTIME PLAYED BY RANGERS: 11 sec. J.P. Parise of the New York Islanders scored at 0:11 of the first overtime, April 11, 1975. Islanders won, 4-3.
SHORTEST ROAD OVERTIME PLAYED BY THE RANGERS: 25 sec. Kevin Haller of the Philadelphia Flyers scored at 0:25 of the first overtime, May 22, 1995 at Philadelphia. Flyers won series, 4-0.
FASTEST GOAL FROM START OF GAME: 27 sec. Ed Hospodar on April 9, 1981 vs. Los Angeles at Los Angeles.
FASTEST GOAL FROM START OF GAME BY OPPONENT: 13 sec. Claude Larose of Montreal on April 11, 1967 at Madison Square Garden.
FASTEST TWO GOALS: 6 sec. Rod Gilbert at 9:32 and 9:38 of second period against Chicago in Quarter-Finals at Chicago, April 11, 1968.
FASTEST THREE GOALS: 38 sec. Jim Wiemer at 12:29, Bob Brooke at 12:43, Ron Greschner at 13:07 of third period against Philadelphia in Division Semi-Finals at Madison Square Garden, April 12, 1986.
LATEST DATE OF PLAYOFF GAME: June 14, 1994 vs. Vancouver.

RANGERS PLAYOFF RECORDS

PLAYER RECORDS

MOST GOALS, ONE GAME: 3 **(11 times),** last- Brian Leetch, May 22, 1995 at Philidelphia. Frank Boucher, 1932. Bryan Hextall, 1940. Pentti Lund, 1950. Vic Hadfield, 1971. Steve Vickers, 1973. Ron Duguay, 1980. Mike Gartner, 1990. Bernie Nicholls, 1990. Mike Gartner, 1992. Mark Messier, 1994.

MOST ASSISTS, ONE GAME: 6 Mikko Leinonen, April 8, 1982 against Philadelphia.

MOST POINTS, ONE GAME: 6 Mikko Leinonen, April 8, 1982 against Philadelphia.

MOST GOALS, ONE YEAR: 12 Mark Messier, 1993-94.

MOST ASSISTS, ONE YEAR: 23 Brian Leetch, 1993-94.

MOST POINTS, ONE YEAR: 34 Brian Leetch, 1993-94.

MOST GOALS, ONE PERIOD: 3 Mark Messier, May 25, 1994 at New Jersey in the third period.

MOST ASSISTS, ONE PERIOD: 3 Brian Leetch, May 9, 1994 vs. Washington at Madison Square Garden in the first period. Jean Ratelle, April 22, 1971 vs. Chicago at Madison Square Garden in the first period. Mikko Leinonen, April 8, 1982 vs. Philadelphia at Madison Square Garden in the first period.

MOST POINTS BY A ROOKIE, ONE YEAR: 20 Don Maloney, 1978-79.

MOST GOALS BY A DEFENSEMAN, ONE YEAR: 11 Brian Leetch, 1993-94.

MOST ASSISTS BY A DEFENSEMAN, ONE YEAR: 23 Brian Leetch, 1993-94.

MOST POINTS BY A DEFENSEMAN, ONE YEAR: 34 Brian Leetch, 1993-94.

MOST POINTS BY A DEFENSEMAN, ONE GAME: 4 Brian Leetch, June 7, 1994 vs. Vancouver at Vancouver (one goal, three assists). Brian Leetch, May 9, 1994 vs. Washington at Madison Square Garden (one goal, three assists). Brad Park, May 4, 1972 vs. Boston at Madison Square Garden (two goals, two assists). Dave Maloney, April 9, 1983 vs. Philadelphia at Madison Square Garden (four assists).

MOST POWER PLAY GOALS, ONE PERIOD: 2 Brian Leetch, May 22, 1995 at Philidelphia in the first period. Mac Colville, March 22, 1942 vs. Toronto at Madison Square Garden in the third period. Brad Park, May 4, 1972 vs. Boston at Madison Square Garden in the first period.

MOST POWER PLAY GOALS, ONE GAME: 2 Brian Leetch, May 22,1995 at Philidelphia. Mac Colville, March 22, 1942 vs. Toronto at Madison Square Garden. Brad Park, May 4, 1972 vs. Boston at Madison Square Garden. Ron Duguay, April 20, 1980 vs. Philadelphia at Madison Square Garden. Robbie Ftorek, April 11, 1982 vs. Philadelphia at Madison Square Garden. Mike Ridley, April 9, 1986 vs. Philadelphia at Philadelphia. Mike Gartner, April 13, 1990 vs. Islanders at New York. Adam Graves, May 6,1995 at Quebec.

MOST POWER PLAY GOALS: ONE YEAR: 5 Alexei Kovalev, 1993-94.

MOST GAME-WINNING GOALS, ONE YEAR: 4 Brian Leetch and Mark Messier, 1993-94.

MOST PENALTY MINUTES, ONE GAME: 39 Ed Hospodar, April 9, 1981 at Los Angeles.

MOST PENALTY MINUTES, ONE YEAR: 93 Ed Hospodar, 1980-81.

MOST WINS BY A GOALTENDER, ONE YEAR: 16 Mike Richter, 1993-94.

MOST SHUTOUTS, ONE YEAR: 4 Mike Richter 1993-94, Dave Kerr, 1936-37.

FASTEST OVERTIME GOAL BY A RANGER: 33 sec. Steve Vickers scored at 0:33 of the first overtime against the Atlanta Flames at Madison Square Garden, April 8, 1980. Rangers won, 2-1.

MOST SHORTHANDED GOALS, ONE GAME: 2 Mark Messier, April 21, 1992 against New Jersey at New York.

CAREER PLAYER RECORDS

MOST GOALS: 34 Rod Gilbert; 28 Ron Duguay; 25 Brian Leetch; 24 Steve Vickers.

MOST ASSISTS: 47 Brian Leetch, 35 Don Maloney, Mark Messier, 33 Rod Gilbert, Jean Ratelle, 32 Brad Park, Walt Tkaczuk, Ron Greschner.

MOST POINTS: 72 Brian Leetch, five playoffs; 67 Rod Gilbert, 10 playoffs; 57, Don Maloney, 9 playoffs; 57 Mark Messier, 3 playoffs 51 Walt Tkaczuk, 10 playoffs.

MOST POINTS BY A DEFENSEMAN: 72 Brian Leetch, five playoffs; 44 Brad Park, 7 playoffs; 37 Ron Greschner, 12 playoffs; 32 Barry Beck, 6 playoffs.

MOST GAMES: 93 Walt Tkaczuk, 85 Don Maloney, 84 Ron Greschner, 79 Rod Gilbert.

MOST POWER PLAY GOALS: 10 Rod Gilbert and Brian Leetch.

MOST PENALTY MINUTES: 159 Ching Johnson.

MOST SHUTOUTS BY A GOALTENDER: 7 Dave Kerr.

PARTICIPATED IN THE MOST PLAYOFFS: 12 Ron Greschner.

PLAYOFF SCORING LEADERS IN RANGERS HISTORY

No.	Player	GP	G	A	PTS
1.	*Brian Leetch	56	25	47	72
2.	Rod Gilbert	79	34	33	67
3.	*Mark Messier	44	22	35	57
	Don Maloney	85	22	35	57
5.	Walt Tkaczuk	93	19	32	51
6.	Steve Vickers	68	24	25	49
	Ron Greschner	84	17	32	49
8.	Ron Duguay	69	28	19	47
9.	Anders Hedberg	58	22	24	46
10.	Brad Park	64	12	32	44
11.	Jean Ratelle	65	9	33	42
12.	Vic Hadfield	61	22	19	41

RANGERS PLAYOFF OVERTIME GAMES

DATE	PLACE	OPP.	GAME/ SERIES	FINAL SCORE	GOAL SCORER	TIME	SERIES WINNER
4-7-28	Mont.	Maroons	2/F	2-1	Frank Boucher	7:05	Rangers
3-21-29	N.Y.	Americans	2/Q	1-0	Butch Keeling	29:50	Rangers
3-26-29	Tor.	Maple Leafs	2/S	2-1	Frank Boucher	2:03	Rangers
3-28-30	Mont.	Canadiens	1/S	1-2	Gus Rivers	68:52	Canadiens
3-26-32	Mont.	Canadiens	2/S	4-3	Bun Cook	59:32	Rangers
4-13-33	Tor.	Maple Leafs	4/S	1-0	Bill Cook*	7:33	Rangers
3-25-37	N.Y.	Maple Leafs	2/Q	2-1	Babe Pratt	13:05	Rangers
3-22-38	N.Y.	Americans	1/Q	1-2	Johnny Sorrell	21:25	Americans
3-27-38	N.Y.	Americans	3/Q	2-3	Lorne Carr	40:40	Americans
3-21-39	N.Y.	Bruins	1/S	1-2	Mel Hill	59:25	Bruins
3-23-39	Bost.	Bruins	2/S	2-3	Mel Hill	8:24	Bruins
3-30-39	Bost.	Bruins	5/S	2-1	Snuffy Smith	17:19	Bruins
4-2-39	Bost.	Bruins	7/S	1-2	Mel Hill	48:00	Bruins
4-2-40	N.Y.	Maple Leafs	1/F	2-1	Alf Pike	15:30	Rangers
4-11-40	Tor.	Maple Leafs	5/F	2-1	Muzz Patrick	11:43	Rangers
4-13-40	Tor.	Maple Leafs	6/F	3-2	Bryan Hextall*	2:07	Rangers
3-20-41	Det.	Red Wings	1/Q	1-2	Gus Giesebrecht	12:01	Red Wings
4-4-50	Mont.	Canadiens	4/S	2-3	Elmer Lach	15:19	Rangers
4-18-50	Det.	Red Wings	4/F	4-3	Don Raleigh	8:34	Red Wings
4-20-50	Det.	Red Wings	5/F	2-1	Don Raleigh	1:38	Red Wings
4-23-50	Det.	Red Wings	7/F	3-4	Pete Babando*	28:31	Red Wings
3-28-57	N.Y.	Canadiens	2/S	4-3	Andy Hebenton	13:38	Canadiens
4-4-57	Mont.	Canadiens	5/S	3-4	Maurice Richard	1:11	Canadiens
3-27-58	N.Y.	Bruins	2/S	3-4	Jerry Toppazzini	4:46	Bruins
4-5-62	Tor.	Maple Leafs	5/S	2-3	Red Kelly	24:23	Maple Leafs
4-13-67	N.Y.	Canadiens	4/S	1-2	John Ferguson	6:28	Canadiens
4-15-71	Tor.	Maple Leafs	6/Q	2-1	Bob Nevin	9:07	Rangers
4-18-71	Chi.	Blackhawks	1/S	2-1	Pete Stemkowski	1:37	Blackhawks
4-27-71	Chi.	Blackhawks	5/S	2-3	Bobby Hull	6:35	Blackhawks
4-29-71	N.Y.	Blackhawks	6/S	3-2	Pete Stemkowski	41:29	Blackhawks
4-16-74	Mont.	Canadiens	5/Q	3-2	Ron Harris	4:07	Rangers
4-28-74	N.Y.	Flyers	4/S	2-1	Rod Gilbert	4:20	Flyers
4-11-75	N.Y.	Islanders	3/P	3-4	J.P. Parise	0:11	Islanders
4-13-78	N.Y.	Sabres	2/P	4-3	Don Murdoch	1:37	Sabres
4-12-79	L.A.	Kings	2/P	2-1	Phil Esposito	6:11	Rangers
4-16-79	Phil.	Flyers	1/Q	2-3	Ken Linseman	0:44	Rangers
4-28-79	Nass.	Islanders	2/SF	3-4	Denis Potvin	8:02	Rangers
5-3-79	N.Y.	Islanders	4/SF	2-3	Bob Nystrom	3:40	Rangers
5-19-79	N.Y.	Canadiens	4/F	3-4	Serge Savard	7:25	Canadiens
4-8-80	N.Y.	Flames	1/P	2-1	Steve Vickers	0:33	Rangers
4-18-82	N.Y.	Islanders	3/DF	3-4	Bryan Trottier	3:00	Islanders
4-10-84	Nass.	Islanders	5/DSF	2-3	Ken Morrow	8:56	Islanders
4-10-85	Phil.	Flyers	1/DSF	4-5	Mark Howe	8:01	Flyers
4-17-86	Wash.	Capitals	1/DF	4-3	Brian MacLellan	1:16	Rangers
4-23-86	N.Y.	Capitals	4/DF	6-5	Bob Brooke	2:40	Rangers
5-5-86	N.Y.	Canadiens	3/CF	3-4	Claude Lemieux	9:41	Canadiens
4-9-90	Nass.	Islanders	3/DSF	3-4	Brent Sutter	20:59	Rangers
4-25-90	Wash.	Capitals	4/DF	3-4	Rod Langway	0:34	Capitals
4-27-90	N.Y.	Capitals	5/DF	1-2	John Druce	6:48	Capitals
4-11-91	N.Y.	Capitals	5/DSF	4-5	Dino Ciccarelli	6:44	Capitals
5-7-92	Pit.	Penguins	3/DF	6-5	Kris King	1:29	Penguins
5-9-92	Pit.	Penguins	4/DF	4-5	Ron Francis	2:47	Penguins
5-15-94	N.Y.	Devils	1/CF	3-4	Stephane Richer	35:23	Rangers
5-19-94	N.J.	Devils	3/CF	3-2	Stephane Matteau	26:13	Rangers
5-27-94	N.Y.	Devils	7/CF	2-1	Stephane Matteau	24:24	Rangers
5-31-94	N.Y.	Canucks	1/F	2-3	Greg Adams	19:26	Rangers
5-12-95	N.Y.	Nordiques	4/Q	3-2	Steve Larmer	8:09	Rangers
5-21-95	Phi.	Flyers	1/CSF	4-5	Eric Desjardins	7:03	Flyers
5-22-95	Phi.	Flyers	2/CSF	3-4	Kevin Haller	0:25	Flyers

P: Preliminaries; Q: Quarter-finals; DSF: Division Semi-Finals; DF: Division-Finals; CSF: Conference Semi-Finals; CF: Conference-Finals; S: Semi-finals; F: Finals.)

*Goal decided Stanley Cup.

RANGERS PLAYOFF RECORD YEAR BY YEAR

Year	Opponent	W-L-T	GF/GA
1926-27	Boston	0-1-1	1/ 3
1927-28	Pittsburgh	1-1-0	6/ 4
	Boston	1-0-1	5/ 2
	Maroons	3-2-0	5/ 6
1928-29	Americans	1-0-1	1/ 0
	Toronto	2-0-0	3/ 1
	Boston	0-2-0	1/ 4
1929-30	Ottawa	1-0-1	6/ 3
	Canadiens	0-2-0	1/ 4
1930-31	Maroons	2-0-0	8/ 1
	Chicago	0-2-0	0/ 3
1931-32	Canadiens	3-1-0	13/ 9
	Toronto	0-3-0	10/18
1932-33	Canadiens	1-0-1	8/ 5
	Detroit	2-0-0	6/ 3
	Toronto	3-1-0	11/ 5
1933-34	Maroons	0-1-1	1/ 2
1934-35	Canadiens	1-0-1	6/ 5
	Maroons	0-1-1	4/ 5
1936-37	Toronto	2-0-0	5/ 1
	Maroons	2-0-0	5/ 0
	Detroit	2-3-0	8/ 9
1937-38	Americans	1-2-0	7/ 8
1938-39	Boston	3-4-0	12/14
1939-40	Boston	4-2-0	15/ 9
	Toronto	4-2-0	14/11
1940-41	Detroit	1-2-0	6/ 6
1941-42	Toronto	2-4-0	12/13
1947-48	Detroit	2-4-0	12/17
1949-50	Montreal	4-1-0	15/ 7
	Detroit	3-4-0	17/22
1955-56	Montreal	1-4-0	9/24
1956-57	Montreal	1-4-0	12/22
1957-58	Boston	2-4-0	16/28
1961-62	Toronto	2-4-0	15/22
1966-67	Montreal	0-4-0	8/14
1967-68	Chicago	2-4-0	12/18
1968-69	Montreal	0-4-0	7/16
1969-70	Boston	2-4-0	16/25
1970-71	Toronto	4-2-0	16/15
	Chicago	3-4-0	14/21
1971-72	Montreal	4-2-0	19/14
	Chicago	4-0-0	17/ 9
	Boston	2-4-0	16/18

Year	Opponent	W-L-T	GF/GA
1972-73	Boston	4-1-0	22/11
	Chicago	1-4-0	11/15
1973-74	Montreal	4-2-0	21/17
	Philadelphia	3-4-0	17/22
1974-75	Islanders	1-2-0	13/10
1977-78	Buffalo	1-2-0	6/11
1978-79	Los Angeles	2-0-0	9/ 2
	Philadelphia	4-1-0	28/ 8
	Islanders	4-2-0	18/13
	Montreal	1-4-0	11/19
1979-80	Atlanta	3-1-0	14/ 8
	Philadelphia	1-4-0	7/14
1980-81	Los Angeles	3-1-0	23/12
	St. Louis	4-2-0	29/22
	Islanders	0-4-0	8/22
1981-82	Philadelphia	3-1-0	19/15
	Islanders	2-4-0	20/27
1982-83	Philadelphia	3-0-0	18/ 9
	Islanders	2-4-0	15/28
1983-84	Islanders	2-3-0	14/13
1984-85	Philadelphia	0-3-0	10/14
1985-86	Philadelphia	3-2-0	18/15
	Washington	4-2-0	20/25
	Montreal	1-4-0	9/15
1986-87	Philadelphia	2-4-0	13/22
1988-89	Pittsburgh	0-4-0	11/19
1989-90	Islanders	4-1-0	22/13
	Washington	1-4-0	15/22
1990-91	Washington	2-4-0	16/16
1991-92	New Jersey	4-3-0	28/25
	Pittsburgh	2-4-0	19/24
1993-94	Islanders	4-0-0	22/3
	Washington	4-1-0	20/12
	New Jersey	4-3-0	18/16
	Vancouver	4-3-0	21/19
1994-95	Quebec	4-2-0	25/19
	Philadelphia	0-4-0	10/18

Totals	W-L-T	GF/GA
Preliminary Round	39-30-0	281/226
Quarter-Finals	44-49-0	296/316
Semi-Finals	62-76-8	350/386
Finals	22-25-0	94/113
Overall	167-180-8	1021/1041

RANGERS PLAYOFF RECORDS

STANLEY CUP WINNING GOALS BY RANGERS

1928	Frank Boucher vs. Montreal Maroons	(at Montreal)
1933	Bill Cook vs. Toronto Maple Leafs	(at Toronto)
1940	Bryan Hextall, Sr. vs. Toronto Maple Leafs	(at Toronto)
1994	Mark Messier vs. Vancouver	(at Madison Square Garden)

AGAINST RANGERS

1929	Bill Carson — Boston Bruins	(at Madison Square Garden)
1932	Ace Bailey — Toronto Maple Leafs	(at Toronto)
1937	Marty Barry — Detroit Red Wings	(at Detroit)
1950	Pete Babando — Detroit Red Wings	(at Detroit)
1972	Bobby Orr — Boston Bruins	(at Madison Square Garden)
1979	Jacques Lemaire — Montreal Canadiens	(at Montreal)

RANGER PLAYOFF HAT TRICKS

Frank Boucher vs. Toronto, 4/9/32 at Toronto, Finals Game 3, 6-4 Maple Leafs, Opposing Goalie: Lorne Chabot.

Bryan Hextall vs. Toronto, 4/3/40 at New York, Finals Game 2, 6-2 Rangers, Opposing Goalie: Turk Broda.

Pentti Lund vs. Montreal, 4/2/50 at New York, Semifinals Game 3, 4-1 Rangers, Opposing Goalie: Bill Durnan.

Vic Hadfield vs. Chicago, 4/22/71 at New York, Semifinals Game 3, 4-1 Rangers, Opposing Goalie: Tony Esposito.

Steve Vickers vs. Boston, 4/10/73 at Boston, Quarterfinals Game 5, 6-3 Rangers, Opposing Goalies: Ross Brooks & Eddie Johnston.

Ron Duguay vs. Philadelphia, 4/20/80 at New York, Quarterfinals Game 4, 4-2 Rangers, Opposing Goalie: Pete Peeters.

Mike Gartner vs. Islanders, 4/13/90 at New York, Division Semifinals Game 5, 6-5 Rangers, Opposing Goalie: Mark Fitzpatrick.

Bernie Nicholls vs. Washington, 4/19/90 at New York, Division Finals Game 1, 7-3 Rangers, Opposing Goalie: Mike Liut.

Mike Gartner vs. New Jersey, 4/27/92 at New York, Division Semifinals Game 5, 8-5 Rangers, Opposing Goalie: Chris Terreri.

Mark Messier vs. New Jersey, 5/27/94 at New Jersey, Conference Finals Game 6, 4-2 Rangers, Opposing Goalie: Martin Brodeur.

Brian Leetch vs. Philadelphia, 5/22/95 at Philadelphia, Conference Semifinals Game 2, 4-3 Flyers, Opposing Goalie: Ron Hextall.

Vic Hadfield tallied three goals against Chicago's Tony Esposito on April 22, 1971.

RANGERS PLAYOFF RECORDS

RANGERS PLAYOFF SHUTOUTS

Lorne Chabot, vs. Boston Bruins, 4/2/27 at Boston, Semifinals Game 1, 0-0.

Lorne Chabot, vs. Pittsburgh Pirates, 3/27/28 at New York, Quarterfinals Game 1, 4-0.

Joe Miller, vs. Montreal Maroons, 4/12/28 at Montreal, Finals Game 4, 1-0.

John Ross Roach, vs. New York Americans, 3/19/29 at New York, Quarterfinals Game 1, 0-0.

John Ross Roach, vs. New York Americans, 3/21/29 at New York, Quarterfinals Game 2, 1-0.

John Ross Roach, vs. Toronto Maple Leafs, 3/24/29 at New York, Semifinals Game 1, 1-0.

John Ross Roach, vs. Montreal Maroons, 3/26/31 at Montreal, Quarterfinals Game 2, 3-0.

John Ross Roach, vs. Montreal Canadiens, 3/27/32 at New York, Semifinals Game 3, 1-0.

Andy Aitkenhead, vs. Detroit Red Wings, 3/30/33 at New York, Semifinals Game 1, 2-0.

Andy Aitkenhead, vs. Toronto Maple Leafs, 4/13/33 at Toronto, Finals Game 4, 1-0.

Andy Aitkenhead, vs. Montreal Maroons, 3/20/34 at Montreal, Quarterfinals Game 1, 0-0.

Dave Kerr, vs. Toronto Maple Leafs, 3/23/37 at Toronto, Quarterfinals Game 1, 3-0.

Dave Kerr, vs. Montreal Maroons, 4/1/37 at New York, Semifinals Game 1, 1-0.

Dave Kerr, vs. Montreal Maroons, 4/3/37 at Montreal, Semifinals Game 2, 4-0.

Dave Kerr, vs. Detroit Red Wings, 4/11/37 at New York, Finals Game 3, 1-0.

Dave Kerr, vs. Boston Bruins, 3/19/40 at New York, Semifinals Game 1, 4-0.

Dave Kerr, vs. Boston Bruins, 3/26/40 at New York, Semifinals Game 4, 1-0.

Dave Kerr, vs. Boston Bruins, 3/28/40 at Boston, Semifinals Game 5, 1-0.

Jim Henry, vs. Toronto Maple Leafs, 3/24/42 at New York, Semifinals Game 3, 3-0.

Chuck Rayner, vs. Montreal Canadiens, 4/6/50 at Montreal, Semifinals Game 6, 3-0.

Eddie Giacomin, vs. Boston Bruins, 4/8/73 at New York, Quarterfinals Game 4, 4-0.

John Davidson, vs. Philadelphia Flyers, 4/22/79 at New York, Quarterfinals Game 4, 6-0.

Glen Hanlon, vs. New York Islanders, 4/5/84 at Nassau Coliseum, Division Semifinals Game 2, 3-0.

John Vanbiesbrouck, vs. Montreal Canadiens, 5/7/86 at New York, Conference Finals Game 4, 2-0.

John Vanbiesbrouck, vs. Philadelphia Flyers, 4/8/87 at Philadelphia, Division Semifinals Game 1, 3-0.

Mike Richter, vs. Washington Capitals, 4/7/91 at Washington, Division Semifinals Game 3, 6-0.

Mike Richter, vs. New Jersey Devils, 4/25/92 at New Jersey, Division Semifinals Game 4, 3-0.

Mike Richter, vs. New York Islanders, 4/17/94 at Madison Square Garden, Conference Quarterfinals Game 1, 6-0.

Mike Richter, vs. New York Islanders, 4/18/94 at Madison Square Garden, Conference Quarterfinals Game 2, 6-0.

Mike Richter, vs. Washington Capitals, 5/5/94 at Washington Conference Semifinals, Game 3, 3-0.

Mike Richter, vs. New Jersey Devils, 5/17/94 at Madison Square Garden Conference Finals, Game 2, 3-0.

Mike Richter has posted the Rangers last six playoff shutouts.

NEW YORK RANGERS
STANLEY CUP CHAMPIONS

1927-28 — Standing (Left to Right)-Ching Johnson, Bill Boyd, Paul Thompson, Lorne Chabot, Lester Patrick (sub-goaltender, manager and coach), Bill Cook, Taffy Abel, Joe Miller (sub-goaltender), Bun Cook. Bottom Row (Left to Right)-Harry Westerby (trainer), Murray Murdoch, Art Chapman, Leo Bourgault, Patsy Gallighen, (unknown), Frank Boucher, Alex Gray.

1932-33 — Standing (Left to Right)-Jimmy Arnott, Gordon Pettinger, Bill Cook, Earl Seibert, Ossie Asmundsen, Lester Patrick (Manager), Babe Siebert, Ching Johnson, Bun Cook, Butch Keeling, Murray Murdoch, Ott Heller, Doug Brennan. Bottom row (Left to Right)-Wilfie Starr, Carl Voss, Cecil Dillon, Harry Westerby (Trainer), Artie Somers, Andy Aitkenhead.

1939-40 — Standing(Left to Right)-Frank Boucher(Coach), Lynn Patrick, Neil Colville, Ott Heller, Art Coulter(Captain), Babe Pratt, Muzz Patrick, Alf Pike, Lester Patrick (Manager). Bottom row (Left to Right)-Alex Shibicky, Phil Watson, Kilby MacDonald, Bryan Hextall, Dave Kerr, Mac Colville, Clint Smith, Dutch Hiller, Harry Westerby(Trainer).

First Row (left to right): Mike Richter, Kevin Lowe, Steve Larmer, Dick Todd - Assistant Coach, Neil Smith - President and General Manager, Mark Messier - Captain, Mike Keenan - Head Coach, Colin Campbell - Associate Coach, Brian Leetch, Adam Graves, Glenn Healy. Second Row: Mike Folga - Trainer, Joe Murphy - Trainer, Glenn Anderson, Joe Kocur, Alexei Kovalev, Craig MacTavish, Sergei Nemchinov, Sergei Zubov, Dave Smith - Trainer, Bruce Lifrieri - Trainer. Third Row: Esa Tikkanen, Greg Gilbert, Jay Wells, Stephane Matteau, Jeff Beukeboom, Doug Lidster, Brian Noonan. Top Row: Mike Hartman, Mike Hudson, Alexander Karpovtsev, Eddie Olczyk, Nick Kypreos.

RANGERS MANAGEMENT

Rangers Presidents

John S. Hammond	(1926 thru 1931-32)
William F. Carey	(1932-33)
John Reed Kilpatrick	(1933-34)
John S. Hammond	(1934-35)
John Reed Kilpatrick	(1935-36 thru 1959-60)
John J. Bergen	(1960-61 thru 1961-62)
William M. Jennings	(1962-63 thru 1980-81)
John H. Krumpe	(1981-82 thru Dec. 31, 1986)
Richard H. Evans	(Jan. 1, 1987 to June 28, 1990)
John C. Diller	(June 29, 1990 to April 22, 1991)
Neil Smith	(June 19, 1992 to present)

Rangers General Managers

Lester Patrick	(1926-27 thru 1945-46)
Frank Boucher	(1946-47 thru 1954-55)
Muzz Patrick	(1955-56 thru 1963-64)
Emile Francis	(1964-65 to Jan. 6, 1976)
John Ferguson	(Jan. 7, 1976 to June 2, 1978)
Fred Shero	(June 2, 1978 to Nov. 21, 1980)
Craig Patrick	(Nov. 21, 1980 to July 14, 1986)
Phil Esposito	(July 14, 1986 to May 24, 1989)
Neil Smith	(July 17, 1989 to present)

Rangers Coaches & Records

	GC	W	L	T	PCT.
Lester Patrick (1926-27 thru 1938-39)	604	281	216	107	.554
Frank Boucher (1939-40 - 12/21/48)	486	166	243	77	.412
Lynn Patrick (12/21/48 thru 1949-50)	107	40	51	16	.449
Neil Colville (1950-51 - 12/6/51)	93	26	41	26	.419
Bill Cook (12/6/51 thru 1952-53)	117	34	59	24	.393
Frank Boucher (1953-54 - 1/6/54)	39	13	20	6	.410
Muzz Patrick (1/6/54 thru 1954-55)	105	35	47	23	.443
Phil Watson (1955-56 - 11/12/59)	294	118	124	52	.490
Alf Pike (11/18/59 thru 1960-61)	123	36	66	21	.378
Doug Harvey (5/30/61 thru 1961-62)	70	26	32	12	.457
Muzz Patrick (9/7/62 - 12/28/62)	34	11	19	4	.382
Red Sullivan (12/28/62 - 12/5/65)	196	58	103	35	.385
Emile Francis (12/5/65 - 6/4/68)	193	81	82	30	.497
Bernie Geoffrion (6/4/68 - 1/17/69)	43	22	18	3	.547
Emile Francis (1/17/69 - 6/4/73)	344	202	88	54	.666
Larry Popein (6/4/73 - 1/11/74)	41	18	14	9	.549
Emile Francis (1/11/74 - 5/19/75)	117	59	39	19	.585
Ron Stewart (5/19/75 - 1/7/76)	39	15	20	4	.436
John Ferguson (1/7/76 - 8/22/77)	121	43	59	19	.434
Jean-Guy Talbot (8/22/77 - 6/2/78)	80	30	37	13	.456
Fred Shero (6/2/78 - 11/22/80)	180	82	74	24	.522
Craig Patrick (11/22/80 - 6/4/81)	60	26	23	11	.525
Herb Brooks (6/4/81 - 1/21/85)	285	131	113	41	.532
Craig Patrick (1/21/85 - 6/19/85)	35	11	22	2	.343
Ted Sator (6/19/85 - 11/21/86)	99	41	48	10	.465
*Phil Esposito (1986-87)	43	24	19	0	.558
*Tom Webster (1986-87)	16	5	7	4	.474
*Wayne Cashman/Ed Giacomin (1986-87)	2	0	2	0	.000
Michel Bergeron (6/18/87 to 4/1/89)	158	73	67	18	.518
Phil Esposito (4/1/89 - 5/24/89)	2	0	2	0	.000
Roger Neilson (8/15/89 - 1/4/93)	280	141	104	35	.566
Ron Smith (1/4/93 - 4/16/93)	44	15	22	7	.421
Mike Keenan (4/17/93-7/24/94)	84	52	24	8	.667
Colin Campbell (8/10/94-present)	48	22	23	3	.490

*(Due to illness to Tom Webster, head coaching situation changed several times during season.)

Dave Maloney served as Rangers captain for two and a half seasons.

Rangers Captains

Bill Cook	(1926-27 thru 1936-37)
Art Coulter	(1937-38 thru 1941-42)
Ott Heller	(1942-43 thru 1944-45)
Neil Colville	(1945-46 thru Dec. 21, 1948)
Buddy O'Connor	(1949-50)
Frank Eddolls	(1950-51 to Dec. 6, 1951)
Allan Stanley	(Dec. 20, 1951 to Nov. 3, 1953)
Don Raleigh	(Nov. 4, 1953 thru 1954-55)
Harry Howell	(1955-56 thru 1956-57)
George Sullivan	(1957-58 thru 1960-61)
Andy Bathgate	(1961-62 to Feb. 22, 1964)
Camille Henry	(Feb. 23, 1964 to Feb. 4, 1965)
Bob Nevin	(Feb. 5, 1965 thru 1970-71)
Vic Hadfield	(1971-72 thru 1973-74)
Brad Park	(1974-75 to Nov. 7, 1975)
Phil Esposito	(Nov. 12, 1975 to Oct. 10, 1978)
Dave Maloney	(Oct. 11, 1978 to Dec. 6, 1980)
Walt Tkaczuk	(Dec. 7, 1980 to Feb. 3, 1981)
Barry Beck	(Feb. 4, 1981 to May 9, 1986)
Ron Greschner	(Oct. 9, 1986 to Dec. 3, 1987)
Kelly Kisio	(Dec. 24, 1987 to May 30, 1991)
Mark Messier	(Oct. 7, 1991 to present)

Rangers Coaching Records

Games Coached

Emile Francis	654
Lester Patrick	604
Frank Boucher	525
Phil Watson	294
Herb Brooks	285
Roger Neilson	280
Red Sullivan	196

Wins

Emile Francis	342
Lester Patrick	281
Frank Boucher	179
Roger Neilson	141
Herb Brooks	131
Phil Watson	118

Losses

Frank Boucher	243
Lester Patrick	216
Emile Francis	209
Phil Watson	124
Herb Brooks	113
Roger Neilson	104

Winning Percentage
(minimum 100 games)

Emile Francis	.602
Roger Neilson	.566
Herb Brooks	.532
Fred Shero	.522
Lester Patrick	.554
Michel Bergeron	.519

Emile Francis leads Rangers coaches in all-time wins, games coached, and winning percentage.

A Brief History of
The New York Rangers

The Rangers' Official Emblem

Celebrating their 70th season in the National Hockey League, the New York Rangers have thrilled fans with exciting hockey and notable achievements, most recently the club's proudest moment — the dramatic 1993-94 Stanley Cup championship.

After finishing atop the NHL during the regular season, the Rangers defeated the New York Islanders and Washington Capitals in the first two playoff rounds, then came from behind to win the Eastern Conference championship on Mark Messier's third period hat trick in Game Six and Stephane Matteau's double overtime goal in Game Seven against the New Jersey Devils. They defeated the Vancouver Canucks in another seven game thriller, with captain Mark Messier scoring the Stanley Cup-winning goal.

The Rangers' fourth Cup and the numerous franchise records set last season continued a long, distinguished history marked by outstanding team and individual performances. In the past five years, those performances have included three division titles and two Presidents' Trophy seasons for the NHL's best regular season record. But success is not new for the Rangers. From the outset, the club was among the best in the NHL.

The NHL granted Madison Square Garden a franchise to operate its own team for the 1926-27 season, following the initial success of the New York Americans, who began play in the Garden for the 1925-26 season and would become the Rangers first arch-rivals. Garden president G.L. "Tex" Rickard chose University of Toronto's Conn Smythe to build his team and Smythe assembled a talented roster, including future Hall of Famers Frank Boucher and Bill Cook, who with Cook's brother Bun formed hockey's top line; Hall of Fame defenseman Ivan "Ching" Johnson, who effectively teamed with Taffy Abel; and second line winger Murray Murdoch, who would become hockey's first "iron man," playing 508 consecutive games. Sportswriters dubbed the team "Tex's Rangers" and that was the origin of the club's name.

Prior to the start of their first season, however, disagreements with the Garden management caused Smythe's exit. On the eve of the club's first season, the task of guiding the Rangers was handed to one of professional hockey's pioneers, Lester Patrick, who grew to be the Big Apple's most visible and quotable hockey man. Patrick directed the Rangers to a first place finish in their opening season (with Bill Cook winning the league scoring title) and, led by Boucher's scoring heroics, their first Stanley Cup in 1927-28. It was the last time an NHL team has won the Cup as quickly as its sophomore campaign. During Game Two of the 1928 Finals against the Montreal Maroons, the 44-year old Patrick substituted for injured goaltender Lorne Chabot in one of hockey's legendary moments.

With hard, clean play and innovative tactics, the Rangers became known as "the classiest team in hockey," going to the Finals four times in six years. Regularly among the leaders in assists, Boucher epitomized the club's style, winning the Lady Byng Trophy so frequently, the league allowed him to keep the original silverware and struck a new award. Bill Cook won a second scoring title in 1932-33 and in April, his overtime goal in Game Four of the Finals gave the Rangers a 1-0 win over Toronto and their second Stanley Cup title. Cecil Dillon's scoring and Andy Aitkenhead's goaltending led the way for Patrick's club.

In their first 16 seasons, the Rangers missed the playoffs only once, and only twice did they fall lower than third place. New York won three regular-season championships in that span, finished second five times and third on six other occasions. The Garden became the place to be on nights the Rangers played, attracting a "dinner-jacket" crowd which often included other sports figures, Broadway entertainers, New York's society elite and City Hall politicians. The Rangers built an empire and New Yorkers loved it.

The Original Rangers gave way to a new group of stars in the late 1930s. Patrick acquired goalie Davey Kerr from the Maroons in 1934 and defenseman Art Coulter from Chicago in 1936 and they became the backbone of the next great Rangers team, which lost a five game Final to Detroit in 1937. Three seasons later, Boucher succeeded Patrick as coach and the Rangers won the Cup again. The 1940 Rangers were led by the dangerous line of Hall of Famer Neil Colville, his brother Mac and Alex Shibicky. Hall of Famer Bryan Hextall, Phil Watson, Dutch Hiller, Alf Pike, Clint Smith, Kilby MacDonald and Lester's son Lynn gave Boucher great depth up front. Lester's other son Muzz helped form a solid defense corps with captain Coulter, Babe Pratt and Ott Heller. Hextall's overtime goal against Toronto in Game Six of the 1940 Finals was the decisive tally in the Rangers third Cup championship.

Two years later, the Rangers finished atop the league with the Watson-Patrick-Hextall line dominating league scoring. But World War II had already begun breaking up this collection of Ranger All-Stars. In the years that followed, the club struggled. In the next 13 seasons, the club only made the playoffs twice. Still the Rangers featured outstanding individual talents. Buddy O'Connor became the first Ranger to win the Hart Trophy as NHL MVP in 1947-48 and goalie Chuck Rayner won the Hart in 1949-50, the year the Rangers lost a seven game overtime Stanley Cup Final to the Red Wings. Edgar Laprade, Hy Buller and Bones Raleigh were standouts in the late Forties and early Fifties.

In the 1950s, a fertile farm system and some deft trades improved the team's fortunes. Hall of Famers Andy Bathgate, Dean Prentice, Harry Howell, Bill Gadsby and Gump Worsley, along with Camille Henry, Andy Hebenton and "Leapin' Louie" Fontinato helped the team back into the playoffs in mid-decade. Bathgate, who became the club's captain and all-time leading scorer, won the Hart Trophy for the 1958-59 season. Hebenton played 560 consecutive games as a Ranger and Howell became recognized as one of hockey's best defensemen and was awarded the Norris Trophy in 1966-67.

A Rangers Renaissance began in 1960s, directed by coach and general manager Emile Francis. Beginning in 1966-67, the club made the playoffs nine consecutive seasons, the only NHL team of the period to accomplish that feat. Led by Rod Gilbert, who eclipsed Bathgate's club scoring records, and his linemates Jean Ratelle and Vic Hadfield, the Rangers were again an NHL powerhouse. All three became All-Stars during the period as did defenseman Brad Park and goalie Ed Giacomin. Reliable two-way players like Pete Stemkowski, Steve Vickers and Walt Tkaczuk helped round out the team. In 1971-72, Hadfield became the first Ranger to score 50 goals in a season and that year the Rangers faced Boston in the Stanley Cup Finals, losing a tough six-game series.

Following a two-year absence from post-season play in the mid-1970s, a new group of Rangers emerged led by stars Anders Hedberg, Ulf Nilsson, Barry Beck, Ron Greschner, Phil Esposito, John Davidson, and the Maloney brothers, Dave and Don. The Rangers dramatically marched to the Stanley Cup Finals in 1979, defeating their new arch-rivals, New York Islanders in the semi-finals before bowing to the Montreal Canadiens in a five game Final. While the Rangers would not reach the Finals again until 1994, they built a good team and it took the best teams to defeat them. Beginning in 1979, the clubs that eliminated the Rangers in the playoffs over each of the next nine seasons all went to the Finals or won the Stanley Cup.

The hiring of Neil Smith as general manager of the Rangers in 1989 began the process which led to the 1994 Stanley Cup championship. Smith acquired center Mark Messier from Edmonton for the 1991-92 season and Messier led the club to the top of the league and was recognized for his efforts by winning the Hart Trophy that season. Messier became the driving force that propelled the Rangers to the Stanley Cup. Through timely trades, keen drafting and opportunistic free agent signings, Smith pieced together as talented a club as the Rangers ever had. The emergence of new superstars like Brian Leetch, Mike Richter and Adam Graves, who broke Hadfield's 50 goal mark in 1993-94, as well as a wealth of potential star players make the future of the New York Rangers brighter than ever.

RANGERS POWER PLAY AND PENALTY KILLING SINCE EXPANSION (1967-68)

Year	Power Play					Penalty Killing		
	PPG	ADV	PCT.	SHG	PPGA	TSH	PCT.	SHGA
1967-68	46	217	21.2	1	42	223	81.2	7
1968-69	56	275	20.4	4	35	223	84.3	9
1969-70	52	295	17.6	7	40	269	85.1	7
1970-71	60	234	25.6	5	41	253	83.8	3
1971-72	60	257	23.3	14	44	282	84.4	10
1972-73	54	238	22.7	5	39	250	84.4	5
1973-74	66	222	29.7	9	45	239	81.2	2
1974-75	84	296	28.4	6	54	295	81.7	7
1975-76	67	323	20.7	3	68	277	75.5	11
1976-77	60	290	20.7	6	55	268	79.5	16
1977-78	78	279	28.0	10	48	244	80.3	6
1978-79	75	306	24.5	9	78	311	74.9	12
1979-80	79	304	26.0	8	54	303	82.2	7
1980-81	63	351	17.9	14	83	392	78.8	12
1981-82	68	306	22.2	7	75	319	76.5	12
1982-83	71	317	22.4	12	75	312	76.0	8
1983-84	74	295	25.1	12	76	347	78.1	11
1984-85	72	305	23.6	9	64	333	80.8	8
1985-86	73	362	20.2	9	81	365	77.8	4
1986-87	75	375	20.0	12	71	379	81.3	15
1987-88	111	491	22.6	6	82	423	80.6	11
1988-89	85	457	18.6	13	85	371	77.1	17
1989-90	103	442	23.3	7	77	362	78.7	8
1990-91	91	389	23.4	9	73	362	79.8	10
1991-92	81	387	20.9	14	60	395	84.8	12
1992-93	77	420	18.3	12	84	446	81.2	18
1993-94	96	417	23.0	20	67	435	84.6	5
1994-95	40	200	20.0	5	34	211	83.9	3

Recent Manpower Games Lost Due to Injuries

Year	Games Lost
1979-80	139
1980-81	296
1981-82	539
1982-83	348
1983-84	139
1984-85	480
1985-86	290
1986-87	339
1987-88	262
1988-89	367
1989-90	334
1990-91	249
1991-92	245
1992-93	208
1993-94	99
1994-95	44

RANGERS YEAR-BY-YEAR SCORING STATISTICS

Year-By-Year Scoring
1926-27—1930-31

1926-27	GP	G	A	PTS	PIM	Playoffs GP	G	A	PTS	PIM
Bill Cook	44	33	4	37	58	2	1	0	1	10
Frank Boucher	44	13	15	28	17	2	0	0	0	4
Bun Cook	44	14	9	23	42	2	0	0	0	6
Taffy Abel	44	8	4	12	78	2	0	1	1	8
Paul Thompson	43	7	3	10	12	2	0	0	0	0
Murray Murdoch	44	6	4	10	12	2	0	0	0	0
Stan Brown	24	6	2	8	14	2	0	0	0	0
Billy Boyd	41	4	1	5	40	–	–	–	–	–
Ching Johnson	27	3	2	5	66	2	0	0	0	8
Leo Bourgault	20	1	1	2	28	2	0	0	0	4
Lester Patrick	1	0	0	0	2	–	–	–	–	–
Ollie Reinikka	16	0	0	0	0	–	–	–	–	–
Reg Mackey	34	0	0	0	16	1	0	0	0	0

1927-28	GP	G	A	PTS	PIM	Playoffs GP	G	A	PTS	PIM
Frank Boucher	44	23	12	35	14	9	7	1	8	2
Bun Cook	44	14	14	28	45	9	2	1	3	8
Bill Cook	43	18	6	24	42	9	2	3	5	26
Ching Johnson	43	10	6	16	146	9	1	1	2	46
Murray Murdoch	44	7	3	10	14	9	2	1	3	12
Paul Thompson	41	4	4	8	22	8	0	0	0	30
Leo Bourgault	37	7	0	7	72	9	0	0	0	10
Alex Gray	43	7	0	7	30	9	1	0	1	0
Billy Boyd	43	4	0	4	11	9	0	0	0	4
Taffy Abel	22	0	1	1	28	9	1	0	1	14
Laurie Scott	23	0	1	1	6	–	–	–	–	–
Patsy Callighen	36	0	0	0	32	9	0	0	0	0

1928-29	GP	G	A	PTS	PIM	Playoffs GP	G	A	PTS	PIM
Frank Boucher	44	10	16	26	8	6	1	0	1	0
Bill Cook	43	15	8	23	41	6	0	0	0	6
Bun Cook	43	13	5	18	70	6	1	0	1	12
Paul Thompson	44	10	7	17	38	6	0	2	2	6
Murray Murdoch	44	8	6	14	18	6	0	0	0	2
Butch Keeling	43	6	3	9	35	6	3	0	3	2
Leo Bourgault	44	2	3	5	59	6	0	0	0	2
Sparky Vail	18	3	0	3	16	6	0	0	0	2
Taffy Abel	44	2	1	3	41	6	0	0	0	8
Myles Lane	24	2	0	2	24	–	–	–	–	–
Russ Oatman	27	1	1	2	10	6	0	0	0	0
Ching Johnson	9	0	0	0	14	6	0	0	0	26
Jerry Carson	10	0	0	0	5	5	0	0	0	0
Billy Boyd	11	0	0	0	5	–	–	–	–	–

1929-30	GP	G	A	PTS	PIM	Playoffs GP	G	A	PTS	PIM
Frank Boucher	42	26	36	62	16	3	1	1	2	0
Bill Cook	44	29	30	59	56	4	0	1	1	11
Bun Cook	43	24	18	42	55	4	2	0	2	10
Butch Keeling	44	19	7	26	34	4	0	3	3	8
Murray Murdoch	44	13	13	26	22	4	3	0	3	6
Paul Thompson	44	7	12	19	36	4	0	0	0	2
Leo Bourgault	44	7	6	13	54	3	1	1	2	6
Ching Johnson	30	3	3	6	82	4	0	0	0	14
Roy Goldsworthy	44	4	1	5	16	4	0	0	0	2
Leo Quenneville	25	0	3	3	10	3	0	0	0	0
Ralph Taylor	24	2	0	2	28	4	0	0	0	10
Sparky Vail	32	1	1	2	2	4	0	0	0	0
Orville Heximer	19	1	0	1	4	–	–	–	–	–
Leo Reise	14	0	1	1	8	4	0	0	0	16
Bill Regan	10	0	0	0	4	4	0	0	0	0
Harry Foster	31	0	0	0	10	–	–	–	–	–

1930-31	GP	G	A	PTS	PIM	Playoffs GP	G	A	PTS	PIM
Bill Cook	44	30	12	42	39	4	3	0	3	4
Frank Boucher	44	12	27	39	20	4	0	2	2	0
Bun Cook	44	18	17	35	72	4	0	0	0	2
Butch Keeling	44	13	9	22	35	4	1	1	2	0
Murray Murdoch	44	7	7	14	8	4	0	2	2	0
Paul Thompson	44	7	7	14	36	4	3	0	3	2
Joe Jerwa	33	4	7	11	72	4	0	0	0	4

Year-By-Year Scoring
1930-31—1934-35

1930-31 (cont'd.)	GP	G	A	PTS	PIM	Playoffs GP	G	A	PTS	PIM
Ching Johnson	44	2	6	8	77	4	1	0	1	17
Henry Maracle	11	1	3	4	2	4	0	0	0	2
Frank Waite	17	1	3	4	4	–	–	–	–	–
Bill Regan	42	2	1	3	49	4	0	0	0	2
Eddie Rodden	24	0	3	3	8	–	–	–	–	–
Gene Carrigan	33	2	0	2	13	–	–	–	–	–
Leo Bourgault	10	0	1	1	6	–	–	–	–	–
Sam McAdam	4	0	0	0	0	–	–	–	–	–
Ernie Kenny	6	0	0	0	0	–	–	–	–	–
Frank Peters	44	0	0	0	59	4	0	0	0	2

1931-32	GP	G	A	PTS	PIM	Playoffs GP	G	A	PTS	PIM
Bill Cook	48	33	14	47	33	7	3	3	6	2
Cecil Dillon	48	23	15	38	22	7	2	1	3	4
Frank Boucher	48	12	23	35	18	7	3	6	9	0
Bun Cook	45	14	20	34	43	7	6	2	8	12
Art Somers	48	11	15	26	45	7	0	1	1	0
Murray Murdoch	48	5	16	21	32	7	0	2	2	2
Butch Keeling	48	17	3	20	38	7	2	1	3	12
Ching Johnson	47	3	10	13	106	7	2	0	2	24
Norman Gainor	46	3	9	12	9	7	0	0	0	2
Earl Seibert	44	4	6	10	88	7	1	2	3	14
Doug Brennan	38	4	3	7	40	7	1	0	1	10
Vic Desjardins	48	3	3	6	16	6	0	0	0	0
Ott Heller	21	2	2	4	9	7	3	1	4	8
Hib Milks	45	0	4	4	12	6	0	0	0	0

1932-33	GP	G	A	PTS	PIM	Playoffs GP	G	A	PTS	PIM
Bill Cook	48	28	22	50	51	8	3	2	5	4
Bun Cook	48	22	15	37	35	8	2	0	2	4
Frank Boucher	46	7	28	35	4	8	2	2	4	6
Cecil Dillon	48	21	10	31	12	8	8	2	10	6
Art Somers	48	7	15	22	28	8	1	4	5	8
Babe Siebert	42	9	10	19	38	8	1	0	1	12
Ching Johnson	48	8	9	17	127	8	1	0	1	14
Murray Murdoch	48	5	11	16	23	8	3	4	7	2
Ozzie Asmundson	48	5	10	15	20	8	0	2	2	4
Butch Keeling	47	8	6	14	22	8	0	2	2	8
Ott Heller	40	5	7	12	31	8	3	0	3	10
Doug Brennan	48	5	4	9	94	8	0	0	0	11
Earl Seibert	45	2	3	5	92	8	1	0	1	14
Carl Voss	10	2	1	3	4	–	–	–	–	–
Gordon Pettinger	35	1	2	3	18	8	0	0	0	0

1933-34	GP	G	A	PTS	PIM	Playoffs GP	G	A	PTS	PIM
Frank Boucher	48	14	30	44	4	2	0	0	0	0
Cecil Dillon	48	13	26	39	10	2	0	1	1	2
Bun Cook	48	18	15	33	36	2	0	0	0	2
Murray Murdoch	48	17	10	27	29	2	0	0	0	0
Bill Cook	48	13	13	26	21	2	0	0	0	2
Earl Seibert	48	13	10	23	66	2	0	0	0	4
Butch Keeling	48	15	5	20	20	2	0	0	0	0
Vic Ripley	35	5	12	17	10	2	1	0	1	4
Ozzie Asmundson	46	2	6	8	8	1	0	0	0	0
Ching Johnson	48	2	6	8	86	2	0	0	0	4
Ott Heller	48	2	5	7	29	2	0	0	0	0
Dan Cox	15	5	0	5	2	–	–	–	–	–
Art Somers	8	1	2	3	5	2	0	0	0	0
Duke Dutkowski	29	0	3	3	16	2	0	0	0	0
Jean Pusie	19	0	2	2	17	–	–	–	–	–
Babe Siebert	13	0	1	1	18	–	–	–	–	–
Albert Leduc	7	0	0	0	6	–	–	–	–	–
Lorne Carr	14	0	0	0	0	–	–	–	–	–
Doug Brennan	37	0	0	0	18	1	0	0	0	0

1934-35	GP	G	A	PTS	PIM	Playoffs GP	G	A	PTS	PIM
Frank Boucher	48	13	32	45	2	4	0	3	3	0
Bill Cook	48	21	15	36	23	4	1	2	3	7
Cecil Dillon	48	25	9	34	4	4	2	1	3	0
Bun Cook	48	13	21	34	26	4	2	0	2	0
Murray Murdoch	48	14	15	29	14	4	0	2	2	4
Earl Seibert	48	6	19	25	86	4	0	0	0	6
Lynn Patrick	48	9	13	22	17	4	2	2	4	0
Bert Connolly	47	10	11	21	23	4	1	0	1	0
Butch Connolly	47	15	4	19	14	4	2	1	3	0
Charlie Mason	46	5	9	14	14	4	0	1	1	0
Ott Heller	47	3	11	14	31	4	0	1	1	4

Year-By-Year Scoring
1934-35—1938-39

1934-35 (cont'd)	GP	G	A	PTS	PIM	Playoffs GP	G	A	PTS	PIM
Ching Johnson	26	2	3	5	34	3	0	0	0	2
Art Somers	41	0	5	5	4	2	0	0	0	2
Alex Levinsky	21	0	4	4	6	–	–	–	–	–
Vic Ripley	4	0	2	2	2	–	–	–	–	–
Bill MacKenzie	20	1	0	1	10	3	0	0	0	0
Harold Starr	30	0	0	0	26	4	0	0	0	2

1935-36	GP	G	A	PTS	PIM
Cecil Dillon	48	18	14	32	12
Frank Boucher	48	11	18	29	2
Lynn Patrick	48	11	14	25	29
Butch Keeling	47	13	5	18	22
Bill Cook	44	7	10	17	16
Glenn Brydson	30	4	12	16	7
Ott Heller	43	2	11	13	40
Murray Murdoch	48	2	9	11	9
Bun Cook	26	4	5	9	12
Ching Johnson	47	5	3	8	58
Howie Morenz	19	2	5	7	6
Alex Shibicky	18	4	2	6	6

*Did not qualify for playoffs

1935-36 (cont'd)	GP	G	A	PTS	PIM
Art Coulter	23	1	5	6	26
Charlie Mason	28	1	5	6	30
Earl Seibert	17	2	3	5	6
Mac Colville	18	1	4	5	6
Bert Connolly	25	2	2	4	10
Thomas Ayres	28	0	4	4	38
Babe Pratt	17	1	1	2	16
Phil Watson	24	0	2	2	24
Neil Colville	1	0	0	0	0
Joe Cooper	1	0	0	0	0
Harold Starr	15	0	0	0	12

1936-37	GP	G	A	PTS	PIM	Playoffs GP	G	A	PTS	PIM
Cecil Dillon	48	20	11	31	13	9	0	3	3	0
Phil Watson	48	11	17	28	22	9	0	2	2	9
Neil Colville	45	10	18	28	33	9	3	3	6	0
Butch Keeling	48	22	4	26	18	9	3	2	5	2
Lynn Patrick	45	8	16	24	23	9	3	0	3	2
Alex Shibicky	47	14	8	22	30	9	1	4	5	0
Frank Boucher	44	7	13	20	5	9	2	3	5	2
Mac Colville	46	7	12	19	10	9	1	2	3	2
Ott Heller	48	5	12	17	42	9	0	0	0	11
Babe Pratt	47	8	7	15	23	9	3	1	4	11
Murray Murdoch	48	0	14	14	16	9	1	1	2	0
Art Coulter	47	1	5	6	27	9	0	3	3	15
Bill Cook	21	1	4	5	6	–	–	–	–	–
Joe Cooper	48	0	3	3	42	9	1	1	2	12
Eddie Wares	2	2	0	2	0	–	–	–	–	–
Clint Smith	2	1	0	1	0	–	–	–	–	–
Bryan Hextall	3	0	1	1	0	–	–	–	–	–
Joe Krol	1	0	0	0	0	–	–	–	–	–
Ching Johnson	34	0	0	0	2	9	0	1	1	4

1937-38	GP	G	A	PTS	PIM	Playoffs GP	G	A	PTS	PIM
Cecil Dillon	48	21	18	39	6	3	1	0	1	0
Clint Smith	48	14	23	37	0	3	2	0	2	0
Neil Colville	45	17	19	36	11	2	0	1	1	0
Alex Shibicky	48	17	18	35	26	3	2	0	2	2
Lynn Patrick	48	15	19	34	24	3	0	1	1	2
Phil Watson	48	7	25	32	52	3	0	2	2	0
Mac Colville	48	14	14	28	18	3	0	2	2	0
Bryan Hextall	48	17	4	21	6	3	2	0	2	0
Babe Pratt	47	5	14	19	56	2	0	0	0	2
Butch Keeling	39	8	9	17	12	3	0	1	1	2
Ott Heller	48	2	14	16	68	3	0	1	1	2
Art Coulter	43	5	10	15	80	–	–	–	–	–
Bobby Kirk	39	4	8	12	14	–	–	–	–	–
Joe Cooper	46	3	2	5	56	3	0	0	0	4
Muzz Patrick	1	0	2	2	0	3	0	0	0	2
Dutch Hiller	9	0	1	1	2	1	0	0	0	0
Frank Boucher	18	0	1	1	2	–	–	–	–	–
Larry Molyneaux	2	0	0	0	2	3	0	0	0	8
Jonny Sherf						1	0	0	0	0

1938-39	GP	G	A	PTS	PIM	Playoffs GP	G	A	PTS	PIM
Clint Smith	48	21	20	41	2	7	1	2	3	0
Neil Colville	47	18	19	37	12	7	0	2	2	2
Phil Watson	48	15	22	37	42	7	1	1	2	7
Bryan Hextall	48	20	15	35	18	7	0	1	1	4
Alex Shibicky	48	24	9	33	24	7	3	1	4	2
Dutch Hiller	48	10	19	29	22	7	1	0	1	9
Lynn Patrick	35	8	21	29	25	7	1	1	2	0
Mac Colville	48	7	21	28	26	7	1	2	3	4
Cecil Dillon	48	12	15	27	6	1	0	0	0	0
Ott Helle	48	0	23	23	42	7	0	1	1	10
Babe Pratt	48	2	19	21	20	7	1	2	3	9
George Allen	19	6	6	12	10	7	0	0	0	4
Art Coulter	4	4	8	12	58	7	1	1	2	6
Muzz Patrick	48	1	10	11	64	7	1	0	1	17

Year-By-Year Scoring
1938-39—1942-43

1938-39 (cont'd.)	GP	G	A	PTS	PIM	GP	G	A	PTS	PIM
								Playoffs		
Joe Krol	1	1	1	2	0	–	–	–	–	–
Bill Carse	1	0	1	1	0	6	1	1	2	0
Larry Molyneaux	43	0	1	1	18	7	0	0	0	0

1939-40	GP	G	A	PTS	PIM	GP	G	A	PTS	PIM
								Playoffs		
Bryan Hextall	48	24	15	39	52	12	4	3	7	11
Neil Colville	48	19	19	38	22	12	2	7	9	18
Phil Watson	48	7	28	35	42	12	3	6	9	16
Alex Shibicky	43	11	21	32	33	11	2	5	7	4
Dutch Hiller	48	13	18	31	57	12	2	4	6	2
Kilby MacDonald	44	15	13	28	19	12	0	2	2	4
Lynn Patrick	48	12	16	28	34	12	2	2	4	4
Clint Smith	41	8	16	24	2	12	1	3	4	2
Mac Colville	47	7	14	21	12	12	3	2	5	6
Ott Heller	47	5	14	19	26	12	0	3	3	12
Alfie Pike	47	8	9	17	38	12	3	1	4	6
Babe Pratt	48	4	13	17	61	12	3	1	4	18
Art Coulter	48	1	9	10	68	12	1	0	1	21
Muzz Patrick	46	2	4	6	44	12	3	0	3	13
Johnny Polich	1	0	0	0	0	–	–	–	–	–
Stan Smith	1	0	0	0	0	1	0	0	0	0
Cliff Barton	3	0	0	0	0	–	–	–	–	–

1940-41	GP	G	A	PTS	PIM	GP	G	A	PTS	PIM
								Playoffs		
Bryan Hextall	48	26	18	44	16	3	0	1	1	0
Lynn Patrick	48	20	24	44	12	3	1	0	1	14
Neil Colville	48	14	28	42	28	3	1	1	2	0
Phil Watson	40	11	25	36	49	3	0	2	2	9
Mac Colville	47	14	17	31	18	3	1	1	2	2
Clint Smith	48	14	11	25	0	3	0	0	0	0
Alex Shibicky	40	10	14	24	14	3	1	0	1	2
Babe Pratt	47	3	17	20	52	3	1	1	2	6
Alfie Pike	48	6	13	19	23	3	0	1	1	2
Art Coulter	35	5	14	19	42	3	0	0	0	14
Dutch Hiller	45	8	10	18	20	3	0	0	0	0
Ott Heller	48	2	16	18	42	3	0	1	1	4
Kilby MacDonald	47	5	6	11	12	3	1	0	1	0
Muzz Patrick	47	2	8	10	21	3	0	0	0	2
Stan Smith	8	2	1	3	0	–	–	–	–	–
Herb Foster	4	1	0	1	5	–	–	–	–	–
Bill Allum	1	0	1	1	0	–	–	–	–	–
Johnny Polich	2	0	1	1	0	–	–	–	–	–
Bill Juzda	5	0	0	0	2	–	–	–	–	–

1941-42	GP	G	A	PTS	PIM	GP	G	A	PTS	PIM
								Playoffs		
Bryan Hextall	48	24	32	56	30	6	1	1	2	4
Lynn Patrick	47	32	22	54	18	6	1	0	1	0
Phil Watson	48	15	37	52	58	6	1	4	5	6
Alex Shibicky	45	20	14	34	16	6	3	2	5	2
Clint Smith	47	10	24	34	4	5	0	0	0	0
Grant Warwick	44	16	17	33	36	6	0	1	1	2
Neil Colville	48	8	25	33	37	6	0	5	5	6
Mac Colville	46	14	16	30	26	6	3	1	4	0
Babe Pratt	47	4	24	28	65	6	1	3	4	24
Alfie Pike	34	8	19	27	16	6	1	0	1	4
Alan Kuntz	31	10	11	21	10	6	1	0	1	2
Art Coulter	47	1	16	17	31	6	0	1	1	4
Bill Juzda	45	4	8	12	29	6	0	1	1	4
Ott Heller	35	6	5	11	22	6	0	0	0	0
Hub Macey	9	3	5	8	0	1	0	0	0	0
Norman Tustin	18	2	4	6	0	–	–	–	–	–
Norman Burns	11	0	4	4	2	–	–	–	–	–

1942-43	GP	G	A	PTS	PIM	1942-43 (cont'd)	GP	G	A	PTS	PIM
Lynn Patrick	50	22	39	61	28	Felix Mancuso	21	6	8	14	13
Bryan Hextall	50	27	32	59	28	Joe Shack	20	5	9	14	6
Phil Watson	46	14	28	42	44	Joe Bell	15	2	5	7	6
Grant Warwick	50	17	18	35	31	Hub Macey	9	3	3	6	0
Clint Smith	47	12	21	33	4	Gordon Davidson	35	2	3	5	4
Bob Kirkpatrick	49	12	12	24	6	Lin Bend	8	3	1	4	2
Hank Goldup	36	11	20	21	33	Billy Gooden	12	0	3	3	0
Alfie Pike	41	6	16	22	48	Dudley Garrett	23	1	1	2	18
Angus Cameron	35	8	11	19	0	Babe Pratt	4	0	2	2	6
Ott Heller	45	4	14	18	14	Billy Warwick	1	0	1	1	4
Vic Myles	45	6	9	15	57	Spence Tatchell	1	0	0	0	0

*Did not qualify for playoffs

Year-By-Year Scoring
1943-44—1947-48

1943-44

	GP	G	A	PTS	PIM
Bryan Hextall	50	21	33	54	41
Dutch Hiller	50	18	22	40	15
Ott Heller	50	8	27	35	29
Ab DeMarco	36	14	19	33	2
John Mahaffy	28	9	20	29	0
Oscar Aubuchon	38	15	12	27	4
Fern Gauthier	33	14	10	24	0
John McDonald	43	10	9	19	6
Billy Gooden	41	9	8	17	15
Grant Warwick	18	8	9	17	14
Kilby MacDonald	24	7	9	16	4
Bob Dill	28	6	10	16	66
Frank Boucher	15	4	10	14	2
Bob McDonald	39	5	6	11	4
Billy Warwick	13	3	2	5	12
Chuck Scherza	24	3	2	5	13
Don Raleigh	15	2	2	4	2
Gordon Davidson	16	1	3	4	4
Roger Leger	7	1	2	3	2
Aldo Palazzari	12	2	0	2	0
Tommy Dewar	9	0	2	2	4
Chuck Sands	9	0	2	2	0
Hank D'Amore	4	1	0	1	2
Jimmy Jamieson	1	0	1	1	0
Archie Fraser	3	0	1	1	0
Tony Demers	1	0	0	0	0
Hank Dyck	1	0	0	0	0
Bob McDonald	1	0	0	0	0
Lloyd Mohns	1	0	0	0	0
Jack Mann	3	0	0	0	0
Max Labovitch	5	0	0	0	0
Art Strobel	7	0	0	0	0

*Did not qualify for playoffs

1944-45

	GP	G	A	PTS	PIM
Ab DeMarco	50	24	30	54	10
Grant Warwick	52	20	22	42	25
Hank Goldup	48	17	25	42	25
Fred Thurier	50	16	19	35	14
Fred Hunt	44	13	9	22	6
Joe Shack	50	4	18	22	14
Ants Atanas	49	13	8	21	40
Phil Watson	45	11	8	19	24
Ott Heller	45	7	12	19	26
Kilby MacDonald	36	9	6	15	12
Bob Dill	48	9	5	14	69
Bucko McDonald	40	2	9	11	0
Jack Mann	6	3	4	7	0
Bill Moe	35	2	4	6	14
Chuck Scherza	22	2	3	5	18
Guy Labrie	27	2	2	4	14
Neil Colville	4	0	1	1	2
Alex Ritson	1	0	0	0	0
Len Wharton	1	0	0	0	0
Jim Drummond	2	0	0	0	0
Hal Cooper	8	0	0	0	2

*Did not qualify for playoffs

1945-46

	GP	G	A	PTS	PIM
Ab DeMarco	50	20	27	47	20
Grant Warwick	45	19	18	37	19
Edgar Laprade	49	15	19	34	0
Phil Watson	49	12	14	26	43
Tony Leswick	50	15	9	24	26
Alfie Pike	33	7	9	16	18
Alex Shibicky	33	10	5	15	12
Lynn Patrick	38	8	6	14	30
Mac Colville	39	7	6	13	8
Cal Gardner	16	8	2	10	2
Neil Colville	49	5	4	9	25
Bill Moe	48	4	4	8	14
Rene Trudell	16	3	5	8	4
Hank Goldup	19	6	1	7	11
Ott Heller	34	2	3	5	14
Bill Juzda	32	1	3	4	17
Church Russell	17	0	5	5	2
Hal Brown	13	2	1	3	2
Muzz Patrick	24	0	2	2	4
Hal Laycoe	17	0	2	2	6
Bryan Hextall	3	0	1	1	0
Alan Kuntz	14	0	1	1	2
Chuck Rayner	40	0	0	0	6

*Did not qualify for playoffs

1946-47

	GP	G	A	PTS	PIM
Tony Leswick	59	27	14	41	51
Grant Warwick	54	20	20	40	24
Edgar Laprade	58	15	25	40	9
Bryan Hextall	60	20	10	30	18
Carl Gardner	52	13	16	29	30
Church Russell	54	20	8	28	8
Rene Trudell	59	8	16	24	38
Neil Colville	60	4	16	20	16
Ab DeMarco	44	9	10	19	4
Alfie Pike	31	7	11	18	2
Phil Watson	48	6	12	18	17
Bill Moe	59	4	10	14	44
Hal Laycoe	58	1	12	13	25
Joe Bill	47	6	4	10	12
Joe Cooper	59	2	8	10	38
Bill Juzda	45	3	5	8	60
Joe Levandoski	8	1	1	2	0
Jean Paul Lamirande	14	1	1	2	14
Harry Bell	1	0	1	1	0
Jean Paul Denis	6	0	1	1	0
Jack Lancien	1	0	0	0	0
Norm Larson	1	0	0	0	0
Sherman White	1	0	0	0	0
Mel Read	6	0	0	0	8
Mac Colville	14	0	0	0	8

*Did not qualify for playoffs

1947-48

	GP	G	A	PTS	PIM	Playoffs GP	G	A	PTS	PIM
Buddy O'Connor	60	24	36	60	8	6	1	4	5	0
Edgar Laprade	59	13	34	47	7	6	1	4	50	
Tony Leswick	60	24	16	40	76	6	3	2	5	8
Phil Watson	54	18	15	33	54	5	2	3	5	2
Don Raleigh	52	15	18	33	2	6	2	0	2	2
Eddie Kullman	51	15	17	32	32	6	1	0	1	2
Grant Warwick	40	17	12	29	30	—	—	—	—	—
Cal Gardner	58	7	18	25	71	5	0	0	0	0
Bryan Hextall	43	8	14	22	18	6	1	3	4	0
Rene Trudell	54	13	7	20	30	5	0	0	0	2
Frank Eddolls	58	6	13	19	16	2	0	0	0	0
Neil Colville	55	4	12	16	25	6	1	0	1	6
Bill Moe	59	1	15	16	31	1	0	0	0	0
Bill Juzda	60	3	9	12	70	6	0	0	0	9
Ed Slowinski	38	6	5	11	2	4	0	0	0	0
Church Russell	19	0	3	3	2	—	—	—	—	—
Ronnie Rowe	5	1	0	1	0	—	—	—	—	—
Fred Shero	19	1	0	1	2	6	0	1	1	6
Jean Lamirande	18	0	1	1	4	6	0	0	0	4

Year-By-Year Scoring
1947-48—1950-51

1947-48 (cont'd)	GP	G	A	PTS	PIM	GP	G	A	PTS	PIM
Herb Foster	1	0	0	0	0	–	–	–	–	–
Larry Kwong	1	0	0	0	0	–	–	–	–	–
Hub Anslow	2	0	0	0	0	–	–	–	–	–
Bing Juckes	2	0	0	0	0	–	–	–	–	–
Fern Perrault	2	0	0	0	0	–	–	–	–	–
Billy Taylor	2	0	0	0	0	–	–	–	–	–
Ken Davies	–	–	–	–	–	1	0	0	0	0
Duncan Fisher	–	–	–	–	–	1	0	1	1	0
Jack Lancien	–	–	–	–	–	2	0	0	0	2
Nick Mickoski	–	–	–	–	–	2	0	1	1	0

1948-49	GP	G	A	PTS	PIM	1948-49 (cont'd)	GP	G	A	PTS	PIM
Buddy O'Connor	46	11	24	35	0	Bill Moe	60	0	9	9	60
Alex Kaleta	56	12	19	31	18	Frank Eddolis	34	4	2	6	10
Edgar Laprade	56	18	12	30	12	Neil Colville	14	0	5	5	2
Penti Lund	59	14	16	30	16	Wes Trainor	17	1	2	3	6
Tony Leswick	60	13	14	27	70	Ed Slowinski	20	1	1	2	2
Don Raleigh	41	10	16	26	8	Ray Manson	1	0	1	1	0
Dunc Fisher	60	9	16	25	40	Red Staley	1	0	1	1	0
Nick Mickoski	54	13	9	22	20	Elwin Morris	18	0	1	1	8
Clint Albright	59	14	5	19	19	Dick Kotanen	1	0	0	0	0
Jack Gordon	31	3	9	12	0	Bucky Buchanan	2	0	0	0	0
Allan Stanley	40	2	8	10	22	Val DeLory	1	0	0	0	0
Ed Kullman	18	4	5	9	14	Odie Lowe	1	0	0	0	0
Fred Shero	59	3	6	9	64	Jack Evans	3	0	0	0	4
Wally Stanowski	60	1	8	9	16	Chuck Rayner	58	0	0	0	2

*Did not qualify for playoffs

1949-50	GP	G	A	PTS	PIM	GP	G	A	PTS	PIM
Edgar Laprade	60	22	22	44	2	12	3	5	8	4
Tony Lewsick	69	19	25	44	85	12	2	4	6	12
Ed Slowinski	63	14	23	37	12	12	2	6	8	6
Don Raleigh	70	12	25	37	11	12	4	5	9	4
Duncan Fisher	70	12	21	33	42	12	3	3	6	14
Buddy O'Connor	66	11	22	33	4	12	4	2	6	4
Alex Kaleta	67	17	14	31	40	10	0	3	3	0
Pentti Lund	64	18	9	27	16	12	6	5	11	0
Nick Mickoski	47	10	10	20	10	12	1	5	6	2
Pat Egan	70	5	11	16	50	12	3	1	4	6
Jack McLeod	38	6	9	15	2	7	0	0	0	0
Fred Shero	67	2	8	10	71	7	0	1	1	2
Bud Poile	28	3	6	9	8	–	–	–	–	–
Allan Stanley	55	4	4	8	58	12	2	5	7	10
Gus Kyle	70	3	5	8	143	12	1	2	3	30
Frank Eddolls	58	2	6	8	20	11	0	1	1	4
Jean Lamirande	16	4	3	7	6	2	0	0	0	0
Jack Lancien	43	1	4	5	27	4	0	1	1	0
Bing Juckes	14	2	1	3	6	–	–	–	–	–
Odie Lowe	3	1	1	2	0	–	–	–	–	–
Don Smith	10	1	1	2	0	1	0	0	0	0
Wally Stanowski	37	1	1	2	10	–	–	–	–	–
Sherman White	3	0	2	2	0	–	–	–	–	–
Doug Adam	4	0	1	1	0	–	–	–	–	–
Jean Denis	4	0	1	1	2	–	–	–	–	–
Jack Gordon	1	0	0	0	0	9	1	1	2	7
Fern Perrault	1	0	0	0	0	–	–	–	–	–
Bill Kyle	2	0	0	0	0	–	–	–	–	–
Jack Evans	3	0	0	0	2	–	–	–	–	–
Bill McDonagh	4	0	0	0	2	–	–	–	–	–
Chick Webster	14	0	0	0	4	–	–	–	–	–
Chuck Rayner	69	0	0	0	6	12	0	0	0	0

1950-51	GP	G	A	PTS	PIM	1950-51 (cont'd)	GP	G	A	PTS	PIM
Reg Sinclair	70	18	21	39	70	Alex Kaleta	58	3	4	7	26
Don Raleigh	64	15	24	39	18	Wally Stanowski	49	1	5	6	28
Buddy O'Connor	66	16	20	36	0	Gus Kyle	64	2	3	5	92
Nick Mickoski	64	20	15	35	12	Bill Kyle	1	0	3	3	0
Ed Slowinski	69	14	18	32	15	Vic Howe	3	1	0	1	0
Ed Kullman	70	14	18	32	88	Ed Harrison	4	1	0	1	2
Zellio Toppanazzi	55	14	13	27	27	Jack Evans	49	1	0	1	95
Tony Leswick	70	15	11	26	112	Jack Gordon	4	0	1	1	0
Edgar Laprade	42	10	13	23	0	Jack Lancien	19	0	1	1	8
Al Stanley	70	7	14	21	75	Dick Kotanen	1	0	0	0	0
Pentti Lund	59	4	16	20	6	Bob Wood	1	0	0	0	0
Jack McLeod	41	5	10	15	2	Bill Wylie	1	0	0	0	0
Pat Egan	70	5	10	15	70	Dunc Fisher	12	0	0	0	0
Frank Eddolis	68	3	8	11	24	Chuck Rayner	66	0	0	0	6

*Did not qualify for playoffs

Year-By-Year Scoring
1951-52—1955-56

1951-52

	GP	G	A	PTS	PIM
Don Raleigh	70	19	42	61	14
Ed Slowinski	64	21	22	43	18
Paul Ronty	65	12	31	43	16
Gaye Stewart	69	15	25	40	22
Wally Hergesheimer	68	26	12	38	6
Edgar Laprade	70	9	29	38	8
Hy Buller	68	12	23	35	96
Reg Sinclair	69	20	10	30	33
Herb Dickenson	37	14	13	27	8
Eddie Kullman	64	11	10	21	59
Nick Mickoski	43	7	13	20	20
Al Stanley	50	5	14	19	52
Steve Kraftcheck	58	8	9	17	30
Jim Ross	51	2	9	11	25
Frank Eddolis	42	3	5	8	18
Jack Evans	52	1	6	7	83
Jack Stoddard	20	4	2	6	2
Jack McLeod	13	2	3	5	2
Zellio Toppazzini	16	1	1	2	4
Clare Martin	15	0	1	1	8
Jim Conacher	16	0	1	1	2
Lloyd Ailsby	3	0	0	0	2
Chuck Rayner	53	0	0	0	4

*Did not qualify for playoffs

1952-53

	GP	G	A	PTS	PIM
Wally Hergesheimer	70	30	29	59	10
Paul Ronty	70	16	38	54	20
Nick Mickoski	70	19	16	35	39
Jack Stoddard	60	12	13	25	29
Hy Buller	70	7	18	25	73
Neil Strain	52	11	13	24	12
Don Raleigh	55	4	18	22	2
Leo Reise	61	4	15	19	53
Ed Kullman	70	8	10	18	61
Allan Stanley	70	5	12	17	52
Harry Howell	67	3	8	11	46
Steve Kraftcheck	69	2	9	11	45
Dean Prentice	55	6	3	9	20
Pete Babando	30	4	5	9	8
Herb Dickenson	11	4	4	8	2
Aldo Guidolin	30	4	4	8	24
Ed Slowinski	37	2	5	7	14
George Senick	13	2	3	5	8
Jim Conacher	17	1	4	5	2
Ron Murphy	15	3	1	4	0
Edgar Laprade	11	2	1	3	2
Gaye Steward	18	1	2	3	8
Jim Ross	11	0	2	2	4
Kelly Burnett	3	1	0	1	0
Dolph Kukulowicz	3	1	0	1	0
Gordie Haworth	2	0	1	1	0
Andy Bathgate	18	0	1	1	6
Frank Bathgate	2	0	0	0	2
Michel Labadie	3	0	0	0	0
Jack McLeod	3	0	0	0	2
Ian Mackintosh	4	0	0	0	4
Chuck Rayner	20	0	0	0	2
Lorne Worsley	50	0	0	0	2

*Did not qualify for playoffs

1953-54

	GP	G	A	PTS	PIM
Paul Ronty	70	13	33	46	18
Don Raleigh	70	15	30	45	14
Wally Hergesheimer	66	27	16	43	42
Camille Henry	66	24	15	39	10
Nick Micoski	68	19	16	35	22
Max Bentley	57	14	18	32	15
Dean Prentice	52	4	13	17	18
Hy Buller	41	3	14	17	40
Harry Howell	67	7	9	16	58
Ed Kullman	70	4	10	14	44
Ivan Irwin	56	2	12	14	109
Ike Hildebrand	31	6	7	13	12
Doug Bentley	20	2	10	12	2
Bob Chrystal	64	5	5	10	44
Jack Evans	44	4	4	8	73
Leo Reise	70	3	5	8	71
Aldo Guidolin	68	2	6	8	51
Edgar Laprade	35	1	6	7	2
Andy Bathgate	20	2	2	4	18
Ron Murphy	27	1	3	4	20
Glen Sonmor	15	2	0	2	17
Billy Dea	14	1	1	2	2
Allan Stanley	10	0	2	2	11
Bill Chalmers	1	0	0	0	0
Vic Howe	1	0	0	0	0
Dolph Kukulowicz	1	0	0	0	0
Bill McCreary	1	0	0	0	0

*Did not qualify for playoffs

1954-55

	GP	G	A	PTS	PIM
Danny Lewicki	70	29	24	53	8
Andy Bathgate	70	20	20	40	37
Don Raleigh	69	8	32	40	19
Dean Prentice	70	16	15	31	20
Ron Murphy	66	14	16	30	36
Larry Popein	70	11	17	28	27
Nick Mickoski	18	0	19	19	6
Pete Conacher	52	10	7	17	10
Bill Gadsby	52	8	8	16	42
Harry Howell	70	2	14	16	87
Bob Chrystal	68	6	9	15	68
Paul Ronty	54	4	11	15	10
Edgar Laprade	60	3	11	14	0
Ivan Irwin	60	0	13	12	85
Camille Henry	21	5	2	7	4
Aldo Guidolin	70	2	5	7	34
Wally Hergesheimer	14	4	2	6	4
Vic Howe	29	2	4	6	10
Jack Evans	47	0	5	5	91
Bill Ezinicki	16	2	2	4	22
Lou Fontinato	28	2	2	4	60
Jackie McLeod	11	1	1	2	2
Bill McCreary	8	0	2	2	0
Allan Stanley	12	0	1	1	2
Dick Bouchard	1	0	0	0	0
Ron Howell	3	0	0	0	0
Glen Sonmor	13	0	0	0	4
Lorne Worsley	65	0	0	0	2

*Did not qualify for playoffs

1955-56

	GP	G	A	PTS	PIM	Playoffs GP	G	A	PTS	PIM
Andy Bathgate	70	19	47	66	59	5	1	2	3	2
Dave Creighton	70	20	31	51	43	5	0	0	0	4
Bill Gadsby	70	9	42	51	84	5	1	3	4	4
Danny Lewicki	70	18	27	45	26	5	0	3	3	0
Ron Murphy	66	16	28	44	71	5	0	1	1	2
Dean Prentice	70	24	18	42	44	5	1	0	1	2
Wally Hergesheimer	70	22	18	40	26	5	1	0	1	0
Larry Popein	64	14	25	39	37	5	0	1	1	2
Andy Hebenton	70	24	14	38	8	5	1	0	1	2
Bronco Horvath	66	12	17	29	40	5	1	2	3	4
Pete Conacher	41	11	11	22	10	5	0	0	0	0
Lou Fontinato	70	3	15	18	202	4	0	0	0	6
Harry Howell	70	3	15	18	77	5	0	1	1	4
Don Raleigh	29	1	12	13	4	—	—	—	—	—
Guy Gendron	63	2	5	7	38	5	2	1	3	2
Jack Evans	70	2	9	11	104	5	1	0	1	18

Year-By-Year Scoring
1956-57—1960-61

1956-57	GP	G	A	PTS	PIM	Playoffs GP	G	A	PTS	PIM
Andy Bathgate	70	27	50	77	60	5	2	0	2	7
Andy Hebenton	70	21	23	44	10	5	2	0	2	2
Dean Prentice	68	19	23	42	38	5	0	2	2	4
Bill Gadsby	70	4	37	41	72	5	1	2	3	2
Dave Creighton	70	18	21	39	42	5	2	2	4	2
Danny Lewicki	70	18	20	38	47	5	0	1	1	2
Larry Popein	67	11	19	30	20	5	0	3	3	0
Camille Henry	36	14	15	29	2	5	2	3	5	0
Red Sullivan	42	6	17	23	36	5	1	2	3	4
Ron Murphy	33	7	12	19	14	5	0	0	0	0
Gerry Foley	69	7	9	16	48	3	0	0	0	0
Guy Gendron	70	9	6	15	40	5	0	1	1	6
Parker MacDonald	45	7	8	15	24	1	1	1	2	0
Lou Fontinato	70	3	12	15	139	5	0	0	0	7
Harry Howell	65	2	10	12	70	5	1	0	1	6
Larry Cahan	61	5	4	9	65	3	0	0	0	2
Jack Evans	70	3	6	9	110	5	0	1	1	4
Bruce Cline	30	2	3	5	10	–	–	–	–	–
Bronco Horvath	7	1	2	3	4	–	–	–	–	–

1957-58	GP	G	A	PTS	PIM	Playoffs GP	G	A	PTS	PIM
Andy Bathgate	65	30	48	78	42	6	5	3	8	6
Camille Henry	70	32	24	56	2	6	1	4	5	5
Dave Creighton	70	17	35	52	40	6	3	3	6	2
Bill Gadsby	65	14	32	46	48	6	0	3	3	4
Red Sullivan	70	11	35	46	61	1	0	0	0	0
Andy Hebenton	70	21	24	45	17	6	2	3	5	4
Larry Popein	70	12	22	34	22	6	1	0	1	4
Danny Lewicki	70	11	19	30	26	6	0	0	0	6
Guy Gendron	70	10	17	27	68	6	1	0	1	11
Dean Prentice	38	13	9	22	14	6	1	3	4	4
Parker MacDonald	70	8	10	18	30	6	1	2	3	2
Jack Evans	70	4	8	12	108	6	0	0	0	17
Harry Howell	70	4	7	11	62	6	1	0	1	8
Lou Fontinato	70	3	8	11	152	6	0	1	1	6
Hank Ciesla	60	2	6	8	16	6	0	2	2	0
Gerry Foley	68	2	5	7	43	6	0	1	1	2
Larry Cahan	34	1	1	2	20	5	0	0	0	4

1958-59	GP	G	A	PTS	PIM	1958-59 (cont'd)	GP	G	A	PTS	PIM
Andy Bathgate	70	40	48	88	48	Hank Diesla	69	6	14	20	21
George Sullivan	70	21	42	63	56	Harry Howell	70	4	10	14	101
Andy Hebenton	70	33	29	62	8	Lou Fontinato	64	7	6	13	149
Camille Henry	70	23	35	58	2	Les Colwill	69	7	6	13	16
Bill Gadsby	70	5	46	51	56	John Hanna	70	1	10	11	83
Dean Prentice	70	17	33	50	11	Wally Hergesheimer	22	3	0	3	6
Larry Popein	61	13	21	34	28	Jack Bowness	35	1	2	3	20
Eddie Schack	67	7	14	21	109	Earl Ingarfield	35	1	2	3	10
James Bartlett	70	11	9	20	118	Larry Cahan	16	1	0	1	8

*Did not qualify for playoffs

1959-60	GP	G	A	PTS	PIM	1959-60 (cont'd)	GP	G	A	PTS	PIM
Andy Bathgate	70	26	48	74	28	Jim Bartlett	44	8	4	12	48
Dean Prentice	70	32	34	66	43	John Hanna	61	4	8	12	87
Andy Hebenton	70	19	27	46	4	Art Stratton	18	2	5	7	2
Red Sullivan	70	12	25	37	81	Jack Bowness	37	2	5	7	34
Larry Popein	66	14	22	36	16	Mel Pearson	23	1	5	6	13
Bill Gadsby	65	9	22	31	60	Earl Ingarfield	20	1	2	3	2
Ken Schinkel	69	13	16	29	27	Irv Spencer	32	1	2	3	20
Brian Cullen	64	8	21	29	6	Bill Sweeney	4	1	0	1	0
Camille Henry	49	12	15	27	6	Ian Cushenan	17	0	1	1	22
Eddie Shack	62	8	10	18	110	Dave Balon	3	0	0	0	0
Bob Kabel	44	5	11	16	32	Parker MacDonald	4	0	0	0	0
Harry Howell	67	7	6	13	58	Noel Price	6	0	0	0	0
Lou Fontinato	64	2	11	13	137						

*Did not qualify for playoffs

1960-61	GP	G	A	PTS	PIM	1960-61 (cont'd)	GP	G	A	PTS	PIM
Andy Bathgate	70	29	48	77	22	Irv Spencer	56	1	8	9	30
Andy Hebenton	70	26	28	54	10	Ken Schinkel	38	2	6	8	18
Camille Henry	53	28	25	53	8	Don Johns	63	1	7	8	34
Dean Prentice	56	20	25	45	17	Jim Morrison	19	1	6	7	6
George Sullivan	70	9	31	40	66	Lou Fontinato	53	2	3	5	100
Bill Gadsby	65	9	26	35	49	Jean Ratelle	3	2	1	3	0
Earl Ingarfield	66	13	21	34	18	Len Ronson	13	2	1	3	10
Brian Cullen	42	11	19	30	6	Eddie Shack	12	1	2	3	17
Johnny Wilson	56	14	12	26	24	Dave Balon	13	1	2	3	8
Pat Hannigan	53	11	9	20	24	Danny Belisle	4	2	0	2	0
Ted Hampson	69	6	14	20	4	Bob Kabel	4	0	2	2	2
Harry Howell	70	7	10	17	62	Al Lebrun	4	0	2	2	4
Floyd Smith	29	5	9	14	0	Rod Gilbert	1	0	1	1	2
John Hanna	46	1	8	9	34	Bob Cunningham	3	0	1	1	0

Year-By-Year Scoring
1960-61—1964-65

1960-61 (cont'd)	GP	G	A	PTS	PIM	1960-61 (cont'd)	GP	G	A	PTS	PIM
Larry Popein	4	0	1	1	0	Phil Latreille	4	0	0	0	2
Noel Price	1	0	0	0	2	Ron Hutchinson	9	0	0	0	0
Wayne Hall	4	0	0	0	0						
*Did not qualify for playoffs											

						Playoffs				
1961-62	GP	G	A	PTS	PIM	GP	G	A	PTS	PIM
Andy Bathgate	70	28	56	84	44	6	1	2	3	4
Dean Prentice	68	22	38	60	20	3	0	2	2	0
Earl Ingarfield	70	26	31	57	18	6	3	2	5	2
Andy Hebenton	70	18	24	42	10	6	1	2	3	0
Camille Henry	60	23	15	38	8	5	0	0	0	0
Doug Harvey	69	6	24	30	42	6	0	1	1	2
Ken Schinkel	65	7	21	28	17	2	1	0	1	0
Ted Hampson	68	4	24	28	10	6	0	1	1	0
Guy Gendron	69	14	11	25	71	6	3	1	4	2
Albert Langlois	69	7	18	25	90	6	0	1	1	2
Pat Hannigan	56	8	14	22	34	4	0	0	0	2
Harry Howell	66	6	15	21	89	6	0	1	1	8
Dave Balon	30	4	11	15	11	6	2	3	5	2
John Wilson	40	11	3	14	14	6	2	2	4	4
Jean Ratelle	31	4	8	12	4	—	—	—	—	—
Irv Spencer	43	2	10	12	31	1	0	0	0	2
Larry Cahan	57	2	7	9	85	6	0	0	0	10
Vic Hadfield	44	3	1	4	22	4	0	0	0	2
Pete Goegan	7	0	2	2	6	—	—	—	—	—
Bob Cunningham	1	0	0	0	0	—	—	—	—	—
Rod Gilbert	1	0	0	0	0	4	2	3	5	4
Mel Pearson	3	0	0	0	2	—	—	—	—	—
Jack Bownass	4	0	0	0	4	—	—	—	—	—

1962-63	GP	G	A	PTS	PIM	1962-63 (cont'd)	GP	G	A	PTS	PIM
Andy Bathgate	70	35	46	81	54	Larry Cahan	56	6	14	20	47
Camille Henry	60	37	23	60	8	Jim Neilson	69	5	11	16	38
Dean Prentice	68	19	34	53	22	Albert Langlois	60	2	14	16	62
Earl Ingarfield	69	19	24	43	40	Ken Schinkel	69	6	9	15	15
Doug Harvey	68	4	35	39	92	Vic Hadfield	36	5	6	11	32
Andy Hebenton	70	15	22	37	8	Leon Rochefort	23	5	4	9	6
Rod Gilbert	70	11	20	31	20	Ted Hampson	46	4	2	6	2
Harry Howell	70	5	20	25	55	Don Johns	6	0	4	4	6
Dave Balon	70	11	13	24	72	Bryan Hextall	21	0	2	2	10
Don McKenney	21	8	16	24	4	Mel Pearson	5	1	0	1	6
Bronco Horvath	41	7	15	22	34	Daune Rupp	2	0	0	0	0
Jean Ratelle	48	11	9	20	8						
*Did not qualify for playoffs											

1963-64	GP	G	A	PTS	PIM	1963-64 (cont'd)	GP	G	A	PTS	PIM
Phil Goyette	67	24	41	65	15	Bob Nevin	14	5	4	9	9
Rod Gilbert	70	24	40	64	62	Richard Duff	14	4	4	8	2
Andy Bathgate	56	16	43	59	26	Richard Meissner	35	3	5	8	0
Camille Henry	68	29	26	55	8	Jean Ratelle	15	0	7	7	6
Harry Howell	70	5	31	36	75	David Richardson	34	3	1	4	21
Jim Neilson	69	5	24	29	93	Ronald Ingram	16	1	3	4	8
Earl Ingarfield	63	16	11	26	26	Doug Harvey	14	0	2	2	10
Don McKenney	55	9	17	26	6	Marc Dufour	10	1	0	1	2
Vic Hadfield	68	14	11	25	151	Howie Glover	25	1	0	1	9
Val Fonteyne	69	7	18	25	4	Rod Seiling	2	0	1	1	0
Don Marshall	70	11	12	23	8	Mike McMahon	18	0	1	1	16
Al Langlois	61	5	8	13	45	Donald McGregor	2	0	0	0	2
Larry Cahan	53	4	8	12	80	Kenneth Schinkel	4	0	0	0	0
Don Johns	57	1	9	10	20	Gordon Labossiere	15	0	0	0	12
*Did not qualify for playoffs											

1964-65	GP	G	A	PTS	PIM	1964-65 (cont'd)	GP	G	A	PTS	PIM
Rod Gilbert	70	25	36	61	52	Larry Cahan	26	0	5	5	32
Phil Goyette	52	12	34	46	6	Jim Mikol	30	1	3	4	46
Vic Hadfield	70	18	20	38	102	Dave Richardson	7	0	1	1	4
Camille Henry	48	21	15	36	20	Don Johns	22	0	1	1	4
Don Marshall	69	20	15	35	2	Val Fonteyne	27	0	1	1	2
Jean Ratelle	54	14	21	35	14	Trevor Fahey	1	0	0	0	0
Bob Nevin	64	16	14	30	28	Jim Johnson	1	0	0	0	0
Earl Ingarfield	69	15	13	28	40	Gord Laboissiere	1	0	0	0	0
Rod Seiling	68	4	22	26	44	Mike McMahon	1	0	0	0	0
Doug Robinson	21	8	14	22	2	Dick Meissner	1	0	0	0	0
Harry Howell	68	2	20	22	63	Marc Dufour	2	0	0	0	0
Lou Angotti	70	9	8	17	20	Billy Taylor	2	0	0	0	0
Bill Hicke	40	6	11	17	26	Ron Ingram	3	0	0	0	2
Jim Nielson	62	0	13	13	58	Sandy Fitzpatrick	4	0	0	0	2
Dick Duff	29	3	9	12	20	Ulf Sterner	4	0	0	0	0
Arnie Brown	58	1	11	12	145	Ted Taylor	4	0	0	0	4
Wayne Hillman	22	1	8	9	26	Mel Pearson	5	0	0	0	4
John Brenneman	22	3	3	6	6	Bob Plager	10	0	0	0	18
*Did not qualify for playoffs											

Year-By-Year Scoring
1965-66—1968-69

1965-66

1965-66	GP	G	A	PTS	PIM
Bob Nevin	69	29	33	62	10
Don Marshall	69	26	28	54	6
Jean Ratelle	67	21	30	51	10
Phil Goyette	60	11	31	42	6
Earl Ingarfield	68	20	16	36	35
Vic Hadfield	67	16	19	35	112
Harry Howell	70	4	29	33	92
Bill Hicke	49	9	18	27	21
Rod Gilbert	34	10	15	25	20
Reggie Fleming	35	10	14	24	122
Jim Neilson	65	4	19	23	84
Doug Robinson	51	8	12	20	8
Wayne Hillman	68	3	17	20	70
Lou Angotti	51	6	12	18	14
Rod Seiling	52	5	10	15	24

*Did not qualify for playoffs

1965-66 (cont'd)	GP	G	A	PTS	PIM
Mike McMahon	41	0	12	12	34
John McKenzie	35	6	5	11	36
Gary Peters	63	7	3	10	42
Arnie Brown	64	1	7	8	106
Bob Piager	18	0	5	5	22
Ray Cullen	8	1	3	4	0
Paul Andrea	4	1	1	2	0
Jim Johnson	5	1	0	1	0
Ted Taylor	4	0	1	1	2
Al Lebrun	2	0	0	0	0
Dunc McCallum	2	0	0	0	0
Allan Hamilton	4	0	0	0	0
Larry Mickey	7	0	0	0	2
John Brenneman	11	0	0	0	14

1966-67

1966-67	GP	G	A	PTS	PIM	Playoffs GP	G	A	PTS	PIM
Phil Goyette	70	12	49	61	6	4	1	0	1	0
Rod Gilbert	64	28	18	46	12	4	2	2	4	6
Don Marshall	70	24	22	46	4	4	0	1	1	2
Bob Nevin	67	20	24	44	6	4	0	3	3	2
Bernie Geoffrion	58	17	25	42	42	4	2	0	2	0
Harry Howell	70	12	28	40	54	4	0	0	0	4
Orland Kurtenbach	60	11	25	36	58	3	0	2	2	0
Earl Ingarfield	67	12	22	34	12	4	1	0	1	2
Vic Hadfield	69	13	20	33	80	4	1	0	1	17
Reg Fleming	61	15	16	31	146	4	0	2	2	11
Jim Neilson	61	4	11	15	65	4	1	0	1	0
Wayne Hillman	67	2	12	14	43	4	0	0	0	2
Arnie Brown	69	2	10	12	61	4	0	0	0	6
Jean Ratelle	41	6	5	11	4	4	0	0	0	2
Bill Hicke	48	3	4	7	11	–	–	–	–	–
Red Berenson	30	0	5	5	2	4	0	1	1	2
Al MacNeil	58	0	4	4	44	4	0	0	0	2
Rod Seiling	12	1	1	2	6	–	–	–	–	–
Larry Mickey	4	0	2	2	–	–	–	–	–	–

1967-68

1967-68	GP	G	A	PTS	PIM	Playoffs GP	G	A	PTS	PIM
Jean Ratelle	74	32	46	78	18	6	0	4	4	2
Rod Gilbert	73	29	48	77	12	6	5	0	5	4
Phil Goyette	73	25	40	65	10	6	0	1	1	4
Bob Nevin	74	28	30	58	20	6	0	3	3	4
Don Marshall	70	19	30	49	2	6	2	1	3	0
Vic Hadfield	59	20	19	39	45	6	1	2	3	6
Orland Kurtenbach	73	15	20	35	82	6	1	0	1	26
Jim Neilson	67	6	29	35	60	6	1	1	2	4
Harry Howell	74	5	24	29	62	6	0	1	1	0
Arnie Brown	74	1	25	26	83	6	0	1	1	8
Reg Fleming	73	17	7	24	132	6	0	2	2	4
Bernie Geoffrion	59	5	16	21	11	1	0	1	1	0
Camille Henry	36	8	12	20	0	6	0	0	0	0
Rod Seiling	71	5	11	16	44	6	0	2	2	4
Ron Stewart	55	7	7	14	19	6	1	1	2	2
Larry Jeffrey	47	2	4	6	15	3	0	0	0	0
Wayne Hillman	62	0	5	5	46	6	0	0	0	0
Red Berenson	19	2	1	3	2	–	–	–	–	–
Larry Mickey	4	0	2	2	0	–	–	–	–	–
Allan Hamilton	2	0	0	0	0	–	–	–	–	–
Walt Tkaczuk	2	0	0	0	0	–	–	–	–	–

1968-69

1968-69	GP	G	A	PTS	PIM	Playoffs GP	G	A	PTS	PIM
Jean Ratelle	75	32	46	78	26	4	1	0	1	0
Rod Gilbert	66	28	49	77	22	4	1	0	1	0
Vic Hadfield	73	26	40	66	108	4	2	1	3	2
Bob Nevin	71	31	25	56	14	4	0	2	2	0
Phil Goyette	67	13	32	45	8	3	0	0	0	4
Jim Neilson	76	10	34	44	95	4	0	3	3	5
Don Marshall	74	20	19	39	12	4	1	0	1	0
Walt Tkaczuk	71	12	24	36	28	4	0	1	1	6
Dave Balon	75	10	21	31	57	4	1	0	1	0
Ron Stewart	75	18	11	29	20	4	0	1	1	0
Brad Park	54	3	23	26	70	4	0	2	2	7
Arnie Brown	74	10	12	22	48	4	0	1	1	0
Rod Seiling	73	4	17	21	73	4	1	0	1	2
Reg Fleming	72	8	12	20	138	3	0	0	0	7
Harry Howell	56	4	7	11	36	2	0	0	0	0
Larry Jeffrey	75	1	6	7	12	4	0	0	0	2
Dennis Hextall	13	1	4	5	25	–	–	–	–	–
Bill Fairbairn	1	0	0	0	0	–	–	–	–	–
Bob Jones	2	0	0	0	0	–	–	–	–	–

Year-By-Year Scoring
1968-69—1971-72

<table>
<thead>
<tr><th>1968-69 (cont'd)</th><th>GP</th><th>G</th><th>A</th><th>PTS</th><th>PIM</th><th colspan="5">Playoffs</th></tr>
<tr><th></th><th></th><th></th><th></th><th></th><th></th><th>GP</th><th>G</th><th>A</th><th>PTS</th><th>PIM</th></tr>
</thead>
<tbody>
<tr><td>Orland Kurtenbach</td><td>2</td><td>0</td><td>0</td><td>0</td><td>2</td><td>—</td><td>—</td><td>—</td><td>—</td><td>—</td></tr>
<tr><td>Guy Trottier</td><td>2</td><td>0</td><td>0</td><td>0</td><td>0</td><td>—</td><td>—</td><td>—</td><td>—</td><td>—</td></tr>
<tr><td>Wayne Rivers</td><td>4</td><td>0</td><td>0</td><td>0</td><td>0</td><td>—</td><td>—</td><td>—</td><td>—</td><td>—</td></tr>
<tr><td>Bob Blackburn</td><td>11</td><td>0</td><td>0</td><td>0</td><td>0</td><td>—</td><td>—</td><td>—</td><td>—</td><td>—</td></tr>
<tr><td>Al Hamilton</td><td>16</td><td>0</td><td>0</td><td>0</td><td>8</td><td>1</td><td>0</td><td>0</td><td>0</td><td>0</td></tr>
</tbody>
</table>

<table>
<thead>
<tr><th>1969-70</th><th>GP</th><th>G</th><th>A</th><th>PTS</th><th>PIM</th><th colspan="5">Playoffs</th></tr>
<tr><th></th><th></th><th></th><th></th><th></th><th></th><th>GP</th><th>G</th><th>A</th><th>PTS</th><th>PIM</th></tr>
</thead>
<tbody>
<tr><td>Walt Tkaczuk</td><td>76</td><td>27</td><td>50</td><td>77</td><td>38</td><td>6</td><td>2</td><td>1</td><td>3</td><td>17</td></tr>
<tr><td>Jean Ratelle</td><td>75</td><td>32</td><td>42</td><td>74</td><td>28</td><td>6</td><td>1</td><td>3</td><td>4</td><td>0</td></tr>
<tr><td>Dave Balon</td><td>76</td><td>33</td><td>37</td><td>70</td><td>100</td><td>6</td><td>1</td><td>1</td><td>2</td><td>32</td></tr>
<tr><td>Bill Fairbairn</td><td>76</td><td>23</td><td>33</td><td>56</td><td>23</td><td>6</td><td>0</td><td>1</td><td>1</td><td>10</td></tr>
<tr><td>Vic Hadfield</td><td>71</td><td>20</td><td>34</td><td>54</td><td>69</td><td>—</td><td>—</td><td>—</td><td>—</td><td>—</td></tr>
<tr><td>Rod Gilbert</td><td>72</td><td>16</td><td>37</td><td>53</td><td>22</td><td>6</td><td>4</td><td>5</td><td>9</td><td>0</td></tr>
<tr><td>Bob Nevin</td><td>68</td><td>18</td><td>19</td><td>37</td><td>8</td><td>6</td><td>1</td><td>1</td><td>2</td><td>2</td></tr>
<tr><td>Brad Park</td><td>60</td><td>11</td><td>26</td><td>37</td><td>98</td><td>5</td><td>1</td><td>2</td><td>3</td><td>11</td></tr>
<tr><td>Arnie Brown</td><td>73</td><td>15</td><td>21</td><td>36</td><td>78</td><td>4</td><td>0</td><td>4</td><td>4</td><td>9</td></tr>
<tr><td>Rod Seiling</td><td>76</td><td>5</td><td>21</td><td>26</td><td>68</td><td>2</td><td>0</td><td>0</td><td>0</td><td>0</td></tr>
<tr><td>Ron Stewart</td><td>76</td><td>14</td><td>10</td><td>24</td><td>14</td><td>6</td><td>0</td><td>0</td><td>0</td><td>2</td></tr>
<tr><td>Don Marshall</td><td>57</td><td>9</td><td>15</td><td>24</td><td>6</td><td>1</td><td>0</td><td>0</td><td>0</td><td>0</td></tr>
<tr><td>Jim Neilson</td><td>62</td><td>3</td><td>20</td><td>23</td><td>75</td><td>6</td><td>0</td><td>1</td><td>1</td><td>8</td></tr>
<tr><td>Orland Kurtenbach</td><td>53</td><td>4</td><td>10</td><td>14</td><td>47</td><td>6</td><td>1</td><td>2</td><td>3</td><td>24</td></tr>
<tr><td>Tim Horton</td><td>15</td><td>1</td><td>5</td><td>6</td><td>16</td><td>6</td><td>1</td><td>1</td><td>2</td><td>28</td></tr>
<tr><td>Allan Hamilton</td><td>59</td><td>0</td><td>5</td><td>5</td><td>54</td><td>5</td><td>0</td><td>0</td><td>0</td><td>2</td></tr>
<tr><td>Jack Egers</td><td>6</td><td>3</td><td>0</td><td>3</td><td>2</td><td>5</td><td>3</td><td>1</td><td>4</td><td>10</td></tr>
<tr><td>Don Luce</td><td>12</td><td>1</td><td>2</td><td>3</td><td>8</td><td>5</td><td>0</td><td>1</td><td>1</td><td>4</td></tr>
<tr><td>Larry Brown</td><td>15</td><td>0</td><td>3</td><td>3</td><td>8</td><td>—</td><td>—</td><td>—</td><td>—</td><td>—</td></tr>
<tr><td>Ted Irvine</td><td>17</td><td>0</td><td>3</td><td>3</td><td>10</td><td>6</td><td>1</td><td>2</td><td>3</td><td>8</td></tr>
<tr><td>Don Blackburn</td><td>3</td><td>0</td><td>0</td><td>0</td><td>0</td><td>1</td><td>0</td><td>0</td><td>0</td><td>0</td></tr>
<tr><td>Ab DeMarco</td><td>3</td><td>0</td><td>0</td><td>0</td><td>0</td><td>5</td><td>0</td><td>0</td><td>0</td><td>2</td></tr>
<tr><td>Mike Robitaille</td><td>4</td><td>0</td><td>0</td><td>0</td><td>8</td><td>—</td><td>—</td><td>—</td><td>—</td><td>—</td></tr>
</tbody>
</table>

<table>
<thead>
<tr><th>1970-71</th><th>GP</th><th>G</th><th>A</th><th>PTS</th><th>PIM</th><th colspan="5">Playoffs</th></tr>
<tr><th></th><th></th><th></th><th></th><th></th><th></th><th>GP</th><th>G</th><th>A</th><th>PTS</th><th>PIM</th></tr>
</thead>
<tbody>
<tr><td>Walter Tkaczuk</td><td>77</td><td>26</td><td>49</td><td>75</td><td>48</td><td>13</td><td>1</td><td>5</td><td>6</td><td>14</td></tr>
<tr><td>Jean Ratelle</td><td>78</td><td>26</td><td>46</td><td>72</td><td>14</td><td>13</td><td>2</td><td>9</td><td>11</td><td>8</td></tr>
<tr><td>Rod Gilbert</td><td>78</td><td>30</td><td>31</td><td>61</td><td>65</td><td>13</td><td>4</td><td>6</td><td>10</td><td>8</td></tr>
<tr><td>Dave Balon</td><td>78</td><td>36</td><td>24</td><td>60</td><td>32</td><td>13</td><td>3</td><td>2</td><td>5</td><td>4</td></tr>
<tr><td>Bob Nevin</td><td>78</td><td>21</td><td>25</td><td>46</td><td>10</td><td>13</td><td>5</td><td>3</td><td>8</td><td>0</td></tr>
<tr><td>Pete Stemkowski</td><td>68</td><td>16</td><td>29</td><td>45</td><td>61</td><td>13</td><td>3</td><td>2</td><td>5</td><td>6</td></tr>
<tr><td>Vic Hadfield</td><td>63</td><td>22</td><td>22</td><td>44</td><td>38</td><td>13</td><td>8</td><td>5</td><td>13</td><td>46</td></tr>
<tr><td>Brad Park</td><td>68</td><td>7</td><td>37</td><td>44</td><td>114</td><td>13</td><td>0</td><td>4</td><td>4</td><td>42</td></tr>
<tr><td>Ted Irvine</td><td>76</td><td>20</td><td>18</td><td>38</td><td>137</td><td>12</td><td>1</td><td>2</td><td>3</td><td>28</td></tr>
<tr><td>Jim Neilson</td><td>77</td><td>8</td><td>24</td><td>32</td><td>69</td><td>13</td><td>0</td><td>3</td><td>3</td><td>30</td></tr>
<tr><td>Bill Fairbairn</td><td>56</td><td>7</td><td>23</td><td>30</td><td>32</td><td>4</td><td>0</td><td>0</td><td>0</td><td>0</td></tr>
<tr><td>Rod Seiling</td><td>68</td><td>5</td><td>22</td><td>27</td><td>34</td><td>13</td><td>1</td><td>0</td><td>1</td><td>12</td></tr>
<tr><td>Bruce MacGregor</td><td>27</td><td>12</td><td>13</td><td>25</td><td>4</td><td>13</td><td>0</td><td>4</td><td>4</td><td>2</td></tr>
<tr><td>Tim Horton</td><td>78</td><td>2</td><td>18</td><td>20</td><td>57</td><td>13</td><td>1</td><td>4</td><td>5</td><td>14</td></tr>
<tr><td>Jack Egers</td><td>60</td><td>7</td><td>10</td><td>17</td><td>50</td><td>3</td><td>0</td><td>0</td><td>0</td><td>2</td></tr>
<tr><td>Arnie Brown</td><td>48</td><td>3</td><td>12</td><td>15</td><td>24</td><td>—</td><td>—</td><td>—</td><td>—</td><td>—</td></tr>
<tr><td>Ron Stewart</td><td>76</td><td>5</td><td>6</td><td>11</td><td>19</td><td>13</td><td>1</td><td>0</td><td>1</td><td>0</td></tr>
<tr><td>Dale Rolfe</td><td>14</td><td>0</td><td>7</td><td>7</td><td>23</td><td>13</td><td>0</td><td>1</td><td>1</td><td>14</td></tr>
<tr><td>Andre Dupont</td><td>7</td><td>1</td><td>2</td><td>3</td><td>21</td><td>—</td><td>—</td><td>—</td><td>—</td><td>—</td></tr>
<tr><td>Syl Apps</td><td>31</td><td>1</td><td>2</td><td>3</td><td>11</td><td>—</td><td>—</td><td>—</td><td>—</td><td>—</td></tr>
<tr><td>Glen Sather</td><td>31</td><td>2</td><td>0</td><td>2</td><td>52</td><td>13</td><td>0</td><td>1</td><td>1</td><td>18</td></tr>
<tr><td>Mike Robitaille</td><td>11</td><td>1</td><td>1</td><td>2</td><td>7</td><td>—</td><td>—</td><td>—</td><td>—</td><td>—</td></tr>
<tr><td>Larry Brown</td><td>31</td><td>1</td><td>1</td><td>2</td><td>16</td><td>11</td><td>0</td><td>1</td><td>1</td><td>0</td></tr>
<tr><td>Jim Krulicki</td><td>27</td><td>0</td><td>2</td><td>2</td><td>6</td><td>—</td><td>—</td><td>—</td><td>—</td><td>—</td></tr>
<tr><td>Ab DeMarco</td><td>2</td><td>0</td><td>1</td><td>1</td><td>0</td><td>—</td><td>—</td><td>—</td><td>—</td><td>—</td></tr>
<tr><td>Don Luce</td><td>9</td><td>0</td><td>1</td><td>1</td><td>0</td><td>—</td><td>—</td><td>—</td><td>—</td><td>—</td></tr>
<tr><td>Don Blackburn</td><td>1</td><td>0</td><td>0</td><td>0</td><td>0</td><td>—</td><td>—</td><td>—</td><td>—</td><td>—</td></tr>
</tbody>
</table>

<table>
<thead>
<tr><th>1971-72</th><th>GP</th><th>G</th><th>A</th><th>PTS</th><th>PIM</th><th colspan="5">Playoffs</th></tr>
<tr><th></th><th></th><th></th><th></th><th></th><th></th><th>GP</th><th>G</th><th>A</th><th>PTS</th><th>PIM</th></tr>
</thead>
<tbody>
<tr><td>Jean Ratelle</td><td>63</td><td>46</td><td>63</td><td>109</td><td>4</td><td>6</td><td>0</td><td>1</td><td>1</td><td>0</td></tr>
<tr><td>Vic Hadfield</td><td>78</td><td>50</td><td>56</td><td>106</td><td>142</td><td>16</td><td>7</td><td>9</td><td>16</td><td>22</td></tr>
<tr><td>Rod Gilbert</td><td>73</td><td>43</td><td>54</td><td>97</td><td>64</td><td>16</td><td>7</td><td>8</td><td>15</td><td>11</td></tr>
<tr><td>Brad Park</td><td>75</td><td>24</td><td>49</td><td>73</td><td>130</td><td>16</td><td>4</td><td>7</td><td>11</td><td>21</td></tr>
<tr><td>Walter Tkaczuk</td><td>76</td><td>24</td><td>42</td><td>66</td><td>65</td><td>16</td><td>4</td><td>6</td><td>10</td><td>35</td></tr>
<tr><td>Bill Fairbairn</td><td>78</td><td>22</td><td>37</td><td>59</td><td>53</td><td>16</td><td>5</td><td>7</td><td>12</td><td>11</td></tr>
<tr><td>Bobby Rousseau</td><td>78</td><td>21</td><td>36</td><td>57</td><td>12</td><td>16</td><td>6</td><td>11</td><td>17</td><td>7</td></tr>
<tr><td>Rod Seiling</td><td>78</td><td>5</td><td>36</td><td>41</td><td>62</td><td>16</td><td>1</td><td>4</td><td>5</td><td>10</td></tr>
<tr><td>Bruce MacGregor</td><td>75</td><td>19</td><td>21</td><td>40</td><td>22</td><td>16</td><td>2</td><td>6</td><td>8</td><td>4</td></tr>
<tr><td>Jim Neilson</td><td>78</td><td>7</td><td>30</td><td>37</td><td>56</td><td>10</td><td>0</td><td>3</td><td>3</td><td>8</td></tr>
<tr><td>Ted Irvine</td><td>78</td><td>15</td><td>21</td><td>36</td><td>66</td><td>16</td><td>4</td><td>5</td><td>9</td><td>19</td></tr>
<tr><td>Pete Stemkowski</td><td>59</td><td>11</td><td>17</td><td>28</td><td>53</td><td>16</td><td>4</td><td>8</td><td>12</td><td>16</td></tr>
<tr><td>Gene Carr</td><td>59</td><td>8</td><td>8</td><td>16</td><td>25</td><td>16</td><td>1</td><td>3</td><td>4</td><td>21</td></tr>
<tr><td>Dale Rolfe</td><td>68</td><td>2</td><td>14</td><td>16</td><td>67</td><td>16</td><td>4</td><td>3</td><td>7</td><td>16</td></tr>
<tr><td>Glen Sather</td><td>75</td><td>5</td><td>9</td><td>14</td><td>77</td><td>16</td><td>0</td><td>1</td><td>1</td><td>22</td></tr>
<tr><td>Ab DeMarco</td><td>48</td><td>4</td><td>7</td><td>11</td><td>4</td><td>4</td><td>0</td><td>1</td><td>1</td><td>0</td></tr>
<tr><td>Gary Doak</td><td>49</td><td>1</td><td>11</td><td>11</td><td>12</td><td>12</td><td>0</td><td>0</td><td>0</td><td>46</td></tr>
<tr><td>Dave Balon</td><td>16</td><td>4</td><td>5</td><td>9</td><td>2</td><td>—</td><td>—</td><td>—</td><td>—</td><td>—</td></tr>
</tbody>
</table>

Year-By-Year Scoring
1971-72—1974-75

1971-72 (cont'd)	GP	G	A	PTS	PIM	Playoffs GP	G	A	PTS	PIM
Pierre Jarry	34	3	3	6	20	–	–	–	–	–
Phil Goyette	8	1	4	5	0	13	1	3	4	2
Jack Egers	17	2	1	3	14	–	–	–	–	–
Ron Stewart	13	0	2	2	2	8	2	1	3	0
Norm Gratton	3	0	1	1	0	–	–	–	–	–
Jim Dorey	1	0	0	0	0	1	0	0	0	0
Mike McMahon	1	0	0	0	0	–	–	–	–	–
Tom Williams	3	0	0	0	0	–	–	–	–	–
Jim Lorentz	7	0	0	0	0	–	–	–	–	–
Steve Andrascik						1	0	0	0	2

1972-73	GP	G	A	PTS	PIM	Playoffs GP	G	A	PTS	PIM
Jean Ratelle	78	41	53	94	12	10	2	7	9	0
Rod Gilbert	76	25	59	84	25	10	5	1	6	2
Walt Tkaczuk	76	27	39	66	59	10	7	2	9	8
Bill Fairbairn	78	30	33	63	23	10	1	8	9	2
Vic Hadfield	63	28	34	62	60	9	2	2	4	11
Pete Stemkowski	78	22	37	59	71	10	4	2	6	6
Steve Vickers	61	30	23	53	37	10	5	4	9	4
Brad Park	52	10	43	53	51	10	2	5	7	8
Bobby Rousseau	78	8	37	45	14	10	2	4	6	2
Rod Seiling	72	9	33	42	36	–	–	–	–	–
Dale Rolfe	72	7	25	32	74	9	0	5	5	4
Bruce MacGregor	52	14	12	26	12	10	2	2	4	2
Glen Sather	77	11	15	26	64	9	0	0	0	7
Ted Irvine	53	8	12	20	54	10	1	3	4	20
Jim Neilson	52	4	16	20	35	10	0	4	4	2
Gene Carr	50	9	10	19	50	1	0	1	1	0
Ab DeMarco	51	3	13	16	15	–	–	–	–	–
Ron Harris	45	3	10	13	17	10	0	3	3	2
Mike Murphy	15	4	4	8	5	10	0	0	0	0
Randy Legge	12	0	2	2	2	–	–	–	–	–
Bill Heindl	4	1	0	1	0	–	–	–	–	–
Jerry Butler	8	1	0	1	4	–	–	–	–	–
Larry Sacharuk	8	1	0	1	0	–	–	–	–	–
Sheldon Kannegeisser	3	0	1	1	0	1	0	0	0	2
Tom Williams	8	0	1	1	0	–	–	–	–	–
Ron Stewart	11	0	1	1	0	–	–	–	–	–
Curt Bennett	16	0	1	1	11	–	–	–	–	–
Bert Marshall	8	0	0	0	14	–	–	–	–	–

1973-74	GP	G	A	PTS	PIM	Playoffs GP	G	A	PTS	PIM
Brad Park	78	25	57	82	148	13	4	8	12	38
Rod Gilbert	75	36	41	77	20	13	3	5	8	4
Pete Stemkowski	78	25	45	70	74	13	6	6	12	35
Jean Ratelle	68	28	39	67	16	13	2	4	6	0
Walt Tkaczuk	71	21	42	63	58	13	0	5	5	22
Bill Fairbairn	78	18	44	62	12	13	3	5	8	6
Steve Vickers	75	34	24	58	18	11	4	4	8	17
Vic Hadfield	77	27	28	55	75	6	1	0	1	0
Bobby Rousseau	72	10	41	51	4	12	1	8	9	4
Ted Irvine	75	26	20	46	105	13	3	5	8	16
Bruce MacGregor	66	17	27	44	6	13	6	2	8	2
Rod Seiling	68	7	23	30	32	13	0	2	2	19
Gilles Marotte	46	2	17	19	28	12	0	1	1	6
Jerry Butler	26	6	10	16	24	12	0	2	2	25
Dale Rolfe	48	3	12	15	56	13	1	8	9	23
Ron Harris	63	2	12	14	25	11	3	0	3	14
Jim Neilson	72	4	7	11	38	12	0	1	1	4
Larry Sacharuk	23	2	4	6	4	–	–	–	–	–
Gene Carr	29	1	5	6	15	–	–	–	–	–
Sheldon Kannegeisser	12	1	3	4	6	–	–	–	–	–
Jack Egers	28	1	3	4	6	8	1	0	1	4
Mike Murphy	16	2	1	3	0	–	–	–	–	–
Tom Williams	14	1	2	3	4	–	–	–	–	–
Bert Wilson	5	1	1	2	2	–	–	–	–	–
Glen Sather	2	0	0	0	2	–	–	–	–	–
Real Lemieux	7	0	0	0	0	–	–	–	–	–

1974-75	GP	G	A	PTS	PIM	Playoffs GP	G	A	PTS	PIM
Rod Gilbert	76	36	61	97	22	3	1	3	4	2
Jean Ratelle	79	36	55	91	26	3	1	5	6	2
Steve Vickers	80	41	48	89	64	3	2	4	6	6
Bill Fairbairn	80	24	37	61	10	3	4	0	4	13
Pete Stemkowski	77	24	35	59	63	3	1	0	1	10
Brad Park	65	13	44	57	104	3	1	4	5	2
Derek Sanderson	75	25	25	50	106	3	0	0	0	0
Ron Greschner	70	8	37	45	93	3	0	1	1	2
Greg Polis	76	26	15	41	55	3	0	0	0	6

Year-By-Year Scoring
1974-75—1977-78

1974-75 (cont'd)

	GP	G	A	PTS	PIM	Playoffs GP	G	A	PTS	PIM
Rick Middleton	47	22	18	40	19	3	0	0	0	2
Walt Tkaczuk	62	11	25	36	34	3	1	2	3	5
Gilles Marotte	77	4	32	36	69	3	0	1	1	4
Ted Irvine	79	17	17	34	66	3	0	1	1	11
Jerry Butler	78	17	16	33	102	3	1	0	1	16
Nick Beverley	54	3	15	18	19	3	0	1	1	0
John Bednarski	35	1	10	11	37	1	0	0	0	17
Dale Rolfe	42	1	8	9	30	–	–	–	–	–
Ron Harris	34	1	7	8	22	3	1	0	1	9
Bert Wilson	61	5	1	6	66	–	–	–	–	–
Bobby Rousseau	8	2	2	4	0	–	–	–	–	–
Bob MacMillan	22	1	2	3	4	–	–	–	–	–
Dave Maloney	4	0	2	2	0	–	–	–	–	–
Joe Zanussi	8	0	2	2	4	–	–	–	–	–
Jerry Holland	1	1	0	1	0	–	–	–	–	–
Rod Seiling	4	0	1	1	0	–	–	–	–	–
Hartland Monahan	6	0	1	1	4	–	–	–	–	–

1975-76

	GP	G	A	PTS	PIM
Rod Gilbert	70	36	50	86	32
Steve Vickers	80	30	53	83	40
Phil Esposito	62	29	38	67	28
Rick Middleton	77	24	26	50	14
Carol Vadnais	64	20	30	50	104
Wayne Dillon	79	21	24	45	10
Pete Stemkowski	75	13	28	41	49
Gerg Polis	79	15	21	36	77
Pat Hickey	70	14	22	36	36
Walt Tkaczuk	78	8	28	36	56
Bill Fairbairn	80	13	15	28	8
Ron Greschner	77	6	21	27	93
Giles Marotte	57	4	17	21	34
Jean Ratelle	13	5	10	15	2

*Did not qualify for playoffs

1975-76 (cont'd)

	GP	G	A	PTS	PIM
Larry Sacharuk	42	6	7	13	14
Jerry Holland	36	7	4	11	6
John Bednarski	59	1	8	9	77
Nick Beverley	63	1	8	9	46
Bill Collins	50	4	4	8	38
Brad Park	6	2	4	6	23
Dave Maloney	21	1	3	4	66
Doug Jarrett	45	0	4	4	19
Eddie Johnstone	10	2	1	3	4
Ron Harris	3	0	1	1	0
Greg Holst	2	0	0	0	0
Dale Lewis	8	0	0	0	0
Derek Sanderson	8	0	0	0	4

1976-77

	GP	G	A	PTS	PIM
Phil Esposito	80	34	46	80	52
Rod Gilbert	77	27	48	75	50
Ken Hodge	78	21	41	62	43
Don Murdoch	59	32	24	56	47
Steve Vickers	75	22	31	53	26
Walt Tkaczuk	80	12	38	50	38
Carol Vadnais	74	11	37	48	131
Ron Greschner	80	11	36	47	89
Wayne Dillon	78	17	29	46	33
Mike McEwen	80	14	29	43	38
Pat Hickey	80	23	17	40	35
Greg Polis	77	16	23	39	44
Bill Goldsworthy	61	10	12	22	43

*Did not qualify for playoffs

1976-77 (cont'd)

	GP	G	A	PTS	PIM
Dave Maloney	66	3	18	21	100
Dave Farrish	80	2	17	19	102
Dan Newman	41	9	8	17	37
Pete Stemkowski	61	2	13	15	8
Nick Fotiu	70	4	8	12	174
Bill Fairbairn	9	1	2	3	0
Mark Heaslip	19	1	0	1	31
Larry Huras	1	0	0	0	0
Larry Sacharuk	2	0	0	0	0
John Bednarski	5	0	0	0	0
Greg Holst	5	0	0	0	0
Nick Beverley	9	0	0	0	2
Doug Jarrett	9	0	0	0	4

1977-78

	GP	G	A	PTS	PIM	Playoffs GP	G	A	PTS	PIM
Phil Esposito	79	38	43	81	53	3	0	1	1	5
Pat Hickey	80	40	33	73	47	3	2	0	2	0
Ron Greschner	78	24	48	72	100	3	0	0	0	2
Walt Tkaczuk	80	26	40	66	30	3	0	2	2	0
Steve Vickers	79	19	44	63	30	3	2	1	3	0
Don Murdoch	66	27	28	55	41	3	1	3	4	4
Carol Vadnais	80	6	40	46	115	3	0	2	2	16
Ron Duguay	71	20	20	40	43	3	1	1	2	2
Lucien DeBlois	71	22	8	30	27	3	0	0	0	2
Ed Johnstone	53	13	13	26	44	3	0	0	0	2
Greg Polis	37	7	16	23	12	3	1	2	3	5
Dave Maloney	56	2	19	21	63	3	0	0	0	11
Dave Farrish	80	2	17	19	102	3	0	0	0	0
Mike McEwen	57	5	13	18	52	3	1	0	1	16
Wayne Dillon	59	5	13	18	52	3	0	1	1	0
Dan Newman	59	5	13	18	22	3	0	0	0	4
Mark Heaslip	29	5	10	15	31	3	0	0	0	0
Rod Gilbert	19	2	7	9	6	–	–	–	–	–
Nick Fotiu	59	2	7	9	105	3	0	0	0	5
Don Awrey	78	2	8	8	38	3	0	0	0	6
Ken Hodge	18	2	4	6	8	–	–	–	–	–
Dallas Smith	29	1	4	5	23	1	0	1	1	0
Jerry Byers	7	2	1	3	0	–	–	–	–	–
Mario Marois	8	1	1	2	15	1	0	0	0	5
Bill Goldsworthy	7	0	1	1	12	–	–	–	–	–
Greg Hickey	1	0	0	0	0	–	–	–	–	–
Mike Keating	1	0	0	0	0	–	–	–	–	–
Bud Stefanski	1	0	0	0	0	–	–	–	–	–
Greg Holst	4	0	0	0	0	–	–	–	–	–
Benoit Gosselin	7	0	0	0	33	–	–	–	–	–

Year-By-Year Scoring
1978-79—1980-81

1978-79	GP	G	A	PTS	PIM		Playoffs GP	G	A	PTS	PIM
Phil Esposito	80	42	36	78	37		18	8	12	20	20
Anders Hedberg	80	33	45	78	33		18	4	5	9	12
Pat Hickey	80	34	41	75	56		18	1	7	8	6
Ulf Nilsson	59	27	39	66	21		2	0	0	0	2
Ron Duguay	79	27	36	63	35		18	5	4	9	11
Mike McEwen	80	20	38	58	35		18	2	11	13	8
Ron Greschner	60	17	36	53	6		18	7	5	12	16
Steve Vickers	66	13	34	47	24		18	5	3	8	13
Carol Vadnais	77	8	37	45	86		18	2	9	11	13
Walt Tkaczuk	77	15	27	42	38		18	4	7	11	10
Don Murdoch	40	15	22	37	6		18	7	5	12	12
Pierre Plante	70	6	25	31	37		18	0	6	6	20
Mario Marois	71	5	26	31	153		18	0	6	6	29
Dean Talafous	68	13	16	29	29		–	–	–	–	–
Lucien DeBlois	62	11	17	28	26		9	2	0	2	4
Dave Maloney	76	11	17	28	151		17	3	4	7	45
Don Maloney	28	9	17	26	39		18	7	13	20	19
David Farrish	71	1	19	20	61		7	0	2	2	14
Ed Johnstone	30	5	3	8	27		17	5	0	5	10
Nick Fotiu	71	3	5	8	190		4	0	0	0	6
Dan Clark	4	0	1	1	6		–	–	–	–	–
Mike Korney	18	0	1	1	18		–	–	–	–	–
Tim Bothwell	1	0	0	0	2		–	–	–	–	–
Mike McDougal	1	0	0	0	0		–	–	–	–	–
Dean Turner	1	0	0	0	0		–	–	–	–	–
Frank Beaton	2	0	0	0	0		–	–	–	–	–
Andre Dore	2	0	0	0	0		–	–	–	–	–
Bobby Sheehan	–	–	–	–	–		15	4	3	7	8

1979-80	GP	G	A	PTS	PIM		Playoffs GP	G	A	PTS	PIM
Phil Esposito	80	34	44	78	73		9	3	3	6	8
Don Maloney	79	25	48	73	97		9	0	4	4	10
Anders Hedberg	80	32	39	71	21		9	3	2	5	7
Steve Vickers	75	29	33	62	38		9	2	2	4	4
Barry Beck	61	14	45	59	98		9	1	4	5	6
Ron Greschner	76	21	37	58	103		9	0	6	6	10
Ulf Nilsson	50	14	44	58	20		9	3	2	5	7
Ron Duguay	73	28	22	50	37		9	5	2	7	11
Walt Tkaczuk	76	12	25	37	36		7	0	1	1	2
Dave Maloney	77	12	25	37	186		8	1	2	3	8
Eddie Johnstone	78	14	21	35	60		9	0	1	1	25
Mario Marois	79	8	23	31	142		9	0	2	2	8
Dean Talafous	55	10	20	30	26		5	1	2	3	9
Carol Vadnais	66	3	20	23	118		9	1	2	3	6
Warren Miller	55	7	6	13	17		6	1	0	1	0
Claude Larose	25	4	7	11	2		–	–	–	–	–
Doug Sulliman	31	4	7	11	2		–	–	–	–	–
Tim Bothwell	45	4	6	10	20		9	0	0	0	8
Jocelyn Guevremont	20	2	5	7	6		–	–	–	–	–
Pat Conacher	17	0	5	5	4		3	0	1	1	2
Cam Conner	12	0	3	3	37		2	0	0	0	2
Ray Markham	14	1	1	2	21		7	1	0	1	24
Frank Beaton	23	1	1	2	43		–	–	–	–	–
Ed Hospodar	20	0	1	1	76		7	0	1	1	42
Andre Dore	2	0	0	0	0		–	–	–	–	–
Dave Silk	2	0	0	0	0		–	–	–	–	–
Jim Mayer	4	0	0	0	0		–	–	–	–	–
Bill Lochead	7	0	0	0	4		–	–	–	–	–

1980-81	GP	G	A	PTS	PIM		Playoffs GP	G	A	PTS	PIM
Anders Hedberg	80	30	40	70	52		14	8	8	16	6
Ed Johnstone	80	30	38	68	100		8	2	2	4	4
Ron Greschner	74	27	41	68	112		14	4	8	12	17
Mike Allison	75	26	38	64	83		14	3	1	4	20
Steve Vickers	73	19	39	58	40		12	4	7	11	14
Don Maloney	61	29	23	52	99		13	1	6	7	13
Dave Maloney	79	11	36	47	132		2	0	2	2	9
Ulf Nilsson	51	14	25	39	42		14	8	8	16	23
Ron Duguay	50	17	21	38	83		14	8	9	17	16
Barry Beck	75	11	23	34	231		14	5	8	13	32
Dean Talafous	50	13	17	30	28		14	3	5	8	2
Tom Laidlaw	80	6	23	29	100		14	1	4	5	18
Walt Tkaczuk	43	6	22	28	28		1	0	0	0	0
Dave Silk	59	14	12	26	58		–	–	–	–	–
Lance Nethery	33	11	12	23	12		14	5	3	8	9
Carol Vadnais	74	3	20	23	91		14	1	3	4	26
Jere Gillis	35	10	10	20	4		14	2	5	7	9
Ed Hospodar	61	5	14	19	214		12	2	0	2	93
Chris Kotsopoulos	54	4	12	16	153		14	0	3	3	63
Nick Fotiu	27	5	6	11	91		2	0	0	0	4
Peter Wallin	12	1	5	6	2		14	2	6	8	6
Doug Sulliman	32	4	1	5	32		3	1	0	1	0
Dan McCarthy	5	4	0	4	4		–	–	–	–	–

Year-By-Year Scoring
1980-81—1983-84

	GP	G	A	PTS	PIM	Playoffs GP	G	A	PTS	PIM
1980-81 (cont'd)										
Gary Burns	11	2	2	4	18	1	0	0	0	2
Cam Connor	15	1	3	4	44	–	–	–	–	–
Andre Dore	15	1	3	4	15	–	–	–	–	–
Mario Marois	8	1	2	3	46	–	–	–	–	–
Jeff Bandura	2	0	1	1	0	–	–	–	–	–
Tim Bothwell	3	0	1	1	0	–	–	–	–	–
Mike McDougal	2	0	0	0	0	–	–	–	–	–
John Hughes	–	–	–	–	–	3	0	1	1	6

	GP	G	A	PTS	PIM	Playoffs GP	G	A	PTS	PIM
1981-82										
Mike Rogers	80	38	65	103	43	9	1	6	7	2
Ron Duguay	72	40	36	76	82	10	5	1	6	31
Mark Pavelich	79	33	43	76	67	6	1	5	6	0
Ed Johnstone	68	30	28	58	57	10	2	6	8	25
Don Maloney	54	22	36	58	73	10	5	5	10	10
Reijo Ruotsalainen	78	18	38	56	27	10	4	5	9	2
Dave Maloney	64	13	36	49	105	10	1	4	5	6
Barry Beck	60	9	29	38	108	10	1	5	6	14
Dave Silk	64	15	20	35	39	9	2	4	6	4
Robbie Ftorek	30	8	25	33	24	10	7	4	11	11
Mikko Leinonen	53	11	19	30	18	7	1	6	7	20
Pat Hickey	53	15	14	29	32	–	–	–	–	–
Mike Allison	48	7	15	22	74	10	1	3	4	18
Tom Laidlaw	79	3	18	21	104	10	0	3	3	14
Andre Dore	56	4	16	20	64	10	1	1	2	16
Nick Fotiu	70	8	10	18	151	10	0	2	2	6
Ron Greschner	29	5	11	16	16	–	–	–	–	–
Rob McClanahan	22	5	9	14	10	10	2	5	7	2
Dean Talafous	29	6	7	13	8	–	–	–	–	–
Jere Gillis	26	3	9	12	16	–	–	–	–	–
Ed Hospodar	41	3	8	11	152	–	–	–	–	–
Peter Wallin	40	2	9	11	12	–	–	–	–	–
Tom Younghans	47	3	5	8	17	2	0	0	0	0
Tim Bothwell	13	0	3	3	10	–	–	–	–	–
Mark Morrison	9	1	1	2	0	–	–	–	–	–
Mike Backman	3	0	2	2	4	1	0	0	0	2
Anders Hedberg	4	0	1	1	0	–	–	–	–	–
Lance Nethery	5	0	0	0	0	–	–	–	–	–
Gary Burns	–	–	–	–	–	4	0	0	0	0
Cam Connor	–	–	–	–	–	10	4	0	4	4

	GP	G	A	PTS	PIM	Playoffs GP	G	A	PTS	PIM
1982-83										
Mike Rogers	71	29	47	76	28	1	0	0	0	0
Mark Pavelich	78	37	38	75	52	9	4	5	9	12
Don Maloney	78	29	40	69	88	5	0	1	1	0
Reijo Ruotsalainen	77	16	53	69	22	9	4	2	6	6
Anders Hedberg	78	25	34	59	12	9	4	8	12	4
Mikko Leinonen	78	17	34	51	23	7	1	3	4	4
Dave Maloney	78	8	42	50	132	7	1	6	7	10
Rob McClanahan	78	22	26	48	46	9	2	5	7	12
Ron Duguay	72	19	25	44	58	9	2	2	4	28
Ed Johnstone	52	15	21	36	27	9	4	1	5	19
Barry Beck	66	12	22	34	112	9	2	4	6	8
Robbie Ftorek	61	12	19	31	41	4	1	0	1	0
Kent-Erik Andersson	71	8	20	28	14	9	0	0	0	0
Nick Fotiu	72	8	13	21	90	5	0	1	1	6
Vaclav Nedomansky	35	12	8	20	0	–	–	–	–	–
Mike Allison	39	11	9	20	37	8	0	5	5	10
Bill Baker	70	4	14	18	64	2	0	0	0	0
Chris Kontos	44	8	7	15	33	–	–	–	–	–
Scot Kleinendorst	30	2	9	11	8	6	0	2	2	2
Tom Laidlaw	80	0	10	10	75	9	1	1	2	10
Ron Greschner	10	3	5	8	0	8	2	2	4	12
Ulf Nilsson	10	2	4	6	2	–	–	–	–	–
Rick Chartraw	26	2	2	4	37	9	0	2	2	6
Mike Backman	7	1	3	4	6	9	2	2	4	0
Dave Silk	16	1	1	2	15	–	–	–	–	–
Pat Conacher	5	0	1	1	4	1	0	0	0	0
Cam Connor	1	0	0	0	0	–	–	–	–	–
Graeme Nicolson	10	0	0	0	9	–	–	–	–	–
George McPhee	–	–	–	–	–	9	3	3	6	6

	GP	G	A	PTS	PIM	Playoffs GP	G	A	PTS	PIM
1983-84										
Mark Pavelich	77	29	53	82	96	5	2	4	6	0
Pierre Larouche	77	48	33	81	22	5	3	1	4	2
Anders Hedberg	79	32	35	67	16	5	1	0	1	0
Don Maloney	79	24	42	66	62	5	1	4	5	0
Mike Rogers	78	23	38	61	45	1	0	0	0	0
Reijo Ruotsalainen	74	20	39	59	26	5	1	1	2	2
Ron Greschner	77	12	44	56	117	2	1	0	1	2
Mark Osborne	73	23	28	51	88	5	0	1	1	7

Year-By-Year Scoring
1983-84—1985-86

1983-84 (cont'd)	GP	G	A	PTS	PIM	Playoffs GP	G	A	PTS	PIM
Peter Sundstrom	77	22	22	44	24	5	1	3	4	0
Barry Beck	72	9	27	36	134	4	1	0	1	6
Dave Maloney	68	7	26	33	168	1	0	0	0	2
Jan Erixon	75	5	25	30	16	5	2	0	2	4
Mikko Leinonen	28	3	23	26	28	5	0	2	2	4
Willie Huber	42	9	14	23	60	4	1	1	2	9
Mike Allison	45	8	12	20	64	5	0	1	1	6
Kent-Erik Andersson	63	5	15	20	8	5	0	1	1	0
Tom Laidlaw	79	3	15	18	62	5	0	0	0	8
Rob McClanahan	41	6	8	14	21	–	–	–	–	–
Nick Fotiu	40	7	6	13	115	–	–	–	–	–
Mike Blaisdell	36	5	6	11	31	–	–	–	–	–
James Patrick	12	1	7	8	2	5	0	3	3	2
Blaine Stoughton	14	5	2	7	4	–	–	–	–	–
Steve Richmond	26	2	5	7	110	4	0	0	0	12
Rob Ftorek	31	3	2	5	22	–	–	–	–	–
Bob Brooke	9	1	2	3	4	5	0	0	0	7
Larry Patey	9	1	2	3	4	4	0	1	1	6
George McPhee	9	1	1	2	11	–	–	–	–	–
Scot Kleinendorst	23	0	2	2	35	–	–	–	–	–
Mike Backman	8	0	1	1	8	–	–	–	–	–
Chris Kontos	46	0	1	1	38	–	–	–	–	–
Mark Morrison	1	0	0	0	0	–	–	–	–	–
Rick Chartraw	4	0	0	0	4	–	–	–	–	–
Dave Barr	6	0	0	0	2	–	–	–	–	–

1984-85	GP	G	A	PTS	PIM	Playoffs GP	G	A	PTS	PIM
Reijo Ruotsalainen	80	28	45	73	32	3	2	0	2	6
Mike Rogers	78	26	38	64	24	3	0	4	4	4
Pierre Larouche	65	24	36	60	8	–	–	–	–	–
Tomas Sandstrom	74	29	29	58	51	3	0	2	2	0
Anders Hedberg	64	20	31	51	10	3	2	1	3	2
Ron Greschner	48	16	29	45	42	2	0	3	3	12
Mark Pavelich	48	14	31	45	29	3	0	3	3	2
Peter Sundstrom	76	18	25	43	34	3	0	0	0	2
James Patrick	75	8	28	36	71	3	0	0	0	4
Steve Patrick	43	11	18	29	63	1	0	0	0	0
Jan Erixon	66	7	22	29	33	2	0	0	0	2
George McPhee	49	12	15	27	139	3	1	0	1	7
Don Maloney	37	11	16	27	32	3	4	0	4	2
Barry Beck	56	7	19	26	75	3	0	1	1	11
Mike Allison	31	9	15	24	17	–	–	–	–	–
Grant Ledyard	42	8	12	20	53	3	0	2	2	4
Robbie Ftorek	48	9	10	19	35	–	–	–	–	–
Bob Brooke	72	7	9	16	79	3	0	0	0	8
Willie Huber	49	3	11	14	55	2	1	0	1	2
Dave Gagner	38	6	6	12	16	–	–	–	–	–
Chris Kontos	28	4	8	12	24	–	–	–	–	–
Tom Laidlaw	61	1	11	12	52	3	0	2	2	4
Nick Fotiu	46	4	7	11	54	–	–	–	–	–
Mark Osborne	23	4	4	8	33	3	0	0	0	4
Jim Wiemer	22	4	3	7	30	1	0	0	0	0
Andre Dore	25	0	7	7	35	–	–	–	–	–
Randy Heath	12	2	3	5	15	–	–	–	–	–
Steve Richmond	34	0	5	5	90	–	–	–	–	–
Dave Maloney	16	2	1	3	10	–	–	–	–	–
Kelly Miller	5	0	2	2	2	3	0	0	0	2
Mike Blaisdell	12	1	0	1	11	–	–	–	–	–
Larry Patey	7	0	1	1	12	1	0	0	0	0
Simo Saarinen	8	0	0	0	8	–	–	–	–	–

1985-86	GP	G	A	PTS	PIM	Playoffs GP	G	A	PTS	PIM
Mike Ridley	80	22	43	65	69	16	6	8	14	26
Reijo Ruotsalainen	80	17	42	59	47	16	0	8	8	6
Tomas Sandstrom	73	25	29	54	109	16	4	6	10	20
Ron Greschner	78	20	28	48	104	5	3	1	4	11
Bob Brooke	79	24	20	44	111	16	6	9	15	28
James Patrick	75	14	29	43	88	16	1	5	6	34
Mark Pavelich	59	20	20	40	82	–	–	–	–	–
Mark Osborne	62	16	24	40	80	15	2	3	5	26
Raimo Helminen	66	10	30	40	10	2	0	0	0	0
Kelly Miller	74	13	20	33	52	16	3	4	7	4
Brian MacLellan	51	11	21	32	47	16	2	4	6	15
Don Maloney	68	11	17	28	56	16	2	1	3	31
Pierre Larouche	28	20	7	27	4	16	8	9	17	2
Peter Sundstrom	53	8	15	23	12	1	0	0	0	2
Jan Erixon	31	2	17	19	4	12	0	1	1	4
Tom Laidlaw	68	6	12	18	103	7	0	2	2	12
Willie Huber	70	7	8	15	85	16	3	2	5	16
Mike Allison	28	2	13	15	22	7	0	2	2	38
Barry Beck	25	4	8	12	7	–	–	–	–	–
Dave Gagner	32	4	6	10	19	4	1	2	3	2
Larry Melnyk	46	1	8	9	65	16	1	2	3	46

Year-By-Year Scoring
1985-86—1988-89

1985-86 (cont'd)	GP	G	A	PTS	PIM	GP	G	A	PTS	PIM
						Playoffs				
George McPhee	30	4	4	8	63	11	0	0	0	32
Wilf Paiement	8	1	6	7	13	16	5	5	10	45
Rob Whistle	32	4	2	6	10	3	0	0	0	2
Chris Jensen	9	1	3	4	0	–	–	–	–	–
Jim Wiemer	7	3	0	3	2	8	1	0	1	6
Bob Crawford	11	1	2	3	10	7	0	1	1	8
Randy Heath	1	0	1	1	0	–	–	–	–	–
Kjell Samuelsson	9	0	0	0	10	9	0	1	1	8
Tony Feltrin	10	0	0	0	21	–	–	–	–	–

1986-87	GP	G	A	PTS	PIM	GP	G	A	PTS	PIM
						Playoffs				
Walt Poddubny	75	40	47	87	49	6	0	0	0	8
Tomas Sandstrom	64	40	34	74	60	6	1	2	3	20
Kelly Kisio	70	24	40	64	73	4	0	1	1	2
Pierre Larouche	73	28	35	63	12	6	3	2	5	4
Don Maloney	72	19	38	57	117	6	2	1	3	6
James Patrick	78	10	45	55	62	6	1	2	3	2
Tony McKegney	64	29	17	46	56	–	–	–	–	–
Ron Greschner	61	6	34	40	62	6	0	5	5	0
Willie Huber	66	8	22	30	70	6	0	2	2	6
Jan Erixon	68	8	18	26	24	6	1	0	1	0
Ron Duguay	34	9	12	21	9	6	2	0	2	4
Curt Giles	61	2	17	19	50	5	0	0	0	6
Larry Melnyk	73	3	12	15	182	6	0	0	0	4
Terry Carkner	52	2	13	15	120	1	0	0	0	0
Chris Jensen	37	6	7	13	21	–	–	–	–	–
Lucien DeBlois	40	3	8	11	27	2	0	0	0	2
Marcel Dionne	14	4	6	10	6	6	1	1	2	2
George McPhee	21	4	4	8	34	6	1	0	1	28
Jeff Jackson	9	5	1	6	15	6	1	1	2	16
Dave Gagner	10	1	4	5	12	–	–	–	–	–
Jay Caufield	13	2	1	3	45	3	0	0	0	12
Mike Donnelly	5	1	1	2	0	–	–	–	–	–
Pat Price	13	0	2	2	37	–	–	–	–	–
Gord Walker	1	1	0	1	2	–	–	–	–	–
Don Jackson	22	1	0	1	91	–	–	–	–	–
Norm Maciver	3	0	1	1	0	–	–	–	–	–
Jim Leavins	4	0	1	1	4	–	–	–	–	–
Mike Siltala	1	0	0	0	0	–	–	–	–	–
Stu Kulak	3	0	0	0	0	3	0	0	0	2
Ron Talakoski	3	0	0	0	24	–	–	–	–	–
Paul Fenton	8	0	0	0	2	–	–	–	–	–

1987-88	GP	G	A	PTS	PIM
Walt Poddubny	77	38	50	88	76
Kelly Kisio	77	23	55	78	88
Tomas Sandstrom	69	28	40	68	95
Marcel Dionne	67	31	34	65	54
James Patrick	70	17	45	62	52
Brian Mullen	74	25	29	54	42
John Ogrodnick	64	22	32	54	16
Ulf Dahlen	70	29	23	52	26
Don Maloney	66	12	21	33	60
Michel Petit	64	9	24	33	223
David Shaw	68	7	25	32	100
Lucien DeBlois	74	9	21	30	103
Jan Erixon	70	7	19	26	33
Norm Maciver	37	9	15	24	14
Paul Cyr	40	4	13	17	41
Jari Gronstrand	62	3	11	14	63
Brian Leetch	17	2	12	14	0
Pierre Larouche	10	3	9	12	13
*Did not qualify for playoffs					

1987-88 (cont'd)	GP	G	A	PTS	PIM
Ron Duguay	48	4	4	8	23
Chris Nilan	22	3	5	8	96
Ron Greschner	51	1	5	6	82
Gord Walker	18	1	4	5	17
Mike Donnelly	17	2	2	4	8
Mark Hardy	19	2	2	4	31
Dave Pichette	6	1	3	4	4
Joe Paterson	21	1	3	4	65
Bruce Bell	13	1	2	3	8
Mark Tinordi	24	1	2	3	50
Steve Nemeth	12	2	0	2	2
Jeff Brubaker	31	2	0	2	78
Simon Wheeldon	5	0	1	1	4
Ron Talakoski	6	0	1	1	12
Chris Jensen	7	0	1	1	2
Mark Janssens	1	0	0	0	0
Rudy Poeschek	1	0	0	0	2
Curt Giles	13	0	0	0	10

1988-89	GP	G	A	PTS	PIM	GP	G	A	PTS	PIM
						Playoffs				
Tomas Sandstrom	79	32	56	88	148	4	3	2	5	12
Brian Leetch	68	23	48	71	50	4	3	2	5	2
Brian Mullen	78	29	35	64	60	3	0	1	1	4
Tony Granato	78	36	27	63	140	4	1	1	2	21
Kelly Kisio	70	26	36	62	91	4	0	0	0	9
Carey Wilson	41	21	34	55	45	4	1	2	3	2
James Patrick	68	11	36	47	41	4	0	1	1	2
Guy Lafleur	67	18	27	45	12	4	1	0	1	0
Ulf Dahlen	56	24	19	43	50	4	0	0	0	0
John Ogrodnick	60	13	29	42	14	3	2	0	2	0
Lucien DeBlois	73	9	24	33	107	4	0	0	0	4
Michel Petit	69	8	25	33	154	4	0	2	2	27
Jason Lafreniere	38	8	16	24	6	3	0	0	0	17
Marcel Dionne	37	7	16	23	20	–	–	–	–	–
Brian Lawton	30	7	10	17	39	–	–	–	–	–
David Shaw	63	6	11	17	88	4	0	2	2	30
Jan Erixon	44	4	11	15	27	4	0	1	1	2
Chris Nilan	38	7	7	14	177	4	0	1	1	28

Year-By-Year Scoring
1988-89—1990-91

1988-89 (cont'd)	GP	G	A	PTS	PIM	Playoffs GP	G	A	PTS	PIM
Mark Hardy	45	2	12	14	45	4	0	1	1	31
Don Maloney	31	4	9	13	16	–	–	–	–	–
Ron Greschner	58	1	10	11	94	4	0	1	1	6
Darren Turcotte	20	7	3	10	4	1	0	0	0	0
Norm Maciver	26	0	10	10	14	–	–	–	–	–
Kevin Miller	24	3	5	8	2	–	–	–	–	–
Normand Rochefort	11	1	5	6	18	–	–	–	–	–
Lindy Ruff	13	0	5	5	31	2	0	0	0	17
Rudy Poeschek	52	0	2	2	199	–	–	–	–	–
Miloslav Horava	6	0	1	1	0	–	–	–	–	–
Simon Wheeldon	6	0	1	1	2	–	–	–	–	–
Joe Paterson	20	0	1	1	84	–	–	–	–	–
Stephane Brochu	1	0	0	0	0	–	–	–	–	–
Paul Cyr	1	0	0	0	2	–	–	–	–	–
Jim Latos	1	0	0	0	0	–	–	–	–	–
Jayson More	1	0	0	0	0	–	–	–	–	–
Mark Janssens	5	0	0	0	0	–	–	–	–	–
Jeff Bloemberg	9	0	0	0	0	1	0	0	0	0
Peter Laviolette	12	0	0	0	6	–	–	–	–	–

1989-90	GP	G	A	PTS	PIM	Playoffs GP	G	A	PTS	PIM
John Ogrodnick	80	43	31	74	44	10	6	3	9	0
Brian Mullen	76	27	41	68	42	10	2	2	4	8
Darren Turcotte	76	32	34	66	32	10	1	6	7	4
Kelly Kisio	68	22	44	66	105	10	2	8	10	8
James Patrick	73	14	43	57	50	10	3	8	11	0
Brian Leetch	72	11	45	56	26	–	–	–	–	–
Bernie Nicholls	32	12	25	37	20	10	7	5	12	16
Troy Mallette	79	13	16	29	305	10	2	2	4	81
Carey Wilson	41	9	17	26	57	10	2	1	3	0
Mike Gartner	12	11	5	16	6	10	5	3	8	12
Mark Hardy	54	0	15	15	94	3	0	1	1	2
Miloslav Horava	45	4	10	14	26	2	0	1	1	0
Kris King	68	6	7	13	286	10	0	1	1	30
Mark Janssens	80	5	8	13	161	9	2	1	3	10
Jan Erixon	58	4	9	13	8	10	1	0	1	2
Randy Moller	60	1	12	13	139	10	1	6	7	32
David Shaw	22	2	10	12	22	–	–	–	–	–
Ron Greschner	55	1	9	10	53	10	0	0	0	16
Lindy Ruff	56	3	6	9	77	8	0	3	3	12
Paul Broten	32	3	5	8	26	6	1	1	2	2
Jeff Bloemberg	28	3	3	6	25	7	0	3	3	5
David Archibald	19	2	3	5	6	–	–	–	–	–
Kevin Miller	16	0	5	5	2	–	–	–	–	–
Normand Rochefort	31	3	1	4	24	1	0	0	0	0
Chris Nilan	25	1	2	3	59	10	2	1	3	26
Ric Bennett	6	1	0	1	5	4	0	1	1	19
Corey Millen	4	0	0	0	2	–	–	–	–	–
Todd Charlesworth	7	0	0	0	6	–	–	–	–	–
Rudy Poeschek	15	0	0	0	55	–	–	–	–	–

1990-91	GP	G	A	PTS	PIM	Playoffs GP	G	A	PTS	PIM
Brian Leetch	80	16	72	88	42	6	1	3	4	0
Bernie Nicholls	71	25	48	73	96	5	4	3	7	8
Mike Gartner	79	49	20	69	53	6	1	1	2	0
Darren Turcotte	74	26	41	67	37	6	1	2	3	0
Brian Mullen	79	19	43	62	43	6	0	2	2	0
James Patrick	74	10	49	59	58	6	0	0	0	6
John Ogrodnick	79	31	23	54	10	4	0	0	0	0
Ray Sheppard	59	24	23	47	21	–	–	–	–	–
Kevin Miller	63	17	27	44	63	–	–	–	–	–
Kelly Kisio	51	15	20	35	58	–	–	–	–	–
Kris King	72	11	14	25	156	6	2	0	2	36
Jan Erixon	53	7	18	25	8	6	1	2	3	0
Randy Moller	61	4	19	23	161	6	0	2	2	11
Troy Mallette	71	12	10	22	252	5	0	0	0	18
Mark Janssens	69	9	7	16	172	6	3	0	3	6
Jody Hull	47	5	8	13	10	–	–	–	–	–
David Shaw	77	2	10	12	89	6	0	0	0	11
Paul Broten	28	4	6	10	10	5	0	0	0	2
Normand Rochefort	44	3	7	10	35	–	–	–	–	–
Miloslav Horava	29	1	6	7	12	–	–	–	–	–
Mark Hardy	70	1	5	6	89	6	0	1	1	30
Corey Millen	4	3	1	4	0	6	1	2	3	0
Steven Rice	11	1	1	2	4	2	2	1	3	6
Jeff Bloemberg	3	0	2	2	0	–	–	–	–	–
Joe Cirella	19	1	0	1	52	6	0	2	2	26
Tie Domi	28	1	0	1	185	–	–	–	–	–
Lindy Ruff	14	0	1	1	27	–	–	–	–	–
Brian McReynolds	1	0	0	0	0	–	–	–	–	–
Joey Kocur	5	0	0	0	36	6	0	2	2	21
Eric Bennett	6	0	0	0	6	–	–	–	–	–
Dennis Vial	21	0	0	0	61	–	–	–	–	–

Year-By-Year Scoring
1990-91—1992-93

1990-91 (cont'd)	GP	G	A	PTS	PIM	Playoffs GP	G	A	PTS	PIM
Tony Amonte	–	–	–	–	–	2	0	2	2	2
Doug Weight	–	–	–	–	–	1	0	0	0	0

1991-92	GP	G	A	PTS	PIM	Playoffs GP	G	A	PTS	PIM
Mark Messier	79	35	72	107	76	11	7	7	14	6
Brian Leetch	80	22	80	102	26	13	4	11	15	4
Mike Gartner	76	40	41	81	55	13	8	8	16	4
James Patrick	80	14	57	71	54	13	0	7	7	12
Tony Amonte	79	35	34	69	55	13	3	6	9	2
Adam Graves	80	26	33	59	139	10	5	3	8	22
Sergei Nemchinov	73	30	28	58	15	13	1	4	5	8
Darren Turcotte	71	30	23	53	57	8	4	0	4	6
John Ogrodnick	55	17	13	30	22	3	0	0	0	0
Doug Weight	53	8	22	30	23	7	2	2	4	0
Kris King	79	10	9	19	224	13	4	1	5	14
Per Djoos	50	1	18	19	40	–	–	–	–	–
Tim Kerr	32	7	11	18	12	8	1	0	1	0
Jan Erixon	46	8	9	17	4	13	2	3	5	2
Joe Cirella	67	3	12	15	121	13	0	4	4	23
Randy Gilhen	40	7	7	14	14	13	1	2	3	2
Joey Kocur	51	7	4	11	121	12	1	1	2	38
Jeff Beukeboom	56	1	10	11	122	13	2	3	5	47
Paul Broten	28	4	6	10	18	13	1	2	3	10
Randy Moller	32	2	7	9	78	–	–	–	–	–
Mark Hardy	52	1	8	9	65	13	0	3	3	31
Tie Domi	42	2	4	6	246	6	1	1	2	32
Corey Millen	11	1	4	5	44	–	–	–	–	–
Rob Zamuner	9	1	2	3	2	–	–	–	–	–
Normand Rochefort	26	0	2	2	31	–	–	–	–	–
Eric Bennett	3	0	1	1	2	–	–	–	–	–
Jeff Bloemberg	3	0	1	1	0	–	–	–	–	–
David Shaw	10	0	1	1	15	–	–	–	–	–
Peter Fiorentino	1	0	0	0	0	–	–	–	–	–
Bernie Nicholls	1	0	0	0	0	–	–	–	–	–
Jody Hull	3	0	0	0	2	–	–	–	–	–
Mark Janssens	4	0	0	0	5	–	–	–	–	–
Jay Wells	11	0	0	0	24	13	0	2	2	10

1992-93	GP	G	A	PTS	PIM
Mark Messier	75	25	66	91	72
Tony Amonte	83	33	43	76	49
Mike Gartner	84	45	23	68	59
Adam Graves	84	36	29	65	148
Sergei Nemchinov	81	23	31	54	34
Darren Turcotte	71	25	28	53	40
Alexei Kovalev	65	20	18	38	79
Brain Leetch	36	6	30	36	26
Sergei Zubov	49	8	23	31	4
Eddie Olczyk	46	13	16	29	26
James Patrick	60	5	21	26	61
Phil Bourque	55	6	14	20	39
Jeff Beukeboom	82	2	17	19	153
Jan Erixon	45	5	11	16	10
Peter Andersson	31	4	11	15	18
Kevin Lowe	49	3	12	15	58
Paul Broten	60	5	9	14	48
Steven King	24	7	5	12	16
Jay Wells	53	1	9	10	107
Joe Cirella	55	3	6	9	85
Joe Kocur	65	3	6	9	131
Mike Hurlbut	23	1	8	9	16
Esa Tikkanen	15	2	5	7	18
Mike Richter	38	0	5	5	2
Per Djoos	6	1	1	2	2
John McIntyre	11	1	0	1	4
Craig Duncanson	3	0	1	1	0
John Vanbiesbrouck	48	0	1	1	18
Dave Marcinyshyn	2	0	0	0	2
Mike Hartman	3	0	0	0	6
Corey Hirsch	4	0	0	0	0
Joby Messier	11	0	0	0	6

* Did not qualify for playoffs

Year-By-Year Scoring
1993-94—1994-95

1993-94	GP	G	A	PTS	PIM		Playoffs			
						GP	G	A	PTS	PIM
Sergei Zubov	78	12	77	89	39	22	5	14	19	0
Mark Messier	76	26	58	84	76	23	12	18	30	33
Adam Graves	84	52	27	79	127	23	10	7	17	24
Brian Leetch	84	23	56	79	67	23	11	23	34	6
Steve Larmer	68	21	39	60	41	23	9	7	16	14
Alexei Kovalev	76	23	33	56	154	23	9	12	21	18
Esa Tikkanen	83	22	32	54	114	23	4	4	8	34
Sergei Nemchinov	76	22	27	49	36	23	2	5	7	6
Kevin Lowe	71	5	14	19	70	22	1	0	1	20
Alexander Karpovtsev	67	3	15	18	58	17	0	4	4	12
Jeff Beukeboom	68	8	8	16	170	22	0	6	6	50
Greg Gilbert	76	4	11	15	29	23	1	3	4	8
Mike Hudson	48	4	7	11	47	–	–	–	–	–
Jay Wells	79	2	7	9	110	23	0	0	0	20
Eddie Olczyk	37	3	5	8	28	1	0	0	0	0
Nick Kypreos	46	3	5	8	102	3	0	0	0	2
Stephane Matteau	12	4	3	7	2	23	6	3	9	20
Glenn Anderson	12	4	2	6	12	23	3	3	6	42
Craig MacTavish	12	4	2	6	11	23	1	4	5	22
Brian Noonan	12	4	2	6	12	22	4	7	11	17
Joe Kocur	71	2	1	3	129	20	1	1	2	17
Mike Hartman	35	1	1	2	70	–	–	–	–	–
Joby Messier	4	0	2	2	0	–	–	–	–	–
Mattias Norstrom	9	0	2	2	6	–	–	–	–	–
Glenn Healy	29	0	2	2	2	2	0	0	0	0
Doug Lidster	34	0	2	2	33	9	2	0	2	10
Jim Hiller	2	0	0	0	7	–	–	–	–	–
Daniel Lacroix	4	0	0	0	0	–	–	–	–	–
Mike Richter	68	0	0	0	2	23	0	0	0	2

1994-95	GP	G	A	PTS	PIM		Playoffs			
						GP	G	A	PTS	PIM
Mark Messier	46	14	39	53	40	10	3	10	13	8
Brian Leetch	48	9	32	41	18	10	6	8	14	8
Sergei Zubov	38	10	26	36	18	10	3	8	11	2
Adam Graves	47	17	14	31	51	10	4	4	8	8
Steve Larmer	47	14	15	29	16	10	2	2	4	6
Alexei Kovalev	48	13	15	28	30	10	4	7	11	10
Brian Noonan	45	14	13	27	26	5	0	0	0	8
Petr Nedved	46	11	12	23	26	10	3	2	5	6
Pat Verbeek	19	10	5	15	18	10	4	6	10	20
Sergei Nemchinov	47	7	6	13	16	10	4	5	9	2
Alexander Karpovtsev	47	4	8	12	30	8	1	0	1	0
Jay Wells	43	2	7	9	36	10	0	0	0	8
Stephane Matteau	41	3	5	8	25	9	0	1	1	10
Kevin Lowe	44	1	7	8	58	10	0	1	1	12
Mark Osborne	37	1	3	4	19	7	1	0	1	2
Nick Kypreos	40	1	3	4	93	10	0	2	2	6
Jeff Beukeboom	44	1	3	4	70	9	0	0	0	10
Joey Kocur	48	1	2	3	71	10	0	0	0	8
Mattias Norstrom	9	0	3	3	2	3	0	0	0	0
Darren Langdon	18	1	1	2	62	–	–	–	–	–
Joby Messier	10	0	2	2	18	–	–	–	–	–
Glenn Healy	17	0	2	2	2	5	0	0	0	0
Jean-Yves Roy	3	1	0	1	2	–	–	–	–	–
Shawn McCosh	5	1	0	1	2	–	–	–	–	–
Mike Hartman	1	0	0	0	4	–	–	–	–	–
Dan Lacroix	1	0	0	0	0	–	–	–	–	–
Troy Loney	4	0	0	0	0	1	0	0	0	0
Nathan LaFayette	12	0	0	0	0	8	0	0	0	2
Mike Richter	35	0	0	0	2	7	0	0	0	0

YEAR-BY-YEAR GOALTENDING STATISTICS

Regular Season

Year	Goaltender	G	W	L	T	GA	AVG	Shutouts
1926-27	Hal Winkler	8	3	4	1	16	2.00	2
	Lorne Chabot	36	22	9	5	56	1.56	10
1927-28	Lorne Chabot	44	19	16	9	79	1.80	11
1928-29	John Ross Roach	44	21	13	10	65	1.48	13
1929-30	John Ross Roach	44	17	17	10	143	3.25	1
1930-31	John Ross Roach	44	19	16	9	87	1.98	7
1931-32	John Ross Roach	48	23	17	8	112	2.33	9
1932-33	Andy Aitkenhead	48	23	17	8	107	2.23	3
1933-34	Andy Aitkenhead	48	21	19	8	113	2.35	7
1934-35	Andy Aitkenhead	10	3	7	0	37	3.70	1
	Percy Jackson	1	0	1	0	8	8.00	0
	Dave Kerr	37	19	12	6	94	2.54	4
1935-36	Dave Kerr	47	18	17	12	95	2.02	8
	Bert Gardiner	1	1	0	0	1	1.00	0
1936-37	Dave Kerr	48	19	20	9	106	2.21	4
1937-38	Dave Kerr	48	27	15	6	96	2.00	8
1938-39	Dave Kerr	48	26	16	6	105	2.19	6
1939-40	Dave Kerr	48	27	11	10	77	1.60	8
1940-41	Dave Kerr	48	21	19	8	125	2.60	2
1941-42	Jim Henry	48	29	17	2	143	2.98	1
1942-43	Jimmy Franks	23	5	14	4	103	4.48	0
	Bill Beveridge	17	4	10	3	89	5.24	1
	Steve Buzinski	9	2	6	1	55	6.11	0
	Lionel Bouvrette	1	0	1	0	6	6.00	0
1943-44	Ken McAuley*	50	6	39	5	310	6.20	0
1944-45	Ken McAuley	46	11	25	10	227	4.94	1
	Doug Stevenson	4	0	4	0	20	5.00	0
1945-46	Chuck Rayner	41	12	21	7	150	3.75	1
	Jim Henry	11	1	7	2	41	4.10	1
1946-47	Chuck Rayner	58	22	30	6	177	3.05	5
	Jim Henry	2	0	2	0	9	4.50	0
1947-48	Jim Henry	48	17	18	13	153	3.19	2
	Chuck Rayner	12	4	8	0	42	3.65	0
	Bob DeCourcy	1	0	0	0	6	12.41	0
1948-49	Chuck Rayner	58	16	31	11	168	2.90	7
	Emile Francis	2	2	0	0	4	2.00	0
1949-50	Chuck Rayner	69	28	30	11	181	2.62	6
	Emile Francis	1	0	1	0	8	8.00	0
1950-51	Chuck Rayner	66	19	27	20	187	2.83	2
	Emile Francis	5	1	2	1	14	2.80	0
1951-52	Chuck Rayner	53	18	25	10	159	3.00	2
	Emile Francis	14	4	7	3	42	3.00	0
	Lorne Anderson	3	1	2	0	18	6.00	0
1952-53	Chuck Rayner	20	4	9	7	58	2.90	1
	Lorne Worsley	50	13	28	9	153	3.06	2
1953-54	Johnny Bower	70	29	31	10	182	2.60	5
1954-55	Lorne Worsley	65	15	33	17	197	3.03	4
	Johnny Bower	5	2	2	1	13	2.60	0
1955-56	Lorne Worsley	70	32	28	10	203	2.90	4
1956-57	Lorne Worsley	68	26	28	14	220	3.24	3
	Johnny Bower	2	0	2	0	7	3.50	0
1957-58	Lorne Worsley	37	21	10	14	86	2.32	4
	Marcel Paille	33	11	15	7	102	3.09	0
1958-59	Lorne Worsley	67	26	9	12	205	3.07	2
	Marcel Paille	1	0	0	1	4	4.00	0
	Bruce Gamble	2	0	2	0	6	3.00	0
	Julian Klymkiw	1	0	0	0	2	6.32	0
1959-60	Lorne Worsley	41	8	25	8	137	3.57	0
	Marcel Paille	17	6	9	2	67	3.94	0
	Al Rollins	8	1	3	4	31	3.88	1
	Jack McCartan	4	2	1	1	7	1.75	0
	Joe Schaefer	1	0	0	0	5	7.69	0
1960-61	Lorne Worsley	59	0	0	0	193	3.29	1
	Marcel Paille	4	0	0	0	16	4.00	0
	Jack McCartan	7	0	0	0	36	4.91	1
	Joe Schaefer	1	0	1	0	3	3.83	0
1961-62	Lorne Worsley	60	22	27	9	174	2.97	2
	Marcel Paille	10	4	4	2	28	2.80	0
	Danny Olesevich	1	0	0	1	2	3.00	0
	Dave Dryden	1	0	1	0	3	4.50	0
1962-63	Lorne Worsley	67	22	34	9	219	3.30	2
	Marcel Paille	3	0	1	2	10	3.33	0
	Marcel Pelletier	2	0	1	1	4	6.00	0
1963-64	Jacques Plante	65	22	35	8	220	3.38	3
	Gilles Villemure	5	0	3	2	18	3.60	0
1964-65	Jacques Plante	33	10	17	5	109	3.37	2
	Marcel Paille	39	10	21	7	135	3.58	0
1965-66	Ed Giacomin	36	8	19	7	128	3.66	0
	Cesare Maniago	28	9	16	3	94	3.50	2
	Don Simmons	11	3	6	3	37	4.52	0

Year	Goaltender	G	W	L	T	GA	AVG	Shutouts
1966-67	Ed Giacomin	68	30	25	11	173	2.61	9
	Cesare Maniago	6	0	3	1	14	3.84	0
1967-68	Ed Giacomin	66	36	20	10	160	2.44	8
	Gilles Villemure	4	1	2	0	8	2.40	0
	Don Simmons	5	2	1	2	13	2.60	0
1968-69	Ed Giacomin	70	37	23	7	175	2.55	7
	Gilles Villemure	4	0	1	0	9	2.25	0
	Don Simmons	5	2	2	1	8	2.33	0
1969-70	Ed Giacomin	70	35	21	14	163	2.36	6
	Terry Sawchuk	8	3	1	2	20	2.91	1
1970-71	Ed Giacomin	45	27	10	7	95	2.16	8
	Gilles Villemure	34	22	8	4	78	2.30	4
1971-72	Ed Giacomin	44	24	10	9	115	2.70	1
	Gilles Villemure	37	24	7	4	74	2.09	3
1972-73	Ed Giacomin	43	26	11	6	125	2.91	4
	Gilles Villemure	34	20	12	2	78	2.29	3
	Peter McDuffe	1	1	0	0	1	1.00	0
1973-74	Ed Giacomin	56	30	15	10	168	3.07	5
	Gilles Villemure	21	7	7	3	62	3.53	0
	Peter McDuffe	6	3	2	1	18	3.18	0
1974-75	Ed Giacomin	37	13	12	8	120	3.48	1
	Gilles Villemure	45	22	14	6	130	3.16	2
	Dunc Wilson	3	1	2	0	13	4.33	1
	Curt Ridley	2	1	1	0	7	5.19	0
1975-76	Ed Giacomin	4	0	3	1	19	4.75	0
	John Davidson	56	22	28	5	212	3.97	3
	Dunc Wilson	20	5	9	3	76	4.22	0
	Doug Soetaert	8	2	2	0	24	5.27	0
1976-77	John Davidson	39	14	14	6	125	3.54	1
	Doug Soetaert	12	3	4	1	58	2.95	1
	Gilles Gratton	41	11	18	7	143	4.22	0
	Dave Tataryn	2	1	1	0	10	7.50	0
1977-78	John Davidson	34	14	13	4	98	3.18	1
	Doug Soetaert	6	2	2	2	20	3.33	0
	Hardy Astrom	4	2	2	0	14	3.50	0
	Wayne Thomas	42	12	20	7	141	3.60	4
1978-79	John Davidson	39	14	13	4	98	3.18	1
	Doug Soetaert	6	2	2	2	20	3.33	0
	Hardy Astrom	4	2	2	0	14	3.50	0
	Wayne Thomas	2	12	20	7	141	3.60	4
1979-80	John Davidson	41	20	15	4	122	3.17	2
	Steve Baker	27	9	8	6	79	3.41	1
	Wayne Thomas	12	4	7	0	44	3.95	0
	Doug Soetaert	8	5	2	0	33	4.55	0
1980-81	Doug Soetaert	39	16	16	7	152	3.93	0
	Steve Baker	21	10	6	5	73	3.48	2
	Wayne Thomas	10	3	6	1	34	3.40	0
	John Davidson	10	1	7	1	48	5.14	0
	Steve Weeks	1	0	1	0	2	2.00	0
1981-82	John Davidson	1	1	0	0	1	1.00	0
	Ed Mio	25	13	6	5	89	3.56	0
	Steve Weeks	49	23	16	9	179	3.77	1
	Steve Baker	6	1	5	0	33	6.03	0
	John Vanbiesbrouck	1	1	0	0	1	1.00	0
1982-83	Ed Mio	41	16	18	6	136	3.45	2
	John Davidson	2	1	1	0	50	2.50	0
	Steve Baker	3	0	1	0	50	2.94	0
	Glen Hanlon	21	9	10	1	670	3.43	0
	Steve Weeks	18	9	5	3	680	3.92	0
1983-84	Glen Hanlon	50	28	14	4	166	3.51	1
	Steve Weeks	26	10	11	2	90	3.97	0
	Ron Scott	9	2	3	3	29	3.59	0
	John Vanbiesbrouck	3	2	1	0	10	3.33	0
1984-85	Glen Hanlon	44	14	20	7	175	4.18	0
	John Vanbiesbrouck	42	12	24	3	166	4.22	1
1985-86	John Vanbiesbrouck	61	31	21	5	184	3.32	3
	Glen Hanlon	23	5	12	1	65	3.33	0
	Ron Scott	4	0	3	0	11	4.23	0
	Terry Kleisinger	4	0	2	0	14	4.40	0
1986-87	Bob Froese	28	14	11	0	92	3.74	0
	John Vanbiesbrouck	50	18	20	5	161	3.63	0
	Ron Scott	1	0	0	1	5	4.62	0
	Doug Soetaert	13	2	7	2	58	3.99	0
1987-88	John Vanbiesbrouck	56	27	22	7	187	3.38	2
	Bob Froese	25	8	11	3	85	2.53	0
	Ron Scott	2	1	1	0	6	4.00	0
1988-89	John Vanbiesbrouck	56	28	21	4	197	3.69	0
	Bob Froese	30	9	14	4	102	3.78	1
1989-90	Mike Richter	23	12	5	5	66	3.00	0
	Bob Froese	15	5	7	1	45	3.33	0
	John Vanbiesbrouck	80	36	31	13	267	3.38	1
1990-91	Mike Richter	45	21	13	7	135	3.12	0
	John Vanbiesbrouck	40	15	18	6	126	3.35	3
1991-92	John Vanbiesbrouck	45	27	13	3	120	2.85	2
	Mike Richter	41	23	12	2	119	3.11	3
1992-93	John Vanbiesbrouck	48	20	18	7	152	3.31	4
	Corey Hirsch	4	1	2	1	14	3.75	0
	Mike Richter	38	13	19	3	134	3.82	1
1993-94	Mike Richter	68	42	12	6	159	2.57	5
	Glenn Healy	29	10	12	2	69	3.03	2

* Harry Lumley, spare Detroit goaltender, substituted for McAuley in one period of one game when McAuley was injured. Lumley allowed no goals.

YEAR-BY-YEAR GOALTENDING STATISTICS

Playoffs

Year	Goaltender	G	W	L	T	GA	AVG	Shutouts
1933-34	Andy Aitkenhead	2	0	1	1	2	1.00	1
1934-35	Dave Kerr	4	1	1	2	10	2.50	0
1936-37	Dave Kerr	9	6	3	0	10	1.11	4
1937-38	Dave Kerr	3	1	2	0	8	2.67	0
1938-39	Dave Kerr	1	0	1	0	2	2.00	0
	Bert Gardiner	6	3	3	0	12	2.00	0
1939-40	Dave Kerr	12	8	4	0	20	1.67	3
1940-41	Dave Kerr	3	1	2	0	6	2.00	0
1941-42	Jim Henry	6	2	4	0	13	2.16	1
1947-48	Chuck Rayner	6	2	4	0	17	2.83	0
1949-50	Chuck Rayner	12	7	5	0	29	2.42	1
1955-56	Lorne Worsley	5	1	4	–	22	4.40	0
1956-57	Lorne Worsley	5	1	4	–	22	4.18	0
1957-58	Lorne Worsley	6	2	4	–	28	4.60	0
1961-62	Lorne Worsley	6	2	4	–	22	3.44	0
1966-67	Ed Giacomin	4	0	4	–	14	3.41	0
1967-68	Ed Giacomin	6	2	4	–	18	3.00	0
1968-69	Ed Giacomin	3	0	3	–	10	3.33	0
	Gilles Villemure	1	0	1	–	4	4.00	0
1969-70	Ed Giacomin	5	2	3	–	19	4.13	0
	Terry Sawchuk	3	0	1	–	6	4.50	0
1970-71	Ed Giacomin	12	7	5	–	28	2.21	0
	Gilles Villemure	2	0	1	–	6	4.50	0
1971-72	Ed Giacomin	10	6	4	–	27	2.70	0
	Gilles Villemure	6	4	2	–	14	2.33	0
1972-73	Ed Giacomin	10	5	4	–	23	2.56	1
	Gilles Villemure	2	0	1	–	2	1.93	0
1973-74	Ed Giacomin	13	7	6	–	37	2.82	0
	Gilles Villemure	1	0	0	–	0	0.00	0
1974-75	Ed Giacomin	2	0	2	–	6	2.79	0
	Gilles Villemure	2	1	0	–	6	2.93	0
1977-78	John Davidson	2	1	1	–	7	3.44	0
	Wayne Thomas	1	0	1	–	4	4.00	0
1978-79	John Davidson	18	11	7	–	42	2.28	1
1979-80	John Davidson	9	4	5	–	21	2.33	0
1980-81	Steve Baker	14	7	7	–	55	4.00	0
	Steve Weeks	1	0	0	–	1	4.29	0
1981-82	John Davidson	1	0	0	–	3	5.45	0
	Ed Mio	8	4	3	–	28	3.79	0
	Steve Weeks	4	1	2	–	9	4.25	0
1982-83	Glen Hanlon	2	0	1	–	5	5.00	0
	Ed Mio	8	5	3	–	32	4.00	0
1983-84	Glen Hanlon	5	2	3	–	13	2.53	1
	John Vanbiesbrouck	1	0	0	–	0	0.00	0
1984-85	Glen Hanlon	3	0	3	–	14	5.00	0
	John Vanbiesbrouck	1	0	0	–	0	0.00	0
1985-86	John Vanbiesbrouck	16	8	8	–	49	3.27	1
	Glen Hanlon	3	0	0	–	6	4.80	0
1986-87	Bob Froese	4	1	1	–	10	3.64	0
	John Vanbiesbrouck	4	1	3	–	11	3.38	1
1988-89	Bob Froese	2	0	2	–	8	6.67	0
	Mike Richter	1	0	1	–	4	4.14	0
	John Vanbiesbrouck	2	0	1	–	6	3.36	0
1989-90	Mike Richter	6	3	2	–	19	3.45	0
	John Vanbiesbrouck	6	2	3	–	15	3.02	0
1990-91	Mike Richter	6	2	4	–	14	2.68	1
	John Vanbiesbrouck	1	0	0	–	1	1.15	0
1991-92	John Vanbiesbrouck	7	2	5	–	23	3.75	0
	Mike Richter	7	4	2	–	24	3.50	1
1993-94	Mike Richter	23	16	7	–	49	2.07	4
	Glenn Healy	2	0	0	–	1	0.88	0
1994-95	Mike Richter	7	2	5	–	23	3.59	0
	Glenn Healy	5	2	1	–	13	3.39	0

ALL TIME RANGERS GAME-BY-GAME RESULTS 1926-27 TO 1994-95

1926-27–1928-29

1926-27

Game No.	Date	Opponent	Score	Result
1	11-16	Maroons	1-0	W
2	11-20	at Toronto	5-1	W
3	11-25	at Pittsburgh	0-2	L
4	11-27	at Canadiens	2-0	W
5	11-30	Chicago	4-3*	W
6	12-4	at Detroit	0-1	L
7	12-7	at Boston	1-0	W
8	12-12	Boston	2-1	W
9	12-15	at Chicago	2-6	L
10	12-19	Detroit	1-1	T
11	12-21	Pittsburgh	1-0	W
12	12-23	at Ottawa	0-1	L
13	12-26	at Americans	2-5	L
14	12-28	Ottawa	2-3*	L
15	1-1	at Chicago	4-0	W
16	1-6	Canadiens	1-0	W
17	1-9	Detroit	4-1	W
18	1-11	at Maroons	3-2	W
19	1-15	Toronto	1-1	T
20	1-16	Chicago	5-4	W
21	1-18	at Boston	3-7	L
22	1-20	Boston	2-2	T

*Overtime

1926-27 (cont'd)

Game No.	Date	Opponent	Score	Result
23	1-23	Americans	2-0	W
24	1-27	at Canadiens	3-2	W
25	1-29	at Detroit	2-0	W
26	2-1	Canadiens	0-1*	L
27	2-6	Pittsburgh	2-1*	W
28	2-10	at Toronto	3-2	W
29	2-12	at Pittsburgh	3-2	W
30	2-15	at Ottawa	2-2	T
31	2-17	Maroons	1-4	L
32	2-20	Boston	3-1	W
33	2-22	Toronto	2-3*	L
34	2-24	Ottawa	0-1*	L
35	2-27	at Americans	4-1	W
36	3-1	at Chicago	0-3	L
37	3-5	at Maroons	0-0	T
38	3-13	Detroit	2-2	T
39	3-15	at Pittsburgh	5-0	W
40	3-17	at Detroit	2-0	W
41	3-20	Americans	2-1	W
42	3-22	Pittsburgh	4-1	W
43	3-25	Chicago	4-0	W
44	3-26	at Boston	3-4	L

1927-28

Game No.	Date	Opponent	Score	Result
1	11-15	at Toronto	4-2	W
2	11-17	Ottawa	3-2	W
3	11-20	at Americans	2-1	W
4	11-22	Maroons	3-4	L
5	11-27	Boston	1-1	T
6	11-29	at Ottawa	2-1	W
7	12-1	at Maroons	1-1	T
8	12-3	at Chicago	2-4	L
9	12-4	at Detroit	3-1	W
10	12-6	at Pittsburgh	2-2	T
11	12-11	Canadiens	0-2	L
12	12-13	at Boston	3-2	W
13	12-15	Detroit	1-2	L
14	12-20	Pittsburgh	2-0	W
15	12-25	Chicago	2-0	W
16	12-27	at Boston	0-2	L
17	12-29	Americans	3-3	T
18	12-31	at Canadiens	0-1	L
19	1-3	Detroit	2-4	L
20	1-8	Chicago	5-0	W
21	1-12	Boston	2-2	T
22	1-14	at Toronto	1-6	L

*Overtime

1927-28 (cont'd)

Game No.	Date	Opponent	Score	Result
23	1-15	at Detroit	2-1	W
24	1-17	Toronto	1-2	L
25	1-22	Pittsburgh	4-1	W
26	1-26	Detroit	3-0	W
27	1-29	at Americans	7-0	W
28	1-31	Maroons	3-1	W
29	2-4	at Pittsburgh	2-4	L
30	2-7	Ottawa	0-0	T
31	2-8	at Ottawa	0-0	T
32	2-12	Chicago	0-3	L
33	2-16	Boston	0-2	L
34	2-23	Pittsburgh	3-0	W
35	2-25	at Chicago	1-0	W
36	2-26	at Detroit	0-0	T
37	2-28	Toronto	1-0	W
38	3-6	at Maroons	1-3	L
39	3-8	at Canadiens	4-3	L
40	3-10	at Boston	3-3	T
41	3-13	Canadiens	1-4	L
42	3-18	Americans	7-3	W
43	3-21	at Chicago	6-1	W
44	3-24	at Pittsburgh	2-4	L

1928-29

Game No.	Date	Opponent	Score	Result
1	11-15	at Detroit	2-0	W
2	11-18	at Americans	1-1	T
3	11-20	Maroons	0-1	L
4	11-22	at Chicago	2-1	W
5	11-25	Pittsburgh	2-0	W
6	11-29	Chicago	2-1*	W
7	12-1	at Maroons	0-3	L
8	12-4	at Boston	0-2	L
9	12-6	at Pittsburgh	0-0	T
10	12-9	at Detroit	2-2	T
11	12-11	Toronto	3-2	W
12	12-13	at Canadiens	3-2*	W
13	12-16	Detroit	3-0	W
14	12-20	Ottawa	1-0	W
15	12-25	Americans	0-1	L
16	12-30	Boston	2-0	W
17	1-1	at Toronto	3-2	W
18	1-3	Pittsburgh	2-2	T
19	1-6	at Americans	0-0	T
20	1-10	at Ottawa	9-3	W
21	1-13	Detroit	1-0	W
22	1-15	at Boston	1-4	L

*Overtime

1928-29 (cont'd)

Game No.	Date	Opponent	Score	Result
23	1-17	Chicago	1-0	W
24	1-19	at Canadiens	0-0	T
25	1-22	Toronto	1-0	W
26	1-24	at Pittsburgh	3-1	W
27	1-27	Boston	1-2	L
28	1-31	Americans	2-1	W
29	2-3	at Chicago	3-2	W
30	2-5	Maroons	1-1	T
31	2-7	at Ottawa	1-2	L
32	2-10	Canadiens	3-3	T
33	2-14	at Toronto	1-3	L
34	2-17	Pittsburgh	2-1	W
35	2-21	Detroit	0-1	L
36	2-23	at Maroons	1-9	L
37	2-26	Ottawa	2-0	W
38	2-28	at Chicago	0-0	T
39	3-3	at Detroit	3-2	W
40	3-5	at Boston	1-2	L
41	3-10	Boston	2-3	L
42	3-14	Chicago	1-1	T
43	3-17	at Pittsburgh	4-3	W
44	3-20	Canadiens	0-1	L

Game-By-Game Results
1929-30—1931-32

Game No.	Date	Opponent	Score	Result
1929-30				
1	11-14	at Maroons	2-1	W
2	11-17	Detroit	5-5	T
3	11-19	at Boston	2-3	L
4	11-21	Maroons	2-1	W
5	11-23	at Pittsburgh	5-3	W
6	11-25	Toronto	3-4	L
7	11-28	at Chicago	3-2	W
8	12-1	at Detroit	3-4	L
9	12-8	Pittsburgh	5-1	W
10	12-12	Canadiens	8-3	W
11	12-14	at Toronto	6-7*	L
12	12-17	Americans	6-2	W
13	12-19	at Canadiens	2-7	L
14	12-22	Chicago	3-1	W
15	12-25	Boston	2-4	L
16	12-28	at Ottawa	3-1	W
17	12-31	Ottawa	1-1	T
18	1-2	at Americans	1-7	L
19	1-5	Pittsburgh	8-3	W
20	1-7	at Boston	0-3	L
21	1-9	Maroons	4-5	L
22	1-12	at Chicago	1-2	L

*Overtime

Game No.	Date	Opponent	Score	Result
1929-30 (cont'd)				
23	1-14	Detroit	3-0	W
24	1-18	at Pittsburgh	6-5	W
25	1-19	Chicago	4-1	W
26	1-23	Ottawa	6-3	W
27	1-26	at Detroit	3-7	L
28	1-28	Americans	4-3*	W
29	2-2	Boston	3-3	T
30	2-4	at Americans	3-5	L
31	2-6	Detroit	1-1	T
32	2-8	at Ottawa	2-2	T
33	2-11	at Maroons	2-5	L
34	2-13	Pittsburgh	4-1	W
35	2-18	Toronto	1-5	L
36	2-23	Boston	2-3	L
37	2-27	Chicago	1-1	T
38	3-1	at Toronto	3-3	T
39	3-2	at Detroit	2-2	T
40	3-4	at Chicago	2-2	T
41	3-8	at Canadiens	0-6	L
42	3-11	Canadiens	3-3	T
43	3-15	at Pittsburgh	4-3*	W
44	3-18	at Boston	2-9	L

Game No.	Date	Opponent	Score	Result
1930-31				
1	11-11	at Philadelphia	3-0	W
2	11-13	at Detroit	0-1	L
3	11-16	at Chicago	1-1	T
4	11-18	Americans	0-0	T
5	11-23	Philadelphia	5-2	W
6	11-25	at Maroons	2-5	L
7	11-27	Chicago	0-4	L
8	11-29	at Philadelphia	6-3	W
9	12-4	at Canadiens	4-5	L
10	12-6	at Toronto	2-4	L
11	12-9	Ottawa	3-2	W
12	12-14	Detroit	3-0	W
13	12-18	Boston	2-4	L
14	12-20	at Boston	2-2	T
15	12-23	Canadiens	5-1	W
16	12-25	at Ottawa	4-1	W
17	12-28	Philadelphia	4-2	W
18	12-30	at Americans	2-2	T
19	1-1	Boston	3-4*	L
20	1-6	Maroons	5-1	W
21	1-8	at Detroit	1-0	W
22	1-11	Chicago	0-2	L

*Overtime

Game No.	Date	Opponent	Score	Result
1930-31 (cont'd)				
23	1-13	at Boston	2-2	T
24	1-15	Toronto	1-1	T
25	1-18	at Chicago	1-2	L
26	1-20	Canadiens	2-3*	L
27	1-25	Detroit	0-1	L
28	1-29	Boston	3-4	L
29	1-31	at Maroons	2-2	T
30	2-3	Maroons	3-0	W
31	2-5	at Americans	2-0	W
32	2-8	Chicago	2-3	L
33	2-10	at Philadelphia	3-1	W
34	2-12	at Detroit	1-1	T
35	2-15	at Chicago	2-1	W
36	2-17	Ottawa	4-5	L
37	2-22	Philadelphia	6-1	W
38	2-26	Toronto	4-1	W
39	3-3	at Boston	1-4	L
40	3-5	at Canadiens	2-1	W
41	3-7	at Toronto	2-5	L
42	3-10	Detroit	3-2	W
43	3-15	Americans	0-0	T
44	3-17	at Ottawa	3-1	W

Game No.	Date	Opponent	Score	Result
1931-32				
1	11-12	at Canadiens	4-1	W
2	11-15	Detroit	1-2	L
3	11-17	at Americans	3-0	W
4	11-19	Boston	2-1	W
5	11-21	at Toronto	5-3	W
6	11-24	Chicago	1-1	T
7	11-29	at Chicago	5-0	W
8	12-3	at Detroit	1-1	T
9	12-8	Toronto	2-4	L
10	12-10	at Maroons	3-2	W
11	12-13	Americans	2-1	W
12	12-15	at Boston	2-2	T
13	12-17	Maroons	5-4*	W
14	12-19	at Canadiens	2-2	T
15	12-22	Canadiens	6-2	W
16	12-25	at Americans	6-0	W
17	12-27	Chicago	3-1	W
18	1-1	Detroit	3-0	W
19	1-3	at Chicago	1-1	T
20	1-5	Maroons	2-0	W
21	1-7	at Maroons	3-4	L
22	1-10	Toronto	2-0	W
23	1-12	at Boston	5-3	W
24	1-14	Boston	3-1	W

*Overtime

Game No.	Date	Opponent	Score	Result
1931-32 (cont'd)				
25	1-17	at Detroit	2-4	L
26	1-19	Canadiens	3-5	L
27	1-24	Detroit	4-3	W
28	1-28	Boston	1-4	L
29	1-30	at Toronto	3-6*	L
30	1-31	at Chicago	3-0	W
31	2-2	Canadiens	1-4	L
32	2-7	Chicago	1-0	W
33	2-9	at Boston	1-2	L
34	2-13	at Canadiens	1-3	L
35	2-16	Detroit	2-2	T
36	2-18	at Toronto	3-5	L
37	2-21	Americans	2-3	L
38	2-23	at Boston	2-0*	W
39	2-25	Boston	3-3*	T
40	3-3	at Detroit	2-1	W
41	3-6	at Chicago	3-4*	L
42	3-8	Chicago	6-1	W
43	3-10	at Americans	1-5	L
44	3-13	Maroons	4-4	T
45	3-15	at Maroons	3-4	L
46	3-17	Toronto	3-6	L
47	3-20	Americans	4-2	W
48	3-22	at Detroit	4-5	L

*Overtime

Game-By-Game Results
1932-33—1934-35

Game No.	Date	Opponent	Score	Result
1932-33				
1	11-10	at Maroons	4-2	W
2	11-12	at Toronto	2-4	L
3	11-20	Toronto	7-0	W
4	11-24	Chicago	1-1	T
5	11-29	at Boston	6-4	W
6	12-1	at Detroit	4-2	W
7	12-4	at Chicago	3-4	L
8	12-6	Canadiens	5-3	W
9	12-8	at Americans	3-1	W
10	12-11	Boston	3-1	W
11	12-13	at Canadiens	1-1	T
12	12-15	Americans	3-2	W
13	12-17	at Ottawa	2-2	T
14	12-20	Detroit	1-4	L
15	12-25	Maroons	2-0	W
16	12-29	Ottawa	4-2	W
17	12-31	at Maroons	2-4	L
18	1-3	Toronto	4-2	W
19	1-8	Americans	2-2	T
20	1-10	at Toronto	2-3	L
21	1-12	Boston	3-1	W
22	1-15	at Chicago	5-0	W
23	1-17	at Detroit	0-2	L
24	1-19	Canadiens	2-1	W
*Overtime				

Game No.	Date	Opponent	Score	Result
1932-33 (cont'd)				
25	1-22	Maroons	0-5	L
26	1-24	at Americans	3-2	W
27	1-26	Chicago	1-3	L
28	1-28	at Ottawa	9-2	W
29	1-31	Detroit	1-2	L
30	2-2	at Maroons	2-2	T
31	2-5	Americans	4-1	W
32	2-7	at Boston	1-2	L
33	2-9	Ottawa	3-3	T
34	2-11	at Toronto	1-2	L
35	2-14	at Ottawa	3-1	W
36	2-16	Toronto	2-5	L
37	2-18	at Canadiens	3-1	W
38	2-21	Chicago	2-2	T
39	2-23	at Detroit	0-3	L
40	2-26	at Chicago	4-1	W
41	3-5	Boston	1-2	L
42	3-9	Detroit	3-2	W
43	3-12	at Americans	8-2	W
44	3-14	Ottawa	3-3	T
45	3-16	at Canadiens	1-2	L
46	3-19	Maroons	3-6	L
47	3-21	at Boston	2-3	L
48	3-23	Canadiens	4-2	W

Game No.	Date	Opponent	Score	Result
1933-34				
1	11-11	at Toronto	3-4	L
2	11-12	at Chicago	0-1	L
3	11-16	Detroit	2-1	W
4	11-19	at Detroit	1-4	L
5	11-21	Toronto	1-1	T
6	11-25	at Maroons	0-1	L
7	12-2	at Boston	3-0	W
8	12-3	Chicago	1-0*	W
9	12-7	Canadiens	0-0	T
10	12-9	at Canadiens	4-2	W
11	12-12	Americans	0-3	L
12	12-14	at Ottawa	4-3	W
13	12-17	Boston	2-2	T
14	12-21	Ottawa	0-0	T
15	12-24	at Americans	3-1	W
16	12-25	Maroons	3-0	W
17	12-28	Toronto	2-2	T
18	12-31	Americans	1-3	L
19	1-2	Canadiens	3-2	W
20	1-4	at Detroit	1-3	L
21	1-7	at Chicago	1-1	T
22	1-9	Detroit	2-1	W
23	1-11	at Ottawa	5-3	W
24	1-14	Maroons	3-1	W
*Overtime				

Game No.	Date	Opponent	Score	Result
1933-34 (cont'd)				
25	1-16	at Americans	1-2	L
26	1-18	Chicago	5-0	W
27	1-20	at Canadiens	4-5	L
28	1-23	Ottawa	5-2	W
29	1-25	at Ottawa	6-3	W
30	1-28	Boston	5-2	W
31	1-30	at Boston	1-2	L
32	2-1	Toronto	5-5	T
33	2-3	at Maroons	4-2	W
34	2-6	Canadiens	3-0	W
35	2-11	Americans	3-4	L
36	2-13	at Boston	6-4	W
37	2-15	at Canadiens	2-5	L
38	2-18	Chicago	1-2	L
39	2-22	Detroit	3-1	W
40	2-24	at Toronto	3-8	L
41	2-27	at Detroit	1-5	L
42	3-1	at Chicago	3-1	W
43	3-6	Ottawa	4-5*	L
44	3-8	at Maroons	2-2	T
45	3-11	Maroons	3-7*	L
46	3-13	at Americans	2-1	W
47	3-15	Boston	2-3	L
48	3-17	at Toronto	2-3	L

Game No.	Date	Opponent	Score	Result
1934-35				
1	11-10	at St. Louis	2-4	L
2	11-15	at Detroit	2-8	L
3	11-18	St. Louis	5-0	W
4	11-22	Detroit	4-3*	W
5	11-25	at Americans	1-3	L
6	11-27	Canadiens	2-3	L
7	12-1	Maroons	2-5	L
8	12-4	at Canadiens	3-5	L
9	12-8	at Toronto	5-2	W
10	12-9	at Chicago	0-4	L
11	12-11	Toronto	4-8	L
12	12-16	Boston	2-1	W
13	12-18	at Boston	3-5	L
14	12-20	Chicago	1-4	L
15	12-22	at Maroons	2-1	W
16	12-25	Americans	3-1	W
17	12-30	Boston	0-0	T
18	1-1	at Boston	2-5	L
19	1-3	Detroit	3-2	W
20	1-8	Maroons	1-1	T
21	1-12	at Americans	3-1	W
22	1-13	St. Louis	3-2	W
23	1-15	Americans	1-1	T
24	1-20	Canadiens	7-1	W
*Overtime				

Game No.	Date	Opponent	Score	Result
1934-35 (cont'd)				
25	1-22	at Canadiens	7-0	W
26	1-24	Chicago	3-3	T
27	1-27	at Americans	4-2	W
28	1-29	Toronto	7-5	W
29	1-31	at Toronto	3-2	W
30	2-3	Detroit	5-3	W
31	2-5	at Maroons	5-4	W
32	2-7	Americans	4-6	L
33	2-10	at Chicago	2-1	W
34	2-12	at St. Louis	5-1	W
35	2-14	Toronto	3-0	W
36	2-16	at Toronto	1-5	L
37	2-17	at Detroit	5-3	W
38	2-19	St. Louis	2-1	W
39	2-24	Boston	0-0	T
40	2-26	at Maroons	1-3	L
41	2-28	Maroons	2-5	L
42	3-5	at Boston	1-3	L
43	3-7	at Detroit	1-6	L
44	3-9	at St. Louis	5-1	W
45	3-10	at Chicago	1-1	T
46	3-12	Canadiens	3-4	L
47	3-14	at Canadiens	4-5	L
48	3-17	Chicago	2-5	L

Game-By-Game Results
1935-36—1937-38

Game No.	Date	Opponent	Score	Result
1935-36				
1	11-10	at Detroit	1-1	T
2	11-12	at Canadiens	2-1*	W
3	11-14	Toronto	0-1	L
4	11-16	at Toronto	2-3	L
5	11-17	at Chicago	0-3	L
6	11-19	Detroit	2-2	T
7	11-24	Boston	1-0	W
8	11-25	at Americans	1-0	W
9	11-28	Chicago	2-1	W
10	12-1	at Boston	0-2	L
11	12-8	Maroons	3-3	T
12	12-12	Americans	5-2*	W
13	12-14	at Maroons	6-2	W
14	12-15	at Detroit	2-4	L
15	12-17	Canadiens	1-1	T
16	12-22	Boston	3-1	W
17	12-25	at Boston	3-2	W
18	12-28	at Toronto	3-9	L
19	12-29	at Chicago	1-3	L
20	12-31	Maroons	1-0	W
21	1-2	Americans	3-6	L
22	1-5	at Americans	0-0	T
23	1-7	Detroit	1-2	L
24	1-12	Boston	3-6	L
*Overtime				

Game No.	Date	Opponent	Score	Result
1935-36 (cont'd)				
25	1-14	at Maroons	2-1	W
26	1-16	Toronto	1-0	W
27	1-18	at Canadiens	1-3	L
28	1-21	Chicago	0-1	L
29	1-23	at Detroit	2-4	L
30	1-26	at Chicago	1-2	L
31	1-28	Canadiens	3-2*	W
32	2-2	Maroons	4-2	W
33	2-4	Detroit	4-4	T
34	2-9	Boston	2-0	W
35	2-11	at Canadiens	1-1	T
36	2-16	Canadiens	1-1	T
37	2-20	Chicago	1-1	T
38	2-23	at Boston	4-3	W
39	2-25	at Toronto	2-2	T
40	2-27	at Detroit	2-4	L
41	3-1	at Chicago	1-2	L
42	3-3	Toronto	0-0	T
43	3-8	Americans	0-1	L
44	3-10	at Maroons	0-0	T
45	3-12	Detroit	4-3*	W
46	3-15	at Americans	2-1	W
47	3-17	Chicago	4-2	W
48	3-22	at Boston	3-1	W

Game No.	Date	Opponent	Score	Result
1936-37				
1	11-8	at Detroit	2-5	L
2	11-10	at Maroons	4-1	W
3	11-15	Americans	1-2	L
4	11-17	at Boston	6-1	W
5	11-19	Detroit	1-0	W
6	11-21	at Canadiens	1-3*	L
7	11-24	Toronto	5-1	W
8	11-26	at Americans	3-1	W
9	11-28	Boston	2-2	T
10	12-3	at Detroit	0-2	L
11	12-6	at Chicago	2-1	W
12	12-8	Chicago	0-0	T
13	12-12	at Toronto	5-3	W
14	12-15	Maroons	2-2	T
15	12-19	at Canadiens	2-4*	L
16	12-20	Canadiens	5-3*	W
17	12-27	Chicago	1-0	W
18	12-29	at Americans	5-1	W
19	12-31	Boston	2-2	T
20	1-3	at Boston	2-3	L
21	1-5	Americans	7-1	W
22	1-9	at Maroons	3-2	W
23	1-10	Montreal	2-5	L
24	1-14	Detroit	0-2	L
*Overtime				

Game No.	Date	Opponent	Score	Result
1936-37 (cont'd)				
25	1-19	Canadiens	1-1	T
26	1-21	at Chicago	0-2	L
27	1-23	at Toronto	0-4	L
28	1-24	Toronto	4-2	W
29	1-26	at Boston	3-0	W
30	1-28	Boston	1-1	T
31	2-2	Detroit	4-4	T
32	2-4	at Detroit	2-2	T
33	2-6	at Maroons	2-4	L
34	2-7	Maroons	1-1	T
35	2-9	at Toronto	5-1	W
36	2-11	at Chicago	2-5	L
37	2-14	Americans	4-5	L
38	2-16	at Boston	2-3	L
39	2-18	Chicago	2-1	W
40	2-23	Toronto	2-1	W
41	2-28	at Chicago	3-4	L
42	3-4	at Detroit	1-2	L
43	3-7	Boston	0-1	L
44	3-9	at Americans	7-8	W
45	3-11	Detroit	2-4	L
46	3-13	at Canadiens	0-1	L
47	3-16	Chicago	3-4	L
48	3-21	Canadiens	3-1	W

Game No.	Date	Opponent	Score	Result
1937-38				
1	11-7	at Detroit	3-0	W
2	11-11	Chicago	1-3	L
3	11-14	at Boston	2-3	L
4	11-16	Americans	1-0	W
5	11-20	at Maroons	3-0	W
6	11-21	Maroons	3-3	T
7	11-25	Toronto	1-3	L
8	11-27	at Canadiens	1-2	L
9	12-2	at Chicago	1-2	L
10	12-5	Boston	4-0	W
11	12-11	at Toronto	6-3	W
12	12-12	at Detroit	5-2	W
13	12-14	Detroit	3-1	W
14	12-16	at Americans	2-0	W
15	12-19	Canadiens	2-2	T
16	12-23	at Maroons	4-0	W
17	12-26	Chicago	1-3	L
18	12-28	at Boston	2-3	L
19	12-31	Boston	5-3	W
20	1-4	Americans	5-5	T
21	1-6	at Chicago	4-1	W
22	1-8	at Toronto	2-3	L
23	1-9	Detroit	4-1	W
24	1-13	Detroit	3-3	T
*Overtime				

Game No.	Date	Opponent	Score	Result
1937-38 (cont'd)				
25	1-16	at Americans	4-0	W
26	1-18	Canadiens	3-1*	W
27	1-23	Maroons	8-2	W
28	1-25	at Boston	3-2	W
29	1-27	at Canadiens	2-4	L
30	1-30	at Chicago	2-2	T
31	2-1	Chicago	6-1	W
32	2-6	Toronto	2-1	W
33	2-10	at Detroit	4-0	W
34	2-12	at Maroons	5-3	W
35	2-13	Maroons	4-1	W
36	2-17	Boston	2-3*	L
37	2-20	at Boston	2-3*	L
38	2-22	Canadiens	1-2	L
39	2-24	Chicago	6-3	W
40	2-26	at Toronto	4-2	W
41	2-27	at Chicago	4-1	W
42	3-3	Detroit	4-3	W
43	3-6	at Americans	1-3	L
44	3-8	Toronto	4-3	W
45	3-13	Boston	1-2	L
46	3-17	Americans	5-3	W
47	3-19	at Canadiens	1-1	T
48	3-20	at Detroit	3-4	L

Game-By-Game Results
1938-39—1940-41

Game No.	Date	Opponent	Score	Result
1938-39				
1	11-13	at Detroit	3-4	W
2	11-15	Detroit	2-0	W
3	11-17	at Chicago	1-0	W
4	11-20	Canadiens	2-1	W
5	11-22	at Boston	2-4	L
6	11-24	Toronto	6-2	W
7	11-27	Chicago	0-1	L
8	12-4	at Americans	6-1	W
9	12-8	at Canadiens	6-5	W
10	12-11	Boston	0-3	L
11	12-15	Americans	1-1	T
12	12-17	at Toronto	3-2	W
13	12-18	at Chicago	0-5	L
14	12-20	Detroit	6-2	W
15	12-22	at Canadiens	5-2	W
16	12-25	at Boston	1-0	W
17	12-28	Toronto	0-2	L
18	12-31	Boston	2-1*	W
19	1-2	Detroit	3-0	W
20	1-5	at Canadiens	2-2	T
21	1-8	Americans	5-2	W
22	1-10	at Americans	0-1*	L
23	1-12	Chicago	6-0	W
24	1-15	at Chicago	1-1	T

*Overtime

Game No.	Date	Opponent	Score	Result
1939-40				
1	11-5	at Detroit	1-1	T
2	11-11	at Toronto	1-1	T
3	11-12	Toronto	0-1	L
4	11-16	Chicago	2-3	L
5	11-18	at Americans	3-1	W
6	11-19	Canadiens	1-2*	L
7	11-23	at Canadiens	1-1	T
8	11-26	at Boston	2-2	T
9	11-28	Detroit	4-1	W
10	11-30	at Chicago	7-2	W
11	12-2	Americans	1-1	T
12	12-10	Boston	3-2	W
13	12-14	Detroit	2-2	T
14	12-16	at Canadiens	4-2	W
15	12-17	at Detroit	0-0	T
16	12-19	Canadiens	5-2	W
17	12-23	Chicago	7-1	W
18	12-25	Toronto	4-1	W
19	12-29	Boston	4-0	W
20	12-31	Americans	5-2	W
21	1-2	at Boston	6-4	W
22	1-4	at Americans	6-2	W
23	1-7	Detroit	3-0	W
24	1-11	Chicago	5-3	W

*Overtime

Game No.	Date	Opponent	Score	Result
1940-41				
1	11-2	at Toronto	4-1	W
2	11-10	at Detroit	2-2	T
3	11-16	Detroit	3-3	T
4	11-19	Americans	3-2	W
5	11-23	Boston	1-2	L
6	11-26	Toronto	2-4	L
7	11-28	at Americans	1-2	L
8	11-30	Canadiens	6-1	W
9	12-1	at Chicago	1-4	L
10	12-5	at Canadiens	3-2	W
11	12-8	Detroit	1-3	L
12	12-10	at Boston	2-6	L
13	12-13	at Detroit	2-3*	L
14	12-15	Americans	6-3	W
15	12-19	Boston	5-3	W
16	12-22	at Chicago	1-3*	L
17	12-25	Chicago	3-3	T
18	12-28	at Toronto	2-3	L
19	12-29	Toronto	3-2	W
20	12-31	at Boston	2-2	T
21	1-1	Canadiens	1-2	L
22	1-4	at Canadiens	1-2	T
23	1-5	at Americans	6-2	W
24	1-7	Chicago	2-3	L

*Overtime

Game No.	Date	Opponent	Score	Result
1938-39 (cont'd)				
25	1-19	at Detroit	3-4	L
26	1-22	Canadiens	7-3	W
27	1-26	Americans	0-1	L
28	1-31	Chicago	3-2	W
29	2-2	at Americans	7-0	W
30	2-4	at Toronto	4-2	W
31	2-5	Toronto	5-5	T
32	2-9	Boston	2-4	L
33	2-12	at Boston	3-2	W
34	2-16	Americans	2-1	W
35	2-18	at Toronto	1-2	L
36	2-21	Detroit	7-3	W
37	2-23	at Detroit	4-2	W
38	2-25	at Canadiens	1-1	T
39	2-26	Canadiens	0-3	L
40	3-2	Chicago	1-3	L
41	3-5	at Boston	3-5*	L
42	3-7	Canadiens	2-2	T
43	3-9	at Chicago	8-3	W
44	3-12	Boston	2-4	L
45	3-14	at Detroit	2-3	L
46	3-16	at Americans	11-5	W
47	3-18	at Toronto	1-2	L
48	3-19	Toronto	6-2	W

Game No.	Date	Opponent	Score	Result
1939-40 (cont'd)				
25	1-13	at Toronto	4-1	W
26	1-14	at Chicago	1-2	L
27	1-18	at Canadiens	1-0	W
28	1-21	Boston	4-2	W
29	1-23	at Americans	5-3	W
30	1-25	Toronto	3-0	W
31	1-28	Americans	4-2	W
32	2-1	at Detroit	0-2	L
33	2-4	Canadiens	9-0	W
34	2-6	at Boston	2-6	L
35	2-8	Toronto	2-1	W
36	2-10	at Toronto	4-4	T
37	2-11	at Chicago	0-3	L
38	2-15	Detroit	3-1	W
39	2-18	at Detroit	0-2	L
40	2-22	at Americans	0-1*	L
41	2-24	at Canadiens	2-0	W
42	2-25	Canadiens	6-2	W
43	2-29	Chicago	1-2	L
44	3-2	at Toronto	1-1	T
45	3-3	at Chicago	2-1	W
46	3-10	Americans	4-2	W
47	3-12	at Boston	1-2	L
48	3-14	Boston	0-0	T

Game No.	Date	Opponent	Score	Result
1940-41 (cont'd)				
25	1-9	at Toronto	2-3*	L
26	1-12	Americans	3-1	W
27	1-14	Detroit	3-3	T
28	1-16	Boston	2-2	T
29	1-19	at Detroit	2-1	W
30	1-21	at Boston	3-4*	L
31	1-26	at Chicago	1-4	L
32	2-2	Canadiens	2-1	W
33	2-4	at Americans	2-2	T
34	2-6	Chicago	6-2	W
35	2-9	at Chicago	2-1	W
36	2-11	at Canadiens	2-6	L
37	2-13	Boston	3-5	L
38	2-15	at Toronto	3-4	L
39	2-16	Toronto	1-4	L
40	2-18	at Americans	5-2	W
41	2-23	Chicago	4-1	W
42	2-25	at Boston	2-0	W
43	2-27	Canadiens	5-2	W
44	3-1	at Canadiens	3-1	W
45	3-2	at Detroit	2-4*	L
46	3-4	Detroit	6-0	W
47	3-9	Toronto	8-5	W
48	3-16	Americans	6-3	W

Game-By-Game Results
1941-42—1943-44

Game No.	Date	Opponent	Score	Result
1941-42				
1	11-1	at Toronto	4-3	W
2	11-9	at Detroit	3-1	W
3	11-15	Boston	1-2	L
4	11-16	at Boston	1-2	L
5	11-18	Toronto	6-8	L
6	11-20	Americans	1-4	L
7	11-22	at Canadiens	7-2	W
8	11-23	Canadiens	4-6	L
9	11-25	Chicago	5-4*	W
10	11-29	Detroit	4-1	W
11	11-30	at Chicago	5-1	W
12	12-7	Boston	5-4	W
13	12-11	at Americans	5-3	W
14	12-13	at Toronto	1-2	L
15	12-16	Americans	3-2*	W
16	12-18	at Chicago	1-5	L
17	12-21	Canadiens	4-3*	W
18	12-23	at Boston	2-3	L
19	12-25	Chicago	5-2	W
20	12-27	at Canadiens	4-2	W
21	12-28	at Detroit	3-1	W
22	12-31	at Americans	4-3	W
23	1-1	Toronto	3-3	T
24	1-6	Detroit	3-2	W

*Overtime

Game No.	Date	Opponent	Score	Result
1941-42 (cont'd)				
25	1-13	Americans	9-2	W
26	1-17	at Canadiens	2-6	L
27	1-18	Canadiens	5-4*	W
28	1-20	at Boston	4-2	W
29	1-24	at Detroit	3-2	W
30	1-25	Detroit	11-2	W
31	2-1	Toronto	7-2	W
32	2-3	at Americans	3-2	W
33	2-5	Boston	4-1	W
34	2-7	at Toronto	4-6	L
35	2-8	at Chicago	4-3	W
36	2-10	Chicago	2-5	L
37	2-14	at Canadiens	3-5	L
38	2-15	Americans	1-5	L
39	2-17	Canadiens	1-2*	L
40	2-22	Chicago	3-2	W
41	2-24	at Boston	4-3	W
42	2-26	Detroit	7-4	W
43	3-3	at Americans	4-4	T
44	3-5	at Detroit	2-5	L
45	3-7	at Toronto	2-4	L
46	3-8	Toronto	2-0	W
47	3-12	Boston	1-2	L
48	3-15	at Chicago	5-1	W

Game No.	Date	Opponent	Score	Result
1942-43				
1	10-31	at Toronto	2-7	L
2	11-5	at Detroit	5-12	L
3	11-7	Canadiens	4-3	W
4	11-8	at Canadiens	4-10	L
5	11-10	Chicago	5-3*	W
6	11-14	at Boston	3-5	L
7	11-15	Boston	3-4	L
8	11-19	Toronto	3-7	L
9	11-22	Detroit	4-4	T
10	11-26	at Chicago	2-1	W
11	11-28	at Toronto	6-8	L
12	11-29	Boston	3-2	W
13	12-3	at Chicago	1-3	L
14	12-6	at Boston	4-5	L
15	12-13	Canadiens	3-7	L
16	12-17	Boston	3-7	L
17	12-19	at Canadiens	1-1	T
18	12-20	Toronto	2-8	L
19	12-25	at Detroit	3-1	W
20	12-27	Toronto	3-1	W
21	12-29	at Boston	5-3	W
22	12-31	Detroit	0-2	L
23	1-1	at Chicago	5-6	L
24	1-3	Chicago	3-3	T
25	1-7	at Detroit	2-2	T

*Overtime

Game No.	Date	Opponent	Score	Result
1942-43 (cont'd)				
26	1-10	Canadiens	4-7	L
27	1-14	Detroit	1-4	L
28	1-16	at Boston	5-7	L
29	1-17	Boston	3-6	L
30	1-21	at Toronto	4-7	L
31	1-23	at Canadiens	5-5	T
32	1-24	at Detroit	0-7	L
33	1-28	at Chicago	1-10	L
34	1-31	Boston	2-7	L
35	2-4	Chicago	1-1	T
36	2-6	at Toronto	2-3	L
37	2-7	at Chicago	4-8	L
38	2-14	Toronto	4-4	T
39	2-18	Detroit	4-5	L
40	2-20	at Canadiens	1-6	L
41	2-21	Canadiens	6-1	W
42	2-25	Chicago	7-4	W
43	2-27	at Detroit	1-7	L
44	2-28	Detroit	1-5	L
45	3-2	at Toronto	4-0	W
46	3-4	Canadiens	2-7	L
47	3-7	Toronto	5-5	T
48	3-14	Chicago	7-5	W
49	3-16	at Boston	5-11	L
50	3-18	at Canadiens	3-6	L

Game No.	Date	Opponent	Score	Result
1943-44				
1	10-30	at Toronto	2-5	L
2	10-31	at Detroit	3-8	L
3	11-2	at Canadiens	1-2	L
4	11-6	Chicago	3-4	L
5	11-7	Toronto	4-7	L
6	11-13	Boston	2-6	L
7	11-14	at Chicago	5-10	L
8	11-18	Detroit	1-3	L
9	11-21	Toronto	2-5	L
10	11-25	at Boston	2-6	L
11	11-27	at Canadiens	3-6	L
12	11-28	Canadiens	2-2	T
13	12-4	at Toronto	4-11	L
14	12-5	at Chicago	6-7	L
15	12-11	at Boston	6-9	L
16	12-12	Boston	6-4	W
17	12-19	Detroit	6-2	W
18	12-23	at Detroit	3-5	L
19	12-25	at Toronto	5-3	W
20	12-26	Chicago	7-6	W
21	12-31	Toronto	0-4	L
22	1-2	Boston	3-13	L
23	1-6	Detroit	0-5	L
24	1-8	at Canadiens	2-8	L
25	1-9	Canadiens	5-6	L

Game No.	Date	Opponent	Score	Result
1943-44 (cont'd)				
26	1-13	Chicago	2-5	L
27	1-15	at Boston	5-7	L
28	1-16	Boston	8-6	W
29	1-22	at Toronto	5-1	W
30	1-23	at Detroit	0-15	L
31	1-27	at Chicago	4-6	L
32	1-30	Canadiens	3-5	L
33	2-3	at Detroit	2-12	L
34	2-5	at Boston	2-7	L
35	2-6	Chicago	4-4	T
36	2-10	Detroit	3-8	L
37	2-13	Toronto	3-6	L
38	2-19	at Canadiens	2-5	L
39	2-20	Canadiens	2-7	L
40	2-22	Chicago	4-8	L
41	2-24	Detroit	3-3	T
42	2-27	at Chicago	2-4	L
43	3-2	at Detroit	5-6	L
44	3-4	at Boston	9-10	L
45	3-5	Boston	4-4	T
46	3-9	Toronto	0-5	L
47	3-11	at Toronto	0-5	L
48	3-12	at Chicago	4-4	T
49	3-18	at Canadiens	2-11	L
50	3-19	Canadiens	1-6	L

Game-By-Game Results
1944-45—1946-47

Game No.	Date	Opponent	Score	Result
1944-45				
1	10-28	at Toronto	1-2	L
2	11-1	at Chicago	3-8	L
3	11-2	at Detroit	3-10	L
4	11-9	Toronto	3-6	L
5	11-11	Detroit	5-3	W
6	11-12	Boston	5-5	T
7	11-18	Detroit	2-2	T
8	11-19	Canadiens	2-6	L
9	11-23	at Chicago	4-4	T
10	11-26	at Boston	4-8	L
11	11-30	at Canadiens	7-5	W
12	12-2	at Toronto	3-4	L
13	12-7	Detroit	2-3	L
14	12-10	Chicago	1-1	T
15	12-12	at Boston	5-7	L
16	12-17	Canadiens	1-4	L
17	12-20	at Chicago	3-1	W
18	12-21	at Detroit	3-11	L
19	12-24	Chicago	3-3	T
20	12-27	Toronto	2-8	L
21	12-30	at Canadiens	1-4	L
22	12-31	Boston	3-2	W
23	1-4	Detroit	4-4	T
24	1-7	Chicago	0-0	T
25	1-9	at Toronto	5-4	W

Game No.	Date	Opponent	Score	Result
1944-45 (cont'd)				
26	1-11	Boston	5-1	W
27	1-14	Canadiens	2-6	L
28	1-18	at Detroit	3-7	L
29	1-20	at Canadiens	2-5	L
30	1-21	at Boston	3-14	L
31	1-24	at Chicago	4-3	W
32	1-27	at Toronto	0-3	L
33	1-28	Toronto	0-7	L
34	2-4	at Boston	3-3	T
35	2-8	at Canadiens	4-9	L
36	2-11	Canadiens	3-4	L
37	2-14	at Detroit	2-4	L
38	2-15	Chicago	6-2	W
39	2-17	at Boston	1-6	L
40	2-18	Boston	2-1	W
41	2-22	Detroit	5-3	W
42	2-24	at Toronto	4-4	T
43	2-25	Boston	4-4	T
44	3-1	Chicago	3-5	L
45	3-4	Toronto	3-6	L
46	3-7	at Chicago	3-6	L
47	3-8	at Detroit	3-7	L
48	3-10	at Canadiens	3-7	L
49	3-11	Canadiens	5-11	L
50	3-18	Toronto	6-5	W

Game No.	Date	Opponent	Score	Result
1945-46				
1	10-31	at Chicago	1-5	L
2	11-3	at Toronto	4-1	W
3	11-4	at Detroit	1-4	L
4	11-8	Chicago	4-5	L
5	11-10	Detroit	2-0	W
6	11-11	Boston	1-7	L
7	11-15	at Canadiens	0-2	L
8	11-17	Canadiens	3-7	L
9	11-18	Toronto	1-3	L
10	11-22	at Chicago	3-3	T
11	11-24	at Toronto	3-4	L
12	11-25	at Detroit	4-1	W
13	11-28	at Boston	1-5	L
14	12-1	at Canadiens	3-4	L
15	12-9	Toronto	2-1	W
16	12-13	Chicago	4-7	L
17	12-16	Canadiens	2-4	L
18	12-19	at Boston	7-8	L
19	12-22	at Toronto	5-5	T
20	12-23	Toronto	3-4	L
21	12-26	Detroit	2-3	L
22	12-30	Chicago	3-2	W
23	12-31	Canadiens	0-0	T
24	1-3	at Detroit	3-3	T
25	1-6	Boston	4-2	W

Game No.	Date	Opponent	Score	Result
1945-46 (cont'd)				
26	1-12	at Canadiens	3-9	L
27	1-13	Chicago	3-2	W
28	1-16	at Boston	2-3	L
29	1-17	Boston	2-4	L
30	1-19	at Toronto	1-3	L
31	1-20	at Chicago	1-9	L
32	1-26	at Canadiens	3-5	L
33	1-27	Detroit	5-2	W
34	2-3	Toronto	6-6	T
35	2-6	at Chicago	2-6	L
36	2-7	at Detroit	2-4	L
37	2-10	Chicago	2-2	T
38	2-14	Boston	2-2	T
39	2-16	at Boston	6-2	W
40	2-17	Canadiens	4-5	L
41	2-21	Detroit	2-2	T
42	2-24	at Chicago	2-2	T
43	2-27	at Toronto	6-4	W
44	2-28	at Detroit	1-4	L
45	3-3	Toronto	2-5	L
46	3-6	at Canadiens	3-7	L
47	3-10	Detroit	3-2	W
48	3-12	Boston	2-3	L
49	3-13	at Boston	5-3	W
50	3-17	Canadiens	8-5	W

Game No.	Date	Opponent	Score	Result
1946-47				
1	10-17	at Canadiens	0-3	L
2	10-20	at Detroit	3-1	W
3	10-23	at Canadiens	4-1	W
4	10-26	at Boston	1-3	L
5	10-30	Boston	3-3	T
6	11-2	Detroit	7-4	W
7	11-3	at Detroit	1-3	L
8	11-6	at Chicago	2-6	L
9	11-9	at Toronto	2-4	L
10	11-10	Boston	0-4	L
11	11-13	Canadiens	4-4	T
12	11-16	Chicago	2-6	L
13	11-17	Toronto	4-5	L
14	11-21	at Detroit	1-3	L
15	11-23	at Canadiens	3-2	W
16	11-24	at Chicago	5-1	W
17	11-27	at Boston	2-5	L
18	12-1	at Chicago	2-1	W
19	12-4	Canadiens	2-1	W
20	12-8	at Boston	6-4	W
21	12-11	Detroit	1-1	T
22	12-14	at Toronto	2-3	L
23	12-15	Canadiens	3-5	L
24	12-18	at Boston	2-3	L
25	12-22	Toronto	1-3	L
26	12-25	Canadiens	2-0	W
27	12-28	at Detroit	2-2	T
28	12-29	Boston	2-2	T
29	12-31	Detroit	4-5	L
30	1-1	at Boston	1-3	L

Game No.	Date	Opponent	Score	Result
1946-47 (cont'd)				
31	1-2	Toronto	4-5	L
32	1-4	at Toronto	2-0	W
33	1-5	Chicago	9-0	W
34	1-8	Boston	1-3	L
35	1-12	Toronto	3-2	W
36	1-15	Detroit	4-3	W
37	1-18	at Canadiens	2-6	L
38	1-19	Chicago	5-3	W
39	1-22	at Chicago	4-2	W
40	1-25	at Toronto	1-0	W
41	2-1	at Canadiens	1-2	L
42	2-2	Canadiens	7-1	W
43	2-5	at Chicago	3-2	W
44	2-9	at Detroit	2-5	L
45	2-12	at Boston	1-10	L
46	2-16	Toronto	6-2	W
47	2-19	Boston	6-0	W
48	2-22	at Toronto	0-2	L
49	2-23	Detroit	2-2	T
50	2-26	Chicago	7-9	L
51	3-2	Boston	2-3	L
52	3-3	Chicago	4-9	L
53	3-5	at Chicago	3-1	W
54	3-9	Toronto	2-4	L
55	3-12	Detroit	2-4	L
56	3-15	at Canadiens	0-1	L
57	3-16	Canadiens	3-4	L
58	3-19	at Detroit	0-2	L
59	3-22	at Toronto	3-5	L
60	3-23	Chicago	4-3	W

Game-By-Game Results
1947-48—1948-49

Game No.	Date	Opponent	Score	Result
1947-48				
1	10-16	at Canadiens	2-1	W
2	10-19	at Boston	1-3	L
3	10-22	at Toronto	1-3	L
4	10-29	Boston	1-3	L
5	11-1	Detroit	4-3	W
6	11-2	Toronto	7-4	W
7	11-6	at Detroit	1-2	L
8	11-8	at Toronto	2-7	L
9	11-9	at Chicago	5-8	L
10	11-12	Boston	2-8	L
11	11-15	Chicago	3-5	L
12	11-16	Canadiens	4-2	W
13	11-19	at Detroit	6-5	W
14	11-22	at Canadiens	5-3	W
15	11-30	at Chicago	6-2	W
16	12-3	Toronto	1-4	L
17	12-6	at Boston	5-5	T
18	12-7	Detroit	3-1	W
19	12-10	Canadiens	4-4	T
20	12-11	at Canadiens	4-2	W
21	12-13	at Toronto	4-1	W
22	12-14	Detroit	1-1	T
23	12-17	Boston	5-2	W
24	12-21	Canadiens	3-4	L
25	12-23	at Chicago	1-7	L
26	12-25	at Detroit	2-0	W
27	12-28	Toronto	1-1	T
28	12-31	Boston	7-3	W
29	1-1	at Boston	1-4	L
30	1-3	at Toronto	5-5	T

Game No.	Date	Opponent	Score	Result
1947-48 (cont'd)				
31	1-4	Chicago	1-4	L
32	1-7	at Detroit	0-6	L
33	1-10	at Canadiens	1-1	T
34	1-11	Canadiens	3-1	W
35	1-14	Chicago	4-2	W
36	1-18	Toronto	2-2	T
37	1-21	Detroit	3-4	L
38	1-25	at Boston	4-6	L
39	1-28	at Chicago	3-2	W
40	1-31	at Canadiens	4-2	W
41	2-1	Chicago	2-2	T
42	2-4	at Detroit	4-4	T
43	2-7	at Toronto	0-3	L
44	2-8	at Chicago	2-2	T
45	2-14	at Boston	4-4	T
46	2-15	Toronto	4-4	T
47	2-18	Detroit	1-3	L
48	2-22	Boston	4-1	W
49	2-25	Chicago	4-7	L
50	2-29	Canadiens	5-3	W
51	3-2	Toronto	1-0	W
52	3-3	at Detroit	2-4	L
53	3-6	at Toronto	1-2	L
54	3-7	Detroit	2-2	T
55	3-10	at Boston	3-6	L
56	3-13	at Canadiens	2-3	L
57	3-14	Canadiens	3-6	L
58	3-16	Boston	2-6	L
59	3-17	at Chicago	5-2	W
60	3-21	Chicago	3-4	L

Game No.	Date	Opponent	Score	Result
1948-49				
1	10-14	at Canadiens	1-1	T
2	10-17	at Detroit	0-7	L
3	10-24	at Boston	1-4	L
4	10-27	Detroit	2-3	L
5	10-31	Boston	2-0	W
6	11-6	at Toronto	3-3	T
7	11-7	at Chicago	2-4	L
8	11-10	Chicago	4-3	W
9	11-13	Canadiens	1-3	L
10	11-14	Toronto	4-4	T
11	11-17	at Detroit	4-4	T
12	11-21	at Boston	4-1	W
13	11-25	at Chicago	4-6	L
14	11-27	at Toronto	0-3	L
15	11-30	Chicago	2-4	L
16	12-4	at Canadiens	1-3	L
17	12-5	Detroit	1-3	L
18	12-7	Boston	2-2	T
19	12-11	at Detroit	3-5	L
20	12-12	Detroit	2-0	W
21	12-15	Toronto	3-1	W
22	12-18	at Toronto	3-3	T
23	12-19	Canadiens	3-2	W
24	12-23	at Chicago	3-2	W
25	12-25	at Canadiens	2-0	W
26	12-26	Chicago	1-2	L
27	12-31	Boston	2-2	T
28	1-1	at Boston	1-4	L
29	1-2	Toronto	4-2	W
30	1-5	Chicago	3-1	W

Game No.	Date	Opponent	Score	Result
1948-49 (cont'd)				
31	1-9	Canadiens	1-1	T
32	1-12	Detroit	1-4	L
33	1-15	at Toronto	1-2	L
34	1-16	Toronto	4-0	W
35	1-19	Boston	2-5	L
36	1-20	at Canadiens	1-2	L
37	1-23	at Chicago	2-2	T
38	1-26	at Detroit	5-1	W
39	1-30	Canadiens	9-0	W
40	2-2	at Boston	3-5	L
41	2-5	at Toronto	1-1	T
42	2-6	at Chicago	2-0	W
43	2-9	at Detroit	0-8	L
44	2-10	Chicago	1-3	L
45	2-12	at Boston	2-4	L
46	2-13	Toronto	0-3	L
47	2-16	Detroit	4-0	W
48	2-19	at Canadiens	1-3	L
49	2-20	Canadiens	3-2	W
50	2-23	Boston	2-3	L
51	2-27	Detroit	3-2	W
52	3-2	at Chicago	2-5	L
53	3-5	at Toronto	1-7	L
54	3-6	Toronto	3-4	L
55	3-9	at Boston	1-8	L
56	3-12	at Canadiens	0-3	L
57	3-13	Canadiens	1-1	T
58	3-15	Boston	2-4	L
59	3-16	at Detroit	2-6	L
60	3-20	Chicago	5-1	W

Game-By-Game Results
1949-50—1950-51

Game No.	Date	Opponent	Score	Result
1949-50				
1	10-15	at Canadiens	1-3	L
2	10-16	at Boston	2-2	T
3	10-19	Detroit	1-6	L
4	10-22	Toronto	2-2	T
5	10-25	at Chicago	2-1	W
6	10-26	at Boston	5-2	W
7	10-29	at Chicago	0-2	L
8	10-30	Toronto	2-4	L
9	11-2	at Toronto	3-3	T
10	11-6	at Detroit	0-7	L
11	11-9	Canadiens	2-2	T
12	11-12	Canadiens	3-5	L
13	11-13	Detroit	1-1	T
14	11-16	Boston	2-1	W
15	11-20	at Chicago	5-2	W
16	11-23	at Detroit	3-4	L
17	11-26	at Canadiens	1-5	L
18	11-27	at Boston	1-1	T
19	11-30	Canadiens	5-2	W
20	12-3	at Toronto	0-2	L
21	12-4	Chicago	4-0	W
22	12-7	Chicago	2-1	W
23	12-10	at Detroit	1-0	W
24	12-11	Detroit	2-1	W
25	12-14	at Chicago	3-5	L
26	12-17	at Boston	3-1	W
27	12-18	Toronto	0-2	L
28	12-21	Canadiens	4-1	W
29	12-24	at Canadiens	0-0	T
30	12-25	Toronto	3-1	W
31	12-28	Chicago	5-2	W
32	12-31	Boston	4-1	W
33	1-1	at Boston	0-6	L
34	1-4	Detroit	2-1	W
35	1-7	at Canadiens	3-1	W

Game No.	Date	Opponent	Score	Result
1950-51				
1	10-11	at Detroit	2-3	L
2	10-15	at Chicago	3-2	W
3	10-19	at Canadiens	0-4	L
4	10-21	at Toronto	0-5	L
5	10-22	at Boston	0-0	T
6	10-25	Boston	1-1	T
7	10-28	at Canadiens	1-5	L
8	10-29	Canadiens	2-2	T
9	11-2	at Detroit	2-2	T
10	11-4	at Toronto	2-2	T
11	11-5	at Chicago	1-3	L
12	11-8	Toronto	3-5	L
13	11-11	at Canadiens	1-1	T
14	11-12	Chicago	1-4	L
15	11-15	Boston	3-4	L
16	11-18	at Toronto	4-5	L
17	11-19	Detroit	3-3	T
18	11-22	Canadiens	3-2	W
19	11-25	at Boston	3-3	T
20	11-26	Toronto	2-3	L
21	11-29	Chicago	1-1	T
22	12-2	at Boston	3-2	W
23	12-3	Boston	3-5	L
24	12-6	Detroit	0-9	L
25	12-9	at Detroit	0-5	L
26	12-10	at Chicago	3-3	T
27	12-13	Canadiens	3-2	W
28	12-16	at Canadiens	1-1	T
29	12-17	Detroit	3-3	T
30	12-20	Boston	4-4	T
31	12-24	Chicago	6-1	W
32	12-25	at Detroit	1-4	L
33	12-27	Toronto	3-1	W
34	12-31	Boston	3-0	W
35	1-1	at Boston	2-3	L

Game No.	Date	Opponent	Score	Result
1949-50 (cont'd)				
36	1-8	Chicago	1-1	T
37	1-11	Toronto	1-2	L
38	1-14	at Detroit	2-4	L
39	1-15	Detroit	0-1	L
40	1-18	Boston	2-4	L
41	1-21	at Toronto	1-2	L
42	1-22	at Chicago	3-4	L
43	1-25	at Toronto	1-5	L
44	1-28	at Boston	2-2	T
45	1-29	Canadiens	2-0	W
46	2-1	at Boston	2-3	L
47	2-2	at Canadiens	1-4	L
48	2-5	at Detroit	5-5	T
49	2-9	at Chicago	5-3	W
50	2-12	Detroit	4-0	W
51	2-15	Boston	2-2	T
52	2-18	at Canadiens	4-2	W
53	2-19	Toronto	2-1	W
54	2-22	Chicago	3-0	W
55	2-23	at Chicago	7-3	W
56	2-25	at Toronto	2-4	L
57	2-26	Boston	4-3	W
58	3-1	Detroit	2-5	L
59	3-4	at Boston	1-5	L
60	3-5	Toronto	5-2	W
61	3-8	at Chicago	4-2	W
62	3-9	Detroit	3-1	W
63	3-11	at Toronto	0-4	L
64	3-12	Canadiens	1-5	L
65	3-15	Boston	1-4	L
66	3-18	at Canadiens	3-5	L
67	3-19	Canadiens	2-4	L
68	3-21	Chicago	3-6	L
69	3-22	at Detroit	7-8	L
70	3-26	Toronto	5-3	W

Game No.	Date	Opponent	Score	Result
1950-51 (cont'd)				
36	1-3	Detroit	5-3	W
37	1-6	at Toronto	4-2	W
38	1-7	Chicago	3-2	W
39	1-10	Canadiens	0-3	L
40	1-13	at Detroit	2-4	L
41	1-14	Toronto	2-1	W
42	1-17	Boston	3-3	T
43	1-20	at Canadiens	2-2	T
44	1-21	at Boston	1-5	L
45	1-25	at Chicago	2-1	W
46	1-27	at Toronto	1-2	L
47	1-28	Detroit	5-3	W
48	2-1	at Detroit	2-3	L
49	2-4	at Chicago	4-4	T
50	2-7	at Boston	2-2	T
51	2-11	Canadiens	3-1	W
52	2-14	Chicago	5-1	W
53	2-15	at Chicago	7-3	W
54	2-17	at Toronto	0-2	L
55	2-18	Toronto	2-5	L
56	2-21	Boston	2-2	T
57	2-24	at Canadiens	2-6	L
58	2-25	Detroit	6-2	W
59	3-1	at Chicago	4-1	W
60	3-3	at Boston	3-3	T
61	3-4	Canadiens	2-2	T
62	3-7	Chicago	3-1	W
63	3-10	at Detroit	2-3	L
64	3-11	Canadiens	5-5	T
65	3-14	Toronto	1-3	L
66	3-15	at Canadiens	3-5	L
67	3-17	at Toronto	1-3	L
68	3-18	Toronto	1-4	L
69	3-21	Detroit	1-4	L
70	3-25	Chicago	5-2	W

Game-By-Game Results
1951-52—1952-53

Game No.	Date	Opponent	Score	Result
1951-52				
1	10-14	at Chicago	2-3	L
2	10-18	at Canadiens	2-3	L
3	10-20	at Toronto	3-2	W
4	10-21	at Boston	1-1	T
5	10-24	Boston	1-3	L
6	10-28	Canadiens	2-1	W
7	10-29	at Canadiens	1-6	L
8	11-1	at Chicago	2-4	L
9	11-3	at Toronto	2-1	W
10	11-4	at Detroit	2-4	L
11	11-7	Detroit	4-4	T
12	11-11	Chicago	3-2	W
13	11-14	Toronto	2-2	T
14	11-17	at Canadiens	2-3	L
15	11-18	Detroit	2-5	L
16	11-21	Boston	3-3	T
17	11-22	at Detroit	1-2	L
18	11-25	Canadiens	2-1	W
19	11-27	at Boston	1-1	T
20	11-28	Chicago	6-3	W
21	12-1	at Toronto	2-8	L
22	12-2	at Chicago	4-6	L
23	12-5	Boston	2-3	L
24	12-9	Toronto	7-2	W
25	12-11	at Boston	2-4	L
26	12-12	Boston	6-3	W
27	12-15	at Toronto	1-4	L
28	12-16	Detroit	1-3	L
29	12-19	Canadiens	4-2	W
30	12-23	Chicago	3-2	W
31	12-25	at Detroit	1-2	L
32	12-26	Detroit	1-0	W
33	12-29	at Canadiens	2-7	L
34	12-30	Toronto	2-2	T
35	1-1	at Boston	4-2	W

Game No.	Date	Opponent	Score	Result
1951-52 (cont'd)				
36	1-2	Detroit	1-0	W
37	1-6	Chicago	3-2	W
38	1-9	Toronto	1-2	L
39	1-10	at Detroit	2-5	L
40	1-13	Canadiens	2-2	T
41	1-16	Chicago	4-6	L
42	1-17	at Chicago	6-6	T
43	1-20	at Detroit	3-2	W
44	1-22	at Boston	3-3	T
45	1-26	at Toronto	3-3	T
46	1-27	Canadiens	3-5	L
47	1-31	at Canadiens	0-1	L
48	2-3	at Detroit	3-4	L
49	2-7	at Chicago	3-1	W
50	2-9	at Boston	4-2	W
51	2-10	Toronto	3-4	L
52	2-13	Boston	6-2	W
53	2-16	at Canadiens	1-5	L
54	2-17	Canadiens	3-2	W
55	2-19	at Toronto	3-3	T
56	2-20	Detroit	1-1	T
57	2-24	Boston	5-2	W
58	2-27	Toronto	1-3	L
59	2-28	at Chicago	2-2	T
60	3-1	at Canadiens	1-3	L
61	3-2	Detroit	4-6	L
62	3-4	at Boston	1-4	L
63	3-6	at Chicago	5-3	W
64	3-9	Canadiens	0-2	L
65	3-12	Chicago	10-2	W
66	3-15	at Toronto	2-5	L
67	3-16	Toronto	2-4	L
68	3-19	Boston	6-4	W
69	3-20	at Detroit	3-7	L
70	3-23	Chicago	6-7	L

Game No.	Date	Opponent	Score	Result
1952-53				
1	10-9	at Detroit	3-5	L
2	10-12	at Chicago	0-2	L
3	10-16	at Canadiens	1-3	L
4	10-18	at Toronto	3-4	L
5	10-19	at Boston	2-2	T
6	10-22	Boston	3-3	T
7	10-26	Detroit	3-2	W
8	10-29	Chicago	1-3	L
9	10-30	at Chicago	3-8	L
10	11-1	at Canadiens	1-4	L
11	11-2	Canadiens	2-2	T
12	11-5	at Toronto	1-4	L
13	11-9	at Detroit	1-3	L
14	11-12	Chicago	5-2	W
15	11-13	at Chicago	2-6	L
16	11-16	Toronto	3-6	L
17	11-19	Detroit	2-2	T
18	11-23	Canadiens	2-2	T
19	11-26	Toronto	4-2	W
20	11-27	at Boston	1-3	L
21	11-30	at Chicago	1-1	T
22	12-3	Chicago	3-5	L
23	12-4	at Detroit	3-5	L
24	12-6	at Toronto	2-2	T
25	12-7	Canadiens	2-2	T
26	12-10	Boston	1-4	L
27	12-14	Toronto	2-2	T
28	12-17	Boston	5-0	W
29	12-18	at Canadiens	2-6	L
30	12-20	at Detroit	1-1	T
31	12-21	Detroit	2-5	L
32	12-25	at Boston	2-1	W
33	12-28	Chicago	3-6	L
34	12-31	Toronto	3-3	T
35	1-4	Boston	5-2	W

Game No.	Date	Opponent	Score	Result
1952-53 (cont'd)				
36	1-7	Chicago	4-6	L
37	1-8	at Canadiens	4-4	T
38	1-11	Canadiens	7-0	W
39	1-14	Detroit	3-2	W
40	1-17	at Toronto	0-1	L
41	1-18	at Chicago	0-2	L
42	1-22	at Detroit	8-2	W
43	1-24	at Boston	0-9	L
44	1-25	at Boston	2-1	W
45	1-28	Canadiens	1-2	L
46	1-29	at Canadiens	2-5	L
47	1-31	at Toronto	0-4	L
48	2-1	at Chicago	1-0	W
49	2-5	at Detroit	3-3	T
50	2-8	Canadiens	1-1	T
51	2-11	Detroit	2-2	T
52	2-14	at Boston	4-5	L
53	2-15	Toronto	1-2	L
54	2-18	Boston	4-2	W
55	2-19	at Chicago	4-2	W
56	2-21	at Canadiens	1-4	L
57	2-22	Detroit	1-2	L
58	2-25	Boston	2-1	W
59	2-28	at Toronto	0-3	L
60	3-1	Toronto	4-2	W
61	3-4	Chicago	1-4	L
62	3-5	at Detroit	1-7	L
63	3-7	at Boston	2-1	W
64	3-8	Canadiens	4-3	W
65	3-11	Detroit	0-2	L
66	3-14	at Canadiens	2-3	L
67	3-15	Toronto	1-1	T
68	3-18	Boston	1-2	L
69	3-21	at Toronto	0-5	L
70	3-22	Chicago	1-3	L

Game-By-Game Results
1953-54—1954-55

Game No.	Date	Opponent	Score	Result
1953-54				
1	10-8	at Detroit	1-4	L
2	10-11	at Chicago	5-3	W
3	10-15	at Canadiens	1-6	L
4	10-17	at Toronto	1-1	T
5	10-18	at Boston	2-3	L
6	10-22	Boston	4-3	W
7	10-25	Canadiens	1-2	L
8	10-28	Chicago	1-6	L
9	10-31	at Toronto	1-4	L
10	11-1	Toronto	2-2	T
11	11-5	at Canadiens	3-4	L
12	11-7	at Chicago	3-1	W
13	11-8	at Detroit	2-2	T
14	11-11	Chicago	3-2	W
15	11-14	Detroit	2-3	L
16	11-15	at Detroit	1-4	L
17	11-18	Chicago	3-1	W
18	11-21	at Toronto	0-1	L
19	11-22	Detroit	2-3	L
20	11-25	Boston	5-3	W
21	11-26	at Boston	2-5	L
22	11-29	Canadiens	2-1	W
23	12-2	Chicago	3-3	T
24	12-3	at Detroit	0-4	L
25	12-5	at Chicago	1-2	L
26	12-6	Toronto	3-3	T
27	12-9	Detroit	3-3	T
28	12-12	at Canadiens	2-7	L
29	12-13	Toronto	1-2	L
30	12-16	Boston	4-3	W
31	12-19	at Toronto	2-3	L
32	12-20	Canadiens	3-1	W
33	12-23	Detroit	2-1	W
34	12-26	at Canadiens	0-2	L
35	12-27	Chicago	1-4	L
1953-54 (cont'd)				
36	12-29	Boston	2-6	L
37	1-1	at Boston	2-1	W
38	1-3	Canadiens	4-3	W
39	1-6	Chicago	4-3	W
40	1-10	Toronto	4-1	W
41	1-13	Detroit	1-3	L
42	1-14	at Chicago	2-0	W
43	1-16	at Toronto	0-4	L
44	1-17	at Detroit	3-2	W
45	1-20	Boston	8-3	W
46	1-23	at Boston	4-3	W
47	1-24	at Boston	1-2	L
48	1-28	at Detroit	3-3	T
49	1-30	at Canadiens	2-1	W
50	2-4	at Chicago	3-2	W
51	2-6	at Canadiens	3-4	L
52	2-7	Canadiens	1-4	L
53	2-10	Detroit	3-2	W
54	2-13	at Boston	0-1	L
55	2-14	Toronto	3-3	T
56	2-17	Boston	2-1	W
57	2-19	at Chicago	3-0	W
58	2-21	Toronto	6-1	W
59	2-24	Boston	3-5	L
60	2-27	at Canadiens	0-5	L
61	2-28	Canadiens	2-0	W
62	3-3	at Toronto	3-3	T
63	3-5	at Chicago	0-0	T
64	3-7	Toronto	0-4	L
65	3-10	Chicago	4-2	W
66	3-11	at Boston	0-1	L
67	3-13	at Detroit	5-2	W
68	3-14	Detroit	2-0	W
69	3-20	at Toronto	5-2	W
70	3-21	Canadiens	1-3	L

Game No.	Date	Opponent	Score	Result
1954-55				
1	10-9	at Detroit	0-4	L
2	10-10	at Chicago	2-1	W
3	10-14	at Boston	3-5	L
4	10-16	at Toronto	4-2	W
5	10-20	Boston	6-2	W
6	10-23	at Canadiens	1-7	L
7	10-24	Canadiens	4-2	W
8	10-27	Detroit	5-2	W
9	10-30	at Toronto	1-3	L
10	10-31	Chicago	1-1	T
11	11-4	at Chicago	1-3	L
12	11-7	at Detroit	0-1	L
13	11-10	Toronto	1-2	L
14	11-13	Chicago	3-5	L
15	11-14	at Chicago	5-0	W
16	11-17	Boston	2-2	T
17	11-20	at Canadiens	1-4	L
18	11-21	Toronto	2-2	T
19	11-24	Boston	3-1	W
20	11-25	at Boston	2-2	T
21	11-27	at Toronto	1-3	L
22	11-28	Canadiens	4-1	W
23	12-1	Detroit	1-6	L
24	12-4	at Boston	3-6	L
25	12-5	Canadiens	3-3	T
26	12-8	Chicago	1-2	L
27	12-9	at Detroit	2-3	L
28	12-11	at Detroit	1-4	L
29	12-12	Toronto	1-1	T
30	12-15	Detroit	3-3	T
31	12-16	at Canadiens	1-5	L
32	12-18	at Toronto	1-3	L
33	12-19	Toronto	3-3	T
34	12-22	Detroit	2-2	T
35	12-25	at Canadiens	1-4	L
1954-55 (cont'd)				
36	12-26	Chicago	4-4	T
37	12-30	Boston	6-1	W
38	1-1	at Boston	0-4	L
39	1-2	Boston	3-3	T
40	1-5	Chicago	2-3	L
41	1-8	at Toronto	0-5	L
42	1-9	Canadiens	1-7	L
43	1-12	Toronto	0-0	T
44	1-14	at Chicago	6-2	W
45	1-16	at Detroit	0-3	L
46	1-19	Detroit	2-0	W
47	1-22	at Boston	1-3	L
48	1-23	at Boston	2-0	W
49	1-27	at Detroit	3-3	T
50	1-29	at Toronto	3-1	W
51	1-30	at Chicago	2-4	L
52	2-5	at Canadiens	1-3	L
53	2-6	Canadiens	3-7	L
54	2-9	Chicago	2-2	T
55	2-12	at Boston	5-5	T
56	2-13	Canadiens	4-1	W
57	2-16	Boston	2-2	T
58	2-19	at Canadiens	2-10	L
59	2-20	Detroit	0-5	L
60	2-23	Toronto	1-3	L
61	2-25	at Chicago	2-2	T
62	2-27	Canadiens	1-7	L
63	3-2	Boston	1-2	L
64	3-5	at Detroit	2-6	L
65	3-6	Detroit	1-2	L
66	3-12	at Toronto	2-1	W
67	3-13	Chicago	5-2	W
68	3-16	at Chicago	1-1	T
69	3-19	at Canadiens	2-4	L
70	3-20	Toronto	3-2	W

Game-By-Game Results
1955-56—1956-57

Game No.	Date	Opponent	Score	Result
1955-56				
1	10-7	at Chicago	7-4	W
2	10-9	at Detroit	3-2	W
3	10-15	at Canadiens	1-4	L
4	10-16	at Boston	1-4	L
5	10-19	Toronto	6-2	W
6	10-22	at Toronto	2-3	L
7	10-23	Chicago	5-4	W
8	10-26	Detroit	6-2	W
9	10-29	Boston	0-1	L
10	11-3	at Detroit	1-1	T
11	11-5	at Toronto	3-0	W
12	11-6	at Chicago	4-2	W
13	11-9	Canadiens	1-1	T
14	11-10	at Boston	1-5	L
15	11-13	Toronto	4-1	W
16	11-16	Detroit	3-3	T
17	11-19	at Canadiens	1-6	L
18	11-20	Canadiens	1-1	T
19	11-23	Boston	4-0	W
20	11-24	at Boston	5-0	W
21	11-27	Canadiens	3-3	T
22	11-30	Chicago	6-1	W
23	12-2	at Chicago	2-1	W
24	12-4	Detroit	7-3	W
25	12-7	Toronto	3-1	W
26	12-10	at Toronto	1-6	L
27	12-11	at Detroit	0-2	L
28	12-14	Chicago	1-4	L
29	12-15	at Canadiens	0-2	L
30	12-18	Toronto	4-1	W
31	12-21	Boston	3-3	T
32	12-25	Canadiens	5-1	W
33	12-29	Chicago	2-4	L
34	12-31	Boston	6-2	W
35	1-1	at Boston	4-2	W

Game No.	Date	Opponent	Score	Result
1955-56 (cont'd)				
36	1-4	Detroit	5-4	W
37	1-8	Chicago	3-5	L
38	1-11	Canadiens	6-1	W
39	1-12	at Detroit	0-6	L
40	1-14	at Toronto	6-5	W
41	1-15	at Chicago	2-0	W
42	1-17	at Chicago	2-2	T
43	1-21	at Canadiens	1-3	L
44	1-22	at Boston	1-3	L
45	1-26	at Detroit	2-3	L
46	1-28	at Toronto	3-1	W
47	1-29	at Chicago	6-2	W
48	2-1	Toronto	5-2	W
49	2-4	at Boston	1-7	L
50	2-5	Canadiens	3-3	T
51	2-8	Boston	3-3	T
52	2-11	at Toronto	0-5	L
53	2-12	Detroit	2-1	W
54	2-14	at Detroit	3-5	L
55	2-15	Chicago	6-1	W
56	2-18	at Canadiens	4-9	L
57	2-19	Boston	0-3	L
58	2-22	Toronto	2-4	L
59	2-23	at Canadiens	2-5	L
60	2-26	Detroit	3-2	W
61	2-28	at Detroit	1-4	L
62	2-29	Boston	4-2	W
63	3-3	at Boston	2-5	L
64	3-4	Chicago	3-2	W
65	3-8	at Chicago	6-4	W
66	3-10	at Toronto	2-5	L
67	3-11	Toronto	4-2	W
68	3-15	Detroit	2-2	T
69	3-17	at Canadiens	2-7	L
70	3-18	Canadiens	1-3	L

Game No.	Date	Opponent	Score	Result
1956-57				
1	10-12	at Chicago	3-0	W
2	10-14	at Detroit	1-2	L
3	10-17	Boston	2-0	W
4	10-20	at Canadiens	0-5	L
5	10-21	Chicago	4-1	W
6	10-24	Canadiens	3-2	W
7	10-28	Toronto	1-1	T
8	10-31	at Toronto	2-7	L
9	11-4	at Boston	1-4	L
10	11-7	Boston	2-4	L
11	11-8	at Canadiens	2-4	L
12	11-10	Detroit	4-6	L
13	11-14	Canadiens	3-5	L
14	11-17	Boston	4-4	T
15	11-18	at Chicago	2-2	T
16	11-21	Toronto	3-3	T
17	11-22	at Boston	4-3	W
18	11-24	at Canadiens	1-6	L
19	11-25	Canadiens	1-1	T
20	11-28	Boston	2-1	W
21	11-29	at Detroit	1-4	L
22	12-2	Toronto	4-2	W
23	12-5	Chicago	2-2	T
24	12-8	at Toronto	0-0	T
25	12-9	Detroit	4-2	W
26	12-13	at Detroit	1-2	L
27	12-15	at Toronto	1-2	L
28	12-16	Canadiens	4-2	W
29	12-21	at Chicago	3-2	W
30	12-23	Toronto	1-3	L
31	12-25	at Detroit	1-8	L
32	12-27	Chicago	3-2	W
33	12-29	at Canadiens	3-6	L
34	12-31	Detroit	0-1	L
35	1-1	at Boston	3-5	L

Game No.	Date	Opponent	Score	Result
1956-57 (cont'd)				
36	1-5	Chicago	4-1	W
37	1-6	Canadiens	2-3	L
38	1-9	Toronto	3-4	L
39	1-11	at Chicago	7-4	W
40	1-12	at Detroit	5-4	W
41	1-13	Detroit	2-3	L
42	1-19	at Canadiens	0-5	L
43	1-20	at Detroit	2-5	L
44	1-23	at Toronto	4-4	T
45	1-26	at Boston	5-3	W
46	1-27	at Chicago	3-2	W
47	1-30	Chicago	2-7	L
48	2-2	Detroit	4-5	L
49	2-3	at Boston	1-4	L
50	2-6	Boston	3-2	W
51	2-7	at Chicago	4-4	T
52	2-9	at Toronto	4-4	T
53	2-10	Canadiens	5-4	W
54	2-14	at Detroit	2-3	L
55	2-16	at Canadiens	2-1	W
56	2-17	Toronto	3-2	W
57	2-20	Boston	5-2	W
58	2-23	at Canadiens	1-4	L
59	2-24	Canadiens	4-3	W
60	2-27	Chicago	6-6	T
61	3-2	at Boston	3-2	W
62	3-3	Detroit	1-1	T
63	3-7	at Chicago	2-2	T
64	3-9	at Toronto	2-1	W
65	3-10	Detroit	4-1	W
66	3-13	Boston	1-2	L
67	3-16	at Toronto	1-14	L
68	3-17	Toronto	3-5	L
69	3-23	at Boston	4-2	W
70	3-24	Chicago	4-4	T

Game-By-Game Results
1957-58—1958-59

Game No.	Date	Opponent	Score	Result
1957-58				
1	10-10	at Detroit	3-2	W
2	10-12	at Canadiens	2-2	T
3	10-13	at Boston	1-3	L
4	10-16	Boston	2-6	L
5	10-20	Chicago	6-1	W
6	10-23	Toronto	3-0	W
7	10-26	at Toronto	0-3	L
8	10-27	Canadiens	4-1	W
9	10-30	Detroit	0-4	L
10	10-31	at Boston	3-0	W
11	11-2	Boston	5-0	W
12	11-3	at Chicago	3-2	W
13	11-5	at Detroit	1-1	T
14	11-6	at Toronto	4-2	W
15	11-9	at Chicago	0-5	L
16	11-13	Chicago	2-2	T
17	11-16	at Canadiens	4-2	W
18	11-17	Canadiens	4-2	W
19	11-20	Detroit	1-1	T
20	11-22	at Chicago	4-2	W
21	11-24	Toronto	1-5	L
22	11-27	Boston	2-5	L
23	11-28	at Boston	0-1	L
24	11-30	Detroit	1-3	L
25	12-1	at Detroit	5-1	W
26	12-4	Chicago	0-2	L
27	12-7	at Toronto	3-3	T
28	12-8	Toronto	1-2	L
29	12-12	at Canadiens	2-3	L
30	12-14	at Detroit	4-4	T
31	12-15	Detroit	4-2	W
32	12-18	Canadiens	5-4	W
33	12-19	at Boston	3-3	T
34	12-21	at Canadiens	4-2	W
35	12-22	Toronto	5-2	W

Game No.	Date	Opponent	Score	Result
1957-58 (cont'd)				
36	12-25	Chicago	1-3	L
37	12-28	at Toronto	1-6	L
38	12-29	Canadiens	3-4	L
39	1-4	Boston	4-7	L
40	1-5	Canadiens	0-4	L
41	1-8	Toronto	5-5	T
42	1-11	at Canadiens	3-9	L
43	1-12	Detroit	2-3	L
44	1-16	at Boston	3-2	W
45	1-18	at Chicago	3-2	W
46	1-19	at Detroit	6-1	W
47	1-25	at Toronto	1-7	L
48	1-26	at Chicago	3-4	L
49	1-29	Boston	1-1	T
50	2-1	Chicago	3-2	W
51	2-2	at Boston	3-4	L
52	2-8	at Detroit	5-2	W
53	2-9	Canadiens	1-3	L
54	2-14	at Chicago	3-1	W
55	2-16	Boston	3-2	W
56	2-19	Chicago	3-2	W
57	2-22	at Canadiens	2-2	T
58	2-23	Toronto	4-2	W
59	2-26	Chicago	4-3	W
60	3-1	at Toronto	5-4	W
61	3-2	Detroit	4-4	T
62	3-8	at Canadiens	3-2	W
63	3-9	Detroit	2-4	L
64	3-11	at Detroit	2-2	T
65	3-12	at Chicago	3-2	W
66	3-15	at Boston	4-0	W
67	3-16	Canadiens	2-3	L
68	3-19	Boston	1-1	T
69	3-22	at Toronto	7-0	W
70	3-23	Toronto	3-2	W

Game No.	Date	Opponent	Score	Result
1958-59				
1	10-8	at Chicago	1-1	T
2	10-11	at Boston	4-4	T
3	10-12	at Detroit	0-3	L
4	10-15	Boston	4-4	T
5	10-18	at Canadiens	2-2	T
6	10-19	Canadiens	3-5	L
7	10-25	Chicago	6-2	W
8	10-26	Toronto	3-2	W
9	10-29	Boston	2-2	T
10	10-30	at Detroit	1-4	L
11	11-1	at Toronto	3-4	L
12	11-2	Detroit	1-2	L
13	11-4	at Chicago	2-4	L
14	11-8	at Canadiens	6-5	W
15	11-9	at Boston	5-1	W
16	11-15	Boston	4-2	W
17	11-16	Canadiens	2-1	W
18	11-19	Toronto	7-4	W
19	11-22	at Toronto	2-2	T
20	11-23	Detroit	1-3	L
21	11-26	Canadiens	5-3	W
22	11-27	at Boston	1-3	L
23	11-29	Boston	1-3	L
24	11-30	at Chicago	2-2	T
25	12-3	Chicago	4-2	W
26	12-6	at Canadiens	0-6	L
27	12-7	Toronto	0-2	L
28	12-10	Detroit	1-2	L
29	12-13	at Toronto	4-4	T
30	12-14	Chicago	3-3	T
31	12-18	at Detroit	2-0	W
32	12-21	Toronto	5-1	W
33	12-25	at Canadiens	1-4	L
34	12-28	Canadiens	5-3	W
35	12-31	Boston	4-3	W

Game No.	Date	Opponent	Score	Result
1958-59 (cont'd)				
36	1-1	at Boston	5-2	W
37	1-3	at Canadiens	1-5	L
38	1-4	Toronto	2-4	L
39	1-7	Chicago	0-4	L
40	1-10	Detroit	3-3	T
41	1-11	at Chicago	4-3	W
42	1-14	at Toronto	3-2	W
43	1-17	at Chicago	1-7	L
44	1-18	at Detroit	4-2	W
45	1-24	at Canadiens	1-3	L
46	1-26	at Boston	8-3	W
47	1-28	Chicago	1-3	L
48	1-31	at Toronto	5-2	W
49	2-1	Detroit	5-4	W
50	2-5	at Detroit	5-0	W
51	2-7	Chicago	3-6	L
52	2-8	at Boston	1-4	L
53	2-11	Boston	3-5	L
54	2-12	at Detroit	0-1	L
55	2-15	Canadiens	1-5	L
56	2-18	at Chicago	2-4	L
57	2-21	at Toronto	1-1	T
58	2-22	Canadiens	5-1	W
59	2-25	Detroit	6-3	W
60	2-28	at Canadiens	1-6	L
61	3-1	Toronto	1-1	T
62	3-7	at Chicago	6-1	W
63	3-8	Detroit	4-2	W
64	3-11	Chicago	3-5	L
65	3-12	at Boston	4-5	L
66	3-14	at Toronto	0-5	L
67	3-15	Toronto	5-6	L
68	3-18	Boston	3-5	L
69	3-21	at Detroit	5-2	W
70	3-22	Canadiens	2-4	L

Game-By-Game Results
1959-60—1960-61

Game No.	Date	Opponent	Score	Result
1959-60				
1	10-7	at Chicago	2-5	L
2	10-10	at Boston	4-6	L
3	10-11	at Detroit	2-4	L
4	10-14	Boston	3-4	L
5	10-17	at Canadiens	4-2	W
6	10-18	Canadiens	5-6	L
7	10-21	Toronto	2-3	L
8	10-24	at Toronto	1-1	T
9	10-25	Chicago	3-1	W
10	10-28	Detroit	3-3	T
11	11-1	Canadiens	1-3	L
12	11-4	at Toronto	1-4	L
13	11-5	at Canadiens	2-8	L
14	11-8	at Detroit	3-3	T
15	11-11	Boston	6-3	W
16	11-14	Detroit	0-4	L
17	11-15	Toronto	2-2	T
18	11-18	at Chicago	3-5	L
19	11-22	Detroit	3-5	L
20	11-25	Boston	3-3	T
21	11-26	at Boston	3-4	L
22	11-28	at Chicago	2-6	L
23	11-29	Chicago	2-2	T
24	12-3	at Canadiens	7-4	W
25	12-5	at Toronto	3-6	L
26	12-6	Toronto	6-0	W
27	12-12	at Boston	4-3	W
28	12-13	Boston	4-3	W
29	12-19	at Canadiens	3-5	L
30	12-20	Canadiens	6-5	W
31	12-23	Chicago	0-3	L
32	12-25	at Detroit	5-2	W
33	12-26	at Toronto	0-4	L
34	12-27	Toronto	3-6	L
35	12-29	Boston	3-4	L

Game No.	Date	Opponent	Score	Result
1959-60 (cont'd)				
36	1-1	at Boston	3-7	L
37	1-3	Canadiens	8-3	W
38	1-6	Chicago	1-2	L
39	1-9	Detroit	3-3	T
40	1-10	at Detroit	4-3	W
41	1-14	at Boston	0-6	L
42	1-16	at Toronto	1-3	L
43	1-17	at Chicago	1-3	L
44	1-21	at Canadiens	2-11	L
45	1-23	at Chicago	1-2	L
46	1-24	at Detroit	2-2	T
47	1-27	Canadiens	2-2	T
48	1-30	at Toronto	2-3	L
49	1-31	Detroit	3-3	T
50	2-3	Toronto	2-4	L
51	2-4	at Detroit	3-1	W
52	2-6	Chicago	1-5	W
53	2-7	Canadiens	4-1	W
54	2-10	at Chicago	1-5	L
55	2-14	at Boston	0-3	L
56	2-17	Chicago	1-5	L
57	2-20	at Canadiens	3-3	T
58	2-21	Boston	7-2	W
59	2-24	Detroit	2-2	T
60	2-27	at Canadiens	2-3	L
61	2-28	Toronto	3-5	L
62	3-5	at Chicago	0-5	L
63	3-6	Detroit	3-1	W
64	3-9	Chicago	1-1	T
65	3-10	at Boston	3-3	T
66	3-12	at Toronto	4-1	W
67	3-13	Toronto	2-2	T
68	3-16	Boston	2-3	L
69	3-19	at Detroit	3-6	L
70	3-20	Canadiens	3-1	W

Game No.	Date	Opponent	Score	Result
1960-61				
1	10-5	Boston	2-1	W
2	10-8	at Toronto	5-2	W
3	10-9	at Chicago	2-3	L
4	10-11	Canadiens	2-3	L
5	10-15	at Canadiens	4-8	L
6	10-16	Toronto	2-7	L
7	10-19	Chicago	2-0	W
8	10-23	Canadiens	2-4	L
9	10-26	Detroit	4-3	W
10	10-27	at Boston	4-6	L
11	10-30	Toronto	1-3	L
12	11-2	at Chicago	4-4	T
13	11-5	at Toronto	3-7	L
14	11-6	at Detroit	2-5	L
15	11-9	Detroit	3-4	L
16	11-10	at Canadiens	7-9	L
17	11-13	Canadiens	1-2	L
18	11-16	Boston	4-3	W
19	11-20	Detroit	3-4	L
20	11-23	Boston	6-3	W
21	11-24	at Boston	5-3	W
22	11-27	Chicago	3-3	T
23	12-3	at Toronto	2-5	L
24	12-4	at Detroit	4-1	W
25	12-7	Detroit	1-3	L
26	12-10	at Boston	3-0	W
27	12-11	Boston	2-2	T
28	12-14	at Chicago	0-4	L
29	12-15	at Detroit	1-1	T
30	12-17	at Canadiens	0-2	L
31	12-18	Toronto	2-3	L
32	12-21	Chicago	2-2	T
33	12-25	Canadiens	4-1	W
34	12-28	Detroit	3-4	L
35	12-31	at Toronto	1-2	L

Game No.	Date	Opponent	Score	Result
1960-61 (cont'd)				
36	1-1	Toronto	1-4	L
37	1-4	Chicago	2-3	L
38	1-7	at Canadiens	3-6	L
39	1-8	Canadiens	4-2	W
40	1-12	at Boston	4-4	T
41	1-14	at Detroit	2-2	T
42	1-15	at Chicago	3-1	W
43	1-18	at Toronto	4-4	T
44	1-21	at Chicago	3-5	L
45	1-22	at Detroit	5-3	W
46	1-25	Boston	2-1	W
47	1-29	Toronto	1-4	L
48	2-1	Chicago	3-1	W
49	2-2	at Canadiens	5-7	L
50	2-4	at Boston	2-1	W
51	2-5	Boston	5-2	W
52	2-8	at Toronto	3-5	L
53	2-9	at Detroit	2-4	L
54	2-11	Canadiens	3-3	T
55	2-12	at Boston	3-8	L
56	2-15	at Chicago	2-5	L
57	2-18	at Canadiens	4-7	L
58	2-19	Toronto	4-2	W
59	2-22	Chicago	4-2	W
60	2-26	Canadiens	1-3	L
61	3-1	Boston	3-1	W
62	3-2	at Chicago	1-7	L
63	3-4	at Toronto	4-5	L
64	3-5	Detroit	8-3	W
65	3-8	Chicago	3-4	L
66	3-9	at Canadiens	1-6	L
67	3-12	Detroit	7-3	W
68	3-14	at Detroit	2-5	L
69	3-15	at Boston	2-6	L
70	3-19	Toronto	2-2	T

Game-By-Game Results
1961-62—1962-63

Game No.	Date	Opponent	Score	Result
1961-62				
1	10-11	at Boston	6-2	W
2	10-12	Boston	6-3	W
3	10-14	at Canadiens	1-3	L
4	10-15	Toronto	2-1	W
5	10-18	Canadiens	2-5	L
6	10—19	at Chicago	4-2	W
7	10-21	at Detroit	4-4	T
8	10-22	Detroit	4-5	L
9	10-25	Chicago	1-1	T
10	10-28	at Toronto	1-5	L
11	10-29	Toronto	4-2	W
12	10-31	at Chicago	4-2	W
13	11-2	at Detroit	0-1	L
14	11-4	at Canadiens	3-3	T
15	11-8	Boston	4-4	T
16	11-12	Chicago	4-1	W
17	11-18	Canadiens	4-4	T
18	11-19	Toronto	5-3	W
19	11-22	Detroit	4-0	W
20	11-23	at Boston	4-3	W
21	11-25	at Toronto	0-6	L
22	11-26	Canadiens	2-2	T
23	12-2	at Boston	1-3	L
24	12-3	Boston	3-1	W
25	12-6	Chicago	3-8	L
26	12-7	at Detroit	3-3	T
27	12-9	at Canadiens	2-2	T
28	12-10	Toronto	2-3	L
29	12-16	at Toronto	2-4	L
30	12-17	at Chicago	1-3	L
31	12-20	Detroit	6-1	W
32	12-23	Chicago	7-3	W
33	12-25	at Detroit	6-4	W
34	12-27	Canadiens	0-3	L
35	12-31	Boston	4-7	L

Game No.	Date	Opponent	Score	Result
1961-62 (cont'd)				
36	1-1	at Boston	4-2	W
37	1-3	at Chicago	1-2	L
38	1-6	at Canadiens	1-5	L
39	1-7	Toronto	3-4	L
40	1-13	at Chicago	2-4	L
41	1-14	at Detroit	1-2	L
42	1-17	at Toronto	2-4	L
43	1-21	at Chicago	1-3	L
44	1-24	Detroit	0-3	L
45	1-27	at Canadiens	1-5	L
46	1-28	Chicago	0-3	L
47	1-31	Boston	5-0	W
48	2-1	at Boston	5-3	W
49	2-3	at Toronto	1-4	L
50	2-4	Canadiens	2-1	W
51	2-7	Detroit	2-2	T
52	2-10	Chicago	2-1	W
53	2-11	at Boston	5-3	W
54	2-14	at Chicago	3-4	L
55	2-15	at Detroit	3-4	L
56	2-17	at Toronto	3-5	L
57	2-18	Toronto	6-2	W
58	2-21	Boston	4-2	W
59	2-24	at Canadiens	2-4	L
60	2-25	Canadiens	3-3	T
61	2-28	Boston	2-2	T
62	3-3	at Toronto	1-3	L
63	3-4	Detroit	2-4	L
64	3-6	at Detroit	5-4	W
65	3-11	Canadiens	1-2	L
66	3-14	Detroit	3-2	W
67	3-17	at Canadiens	0-2	L
68	3-18	Toronto	2-2	T
69	3-22	at Boston	4-3	W
70	3-25	Chicago	4-1	W

Game No.	Date	Opponent	Score	Result
1962-63				
1	10-11	Detroit	1-2	L
2	10-13	at Canadiens	3-6	L
3	10-14	Toronto	5-3	W
4	10-17	Chicago	1-5	L
5	10-21	Canadiens	3-3	T
6	10-27	at Toronto	5-1	W
7	10-28	Chicago	3-5	L
8	10-30	at Chicago	3-5	L
9	11-1	at Detroit	0-4	L
10	11-3	at Canadiens	3-3	T
11	11-4	at Boston	4-3	W
12	11-7	Toronto	1-5	L
13	11-10	at Toronto	3-5	L
14	11-11	Detroit	2-3	L
15	11-14	Boston	6-2	W
16	11-17	Chicago	3-4	L
17	11-18	Toronto	3-1	W
18	11-21	Boston	4-2	W
19	11-22	at Boston	7-1	W
20	11-24	at Toronto	1-4	L
21	11-25	Canadiens	1-3	L
22	11-29	at Detroit	5-0	W
23	12-2	at Chicago	1-5	L
24	12-5	Detroit	3-3	T
25	12-8	at Boston	3-3	T
26	12-9	Boston	2-4	L
27	12-12	at Chicago	3-4	L
28	12-13	at Detroit	2-3	L
29	12-15	at Canadiens	4-2	W
30	12-16	Detroit	5-2	W
31	12-22	at Toronto	2-4	L
32	12-23	Chicago	1-3	L
33	12-25	at Boston	2-6	L
34	12-27	Boston	9-3	W
35	12-30	Canadiens	4-4	T

Game No.	Date	Opponent	Score	Result
1962-63 (cont'd)				
36	12-31	at Detroit	1-1	T
37	1-2	Toronto	3-2	W
38	1-5	at Canadiens	2-2	T
39	1-6	Canadiens	0-6	L
40	1-12	at Chicago	1-3	L
41	1-13	at Detroit	2-4	L
42	1-19	at Boston	5-3	W
43	1-20	at Chicago	2-6	L
44	1-23	Chicago	3-3	T
45	1-26	at Canadiens	4-2	W
46	1-27	Toronto	2-4	L
47	1-30	Detroit	1-6	L
48	2-2	at Toronto	2-2	T
49	2-3	Boston	4-6	L
50	2-6	Canadiens	6-3	W
51	2-9	Chicago	3-3	T
52	2-10	at Chicago	2-4	L
53	2-12	at Boston	3-6	L
54	2-16	at Toronto	2-4	L
55	2-17	Toronto	4-1	W
56	2-20	Boston	3-3	T
57	2-23	at Canadiens	3-6	L
58	2-24	Detroit	2-3	L
59	2-26	at Detroit	4-3	W
60	2-28	at Chicago	6-1	W
61	3-2	at Toronto	3-4	L
62	3-3	Detroit	2-3	L
63	3-6	Chicago	5-2	W
64	3-9	at Canadiens	5-2	W
65	3-10	Canadiens	1-5	L
66	3-14	at Detroit	4-9	L
67	3-17	Toronto	1-2	L
68	3-20	Boston	5-1	W
69	3-21	at Boston	2-2	T
70	3-24	Canadiens	5-0	W

Game-By-Game Results
1963-64—1964-65

Game No.	Date	Opponent	Score	Result
1963-64				
1	10-9	at Chicago	1-3	L
2	10-12	at Canadiens	2-6	L
3	10-16	Detroit	3-0	W
4	10-20	Boston	5-1	W
5	10-24	at Boston	2-0	W
6	10-26	at Toronto	4-6	L
7	10-27	Chicago	1-4	L
8	10-30	Boston	4-3	W
9	10-31	at Detroit	1-4	L
10	11-3	Canadiens	3-5	L
11	11-5	at Chicago	2-3	L
12	11-7	at Detroit	0-1	L
13	11-9	at Canadiens	2-4	L
14	11-14	Toronto	4-5	L
15	11-16	at Toronto	4-5	L
16	11-17	Detroit	5-2	W
17	11-20	Boston	1-1	T
18	11-24	Toronto	3-3	T
19	11-27	Detroit	3-2	W
20	11-28	at Boston	3-5	L
21	11-30	Chicago	2-3	L
22	12-1	at Chicago	3-3	T
23	12-5	at Canadiens	2-4	L
24	12-7	at Boston	6-8	L
25	12-8	Boston	2-2	T
26	12-11	Chicago	2-6	L
27	12-12	at Canadiens	4-6	L
28	12-14	at Toronto	3-5	L
29	12-15	Canadiens	4-2	W
30	12-18	Detroit	1-1	T
31	12-22	Toronto	1-1	T
32	12-25	at Detroit	3-4	L
33	12-27	Chicago	4-2	W
34	12-29	Canadiens	2-6	L
35	1-1	at Chicago	5-2	W

Game No.	Date	Opponent	Score	Result
1963-64 (cont'd)				
36	1-4	Detroit	5-2	W
37	1-5	Toronto	3-2	W
38	1-9	at Boston	5-3	W
39	1-12	at Detroit	3-5	L
40	1-15	at Toronto	5-4	W
41	1-18	at Chicago	1-6	L
42	1-19	at Detroit	3-1	W
43	1-22	Boston	6-4	W
44	1-23	at Canadiens	2-4	L
45	1-25	at Toronto	1-1	T
46	1-26	Detroit	3-2	W
47	1-30	at Boston	3-1	W
48	2-1	Chicago	2-2	T
49	2-2	Chicago	4-2	W
50	2-5	Boston	2-3	L
51	2-6	at Boston	0-4	L
52	2-8	Canadiens	2-8	L
53	2-9	at Detroit	2-4	L
54	2-12	at Chicago	2-5	L
55	2-16	Toronto	4-2	W
56	2-19	Chicago	2-7	L
57	2-22	at Toronto	2-5	L
58	2-23	Toronto	3-4	L
59	2-27	at Boston	4-2	W
60	2-29	at Canadiens	0-4	L
61	3-1	Detroit	2-2	T
62	3-4	Chicago	4-3	W
63	3-7	at Canadiens	3-2	W
64	3-8	Canadiens	0-0	T
65	3-11	Boston	3-5	L
66	3-14	at Toronto	3-7	L
67	3-15	Toronto	1-3	L
68	3-17	at Chicago	0-4	L
69	3-19	at Detroit	3-9	L
70	3-22	Canadiens	1-2	L

Game No.	Date	Opponent	Score	Result
1964-65				
1	10-12	at Boston	6-2	W
2	10-13	Canadiens	0-3	L
3	10-17	at Canadiens	2-2	T
4	10-18	Toronto	3-3	T
5	10-21	Detroit	0-1	L
6	10-24	at Toronto	1-1	T
7	10-25	Chicago	2-5	L
8	10-28	Boston	3-1	W
9	11-1	Canadiens	3-1	W
10	11-3	at Chicago	1-2	L
11	11-5	at Detroit	1-3	L
12	11-7	at Toronto	1-0	W
13	11-11	Boston	4-2	W
14	11-15	Detroit	2-6	L
15	11-17	at Detroit	2-1	W
16	11-22	Detroit	3-3	T
17	11-25	Toronto	6-3	W
18	11-26	at Boston	1-6	L
19	11-28	at Toronto	4-1	W
20	11-29	Canadiens	2-5	L
21	12-2	Chicago	3-3	T
22	12-5	at Boston	3-3	T
23	12-6	at Chicago	4-1	W
24	12-9	Chicago	1-6	L
25	12-12	at Canadiens	1-7	L
26	12-13	Toronto	3-3	T
27	12-16	Detroit	3-7	L
28	12-19	at Toronto	3-6	L
29	12-20	Canadiens	2-3	L
30	12-23	at Canadiens	0-2	L
31	12-25	at Boston	3-0	W
32	12-26	Boston	0-2	L
33	12-27	at Detroit	1-3	L
34	12-29	Chicago	2-4	L
35	1-1	at Chicago	1-2	L

Game No.	Date	Opponent	Score	Result
1964-65 (cont'd)				
36	1-3	Toronto	3-3	T
37	1-6	Boston	5-2	W
38	1-9	at Canadiens	6-5	W
39	1-10	Toronto	0-6	L
40	1-14	at Boston	2-5	L
41	1-16	at Chicago	6-3	W
42	1-17	at Detroit	4-2	W
43	1-23	at Toronto	1-1	T
44	1-24	at Chicago	2-7	L
45	1-27	Boston	5-2	W
46	1-30	at Canadiens	1-5	L
47	1-31	Detroit	1-4	L
48	2-3	Chicago	1-4	L
49	2-6	at Boston	2-3	L
50	2-7	Boston	8-3	W
51	2-13	Chicago	0-3	L
52	2-14	at Detroit	2-6	L
53	2-17	at Chicago	4-5	L
54	2-20	at Detroit	2-3	L
55	2-21	Canadiens	2-2	T
56	2-24	at Canadiens	1-6	L
57	2-27	at Toronto	4-3	W
58	2-28	Toronto	6-2	W
59	3-3	Boston	1-6	L
60	3-4	at Boston	4-3	W
61	3-6	at Canadiens	1-2	L
62	3-7	Detroit	5-6	L
63	3-10	Chicago	1-1	T
64	3-14	Canadiens	4-6	L
65	3-19	Detroit	6-6	T
66	3-20	at Toronto	1-4	L
67	3-21	Toronto	1-10	L
68	3-23	at Chicago	3-2	W
69	3-25	at Detroit	4-7	L
70	3-28	Canadiens	3-5	L

Game-By-Game Results
1965-66—1966-67

Game No.	Date	Opponent	Score	Result
1965-66				
1	10-24	Canadiens	3-4	L
2	10-27	at Canadiens	3-4	L
3	10-30	at Boston	8-2	W
4	11-3	Toronto	2-2	T
5	11-6	at Toronto	4-2	W
6	11-7	Detroit	3-2	W
7	11-10	Boston	2-2	T
8	11-11	at Detroit	3-3	T
9	11-13	at Toronto	2-5	L
10	11-14	at Chicago	4-2	W
11	11-17	Chicago	3-5	L
12	11-20	at Canadiens	3-9	L
13	11-21	Detroit	3-3	T
14	11-24	Boston	4-1	W
15	11-25	at Boston	2-6	L
16	11-27	Chicago	0-1	L
17	11-28	Toronto	2-4	L
18	12-1	Toronto	2-2	T
19	12-4	at Canadiens	3-4	L
20	12-5	Chicago	2-6	L
21	12-8	at Chicago	2-2	T
22	12-9	at Detroit	3-7	L
23	12-11	Detroit	2-4	L
24	12-12	Toronto	1-1	T
25	12-18	at Toronto	4-8	L
26	12-19	Canadiens	3-2	W
27	12-22	at Chicago	3-4	L
28	12-23	at Detroit	2-4	L
29	12-25	at Boston	2-4	L
30	12-26	Boston	6-4	W
31	12-29	Chicago	0-3	L
32	1-1	at Canadiens	1-5	L
33	1-2	Canadiens	3-6	L
34	1-8	Chicago	6-4	W
35	1-9	Boston	1-3	L

Game No.	Date	Opponent	Score	Result
1965-66 (cont'd)				
36	1-15	at Detroit	4-4	T
37	1-16	at Chicago	6-5	W
38	1-19	at Toronto	2-6	L
39	1-22	at Boston	3-5	L
40	1-23	at Detroit	1-5	L
41	1-26	Detroit	4-3	W
42	1-29	at Canadiens	2-6	L
43	1-30	Toronto	8-4	W
44	2-2	at Chicago	3-4	L
45	2-5	at Boston	3-5	L
46	2-6	Canadiens	0-4	L
47	2-9	at Toronto	0-3	L
48	2-10	at Detroit	2-6	L
49	2-12	Boston	9-2	W
50	2-13	at Chicago	1-6	L
51	2-16	Chicago	2-5	L
52	2-19	at Toronto	3-1	W
53	2-20	Canadiens	3-5	L
54	2-23	Detroit	5-0	W
55	2-26	at Canadiens	3-4	L
56	2-27	Toronto	2-2	T
57	3-2	Boston	5-3	W
58	3-3	at Boston	5-4	W
59	3-6	Detroit	1-1	T
60	3-9	Chicago	1-0	W
61	3-12	at Chicago	2-4	L
62	3-13	Canadiens	3-2	W
63	3-16	Boston	1-3	L
64	3-19	at Canadiens	2-6	L
65	3-20	at Boston	3-4	L
66	3-23	Detroit	1-2	L
67	3-27	Toronto	1-5	L
68	3-31	at Detroit	3-5	L
69	4-2	at Toronto	3-3	T
70	4-3	Canadiens	4-1	W

Game No.	Date	Opponent	Score	Result
1966-67				
1	10-19	Chicago	3-6	L
2	10-22	at Toronto	4-4	T
3	10-23	Toronto	1-0	W
4	10-27	at Detroit	3-5	L
5	10-29	at Canadiens	0-3	L
6	11-3	at Boston	7-1	W
7	11-5	at Toronto	1-3	L
8	11-6	Toronto	3-3	T
9	11-8	at Chicago	1-3	L
10	11-9	Boston	3-3	T
11	11-12	at Canadiens	6-3	W
12	11-13	Detroit	5-2	W
13	11-16	Chicago	2-2	T
14	11-19	at Boston	3-3	T
15	11-20	Canadiens	1-2	L
16	11-23	Boston	5-4	W
17	11-26	Chicago	4-1	W
18	11-27	Toronto	5-0	W
19	11-30	at Chicago	5-0	W
20	12-3	at Boston	2-2	T
21	12-4	Canadiens	1-3	L
22	12-7	Boston	4-2	W
23	12-8	at Detroit	4-2	W
24	12-11	Canadiens	4-2	W
25	12-14	Detroit	4-1	W
26	12-17	at Toronto	3-1	W
27	12-18	at Detroit	0-5	L
28	12-21	Boston	5-1	W
29	12-24	at Canadiens	4-3	W
30	12-25	at Chicago	1-0	W
31	12-27	Chicago	2-3	L
32	12-29	Detroit	4-2	W
33	12-31	at Canadiens	0-3	L
34	1-1	Toronto	1-2	L
35	1-4	at Toronto	1-1	T

Game No.	Date	Opponent	Score	Result
1966-67 (cont'd)				
36	1-8	Canadiens	2-1	W
37	1-12	at Boston	3-0	W
38	1-14	at Chicago	3-5	L
39	1-15	at Detroit	2-0	W
40	1-21	at Boston	2-6	L
41	1-22	at Detroit	2-7	L
42	1-25	Boston	2-1	W
43	1-28	at Canadiens	2-3	L
44	1-29	Detroit	2-4	L
45	2-4	at Boston	4-3	W
46	2-5	Toronto	4-1	W
47	2-8	Boston	1-2	L
48	2-11	at Detroit	3-6	L
49	2-12	Canadiens	4-4	T
50	2-15	at Toronto	0-6	L
51	2-18	Chicago	4-1	W
52	2-19	at Chicago	3-2	W
53	2-22	Detroit	1-0	W
54	2-25	at Canadiens	5-0	W
55	2-26	Toronto	2-4	L
56	3-1	at Chicago	1-6	L
57	3-4	at Boston	4-4	T
58	3-5	Canadiens	0-2	L
59	3-8	Detroit	1-3	L
60	3-11	at Toronto	2-2	T
61	3-12	Canadiens	2-2	T
62	3-15	Chicago	1-3	L
63	3-18	at Canadiens	2-4	L
64	3-19	Boston	3-1	W
65	3-22	at Chicago	3-3	T
66	3-23	at Detroit	1-4	L
67	3-26	Toronto	4-0	W
68	3-29	Detroit	10-5	W
69	4-1	at Toronto	1-5	L
70	4-2	Chicago	0-8	L

Game-By-Game Results
1967-68—1968-69

1967-68

Game No.	Date	Opponent	Score	Result
1	10-11	at Chicago	6-3	W
2	10-15	at Detroit	2-3	L
3	10-18	Canadiens	2-2	T
4	10-21	at Toronto	5-3	W
5	10-22	Pittsburgh	6-4	W
6	10-25	Chicago	2-2	T
7	10-26	at Canadiens	1-1	T
8	10-29	Toronto	3-2	W
9	10-31	at Los Angeles	6-1	W
10	11-1	at California	2-0	W
11	11-4	at Toronto	2-4	L
12	11-8	Boston	3-6	L
13	11-12	Oakland	5-3	W
14	11-16	at Philadelphia	2-3	L
15	11-18	at Boston	1-3	L
16	11-19	Minnesota	5-2	W
17	11-22	Chicago	1-7	L
18	11-23	at Boston	2-4	L
19	11-26	St. Louis	1-0	W
20	11-29	Detroit	1-3	L
21	12-2	at Pittsburgh	4-1	W
22	12-3	Los Angeles	4-2	W
23	12-6	Detroit	3-3	T
24	12-7	at Boston	1-3	L
25	12-9	at Detroit	2-3	L
26	12-10	Canadiens	3-2	W
27	12-13	at Chicago	2-5	L
28	12-16	at Toronto	2-4	L
29	12-17	St. Louis	5-3	W
30	12-20	Detroit	2-0	W
31	12-23	Boston	0-4	L
32	12-25	at Philadelphia	3-1	W
33	12-27	Minnesota	3-3	T
34	12-30	Chicago	3-3	T
35	12-31	Toronto	4-0	W
36	1-3	Boston	5-5	T
37	1-6	at Canadiens	2-5	L
38	1-7	Toronto	6-2	W
39	1-10	at Chicago	3-3	T
40	1-13	at St. Louis	3-1	W
41	1-17	at Chicago	4-2	W
42	1-19	at Los Angeles	2-5	L
43	1-20	at Oakland	3-0	W
44	1-24	Boston	2-1	W
45	1-27	at St. Louis	3-4	L
46	1-28	Oakland	4-2	W
47	1-31	Chicago	2-3	L
48	2-1	at Canadiens	2-5	L
49	2-3	at Boston	3-3	T
50	2-4	Canadiens	3-0	W
51	2-8	at Detroit	3-2	W
52	2-10	at Pittsburgh	2-2	T
53	2-11	Detroit	3-3	T
54	2-15	at Minnesota	6-2	W
55	2-17	at Toronto	3-2	W
56	2-18	Philadelphia	3-1	W
57	2-21	Canadiens	2-7	L
58	2-24	at Canadiens	6-1	W
59	2-25	Toronto	3-1	W
60	2-29	at Detroit	4-2	W
61	3-2	Philadelphia	4-0	W
62	3-3	Chicago	4-0	W
63	3-6	Detroit	6-1	W
64	3-9	at Minnesota	1-1	T
65	3-10	Los Angeles	3-4	L
66	3-13	Boston	1-2	L
67	3-14	at Canadiens	1-3	L
68	3-17	Pittsburgh	3-0	W
69	3-20	at Chicago	5-3	W
70	3-23	at Toronto	1-3	L
71	3-24	Toronto	4-2	W
72	3-28	at Boston	5-4	W
73	3-30	at Detroit	3-1	W
74	3-31	Canadiens	4-2	W

1968-69

Game No.	Date	Opponent	Score	Result
1	10-13	at Chicago	2-5	L
2	10-16	Philadelphia	3-1	W
3	10-17	at Detroit	2-7	L
4	10-20	Los Angeles	7-0	W
5	10-23	Oakland	6-1	W
6	10-26	at Minnesota	3-0	W
7	10-27	Toronto	3-5	L
8	10-30	Pittsburgh	7-3	W
9	10-31	at Philadelphia	2-1	W
10	11-3	Minnesota	2-1	W
11	11-6	at Los Angeles	0-2	L
12	11-8	at Oakland	3-2	W
13	11-10	at Chicago	4-2	W
14	11-13	St. Louis	1-3	L
15	11-16	at Pittsburgh	2-1	W
16	11-17	Montreal	3-2	W
17	11-20	Los Angeles	4-2	W
18	11-23	at Boston	1-5	L
19	11-24	Oakland	3-2	W
20	11-27	Chicago	2-4	L
21	11-30	at Boston	4-1	W
22	12-1	Toronto	3-1	W
23	12-4	at Montreal	4-2	W
24	12-5	at Detroit	2-4	L
25	12-7	at Toronto	2-5	L
26	12-8	Detroit	2-5	L
27	12-11	Boston	2-2	T
28	12-14	at Minnesota	1-4	L
29	12-15	Philadelphia	1-3	L
30	12-18	Chicago	1-3	L
31	12-21	at St. Louis	2-2	T
32	12-22	Minnesota	4-2	W
33	12-25	at Philadelphia	2-2	T
34	12-26	Oakland	3-1	W
35	12-28	at Montreal	3-5	L
36	12-29	Montreal	3-1	W
37	1-2	Boston	2-4	L
38	1-4	at Toronto	3-5	L
39	1-5	Minnesota	5-1	W
40	1-9	at Philadelphia	3-1	W
41	1-11	at Detroit	2-3	L
42	1-14	at Los Angeles	1-3	L
43	1-17	at Oakland	3-1	W
44	1-18	at St. Louis	2-2	T
45	1-23	Los Angeles	3-1	W
46	1-25	Chicago	3-0	W
47	1-26	Montreal	3-2	W
48	1-29	Detroit	2-0	W
49	1-30	at St. Louis	4-3	W
50	2-1	at Montreal	2-6	L
51	2-2	Pittsburgh	7-3	W
52	2-5	at Pittsburgh	2-3	L
53	2-8	St. Louis	2-0	W
54	2-9	Philadelphia	3-3	T
55	2-12	at Oakland	2-3	L
56	2-13	at Los Angeles	1-4	L
57	2-15	at Toronto	2-6	L
58	2-16	Toronto	4-2	W
59	2-19	Detroit	1-1	T
60	2-23	Boston	9-0	W
61	2-26	Chicago	5-3	W
62	3-1	at Boston	5-8	L
63	3-2	St. Louis	2-1	W
64	3-5	at Chicago	4-4	T
65	3-6	at Detroit	4-1	W
66	3-8	at Pittsburgh	5-3	W
67	3-9	Montreal	2-2	T
68	3-12	Pittsburgh	4-3	W
69	3-16	Detroit	6-4	W
70	3-19	at Minnesota	4-2	W
71	3-22	at Montreal	1-3	L
72	3-23	Boston	4-2	W
73	3-26	at Chicago	4-6	L
74	3-27	at Boston	3-3	T
75	3-29	at Toronto	4-2	W
76	3-30	Toronto	4-0	W

Game-By-Game Results
1969-70—1970-71

Game No.	Date	Opponent	Score	Result
1969-70				
1	10-12	at Boston	1-2	L
2	10-15	Minnesota	4-3	W
3	10-18	at Montreal	3-7	L
4	10-19	Toronto	1-0	W
5	10-22	Chicago	1-1	T
6	10-25	at Detroit	4-1	W
7	10-26	Montreal	3-8	L
8	10-29	at Pittsburgh	3-1	W
9	10-30	at Philadelphia	3-3	T
10	11-1	at Toronto	3-2	W
11	11-2	St. Louis	6-4	W
12	11-5	at Chicago	1-3	L
13	11-7	at Oakland	8-1	W
14	11-8	at Los Angeles	4-1	W
15	11-12	Detroit	4-2	W
16	11-15	at Boston	6-5	W
17	11-16	St. Louis	4-2	W
18	11-19	at Chicago	1-1	T
19	11-22	at St. Louis	5-0	W
20	11-23	Oakland	5-2	W
21	11-26	Boston	3-0	W
22	11-29	Philadelphia	2-2	T
23	11-30	Minnesota	2-2	T
24	12-3	Chicago	3-3	T
25	12-7	Montreal	6-3	W
26	12-10	Boston	5-2	W
27	12-11	at Boston	1-2	L
28	12-13	at Minnesota	5-2	W
29	12-14	Toronto	1-3	L
30	12-17	Philadelphia	2-2	T
31	12-20	at Toronto	5-2	W
32	12-21	Oakland	3-1	W
33	12-26	Pittsburgh	2-3	L
34	12-28	Los Angeles	3-3	T
35	12-31	Chicago	2-1	W
36	1-3	at Minnesota	3-3	T
37	1-4	Oakland	5-2	W
38	1-7	at Pittsburgh	5-3	W

Game No.	Date	Opponent	Score	Result
1969-70 (cont'd)				
39	1-11	at Montreal	1-4	L
40	1-14	at Toronto	7-1	W
41	1-15	at Philadelphia	4-4	T
42	1-17	at Minnesota	3-1	W
43	1-22	at St. Louis	3-4	L
44	1-24	Boston	8-1	W
45	1-25	Los Angeles	3-2	W
46	1-28	at Los Angeles	4-5	L
47	1-30	at Oakland	2-1	W
48	2-1	Pittsburgh	6-0	W
49	2-4	Detroit	5-1	W
50	2-8	Los Angeles	5-1	W
51	2-11	at Los Angeles	6-2	W
52	2-13	at Oakland	2-4	L
53	2-15	Montreal	2-0	W
54	2-18	Philadelphia	3-3	T
55	2-19	at Detroit	3-3	T
56	2-21	at Chicago	2-4	L
57	2-22	Toronto	5-3	W
58	2-25	St. Louis	2-1	W
59	2-26	at Boston	3-5	L
60	2-28	at Detroit	3-3	T
61	3-1	Chicago	1-3	L
62	3-4	Detroit	0-2	L
63	3-6	at St. Louis	1-3	L
64	3-8	Pittsburgh	0-0	T
65	3-11	at Montreal	3-5	L
66	3-14	at Chicago	4-7	L
67	3-15	Minnesota	2-4	L
68	3-18	at Pittsburgh	2-0	W
69	3-19	at Philadelphia	2-2	T
70	3-22	Toronto	2-5	L
71	3-25	Boston	1-3	L
72	3-28	at Montreal	1-1	T
73	3-29	Montreal	4-1	W
74	4-1	at Toronto	2-1	W
75	4-4	at Detroit	2-6	L
76	4-5	Detroit	9-5	W

Game No.	Date	Opponent	Score	Result
1970-71				
1	10-10	at St. Louis	1-3	L
2	10-14	Buffalo	3-0	W
3	10-17	at Toronto	6-2	W
4	10-18	Montreal	1-0	W
5	10-21	Toronto	3-2	W
6	10-24	at Minnesota	4-1	W
7	10-25	California	2-2	T
8	10-28	Detroit	4-1	W
9	10-31	at Boston	0-6	L
10	11-1	Chicago	5-2	W
11	11-4	at California	1-3	L
12	11-7	at Los Angeles	6-2	W
13	11-11	Pittsburgh	3-3	T
14	11-14	at Chicago	1-2	L
15	11-15	Toronto	4-2	W
16	11-18	at Los Angeles	5-3	W
17	11-21	at Montreal	5-4	W
18	11-22	Minnesota	2-0	W
19	11-25	at Philadelphia	1-3	L
20	11-26	at Buffalo	2-2	T
21	11-28	Boston	3-3	T
22	11-29	Pittsburgh	6-2	W
23	12-2	St. Louis	4-2	W
24	12-5	at Toronto	1-0	W
25	12-6	Vancouver	4-1	W
26	12-8	at Vancouver	1-4	L
27	12-9	Los Angeles	2-2	T
28	12-11	at California	2-1	W
29	12-13	Los Angeles	4-0	W
30	12-16	Buffalo	4-0	W
31	12-19	at Minnesota	5-3	W
32	12-20	Vancouver	5-1	W
33	12-22	at Buffalo	7-2	W
34	12-23	Pittsburgh	6-1	W
35	12-26	at Detroit	4-7	L
36	12-27	St. Louis	4-4	T
37	12-29	California	3-2	W
38	1-2	at Pittsburgh	3-1	W
39	1-3	Montreal	6-5	W

Game No.	Date	Opponent	Score	Result
1970-71 (cont'd)				
40	1-9	at Minnesota	1-0	W
41	1-10	at St. Louis	4-2	W
42	1-12	at Vancouver	4-2	W
43	1-15	at California	1-3	L
44	1-17	at Chicago	3-4	L
45	1-20	Philadelphia	3-3	T
46	1-21	at Buffalo	5-5	T
47	1-24	Minnesota	6-2	W
48	1-27	Boston	2-2	T
49	1-30	at Philadelphia	2-5	L
50	1-31	Los Angeles	2-2	T
51	2-3	Chicago	2-4	L
52	2-4	at Detroit	1-0	W
53	2-6	at Vancouver	5-4	W
54	2-9	at Boston	3-6	L
55	2-10	Minnesota	4-3	W
56	2-13	at St. Louis	1-2	L
57	2-14	St. Louis	2-1	W
58	2-17	at Montreal	0-3	L
59	2-20	at Pittsburgh	2-0	W
60	2-21	Detroit	4-1	W
61	2-24	Philadelphia	4-2	W
62	2-27	at Pittsburgh	4-0	W
63	2-28	Vancouver	4-2	W
64	3-3	California	8-1	W
65	3-6	at Detroit	2-2	T
66	3-7	Los Angeles	4-2	W
67	3-10	at Chicago	4-2	W
68	3-12	Philadelphia	7-2	W
69	3-14	Toronto	1-0	W
70	3-18	at Philadelphia	1-2	L
71	3-20	at Toronto	1-3	L
72	3-21	Montreal	2-6	L
73	3-23	Buffalo	7-2	W
74	3-27	at Boston	6-3	W
75	3-28	Boston	2-1	W
76	3-31	Chicago	4-2	W
77	4-3	at Montreal	2-7	L
78	4-4	Detroit	6-0	W

Game-By-Game Results
1971-72—1972-73

1971-72

Game No.	Date	Opponent	Score	Result
1	10-9	at Montreal	4-4	T
2	10-10	at Boston	4-1	W
3	10-13	Boston	1-6	L
4	10-16	at Toronto	5-3	W
5	10-17	Montreal	8-4	W
6	10-20	Chicago	3-1	W
7	10-23	at St. Louis	4-3	W
8	10-24	Pittsburgh	1-1	T
9	10-27	Detroit	7-4	W
10	10-30	at Pittsburgh	1-1	T
11	10-31	Toronto	3-3	T
12	11-3	at Los Angeles	7-1	W
13	11-5	at California	8-1	W
14	11-6	at Vancouver	3-1	W
15	11-10	Los Angeles	7-1	W
16	11-13	Buffalo	5-2	W
17	11-14	Vancouver	6-1	W
18	11-20	at Minnesota	1-4	L
19	11-21	California	12-1	W
20	11-24	St. Louis	8-3	W
21	11-27	at Detroit	1-3	L
22	11-28	at Philadelphia	4-2	W
23	12-1	Buffalo	7-2	W
24	12-4	at Pittsburgh	2-4	L
25	12-5	Vancouver	6-3	W
26	12-8	at Chicago	2-2	T
27	12-9	at Philadelphia	5-0	W
28	12-12	Pittsburgh	6-1	W
29	12-15	Philadelphia	6-2	W
30	12-16	at Boston	1-8	L
31	12-18	at St. Louis	5-2	W
32	12-19	Minnesota	1-1	T
33	12-22	Pittsburgh	4-2	W
34	12-25	at Minnesota	2-1	W
35	12-26	Montreal	5-1	W
36	12-29	Philadelphia	5-1	W
37	1-2	Boston	1-4	L
38	1-5	St. Louis	9-1	W
39	1-9	Los Angeles	8-0	W

1971-72 (cont'd)

Game No.	Date	Opponent	Score	Result
40	1-12	at Chicago	5-5	T
41	1-13	at Buffalo	5-2	W
42	1-15	at Toronto	3-4	L
43	1-19	at Los Angeles	5-1	W
44	1-21	at California	5-0	W
45	1-22	at Vancouver	2-5	L
46	1-26	Buffalo	5-1	W
47	1-29	at Minnesota	2-4	L
48	1-30	Minnesota	1-1	T
49	2-2	Boston	0-2	L
50	2-3	at Buffalo	4-2	W
51	2-5	at St. Louis	5-6	L
52	2-6	Toronto	2-2	T
53	2-9	Chicago	4-1	W
54	2-12	at Pittsburgh	8-3	W
55	2-13	Los Angeles	4-2	W
56	2-15	at Vancouver	5-1	W
57	2-17	at Los Angeles	6-4	W
58	2-18	at California	2-2	T
59	2-20	Detroit	4-3	W
60	2-22	at Montreal	7-3	W
61	2-23	Philadelphia	4-3	W
62	2-27	St. Louis	2-0	W
63	3-1	California	4-1	W
64	3-2	at Buffalo	4-3	W
65	3-5	Vancouver	6-1	W
66	3-8	Chicago	3-3	T
67	3-11	at Detroit	4-2	W
68	3-12	California	3-7	L
69	3-15	at Chicago	1-3	L
70	3-16	at Detroit	2-1	W
71	3-18	at Philadelphia	5-3	W
72	3-19	Toronto	5-3	W
73	3-23	at Boston	1-4	L
74	3-25	at Montreal	3-3	T
75	3-26	Minnesota	0-5	L
76	3-29	Detroit	2-2	T
77	4-1	at Toronto	1-2	L
78	4-2	Montreal	5-6	L

1972-73

Game No.	Date	Opponent	Score	Result
1	10-7	at Detroit	3-5	L
2	10-8	at Chicago	1-5	L
3	10-11	Vancouver	5-3	W
4	10-14	at Montreal	1-6	L
5	10-15	Minnesota	6-2	W
6	10-18	Boston	7-1	W
7	10-21	at Islanders	2-1	W
8	10-22	Montreal	1-1	T
9	10-25	Philadelphia	6-1	W
10	10-29	Chicago	7-1	W
11	11-1	at Chicago	3-2	W
12	11-4	at Pittsburgh	4-6	L
13	11-5	at Philadelphia	3-2	W
14	11-8	Vancouver	5-2	W
15	11-11	California	7-2	W
16	11-12	Los Angeles	5-1	W
17	11-15	Philadelphia	7-3	W
18	11-18	at St. Louis	3-1	W
19	11-19	Pittsburgh	3-5	L
20	11-21	at Atlanta	3-1	W
21	11-23	at Buffalo	3-5	L
22	11-26	Toronto	7-4	W
23	11-28	at Vancouver	1-2	L
24	11-29	at Los Angeles	2-2	T
25	12-1	at California	3-3	T
26	12-3	Atlanta	3-2	W
27	12-6	Buffalo	2-3	L
28	12-9	at Islanders	4-1	W
29	12-10	Islanders	4-1	W
30	12-13	at Toronto	4-3	W
31	12-14	at Boston	2-4	L
32	12-16	at Minnesota	1-5	L
33	12-17	Pittsburgh	9-1	W
34	12-20	at St. Louis	5-4	W
35	12-21	Atlanta	2-5	L
36	12-24	Detroit	5-0	W
37	12-27	Buffalo	1-4	L
38	12-31	St. Louis	6-1	W
39	1-3	Los Angeles	3-0	W

1972-73 (cont'd)

Game No.	Date	Opponent	Score	Result
40	1-6	Buffalo	1-4	L
41	1-7	Pittsburgh	3-0	W
42	1-11	at Buffalo	4-2	W
43	1-13	at St. Louis	5-3	W
44	1-14	at Philadelphia	5-2	W
45	1-17	at Los Angeles	4-4	T
46	1-19	at California	6-0	W
47	1-20	at Vancouver	4-3	W
48	1-24	Boston	4-2	W
49	1-27	at Detroit	6-3	W
50	1-28	Toronto	5-2	W
51	1-31	California	3-1	W
52	2-3	at Boston	7-3	W
53	2-4	Atlanta	6-0	W
54	2-7	Islanders	6-0	W
55	2-10	at Islanders	6-0	W
56	2-11	Montreal	2-2	T
57	2-14	at Montreal	3-6	L
58	2-15	at Buffalo	1-4	L
59	2-18	Islanders	3-2	W
60	2-21	at Los Angeles	4-3	W
61	2-23	at California	3-5	L
62	2-25	Minnesota	6-5	W
63	2-28	Chicago	3-3	T
64	3-3	at Detroit	6-3	W
65	3-4	Vancouver	3-4	L
66	3-7	Philadelphia	2-2	T
67	3-10	at Pittsburgh	5-4	W
68	3-11	Toronto	4-2	W
69	3-14	at Chicago	2-4	L
70	3-17	at Toronto	5-7	L
71	3-18	St. Louis	3-1	W
72	3-20	at Minnesota	6-1	W
73	3-22	at Atlanta	4-1	W
74	3-24	at Boston	0-3	L
75	3-25	Minnesota	1-2	L
76	3-28	Boston	3-6	L
77	3-31	at Montreal	1-5	L
78	4-1	Detroit	3-3	T

Game-By-Game Results
1973-74—1974-75

Game No.	Date	Opponent	Score	Result
1973-74				
1	10-10	Detroit	4-1	W
2	10-13	at Pittsburgh	8-2	W
3	10-14	Los Angeles	1-1	T
4	10-17	St. Louis	4-0	W
5	10-20	at Toronto	2-3	L
6	10-21	Montreal	2-3	L
7	10-27	at Islanders	2-3	L
8	10-28	Pittsburgh	2-7	L
9	10-30	at Vancouver	3-3	T
10	11-1	at Los Angeles	1-2	L
11	11-4	at Chicago	1-4	L
12	11-7	Boston	7-3	W
13	11-9	at Atlanta	3-3	T
14	11-11	Islanders	5-2	W
15	11-14	Chicago	4-4	T
16	11-15	at Boston	2-10	L
17	11-17	at Minnesota	6-3	W
18	11-18	Pittsburgh	7-0	W
19	11-21	California	3-0	W
20	11-22	at Buffalo	7-6	W
21	11-24	Los Angeles	5-5	T
22	11-25	Vancouver	5-0	W
23	11-29	at Philadelphia	2-2	T
24	12-1	at St. Louis	4-4	T
25	12-2	Toronto	6-4	W
26	12-5	St. Louis	5-1	W
27	12-6	at Buffalo	4-8	L
28	12-9	California	6-3	W
29	12-12	Buffalo	1-1	T
30	12-15	at Toronto	2-2	T
31	12-16	Chicago	1-6	L
32	12-20	Detroit	5-2	W
33	12-22	at Pittsburgh	4-1	W
34	12-23	at Atlanta	1-3	L
35	12-26	Philadelphia	2-1	W
36	12-29	at Montreal	1-7	L
37	12-30	Minnesota	4-3	W
38	1-3	at Philadelphia	2-4	L
39	1-4	Boston	2-4	L

Game No.	Date	Opponent	Score	Result
1973-74 (cont'd)				
40	1-6	Atlanta	5-2	W
41	1-10	at Buffalo	2-7	L
42	1-12	at Vancouver	6-1	W
43	1-13	at California	7-2	W
44	1-16	at Detroit	4-4	T
45	1-17	at St. Louis	2-3	L
46	1-19	at Chicago	3-2	W
47	1-23	Atlanta	4-1	W
48	1-27	Los Angeles	5-3	W
49	1-30	at Pittsburgh	4-2	W
50	2-2	at Minnesota	3-1	W
51	2-3	Minnesota	5-5	T
52	2-6	Islanders	6-0	W
53	2-9	at Montreal	2-7	L
54	2-10	St. Louis	4-2	W
55	2-14	at Philadelphia	4-4	T
56	2-16	at Vancouver	9-4	W
57	2-21	at Los Angeles	5-3	W
58	2-22	at California	4-3	W
59	2-24	Philadelphia	3-2	W
60	2-27	Vancouver	4-2	W
61	3-2	at Minnesota	3-1	W
62	3-3	California	8-2	W
63	3-6	Montreal	9-2	W
64	3-9	at Montreal	2-4	L
65	3-10	Islanders	4-2	W
66	3-14	Chicago	2-5	L
67	3-16	at Islanders	3-1	W
68	3-17	at Boston	2-5	L
69	3-20	Vancouver	5-7	L
70	3-21	at Atlanta	5-5	T
71	3-23	at Detroit	3-5	L
72	3-24	Buffalo	5-3	W
73	3-27	Boston	2-3	L
74	3-30	at Toronto	3-7	L
75	3-31	Toronto	3-3	T
76	4-3	Detroit	5-3	W
77	4-6	at Detroit	3-8	L
78	4-7	Montreal	6-4	W

Game No.	Date	Opponent	Score	Result
1974-75				
1	10-9	Washington	6-3	W
2	10-12	at Toronto	3-7	L
3	10-16	California	5-5	T
4	10-19	at Islanders	4-2	W
5	10-20	Vancouver	0-1	L
6	10-23	St. Louis	5-1	W
7	10-26	at Pittsburgh	5-4	W
8	10-27	Atlanta	4-1	W
9	10-30	Islanders	1-1	T
10	10-31	at Philadelphia	1-5	L
11	11-3	Buffalo	3-4	L
12	11-5	at Vancouver	1-2	L
13	11-6	at California	7-3	W
14	11-9	at Los Angeles	2-2	T
15	11-13	Philadelphia	2-3	L
16	11-16	at Montreal	4-4	T
17	11-17	California	10-0	W
18	11-20	at Detroit	5-4	W
19	11-23	Boston	2-5	L
20	11-24	Pittsburgh	7-5	W
21	11-27	Toronto	4-1	W
22	11-29	at Atlanta	2-3	L
23	12-1	St. Louis	4-4	T
24	12-4	Detroit	4-2	W
25	12-7	at Chicago	7-4	W
26	12-8	Montreal	3-3	T
27	12-12	at Washington	6-6	T
28	12-14	at St. Louis	2-6	L
29	12-15	Los Angeles	3-3	T
30	12-18	Minnesota	7-0	W
31	12-19	at Boston	3-11	L
32	12-22	Atlanta	3-4	L
33	12-27	Buffalo	9-5	W
34	12-29	Kansas City	2-1	W
35	12-30	at Minnesota	8-1	W
36	1-1	Chicago	6-2	W
37	1-4	at Islanders	5-3	W
38	1-5	Vancouver	6-2	W
39	1-8	at Kansas City	6-1	W
40	1-11	at St. Louis	5-3	W

Game No.	Date	Opponent	Score	Result
1974-75 (cont'd)				
41	1-12	at Chicago	2-4	L
42	1-15	at Minnesota	5-3	W
43	1-17	at California	4-4	T
44	1-18	at Vancouver	3-2	W
45	1-23	Atlanta	5-2	W
46	1-25	at Pittsburgh	2-5	L
47	1-26	Los Angeles	3-2	W
48	1-28	at Los Angeles	2-5	L
49	1-30	at Buffalo	3-6	L
50	2-1	at Chicago	4-1	W
51	2-2	Detroit	5-5	T
52	2-5	Philadelphia	3-4	L
53	2-6	at Philadelphia	3-1	W
54	2-8	at Montreal	1-7	L
55	2-9	Washington	7-3	W
56	2-11	at Washington	4-7	L
57	2-15	at Minnesota	9-2	W
58	2-16	Toronto	5-5	T
59	2-18	at Kansas City	2-2	T
60	2-19	Chicago	2-2	T
61	2-22	at Toronto	2-5	L
62	2-23	Philadelphia	2-1	W
63	2-26	St. Louis	5-1	W
64	3-2	Pittsburgh	6-8	L
65	3-5	Buffalo	3-6	L
66	3-7	at Kansas City	5-2	W
67	3-9	Montreal	3-5	L
68	3-11	at Boston	3-6	L
69	3-12	Islanders	5-3	W
70	3-14	at Atlanta	0-1	L
71	3-19	Vancouver	3-0	W
72	3-20	at Buffalo	3-6	L
73	3-22	at Detroit	4-7	L
74	3-23	Boston	7-5	W
75	3-26	Minnesota	2-4	L
76	3-29	at Islanders	4-6	L
77	3-30	Kansas City	8-2	W
78	4-3	at Philadelphia	1-1	T
79	4-4	at Atlanta	3-2	W
80	4-6	Islanders	4-6	L

Game-By-Game Results
1975-76—1976-77

Game No.	Date	Opponent	Score	Result
1975-76				
1	10-8	Chicago	2-2	T
2	10-10	at Atlanta	2-1	W
3	10-12	Los Angeles	4-6	L
4	10-15	Atlanta	3-1	W
5	10-18	at Toronto	1-4	L
6	10-19	Vancouver	8-1	W
7	10-22	at Buffalo	1-9	L
8	10-25	at Islanders	1-7	L
9	10-26	Philadelphia	2-7	L
10	10-29	St. Louis	3-1	W
11	11-1	at Montreal	0-4	L
12	11-2	Detroit	4-6	L
13	11-4	at Vancouver	4-2	W
14	11-7	at California	5-7	L
15	11-8	at Los Angeles	1-3	L
16	11-11	at St. Louis	3-5	L
17	11-12	Chicago	4-4	T
18	11-15	at Minnesota	5-2	W
19	11-16	Detroit	3-0	W
20	11-19	Kansas City	4-6	L
21	11-22	at Philadelphia	2-4	L
22	11-23	California	3-2	W
23	11-26	Boston	4-6	L
24	11-29	at Pittsburgh	3-8	L
25	11-30	St. Louis	5-2	W
26	12-4	at Buffalo	6-6	T
27	12-5	at Kansas City	3-2	W
28	12-7	Washington	5-2	W
29	12-10	Buffalo	2-2	T
30	12-11	at Boston	5-1	W
31	12-13	at Detroit	5-2	W
32	12-14	Toronto	1-6	L
33	12-17	Islanders	0-3	L
34	12-19	at Atlanta	3-8	L
35	12-21	Minnesota	2-0	W
36	12-23	Pittsburgh	4-3	W
37	12-31	Atlanta	1-8	L
38	1-4	Toronto	6-8	L
39	1-6	at St. Louis	2-5	L
40	1-10	at Kansas City	8-4	W

Game No.	Date	Opponent	Score	Result
1975-76 (cont'd)				
41	1-11	at Chicago	6-2	W
42	1-14	at Vancouver	1-5	L
43	1-16	at California	0-7	L
44	1-18	at Pittsburgh	3-8	L
45	1-21	Chicago	3-3	T
46	1-23	at Washington	5-7	L
47	1-25	Los Angeles	1-4	L
48	1-28	Buffalo	3-3	T
49	1-29	at St. Louis	6-3	W
50	1-31	at Toronto	4-6	L
51	2-1	Minnesota	3-2	W
52	2-4	Islanders	5-6	L
53	2-7	at Detroit	5-4	W
54	2-8	Montreal	0-3	L
55	2-12	at Philadelphia	1-6	L
56	2-13	Philadelphia	3-5	L
57	2-15	Kansas City	5-1	W
58	2-17	at Islanders	3-1	W
59	2-18	Washington	11-4	W
60	2-20	at Montreal	3-5	L
61	2-22	Boston	2-5	L
62	2-25	California	4-6	L
63	2-28	at Minnesota	3-5	L
64	2-29	Montreal	1-1	T
65	3-3	Vancouver	3-3	T
66	3-5	at Atlanta	3-8	L
67	3-7	Atlanta	6-6	T
68	3-11	at Los Angeles	3-4	L
69	3-13	at Vancouver	7-3	W
70	3-16	at Washington	2-5	L
71	3-17	Minnesota	3-1	W
72	3-20	at Boston	1-8	L
73	3-21	Pittsburgh	2-4	L
74	3-24	at Buffalo	3-7	L
75	3-25	at Philadelphia	1-4	L
76	3-27	at Chicago	6-5	W
77	3-28	Kansas City	4-2	W
78	3-31	Islanders	3-1	W
79	4-3	at Islanders	2-10	L
80	4-4	Philadelphia	2-0	W

Game No.	Date	Opponent	Score	Result
1976-77				
1	10-6	Minnesota	6-5	W
2	10-8	at Colorado	5-3	W
3	10-9	at St. Louis	1-2	L
4	10-12	at Minnesota	10-4	W
5	10-13	Boston	1-5	L
6	10-16	at Montreal	4-7	L
7	10-17	Colorado	4-3	W
8	10-20	Los Angeles	2-4	L
9	10-24	Vancouver	4-5	L
10	10-26	at Cleveland	5-2	W
11	10-27	Boston	3-4	L
12	10-30	at Pittsburgh	2-2	T
13	10-31	Detroit	5-6	L
14	11-3	at Vancouver	6-1	W
15	11-6	at Los Angeles	3-3	T
16	11-10	Washington	5-7	L
17	11-13	Buffalo	2-6	L
18	11-14	Pittsburgh	1-5	L
19	11-17	Chicago	3-2	W
20	11-20	at St. Louis	1-3	L
21	11-22	at Vancouver	3-2	W
22	11-24	at Philadelphia	2-2	T
23	11-27	at Detroit	5-0	W
24	11-28	Minnesota	4-1	W
25	11-30	at Atlanta	2-2	T
26	12-1	Washington	4-1	W
27	12-4	at Minnesota	11-4	W
28	12-5	Toronto	5-5	T
29	12-8	St. Louis	4-4	T
30	12-11	at Toronto	1-4	L
31	12-12	Montreal	5-2	W
32	12-14	at Islanders	4-4	T
33	12-16	at Buffalo	2-7	L
34	12-18	at Chicago	3-3	T
35	12-19	Cleveland	3-2	W
36	12-22	Philadelphia	3-3	T
37	12-23	at Boston	3-3	T
38	12-26	Islanders	1-2	L
39	12-28	at Washington	5-2	W
40	12-31	Atlanta	2-4	L

Game No.	Date	Opponent	Score	Result
1976-77 (cont'd)				
41	1-2	Vancouver	5-3	W
42	1-5	Philadelphia	4-4	T
43	1-7	at Colorado	4-4	T
44	1-9	Los Angeles	4-5	L
45	1-12	at Atlanta	1-6	L
46	1-13	at Buffalo	5-7	L
47	1-16	at Chicago	5-2	W
48	1-19	at Cleveland	3-3	T
49	1-22	at Los Angeles	0-6	L
50	1-23	at Vancouver	2-6	L
51	1-27	Pittsburgh	0-3	L
52	1-30	St. Louis	5-2	W
53	2-1	at Colorado	2-5	L
54	2-3	at Islanders	3-6	L
55	2-6	Islanders	4-0	W
56	2-9	Buffalo	1-2	L
57	2-10	at Detroit	5-4	W
58	2-13	Toronto	8-3	W
59	2-17	at Philadelphia	1-7	L
60	2-19	at Islanders	2-5	L
61	2-20	Detroit	3-2	W
62	2-23	at Toronto	5-4	W
63	2-26	at Chicago	1-2	L
64	2-27	Montreal	1-8	L
65	3-3	Boston	1-4	L
66	3-5	at Montreal	2-7	L
67	3-6	Cleveland	4-3	W
68	3-9	Minnesota	6-4	W
69	3-10	at Boston	3-10	L
70	3-12	at Atlanta	3-6	L
71	3-13	Atlanta	3-5	L
72	3-16	Philadelphia	4-4	T
73	3-19	at Pittsburgh	5-2	W
74	3-20	St. Louis	5-3	W
75	3-23	Colorado	5-3	W
76	3-25	at Washington	2-7	L
77	3-27	Chicago	3-5	L
78	3-30	Atlanta	4-3	W
79	4-2	at Philadelphia	1-4	L
80	4-3	Islanders	2-5	L

Game-By-Game Results
1977-78—1978-79

Game No.	Date	Opponent	Score	Result
1977-78				
1	10-12	Vancouver	6-3	W
2	10-15	at Montreal	0-5	L
3	10-16	Islanders	4-2	W
4	10-19	Pittsburgh	3-3	T
5	10-22	at Islanders	2-7	L
6	10-23	Montreal	2-6	L
7	10-25	at Cleveland	5-0	W
8	10-26	St. Louis	6-2	W
9	10-29	at Atlanta	3-4	L
10	10-30	Los Angeles	3-5	L
11	11-2	at Colorado	2-6	L
12	11-4	at Vancouver	5-1	W
13	11-5	at Los Angeles	1-3	L
14	11-9	Buffalo	8-4	W
15	11-12	at Detroit	1-3	L
16	11-13	Atlanta	2-5	L
17	11-16	Chicago	5-2	W
18	11-19	at Pittsburgh	5-5	T
19	11-20	Vancouver	0-3	L
20	11-23	Colorado	6-3	W
21	11-26	at Boston	2-3	L
22	11-27	at Buffalo	2-3	L
23	11-30	at St. Louis	4-0	W
24	12-3	at Minnesota	4-0	W
25	12-4	Minnesota	4-4	T
26	12-7	Philadelphia	3-3	T
27	12-8	at Philadelphia	4-7	L
28	12-11	Boston	2-8	L
29	12-14	at Chicago	2-2	T
30	12-15	at Detroit	5-5	T
31	12-17	at Cleveland	2-4	L
32	12-18	Detroit	6-2	W
33	12-21	Washington	5-5	T
34	12-23	Cleveland	5-4	W
35	12-28	Philadelphia	3-4	L
36	12-30	at Washington	3-3	T
37	12-31	Buffalo	2-2	T
38	1-4	at Minnesota	5-3	W
39	1-7	at Colorado	1-3	L
40	1-9	Pittsburgh	3-5	L

Game No.	Date	Opponent	Score	Result
1977-78 (cont'd)				
41	1-10	at Boston	3-2	W
42	1-14	at Philadelphia	1-4	L
43	1-17	at Vancouver	5-4	W
44	1-18	at Los Angeles	3-0	W
45	1-20	at Atlanta	3-5	L
46	1-22	at Pittsburgh	1-3	L
47	1-25	Toronto	3-4	L
48	1-28	at Islanders	2-6	L
49	1-29	Los Angeles	1-4	L
50	2-1	Islanders	6-7	L
51	2-4	at St. Louis	2-2	T
52	2-5	Colorado	6-3	W
53	2-8	Minnesota	3-0	W
54	2-9	at Buffalo	0-2	L
55	2-11	at Toronto	2-3	L
56	2-12	Montreal	3-5	L
57	2-15	Vancouver	6-3	W
58	2-19	Colorado	4-4	T
59	2-22	at Chicago	2-3	L
60	2-23	Chicago	6-2	W
61	2-25	at Montreal	6-3	W
62	2-27	Atlanta	3-5	L
63	3-1	Detroit	3-2	W
64	3-5	Toronto	1-4	L
65	3-8	Cleveland	6-1	W
66	3-12	Washington	8-2	W
67	3-15	Philadelphia	2-2	T
68	3-18	Boston	3-6	L
69	3-19	at Minnesota	7-7	T
70	3-22	at St. Louis	6-1	W
71	3-24	at Washington	11-4	W
72	3-25	at Toronto	5-2	W
73	3-27	St. Louis	5-2	W
74	3-29	Islanders	5-1	W
75	4-1	at Atlanta	0-6	L
76	4-2	at Boston	3-8	L
77	4-5	Atlanta	2-4	L
78	4-6	at Philadelphia	0-3	L
79	4-8	at Islanders	2-7	L
80	4-9	Chicago	3-2	W

Game No.	Date	Opponent	Score	Result
1978-79				
1	10-12	Philadelphia	3-3	T
2	10-15	Colorado	4-1	W
3	10-18	Detroit	3-3	T
4	10-19	at Detroit	2-2	T
5	10-21	at Islanders	3-5	L
6	10-22	Toronto	5-2	W
7	10-25	Vancouver	6-2	W
8	10-28	at Montreal	2-1	W
9	10-29	Pittsburgh	3-2	W
10	11-2	at Colorado	3-0	W
11	11-4	at Los Angeles	7-3	W
12	11-5	at Vancouver	5-2	W
13	11-8	Minnesota	3-5	L
14	11-11	at Pittsburgh	2-1	W
15	11-12	Islanders	3-5	L
16	11-15	Chicago	8-1	W
17	11-18	at Minnesota	7-2	W
18	11-19	Atlanta	1-3	L
19	11-22	Toronto	3-3	T
20	11-26	Washington	9-4	W
21	11-29	at Atlanta	5-3	W
22	12-2	at Toronto	2-5	L
23	12-3	Boston	2-3	L
24	12-6	St. Louis	7-4	W
25	12-7	at Philadelphia	5-2	W
26	12-9	at Detroit	4-5	L
27	12-10	Philadelphia	0-4	L
28	12-13	Los Angeles	8-7	W
29	12-16	at Boston	1-4	L
30	12-17	Boston	1-4	L
31	12-20	Buffalo	6-3	W
32	12-22	Detroit	4-2	W
33	12-23	at Islanders	4-9	L
34	12-26	at Atlanta	5-3	W
35	12-28	at Philadelphia	5-6	L
36	12-30	at Chicago	5-4	W
37	12-31	Atlanta	5-6	L
38	1-3	Montreal	6-2	W
39	1-5	Vancouver	6-4	W
40	1-9	at St. Louis	5-3	W

Game No.	Date	Opponent	Score	Result
1978-79 (cont'd)				
41	1-10	at Colorado	5-3	W
42	1-14	at Atlanta	6-4	W
43	1-15	Minnesota	1-8	L
44	1-17	Islanders	5-3	W
45	1-20	at St. Louis	2-3	L
46	1-21	Philadelphia	5-5	T
47	1-24	at Washington	1-5	L
48	1-25	at Buffalo	5-4	W
49	1-27	at Islanders	7-2	W
50	1-30	at Vancouver	5-3	W
51	1-31	at Colorado	4-5	L
52	2-3	at Los Angeles	2-4	L
53	2-14	Boston	5-1	W
54	2-15	at Buffalo	3-4	L
55	2-17	at Philadelphia	4-2	W
56	2-18	Washington	6-6	T
57	2-21	St. Louis	7-3	W
58	2-24	at Toronto	4-2	W
59	2-25	Islanders	3-2	W
60	2-27	at St. Louis	1-4	L
61	2-28	at Minnesota	4-4	T
62	3-3	Buffalo	2-2	T
63	3-4	Toronto	2-4	L
64	3-7	Colorado	5-3	W
65	3-10	at Montreal	6-3	W
66	3-11	Chicago	5-2	W
67	3-14	Atlanta	4-6	L
68	3-15	at Boston	7-4	W
69	3-17	at Islanders	2-5	L
70	3-18	Pittsburgh	1-5	L
71	3-20	at Washington	2-2	T
72	3-21	at Chicago	7-6	W
73	3-25	Montreal	0-1	L
74	3-27	Philadelphia	4-4	T
75	3-28	at Pittsburgh	1-7	L
76	4-1	at Philadelphia	3-7	L
77	4-2	Los Angeles	5-4	W
78	4-4	Atlanta	3-3	T
79	4-6	at Atlanta	2-9	L
80	4-8	Islanders	2-5	L

Game-By-Game Results
1979-80—1980-81

Game No.	Date	Opponent	Score	Result
1979-80				
1	10-10	at Toronto	6-3	W
2	10-14	Washington	3-5	L
3	10-18	Vancouver	6-3	W
4	10-20	at Montreal	4-5	L
5	10-21	Pittsburgh	6-3	W
6	10-24	Edmonton	10-2	W
7	10-25	at Philadelphia	2-5	L
8	10-27	at Minnesota	2-7	L
9	10-28	Hartford	2-2	T
10	11-1	at Los Angeles	2-4	L
11	11-3	at Colorado	2-7	L
12	11-4	at Vancouver	4-2	W
13	11-7	Los Angeles	8-4	W
14	11-10	Quebec	5-4	W
15	11-11	Pittsburgh	1-4	L
16	11-13	at Islanders	5-10	L
17	11-14	Detroit	3-2	W
18	11-16	at Atlanta	2-4	L
19	11-18	St. Louis	5-3	W
20	11-21	Winnipeg	4-6	L
21	11-24	at Pittsburgh	3-5	L
22	11-25	Toronto	3-4	L
23	11-28	Minnesota	4-4	T
24	11-29	at Buffalo	1-2	L
25	12-1	at St. Louis	2-0	W
26	12-3	Montreal	3-3	T
27	12-5	Chicago	3-3	T
28	12-7	at Hartford	7-4	W
29	12-9	Islanders	5-4	W
30	12-11	at Detroit	2-1	W
31	12-12	at Chicago	5-2	W
32	12-15	at Washington	4-5	L
33	12-16	Philadelphia	1-1	T
34	12-19	Vancouver	5-3	W
35	12-22	at Pittsburgh	4-3	W
36	12-23	Boston	3-4	L
37	12-30	Washington	5-2	W
38	1-2	at Quebec	3-3	T
39	1-4	Philadelphia	3-5	L
40	1-6	Atlanta	5-5	T

Game No.	Date	Opponent	Score	Result
1979-80 (cont'd)				
41	1-7	Hartford	5-2	W
42	1-9	at Detroit	0-4	L
43	1-11	at Edmonton	6-2	W
44	1-12	at Winnipeg	3-0	W
45	1-14	Colorado	6-6	T
46	1-16	Winnipeg	4-1	W
47	1-19	at Boston	3-6	L
48	1-20	Chicago	1-2	L
49	1-22	at Los Angeles	5-4	W
50	1-23	at Vancouver	6-4	W
51	1-27	at Colorado	3-3	T
52	1-31	at Buffalo	2-6	L
53	2-2	at Washington	6-3	W
54	2-3	at Quebec	4-5	L
55	2-10	Quebec	3-1	W
56	2-13	at Chicago	1-3	L
57	2-17	Toronto	4-6	L
58	2-18	at Hartford	4-6	L
59	2-20	Edmonton	4-1	W
60	2-23	at Minnesota	3-6	L
61	2-24	Islanders	8-2	W
62	2-27	Los Angeles	5-4	W
63	2-28	at Boston	5-2	W
64	3-2	Boston	2-1	W
65	3-5	Buffalo	4-2	W
66	3-8	at Montreal	2-5	L
67	3-9	Minnesota	4-2	W
68	3-12	Colorado	6-0	W
69	3-15	at Toronto	8-4	W
70	3-16	St. Louis	5-2	W
71	3-19	at Edmonton	2-4	L
72	3-21	at Winnipeg	2-4	L
73	3-23	Montreal	1-6	L
74	3-25	Buffalo	3-3	T
75	3-28	at Atlanta	2-4	L
76	3-29	at St. Louis	4-3	W
77	3-31	Detroit	7-5	W
78	4-2	Atlanta	3-7	L
79	4-5	at Islanders	1-2	L
80	4-6	at Philadelphia	8-3	W

Game No.	Date	Opponent	Score	Result
1980-81				
1	10-9	at Boston	2-7	L
2	10-11	at Toronto	8-3	W
3	10-12	Pittsburgh	3-6	L
4	10-15	St. Louis	1-2	L
5	10-18	at Washington	2-8	L
6	10-19	Edmonton	2-4	L
7	10-22	Vancouver	3-2	W
8	10-25	at Detroit	2-4	L
9	10-26	Detroit	7-6	W
10	10-28	at St. Louis	4-5	L
11	10-30	at Philadelphia	3-3	T
12	11-1	at Montreal	4-7	L
13	11-2	Los Angeles	3-6	L
14	11-5	at Chicago	3-3	T
15	11-8	at Vancouver	4-6	L
16	11-10	at Los Angeles	1-4	L
17	11-11	at Calgary	3-7	L
18	11-14	Pittsburgh	3-3	T
19	11-16	Hartford	7-3	W
20	11-19	Philadelphia	1-5	L
21	11-22	at Islanders	4-6	L
22	11-23	Vancouver	2-2	T
23	11-26	Boston	6-4	W
24	11-29	at Pittsburgh	4-2	W
25	12-1	Minnesota	3-5	L
26	12-3	at Winnipeg	4-3	W
27	12-5	at Edmonton	5-1	W
28	12-7	Chicago	5-4	W
29	12-10	Washington	6-2	W
30	12-12	at Colorado	4-3	W
31	12-14	at Chicago	1-2	L
32	12-17	Winnipeg	8-2	W
33	12-20	at Minnesota	3-3	T
34	12-22	Calgary	2-3	L
35	12-26	at Washington	3-7	L
36	12-28	Montreal	2-5	L
37	12-30	at Quebec	6-3	W
38	12-31	Colorado	4-6	L
39	1-2	Islanders	3-1	W
40	1-4	Quebec	2-2	T

Game No.	Date	Opponent	Score	Result
1980-81 (cont'd)				
41	1-9	Buffalo	3-3	T
42	1-11	Toronto	3-5	L
43	1-13	at Calgary	4-4	T
44	1-15	at Colorado	3-4	L
45	1-18	at Buffalo	0-4	L
46	1-19	Calgary	6-3	W
47	1-21	at Winnipeg	1-5	L
48	1-23	at Edmonton	7-4	W
49	1-24	at Vancouver	7-5	W
50	1-28	at Los Angeles	6-2	W
51	1-31	at Minnesota	7-3	W
52	2-2	Los Angeles	2-3	L
53	2-4	Islanders	9-3	W
54	2-5	at Boston	3-6	L
55	2-8	Minnesota	3-3	T
56	2-12	Winnipeg	8-6	W
57	2-14	at Toronto	3-6	L
58	2-15	St. Louis	4-5	L
59	2-18	Toronto	8-3	W
60	2-19	at Detroit	3-7	L
61	2-21	Washington	6-4	W
62	2-22	at Hartford	5-6	L
63	2-25	Buffalo	6-3	W
64	2-28	at Pittsburgh	4-6	L
65	3-1	Montreal	4-4	T
66	3-4	Edmonton	5-5	T
67	3-7	at St. Louis	2-7	L
68	3-8	Detroit	4-4	T
69	3-10	at Quebec	4-6	L
70	3-11	Colorado	3-4	L
71	3-14	Hartford	6-2	W
72	3-18	Boston	3-2	W
73	3-21	at Hartford	6-4	W
74	3-22	Quebec	7-7	T
75	3-25	at Buffalo	2-4	L
76	3-28	at Montreal	6-2	W
77	3-30	Philadelphia	0-0	T
78	4-2	at Islanders	1-2	L
79	4-3	Chicago	3-1	W
80	4-5	at Philadelphia	2-0	W

Game-By-Game Results
1981-82—1982-83

Game No.	Date	Opponent	Score	Result
1981-82				
1	10-6	Detroit	2-5	L
2	10-9	at Winnipeg	3-8	L
3	10-10	at Minnesota	0-7	L
4	10-14	Vancouver	2-1	W
5	10-17	at Islanders	4-5	L
6	10-18	St. Louis	5-3	W
7	10-21	Los Angeles	2-5	L
8	10-24	at Toronto	5-3	W
9	10-25	Montreal	2-4	L
10	10-28	Edmonton	3-5	L
11	10-31	at Boston	3-7	L
12	11-1	Calgary	4-2	W
13	11-4	at Pittsburgh	3-6	L
14	11-5	at Philadelphia	6-2	W
15	11-7	at Washington	3-1	W
16	11-11	Buffalo	7-3	W
17	11-13	at Buffalo	3-3	T
18	11-15	Edmonton	3-5	L
19	11-18	Philadelphia	5-2	W
20	11-21	at Islanders	3-4	L
21	11-22	Islanders	2-7	L
22	11-25	Toronto	3-3	T
23	11-28	at Quebec	4-7	L
24	11-29	Quebec	4-4	T
25	12-2	at Los Angeles	4-3	W
26	12-5	at Colorado	2-1	W
27	12-6	Hartford	3-5	L
28	12-9	Boston	3-4	L
29	12-12	at Philadelphia	5-3	W
30	12-14	Pittsburgh	5-4	W
31	12-16	Philadelphia	3-7	L
32	12-19	at Pittsburgh	3-3	T
33	12-20	Washington	2-3	W
34	12-23	Winnipeg	5-2	W
35	12-26	at Washington	4-4	T
36	12-27	Pittsburgh	5-3	W
37	12-30	Islanders	6-4	W
38	1-2	at Montreal	6-5	W
39	1-3	Washington	3-4	L
40	1-7	Vancouver	4-1	W

Game No.	Date	Opponent	Score	Result
1981-82 (cont'd)				
41	1-9	Chicago	7-5	W
42	1-11	Minnesota	5-3	W
43	1-13	at Minnesota	2-0	W
44	1-15	at Winnipeg	4-4	T
45	1-18	at Toronto	2-6	L
46	1-20	Islanders	3-2	W
47	1-23	at Islanders	1-6	L
48	1-24	Washington	4-4	T
49	1-27	at Washington	5-4	W
50	1-29	at Colorado	5-2	W
51	1-31	at Los Angeles	6-3	W
52	2-2	at Vancouver	4-3	W
53	2-4	at Calgary	4-4	T
54	2-7	at Edmonton	4-8	L
55	2-10	at St. Louis	3-3	T
56	2-13	at Hartford	3-2	W
57	2-14	Quebec	5-2	W
58	2-17	at Pittsburgh	5-3	W
59	2-18	Colorado	4-4	T
60	2-21	Montreal	2-4	L
61	2-24	Chicago	6-4	W
62	2-27	at Boston	6-4	W
63	2-28	Pittsburgh	2-4	L
64	3-3	Calgary	4-2	W
65	3-4	at Philadelphia	4-4	T
66	3-6	at Islanders	4-6	L
67	3-8	Detroit	6-3	W
68	3-10	Philadelphia	5-5	T
69	3-11	at Detroit	4-1	W
70	3-14	Washington	5-5	T
71	3-17	Philadelphia	5-2	W
72	3-20	at Washington	4-3	W
73	3-21	St. Louis	8-5	W
74	3-24	at Pittsburgh	7-2	W
75	3-26	at Buffalo	8-5	W
76	3-28	at Philadelphia	1-3	L
77	3-29	Islanders	3-7	L
78	3-31	at Chicago	4-1	W
79	4-2	Pittsburgh	5-7	L
80	4-3	at Hartford	3-3	T

Game No.	Date	Opponent	Score	Result
1982-83				
1	10-6	Washington	4-5	L
2	10-8	at New Jersey	2-3	L
3	10-9	at Pittsburgh	5-3	W
4	10-11	Islanders	3-4	L
5	10-13	Philadelphia	5-2	W
6	10-16	at Montreal	2-8	L
7	10-17	Los Angeles	3-5	L
8	10-20	Vancouver	6-5	W
9	10-23	at Islanders	2-5	L
10	10-24	Minnesota	4-2	W
11	10-27	Calgary	7-4	W
12	10-30	at Quebec	4-5	L
13	10-31	Pittsburgh	6-2	W
14	11-5	at Edmonton	1-5	L
15	11-6	at Calgary	2-2	T
16	11-10	St. Louis	5-4	W
17	11-11	at Philadelphia	3-7	L
18	11-14	Edmonton	2-7	L
19	11-17	Toronto	6-1	W
20	11-20	at Toronto	6-3	W
21	11-21	Islanders	7-3	W
22	11-24	Minnesota	8-5	W
23	11-27	at Islanders	3-0	W
24	11-28	at Buffalo	3-7	L
25	12-1	Hartford	6-1	W
26	12-4	at Hartford	2-5	L
27	12-5	Toronto	6-5	W
28	12-8	at Chicago	2-7	L
29	12-10	at Washington	4-4	T
30	12-12	New Jersey	4-0	W
31	12-15	Los Angeles	7-1	W
32	12-17	Islanders	2-5	L
33	12-18	at Detroit	3-3	T
34	12-20	Pittsburgh	6-3	W
35	12-22	Buffalo	1-3	L
36	12-26	at Pittsburgh	3-4	L
37	12-30	at New Jersey	5-2	W
38	1-1	at Washington	7-2	W
39	1-3	Detroit	6-2	W
40	1-5	Buffalo	3-3	T

Game No.	Date	Opponent	Score	Result
1982-83 (cont'd)				
41	1-7	Quebec	5-1	W
42	1-9	New Jersey	4-3	W
43	1-12	Winnipeg	5-5	T
44	1-15	at Boston	0-2	L
45	1-16	Philadelphia	0-4	L
46	1-18	at Vancouver	3-3	T
47	1-21	at Winnipeg	1-4	L
48	1-23	at Philadelphia	1-3	L
49	1-24	Boston	1-3	L
50	1-27	Montreal	1-4	L
51	1-29	at Pittsburgh	2-1	W
52	1-30	Chicago	4-5	L
53	2-1	at Los Angeles	5-5	T
54	2-5	at St. Louis	2-2	T
55	2-6	at Chicago	1-4	L
56	2-10	at Minnesota	5-7	L
57	2-12	at Montreal	3-2	W
58	2-16	Washington	5-4	W
59	2-19	at Philadelphia	5-8	L
60	2-20	Winnipeg	9-4	W
61	2-23	Hartford	11-3	W
62	2-26	at Quebec	3-6	L
63	2-28	Pittsburgh	9-3	W
64	3-1	at Pittsburgh	3-3	T
65	3-3	Washington	3-4	L
66	3-6	New Jersey	4-6	L
67	3-8	at Vancouver	3-7	L
68	3-11	at Edmonton	1-3	L
69	3-12	at Calgary	4-1	W
70	3-14	Philadelphia	8-2	W
71	3-16	Islanders	2-1	W
72	3-20	Boston	0-4	L
73	3-21	at New Jersey	2-4	L
74	3-23	at Detroit	7-1	W
75	3-26	at Islanders	2-3	L
76	3-27	Washington	5-4	W
77	3-29	at St. Louis	4-3	W
78	3-31	at Philadelphia	4-2	W
79	4-1	New Jersey	3-3	T
80	4-3	at Washington	0-3	L

Game-By-Game Results
1983-84—1984-85

Game No.	Date	Opponent	Score	Result
1983-84				
1	10-5	New Jersey	6-2	W
2	10-7	at New Jersey	3-1	W
3	10-8	at Pittsburgh	6-1	W
4	10-10	Los Angeles	2-1	W
5	10-13	Washington	4-3	W
6	10-15	at St. Louis	5-6	L
7	10-16	Philadelphia	5-4	W
8	10-19	Calgary	3-1	W
9	10-22	at Islanders	3-2	W
10	10-23	Islanders	6-5*	W
11	10-26	Winnipeg	5-7	L
12	10-28	Toronto	3-5	L
13	10-30	Edmonton	4-5*	L
14	11-2	at Buffalo	3-3	T
15	11-5	at Quebec	4-4	T
16	11-8	at New Jersey	5-1	W
17	11-9	Calgary	4-3	W
18	11-12	at Washington	4-7	L
19	11-13	Detroit	6-3	W
20	11-16	Washington	4-1	W
21	11-19	at Boston	6-6	T
22	11-20	Quebec	6-5*	W
23	11-23	Buffalo	4-6	L
24	11-25	at Washington	1-3	L
25	11-26	at Hartford	3-4*	L
26	11-28	Vancouver	3-3	T
27	11-30	Chicago	0-4	L
28	12-3	at Detroit	4-2	W
29	12-4	Minnesota	6-4	W
30	12-7	Washington	7-5	W
31	12-12	New Jersey	3-7	L
32	12-14	Edmonton	4-9	L
33	12-17	at Islanders	1-7	L
34	12-21	Pittsburgh	6-1	W
35	12-23	Chicago	3-2	W
36	12-26	at Pittsburgh	4-7	L
37	12-28	at Chicago	7-4	W
38	12-30	Philadelphia	6-3	W
39	12-31	at Buffalo	3-2	W
40	1-2	at Washington	2-2	T

*Overtime

Game No.	Date	Opponent	Score	Result
1983-84 (cont'd)				
41	1-4	New Jersey	4-3*	W
42	1-7	at Boston	2-5	L
43	1-8	Islanders	5-4	W
44	1-12	at Philadelphia	2-1	W
45	1-14	at Islanders	2-4	L
46	1-16	Detroit	8-5	W
47	1-18	St. Louis	6-2	W
48	1-20	Pittsburgh	3-6	L
49	1-21	at Toronto	6-3	W
50	1-25	at Pittsburgh	6-3	W
51	1-26	Montreal	2-4	L
52	1-29	St. Louis	3-2	W
53	2-2	at Calgary	1-8	L
54	2-4	at Vancouver	5-4	W
55	2-5	at Los Angeles	3-3	T
56	2-8	at Winnipeg	3-1	W
57	2-9	at Minnesota	4-4	T
58	2-11	at Los Angeles	6-6	T
59	2-15	Islanders	3-2	W
60	2-18	at Islanders	3-4	L
61	2-19	Philadelphia	2-3*	L
62	2-23	Quebec	4-2	W
63	2-25	at Montreal	4-7	L
64	2-26	Pittsburgh	4-3*	W
65	2-28	at New Jersey	3-3	T
66	2-29	at Toronto	1-3	L
67	3-3	at Washington	1-5	L
68	3-4	Vancouver	4-5	L
69	3-7	at Minnesota	3-6	L
70	3-9	at Winnipeg	6-5*	W
71	3-10	at Edmonton	3-2	W
72	3-14	Philadelphia	6-3	W
73	3-17	at Philadelphia	4-6	L
74	3-20	Boston	4-6	L
75	3-22	at New Jersey	5-3	W
76	3-24	at Philadelphia	5-6	L
77	3-25	Montreal	3-2	W
78	3-29	Pittsburgh	6-4	W
79	3-31	at Hartford	3-5	L
80	4-1	Hartford	2-0	W

Game No.	Date	Opponent	Score	Result
1984-85				
1	10-11	Hartford	4-4	T
2	10-13	at Minnesota	1-3	L
3	10-14	Minnesota	1-3	L
4	10-20	at Washington	6-5	W
5	10-21	Islanders	6-5	W
6	10-25	at New Jersey	11-2	W
7	10-27	at Quebec	5-2	W
8	10-28	Boston	4-6	L
9	10-30	at Islanders	3-7	L
10	11-3	at Pittsburgh	7-5	W
11	11-7	Washington	4-3	W
12	11-9	Islanders	5-4*	W
13	11-11	Los Angeles	2-4	L
14	11-14	at Chicago	4-6	L
15	11-17	at Islanders	4-10	L
16	11-18	New Jersey	0-6	L
17	11-21	Buffalo	3-2	W
18	11-24	at Quebec	3-8	L
19	11-25	Quebec	2-3*	L
20	11-28	Washington	1-2	L
21	11-30	Toronto	3-3	T
22	12-1	at Toronto	4-1	W
23	12-3	Philadelphia	2-6	L
24	12-5	Calgary	4-4	T
25	12-7	Pittsburgh	3-4*	L
26	12-8	at Philadelphia	2-4	L
27	12-10	Los Angeles	4-2	W
28	12-12	Boston	3-3	T
29	12-15	at Washington	2-4	L
30	12-16	Washington	3-6	L
31	12-19	Winnipeg	4-5	L
32	12-22	at New Jersey	5-3	W
33	12-23	Montreal	3-3	T
34	12-26	at Detroit	2-5	L
35	12-29	at Montreal	3-7	L
36	12-30	St. Louis	6-2	W
37	1-2	Vancouver	6-0	W
38	1-5	at Boston	3-3	T
39	1-6	New Jersey	5-4*	W
40	1-9	at Winnipeg	5-6*	L

*Overtime

Game No.	Date	Opponent	Score	Result
1984-85 (cont'd)				
41	1-12	at St. Louis	4-4	T
42	1-14	New Jersey	1-2	L
43	1-16	Buffalo	2-2	T
44	1-18	at New Jersey	9-6	W
45	1-19	at Washington	1-7	L
46	1-24	Detroit	3-1	W
47	1-26	at Montreal	2-3	L
48	1-27	Minnesota	3-2	W
49	1-31	at Calgary	2-7	L
50	2-2	at Edmonton	1-5	L
51	2-3	at Vancouver	1-4	L
52	2-5	at Los Angeles	5-7	L
53	2-7	at Islanders	5-7	L
54	2-9	at Hartford	2-2	T
55	2-10	at Philadelphia	2-3	L
56	2-15	Edmonton	8-7	W
57	2-17	Islanders	9-3	W
58	2-21	Hartford	3-4*	L
59	2-22	at Pittsburgh	8-3	W
60	2-25	Winnipeg	5-12	L
61	2-28	Washington	4-5	L
62	3-2	at Pittsburgh	4-5	L
63	3-3	Pittsburgh	7-3	W
64	3-6	at Vancouver	6-3	W
65	3-7	at Calgary	5-11	L
66	3-9	at Edmonton	3-3	T
67	3-11	Chicago	3-4*	L
68	3-13	Philadelphia	2-5	L
69	3-16	at Pittsburgh	0-5	L
70	3-17	New Jersey	7-3	W
71	3-21	at Philadelphia	4-8	L
72	3-22	at Detroit	3-5	L
73	3-24	Islanders	2-5	L
74	3-26	Pittsburgh	5-4	W
75	3-27	at Buffalo	2-3	L
76	3-30	at Philadelphia	0-3	L
77	3-31	Toronto	7-5	W
78	4-2	Philadelphia	1-9	L
79	4-4	at St. Louis	5-4	W
80	4-7	at Chicago	1-3	L

Game-By-Game Results
1985-86—1986-87

Game No.	Date	Opponent	Score	Result
1985-86				
1	10-10	Washington	4-2	W
2	10-12	at Hartford	2-8	L
3	10-13	New Jersey	2-3*	L
4	10-16	at Los Angeles	3-4	L
5	10-19	at Islanders	4-5	L
6	10-20	Vancouver	4-3	W
7	10-23	New Jersey	5-1	W
8	10-25	Los Angeles	5-0	W
9	10-27	Boston	2-1	W
10	11-2	at New Jersey	5-6*	L
11	11-4	at Pittsburgh	4-2	W
12	11-6	Philadelphia	2-5	L
13	11-8	at Winnipeg	7-3	W
14	11-9	at Minnesota	3-4*	L
15	11-11	Chicago	4-5*	L
16	11-13	Montreal	5-2	W
17	11-16	at Montreal	2-2	T
18	11-17	Edmonton	2-3*	L
19	11-20	Toronto	7-3	W
20	11-23	at Islanders	5-0	W
21	11-24	Islanders	3-4*	L
22	11-27	Calgary	2-5	L
23	11-29	at Washington	5-2	W
24	11-30	at Pittsburgh	4-5	L
25	12-2	Pittsburgh	0-6	L
26	12-4	Winnipeg	7-4	W
27	12-7	at Philadelphia	0-4	L
28	12-8	Philadelphia	3-1	W
29	12-11	at New Jersey	4-2	W
30	12-14	at Boston	2-4	L
31	12-15	Pittsburgh	2-5	L
32	12-18	Buffalo	4-5	L
33	12-20	Islanders	2-2	T
34	12-21	at Islanders	5-4	W
35	12-23	Detroit	10-2	W
36	12-26	at Buffalo	1-6	L
37	12-28	at Minnesota	1-3	L
38	12-29	Washington	6-5	W
39	1-1	at Washington	0-3	L
40	1-5	Quebec	4-5	L

*Overtime

Game No.	Date	Opponent	Score	Result
1985-86 (cont'd)				
41	1-10	Montreal	6-4	W
42	1-12	St. Louis	2-2	T
43	1-14	at Vancouver	2-1	W
44	1-15	at Los Angeles	4-3	W
45	1-18	at Edmonton	5-4	W
46	1-20	Hartford	0-5	L
47	1-22	at Toronto	4-2	W
48	1-23	Quebec	0-4	L
49	1-27	at Quebec	6-6	T
50	1-29	at Chicago	4-5	L
51	1-31	at Buffalo	3-5	L
52	2-1	at Hartford	3-1	W
53	2-5	at St. Louis	3-4	L
54	2-8	at Boston	3-2	W
55	2-12	Vancouver	5-2	W
56	2-14	at Detroit	7-5	W
57	2-16	Detroit	3-1	W
58	2-20	St. Louis	3-2	W
59	2-24	Minnesota	5-1	W
60	2-25	at Toronto	3-7	L
61	2-27	Pittsburgh	8-3	W
62	3-1	at Washington	0-4	L
63	3-2	Washington	2-4	L
64	3-5	at Winnipeg	1-4	L
65	3-6	at Calgary	5-2	W
66	3-9	Philadelphia	1-4	L
67	3-11	at New Jersey	6-3	W
68	3-12	Calgary	2-3	L
69	3-15	at Pittsburgh	2-2	T
70	3-16	Islanders	3-1	W
71	3-18	at Islanders	2-6	L
72	3-22	at Philadelphia	2-4	L
73	3-23	Chicago	3-5	L
74	3-25	at New Jersey	5-4	W
75	3-28	Edmonton	4-2	W
76	3-29	at Philadelphia	2-8	L
77	3-31	New Jersey	9-0	W
78	4-2	Philadelphia	2-3	L
79	4-5	at Washington	4-4	T
80	4-6	Pittsburgh	4-5*	L

Game No.	Date	Opponent	Score	Result
1986-87				
1	10-9	New Jersey	3-5	L
2	10-11	at Pittsburgh	5-6*	L
3	10-13	Washington	6-7*	L
4	10-15	at Chicago	5-5	T
5	10-18	at Islanders	3-2	W
6	10-19	Islanders	2-2	T
7	10-22	Los Angeles	5-4*	W
8	10-25	at Montreal	3-3	T
9	10-26	Toronto	3-3	T
10	10-29	at St. Louis	2-7	L
11	11-2	Winnipeg	4-5*	L
12	11-5	at Detroit	4-5*	L
13	11-8	at Philadelphia	3-2	W
14	11-9	at Quebec	5-6	L
15	11-12	Buffalo	2-1*	W
16	11-14	Philadelphia	2-1	W
17	11-16	Edmonton	6-8	L
18	11-17	at New Jersey	2-3	L
19	11-19	at Edmonton	4-5*	L
20	11-21	at Vancouver	8-5	W
21	11-22	at Calgary	5-8	L
22	11-26	Quebec	4-2	W
23	11-29	at Pittsburgh	5-5	T
24	11-30	Pittsburgh	2-2	T
25	12-2	at New Jersey	5-8	L
26	12-5	at Winnipeg	6-3	W
27	12-10	Los Angeles	5-4	W
28	12-11	at Montreal	2-6	L
29	12-14	at Washington	3-1	W
30	12-15	Minnesota	3-4	L
31	12-17	Washington	6-1	W
32	12-20	at Islanders	2-5	L
33	12-21	Hartford	3-4*	L
34	12-23	New Jersey	8-5	W
35	12-26	at New Jersey	7-4	W
36	12-27	at St. Louis	2-3	L
37	12-30	at Pittsburgh	5-3	W
38	12-31	Islanders	4-3*	W
39	1-3	at Quebec	5-2	W
40	1-5	Minnesota	3-3	T

*Overtime

Game No.	Date	Opponent	Score	Result
1986-87 (cont'd)				
41	1-7	Philadelphia	3-6	L
42	1-9	Islanders	1-2	L
43	1-11	Vancouver	8-3	W
44	1-12	at Boston	1-4	L
45	1-14	at Calgary	8-5	W
46	1-19	at Los Angeles	2-2	T
47	1-21	at Vancouver	3-5	L
48	1-23	at Edmonton	4-7	L
49	1-26	New Jersey	6-3	W
50	1-28	Winnipeg	1-2	L
51	1-31	at Philadelphia	3-1	W
52	2-1	Boston	5-4	W
53	2-4	Washington	3-2	W
54	2-7	at Washington	5-4*	W
55	2-8	Toronto	4-5	L
56	2-15	Pittsburgh	4-1	W
57	2-17	Detroit	6-2	W
58	2-19	at Chicago	2-5	L
59	2-20	Buffalo	3-6	L
60	2-22	Pittsburgh	2-4	L
61	2-24	at Buffalo	6-3	W
62	2-25	at Toronto	4-2	W
63	2-28	at Detroit	1-4	L
64	3-1	at Washington	3-7	L
65	3-4	Islanders	7-5	W
66	3-8	Calgary	4-7	L
67	3-11	Boston	3-2	W
68	3-12	at Philadelphia	6-1	W
69	3-14	at Pittsburgh	3-2*	W
70	3-15	Philadelphia	2-5	L
71	3-17	at Philadelphia	1-4	L
72	3-18	Hartford	3-5	L
73	3-21	at Islanders	3-4	L
74	3-22	Chicago	5-3	W
75	3-25	New Jersey	2-8	L
76	3-27	St. Louis	6-4	W
77	3-30	at Minnesota	6-5	W
78	4-1	Washington	1-5	L
79	4-4	at Hartford	3-5	L
80	4-5	Montreal	2-8	L

Game-By-Game Results
1987-88—1988-89

Game No.	Date	Opponent	Score	Result
1987-88				
1	10-8	Pittsburgh	4-4	T
2	10-10	at Hartford	6-2	W
3	10-12	Minnesota	4-2	W
4	10-15	at Pittsburgh	6-6	T
5	10-17	at Washington	3-4	L
6	10-19	Washington	2-4	L
7	10-21	Calgary	4-5	L
8	10-23	Chicago	7-3	W
9	10-24	at Philadelphia	5-3	W
10	10-26	Philadelphia	2-2	T
11	10-28	Los Angeles	3-4	L
12	10-31	at NY Islanders	2-8	L
13	11-1	Edmonton	6-7	L
14	11-3	at Calgary	3-5	L
15	11-4	at Edmonton	2-7	L
16	11-7	at Los Angeles	4-5	L
17	11-10	New Jersey	2-3	L
18	11-14	at Pittsburgh	2-3*	L
19	11-15	Winnipeg	6-4	W
20	11-19	at Minnesota	3-4	L
21	11-20	at Winnipeg	4-3	W
22	11-25	Toronto	5-3	W
23	11-28	at NY Islanders	4-5	L
24	11-29	NY Islanders	3-1	W
25	12-3	at Boston	3-4	L
26	12-5	at St. Louis	3-2	W
27	12-9	Montreal	2-2	T
28	12-10	at Philadelphia	3-5	L
29	12-12	at Toronto	3-4	L
30	12-14	Detroit	4-3	W
31	12-16	New Jersey	9-3	W
32	12-19	at Pittsburgh	3-4	L
33	12-20	Pittsburgh	4-8	L
34	12-22	Philadelphia	4-6	L
35	12-26	at New Jersey	5-3	W
36	12-27	Boston	4-1	W
37	12-29	at NY Islanders	3-3	T
38	12-31	Quebec	6-1	W
39	1-2	at Minnesota	5-3	W
40	1-4	St. Louis	6-2	W

*Overtime

Game No.	Date	Opponent	Score	Result
1987-88 (cont'd)				
41	1-6	Vancouver	4-2	W
42	1-8	at Washington	4-8	L
43	1-10	at Buffalo	3-4	L
44	1-11	Chicago	2-2	T
45	1-13	Detroit	4-7	L
46	1-16	at Montreal	3-4	L
47	1-17	Philadelphia	1-2	L
48	1-19	at Los Angeles	3-6	L
49	1-22	at Vancouver	6-3	W
50	1-28	at Philadelphia	5-2	W
51	1-30	at Boston	4-2	W
52	2-2	at NY Islanders	2-2	T
53	2-4	at Quebec	2-3	L
54	2-6	at Washington	3-0	W
55	2-7	Pittsburgh	6-3	W
56	2-11	Washington	3-5	L
57	2-14	NY Islanders	3-1	T
58	2-15	Montreal	3-1	W
59	2-17	Calgary	5-3	W
60	2-19	at New Jersey	3-6	L
61	2-21	Vancouver	4-6	L
62	2-25	Pittsburgh	2-1	W
63	2-26	at New Jersey	2-1	W
64	2-29	St. Louis	5-2	W
65	3-2	NY Islanders	3-1	W
66	3-4	at Buffalo	3-6	L
67	3-5	at Hartford	1-3	L
68	3-8	New Jersey	7-4	W
69	3-12	at Washington	4-2	W
70	3-15	Philadelphia	3-1	W
71	3-16	Washington	4-8	L
72	3-19	at Toronto	4-3	W
73	3-20	Hartford	2-1	W
74	3-22	Buffalo	2-3	L
75	3-24	Edmonton	6-1	W
76	3-26	at Detroit	4-4	T
77	3-27	at New Jersey	2-7	L
78	3-30	at Chicago	4-3	W
79	4-1	at Winnipeg	6-6	T
80	4-3	Quebec	3-0	W

Game No.	Date	Opponent	Score	Result
1988-89				
1	10-6	at Chicago	2-2	T
2	10-8	at St. Louis	4-2	W
3	10-10	New Jersey	0-5	L
4	10-12	Hartford	3-4	L
5	10-16	Vancouver	3-2	W
6	10-19	Washington	5-1	W
7	10-21	at Washington	4-1	W
8	10-23	Quebec	8-2	W
9	10-26	Philadelphia	4-3	W
10	10-29	at Philadelphia	6-5	W
11	10-30	Pittsburgh	9-2	W
12	11-2	at Buffalo	4-6	L
13	11-6	at New Jersey	5-6	L
14	11-8	at NY Islanders	3-4	L
15	11-9	Philadelphia	5-3	W
16	11-11	Boston	4-4	T
17	11-13	Detroit	3-5	L
18	11-15	at Philadelphia	3-3	T
19	11-17	at Los Angeles	6-5	W
20	11-19	at Minnesota	4-1	W
21	11-21	Montreal	2-4	L
22	11-23	at Pittsburgh	2-8	L
23	11-26	at NY Islanders	6-4	W
24	11-27	NY Islanders	5-3	W
25	11-29	at Winnipeg	4-3	W
26	12-1	at Calgary	3-6	L
27	12-4	at Edmonton	6-10	L
28	12-6	at Vancouver	5-3	W
29	12-8	at Hartford	4-5	L
30	12-10	at Boston	1-1	T
31	12-12	Los Angeles	2-5	L
32	12-14	NY Islanders	2-1	W
33	12-17	at Montreal	3-6	L
34	12-19	Washington	3-1	W
35	12-21	Buffalo	2-5	L
36	12-23	at Washington	2-2	T
37	12-26	New Jersey	5-1	W
38	12-27	at New Jersey	7-5	W
39	12-31	Chicago	4-1	W
40	1-2	Hartford	5-4	W

*Overtime

Game No.	Date	Opponent	Score	Result
1988-89 (cont'd)				
41	1-4	Washington	3-3	T
42	1-7	at NY Islanders	5-1	W
43	1-9	New Jersey	4-5	L
44	1-14	at Pittsburgh	4-4	T
45	1-15	Pittsburgh	6-4	W
46	1-18	at Chicago	6-4	W
47	1-19	at St. Louis	5-0	W
48	1-21	at Vancouver	5-4*	W
49	1-23	at Edmonton	3-2	W
50	1-26	at Calgary	3-5	L
51	1-28	at Toronto	1-1	T
52	1-30	NY Islanders	7-3	W
53	2-1	Washington	3-4*	L
54	2-4	at Montreal	5-7	L
55	2-5	Minnesota	3-5	L
56	2-9	Winnipeg	4-3	W
57	2-12	Edmonton	1-3	L
58	2-14	at Philadelphia	1-3	L
59	2-17	Toronto	6-10	L
60	2-18	at Pittsburgh	5-3	W
61	2-20	New Jersey	7-4	W
62	2-22	Philadelphia	4-6	L
63	2-25	at Quebec	7-2	W
64	2-27	Los Angeles	6-4	W
65	3-1	Toronto	7-4	W
66	3-3	at New Jersey	3-6	L
67	3-5	Boston	0-5	L
68	3-8	Buffalo	0-2	L
69	3-9	at Detroit	2-3	L
70	3-11	at Washington	2-4	L
71	3-13	Calgary	4-3	W
72	3-15	Winnipeg	3-6	L
73	3-18	at Quebec	3-8	L
74	3-20	St. Louis	7-4	W
75	3-22	Minnesota	3-1	W
76	3-25	at Philadelphia	1-6	L
77	3-26	Pittsburgh	4-6	L
78	3-29	at Detroit	3-4	L
79	4-1	at Pittsburgh	2-5	L
80	4-2	NY Islanders	4-6	L

Game-By-Game Results
1989-90—1990-91

Game No.	Date	Opponent	Score	Result
1989-90				
1	10-6	at Winnipeg	4-1	W
2	10-8	at Chicago	5-3	W
3	10-11	Calgary	5-4	W
4	10-13	at Washington	4-7	L
5	10-15	Pittsburgh	4-2	W
6	10-17	Chicago	3-3	T
7	10-19	Hartford	7-3	W
8	10-21	at Philadelphia	3-1	W
9	10-23	Vancouver	5-3	W
10	10-25	Edmonton	3-3	T
11	10-27	Islanders	5-5	T
12	10-28	at Islanders	4-1	W
13	10-30	Philadelphia	1-3	L
14	11-2	Quebec	6-1	W
15	11-4	at Montreal	2-3	L
16	11-6	Detroit	6-1	W
17	11-8	Montreal	2-3	L
18	11-12	Islanders	4-2	W
19	11-14	at Pittsburgh	0-6	L
20	11-17	at New Jersey	4-5*	L
21	11-18	at Hartford	3-2	W
22	11-20	Winnipeg	3-3	T
23	11-22	at Buffalo	1-4	L
24	11-25	at Toronto	4-7	L
25	11-26	Quebec	3-1	W
26	11-29	at Winnipeg	4-5	L
27	12-1	at Vancouver	4-3	W
28	12-2	at Los Angeles	0-6	L
29	12-6	New Jersey	5-3	W
30	12-9	at Islanders	0-0	T
31	12-10	Philadelphia	2-4	L
32	12-13	St. Louis	1-3	L
33	12-16	at Islanders	3-4	L
34	12-17	Montreal	0-2	L
35	12-20	Buffalo	2-2	T
36	12-23	at Washington	2-3	L
37	12-26	New Jersey	4-4	T
38	12-27	at Pittsburgh	4-7	L
39	12-29	at New Jersey	2-3	L
40	12-31	Pittsburgh	4-5	L

*Overtime

Game No.	Date	Opponent	Score	Result
1989-90 (cont'd)				
41	1-3	Washington	2-1	W
42	1-4	at Minnesota	2-8	L
43	1-6	at St. Louis	3-4	L
44	1-8	Pittsburgh	5-7	L
45	1-10	Chicago	2-2	T
46	1-13	at Boston	3-2	W
47	1-14	Philadelphia	4-3*	W
48	1-18	at Pittsburgh	3-3	T
49	1-23	at Edmonton	4-3	W
50	1-25	at Calgary	5-8	L
51	1-27	at Los Angeles	3-1	W
52	1-31	St. Louis	2-2	T
53	2-3	at Boston	2-1	W
54	2-4	Minnesota	4-3	W
55	2-7	Edmonton	5-2	W
56	2-9	at Buffalo	2-3	L
57	2-11	Calgary	2-5	L
58	2-13	at Philadelphia	4-3	W
59	2-14	Pittsburgh	3-4*	L
60	2-16	at New Jersey	2-1	W
61	2-19	New Jersey	4-3*	W
62	2-21	at Detroit	4-4	T
63	2-23	at Washington	6-3	W
64	2-26	Boston	6-1	W
65	2-28	Washington	3-2	W
66	3-2	Islanders	6-3	W
67	3-3	at Hartford	4-6	L
68	3-5	Detroit	3-2	W
69	3-8	at Philadelphia	7-5	W
70	3-10	at Minnesota	2-2	T
71	3-12	Los Angeles	2-6	L
72	3-14	at Toronto	8-2	W
73	3-17	at Islanders	3-6	L
74	3-18	Vancouver	4-2	W
75	3-21	Toronto	5-5	T
76	3-25	Philadelphia	7-3	W
77	3-27	at Quebec	7-4	W
78	3-29	at New Jersey	4-6	L
79	3-31	at Washington	1-2	L
80	4-1	Washington	2-3	L

Game No.	Date	Opponent	Score	Result
1990-91				
1	10-4	at Chicago	3-4	L
2	10-6	at Hartford	4-5	L
3	10-8	Minnesota	6-3	W
4	10-10	Washington	4-2	W
5	10-12	Montreal	3-0	W
6	10-13	at Washington	5-2	W
7	10-17	Winnipeg	5-3	W
8	10-19	at New Jersey	2-3	L
9	10-20	at Pittsburgh	4-3	W
10	10-22	Toronto	5-1	W
11	10-25	Philadelphia	5-3	W
12	10-27	at Quebec	4-1	W
13	10-29	Quebec	5-0	W
14	10-31	Los Angeles	9-4	W
15	11-2	Islanders	2-3	L
16	11-3	at Pittsburgh	1-3	L
17	11-5	Boston	2-3*	L
18	11-7	Buffalo	6-2	W
19	11-9	at New Jersey	3-2	W
20	11-11	Calgary	4-4	T
21	11-13	at Philadelphia	1-1	T
22	11-15	at Minnesota	4-2	W
23	11-16	at Winnipeg	6-4	W
24	11-19	Minnesota	2-2	T
25	11-21	at Buffalo	5-5	T
26	11-24	at Islanders	2-2	T
27	11-26	Buffalo	5-0	W
28	11-28	Washington	3-6	L
29	11-30	at Philadelphia	1-5	L
30	12-1	at Boston	5-4	W
31	12-3	Pittsburgh	4-9	L
32	12-5	at Calgary	1-4	L
33	12-7	at Edmonton	3-4	L
34	12-11	at Los Angeles	6-4	W
35	12-14	at Vancouver	5-3	W
36	12-17	Washington	5-3	W
37	12-19	Toronto	1-4	L
38	12-22	at Montreal	1-3	L
39	12-23	Boston	5-5	T
40	12-28	at Washington	5-3	W

*Overtime

Game No.	Date	Opponent	Score	Result
1990-91 (cont'd)				
41	12-30	New Jersey	2-2	T
42	1-2	Los Angeles	4-1	W
43	1-3	at Pittsburgh	7-5	W
44	1-5	at St. Louis	3-2*	W
45	1-7	Philadelphia	3-2	W
46	1-9	St. Louis	2-3	L
47	1-11	at Detroit	3-6	L
48	1-13	Hartford	4-3	W
49	1-15	Edmonton	2-2	T
50	1-17	Chicago	2-3	L
51	1-22	at Islanders	2-3	L
52	1-25	at Edmonton	4-3	W
53	1-30	at Calgary	1-5	L
54	1-31	at Vancouver	3-3	T
55	2-3	Winnipeg	3-4	L
56	2-6	Islanders	5-2	W
57	2-8	Vancouver	8-1	W
58	2-9	at Montreal	4-6	L
59	2-13	New Jersey	6-3	W
60	2-15	Hartford	5-3	W
61	2-18	Islanders	4-5	L
62	2-21	at Philadelphia	4-4	T
63	2-22	at Washington	2-3	L
64	2-24	New Jersey	5-2	W
65	2-27	Washington	4-4	T
66	2-28	at St. Louis	4-4	T
67	3-2	at Toronto	5-2	W
68	3-4	Philadelphia	6-2	W
69	3-7	at Quebec	2-4	L
70	3-9	at Islanders	4-6	L
71	3-10	at Chicago	2-5	L
72	3-13	Detroit	1-4	L
73	3-15	at New Jersey	2-5	L
74	3-17	Pittsburgh	2-4	L
75	3-21	at Pittsburgh	4-5*	L
76	3-23	at Philadelphia	4-7	L
77	3-24	Islanders	3-1	W
78	3-26	New Jersey	3-3	T
79	3-30	at Detroit	5-6	L
80	3-31	Pittsburgh	6-3	W

Game-By-Game Results
1991-92—1992-93

Game No.	Date	Opponent	Score	Result
1991-92				
1	10-3	at Boston	3-5	L
2	10-5	at Montreal	2-1	W
3	10-7	Boston	2-1	W
4	10-9	Islanders	5-3	W
5	10-11	at Washington	1-5	L
6	10-12	at Hartford	2-5	L
7	10-14	Washington	3-5	L
8	10-16	New Jersey	4-2	W
9	10-19	at Pittsburgh	5-4	W
10	10-20	Edmonton	3-4	L
11	10-23	Los Angeles	7-2	W
12	10-26	at Quebec	5-3	W
13	10-29	Minnesota	3-2	W
14	10-31	Quebec	5-4	W
15	11-2	at Philadelphia	4-2	W
16	11-4	Calgary	4-0	W
17	11-6	Montreal	1-4	L
18	11-8	Toronto	3-3	T
19	11-11	Pittsburgh	3-1	W
20	11-13	Washington	3-5	L
21	11-16	at Islanders	2-4	L
22	11-19	at Vancouver	4-3	W
23	11-21	at Los Angeles	1-6	L
24	11-23	at St. Louis	3-0	W
25	11-27	at Winnipeg	2-3	L
26	11-29	at Buffalo	5-4	W
27	12-2	Philadelphia	4-2	W
28	12-6	at Detroit	5-6	L
29	12-8	Boston	4-0	W
30	12-10	at Pittsburgh	3-5	L
31	12-13	at Washington	5-3	W
32	12-14	at Hartford	6-2	W
33	12-16	San Jose	4-3	W
34	12-18	Philadelphia	6-3	W
35	12-21	at Pittsburgh	7-5	W
36	12-23	New Jersey	3-0	W
37	12-26	at Washington	8-6	W
38	12-28	at Islanders	4-5	L
39	12-29	Pittsburgh	3-6	L
40	12-31	at Winnipeg	5-2	W

Game No.	Date	Opponent	Score	Result
1991-92 (cont'd)				
41	1-2	at Chicago	4-3	W
42	1-4	at New Jersey	4-6	L
43	1-6	Winnipeg	4-2	W
44	1-8	St. Louis	3-5	L
45	1-11	at Quebec	7-2	W
46	1-12	at Buffalo	3-6	L
47	1-14	Buffalo	6-2	W
48	1-16	Calgary	6-4	W
49	1-22	at Calgary	4-4	T
50	1-23	at Edmonton	3-1	W
51	1-28	at San Jose	4-2	W
52	1-30	at Los Angeles	4-1	W
53	2-1	at Minnesota	2-1	W
54	2-5	Pittsburgh	4-3	W
55	2-7	at Washington	2-6	L
56	2-9	Detroit	5-5	T
57	2-12	Vancouver	5-2	W
58	2-14	Islanders	9-2	W
59	2-16	at New Jersey	2-4	L
60	2-17	Vancouver	3-3	T
61	2-20	at Islanders	2-6	L
62	2-21	Minnesota	5-4	W
63	2-23	Philadelphia	2-1	W
64	2-25	Chicago	4-1	W
65	3-1	Hartford	9-4	W
66	3-2	at New Jersey	7-1	W
67	3-4	New Jersey	4-5	L
68	3-7	at Philadelphia	4-5	L
69	3-9	Washington	2-5	L
70	3-11	Chicago	7-1	W
71	3-14	at St. Louis	6-0	W
72	3-16	Montreal	4-1	W
73	3-18	Islanders	1-1	T
74	3-20	at Detroit	4-2	W
75	3-22	New Jersey	6-3	W
76	3-23	at Philadelphia	4-3	W
77	3-24	Philadelphia	4-1	W
78	3-28	at Islanders	1-4	L
79	4-15	at Toronto	2-4	L
80	4-16	Pittsburgh	7-1	W

Game No.	Date	Opponent	Score	Result
1992-93				
1	10/9	at Washington	4-2	W
2	10/10	at New Jersey	2-4	L
3	10/12	Hartford	6-2	W
4	10/14	New Jersey	6-1	W
5	10/17	at Islanders	3-6	L
6	10/18	Islanders	4-3	W
7	10/21	Washington	2-1	W
8	10/23	Montreal	3-3	T
9	10/24	at Ottawa	3-2	W
10	10/26	Philadelphia	8-4	W
11	10/29	Quebec	3-6	L
12	10/31	at Montreal	3-4	L
13	11/2	Buffalo	7-6	W
14	11/4	Philadelphia	3-1	W
15	11/7	at Boston	2-2	T
16	11/9	Tampa Bay	1-5	L
17	11/11	Washington	4-7	L
18	11/14	at Quebec	3-6	L
19	11/19	at Philadelphia	3-7	L
20	11/21	at Winnipeg	5-4	W
21	11/23	Pittsburgh	2-5	L
22	11/25	at Pittsburgh	11-3	W
23	11/27	at Minnesota	4-4	T
24	11/30	Minnesota	2-4	L
25	12/2	Detroit	5-3	W
26	12/4	at Washington	4-8	L
27	12/6	Toronto	6-0	W
28	12/9	Tampa Bay	6-5	W
29	12/11	at Tampa Bay	5-4	W
30	12/13	Montreal	10-5	W
31	12/15	Calgary	0-3	L
32	12/17	at St. Louis	4-3	W
33	12/19	at Hartford	4-4	T
34	12/21	at New Jersey	3-0	W
35	12/23	New Jersey	4-5	L
36	12/26	at Islanders	4-6	L
37	12/27	Boston	6-5	W
38	12/29	at Washington	3-4	L
39	12/31	at Buffalo	6-11	L
40	1/2	at Pittsburgh	2-5	L
41	1/4	New Jersey	3-3	T
42	1/6	Ottawa	6-2	W

Game No.	Date	Opponent	Score	Result
1992-93 (cont'd)				
43	1/9	at Philadelphia	3-4	L
44	1/11	Vancouver	3-3	T
45	1/13	Washington	5-4	W
46	1/16	at Montreal	0-3	L
47	1/19	at Detroit	2-2	T
48	1/23	at Los Angeles	8-3	W
49	1/27	Winnipeg	5-2	W
50	1/29	at Buffalo	4-6	L
51	1/30	at Toronto	1-3	L
52	2/1	at Islanders	4-4	T
53	2/3	Philadelphia	2-2	T
54	2/8	at New Jersey	4-5	L
55	2/10	Pittsburgh	0-3	L
56	2/12	Islanders	4-3	W
57	2/13	at Islanders	2-5	L
58	2/15	St. Louis	4-1	W
59	2/20	at San Jose	6-4	W
60	2/22	at San Jose	4-0	W
61	2/24	at Vancouver	4-5	L
62	2/26	at Calgary	4-4	T
63	2/27	at Edmonton	1-0	W
64	3/3	Buffalo	2-2	T
65	3/5	Pittsburgh	3-1	W
66	3/6	at Quebec	2-10	L
67	3/9	Los Angeles	4-3	W
68	3/11	at Chicago	4-1	W
69	3/15	Boston	1-3	L
70	3/17	Edmonton	3-4	L
71	3/19	San Jose	8-1	W
72	3/22	at Ottawa	5-4	W
73	3/24	Philadelphia	4-5	L
74	3/26	Chicago	1-3	L
75	3/28	Quebec	2-3	L
76	4/2	Islanders	2-3	L
77	4/4	at Washington	4-0	W
78	4/5	Hartford	4-5	L
79	4/7	at New Jersey	2-5	L
80	4/9	Pittsburgh	4-10	L
81	4/10	at Pittsburgh	2-4	L
82	4/12	at Philadelphia	0-1	L
83	4/14	Washington	0-2	L
84	4/16	at Washington	2-4	L

Game-By-Game Results
1993-94—1994-95

Game No.	Date	Opponent	Score	Result
1993-94				
1	10-5	Boston	3-4	L
2	10-7	Tampa Bay	5-4	W
3	10-9	@ Pittsburgh	2-3	L
4	10-11	Washington	5-2	W
5	10-13	Quebec	6-4	W
6	10-15	@ Buffalo	5-2	W
7	10-16	@ Philadelphia	3-4	L
8	10-19	Anaheim	2-4	L
9	10-22	@ Tampa Bay	1-4	L
10	10-24	Los Angeles	3-2	W
11	10-28	Montreal	3-3(OT)	T
12	10-30	@ Hartford	4-1	W
13	10-31	New Jersey*	4-1	W
14	11-3	Vancouver	6-3	W
15	11-6	@ Quebec	4-2	W
16	11-8	Tampa Bay	6-3	W
17	11-10	Winnipeg	2-1	W
18	11-13	@ Washington	2-0	W
19	11-14	San Jose	3-3(OT)	T
20	11-16	@ Florida	4-2	W
21	11-19	@ Tampa Bay	5-3	W
22	11-23	Montreal	5-4	W
23	11-24	@ Ottawa	7-1	W
24	11-27	@ Islanders	4-6	L
25	11-28	Washington	3-1	W
26	11-30	@ New Jersey	3-1	W
27	11-4	@ Toronto	4-3	W
28	11-5	New Jersey	2-1	W
29	12-8	Edmonton	1-1(OT)	T
30	12-13	Buffalo	2-0	W
31	12-15	Hartford	5-2	W
32	12-17	@ Detroit	4-6	L
33	12-19	Ottawa	6-3	W
34	12-22	@ Florida	2-3	L
35	12-23	@ Washinton	1-0	W
36	12-26	New Jersey	8-3	W
37	12-29	@ St. Louis	4-3	W
38	12-31	@ Buffalo	1-4	L
39	1-3	Florida	3-2	W
40	1-5	Calgary	1-4	L
41	1-8	@ Montreal	2-3	L
42	1-10	Tampa Bay	2-5	L

* indicates neutral site games in Halifax

Game No.	Date	Opponent	Score	Result
1993-94 (cont'd)				
43	1-14	Philadelphia	5-2	W
44	1-16	@ Chicago	5-1	W
45	1-18	St. Louis	4-1	W
46	1-25	@ San Jose	8-3	W
47	1-27	@ Los Angeles	5-4(OT)	W
48	1-28	@ Anaheim	2-3	L
49	1-31	Pittsburgh	5-3	W
50	2-2	Islanders	4-4(OT)	T
51	2-3	@ Boston	3-0	W
52	2-7	Washngton	1-4	L
53	2-9	@ Montreal	3-4(OT)	L
54	2-12	@ Ottawa	4-3(OT)	W
55	2-14	@ Quebec	4-2	W
56	2-18	Ottawa	3-0	W
57	2-19	@ Hartford	2-4	L
58	2-21	Pittsburgh	4-3(OT)	W
59	2-23	Boston	3-6	L
60	2-24	@ New Jersey	3-1	W
61	2-26	@Dallas	1-3	L
62	2-28	Philadelphia	4-1	W
63	3-2	Quebec	5-2	W
64	3-4	Islanders	3-3	T
65	3-5	@ Islanders	5-4	W
66	3-7	Detroit	3-6	L
67	3-9	Washington*	7-5	W
68	3-10	@ Boston	2-2	T
69	3-12	@ Pittsburgh	2-6	L
70	3-14	@ Florida	1-2	L
71	3-16	Hartford	4-0	W
72	3-18	Chicago	3-7	L
73	3-22	@ Calgary	4-4	T
74	3-23	@ Edmonton	5-3	W
75	3-25	@ Vancouver	5-2	W
76	3-27	@ Winnipeg	1-3	L
77	3-29	@ Philadelphia	4-3	W
78	4-1	Dallas	3-0	W
79	4-2	@ New Jersey	4-2	W
80	4-4	Florida	3-2	W
81	4-8	Toronto	5-3	W
82	4-10	@ Islanders	4-5	L
83	4-12	Buffalo	3-2	W
84	4-14	Philadelphia	2-2	T

Game No.	Date	Opponent	Score	Result
1994-95				
1	1-20	Buffalo	1-2	L
2	1-21	Montreal	5-2	W
3	1-23	Boston	1-2	L
4	1-25	Pittsburgh	2-3	L
5	1-28	@ Quebec	0-2	L
6	1-30	Ottawa	6-2	W
7	2-1	@ Pittsburgh	3-4	L
8	2-2	Tampa Bay	3-3	T
9	2-4	@ Ottawa	2-1	W
10	2-8	Washington	5-4	W
11	2-9	@ New Jersey	1-4	L
12	2-11	@ Tampa Bay	3-2	W
13	2-15	@ Buffalo	2-1	W
14	2-16	Montreal	2-2	T
15	2-18	@ Montreal	2-5	L
16	2-20	@ Tampa Bay	3-1	W
17	2-21	@ Florida	5-3	W
18	2-24	Hartford	1-2	L
19	2-26	@ Buffalo	4-2	W
20	2-28	Florida	0-0	T
21	3-1	@ Hartford	5-2	W
22	3-3	Philadelphia	5-3	W
23	3-5	@ Washington	2-4	L
24	3-6	Ottawa	4-3	W

Game No.	Date	Opponent	Score	Result
1994-95 (cont'd)				
25	3-8	New Jersey	6-4	W
26	3-11	@ Montreal	1-3	L
27	3-15	Philadelphia	3-4	L
28	3-18	@ Washington	1-4	L
29	3-2	New Jersey	2-5	L
30	3-23	@ Islanders	0-1	L
31	3-25	@ Quebec	1-2	L
32	3-30	Quebec	4-5	L
33	4-1	@ Boston	3-2	W
34	4-2	@ Philadelphia	2-4	L
35	4-5	@ Florida	5-0	W
36	4-7	Islanders	3-4	L
37	4-9	@ New Jersey	0-2	L
38	4-12	Buffalo	3-1	W
39	4-14	Boston	5-3	W
40	4-16	@ Islanders	3-2	W
41	4-18	@ Pittsburgh	5-6	L
42	4-20	Hartford	3-2	W
43	4-23	@ Boston	4-5	L
44	4-24	Washington	5-4	W
45	4-26	Tampa Bay	6-4	W
46	4-28	Islanders	2-4	L
47	4-30	@ Philadelphia	2-0	W
48	5-2	Florida	3-4	L

STEVEN McDONALD AWARD

Following the 1987-88 season, the Rangers, in conjunction with Mitsubishi Motors, established a new award dedicated to paralyzed New York City police officer Steven McDonald. The award was named the Steven McDonald "Extra Effort Award", and is presented annually to the Rangers player "who goes above and beyond the call of duty," as Steven did as a New York City police officer. The winner is chosen by Rangers fans who vote on the award from February through April.

McDonald, a lifelong Rangers fan, was shot in the line of duty on July 12, 1986, in Central Park. He spent 18 months in the hospital and watched video tapes of each Rangers game during his recovery. Several Rangers players visited him in the hospital and presented him with a jersey.

He grew up listening to Rangers games on the radio and watching on television but had never been to a game in person. His heroes included Eddie Giacomin, Brad Park, and Jean Ratelle. He now attends a good number of games during the season, sitting at ice level in the zamboni entrance.

The inaugural winner of the award was Jan Erixon in 1987-88. NHL rookie-of-the-year finalist Tony Granato captured the award in 1988-89 before Kelly Kisio and John Vanbiesbrouck were named co-winners in 1989-90. Jan Erixon became the first repeat winner of the award in 1990-91. Adam Graves captured the prestigious award for three consecutive seasons, from 1991-92 to 1993-94.

The 1994-95 recipient was team captain, Mark Messier. Messier led the club in scoring with 53 points in his fourth season with the club. Along with the trophy, Messier received a 1995 Mitsubishi Eclipse, courtesy of Mitsubishi Motors, while Mitsubishi also presented their annual check for $15,000 to the Steven McDonald Foundation.

Mark Messier accepts the Steven McDonald Award. Pictured left to right are Mark Messier, Patty Ann McDonald, the McDonalds' son Conor, and Steven.

LARS-ERIK SJOBERG AWARD

For the sixth consecutive year, the New York Rangers, in conjunction with the Professional Hockey Writer's Association, presented the Lars-Erik Sjoberg Award, symbolic of the best rookie in training camp.

Sjoberg a, 180-pound defenseman, came to North America in 1974 after a distinguished nine-year career in Sweden, along with fellow countrymen Anders Hedberg and Ulf Nilsson. The trio were three of an unprecedented six Europeans signed by the Winnipeg Jets of the World Hockey Association, that year helping blaze the trail for Europeans to play in the NHL. Sjoberg, who served as Jets team captain for five seasons, led the Jets to three WHA Championships during the 1970's. "Pound-for-pound, he was one of the best defensemen who has ever played the game," said Jets teammate Bobby Hull.

Sjoberg joined the Rangers staff on July 22, 1980 when he was named as the team's European Scout. He held that position until he passed away in October of 1987. In his time with New York, the Rangers drafted several European players who went on to play in the National Hockey League including, Reijo Ruotsalainen, Jan Erixon, Peter Sundstrom, Tomas Sandstrom, Kjell Samuelsson and Ulf Dahlen.

The 1994 recipient of the award was defenseman Mattias Norstrom. The native of Stockholm, Sweden captured the award for the second consecutive season while appearing in his second training camp with the Rangers. Norstrom was selected in the second round, 48th overall in the 1992 NHL Entry Draft.

Previous winners of the award include Peter Andersson in 1992, Tony Amonte 1991, Steven Rice in 1990 and Troy Mallette in 1989. The inaugural winner of the award was Mike Richter in 1988.

Walt MacPeek of the Newark Star-Ledger presents Mattias Norstrom with the Lars-Erik Sjoberg award symbolic of the best rookie in training camp.

RANGERS AWARD WINNERS

NHL AWARDS

LADY BYNG TROPHY

Frank Boucher...................................... 1927-28
Frank Boucher...................................... 1928-29
Frank Boucher...................................... 1929-30
Frank Boucher...................................... 1930-31
Frank Boucher...................................... 1932-33
Frank Boucher...................................... 1933-34
Frank Boucher...................................... 1934-35
Clint Smith... 1938-39
Buddy O'Connor.................................. 1947-48
Edgar Laprade 1949-50
Camille Henry...................................... 1957-58
Jean Ratelle 1971-72

NORRIS TROPHY

Doug Harvey 1961-62
Harry Howell... 1966-67
Brian Leetch.. 1991-92

HART TROPHY

Buddy O'Connor.................................. 1947-48
Chuck Rayner 1949-50
Andy Bathgate..................................... 1958-59
Mark Messier....................................... 1991-92

KING CLANCY TROPHY

Adam Graves 1993-94

CONN SMYTHE TROPHY

Brian Leetch   1994

CALDER TROPHY

Kilby MacDonald 1939-40
Grant Warwick...................................... 1941-42
Edgar Laprade 1945-46
Pentti Lund 1948-49
Lorne Worsley 1952-53
Camille Henry...................................... 1953-54
Steve Vickers 1972-73
Brian Leetch 1988-89

VEZINA TROPHY

Dave Kerr 1939-40
Ed Giacomin, Gilles Villemure.............. 1970-71
John Vanbiesbrouck............................. 1985-86

ROSS TROPHY

Bill Cook 1926-27
Bill Cook 1932-33
Bryan Hextall.. 1941-42

PATRICK TROPHY

William Jennings   1971
Phil Esposito   1978
Fred Shero   1980
Rod Gilbert   1991

MASTERTON TROPHY

Jean Ratelle 1970-71
Rod Gilbert 1975-76
Anders Hedberg................................... 1984-85

Mark Messier displays the Hart Trophy which he was awarded following the 1991–92 season.

RANGERS AWARD WINNERS

WEST SIDE ASSN. TROPHY AS RANGERS' MVP

Lynn Patrick	1941-42
Lynn Patrick	1942-43
Ott Heller and	
Bryan Hextall	1943-44
Ab DeMarco	1944-45
Chuck Rayner	1945-46
Chuck Rayner	1946-47
Buddy O'Connor	1947-48
Edgar Laprade and	
Chuck Rayner	1948-49
Edgar Laprade	1949-50
Don Raleigh	1950-51
Hy Buller	1951-52
Paul Ronty	1952-53
Wally Hergesheimer	1953-54
Danny Lewicki	1954-55
Bill Gadsby	1955-56
Andy Bathgate	1956-57
Andy Bathgate	1957-58
Andy Bathgate	1958-59
Dean Prentice	1959-60
Lorne Worsley	1960-61
Andy Bathgate	1961-62
Lorne Worsley	1962-63
Harry Howell	1963-64
Don Marshall	1964-65
Bob Nevin	1965-66
Ed Giacomin	1966-67
Rod Gilbert	1967-68
Ed Giacomin	1968-69
Walter Tkaczuk	1969-70
Ed Giacomin	1970-71
Jean Ratelle	1971-72
Jean Ratelle	1972-73
Brad Park	1973-74
Rod Gilbert	1974-75
Rod Gilbert	1975-76
Dave Maloney	1976-77
Walter Tkaczuk	1977-78
Phil Esposito	1978-79
Anders Hedberg	1979-80
Eddie Johnstone	1980-81
Barry Beck and	
Mike Rogers	1981-82
Mark Pavelich	1982-83
Barry Beck	1983-84
Tomas Sandstrom	1984-85
John Vanbiesbrouck	1985-86
Walt Poddubny	1986-87
James Patrick	1987-88
Brian Leetch	1988-89
John Ogrodnick	1989-90
Brian Leetch	1990-91
Mark Messier	1991-92
Adam Graves	1992-93
Adam Graves	1993-94
Mark Messier	1994-95

WEST SIDE ASSOCIATION PLAYERS' PLAYER AWARD

Andy Hebenton	1958-59
Red Sullivan and	
Andy Hebenton	1959-60
Andy Hebenton	1960-61
Earl Ingarfield	1961-62
Andy Bathgate	1962-63
Rod Gilbert and	
Phil Goyette	1963-64
Harry Howell	1964-65
Wayne Hillman and	
Don Marshall	1965-66
Harry Howell	1966-67
Jean Ratelle	1967-68
Jean Ratelle	1968-69
Jean Ratelle	1969-70
Jean Ratelle	1970-71
Vic Hadfield	1971-72
Walter Tkaczuk	1972-73
Ted Irvine	1973-74
Jean Ratelle	1974-75
John Davidson	1975-76
John Davidson and	
Phil Esposito	1976-77
John Davidson and	
Ron Greschner	1977-78
Ulf Nilsson	1978-79
Don Maloney	1979-80
Don Maloney	1980-81
Tom Laidlaw and	
Mark Pavelich	1981-82
Tom Laidlaw	1982-83
Glen Hanlon	1983-84
Reijo Ruotsalainen	1984-85
John Vanbiesbrouck	1985-86
Don Maloney	1986-87
James Patrick	1987-88
Guy Lafleur	1988-89
Kelly Kisio	1989-90
Mike Richter	1990-91
Adam Graves	1991-92
Adam Graves	1992-93
Eddie Olczyk	1993-94
Adam Graves	1994-95

TOOTS SHOR "CRUMB BUM" AWARD, FOR SERVICE TO NEW YORK YOUNGSTERS

Ed Hospodar	1981
Barry Beck	1982
Nick Fotiu	1983
Dave and Don Maloney	1984
Ron Greschner	1985
John Vanbiesbrouck	1987
Pierre Larouche	1988
Guy Lafleur	1989
Carey Wilson	1990
Mike Gartner	1991
Kris King	1992
Adam Graves	1993
Brian Leetch	1994
Mark Messier	1995

RANGERS AWARD WINNERS

RANGERS FAN CLUB'S
FRANK BOUCHER TROPHY

Don Raleigh	1951-52
Wally Hergesheimer	1952-53
Johnny Bower	1953-54
Edgar Laprade	1954-55
Lorne Worsley	1955-56
Andy Bathgate	1956-57
Andy Bathgate	1957-58
Andy Bathgate	1958-59
Dean Prentice	1959-60
Lorne Worsley	1960-61
Andy Bathgate	1961-62
Lorne Worsley	1962-63
Rod Gilbert	1963-64
Harry Howell	1964-65
Harry Howell	1965-66
Harry Howell	1966-67
Rod Gilbert	1967-68
Ed Giacomin	1968-69
Walter Tkaczuk	1969-70
Dave Balon	1970-71
Jean Ratelle	1971-72
Jean Ratelle	1972-73
Brad Park	1973-74
Rod Gilbert	1974-75
Rod Gilbert	1975-76
Rod Gilbert	1976-77
Pat Hickey	1977-78
Phil Esposito	1978-79
Phil Esposito	1979-80
Eddie Johnstone	1980-81
Nick Fotiu	1981-82
Mark Pavelich	1982-83
Barry Beck and Nick Fotiu	1983-84
Anders Hedberg and Mike Rogers	1984-85
John Vanbiesbrouck	1985-86
Walt Poddubny	1986-87
Walt Poddubny	1987-88
Guy Lafleur	1988-89
Brian Mullen	1989-90
Mike Richter	1990-91
Mark Messier	1991-92
Mike Gartner	1992-93
Adam Graves	1993-94
Adam Graves	1994-95

STEVEN McDONALD
EXTRA EFFORT AWARD

Jan Erixon	1987-88
Tony Granato	1988-89
John Vanbiesbrouck and Kelly Kisio	1989-90
Jan Erixon	1990-91
Adam Graves	1991-92
Adam Graves	1992-93
Adam Graves	1993-94
Mark Messier	1994-95

RANGERS GOOD GUY AWARD, FOR COOPERATION WITH MEDIA AS VOTED BY THE PROFESSIONAL HOCKEY WRITERS ASSOCIATION

Ted Irvine	1974-75
Ron Harris	1975-76
John Davidson	1976-77
Rod Gilbert	1977-78
Dave Maloney	1978-79
Anders Hedberg	1979-80
Don Maloney	1980-81
Barry Beck	1981-82
Rob McClanahan	1982-83
Pierre Larouche	1983-84
John Vanbiesbrouck	1984-85
Ron Greschner	1985-86
James Patrick	1986-87
Bob Froese	1987-88
Tony Granato	1988-89
Kelly Kisio	1989-90
Mike Richter	1990-91
Mark Messier	1991-92
Adam Graves	1992-93
Neil Smith	1993-94
Kevin Lowe	1994-95

RANGERS FAN CLUB
ROOKIE OF THE YEAR

John Vanbiesbrouck	1984-85
Mike Ridley	1985-86
Terry Carkner	1986-87
Ulf Dahlen	1987-88
Brian Leetch and Tony Granato	1988-89
Darren Turcotte	1989-90
Mike Richter	1990-91
Tony Amonte	1991-92
Sergei Zubov	1992-93
Alexander Karpovtsev	1993-94
No winner	1994-95

LARS-ERIK SJOBERG AWARD
(BEST ROOKIE OF TRAINING CAMP)

Mike Richter	1988
Troy Mallette	1989
Steven Rice	1990
Tony Amonte	1991
Peter Andersson	1992
Mattias Norstrom	1993
Mattias Norstrom	1994

RANGERS FAN CLUB
CEIL SAIDEL AWARD

Adam Graves	1994-95

RANGERS MILESTONE WINNERS / HALL OF FAMERS

RANGERS NHL MILESTONE WINNERS

Andy Bathgate	624 assists	Vic Hadfield	1002 games
	1069 games	Harry Howell	1411 games
Marcel Dionne	731 goals	Steve Larmer	441 goals
	1040 assists		871 assists
	1771 points		1012 points
Phil Esposito	717 goals		1006 games
	873 assists	Kevin Lowe	1130 games
	1590 points	Mark Messier	492 goals
	1282 games		877 assists
Mike Gartner	611 goals		1369 points
	548 assists		1127 games
	1159 points	Jim Neilson	1023 games
	1160 games	Bob Nevin	1128 games
Ed Giacomin	54 shutouts	Dean Prentice	1378 games
	610 games	Chuck Rayner	25 shutouts
Rod Gilbert	406 goals	Jay Wells	1001 games
	615 assists		
	1021 points		
	1065 games		

RANGERS IN U.S. HOCKEY HALL OF FAME

Robert E. Dill	William M. Jennings
Victor Des Jardins	John W. McCartan

RANGERS IN HOCKEY HALL OF FAME
PLAYERS (33)

Howie Morenz ....(April, 1945)	Art Coulter ....(August, 1974)
Lester Patrick ....(April, 1945)	Andy Bathgate ....(September, 1978)
Bill Cook ....(August, 1952)	Jacques Plante ....(September, 1978)
Frank Boucher.....................(April, 1958)	Harry Howell ....(September, 1979)
Ching Johnson ....(April, 1958)	Lynn Patrick ....(September, 1980)
Babe Siebert........................(June, 1961)	Gump Worsley ....(September, 1980)
Earl Seibert ....(June, 1963)	Rod Gilbert.................(September, 1982)
Doug Bentley ....(June, 1964)	Phil Esposito ....(September, 1984)
Max Bentley ....(August, 1966)	Jean Ratelle ....(September, 1985)
Babe Pratt ....(August, 1966)	Ed Giacomin ....(June, 1987)
Neil Colville ....(September, 1967)	Guy Lafleur ....(September, 1988)
Bryan Hextall ....(June, 1969)	Buddy O'Connor ....(September, 1988)
Bill Gadsby ....(June, 1970)	Brad Park ....(September, 1988)
Terry Sawchuk ....(August, 1971)	Clint Smith..................(September, 1991)
Bernie Geoffrion ....(August, 1972)	Marcel Dionne............(September, 1992)
Doug Harvey ....(August, 1973)	Edgar Laprade ....(September, 1993)
Chuck Rayner ....(August, 1973)	Fred "Bun" Cook ....(September, 1995)

BUILDERS

Emile Francis ....(1982)

RANGERS ALL-TIME DRAFT

1963

Round/Overall	Name	Pos.	Team, League
1/4	Al Osborne	RW	Weston, Jr. B
2/10	Terry Jones	C	Weston, Midg.
3/15	Mike Cummings	LW	Georgetown, OHL Midget
4/20	Campbell Alleson	D	Portage La Praire, Jr. B

1964

Round/Overall	Name	Pos.	Team, League
1/3	Robert Graham	D	Toronto, Midget
2/9	Tim Ecclestone	C	Etobicoke, Jr. B
3/15	Gordon Lowe	D	Toronto, Midget
4/21	Syl. Apps Jr.	C	Kingston, Midget

1965

Round/Overall	Name	Pos.	Team, League
1/1	Andre Veilleux	RW	Montreal, Jr. B
2/6	George Surmay	G	Winnipeg, MJHL
3/10	Michel Parizeau	LW	Montreal, Jr. B

1966

Round/Overall	Name	Pos.	Team, League
1/2	Brad Park	D	Toronto, OHA
2/8	Joey Johnston	C	Peterborough, OHA
3/14	Don Luce	C	Kitchener, OHA
4/20	Jack Egers	LW	Kitchener, Jr. B

1967

Round/Overall	Name	Pos.	Team, League
1/6	Robert Dickson	LW	Chatham, OHL
2/15	Brian Tosh	D	Smith Falls, Jr. A

1968

Round/Overall	Name	Pos.	Team, League
3/19	Bruce Buchanan	D	Weyburn, WHL

1969

Round/Overall	Name	Pos.	Team, League
1/8	Andre Dupont	D	Montreal, OHA
2/12	Pierre Jarry	C	Ottawa, OHA
3/23	Bert Wilson	LW	London, OHA
4/35	Kevin Morrison	RW	St. Jerome, QMJHL
5/47	Bruce Hellemond	D	Moose Jaw, WHL
6/59	Gordon Smith	D	Cornwall, QMJHL

1970

Round/Overall	Name	Pos.	Team, League
1/11	Normand Gratton	RW	Montreal, OHA
2/25	Mike Murphy	RW	Toronto, OHA
3/39	Wendell Bennett	RW	Weyburn, SJHL
4/53	Andre St. Pierre	D	Drummondville, QMJHL
5/67	Gary Coalter	RW	Hamilton, OHA
6/81	Duane Wylie	C	St. Catharines, OHA
7/94	Wayne Bell	G	Estevan, WHL
8/106	Pierre Brind'Amour	LW	Montreal, OHA

1971

Round/Overall	Name	Pos.	Team, League
1/10	Steve Vickers	LW	Toronto, OHA
1/13	Steve Durbano	D	Toronto, OHA
2/27	Tom Williams	LW	Hamilton, OHA
3/41	Terry West	C	London, OHA
4/55	Jerry Butler	RW	Hamilton, OHA
5/69	Fraser Robertson	D	Lethbridge, AJHL
6/83	Wayne Wood	G	Montreal, OHA
7/96	Doug Keeler	C	Ottawa, OHA
7/97	Jean-Denis Royal	D	St. Jerome, QMJHL
9/109	Eugene Sobchuk	C	Regina, WHL
10/110	Jim Ivison	D	Brandon, WHL
11/111	Andre Peloffy	C	Rosemount, QMJHL
12/112	Elston Evoy	C	Sault Ste. Marie, OHA
13/114	Gerald Lacompte	D	Sherbrooke, QMJHL
14/115	Wayne Forsey	LW	Swift Current, WHL
15/116	Bill Forrest	D	Hamilton, OHA

1972

Round/Overall	Name	Pos.	Team, League
1/10	Al Blanchard	RW	Kitchener, OHA
1/15	Bob MacMillan	C	St. Catharines, OHA
2/21	Larry Sacharuk	D	Saskatoon, WHL
2/31	Rene Villemure	LW	Shawinigan, QMJHL
3/48	Gerry Teeple	C	Cornwall, QMJHL
4/63	Doug Horbul	LW	Calgary, WHL
5/78	Marty Gateman	D	Hamilton, OHA
6/95	Ken Ireland	C	New Westminster, WHL
7/111	Jeff Hunt	RW	Winnipeg, WHL
8/127	Yvon Blais	LW	Cornwall, QMJHL
9/137	Pierre Archambault	D	St. Jerome, QMJHL

1973

Round/Overall	Name	Pos.	Team, League
1/14	Rick Middleton	RW	Oshawa, OHA
2/30	Pat Hickey	RW	Hamilton, OHA
3/46	John Campbell	LW	Sault Ste. Marie, OHA
4/62	Brian Movik	D	Calgary, WHL
5/78	Pierre Laganiere	RW	Sherbrooke, QMJHL
6/94	Dwayne Pentland	D	Brandon, WHL

1974

Round/Overall	Name	Pos.	Team, League
1/14	Dave Maloney	D	Kitchener, OHA
2/32	Ron Greschner	D	New Westminster, WHL
3/50	Jerry Holland	LW	Calgary, WHL
4/68	Boyd Anderson	LW	Medicine Hat, WHL
5/86	Dennis Olmstead	C	Univ. of Wisc., WCHA
6/104	Eddie Johnstone	RW	Medicine Hat, WHL
7/122	John Memryk	G	Winnipeg, WHL
8/139	Greg Holst	C	Kingston, OHA
9/156	Claude Arvisais	C	Shawinigan, QMJHL
10/171	Ken Dodd	LW	New Westminster, WHL
11/186	Ralph Krentz	LW	Brandon, WHL
12/198	Larry Jacques	RW	Ottawa, OHA
13/208	Tom Gastle	LW	Peterborough, OHA
14/218	Eric Brubacher	C	Kingston, OHA
15/224	Russell Hall	RW	Winnipeg, WHL
16/227	Bill Kriski	G	Winnipeg, WHL
17/230	Kevin Treacy	RW	Cornwall, QMJHL
18/233	Ken Gassoff	C	Medicine Hat, WHL
19/236	Clifford Bast	D	Medicine Hat, WHL
20/239	Jim Mayer	RW	Mich. Tech, WCHA
21/241	Warren Miller	RW	Univ. of Minn., WCHA
22/243	Kevin Walker	D	Cornell University, ECAC
23/245	Jim Warner	RW	Minnesota, Midwest Jr.

RANGERS ALL-TIME DRAFT

1975

Round/Overall	Name	Pos.	Team, League
1/12	Wayne Dillon	C	Toronto, WHA
2/30	Doug Soetaert	G	Edmonton, WHL
3/48	Greg Hickey	LW	Hamilton, OHA
4/66	Bill Cheropita	G	St. Catharines, OHA
5/84	Larry Huras	D	Kitchener, OHA
6/102	Randy Koch	LW	Univ. of Vermont, ECAC
7/120	Claude Larose	LW	Sherbrooke, QMJHL
8/138	Bill Hamilton	RW	St. Catherine's, OHA
9/154	Bud Stefanski	C	Oshawa, OHA
10/169	Dan Beaulieu	LW	Quebec, QMJHL
11/184	John McMorrow	C	Providence Coll., ECAC
12/195	Tom McNamara	G	Univ. of Vermont, ECAC
13/200	Steve Roberts	D	Providence Coll., ECAC
13/201	Paul Dionne	D	Princeton Univ., ECAC
14/205	Cecil Luckern	RW	U. of New Hamp., ECAC
15/209	John Corriveau	RW	U. of New Hamp., ECAC
16/212	Tom Funke	LW	Fargo, Midwest Jr.

1976

Round/Overall	Name	Pos.	Team, League
1/6	Don Murdoch	RW	Medicine Hat, WHL
2/24	Dave Farrish	D	Sudbury, OHA
3/42	Mike McEwen	D	Toronto, OHA
4/60	Claude Periard	LW	Trois Rivieres , QMJHL
5/78	Doug Gaines	C	St. Catharines, OHA
6/96	Barry Scully	RW	Kingston, OHA
7/112	Remi Levesque	LW	Quebec, QMJHL

1977

Round/Overall	Name	Pos.	Team, League
1/8	Lucien DeBlois	RW	Sorel, QMJHL
1/13	Ron Duguay	C	Sudbury, OHA
2/26	Mike Keating	LW	St. Catharines, OHA
3/44	Steve Baker	G	Union College, Ind.
4/62	Mario Marois	D	Quebec, QMJHL
5/80	Benoit Gosselin	LW	Trois Rivieres, QMJHL
6/98	John Bethel	LW	Boston University, ECAC
7/116	Robert Sullivan	C	Chicoutimi, QMJHL
8/131	Lance Nethery	LW	Cornell University, ECAC
9/146	Alex Jeans	RW/C	Univ. of Toronto, OUAA
10/157	Peter Raps	LW	West. Mich. Univ., CCHA
11/164	Mike Brown	RW	West. Mich. Univ., CCHA
12/171	Mark Miler	LW	Univ. of Michigan, WCHA

1978

Round/Overall	Name	Pos.	Team, League
2/26	Don Maloney	LW	Kitchener, OHA
3/43	Ray Markham	C	Flin Flon, WHL
3/44	Dean Turner	D	Univ. of Michigan, WCHA
4/59	Dave Silk	RW	Boston University, ECAC
4/60	Andre Dore	D	Quebec, OHL
5/76	Mike McDougal	RW	Port Huron, IHL
6/93	Tom Laidlaw	D	North. Mich Univ., CCHA
7/110	Dan Clark	D	Milwaukee, IHL
8/127	Greg Kostenko	D	Ohio State Univ., CCHA
8/144	Brian McDavid	D	Sudbury, OHA
9/161	Mark Rodrigues	G	Yale University, ECAC
10/176	Steve Weeks	G	North. Mich. Univ., CCHA
11/192	Pierre Daigneault	LW	St. Laurent Coll., QUAA
12/206	Chris McLaughlin	D	Dartmouth Coll. , ECAC
13/217	Todd Johnson	C	Boston University, ECAC
13/223	Dan McCarthy	C	Sudbury, OHA

1979

Round/Overall	Name	Pos.	Team, League
1/13	Doug Sulliman	LW	Kitchener, OHA
2/34	Ed Hospodar	D	Ottawa, OHA
4/76	Pat Conacher	C	Saskatoon, WHL
5/97	Dan Makuch	RW	Clarkson College, ECAC
6/118	Stan Adams	C	Niagara Falls, OHA

1980

Round/Overall	Name	Pos.	Team, League
1/14	Jim Malone	C	Toronto, OHA
2/35	Mike Allison	C	Sudbury, OHA
4/77	Kurt Kleinendorst	C	Providence Coll., ECAC
5/98	Scot Kleinendorst	D	Providence Coll., ECAC
6/119	Reijo Ruotsalainen	D	Karpat Finnish
7/140	Bob Scurfield	C	West. Mich. Univ., CCHA
8/161	Bart Wilson	D	Toronto, OHA
9/182	Chris Wray	RW	Boston College, ECAC
10/203	Anders Backstrom	D	Brynas, Swedish

1981

Round/Overall	Name	Pos.	Team, League
1/9	James Patrick	D	Prince Albert, SJHL
2/30	Jan Erixon	RW	Skelleftea, Swedish
3/50	Peter Sundstrom	LW	Bjorkloven, Swedish
3/51	Mark Morrison	C	Victoria, WHL
4/72	John Vanbiesbrouck	G	Sault Ste. Marie, OHA
6/114	Eric Magnuson	D	RPI, ECAC
7/135	Mike Guentzel	D	Coleraine H.S., (MN)
8/156	Ari Lahtenmaki	RW	IFK Helsinki, Finnish
9/177	Paul Reifenberger	RW/C	Anoka H.S., (MN),
10/198	Mario Proulx	G	Providence Coll., ECAC

1982

Round/Overall	Name	Pos.	Team, League
1/15	Chris Kontos	C	Toronto , OHL
2/36	Tomas Sandstrom	RW	Farjestads, Swedish
3/57	Corey Millen	C	Cloquet H.S., (MN)
4/78	Chris Jensen	C	Kelowna, BCJHL
6/120	Tony Granato	C	Northwood Prep, (NY)
7/141	Sergei Kapustin	LW	Central Red Army, USSR
8/160	Brian Glynn	C	Buffalo, NAJHL
8/162	Jan Karlsson	D	Kiruna, Swedish
9/183	Kelly Miller	C	Mich. St. Univ., CCHA
10/193	Simo Saarinen	D	IFK Helsinki, Finnish
10/204	Bob Lowes	C	Prince Albert, SJHL
11/225	Andy Otto	D	Northwood Prep, (NY)
12/246	Dwayne Robinson	D	U. of N. Hamp., Hockey E.

1983

Round/Overall	Name	Pos.	Team, League
1/12	Dave Gagner	C	Brantford, OHL
2/33	Randy Heath	LW	Portland, WHL
3/49	Vesa Salo	D	Lukko, Finnish
3/53	Gordon Walker	LW	Portland, WHL
4/73	Peter Andersson	D	Orebo IK, Swedish
5/93	Jim Andonoff	RW	Belleville, OHL
6/113	Bob Alexander	D	Rosemount H.S., (MN)
7/133	Steve Orth	C	St. Cloud Tech H.S., (MN)
8/153	Peter Marcov	LW	Welland, Ont. Jr. B
9/173	Paul Jerrard	D/RW	Notre Dame H.S., (Sask.)
11/213	Bryan Walker	D	Portland, WHL
12/233	Ulf Nilsson	G	Skelleftea, Sweden

RANGERS ALL-TIME DRAFT

1984

Round/Overall	Name	Pos.	Team, League
1/14	Terry Carkner	D	Peterborough, OHL
2/35	Raimo Helminen	C	Ilves, Finnish
4/77	Paul Broten	C	Roseau H.S., (MN)
5/98	Clark Donatelli	LW	Stratford, Ont. Jr. B
6/119	Kjell Samuelsson	D	Leksand, Swedish
7/140	Tom Hussey	LW	St. Andrew's H.S., (Ont.)
8/161	Brian Nelson	C	Wilmar H.S., (MN)
9/182	Ville Kentala	LW	IFK Helsinki, Finnish
9/188	Heinz Ehlers	C	Leksand, Swedish
10/202	Kevin Miller	C	Redford, NAJHL
11/223	Tom Lorentz	C	Brady H.S., (MN)
12/243	Scott Brower	G	Lloydminster, SJHL

1985

Round/Overall	Name	Pos.	Team, League
1/7	Ulf Dahlen	C	Ostersund, Swedish
2/28	Mike Richter	G	Northwood Prep, (NY)
3/49	San Lindstahl	G	Sodertalje, Swedish
4/70	Pat Janostin	D	Notre Dame H.S. (Sask.)
5/91	Brad Stepan	LW	Hastings H.S., (MN)
6/112	Brian McReynolds	C	Orillia, OHL
7/133	Neil Pilon	D	Kamloops, WHL
8/154	Larry Bernard	LW	Seattle, WHL
9/175	Stephane Brochu	D	Quebec, QMJHL
10/196	Steve Nemeth	C	Lethbridge, WHL
11/217	Robert Burakovski	LW	Leksand, Swedish
12/238	Rudy Poeschek	D	Kamloops, WHL

1986

Round/Overall	Name	Pos.	Team, League
1/9	Brian Leetch	D	Avon Old Farms HS, (CT)
3/51	Bret Walter	C	Univ. of Alberta, CWUAA
3/53	Shaun Clouston	RW	Univ. of Alberta, CWUAA
4/72	Mark Janssens	C	Regina, WHL
5/93	Jeff Bloemberg	D	North Bay, OHL
6/114	Darren Turcotte	C	North Bay, OHL
7/135	Robb Graham	RW	Guelph, OHL
8/156	Barry Chyzowski	C	St. Albert, AJHL
9/177	Pat Scanlon	LW/C	Cretin H.S., (MN)
10/198	Joe Ranger	D	London, OHL
11/219	Russell Parent	D	S. Winnipeg, MJHL
12/240	Soren True	LW	Skobakken, Denmark

1987

Round/Overall	Name	Pos.	Team, League
1/10	Jayson More	D	New Westminster, WHL
2/31	Daniel Lacroix	LW	Granby, QMJHL
3/46	Simon Gagne	RW	Laval, QMJHL
4/69	Michael Sullivan	C	Boston Univ., Hockey E.
5/94	Erik O'Borsky	C	Yale University, ECAC
6/115	Ludek Cajka	D	Dukla Jihlava, Czech.
7/136	Clint Thomas	D	RPI, ECAC
8/157	Chuck Wiegand	C	Essex Junction HS, (VT)
9/178	Eric Burrill	RW	Tartan H.S., (MN)
10/199	David Porter	LW	North. Mich. U., WCHA
10/205	Bret Barnett	RW	Wexford, Ont. Jr. B
11/220	Lance Marciano	D	Choate H.S., (CT)

1988

Round/Overall	Name	Pos.	Team, League
2/22	Troy Mallette	C	Sault Ste. Marie, OHL
2/26	Murray Duval	D	Spokane, WHL
4/68	Tony Amonte	RW	Thayer Academy, (MA)
5/99	Martin Bergeron	C	Drummondville, QMJHL
6/110	Dennis Vial	D	Hamilton, OHL
7/131	Mike Rosati	G	Hamilton, OHL
8/152	Eric Couvrette	LW	St. Jean, QMJHL
9/173	Patrick Forrest	D	St. Cloud State
10/194	Paul Cain	C	Cornwall, OHL
10/202	Eric Fenton	C	N. Yarmouth Prep, (MA).
11/215	Peter Fiorentino	D	Sault Ste. Marie, OHL
12/236	Keith Slifstein	RW	Choate H.S., (CT)

1989

Round/Overall	Name	Pos.	Team, League
1/20	Steven Rice	RW	Kitchene, OHL
2/40	Jason Prosofsky	RW	Medicine Hat, WHL
3/45	Rob Zamuner	C	Guelph, OHL
3/49	Louie DeBrusk	LW	London, OHL
4/67	Jim Cummins	RW	Michigan State, CCHA
5/88	Aaron Miller	D	Niagara Scenics, NAHL
6/118	Joby Messier	D	Michigan State, CCHA
7/139	Greg Leahy	C	Portland, WHL
8/160	Greg Spenrath	LW	Tri-City, WHL
9/181	Mark Bavis	C	Cushing Academy, USS
10/202	Roman Oksiuta	RW	Khimik Voskresensk, Rus.
11/223	Steve Locke	LW	Niagara Falls, OHL
12/244	Ken MacDermid	LW	Hull, QMJHL

1990

Round/Overall	Name	Pos.	Team, League
1/13	Michael Stewart	D	Michigan State, CCHA
2/34	Doug Weight	C	Lake Superior St., CCHA
3/55	John Vary	D	North Bay, OHL
4/69	Jeff Nielsen	RW	Grand Rapids H.S., (MN)
4/76	Rick Willis	LW	Pingree Prep, (MA)
5/85	Sergei Zubov	D	CSKA, Sov. Elite
5/99	Lubos Rob	C	Budejovice, Czech.
6/118	Jason Weinrich	D	Springfield H.S., (MA)
7/139	Bryan Lonsinger	D	Choate H.S., (CT)
8/160	Todd Hedlund	RW	Roseau H.S., (MN)
9/181	Andrew Silverman	D	Beverly H.S., (MA)
10/202	Jon Hillebrandt	G	Monona Grove H.S., (WI)
11/223	Brett Lievers	C	Wayzata H.S., (MN)
12/244	Sergei Nemchinov	C	Soviet Wings, Sov. Elite

1991

Round/Overall	Name	Pos.	Team, League
1/15	Alexei Kovalev	LW	Dynamo Moscow, USSR
2/37	Darcy Werenka	D	Lethbridge, WHL
5/96	Corey Machanic	D	U. of Vermont, USC
6/125	Fredrik Jax	RW	Leksand, Swe.
6/128	Barry Young	D	Sudbury, OHL
7/147	John Rushin	C	Kennedy, USS
8/169	Corey Hirsch	G	Kamloops, WHL
9/191	Vjateslav Uvaev	D	Spartkak Moscow, USSR
10/213	Jamie Ram	G	Mich. Tech Univ., USC
11/235	Vitali Chinakov	C	Torpedo Jaroslav, USSR
12/257	Brian Wiseman	C	Univ. of Michigan, USC

RANGERS ALL-TIME DRAFT

1992

Round/Overall	Name	Pos.	Team, League
1/24	Peter Ferraro	C/R	Waterloo, USJHL
2/48	Mattias Norstrom	D/L	AIK, Swe. El.
3/72	Eric Cairns	D/L	Detroit, OHL
4/85	Chris Ferraro	RW/R	Waterloo, USJHL
5/120	Dimitri Starostenko	RW/L	CSKA Moscow, CIS
6/144	Davide Dal Grande	D/L	Ottawa, Tier 2,
7/168	Matt Oates	LW/L	Miami of Ohio, WCHA
8/192	Mickey Elick	D	Univ. of Wisc., WCHA
9/216	Dan Brierley	D/L	Choate H.S., (CT)
10/240	Vladimir Vorobiev	RW/L	Met. Cherepovets, CIS

1993

Round/Overall	Name	Pos.	Team, League
1/8	Niklas Sundstrom	C	Modo, Swe. El.
2/34	Lee Sorochan	D	Lethbridge, WHL
3/61	Maxim Galanov	D	Lada Togilatti, CIS
4/86	Sergei Olympijev	C	Dynamo Minsk, CIS
5/112	Gary Roach	D	Sault Ste. Marie, OHL
6/138	Dave Trofimenkoff	G	Lethbridge, WHL
7/162	Serei Kondrashkin	RW	Cheropovets, CIS
7/164	Todd Marchant	C	Clarkson Univ., ECAC
8/190	Eddy Campbell	D	Omaha Jr. A, Tier 2
9/216	Ken Shepard	G	Oshawa, OHL
10/242	Andrei Kudinov	C	Chelyabinsk, CIS
11/261	Pavel Komarov	D	Nizhni Novgorod, CIS
11/268	Maxim Smelnitski	C	Chelyabinsk, CIS

1994

Round/Overall	Name	Pos.	Team, League
1/26	Dan Cloutier	G	Sault Ste. Marie, OHL
2/52	Rudolf Vercik	LW	Slovan Bratislava, Slovakia
3/78	Adam Smith	D	Tacoma, WHL
4/100	Alexander Korobolin	D	Chelyabinsk, Rus. El.
4/104	Sylvain Blouin	D	Laval, QMJHL
5/130	Martin Ethier	D	Beauport, QMJHL
6/135	Yuri Litvinov	C	Krylja Sovetov, Rus. El.
6/156	David Brosseau	C	Shawinigan, QMJHL
7/182	Alexei Lazarenko	W	CSKA, Rus. El.
8/208	Craig Anderson	D	Park Center H.S., MN
9/209	Vitali Yeremeyev	G	Ust-Kamenogorsk, Rus.
10/260	Radoslav Kropac	RW	Slovan Bratislava, Slovakia
11/267	Jamie Butt	LW	Tacoma, WHL
11/286	Kim Johnsson	D	Malmo, Swe. El.

1995

Round/Overall	Name	Pos.	Team, League
2/39	Christian Dube	C	Sherbrooke, QMJHL
3/65	Mike Martin	D	Windsor, OHL
4/91	Marc Savard	C	Oshawa, OHL
5/110	Alexei Vasiljev	D	Yaroslavl, CIS
5/117	Dale Purinton	D	Tacoma, WHL
6/143	Peter Slamiar	RW	Zvolen, Jr., Slovakia
7/169	Jeff Heil	G	Wisconsin-River Falls, NCHA
8/195	Ilja Gorohov	D	Yaroslavl, CIS
9/221	Bob Maudie	C	Kamloops, WHL

Neil Smith welcomes Christian Dube, the Rangers first selection in the 1995 NHL Entry Draft.

RANGERS ALL-TIME REGISTER

(A complete listing of everyone who has played for the New York Rangers from 1926-27 through 1994-95)

Number	Name & Position	Yrs. Played	GP	G	A	PTS	PIM
					Statistics		

A

Number	Name & Position	Yrs. Played	GP	G	A	PTS	PIM
4	Taffy Abel (D)	1926-27—1928-29	110	10	6	16	147
19	Doug Adam (LW)	1949-50	4	0	1	1	0
17	Lloyd Ailsby (D)	1951-52	3	0	0	0	2
15	Clint Albright (C)	1948-49	59	14	5	19	19
17	George Allen (C)	1938-39	19	6	6	12	10
14	Mike Allison (C)	1980-81—1985-86	266	63	102	165	297
18	Bill Allum (D)	1940-41	1	0	1	1	0
33, 31	Tony Amonte (RW)	1991-92—1993-94	234	84	99	183	135
36	Glenn Anderson (RW)	1993-94	12	4	2	6	12
24	Kent-Erik Andersson (RW)	1982-83—1983-84	134	13	35	48	22
5	Peter Andersson (D)	1992-93—1993-94	39	5	12	17	20
25	Steve Andrascik**(RW)	1971-72	**1	0	0	0	0
18	Paul Andrea (RW)	1965-66	4	1	1	2	0
17	Lou Angotti (C)	1964-65—1965-66	91	11	10	21	22
20	Hub Anslow (LW)	1947-48	2	0	0	0	0
6	Syl Apps (C)	1970-71	31	1	2	3	11
10	Dave Archibald (C)	1989-90	19	2	3	5	6
16	Oscar Asmundson (C)	1932-33—1933-34	94	7	16	23	28
9	Walt Atanas (RW)	1944-45	49	13	8	21	40
24	Ron Attwell (C)	1967-68	4	0	0	0	2
10	Oscar Aubuchon (LW)	1943-44	38	16	12	28	4
6	Don Awrey (D)	1977-78	78	2	8	10	38
2	Thomas Ayres (D)	1935-36	28	0	4	4	38

B

Number	Name & Position	Yrs. Played	GP	G	A	PTS	PIM
15	Pete Babando (LW)	1952-53	29	4	4	8	4
21	Mike Backman (RW)	1981-82—1983-84	18	1	6	7	18
6	Bill Baker (D)	1982-83	70	4	14	18	64
11, 22, 8, 17	Dave Balon (LW)	1959-60—1962-63; 1968-69—1971-72	361	99	113	212	284
25	Jeff Bandura (D)	1980-81	2	0	1	1	0
11	Dave Barr (C)	1983-84	6	0	0	0	2
22, 14, 17	Jimmy Bartlett (LW)	1955-56; 1958-59—1959-60	126	19	14	33	174
	Cliff Barton (RW)	1939-40	3	0	0	0	0
12, 10, 9, 16,	Andy Bathgate (RW)	1952-53—1963-64	719	272	457	729	444
16	Frank Bathgate (C)	1952-53	2	0	0	0	2
21	Frank Beaton (LW)	1978-79—1979-80	25	1	1	2	43
5, 3	Barry Beck (D)	1979-80—1985-86	415	66	173	239	775
23	John Bednarski (D)	1974-75—1976-77	99	2	18	20	114
19	Danny Belisle (RW)	1960-61	4	2	0	2	0
29	Bruce Bell (D)	1987-88	13	1	2	3	8
2	Harry Bell (D)	1946-47	1	0	1	1	0
20, 5	Joe Bell (LW)	1942-43; 1946-47	62	8	9	17	18
15	Lin Bend (C)	1942-43	8	3	1	4	2
20	Curt Bennett (C)	1972-73	16	0	1	1	11
17, 27	Ric Bennett (LW)	1989-90—1991-92	15	1	1	2	13
14	Doug Bentley (LW)	1953-54	20	2	10	12	2
22, 10	Max Bentley (C)	1953-54	57	14	18	32	15
24	Gordon Berenson (C)	1966-67—1967-68	49	2	6	8	4
23	Jeff Beukeboom (D)	1991-92—1994-95	250	12	38	50	515
25	Nick Beverley (D)	1974-75—1976-77	126	4	23	27	67
6	Bob Blackburn (D)	1968-69	11	0	0	0	0
23	Don Blackburn (LW)	1969-70—1970-71	4	0	0	0	0
18	Mike Blaisdell (RW)	1983-84—1984-85	48	6	6	12	42
38	Jeff Bloemberg (D)	1988-89—1991-92	43	3	6	9	25
6, 3	Tim Bothwell (D)	1978-79—1981-82	62	4	10	14	32
21	Dick Bouchard (RW)	1954-55	1	0	0	0	0
17, 7	Frank Boucher (C)	1926-27—1937-38; 1943-44	533	152	261	413	114
2, 12	Leo Bourgault (D)	1926-27—1930-31	155	17	11	28	219

**Denotes playoff statistics

RANGERS ALL-TIME REGISTER

Number	Name & Position	Yrs. Played	GP	G	A	PTS	PIM
29	Phil Bourque (LW)	1992-93—1993-94	71	6	15	21	47
27	Paul Boutilier (D)	1987-88	4	0	1	1	6
15, 2	Jack Bownass (D)	1958-59—1959-60;					
		1961-62	76	3	7	10	58
8	William Boyd (RW)	1926-27—1928-29	95	8	1	9	56
15	Doug Brennan (D)	1931-32—1933-34	123	9	7	16	152
18	John Brenneman (LW)	1964-65—1965-66	33	3	3	6	20
32	Stephane Brochu (D)	1988-89	1	0	0	0	0
13	Bob Brooke (C)	1983-84—1986-87	175	35	36	71	214
37	Paul Broten (RW)	1989-90—1992-93	194	27	33	60	194
4	Arnie Brown (D)	1964-65—1970-71	460	33	98	131	545
16	Harold Brown (RW)	1945-46	13	2	1	3	2
4, 21	Larry Brown (D)	1969-70—1970-71	46	1	4	5	18
14	Stanley Brown (LW)	1926-27	24	6	2	8	14
17, 24	Jeff Brubaker (LW)	1987-88	31	2	0	2	78
12	Glenn Brydson (RW)	1935-36	30	4	12	16	9
19	Bucky Buchanan (C)	1948-49	2	0	0	0	0
4	Hy Buller (D)	1951-52—1953-54	179	22	55	77	209
14	Kelly Burnett (C)	1952-53	3	1	0	1	0
24, 27	Gary Burns (LW)	1980-81—1981-82	11	2	2	4	18
15	Norman Burns (C)	1941-42	11	0	4	4	2
17, 20	Jerry Butler (RW)	1972-73—1974-75	112	24	26	50	130
15	Jerry Byers (LW)	1977-78	7	2	1	3	0

C

Number	Name & Position	Yrs. Played	GP	G	A	PTS	PIM
5, 2	Larry Cahan (D)	1956-57—1958-59;					
		1961-62—1964-65	303	19	39	58	337
14	Patsy Callighen (D)	1927-28	36	0	0	0	32
14	Angus Cameron (C)	1942-43	35	8	11	19	0
38	Terry Carkner (D)	1986-87	52	2	13	15	120
11	Bob Carpenter (C)	1986-87	28	2	8	10	20
9, 20	Gene Carr (C)	1971-72—1973-74	138	18	23	41	90
11	Lorne Carr (RW)	1933-34	14	0	0	0	0
14	Gene Carrigan (C)	1930-31	33	2	0	2	13
18	Bill Carse (C)	1938-39	1	0	1	1	0
	Gerald Carson (C)	1928-29	14	0	0	0	5
26	Jay Caufield (RW)	1986-87	13	2	1	3	45
	Bill Chalmers (C)	1953-54	1	0	0	0	0
36	Todd Charlesworth (D)	1989-90	7	0	0	0	6
11	Rick Chartraw (D)	1982-83—1983-84	30	2	2	4	41
6	Bob Chrystal (D)	1953-54—1954-55	132	11	14	25	112
15	Hank Ciesla (C)	1957-58—1958-59	129	8	20	28	37
18, 6	Joe Cirella (D)	1990-91—1992-93	141	7	18	25	258
32	Dan Clark (D)	1978-79	4	0	1	1	6
6	Bruce Cline (RW)	1956-57	30	2	3	5	10
15	Bill Collins (RW)	1975-76	50	4	4	8	38
5, 16	Mac Colville (RW)	1935-36—1941-42;					
		1945-46—1946-47	353	71	104	175	132
6	Neil Colville (C)	1935-36—1941-42;					
		1944-45—1948-49	464	99	166	265	213
16	Les Colwill (RW)	1958-59	69	7	6	13	16
6, 16	Charles Conacher, Jr. (LW)	1954-55—1955-56	93	21	18	39	22
15, 5	Jim Conacher (C)	1951-52—1952-53	33	2	5	7	4
28	Pat Conacher (C)	1979-80; 1982-83	22	0	6	6	8
15	Bert Connolly (LW)	1934-35—1935-36	72	12	13	25	33
20	Cam Connor (RW)	1979-80—1982-83	28	1	6	7	81
5	Bill Cook (RW)	1926-27—1936-37	475	228	138	366	386
6	Fred "Bun" Cook (LW)	1926-27—1935-36	433	154	139	293	436
10	Hal Cooper (RW)	1944-45	8	0	0	0	2
11, 12	Joe Cooper (D)	1935-36—1937-38;					
		1946-47	154	5	13	18	136
2, 17	Art Coulter (D)	1935-36—1941-42	287	18	67	85	332
18	Danny Cox (LW)	1933-34	15	5	0	5	2
32	Bob Crawford (RW)	1985-86—1986-87	14	1	2	3	12
16	Dave Creighton (C)	1955-56—1957-58	210	55	87	142	125
14	Brian Cullen (C)	1959-60—1960-61	106	19	40	59	12
17	Ray Cullen (C)	1965-66	8	1	3	4	0
19	Bob Cunningham (C)	1960-61—1961-62	4	0	1	1	0

RANGERS ALL-TIME REGISTER

Number	Name & Position	Yrs. Played	GP	G	A	PTS	PIM
2	Ian Cushenan (D)	1959-60	17	0	1	1	12
22	Paul Cyr (LW)	1987-88—1988-89	41	4	13	17	43

D

Number	Name & Position	Yrs. Played	GP	G	A	PTS	PIM
16, 9	Ulf Dahlen (LW)	1987-88—1989-90	189	71	60	131	106
5	Hank Damore (C)	1943-44	4	1	0	1	2
4	Gordon Davidson (D)	1942-43—1943-44	51	3	6	9	8
8	Ken Davies** (C)	1947-48	**1	0	0	0	0
16	Billy Dea (LW)	1953-54	14	1	1	2	2
35, 23, 23, 32	Lucien DeBlois (RW)	1977-78—1979-80; 1986-87—1988-89	326	57	79	136	297
16	Val Delory (LW)	1948-49	1	0	0	0	0
24	Ab DeMarco, Jr. (D)	1969-70—1972-73	104	8	21	29	19
15	Ab DeMarco, Sr. (D)	1943-44—1946-47	182	67	86	153	36
5	Tony Demers (RW)	1943-44	1	0	0	0	0
14	Jean Paul Denis (RW)	1946-47; 1949-50	10	0	2	2	2
11	Victor Desjardins (C)	1931-32	48	3	3	6	16
2	Tommy Dewar (D)	1943-44	9	0	2	2	4
14	Herb Dickenson (LW)	1951-52—1952-53	48	18	17	35	10
4	Bob Dill (D)	1943-44—1944-45	76	15	15	30	135
8, 15	Cecil Dillon (RW)	1930-31—1938-39	409	160	121	281	93
9, 11	Wayne Dillon (C)	1975-76—1977-78	216	43	66	109	58
16	Marcel Dionne (C)	1986-87—1988-89	118	42	56	98	80
44	Per Djoos (D)	1991-92—1992-93	56	2	19	21	42
3	Gary Doak (D)	1971-72	49	1	10	11	2
28	Tie Domi (RW)	1990-91—1992-93	82	5	4	9	526
22	Mike Donnelly (LW)	1986-87—1987-88	22	3	3	6	8
27, 2, 33	Andre Dore (D)	1978-79—1982-83; 1984-85	139	8	38	46	153
8	Jim Dorey (D)	1971-72	1	0	0	0	0
16	Jim Drummond (D)	1944-45	2	0	0	0	0
9	Dick Duff (LW)	1963-64—1964-65	43	7	13	20	22
6	Marc Dufour (RW)	1963-64—1964-65	12	1	0	1	2
44, 10	Ron Duguay (RW)	1977-78—1982-83; 1986-87—1987-88	499	164	176	340	370
19	Craig Duncanson (RW)	1992-93	3	0	1	1	0
25	Andre Dupont (D)	1970-71	7	1	2	3	21
18	Duke Dutkowski (D)	1933-34	29	0	3	3	16
	Henry Dyck (LW)	1943-44	1	0	0	0	0

E

Number	Name & Position	Yrs. Played	GP	G	A	PTS	PIM
2	Frank Eddolls (D)	1947-48—1951-52	260	18	34	52	88
6	Pat Egan (D)	1949-50—1950-51	140	10	21	31	120
20	Jack Egers (RW)	1969-70—1971-72; 1973-74	111	13	14	27	72
20	Jan Erixon (LW)	1983-84—1992-93	556	57	159	216	167
77, 12, 5	Phil Esposito (C)	1975-76—1980-81	422	184	220	404	263
5, 30, 3	Jack Evans (D)	1948-49—1951-52; 1953-54—1957-58	407	15	38	53	670
5	Bill Ezinicki (RW)	1954-55	16	2	2	4	22

F

Number	Name & Position	Yrs. Played	GP	G	A	PTS	PIM
24	Trevor Fahey (LW)	1964-65	1	0	0	0	0
10, 14	Bill Fairbairn (RW)	1968-69—1976-77	536	138	224	362	161
3	Dave Farrish (D)	1976-77—1978-79	217	6	41	47	225
6	Glen Featherstone (D)	1994-95	6	1	0	1	18
32	Tony Feltrin (D)	1985-86	10	0	0	0	21
42, 25	Paul Fenton (LW)	1986-87	8	0	0	0	2
41	Peter Fiorentino (D)	1991-92	1	0	0	0	0
12	Dunc Fisher (RW)	1947-48—1950-51	142	21	37	58	82
6	Sandy Fitzpatrick (C)	1964-65	4	0	0	0	2
9	Reg Fleming (LW)	1965-66—1968-69	241	50	49	99	540
18	Gerry Foley (RW)	1956-57—1957-58	137	9	14	23	91
14	Val Fonteyne (LW)	1963-64—1964-65	96	7	19	26	6
8	Lou Fontinato (D)	1954-55—1960-61	418	22	57	79	939

**Denotes playoff statistics

RANGERS ALL-TIME REGISTER

Number	Name & Position	Yrs. Played	GP	G	A	PTS	PIM
4	Harry "Yip" Foster (D)	1929-30	31	0	0	0	10
18	Herb Foster (LW)	1940-41; 1947-48	5	1	0	1	5
22	Nick Fotiu (LW)	1976-77—1978-79; 1980-81—1984-85	455	41	62	103	970
6	Archie Fraser (C)	1943-44	3	0	1	1	0
8,38	Robbie Ftorek (C)	1981-82—1984-85	170	32	55	87	112

G

Number	Name & Position	Yrs. Played	GP	G	A	PTS	PIM
4	Bill Gadsby (D)	1954-55—1960-61	457	58	212	270	411
9	Dave Gagner (C)	1984-85—1986-87	80	11	16	27	47
8	Dutch Gainor (C)	1931-32	46	3	9	12	9
17, 12	Cal Gardner (C)	1945-46—1947-48	126	28	36	64	103
15	Dudley Garrett (D)	1942-43	23	1	1	2	18
22	Mike Gartner (RW)	1989-90—1993-94	322	173	113	286	231
9	Fern Gauthier (RW)	1943-44	33	14	10	24	0
7, 10	Guy Gendron (LW)	1955-56—1957-58; 1961-62	272	38	41	79	217
5	Bernie Geoffrion (RW)	1966-67—1967-68	117	22	41	63	53
17	Greg Gilbert (LW)	1993-94	76	4	11	15	29
7, 16	Rod Gilbert (RW)	1960-61—1977-78	1065	406	615	1021	508
6	Curt Giles (D)	1986-87—1987-88	74	2	17	19	60
16	Randy Gilhen (C)	1991-92—1992-93	73	10	9	19	22
6	Jere Gillis (LW)	1980-81—1981-82	61	13	19	32	20
8	Howie Glover (RW)	1963-64	25	1	0	1	9
19	Pete Goegan (D)	1961-62	7	0	2	2	6
12	Bill Goldsworthy (RW)	1976-77—1977-78	68	10	13	23	55
14	Leroy Goldsworthy (D)	1929-30	44	4	1	5	16
11	Hank Goldup (LW)	1942-43—1945-46	103	34	46	80	69
16	Billy Gooden (LW)	1942-43—1943-44	53	9	11	20	15
19, 16	Jack Gordon (RW)	1948-49—1950-51	36	3	10	13	0
11	Benoit Gosselin (LW)	1977-78	7	0	0	0	33
9, 20	Phil Goyette (C)	1963-64—1968-69; 1971-72	397	98	231	329	51
18, 39	Tony Granato (RW)	1988-89—1989-90	115	43	45	88	217
23	Norm Gratton (LW)	1971-72	3	0	1	1	0
9, 11	Adam Graves (LW)	1991-92—1994-95	295	131	103	234	465
2	Alex Gray (RW)	1927-28	43	7	0	7	28
4	Ron Greschner (D)	1974-75—1989-90	982	179	431	610	1226
5	Jari Gronstrand (D)	1987-88	62	3	11	14	63
2	Jocelyn Guevremont (D)	1979-80	20	2	5	7	6
20, 12	Aldo Guidolin (D)	1952-53—1955-56	182	9	15	24	117

H

Number	Name & Position	Yrs. Played	GP	G	A	PTS	PIM
11	Vic Hadfield (LW)	1961-62—1973-74	839	262	310	572	1036
19	Wayne Hall (LW)	1960-61	4	0	0	0	0
6, 25	Allan Hamilton (D)	1965-66; 1967-68—1969-70	81	0	5	5	54
6	Ken Hammond (D)	1988-89	3	0	0	0	0
22	Ted Hampson (C)	1960-61—1962-63	183	14	40	54	16
2, 6	John Hanna (D)	1958-59—1960-61	177	6	26	32	204
6	Pat Hannigan (RW)	1960-61—1961-62	109	19	23	42	58
14	Mark Hardy (D)	1987-88—1992-93	284	7	52	59	409
3	Ron Harris (D)	1972-73—1975-76	146	6	30	36	64
17	Ed Harrison (LW)	1950-51	4	1	0	1	2
18	Mike Hartman (RW)	1992-93—1994-95	39	1	1	2	80
2	Doug Harvey (D)	1961-62—1963-64	151	10	61	71	144
12	Gordie Haworth (C)	1952-53	2	0	1	1	0
19	Mark Heaslip (RW)	1976-77—1977-78	48	6	10	16	65
26, 40	Randy Heath (LW)	1984-85—1985-86	13	2	4	6	15
12	Andy Hebenton (RW)	1955-56—1962-63	560	177	191	368	75
15	Anders Hedberg (RW)	1978-79—1984-85	465	172	225	397	144
23	Bill Heindl (LW)	1972-73	4	1	0	1	0
3, 14	Ott Heller (D)	1931-32—1945-46	647	55	176	231	465
23	Raimo Helminen (C)	1985-86—1986-87	87	12	34	46	12
21	Camille Henry (C)	1953-54—1954-55; 1956-57—1964-65; 1967-68	637	256	222	478	78

RANGERS ALL-TIME REGISTER

Number	Name & Position	Yrs. Played	GP	G	A	PTS	PIM
18	Wally Hergesheimer (RW)	1951-52—1955-56;					
		1958-59	310	112	77	189	94
15	Orville Heximer (LW)	1929-30	19	1	0	1	4
6	Bryan Hextall, Jr. (C)	1962-63	21	0	2	2	10
12, 19	Bryan Hextall, Sr. (RW)	1936-37—1943-44;					
		1945-46—1947-48	449	187	175	362	227
21	Dennis Hextall (C)	1967-68—1968-69	13	1	4	5	25
17, 12	Bill Hicke (RW)	1964-65—1966-67	137	18	33	51	58
28	Greg Hickey (LW)	1977-78	1	0	0	0	0
16, 14	Pat Hickey (LW)	1975-76—1979-80;					
24		1981-82	370	128	129	257	216
14	Ike Hildebrand (RW)	1953-54	31	6	7	13	12
8, 18	Dutch Hiller (LW)	1937-38—1940-41;					
		1943-44	200	49	70	119	116
16	Jim Hiller (RW)	1993-94	2	0	0	0	7
2	Wayne Hillman (D)	1964-65—1967-68	219	6	42	48	185
88	Ken Hodge (RW)	1976-77—1977-78	96	23	45	68	51
22	Jerry Holland (LW)	1974-75—1975-76	37	8	4	12	6
17	Greg Holst (C)	1975-76—1977-78	11	0	0	0	0
6	Miloslav Horava (D)	1988-89—1990-91	79	5	17	22	38
3	Tim Horton (D)	1969-70—1970-71	93	3	23	26	73
6, 11	Bronco Horvath (C)	1955-56—1956-57;					
		1962-63	114	20	34	54	78
23	Ed Hospodar (D)	1979-80—1980-81	122	8	23	31	442
16, 11	Vic Howe (RW)	1950-51;					
		1953-54—1954-55	33	3	4	7	10
3	Harry Howell (D)	1952-53—1968-69	1160	82	263	345	1147
21, 5	Ron Howell (D-F)	1954-55—1955-56	4	0	0	0	4
27	Willie Huber (D)	1983-84—1987-88	238	28	58	86	284
15	Mike Hudson (C)	1993-94	48	4	7	11	47
28	John Hughes** (D)	1980-81	**3	0	1	1	6
21	Jody Hull (RW)	1990-91—1991-92	50	5	8	13	12
5	Fred Hunt (RW)	1944-45	44	13	9	22	6
25	Larry Huras (D)	1976-77	1	0	0	0	0
32	Mike Hurlbut (D)	1992-93	23	1	8	9	16
11	Ron Hutchinson (C)	1960-61	9	0	0	0	0

I

Number	Name & Position	Yrs. Played	GP	G	A	PTS	PIM
10	Earl Ingarfield (C)	1958-59—1966-67	527	122	142	264	201
4	Ron Ingram (D)	1963-64—1964-65	19	1	3	4	10
27	Ted Irvine (LW)	1969-70—1974-75	378	86	91	177	438
2	Ivan Irwin (D)	1953-54—1955-56;					
		1957-58	151	2	26	28	214

J

Number	Name & Position	Yrs. Played	GP	G	A	PTS	PIM
29	Don Jackson (D)	1986-87	22	1	0	1	91
14	Jeff Jackson (LW)	1986-87	9	5	1	6	15
14	Jimmy Jamieson (D)	1943-44	1	0	1	1	0
15, 47, 27	Mark Janssens (C)	1987-88—1991-92	157	14	15	29	338
28	Doug Jarrett (D)	1975-76—1976-77	54	0	4	4	23
8	Pierre Jarry (LW)	1971-72	34	3	3	6	20
10, 17	Larry Jeffrey (LW)	1967-68—1968-69	122	3	10	13	27
15, 39	Chris Jensen (RW)	1985-86—1987-88	53	7	11	18	23
2	Joe Jerwa (D)	1930-31	33	4	7	11	72
6, 5	Don Johns (D)	1960-61;	148	2	21	23	70
		1962-63—1964-65					
3	Ching Johnson (D)	1926-27—1936-37	403	38	48	86	798
24	Jim Johnson (C)	1964-65—1966-67	8	1	0	1	0
17, 14	Ed Johnstone (RW)	1975-76;					
		1977-78—1982-83	371	109	125	234	319
6	Bob Jones (LW)	1968-69	2	0	0	0	0
16	Bing Juckes (LW)	1947-48; 1949-50	16	2	1	3	6
19	Bill Juzda (D)	1940-41—1941-42;					
		1945-46—1947-48	187	11	25	36	178

RANGERS ALL-TIME REGISTER

Number	Name & Position	Yrs. Played	GP	G	A	PTS	PIM
					Statistics		

K

Number	Name & Position	Yrs. Played	GP	G	A	PTS	PIM
11, 15	Bob Kabel (C)	1959-60—1960-61	48	5	13	18	34
17	Alex Kaleta (LW)	1948-49—1950-51	181	32	37	69	84
26	Sheldon Kannegiesser (D)	1972-73—1973-74	12	1	3	4	6
25	Alexander Karpovtsev (D)	1993-94—1994-95	114	7	23	30	88
21	Mike Keating (LW)	1977-78	1	0	0	0	0
10, 11	Butch Keeling (LW)	1928-29—1937-38	455	136	55	191	250
6	Ralph Keller (D)	1962-63	3	1	0	1	6
6	Dean Kennedy (D)	1988-89	16	0	1	1	40
16	Bill Kenny (D)	1930-31	6	0	0	0	0
12	Tim Kerr (RW)	1991-92	32	7	11	18	12
19, 12	Kris King (LW)	1989-90—1992-93	249	27	33	60	733
25	Steven King (RW)	1992-93	24	7	5	12	16
16	Bobby Krik (RW)	1937-38	39	4	8	12	14
6	Bob Kirkpatrick (C)	1942-43	49	12	12	24	6
11, 16	Kelly Kisio (C)	1986-87—1990-91	336	110	195	305	415
3	Scot Kleinendorst (D)	1982-83—1983-84	53	2	11	13	43
26	Joe Kocur (RW)	1990-91—1994-95	240	13	13	26	488
23	Chris Kontos (C)	1982-83—1984-85	78	12	16	28	65
6	Mike Korney (RW)	1978-79	18	0	1	1	18
16	Dick Kotanen (D)	1948-49; 1950-51	2	0	0	0	0
24	Chris Kotsopoulos (D)	1980-81	54	4	12	16	153
27	Alexei Kovalev (RW)	1992-93—1994-95	189	56	66	122	263
6	Steve Kraftcheck (D)	1951-52—1952-53	127	10	18	28	75
12	Joe Krol (LW)	1936-37; 1938-39	2	1	1	2	0
22	Jim Krulicki (LW)	1970-71	27	0	2	2	6
15	Dolph Kukulowicz (C)	1952-53—1953-54	4	1	0	1	0
18	Stu Kulak (RW)	1986-87	3	0	0	0	0
19, 14	Eddie Kullman (RW)	1947-48—1948-49; 1950-51—1953-54	343	56	70	126	298
17	Alan Kuntz (LW)	1941-42; 1945-46	45	10	12	22	12
25	Orland Kurtenbach (C)	1960-61; 1966-67—1969-70	198	30	61	91	191
	Larry Kwong	1947-48	1	0	0	0	0
19	Bill Kyle(C)	1949-50—1950-51	3	0	3	3	0
15, 6	Gus Kyle (D)	1949-50—1950-51	134	5	8	13	235
19	Nick Kypreos (LW)	1993-94—1994-95	86	4	8	12	195

L

Number	Name & Position	Yrs. Played	GP	G	A	PTS	PIM
15	Michel Labadie (RW)	1952-53	3	0	0	0	0
18, 19	Gordon Labossiere (C)	1963-64—1964-65	16	0	0	0	12
17	Max Labovitch (RW)	1943-44	5	0	0	0	4
20	Guy Labrie (D)	1944-45	27	2	2	4	14
32, 37	Daniel Lacroix (C)	1993-94—1994-95	5	0	0	0	0
22	Nathan LaFayette (C)	1994-95	12	0	0	0	0
10	Guy Lafleur (RW)	1988-89	67	18	29	45	12
15	Jason Lafreneiere (C)	1988-89	38	8	16	24	6
2	Tom Laidlaw (D)	1980-81—1986-87	510	20	99	119	561
14	Lane Lambert (RW)	1986-87	18	2	2	4	33
21, 16, 22	Jean Paul Lamirande (D)	1946-47—1947-48; 1949-50	48	5	5	10	26
16	Jack Lancien (D)	1946-47—1947-48; 1949-50—1950-51	63	1	5	6	35
12	Myles Lane (D)	1928-29	24	2	0	2	24
15	Darren Langdon (LW)	1994-95	18	1	1	2	62
4	Al Langlois (D)	1961-62—1963-64	173	13	34	47	184
10	Edgar Laprade (C)	1945-46—1954-55	500	108	172	280	42
28	Steve Larmer (RW)	1993-94—1994-95	115	35	54	89	57
20	Claude Larose (C)	1979-80—1981-82	25	4	7	11	2
10, 24, 10	Pierre Larouche (RW)	1983-84—1987-88	253	123	120	243	59
19	Norm Larson (RW)	1946-47	1	0	0	0	0
44	Jim Latos (RW)	1988-89	1	0	0	0	0
18	Phil Latreille (RW)	1960-61	4	0	0	0	2
39	Peter Laviolette (D)	1988-89	12	0	0	0	6
17	Brian Lawton (C)	1988-89	30	7	10	17	39
2	Hal Laycoe (D)	1945-46—1946-47	75	1	14	15	31
24	Jim Leavins (D)	1986-87	4	0	1	1	4

RANGERS ALL-TIME REGISTER

					Statistics		
Number	Name & Position	Yrs. Played	GP	G	A	PTS	PIM
18	Al Lebrun (D)	1960-61; 1965-66	6	0	2	2	4
18	Albert Leduc (D)	1933-34	10	0	0	0	6
30	Grant Ledyard (D)	1984-85—1985-86	69	10	21	31	73
2	Brian Leetch (D)	1987-88—1994-95	485	112	375	487	255
5	Roger Leger (D)	1943-44	7	1	2	3	2
4	Randy Legge (D)	1972-73	12	0	2	2	2
28	Mikko Leinonen (C)	1981-82—1983-84	159	31	77	108	69
14, 9	Real Lemieux (LW)	1969-70; 1973-74	62	4	6	10	51
18	Tony Leswick (LW)	1945-46—1950-51	368	113	89	202	420
14	Joe Levandoski (RW)	1946-47	8	1	1	2	0
11	Alex Levinsky (D)	1934-35	21	0	4	4	6
22	Danny Lewicki (LW)	1954-55—1957-58	280	76	90	166	107
27	Dale Lewis (LW)	1975-76	8	0	0	0	0
26	Igor Liba (LW)	1988-89	10	2	5	7	15
6	Doug Lidster (D)	1993-94	34	0	2	2	33
28	Bill Lochead (LW)	1979-80	7	0	0	0	4
14	Troy Loney (LW)	1994-95	4	0	0	0	0
25	Jim Lorentz (C)	1971-72	5	0	0	0	0
4	Kevin Lowe (D)	1992-93—1994-95	164	9	33	42	186
19	Odie Lowe (C)	1948-49—1949-50	4	1	1	2	0
14	Don Luce (C)	1969-70—1970-71	21	1	3	4	8
9	Pentti Lund (RW)	1948-49—1950-51	182	36	41	77	38

M

2, 8, 14	Kilby MacDonald (LW)	1939-40—1940-41; 1943-44—1944-45	151	36	34	70	47
14	Parker MacDonald (LW)	1956-57—1957-58; 1959-60	119	15	18	33	54
19, 17	Hub Macey (LW)	1941-42—1942-43	18	6	8	14	0
12, 14	Bruce MacGregor (RW)	1970-71—1973-74	220	62	73	135	44
37	Norm Maciver (D)	1986-87—1988-89	66	9	26	35	28
11	Bill MacKenzie (D)	1934-35	20	1	0	1	10
2	Reg Mackey (D)	1926-27	34	0	0	0	16
14	Mickey MacIntosh (F)	1952-53	4	0	0	0	4
26	Brian MacLellan (LW)	1985-86	51	11	21	32	47
12	Bob MacMillan (RW)	1974-75	22	1	2	3	4
6	Al MacNeil (D)	1966-67	58	0	4	4	44
14	Craig MacTavish (C)	1993-94	12	4	2	6	11
2	John Mahaffy (C)	1943-44	28	9	20	29	0
16, 26	Troy Mallette (LW)	1989-90—1990-91	150	25	26	51	557
26	Dave Maloney (D)	1974-75—1984-85	605	70	225	295	1113
12	Don Maloney (LW)	1978-79—1988-89	653	195	307	502	739
5	Felix Mancuso (RW)	1942-43	21	6	8	14	13
16	Jack Mann (C)	1943-44—1944-45	9	3	4	7	0
19	Ray Manson (LW)	1948-49	1	0	1	1	0
14	Henry Maracle (F)	1930-31	11	1	3	4	4
39	Todd Marchant (C)	1993-94	1	0	0	0	0
42	Dave Marcinyshyn (D)	1992-93	2	0	0	0	2
29	Ray Markham (C)	1979-80	14	1	1	2	21
25	Mario Marios (D)	1977-78—1980-81	166	15	52	67	356
6	Gilles Marotte (D)	1973-74—1975-76	180	10	66	76	131
4	Bert Marshall (D)	1972-73	8	0	0	0	14
22	Don Marshall (LW)	1963-64—1969-70	479	129	141	270	40
17	Clare Martin (D)	1951-52	15	0	1	1	8
16	Charles Mason (D)	1934-35—1935-36	74	6	14	20	44
32	Stephane Matteau (LW)	1993-94—1994-95	53	7	8	15	27
26	Brad Maxwell (D)	1986-87	9	0	4	4	6
34	Jim Mayer (RW)	1979-80	4	0	0	0	0
12	Sam McAdam (LW)	1930-31	4	0	0	0	0
20	Dunc McCallum (D)	1965-66	2	0	0	0	2
28	Dan McCarthy (C)	1980-81	5	4	0	4	4
9, 39	Rob McClanahan (LW)	1981-82—1983-84	141	33	43	76	77
39	Shawn McCash (C)	1994-95	5	1	0	1	2
21	Bill McCreary (C)	1953-54—1954-55	10	0	2	2	2
19	Bill McDonagh (LW)	1949-50	4	0	0	0	2
14	Bob McDonald (RW)	1943-44	1	0	0	0	0
6	Bucko McDonald (D)	1943-44—1944-45	81	7	15	22	14
11	John McDonald (RW)	1943-44	43	10	9	19	6
22, 28	Mike McDougal (RW)	1978-79; 1980-81	3	0	0	0	0

RANGERS ALL-TIME REGISTER

Number	Name & Position	Yrs. Played	GP	G	A	PTS	PIM
6, 27	Mike McEwen (D)	1976-77—1979-80; 1985-86	242	42	92	134	141
18	Sandy McGregor (RW)	1963-64	2	0	0	0	2
14	John McIntyre (C)	1992-93	11	1	0	1	4
25	Tony McKegney (RW)	1986-87	64	29	17	46	56
17	Don McKenney (C)	1962-63—1963-64	76	17	33	50	10
14	John McKenzie (RW)	1965-66	35	6	5	11	36
14, 19 18, 12	Jack McLeod (RW)	1949-50 —1952-53;106 1954-55	14	23	37	12	
4, 6	Mike McMahon (D)	1963-64—1965-66; 1971-72	61	0	13	13	50
21, 37	George McPhee (LW)	1982-83—1986-87	109	21	24	45	247
16	Brian McReynolds (C)	1990-91	1	0	0	0	0
12	Dick Meissner (RW)	1963-64—1964-65	36	3	5	8	9
30	Larry Melnyk (D)	1985-86—1987-88	133	4	21	25	281
28, 29	Joby Messier (D)	1992-93—1994-95	25	0	4	4	24
11	Mark Messier (C)	1991-92—1994-95	276	100	235	335	264
18, 12, 9	Larry Mickey (RW)	1965-66—1967-68	19	0	2	2	2
11	Nick Mickoski (LW)	1947-48—1954-55	362	88	93	181	129
9	Rick Middleton (RW)	1974-75—1975-76	124	46	44	90	33
12	Jim Mikol (D)	1964-65	30	1	3	4	6
4	Hib Milks (LW)	1931-32	45	0	4	4	12
32, 23	Corey Millen (C)	1989-90—1991-92	19	4	5	9	12
40, 10	Kelly Miller (RW)	1984-85—1986-87	117	19	36	55	76
32, 26	Kevin Miller (RW)	1988-89—1990-91	103	20	37	57	67
24	Warren Miller (RW)	1979-80	55	7	6	13	17
21	Bill Moe (D)	1944-45—1948-49	261	11	42	53	163
5	Lloyd Mohns (D)	1943-44	1	0	0	0	0
24	Randy Moller (D)	1989-90—1991-92	164	7	38	49	378
16	Larry Molyneaux (D)	1937-38—1938-39	45	0	1	1	20
15	Hartland Monahan (RW)	1974-75	6	0	1	1	4
40	Jayson More (D)	1988-89	1	0	0	0	0
11	Howie Morenz (C)	1935-36	19	2	5	7	6
8	Elwin Morris (D)	1948-49	18	0	1	1	8
2	Jim Morrison (D)	1960-61	19	1	6	7	6
21	Mark Morrison (C)	1981-82; 1983-84	10	1	1	2	0
19	Brian Mullen (RW)	1987-88—1990-91	307	100	148	248	188
14	Don Murdoch (RW)	1976-77—1979-80	221	97	93	190	110
9	Murray Murdoch (LW)	1926-27—1936-37	508	84	108	192	197
14	Mike Murphy (RW)	1972-73—1973-74	31	6	5	11	5
15, 10	Ron Murphy (LW)	1952-53—1956-57	207	41	60	101	141
18	Vic Myles (D)	1942-43	45	6	9	15	57

N

Number	Name & Position	Yrs. Played	GP	G	A	PTS	PIM
34	Vaclav Nedomansky (RW)	1982-83	35	12	8	20	0
10	Petr Nedved (C)	1994-95	46	11	12	23	26
15	Jim Neilson (D)	1962-63—1973-74	810	60	238	298	766
13	Sergei Nemchinov (C)	1991-92—1994-95	287	82	92	174	101
47	Steve Nemeth (C)	1987-88	12	2	0	2	2
21	Lance Nethery (C)	1980-81—1981-82	38	11	12	23	12
8	Bob Nevin (RW)	1963-64—1970-71	505	168	174	342	105
24	Dan Newman (LW)	1976-77—1977-78	100	14	21	35	59
9	Bernie Nicholls (C)	1989-90—1991-92	104	37	73	110	116
25	Graeme Nicolson (D)	1982-83	10	0	0	0	9
30	Chris Nilan (RW)	1987-88—1989-90	85	11	14	25	332
19, 11	Ulf Nilsson (C)	1978-79—1982-83	170	57	112	169	85
16	Brian Noonan (RW)	1993-94—1994-95	57	18	15	33	38
14, 5	Mattias Norstrom (D)	1993-94—1994-95	18	0	5	5	8

O

Number	Name & Position	Yrs. Played	GP	G	A	PTS	PIM
14	Warren Oatman (F)	1928-29	27	1	1	2	10
5	Buddy O'Connor (C)	1947-48	238	62	102	164	12
25	John Ogrodnick (LW)	1987-88—1991-92	338	126	128	254	106
12	Eddie Olczyk (LW)	1992-93—1994-95	103	18	22	40	58
19, 20	Mark Osborne (LW)	1983-84—1986-87 1994-95	253	61	74	135	321

RANGERS ALL-TIME REGISTER

Number	Name & Position	Yrs. Played	GP	G	A	PTS	PIM
P							
11	Wilf Paiement (RW)	1985-86	8	1	6	7	13
14	Aldo Palazzari (RW)	1943-44	12	2	0	2	0
2	Brad Park (D)	1968-69—1975-76	465	95	283	378	738
27	Joe Paterson (LW)	1987-88—1988-89	41	1	4	5	149
6	Larry Patey (C)	1983-84—1984-85	16	1	3	4	16
3	James Patrick (D)	1983-84—1993-94	671	104	363	467	541
9, 18	Lynn Patrick (LW)	1934-35—1942-43; 1945-46	455	145	190	335	270
2, 15	Muzz Patrick (D)	1937-38—1940-41; 1945-46	166	5	26	31	133
11	Stephen Patrick (RW)	1984-85—1985-86	71	15	21	36	100
16, 40	Mark Pavelich (C)	1981-82—1985-86	341	133	185	318	326
18	Jim Pavese (D)	1987-88	14	0	1	1	48
12, 16	Mel Pearson (LW)	1959-60; 1961-62 1962-63—1964-65	36	2	5	7	25
3	Fern Perreault (LW)	1947-48; 1949-50	3	0	0	0	0
4	Frank Peters (D)	1930-31	44	0	0	0	59
21	Gary Peters (C)	1965-66	63	7	3	10	42
24, 17	Michel Petit (D)	1987-88—1988-89	133	17	49	66	377
11	Gordon Pettinger (C)	1932-33	35	1	2	3	18
32	Dave Pichette (D)	1987-88	6	1	3	4	4
2, 16	Alf Pike (C)	1939-40—1942-43; 1945-46—1946-47	234	42	77	119	145
2, 25	Bob Plager (D)	1964-65—1966-67	29	0	5	5	40
24	Pierre Plante (RW)	1978-79	70	6	25	31	37
8	Walt Poddubny (C)	1986-87—1987-88	152	78	97	175	125
29, 41	Rudy Poeschek (RW)	1987-88—1989-90	68	0	2	2	256
14	Bud Poile (RW)	1949-50	28	3	6	9	8
19	Johnny Polich (RW)	1939-40—1940-41	3	0	1	1	0
20	Greg Polis (LW)	1974-75—1978-79	275	65	76	141	196
19	Larry Popein (C)	1954-55—1960-61	402	75	127	202	150
11, 2	Babe Pratt (D)	1935-36—1942-43	307	27	97	124	299
17	Dean Prentice (LW)	1952-53—1962-63	666	186	236	422	263
15	Noel Price (D)	1959-60—1960-61	7	0	0	0	4
47	Pat Price (D)	1986-87	13	0	2	2	49
17	Jean Pusie (D)	1933-34	19	0	2	2	17
Q							
12	Leo Quenneville (F)	1929-30	25	0	3	3	10
R							
7, 9	Don Raleigh (C)	1943-44; 1947-48—1955-56	535	101	219	320	96
19, 14	Jean Ratelle (C)	1960-61—1975-76	862	336	481	817	192
5	Mel Read (C)	1946-47	6	0	0	0	8
11	William Regan (D)	1929-30—1930-31	52	2	1	3	53
11	Oliver Reinikka (F)	1926-27	16	0	0	0	0
5	Leo Reise, Jr. (D)	1952-53—1953-54	131	7	20	27	124
2	Leo Reise, Sr. (D)	1929-30	14	0	1	1	8
10	Steven Rice (RW)	1990-91	11	1	1	2	4
18	Dave Richardson (LW)	1963-64—1964-65	41	3	2	5	25
41	Steve Richmond (D)	1983-84—1985-86	77	2	12	14	263
18	Mike Ridley (C)	1985-86—1986-87	118	38	63	101	89
4	Vic Ripley (LW)	1933-34—1934-35	39	5	14	19	12
19	Alex Ritson (LW)	1944-45	1	0	0	0	0
21	Wayne Rivers (RW)	1968-69	4	0	0	0	0
5	Doug Robinson (LW)	1964-65—1966-67	73	16	26	42	10
25, 24	Mike Robitaille (D)	1969-70—1970-71	15	1	1	2	15
16	Leon Rochefort (RW)	1960-61; 1962-63	24	5	4	9	6
5	Normand Rochefort (D)	1988-89—1991-92	112	7	15	22	108
12	Edmond Rodden (F)	1930-31	24	0	3	3	8
17, 27	Mike Rogers (C)	1981-82—1985-86	316	117	191	308	142
5	Dale Rolfe (D)	1970-71—1974-75	244	13	66	79	190
19	Len Ronson (LW)	1960-61	13	2	1	3	10

RANGERS ALL-TIME REGISTER

Number	Name & Position	Yrs. Played	GP	G	A	PTS	PIM
9	Paul Ronty (C)	1951-52—1954-55	260	45	114	159	62
2, 15	Jim Ross (D)	1951-52—1952-53	62	2	11	13	29
22	Bobby Rousseau (RW)	1971-72—1974-75	236	41	116	157	30
15	Ronnie Rowe (LW)	1947-48	5	1	0	1	0
8	Jean-Yves Roy (RW)	1994-95	3	1	0	1	2
44	Lindy Ruff (D)	1988-89—1990-91	83	3	12	15	135
29	Reijo Ruotsalainen (D)	1981-82—1985-86	389	99	217	316	154
19	Duane Rupp (D)	1962-63	2	0	0	0	0
16	Church Russell (LW)	1945-46—1947-48	90	20	16	36	12

S

Number	Name & Position	Yrs. Played	GP	G	A	PTS	PIM
21	Simo Saarinen (D)	1984-85	8	0	0	0	8
4, 3 2, 5	Larry Sacharuk (D)	1972-73—1973-74; 1975-76—1976-77	75	9	11	20	18
26, 8	Kjell Samuelsson (D)	1985-86—1986-87	39	2	6	8	60
16, 4	Derek Sanderson (C)	1974-75—1975-76	83	25	25	50	110
5	Chuck Sands (C)	1943-44	9	0	2	2	0
28	Tomas Sandstrom (RW)	1984-85—1989-90	407	173	207	380	563
6	Glen Sather (LW)	1970-71—1973-74	188	18	24	42	193
17	Chuck Scherza (C)	1943-44—1944-45	27	5	5	10	29
18	Ken Schinkel (RW)	1959-60—1963-64; 1966-67	265	34	55	89	77
11	Lawrence Scott (F)	1927-28	23	0	1	1	6
21, 2	Earl Seibert (D)	1931-32—1935-36	202	27	41	68	338
16	Rod Seiling (D)	1963-64—1974-75	644	50	198	248	425
16	George Senick (LW)	1952-53	13	2	3	5	8
6, 5	Eddie Shack (RW)	1958-59—1960-61	141	16	26	42	236
18	Joe Shack (LW)	1942-43; 1944-45	70	9	27	36	20
27, 21	David Shaw (D)	1987-88—1991-92	240	17	57	74	314
6	Bobby Sheehan** (C)	1978-79	15	4	3	7	2
23	Ray Sheppard (RW)	1990-91	59	24	23	47	21
	Johnny Sherf** (LW)	1937-38	1	0	0	0	0
3	Fred Shero (D)	1947-48—1949-50	145	6	14	20	137
4	Alex Shibicky (LW)	1935-36—1941-42; 1945-46	322	110	91	201	161
4	Alex "Babe" Siebert (LW)	1932-33—1933-34	55	9	11	20	56
16	Dave Silk (RW)	1979-80—1982-83	141	30	33	63	112
41	Mike Siltala (RW)	1986-87—1987-88	4	0	0	0	0
21	Reg Sinclair (RW)	1950-51—1951-52	139	38	31	69	103
20, 11	Ed Slowinski (RW)	1947-48—1952-53	291	58	74	132	63
14, 20, 10	Clint Smith (C)	1936-37—1942-43	281	80	115	195	12
15	Dallas Smith (D)	1977-78	29	1	4	5	23
21	Don Smith (RW)	1949-50	10	1	1	2	0
19	Floyd Smith (RW)	1960-61	29	5	9	14	0
17	Stan Smith (C)	1939-40—1940-41	9	2	1	3	0
12	Art Somers (LW)	1931-32—1934-35	145	19	37	56	82
16	Glen Sonmor (LW)	1953-54—1954-55	28	2	0	2	21
15, 16, 21	Irv Spencer (D)	1959-60—1961-62	131	4	20	24	81
19	Red Staley (C)	1948-49	1	0	1	1	0
8	Allan Stanley (D)	1948-49—1954-55	307	23	56	79	272
4	Wally Stanowski (D)	1948-49—1950-51	146	3	14	17	54
4	Harold Starr (D)	1934-35—1935-36	45	0	0	0	38
21	Bud Stefanski (C)	1977-78	1	0	0	0	0
21	Pete Stemkowski (C)	1970-71—1976-77	496	113	204	317	379
5	Ulf Sterner (LW)	1964-65	4	0	0	0	0
16	Gaye Stewart (LW)	1951-52—1952-53	87	16	27	43	30
12	Ron Stewart (RW)	1967-68—1972-73	306	44	37	81	74
13	Jack Stoddard (RW)	1951-52—1952-53	80	16	15	31	31
21	Blaine Stoughton (RW)	1983-84	14	5	2	7	4
21	Neil Strain (LW)	1952-53	52	11	13	24	12
15, 10	Art Stratton (C)	1959-60	18	2	5	7	2
10	Art Strobel (LW)	1943-44	7	0	0	0	0
9	Doug Sulliman (RW)	1979-80—1980-81	63	8	8	16	34
7	Red Sullivan (C)	1956-57—1960-61	322	59	150	209	300
25	Peter Sundstrom (RW)	1983-84—1985-86	206	48	62	110	70
5	Bill Sweeney (C)	1959-60	4	1	0	1	0

RANGERS ALL-TIME REGISTER

Number	Name & Position	Yrs. Played	GP	G	A	PTS	PIM
					Statistics		

T

Number	Name & Position	Yrs. Played	GP	G	A	PTS	PIM
19	Dean Talafous (RW)	1978-79—1981-82	202	42	60	102	91
26, 35	Ron Talakoski (RW)	1986-87—1987-88	9	0	1	1	33
15	Bill Taylor (C)	1947-48	2	0	0	0	0
19	G. Bill Taylor (C)	1964-65	2	0	0	0	0
12	Ralph Taylor (D)	1929-30	24	2	0	2	28
18, 5	Ted Taylor (LW)	1964-65—1965-66	8	0	1	1	6
17	Spence Thatchell (D)	1942-43	1	0	0	0	0
8, 10	Paul Thompson (LW)	1926-27—1930-31	216	35	33	68	144
14	Fred Thurier (C)	1944-45	50	16	19	35	14
10	Esa Tikkanen (LW)	1992-93—1993-94	98	24	37	61	132
6	Mark Tinordi (D)	1987-88	24	1	2	3	50
18, 17	Walt Tkaczuk (C)	1967-68—1980-81	945	227	451	678	556
12	Zellio Toppazzini (RW)	1950-51—1951-52	71	15	14	29	31
14	Wes Trainor (RW)	1948-49	17	1	2	3	6
14	Guy Trottier (RW)	1968-69	2	0	0	0	0
4	Rene Trudell (RW)	1945-46—1947-48	129	24	28	52	72
8	Darren Turcotte (C)	1988-89—1993-94	325	122	133	255	183
6	Dean Turner (D)	1978-79	1	0	0	0	0
17	Norm Tustin (LW)	1941-42	18	2	4	6	0

V

Number	Name & Position	Yrs. Played	GP	G	A	PTS	PIM
5, 2	Carol Vadnais (D)	1975-76—1981-82	485	56	190	246	690
11	Sparky Vail	1928-29—1929-30	50	4	1	5	18
17	Pat Verbeek (RW)	1994-95	19	10	5	15	18
40	Dennis Vial (D)	1990-91	21	0	0	0	61
8	Steve Vickers (LW)	1972-73—1981-82	698	246	340	586	330
11	Carl Voss (C)	1932-33	9	2	1	3	4

W

Number	Name & Position	Yrs. Played	GP	G	A	PTS	PIM
15	Frank Waite (F)	1930-31	17	1	3	4	4
14, 36	Gord Walker (LW)	1986-87—1987-88	19	2	4	6	19
25	Peter Wallin (RW)	1980-81—1981-82	52	3	14	17	14
	Eddie Wares (RW)	1936-37	2	2	0	2	0
14	Billy Warwick (LW)	1942-43—1943-44	14	3	3	6	16
8	Grant Warwick (RW)	1941-42—1947-48	293	117	116	233	179
7, 15	Phil Watson (RW)	1935-36—1942-43; 1944-45—1947-48	546	127	233	360	471
21	John Webster (LW)	1949-50	14	0	0	0	4
39	Doug Weight (C)	1991-92—1992-93	118	23	47	70	78
24	Jay Wells (D)	1991-92—1994-95	186	5	23	28	277
12	Len Wharton (D)	1944-45	1	0	0	0	0
41	Simon Wheeldon (C)	1987-88—1988-89	11	0	2	2	6
17, 39	Rob Whistle (D)	1985-86	32	4	2	6	10
19	Sherman White (C)	1946-47; 1949-50	4	0	2	2	0
14	Doug Wickenheiser (C)	1988-89	1	1	0	1	0
20	Juha Widing (C)	1969-70	44	7	7	14	10
6, 24	Jim Wiemer (D)	1984-85—1985-86	29	7	3	10	32
17	Tom Williams (LW)	1971-72—1973-74	25	1	3	4	6
14	Bert Wilson (LW)	1973-74—1974-75	66	6	2	8	68
17	Carey Wilson (C)	1988-89—1989-90	82	30	51	81	102
16	Johnny Wilson (LW)	1960-61—1961-62	96	25	15	40	38
4	Bob Wood (D)	1950-51	1	0	0	0	0
14	Bill Wylie (C)	1950-51	1	0	0	0	0

Y

Number	Name & Position	Yrs. Played	GP	G	A	PTS	PIM
19, 39	Tom Younghans (RW)	1981-82	47	3	5	8	17

Z

Number	Name & Position	Yrs. Played	GP	G	A	PTS	PIM
31	Rob Zamuner (C)	1991-92	9	1	2	3	2
24	Joe Zanussi (D)	1974-75	8	0	2	2	4
21	Sergei Zubov (D)	1992-93—1994-95	165	30	126	156	51

RANGERS ALL-TIME REGISTER

Goaltenders

Number	Name	Yrs. Played	W-L-T	GP	MINS	GA	AVG	SO
1	Andy Aitkenhead	1932-33—1934-35	47-43-16	106	6570	257	2.42	11
1	Lorne Anderson	1951-52	1-2-0	3	180	18	6.00	0
31	Hardy Astrom	1977-78	2-2-0	4	240	14	3.50	0
35	Steve Baker	1979-80—1982-83	20-20-11	57	3081	190	3.70	3
1	Gordie Bell**	1955-56	**1-1-0	2	120	9	4.50	0
1	Bill Beveridge	1942-43	4-10-3	17	1020	89	5.24	1
1	Lionel Bouvrette	1942-43	0-1-0	1	60	6	6.00	0
1	Johnny Bower	1953-54—1954-55; 1956-57	31-35-11	77	4620	202	2.62	5
1	Steve Buzinski	1942-43	2-6-1	9	560	55	5.89	0
1	Lorne Chabot	1926-27—1927-28	41-25-14	80	5037	135	1.61	21
30, 00, 35	John Davidson	1975-76—1982-83	93-90-25	222	12,449	742	3.58	7
1	Bob DeCourcy	1947-48	0-0-0	1	29	6	12.41	0
1	Dave Dryden	1961-62	0-1-0	1	40	3	4.50	0
1, 16	Emile Francis	1948-49—1951-52	7-9-5	22	1280	68	3.19	0
1	Jimmy Franks	1942-43	5-14-4	23	1380	103	4.48	0
33	Bob Froese	1986-87—1989-90	36-43-8	98	5350	324	3.63	1
1	Bruce Gamble	1958-59	0-2-0	2	120	6	3.00	0
1	Bert Gardiner	1935-36; 1938-39	1-0-0	1	60	1	1.00	0
1, 30	Ed Giacomin	1965-66—1975-76	266-169-90	539	31,646	1441	2.73	49
33	Gilles Gratton	1976-77	11-18-7	41	2034	143	4.22	0
1	Glen Hanlon	1982-83—1985-86	56-56-13	138	7690	473	3.69	0
30	Glenn Healy	1993-94—1994-95	18-18-3	46	2256	104	2.77	3
1,20	Jim Henry	1941-42—1945-46; 1947-48	47-44-17	109	6583	346	3.15	4
31	Corey Hirsch	1992-93	1-2-1	4	224	14	3.75	0
1	Percy Jackson	1934-35	0-1-0	1	60	8	8.00	0
1	Dave Kerr	1934-35—1940-41	157-110-57	324	20,230	698	2.07	40
44	Terry Kleisinger	1985-86	0-2-0	4	191	14	4.40	0
1	Julian Klymkiew	1958-59	0-0-0	1	19	2	6.32	0
1	Harry Lumley	1943-44	0-0-0	1	20	0	0.00	0
30	Cesare Maniago	1965-66—1966-67	9-19-4	34	1832	108	3.54	2
1	Ken McAuley	1943-44—1944-45	17-64-15	96	5740	537	5.61	1
1	Jack McCartan	1959-60—1960-61	3-7-2	12	680	43	3.79	1
31	Peter McDuffe	1972-73—1973-74	4-2-1	7	400	19	2.85	0
1	Joe Miller**	1927-28	**2-1-0	3	180	3	1.00	1
41	Ed Mio	1981-82—1982-83	29-24-11	66	3865	225	3.49	2
1	Dan Olesevich	1961-62	0-0-1	1	40	2	3.00	0
23,1	Marcel Paille	1957-58—1962-63; 1964-65	33-52-21	107	6342	362	3.42	2
16	Lester Patrick**	1927-28	**1-0-0	1	46	1	1.30	0
	Marcel Pelletier	1962-63	0-1-1	2	40	4	6.00	0
1	Jacques Plante	1963-64—1964-65	32-52-13	98	5838	329	3.38	5
1	Chuck Rayner	1945-46—1952-53	123-181-73	377	22,488	1122	2.99	24
35	Mike Richter	1989-90—1994-95	125-78-25	250	14,022	710	3.04	11
35	Curt Ridley	1974-75	1-1-0	2	81	7	5.19	0
1	John Ross Roach	1928-29—1931-32	80-63-37	180	11,310	407	2.16	30
1	Al Rollins	1959-60	1-3-4	8	480	31	3.88	0
30	Terry Sawchuk	1969-70	3-1-2	8	412	20	2.91	1
1	Joe Schaefer	1959-60—1960-61	0-1-0	2	86	8	5.58	0
31, 35	Ron Scott	1983-84—1987-88	3-7-4	16	796	51	3.84	0
30	Don Simmons	1965-66; 1967-68—1968-69	7-9-4	21	997	58	3.49	0
1, 31, 1, 33	Doug Soetaert	1975-76—1980-81; 1986-87	35-40-15	103	5226	372	4.27	1
1	Doug Stevenson	1944-45	0-4-0	4	240	20	5.00	0
25	Dave Tataryn	1976-77	1-1-0	2	80	10	7.50	0
1	Wayne Thomas	1977-78—1980-81	34-43-11	94	5288	320	3.63	5
34	John Vanbiesbrouck	1981-82; 1983-84—1992-93	200-177-47	449	25,380	1458	3.45	16
30, 1	Gilles Villemure	1963-64—1967-68; 1970-71—1975-76	96-54-21	184	10,472	457	2.62	13
31	Steve Weeks	1980-81—1983-84	42-33-14	94	5313	339	3.83	1
1, 31	Dunc Wilson	1974-75—1975-76	6-11-3	23	1260	89	4.24	0
1	Hal Winkler	1926-27	3-4-1	8	514	16	1.87	2
1	Lorne Worsley	1952-53—1962-63	204-271-101	583	34,675	1789	3.10	24

**Denotes Playoff Statistics